GOD'S PLAYGROUND
A History of Poland

GOD'S PLAYGROUND

A History of Poland

IN TWO VOLUMES
VOLUME I
THE ORIGINS TO 1795

by

NORMAN DAVIES

COLUMBIA UNIVERSITY PRESS
NEW YORK 1982

Library of Congress Cataloging in Publication Data
Davies, Norman.
   A history of Poland, God's playground.

   Bibliography: p.
   Includes indexes.
   Contents: v. 1. The origins to 1795 —
v. 2. 1795 to the present.
   1. Poland — History. I. Title. II. Title: Gods playground.
DK4140.D38   943.8   81-10241
ISBN 0-231-04326-0 (set)
ISBN 0-231-05350-9 (v. 1)   AACR2
ISBN 0-231-05352-5 (v. 2)

Set in IBM Press Roman
in Great Britain by
Express Litho Service (Oxford)

for DANIEL

So that he may know and love the land of his birth,

(if he wants to.)

PREFACE

To write the history of someone else's country is, no doubt, to take a terrible liberty. Judging by the reticence which professional scholars show before pronouncing on minor episodes in the past of their own country, it would seem that only the young and foolhardy might attempt to publish their thoughts on other people's millennia. A proper appreciation of the complexities of the task deters most of those best qualified to perform it. An Englishman who has dared to write a *History of Poland,* therefore, must be aware that any number of Polish scholars know vastly more about the subject than he does. At the same time, free from the burdens of their knowledge and from political circumstances which inhibit the expression of independent views, he can still hope to contribute perspectives and insights of value. Fortitude, no less than Modesty, must be his constant companions.

This study is not inspired by any particular ideology. It cannot claim to be objective, of course, since objectivity is always impossible. Like all history books, it had to be written through the distorting medium of the mind of the historian, whose private quirks necessarily select a finite quantity of information from the infinite details of past reality. It can faithfully reproduce that reality no more than a two-dimensional photograph, formed through the refracting glass of the camera's lens, can produce an accurate picture of the three-dimensional world. The historian, like the camera, always lies. He is incapable of telling the whole truth. All he can do is to recognize the particular distortions to which his work is inevitably subject, and to avoid the grosser forms of retouching and excision. Like the photographer who demonstrates the effect on his picture of all the available light filters, he can present the various interpretations of controversial issues with equal prominence, and refrain from arbitrary judgements. By so doing, he can hope if not to be objective, then at least to be impartial.

In this regard, a note on the historian's private philosophy of history may not be entirely irrelevant. Two formative influences have tended to pull me in opposite directions. A period of study at the Jagiellonian University in Cracow, where the requirements for the doctoral examinations included reading matter of a distinctly ideological nature, certainly aroused my curiosity about the problem of Causality. Whilst not converting me to the cogency of Marxism, Leninism, or Marxism—Leninism, it did reinforce my earlier suspicions that something akin to 'historical forces' might exist, and might be responsible in part for the way that things happen. Concurrently, an earlier period of study in the School of Modern History at Oxford under the tuition of Mr A. J. P. Taylor did not pass entirely into oblivion. Unlike our illustrious predecessor at Magdalen College, Edward Gibbon, I cannot pretend that my years at Oxford 'were the most idle and unprofitable of my whole life'. I did not accept that Mr Taylor's inimitable opinions are invariably perverse, and I respect his promptings that both chance, and the will of individual human beings, play their part in directing the course of events. As a result, in trying to reconcile the contrary influences, I have come to hold that Causality is not composed exclusively of determinist, individualist, or random elements, but from a combination of all three. In any given historical situation, I insist at the start on identifying a matrix of social, economic, cultural, institutional, military, personal, and dynamic political factors which are pertinent to all further developments. But there I draw the line. I think that the matrix of historical forces determines the limits of the possible, but does not, and cannot determine what course events will subsequently take within those given limits. I believe that a range of choices is always available to individuals, especially to those set in positions of authority, and that their response to the options before them can influence mankind's fate decisively. In the realm of human motivation, I happen to believe in the primacy of the irrational, seeing Reason as the servant, not as the master of our fears, emotions, and instincts. Finally, I believe that all human beings are fallible; that all leaders of men are inadequate to their calling: and that the results of their actions are rarely an exact measure of what they intended. As Bismarck once remarked, they are not so much in full control of events, as in a position occasionally to deflect them. When they fail to do either, they lay themselves open to what the ancients called Fate or Providence, what the moderns call Accidents, and what the British call 'muddling through'. In short, life is not entirely absurd; but it is not entirely rational either. Among British and American scholars, attitudes of this sort are not uncommon; but whether they find any coherent expression in the text only the reader can judge.

In writing the history of a modern country, however, philosophical reflections must often take second place to more practical problems. Among them is the problem of hindsight. On the one hand, the cautious historian is bound to wonder whether the teleological exercise of tracing the origins of a modern state or nation from the present into the past is essentially unhistorical. It tends to confuse antecedent and postcedent with cause and effect, and obliterates the multifarious alternatives which faced the actors of the drama at each stage of their progress. It justifies the course of events in terms of their outcome. In the Polish case, it suggests that the present People's Republic of Poland is the one and only conceivable product of the historical process. On the other hand, the historian is unable to deny that he is living in the fourth quarter of the twentieth century, and not in the Dark Ages, and that he is blessed with the benefit of hindsight whether he likes it or not. Nor can he ignore the interests of his readers, whose curiosity about a modern country will have more probably been aroused by the happenings of their own times than by any thirst for knowledge about the remoter past. He is bound to pay some special attention to those aspects of his subject most closely connected to the world in which we live.

There is, above all, the capital problem of definition. For the historian who aims to write a comprehensive survey of a European country, the really difficult task lies less in the interpretation of historical facts than in defining what facts are supposed to be interpreted. In this regard, it is much easier to discredit the syntheses of rivals and predecessors than to construct a coherent scheme for oneself. Oddly enough, modern Marxist—Leninist historians in Poland have swallowed the old nationalist ideology hook, line, and sinker. Although their socio-economic analysis of the development of the Polish national community represents a new tack in modern historio-graphy, their unquestioning acceptance of the permanent existence of that community throughout recorded history stands in complete agreement with the definition of Polish History as assumed by pre-war nationalist scholars. Very few Polish historians have doubted the contention that the Polish community of their own day was the sole legitimate claimant to the soil on which they live, and that they are the natural and exclusive heirs of all those earlier communities who occupied those same lands. Yet such a contention, though politically convenient, is demonstrably false. The citizens of the People's Republic do not have the same things in common as the citizens of pre-war Poland, still less with the subjects of the stateless Polish nation of the nineteenth century or of the Kingdom and Republic of earlier times.

A more cautious approach would suggest that nothing in our present understanding of European History permits us to view the growth of its constituent nations as an 'autonomous . . . organic . . . process'. There is something to be said for analysing the development of states and institutions from that point of view, but nothing for applying it to the development of nations. In Poland's case, where the existence of the state has been intermittent, and only partly coincidental with the life of the nation, it would seem to be quite inappropriate.

In my view, the historian has no safe choice but to examine the pieces of the puzzle separately, with no hope of fitting Society, State, and Nation into some neat and consequential pattern. I do not maintain, of course, that Polish History is completely fortuitous or disjointed. What I do say is, firstly that the role of arbitrary external influences and of foreign powers has been no less important than that of coherent domestic forces; and, secondly, that the instances of dis-continuity are no less in evidence than the strands of continuity.

In the history of the Polish State, the established order has been overturned on at least five occasions – in 1138, in 1795, in 1813, in 1864, and in 1939. On each occasion, all concrete manifestations of a unified political community were lost. At the end of each disembodiment – in 1320, 1807, 1815, 1918, and 1944 – the new order which came into being owed little to its predecessors, and was obliged to make a fresh start, in new conditions and under new management. Similarly, in the history of the Polish nation, the destiny of its members has been fused for long periods and in the most intimate way with that of other peoples – in the early centuries with the Czechs and other Slavs; from 1385 to 1793 with the peoples of the Grand Duchy of Lithuania; from 1772 to 1918, with the peoples of the Russian, German, and Austrian Empires; and over the entire span of recorded history to the Final Solution of 1941–4 with the Askenazy Jews. In strong contrast to conditions which prevailed for centuries prior to the Second World War, the present situation, where the limits of the Polish People's Republic are virtually coterminous with the homeland of a homogeneous and nationally-conscious Polish nation, is unprecedented. It represents a radical break with the past.

A volume which aims to occupy a neutral position on the national question, is unlikely to win the acclaim of its Polish readers. Equally, it goes without saying that the political authorities in Warsaw will fail to praise a work that tries to treat Poland's relationship with each of her neighbours in an even-handed manner. The ideologists of the regime will be unable to approve an account which rejects the organic nature of the historical process. More importantly, the great majority of Poles, irrespective of their political persuasions, will be disappointed to read a work which fails to confirm their most cherished beliefs. For them, Polish History is a cause, an ideal, a political instrument. For the independent historian, it is merely an object of study. Whatever his private feelings, the historian cannot assume that Poland has any special moral worth, or superior mission, or even any absolute right to exist. He must simply describe how it arose; how it has changed; what it has contributed to European civilization; and what it has meant to different people at different times. For my part, I see Poland as an immensely complex phenomenon – both land, and state, and nation, and culture: a community in constant flux, forever transmuting its composition, its view of itself, and its *raison d'être:* in short, a puzzle with no clear solution. As one of my audience so bitterly complained when I once tried to explain this point of view to a seminar at Harvard University: 'You make it sound as if Polish History were *normal*'.

For British and American readers, of course, an impartial 'History of Poland' needs no apology. A country which has occupied such a central place in European affairs, which has supplied some of Britain and America's most prominent ethnic minorities, and which has endured more than its share of Europe's troubles, has regularly escaped the due attention of historical scholars. Polish affairs, like those of many countries beyond the frontier of power and prestige, have usually been reduced to an intermittent flow of news items – inadequately researched, briefly mentioned at moments of crisis, and quickly forgotten. They have usually been presented to the English-speaking world, either by Germans or Russians seeking to justify their malpractices, or by Poles and Jews pleading their special causes. They have been shrouded behind the veils of political interest, national pride, and linguistic obscurity, and have rarely been revealed in the flesh. Polish History books, written by Polish scholars for a Polish audience, make strange reading when translated into English. Large composite works such as the *Cambridge History of Poland* of 1941–50 launched by W. F. Reddaway,[1] or the *History of Poland* edited by Stefan Kieniewicz and others in 1968,[2] are not readily digestible; whilst tracts inspired by the two World Wars such as those of Allison Philips, Lord Eversley, or W. J. Rose, have not outlived the political necessities which gave them birth.[3] Yet very few comprehensive surveys of Polish History, written by British or American scholars with the British and American readership in mind, have ever been attempted. When the present volume finds its way into print, it will be one of the very few products of its kind since Professor W. F. Morfill's pioneering effort in 1893.[4]

Furthermore, Polish History displays many qualities of intrinsic interest. The decline and fall of the old Republic, from grandeur to annihilation, is both terrible and pathetic. As Ferdinand Lot remarked in relation to a more familiar stricken civilization: 'the tragedy of a world which did not wish to die presents a spectacle as entrancing as anything which the historian or sociologist is ever likely to see'. In more recent times, Polish experiences have stood in marked contrast to the events which moulded the British and American traditions. The Poles have been politically defeated, and economically deprived for longer than anyone can remember. For the British and Americans who until recently tended to assume that victory and prosperity were their birthright, the Polish example offers ample food for thought. On the European scale, Poland is the underdog of them all. In Michelet's words, 'it is the most human of nations'.[5]

A sceptical stance towards methodology has necessarily conditioned the contents and structure of the following study. It has meant, for instance, that no claim can be made for it to be a 'synthesis', but only a 'survey' or 'outline'. It has given the comments a heterodox character, redolent of the hopeless habits of English empiricism, mixed with a dash of *Angst* and perhaps with a grain of Charity. The doubts are fully justified. It is all very unsatisfactory. It would be nice to have a theory; but I do not have one. It would be nice to give simple answers to simple questions such as 'Where was Poland?', or 'Who is a Pole, and who is not?'. But I cannot. All I have to offer are a few facts, and a few observations.

By way of consolation, close attention has been paid to the practical aspects of structure and arrangement. Equal space has been given to thematic and chronological chapters. After a series of introductory essays discussing Historiography, Historical Geography, and the early Polish dynasties up to 1572, the body of the book is divided into two main blocks, separated at the crucial breaking-point of 1795. The first block, entitled *The Life and Death of the Polish–Lithuanian Republic* traces the history of the Polish–Lithuanian Union from its initiation in 1569 to its collapse at the Third Partition. The second block entitled *The Growth of the Modern Nation* traces the attempts to build a nation from the fragments of the old Republic and to restore a measure of national sovereignty. It runs from the Third Partition to the end of the Second World War in 1945, when the existence of a Polish national state was finally confirmed. Each block contains a group of chapters discussing the principal religious, social, economic, constitutional, and diplomatic themes of longer duration, followed by a group of narrative chapters. Together they constitute the warp and the woof of a close-knit texture designed to convey a sense of the complex relationships, and confused reverberations, of public and social life. The final chapter presents a review of events in the Polish People's Republic in the years since the Second World War. Its concluding section, a personal and impressionistic piece, is based on an article which first appeared in *The Times* of 27 October 1972 as 'A Magical Mystery Tour of Poland'.

The content matter is as catholic as space allows. In view of the unfamiliarity of Polish History to most British and American readers, the treatment of weighty events has been sweetened with a mild infusion of anecdotes, epitaphs, *bons mots,* ditties, hymns, songs, poems, travelogues, lyrical evocations, and antiquarian curiosities — in short with a selection of all those historical whimsicalities which scientific scholars judge unworthy of their genius.

Space has been found for historical documents and literary extracts to be quoted at length in each chapter. The purpose here was to provide some concrete details to interrupt the flow of tedious summaries which would otherwise dominate this outline of a very large subject. The selection of texts cannot be fully representative, of course. But an account which evokes some sense of the infinite specifics of human affairs is less likely to deform than one that talks exclusively in sweeping generalizations. Given due warning of the dangers of selectivity, the reader will reach no harm if he glimpses the rich profusion of source materials on which students of Polish History can draw.

Space has also been found for a limited quantity of encyclopaedic information. Here, the interests of form and readability have had to be reconciled with the need to provide suitable leads for further investigation, and to remedy the disgraceful gaps with regard to Polish affairs in many standard British and American reference works.

Notes have been kept to a minimum. Bibliographical references have been provided at the end of the book for passages which draw heavily on secondary materials or on recent research. Needless to say, the mention of source materials does not necessarily imply agreement with any of the opinions expressed therein.

Due warning was given by the publishers that the modern reader is easily frightened by foreign languages. This is a great pity, since much of the flavour of East European History

comes from the rich linguistic variety of the sources. None
the less, all foreign texts and quotations have been put into
English, and only a few have been left with the original text
in parallel. Wherever possible, foreign verse has been versified
in English. Except where indicated, all translations from the
Latin, Polish, Russian, French, German, and Italian, are my
own work.

Place-names cause endless trouble and fascination. In a work
of Polish History, it would have been relatively simple to put
all such names into their Polish form. But such a policy would
have led to many anachronisms; and an attempt has been
made in each instance to find the form most appropriate to the
relevant time and historical context. The main lines of this exercise are summarized in the course of Volume II, Chapter 21.

No work of this size and scope could be written without
the assistance of friends and colleagues. Many of the contro-
versial passages have been read in draft by specialists who
were kind enough to offer the benefit of their critical advice.
In this regard, the author's thanks are due to the following:
Robert Auty, James Bolton, Maureen Burke, Jan Ciechanowski,
Olga Crisp, Bohdan Czaykowski, Daniel Davies, Tony French,
Józef Gierowski, Alexander Gieysztor, Maria Gimbutas, Karol
Górski, Ian Hamilton, Gershon Hundert, Wacław Jędrzejewicz,
Richard Jenkins, Dolek Juzwenko, Stefan Kieniewicz, Antoni
Mączak, Isabel de Madariaga, Bolesław Mazur, David Morgan,
Laszlo Peter, Hugh Seton-Watson, Janusz Tomiak, Eva Travers,
Angus Walker, and Piotr Wandycz. The author's apologies are
due to those whose advice has been respectfully ignored.

The subtitle of this study — *'God's Playground'* — may raise
some eyebrows. It is one of several possible English translations of an old Polish phrase, *Boże Igrzysko* which first appears
in the 1580s as the title of Kochanowski's verse *Człowiek-Boże
Igrzysko* (Mankind — Bauble of the Gods), where it is generally
thought to be a calque of Plautus's *pila deorum*.[6] *Boże*,
meaning 'divine', refers in a pagan context to the 'Gods', and
in a Christian context to 'God'. *Igrzysko*, being a diminutive
noun derived from an old form of the verb *igrać*, 'to play',
can be variously translated as a 'bauble' or 'plaything' (with
which one plays): as a 'comedy' or 'drama' (that is played);
as the 'actor', 'comedian', or 'jester' (who does the playing);

or else as 'the stage' or 'playground' (where things are played).
In this last sense, it recurs at several points in Polish literature,
and can be aptly used as an epithet for a country where fate
has frequently played mischievous tricks, and where a lively
sense of humour has always formed an essential item of equipment in the national survival kit. It may not be unduly scientific, but among readers in general, even among historians, it
may conceivably recall Montesquieu's view that all forms of
folly are permissible so long as they are not expressed with
solemnity. In Polish circles, the national history is sometimes
discussed in markedly reverential tones; and the 'high-priests'
of official ideology are not noted for their wit. Even so, it is
hoped that a good-humoured and open-minded approach is
not necessarily lacking in respect, and that it may find some
understanding among those who have always viewed the
'jesters', from Stańczyk, Potocki, and Zabłocki onwards, as
skilled purveyors of the Polish tradition.[7]

In the twelve months since the text of the present volume
was completed, little has happened to disturb its main con-
tentions. The political stalemate in Poland stays unresolved.
The food queues and the opposition groups still loom large;
but the authorities have done nothing to disperse either the
one or the other. The direr prophecies of open insurrection
or of Soviet intervention have not been fulfilled. In November
1978, the Sixtieth Anniversary of National Independence was
marked by a series of offical and unofficial celebrations. The
state-controlled media gave prominence to the 7—8 November
— the anniversaries of the Russian Revolution and of Daszyń-
ski's improvised People's Government in Lublin; whilst the
Church and the populace at large saved their rejoicings for
the traditional date of 11 November. Numerous academic
gatherings debated the significance of the events of 1918.
Party apologists spared no chance to minimize the role of
Józef Piłsudski and to conceal the fact that the Polish communist movement had been opposed to national independence
at that juncture. Almost all the commentators followed a
characteristically sanguine line of argumentation, assuming
that the will of the Polish people had somehow been sufficient
in itself to realize the nation's supposedly uniform aspirations. It was a rare voice indeed which tried to balance a sober

assessment of the international situation in 1918 with a proper appreciation of the complicated state of Polish public opinion.

In terms of personal achievement, 1978 saw two events worthy of note. In June, the State and Party authorities widely publicized the propulsion into orbit by a Soviet spaceship of Colonel Mierosław Hermaszewski. On 16 October, the entire Polish nation swelled with joy and pride at the elevation of Cardinal Karol Wojtyła, Archbishop of Cracow, to be Pope John Paul II. The contrast between the stage-managed festivities surrounding the first Pole in the cosmos and the spontaneous delirium surrounding the first Pole at the head of the Papacy spoke worlds about the true condition of Poland today. The obvious symbolism − of the Polish passenger in an artificial Soviet satellite and of the vibrant Polish leader at the helm of the Vatican − was lost on nobody. The one, in succession to Lajka, was furthering the cause of modern science and of military technology; the other, in the steps of St. Peter, was strengthening the cause of traditional religion and spirituality.

The full impact of John Paul II's pontificate cannot possibly be gauged at this early date; but there can be little doubt that it has already done more to reinforce Poland's Catholic and western identity, than any other event in living memory. The simple fact that this self-confessed son of the Polish soil has been proved *papabile* will serve to raise the self-esteem of all his compatriots, to boost their morale, and to strengthen their resolve in all their international dealings. The new Pope is well aware of the implications. In his inaugural statement on 23 October 1978, he addressed himself to his compatriots irrespective of their beliefs, and drew their attention to the true meaning of Patriotism, which he specifically disassociated from all forms of 'narrow nationalism and chauvinism'. 'The love of our country unites us all', he declared, 'and must act as a bond over and above all our differences.' Earlier in the year, in his last sermon in Cracow in celebration of the Third of May, he had expounded the theme still more explicitly:

For everything that we have lived through in the course of our history, especially in the most painful periods of partition, occupation, insurrection, struggle, and suffering, has had the effect of pumping both the historical and the contemporary life of the entire Nation through the heart of every Pole. Nothing which is Polish can be alien or indifferent to Him. It was the great poet Stanisław Wyspiański who asked his listeners to gather round a little girl, to whom he said, 'What can you hear beating there inside you? It's your heart. And that heart is what Poland really is.' . . .

After all, each one of us possesses a heritage within us — a heritage to which generations and centuries of achievement and calamity, of triumph and failure, have contributed: a heritage which somehow takes deeper root and grows new tissues from every one of us. We cannot live without it. It is our soul. It is this heritage, variously labelled the Fatherland or the Nation, by which we live. As Christians, we live by this Polish heritage, this Polish Millennium, this Polish Christianity of ours. Such is the law of reality . . .

For believers and unbelievers alike, these were powerful words indeed, to be heeded by some, to be feared by others, but to be respected by all.

*   *   *   *   *

The final preparation of a large typescript further increases an author's indebtedness to collaborators and patrons. In this regard, I wish to acknowledge the assistance of Mr. Ken Wass of University College, London, who undertook the technical drawing of most of my maps and diagrams: of Andrzej Suchcitz and Marek Siemaszko, who compiled the index: of the Publications Committee of the School of Slavonic and East European Studies: and especially of the De Brzezie Lanckoroński Foundation, which provided a generous subsidy.

Norman Davies.
Wolvercote, 3 May 1979.

CONTENTS

Maps and Diagrams   xxi

Illustrations   xxiii

Notes on the Illustrations   xxv

Chronology   xxix

I *Introduction. The Origins to 1572*

  1. MILLENIUM: A Thousand Years of History (Historiography)   3

  2. POLSKA: The Polish Land (Historical Geography)   23

  3. PIAST: The Polanian Dynasty (to 1370)   61

  4. ANJOU: The Hungarian Connection (1370–1386)   106

  5. JOGAILA: The Lithuanian Union (1386–1572)   115

II *The Life and Death of the Polish–Lithuanian Republic (1569–1795)*

  6. ANTEMURALE: The Bulwark of Christendom (Religion)   159

  7. SZLACHTA: The Nobleman's Paradise (Society)   201

  8. HANDEL: The Baltic Grain Trade (Economy)   256

  9. MIASTO: The Vicissitudes of Urban Life (The Cities)   293

  10. ANARCHIA: The Noble Democracy (Constitution)   321

  11. SERENISSIMA: Diplomacy in Poland–Lithuania (Foreign Affairs)   373

  12. VALOIS: The French Experiment (1572–1575)   413

  13. BATHORY: The Transylvanian Victor (1576–1586)   421

  14. VASA: The Swedish Connection (1587–1668)   433

15. MICHAŁ: The Austrian Candidate
                 (1669—1673)   470
16. SOBIESKI: Terror of the Turk (1674—1696)   473
17. WETTIN: The Saxon Era (1697—1763)   492
18. AGONIA: The End of the Russian
                 Protectorate (1764—1795)   511

Notes on the text   547
Index   573

MAPS AND DIAGRAMS

Page

Maps 1. The Polish Lands   2

2. Poland's Changing Territory   25

3. Polish Prehistory:
   A. The Autochthonous View   41
   B. The Non-autochthonous View   41

4. The Realm of the Early Piasts
   (10th to 11th Centuries)   68

5. The Period of Fragmentation (c. 1250)   73

6. The Teutonic State (1230–1561)   89

7. Poland under Casimir the Great (1330–70)   97

8. The Angevin Realm (c. 1380)   110

9. The Jagiellonian Realm (c. 1500)   140

10. Ecclesiastical Dioceses (17th Century)   169

11. Reformation Centres in Poland–Lithuania   178

12. The Distribution of Landed Property in
    Royal Prussia (c. 1570)
    A. Palatinate of Chełmno   222
    B. Palatinate of Malbork   223

13. The Vistula Trade   259

14. Owieczki – A Nobleman's Manor (1797)   283

15. The Incorporated Cities of Mazovia   296

16. Warsaw – the Growth of the City to 1800   309

17. The Vasa Realm (c. 1600)   438

18. Poland–Lithuania at its greatest extent
    (1634–35)   449

19. The Deluge – the invasions of Poland–
    Lithuania, 1648–67   464

20. Saxony–Poland (c. 1750)   494

21. International Wars in the Eighteenth-
    Century   498

22. The Partitions of Poland (1773–95)   512

Page

Diagrams A. Periodization Schemes of Polish History   8

B. Poland — Physical Structure   36

C. The Ancestral Homeland of the Slavs   42

D. The Slavonic Languages   48

E. The Piast Dynasty
   (Genealogical Table)   64/65

F. The Jagiellons and the Vasas
   (Genealogical Table)   136/137

G. The Religious Communities of Poland—
   Lithuania
   a) in 1660   b) in 1772   162

H. The Social Estates of Poland—Lithuania
   a) 16th Century   b) in 1791   202

I. Social Groups in the Sixteenth Century
   a) According to the Poll-tax of 1520
   b) Tax Brackets (after A. Wyczański)   204

J. Economic strata within the Noble Estate
   (*Szlachta*)   220

K. Central Institutions of the
   Rzeczpospolita   324/325

L. The Organs of Jewish Autonomy
   (c. 1550—1764)   442/443

M. The Partitions of Poland   522

LIST OF ILLUSTRATIONS

Plates follow page 286

Plate I OUTPOST OF LATIN CHRISTENDOM
Regina Poloniae (Queen of Poland) – The Black Madonna of Częstochowa
The Epitaph of Jan z Ujazdu, (c. 1450)

Plate II THE END OF THE JAGIELLONS
J. Simmler, *The Death of Barbara Radziwiłł, (1551)*
(Anon.) *Anna Jagiellonka, (1523–96)*

Plate III THANKS BE TO GOD
(Anon.) *'God and Corn will repay',* The Vistula Grain Trade
The Crown of the Law – Jewish Ark Curtain from Przedbórz

Plate IV THE UNION OF FREE PEOPLES
J. Matejko, *The Union of Lublin, 1569*
B. Bellotto (Canaletto), *Royal Election at Wola, 1764*

Plate V A POWER IN THE EAST
J. Matejko, *Stefan Bathory before Pskov, 1581*
(Miniature.) *Gniński's Embassy to the Porte, 1677*

Plate VI THE NOBLES' PARADISE
(Anon.) *Sebastian Lubomirski, 1536–1613*
(Anon.) *Katarzyna Ostrogska, neé Lubomirska*

Plate VII MONARCHS OF A REPUBLIC
L. de Silvestre, *Augustus the Strong, 1670–1733*
M. Bacciarelli, *Stanislas-Augustus in Coronation Robes, 1764*

Plate VIII RESISTANCE AND DESPAIR
J. Chełmoński, *'Casimir Pułaski at Częstochowa, 1771'*
J. Matejko, *'Rejtan', 1773*

xxiii

NOTES ON THE ILLUSTRATIONS

Vol I

Plate I

The 'Black Madonna of Częstochowa', the most venerated symbol of Polish Catholicism, is probably of Byzantine origin, brought to the monastery of Jasna Góra (founded 1382) in the late fourteenth century. Ever since its providential deliverance from the Swedish siege of 1655, the shrine has been the centre of the national Marian cult.
Sikorski Museum (London).

(Anon.) *Epitafium* (Funeral Portrait) of Jan z Ujazdu, (John of Ujazd), a knight of the heraldic clan of *Drużyna* (see coat-of-arms), dated 1450, formerly in the parish church of Czchów and in the Lubomirski Collection at Lwów.
Kraków (Wawel Collection).

Plate II

Józef Simmler (1823–68), *Śmierć Barbary Radziwiłłówna*, (1860). This sentimental study of Queen Barbara's death in 1551, painted by a member of the German 'Nazarene' School, was immensely popular in nineteenth-century Poland.
Muzeum Narodowe (Warsaw).

(Anon.) Portrait of *Anna Jagiellonka* (1523–96), the last of the Jagiellons – daughter of Sigismund I and Bona Sforza, sister of Sigismund-August, queen of Stefan Bathory, aunt of Sigismund III Vasa.
Muzeum Narodowe (Wilanów).

Plate III

(Anon.) *Zboże zapłaci* (17th century), Toruń – a scene from the Vistula Grain Trade. The title is a pun on the Polish words for 'God' and 'Corn'.
Muzeum Toruńskie, MT/M/92/SN.

A *parokhet* (Curtain of the Ark) from the synagogue at Przedbórz, near Piotrków, date illegible. The design incorporates the *Keter Torah* (Crown of the Law) over three Polish eagles. The dedication is to one, Zvi Hirsch, deceased and his wife . . .
Orbis Books (London)

Plate IV   J. Matejko (1838–93), *Unia Lubelska,* (1869). A reconstruction of the submission of the Lithuanian princes painted for the 300th Anniversary of the Union of Lublin. King Sigismund-August holds the crucifix aloft as Primate Uchański proffers the oath to Hetman Mielecki, Chancellor Mikołaj Radziwiłł, and Jan Chodkiewicz, (with head in hands). Also present – Frycz Modrzewski, Prince Roman Sanguszko, Prince Michał Wiśniowiecki, Anna Jagiellonka, Cardinal Hosiusz, Prince Ostrogski, Duke Albrecht von Hohenzollern of Prussia.
Muzeum Narodowe (Warsaw).

Bernardo Bellotto (1721–80), called 'Caneletto the Younger', *Elekcja Stanisława Augusta* (1776), one of two versions of the Royal Election of 1764 painted a dozen years after the event.
Muzeum Narodowe (Warsaw).

Plate V   J. Matejko, *Batory pod Pskowem* (1872). King Stefan Bathory receives the traditional welcome of bread and salt from a deputation of Muscovite boyars; in attendance – Chancellor Zamoyski, Prince Ostrogski, the Papal Legate Possevino, Hetman Żółkiewski in hussar's armour, Cossack Ataman Oryszowski.
Muzeum Narodowe (Warsaw).

(Miniature), *Gniński's Embassy to the Porte* (1677). Sobieski's luckless ambassador is ushered into the presence of Sultan Mehmet IV after a long wait.
Kraków (Czartoryski Collection).

Plate VI   (Anon.) *Sebastian Lubomirski* (1536–1613), founder of the Lubomirski fortunes – castellan of Wojnicz, *żupnik* (leaseholder) of the royal salt mines at Wieliczka, *starosta* of Spisz.
Muzeum Narodowe (Warsaw).

(Anon.) *Katarzyna z Lubomirskich Ostrogska,* (c. 1600), daughter of Sebastian Lubomirski and Anna Branicka, second wife of Prince Janusz Ostrogski (1554–1620), *Wojewoda* of Volhynia, Castellan of Cracow, and a Catholic convert from Orthodoxy.
Muzeum Narodowe (Warsaw).

Plate VII   Louis de Silvestre (1675–1760), court painter at Dresden and Warsaw, 1716–48, decorator of the Saxon Palace. Portrait of *August II in armour.*
Muzeum Narodowe (Wilanów).

Marcello Bacciarelli (1731–1818), principal artistic director of the royal court from 1766. Portrait of *Stanisław-August in Coronation Robes,* painted c. 1700. *Muzeum Narodowe (Warsaw).*

Plate VIII   Józef Chełmoński (1849–1914). Polish realist painter, best known for his scenes of country life, eg. *Żórawie* (The Cranes, 1870) and of horses, eg. *Czwórka* (The Foursome, 1881). *Pułaski pod Częstochową* records one of the actions of the Confederates of Bar. In the background, the monastery of Jasna Góra. *Muzeum Narodowe (Warsaw).*

J. Matejko, *Rejtan* (1866). Tadeusz Rejtan (1746–80), Envoy of Nowogródek, bars the entrance to the Senate in protest against the confirmation of the First Partition, 1773. Prince Adam Poniński, Marshal of the Sejm, flanked by Feliks Potocki in white and Hetman Branicki, orders him to desist. In the balcony, Prince Repnin; on the wall, a portrait of Catherine II. *Muzeum Narodowe (Warsaw).*

CHRONOLOGY

Prehistory

BC *c.* 180,000	Earliest trace of Man, in the Ojców Caves near Cracow
4000–1800	Neolithic cultures
c. 2500	Beginnings of primitive agriculture
1800–400	Bronze Age cultures
c. 600	Iron Age cultures begin
c. 550	Earliest construction of island fortress at Biskupin
c. 500	Invasion of nomadic Scythians
c. 400	Presence of Celtic tribes
AD 1st Century	Presence of Germanic tribes – Goths, Gepids, Markomans, Burgundians, etc.
2nd Century	Ptolemy's Geography mentions Kalixia (Kalisz)
3rd Century	Emigration of Goths and Gepids to Black Sea Coast
5th Century	Supremacy of the Huns
6th Century	Supremacy of the Avars: Expansion of the Slavs begins
c. 844	Anonymous Bavarian Geographer's List of Slavonic tribes east of Elbe

History

9th Century to 1370(–85) THE PIAST KINGDOM

c. 850	Founding of Piast dynasty in the Polanian realm
	Vislanian tribe within the sphere of the Great Moravian Empire
pre-963–992	Reign of Mieszko I
966	Baptism of Mieszko I: Introduction of Latin Christianity
991	*Dagome ludex:* oldest manuscript from Poland

992–1025	Reign of Bolesław I Chrobry
997	Martyrdom of St. Wojciech (Adalbert)
1000	Congress of Gniezno: Founding of Polish See
1025	Coronation of Bolesław I
1079	Execution of St. Stanisław, Bishop of Cracow
1116	Chronicle of Gallus Anonimus written
1138	Testament of Bolesław III Krzywousty: initiation of the 'principate'
1138–1295	Period of fragmentation of Piast realm
1180	Congress of Łeczyca: ecclestiastical immunities granted
c. 1220	Chronicle of Wincenty Kadłubek.
1226	Installation of Teutonic Order in Prussia
1241	First Mongol Invasion: Battle of Legnica
1242	Incorporation of first Polish municipality, Wrocław (Breslau)
1264	Statute of Jewish liberties at Kalisz
1295	Coronation of Przemysł II: Restoration of Polish kingdom
1300–1305	Union of Poland and Bohemia under Vaclav II
1306–1333	Reign of Władysław II Łokietek
1308	Seizure of Gdańsk by Teutonic Knights
1320	Coronation of Łokietek
1333–1370	Reign of Kazimierz III (Casimir the Great)
1335	Cession of Silesia to Bohemia
1340	Polish Conquest of Red Ruthenia begins
1364	Congress of Cracow. Foundation of *Stadium generale*
1370	Death of Casimir the Great
1370–1385	Union of Poland and Hungary under Louis of Anjou
1374	Statute of Košice: noble immunities granted
1385–1572	*JAGIELLONIAN PERIOD:* personal union of Poland and Lithuania
1385	Union of Krewo: betrothal of Jadwiga and Jagiełło

1386–1434	Reign of Władysław Jagiełło
1400	Refounding of Jagiellonian University
1410	Battle of Grunwald
1413	Union of Horodło
1425	*Neminem captivabimus:* statute of noble immunity
1434–1444	Reign of Władysław Warneńczyk, King of Poland and Hungary
1444	Battle of Varna
1444–1492	Reign of Kazimierz Jagiellończyk
1454	Incorporation of Royal Prussia
1466	Peace of Toruń: partition of Prussia
1474	Earliest printing press in Cracow
1493	Establishment of bicameral sejm
1505	Statute of *Nihil Novi*
1506–1548	Reign of Zygmunt I Stary
1525	Secularization of Teutonic Order: Homage of Albrecht von Hohenzollern
1529	Incorporation of Mazovia
1543	Death of Copernicus
1548–1572	Reign of Zygmunt II August
1561	Incorporation of Livonia: Polish entry into Livonian wars
1562–3	Piotrków Sejm: Executionist Movement
1563	Schism among Polish Calvinists: 'Arians' breakaway: Brest Bible
1564	Arrival of Jesuits in Poland
1569	Transfer of Ukraine to the Kingdom of Poland: Union of Lublin signed

1569–1795 'RZECZPOSPOLITA' OF POLAND–LITHUANIA	
1573	Confederation of Warsaw: Religious toleration guaranteed
1573	First Royal Election of Henry Valois: *Pacta Conventa*
1576–1586	Reign of Stefan Bathory
1578	Creation of legal Tribunals
1584	Death of Jan Kochanowski
1587–1632	Reign of Zygmunt III Vasa
1596	Union of Brest: creation of Uniate Church

1605	Polish intervention in Moscow's 'Time of Troubles'
1606–8	Rokosz of M. Zebrzydowski
1617–29	First Swedish war
1620–1	First Turkish war: Cecora (1620), Chocim (1621)
1632–1648	Reign of Władysław IV Vasa
1634	Peace of Polanów with Muscovy
1635	Peace of Stumsdorf with Sweden
	Re-establishment of Orthodox hierarchy
1648–1668	Reign of Jan Kazimierz Vasa
1648–57	Chmielnicki's Revolt in Ukraine
1652	First *Liberum Veto*
1654–60	First Northern War, with Sweden. Peace of Oliva (1660)
1655–67	Muscovite War: Truce of Andrusovo (1667)
1657	Treaty of Wehlau: independence of Duchy of Prussia
1661	Merkuriusz Polski: first Polish newspaper
1665–7	Rebellion of Jerzy Lubomirski
1672	Second Turkish War
1674–1696	Reign of Jan Sobieski
1675	Treaty of Jaworów with France
1683	Siege of Vienna
1686	Grzymułtowski Peace (unratified) with Muscovy
1697–1764	Reign of Saxon Kings: August II (to 1733), August III (to 1764)
1700–21	Great Northern War
1704–10	Stanisław Leszczyński, elected King under Swedish protection
1717	Silent Sejm: start of Russian Protectorate
1724	Tumult of Thorn
1733–5	War of the Polish Succession
1747	Załuski Library opened to public
1764–1795	Reign of Stanisław-August Poniatowski
1768–72	Confederation of Bar
1772	First Partition of Poland

1780   Adam Naruszewicz's *Historiya Narodu Polskiego*
1788–92   Four Years' Sejm
1791   Constitution of 3 May
1792   Confederation of Targowica: Russo-Polish War
1793   Second Partition of Poland: last Sejm at Grodno
1794   Kościuszko's National Rising
1795   Third Partition of Poland: King's deportation and abdication

Part One
INTRODUCTION.
THE ORIGINS
TO 1572

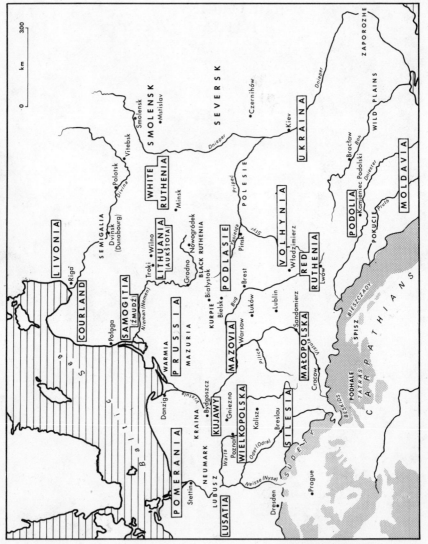

Map 1.   The Polish Lands

CHAPTER ONE

MILLENIUM

A Thousand Years of History

The earliest documentary record from that part of Europe which is now called Poland, dates from AD 965 to 966. In those years, Ibrahim-Ibn-Jakub, a Moorish Jew from Tortosa in Spain, accompanied the Khalif of Cordoba on an embassy to central Europe. He visited Prague, and possibly Cracow, which lay at the time within the kingdom of the Czechs. Fragments of his report were known to later Arab geographers:

The lands of the Slavs stretch from the Syrian Sea to the Ocean in the north ... They comprise numerous tribes, each different from the other ... At present, there are four kings: the king of the Bulgars; Bojeslav, King of Faraga, Boiema and Karako; Mesko, King of the North; and Nakon on the border of the West ...

As far as the realm of Mesko is concerned, this is the most extensive of their lands. It produces an abundance of food, meat, honey, and fish. The taxes collected by the King from commercial goods are used for the support of his retainers. He keeps three thousand armed men divided into detachments ... and provides them with everything they need, clothing, horses, and weapons ... The dowry system is very important to the Slavs, and is similar to the customs of the Berbers. When a man possesses several daughters or a couple of sons, the former become a source of wealth, the latter a source of great prestige.

In general, the Slavs are violent, and inclined to aggression. If not for the disharmony amongst them, caused by the multiplication of factions and by their fragmentation into clans, no people could match their strength. They inhabit the richest limits of the lands suitable for settlement, and most plentiful in means of support. They are specially energetic in agriculture ... Their trade on land and sea reaches to the Ruthenians and to Constantinople ...

Their women, when married, do not commit adultery. But a girl, when she falls in love with some man or other, will go to him and quench her lust. If a husband marries a girl and finds her to be a virgin, he says to her, 'If there were something good in you, men would have desired you, and you would certainly have found someone to take your virginity'. Then he sends her back, and frees himself from her.

The lands of the Slavs are the coldest of all. When the nights are moonlit and the days clear, the most severe frosts occur ... The wells and ponds are covered with a hard shell of ice, as if made of stone. When people breathe, icicles form on their beards, as if made of glass ...

They have no bath-houses as such, but they do make use of wooden huts (for bathing). They build a stone stove, on which, when it is heated, they pour water ... They hold a bunch of grass in their hands, and waft the steam around. Then their pores open, and all excess matter escapes from their bodies. This hut is called *al-istba*.

Their kings travel in great carriages, on four wheels. From the corners of the carriage a cradle is slung on chains, so that the passenger is not shaken by the motion. They prepare similar carriages for the sick and injured ...

The Slavs wage war with the Byzantines, with the Franks and Langobards, and with other peoples, conducting themselves in battle with varying success.[1]

Mieszko I, King of the North, or 'Mesko' as Ibrahim's Czech hosts called him, was understandably of special interest to the visitor from Spain. In that same year, when the Corbodan embassy arrived in Prague, Mieszko betrothed the Czech king's daughter, Dubravka, and took her to his Polish home in Poznań. In the following year, as part of the marriage agreement, he renounced the pagan religion of his ancestors, and was baptized into the Christian faith. Mieszko was in no sense a national monarch of the sort imagined by nineteenth-century romantics. He was chief of the *Polanie* or Polanians, one of the numerous Slav tribes of the period. He was a war-lord, whose fluctuating territory reflected little else but the ebb and flow of military success. He was as ready to plunder his various Slav neighbours as he was, on occasion, to make common cause with Germans or Czechs alike. Of all his feats, like those of his grandson Canute in Denmark and England, none but his baptism was permanent. By this one act, he brought his people into the world of western culture and Latin literacy. He prepared the way for the creation in the succeeding reign of the ecclesiastical province of Poland with its see at Gniezno. He started the recorded history of the Poles which has continued without a break from that day to this.

* * * * *

The events of a thousand years are as daunting to the historian who has to expound them, as to the reader who wants

to learn about them. They are too complex to be com-
prehended in bulk; and served in one lump, are entirely
indigestible. As a result, they are customarily divided into
chronological groups, or periods. For some historians, this
'periodization' is no more than an empirical exercise, like the
work of a chef who divides the meal into separate dishes,
arranging the ingredients according to his individual art and
the dictates of digestion. For others, it is a matter of high
seriousness, guided by the laws of philosophy and science. It
is one of the unavoidable tasks of the trade. The manner in
which it is undertaken reveals much, not only about History
but also about the historian.

The earliest writers on historical matters did not attempt
to periodize their subject. As chroniclers they are often dismissed as men whose fragments, fables, and ecclesiastical
tales 'abused the privilege of fiction'. In Poland, as elsewhere
in Europe, they were mainly learned clerics, writing in Latin
about the heroes of the Faith or the glories of the ruling
house. Gallus Anonimus, 'the Anonymous Gaul' (d. 1118),
was a Benedictine monk from France who related the reign
of Boleslaus the Wry-mouthed. Wincenty Kadłubek, also
known as Master Vincent (d. 1223), sometime student of the
Sorbonne and Bishop of Cracow, composed a chronicle on
the model of Livy, filling the considerable gaps in his knowledge with moral homilies or with recherché and entirely
inappropriate classical digressions. His terms of reference as
laid down by his patron, Casimir the Just, were 'to endow
posterity with the honesty of their ancestors'. Janko of
Czarnków, (d. 1387) was more political, detailing the events
of his own lifetime, and, as he saw it, the misdemeanours of
Louis of Anjou.[2]

Jan Długosz (Longinus, 1415–80), Canon of Cracow and
royal tutor, is often regarded as Poland's first historian. He
has also been described as the 'greatest medieval publicist',
using his vast literary output to defend the position and
privileges of the Church and clergy. He was one of the pioneers in collecting and recording historical sources, both
documentary and oral. He spent many years of his life touring the monastic libraries and cathedral chapters of the
country, copying manuscripts, and interviewing eyewitnesses

of prominent events. He was certainly one of the most endearing of chroniclers, and laced his learned panegyrics to the Polish kings with intimate, personal anecdotes. Of the twelfth-century monarch, Władysław II, for example, he tells how the Prince, preparing to bivouac in the forest, turned to his hunting companion with the words: 'It's as soft as for your lady with her knight', and received the reply: 'or for your queen with her bishop'. The twelve books of his *Historia Polonica* (Polish History) contain little sense of analysis. His aim, as he said, was simply 'to recover the memory of great men from their ashes'. He lived in a world where Causality was still ruled by Providence: where the concept of Progress had not been invented: and where History, as the science of the development of human affairs, would have been thought quite pointless. In the medieval view, mankind does not advance. Rather, with every year that passes, it retreats ever further from that original state of grace whose recovery is the only conceivable goal of our existence. Even so, Długosz was well aware that historical study has moral and didactic value. 'Unlike philosophy', he wrote, 'which merely arouses people and excites them, History . . . permits us to look, as through a mirror, on everything relating to heroism, wisdom, modesty, piety, and human folly.'[3]

The sixteenth-century chroniclers did not question earlier assumptions. Maciej Miechowita's *Chronica Polonorum* (Chronicle of the Poles) of 1519 continued Długosz's narrative up to his own day. The *Kronika wszystkiego świata* (Chronicle of the Whole World, 1551) of Marcin Bielski (1495–1575) was the earliest historical work composed in the Polish vernacular. The *Chronica Polonica* (Polish Chronicle, 1555) of Marcin Kromer (1512–89), Bishop of Warmia, was full of fables and fine illustrations, and was a best-seller.

The seventeenth and eighteenth centuries saw the art of the chronicler adorned with extravagant poetic flourishes and with increasing social interest. A justly renowned Polish translation of Tasso's *Gerusalemme Liberata,* published in 1618 by Piotr Kochanowski, nephew of the poet, set the style for numerous works of contemporary history. Samuel Twardowski (1600–60) recorded outstanding events in the reigns of the Vasa kings in 35,000 tredecimosyllabic verses.

The Arian, Wacław Potocki (1621–96), composed a lesser quantity of epic verse of still greater literary and historical value, notably in his *Wojna chocimska* (The War of Chocim, 1670). Wespazjan Kochowski (1633–1700) combined Polish psalmody with important work in Latin on current affairs. His *Annalium Poloniae . . . Climacter Primus* (1683), *Secundus* (1688), and *Tertius* (1698) contain a mine of detailed information on the political and international crises of his lifetime. The earlier Renaissance tradition of social comment and satire was developed by Szymon Starowolski (1588–1656), and by the two Opaliński brothers, Krzysztof (1610–56) and Łukasz (1612–84). Personal memoirs, rich in social and political observation, were written by Jan Pasek (1636–1701), Marcin Matuszewicz (d. 1784), and Jędrzej Kitowicz (1728–1804).

The first historians in the modern sense appeared during the Enlightenment, among them Adam Naruszewicz (1733–96), Bishop of Smolensk. Despite his episcopal dignity, he subjected the workings of Providence to critical examination and launched a campaign for the collection and publication of historical documents. Although he was preparing the ground for work on the whole of Polish History, his own six volumes of *Historia narodu polskiego* (A History of the Polish Nation), which began to appear in 1780, did not reach beyond the fourteenth century. As with other monarchists of the pre-nationalist era, he divided the past along dynastic lines. Naruszewicz identified the Piast Period from earliest times to 1386, the Jagiellonian Period from 1387 to 1572, and the period of Elective Monarchy from 1572 to his own day.[4] (See Diagram A.)

Naruszewicz died at the time when the Polish monarchy had just been destroyed, and his simple, monarchist outlook could not long satisfy his successors. His mantle was assumed in due course by a man of a completely different stamp. Joachim Lelewel (1786–1861) was an active republican, who in 1824 was removed by the Tsarist authorities from the Chair of History at Wilno. In 1830–1, he was a Minister in Warsaw in the insurrectionary government. Thereafter, he lived in exile in Brussels. In 1847, he was elected vice-president of an International Democratic Society, relinquishing his

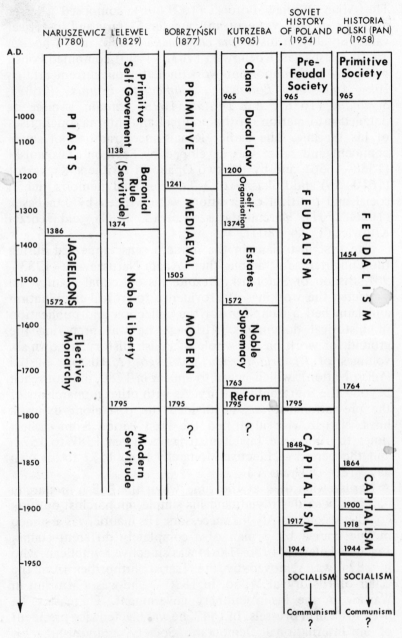

Diagram A.   Periodization Schemes of Polish History

office in the following year to Karl Marx. Like Marx, Lelewel's view of history contained a strong messianic streak, but with time assumed a much more bizarre and speculative character. He elaborated a theory of Slavic *'Gminowładstwo'* (communal self-government) whereby the Poles were seen to possess a natural predilection for democracy, and the whole of their history was interpreted as a struggle for freedom. Hence he divided Polish History into alternating periods of Liberty, and of Servitude. The first period, from earliest times to the Testament of Boleslaus the Wry-mouthed in 1138, was one of primitive self-government where the immemorial customs of the race were preserved by the rule of benevolent princes. In the second period from 1139 to the Statute of Košice of 1374, the Polish nation fell beneath the tyranny of baronial rule, thereby losing control of its destiny. From 1374 to the Third Partition of 1795, Liberty reasserted itself in the form of the Noble Democracy of the old Kingdom and Republic. The final period of Servitude was initiated by the Partitions, and lasted until the time when Lelewel was writing. Needless to say, Lelewel's historical scheme was closely allied to his political programme. His *Dzieje Polski potocznym sposobem opowiedziane* (Poland's Past Recounted in a Familiar Way, 1829) became a bible for the thousands of insurrectionaries and émigrés of his generation. In it, he described the role of the Polish nation as that of an 'ambassador to humanity', whose sufferings were meant to inspire the world and whose special mission demanded the rejection of worldly trappings and success. In short, he invented a historiosophical variant of Mickiewicz's allegory of Poland as the 'Christ among Nations'.[5]

Lelewel's theories proved particularly seductive for his contemporaries, and the disasters of two abortive Risings, in 1830 and in 1863, were needed before Polish historians were weaned away from them. In the interval, much of the pioneering work on Polish History was undertaken in Germany. Among the Poles, it was left to the Cracow School forming round the 'Stańczyk Group' of Józef Szujski (1835–83), Walerian Kalinka (1826–86), and Michał Bobrzyński (1849–1935) to bring the subject back to earth.[6]

Of all the Stańczyks, Bobrzyński perhaps did most to popularize their point of view. As Professor at the Jagiellonian

University he was a leading specialist in medieval law; and as
Governor of Galicia, he was one of the highest placed Poles in
the public life of his day. As author of *Dzieje Polski w zarysie*
(Poland's Past in Outline), which between 1877 in Cracow
and 1944 in Jerusalem ran through at least five editions, he
exercised considerable influence over the Polish reading
public. Among his many contributions, he realized that
periodization was an important and neglected subject, and
discussed it in a number of methodological articles. In his
own work, he adopted a common-sense scheme based mainly
on political considerations, and proposed three simple periods
— Primitive, Medieval, and Modern. He placed his dividing
lines at 1241, the date of the Mongol invasion; at 1505 with the
constitution of *Nihil Novi*; and finally at 1795 at the Third Partition. The Primitive Period was characterized by the patriarchal governments of tribal lords and early Piast dynasts; the
Medieval Period by the independent development of society;
and the Modern Period by the indefatigable struggle between
the adherents and the opponents of noble privilege.[7]

Bobrzyński's scheme led to a wave of polemics. 'Sub-
periods' and 'transitional periods' were proposed by those
who could not bear the arbitrariness of simple divisions. The
nature and the relevance of the 'turning-point' and the 'dividing line' were thoroughly examined. Szujski confined his
criticisms to the ineptness of Bobrzyński's scheme in the
realm of foreign affairs; whilst Tadeusz Wojciechowski
(1838–1919), Professor at Lemberg (Lwów) and the founding President of the Polish Historical Society (PTH), argued
that the Modern Period of Polish History should begin with
the outbreak of Chmielnicki's Rebellion in the Ukraine in
1648. In effect the most far-reaching revisions were proposed
by constitutional historians. Restricting their arguments to
the documents of Polish legal history, they were able to argue
their case more precisely than any of their rivals. The scheme
proposed by Stanisław Kutrzeba (1876–1946), Bobrzyński's
younger colleague at Cracow, as elaborated in his *Historia
ustroju Polski w zarysie* (History of Polish Government in
Outline, 1905), was one of the more cogent:

Up to AD 965   The Period of Tribal Organization
965–1200   The Period of Princely Law

1200–1374	The Period of Independent Jurisdictions
1374–1569	The Period of the Estates
1569–1763	The Period of Noble Supremacy
1764–1795	The Period of Reform.[8]

Methodological debates of this sort were taking place all over Europe at that time, and show that Polish scholars played their part in the establishment of History as a coherent academic discipline.

However, the work of the Stańczyk Group — who took their name from that of the mordant jester of King Sigismund I — also provoked discussions of more specific relevance to Polish affairs. The Group had come together in the years following the failure of the January Rising of 1863, and had made its initial impact by denouncing what appeared to them as the ridiculously romantic pretensions of the insurrectionaries. In particular, they attacked the notion that Poland's ills were exclusively due to foreign oppression, and urged their colleagues to examine the causes of Poland's own internal weakness. As Bobrzyński himself declared, 'We had no proper government, and that is the one and only cause of our collapse'. Szuyski attacked the motives of his contemporaries more directly. 'History is a surgeon for the fallen warrior', he wrote, 'not a nurse for the spoiled child'. In this way, the Stańczyks reserved their special brand of caustic wit for all who sought to romanticize Poland's past for the sake of modern insurrectionary politics. They compared the irresponsible Golden Freedom of the eighteenth-century nobility with the frivolous intrigues and self-righteous rhetoric of contemporary patriots. In their view, the *Liberum Veto* (the right of the individual to obstruct the will of the community as a whole), the *Liberum Conspiro* (the freedom to conspire against authority), and the *Liberum Defaecatio* (the right to vilify one's opponents) were all Polish traits in the same, unfortunate tradition. They held that the destruction of the old republic had occurred in the natural course of events, and that all attempts to revive it were pointless. In this sense, in their critical stance towards Poland's viability as an independent state, they were dubbed 'Pessimists'. The reaction against them gained ground in the 1880s, and continued to develop until the First World War.

Under the leadership of Tadeusz Korzon (1839–1918) and Władysław Smoleński (1851–1926), the Warsaw Positivists subjected the findings of the Cracovian School to detailed examination, and produced some strikingly different conclusions.[9] Korzon's *Dzieje wewnętrzne Polski za Stanisława-Augusta* (Poland's Internal History under Stanisław-August, 1880–6) and Smoleński's writings on the Polish Enlightenment contrived to stress Poland's economic and cultural achievements in the era of political failure. In Cracow, Kalinka diverged from his Stańczyk colleagues, believing like De Tocqueville in France that the destruction of the *Ancien Régime* was provoked by the very success of Reform. In their separate ways, they all stressed that Poland's tragedies had not been caused exclusively by her own failings. To that extent, they gave encouragement to people who were working for a national, political revival, and deserved their label of 'Optimists'. Korzon's *Historiya nowożytna* (Modern History, 1889) treated Polish affairs as an integral part of European developments, contrasting sharply with Bobrzyński's both in tone and in substance.[10] These rivalries, between the Pessimists and the Optimists, have continued to dominate Polish historiography from that day to this.[11]

The same positivist era laid the foundations of Polish History as a modern science. The systematic collection and publication of source materials, first started by Bishop Naruszewicz, reached impressive proportions. Archives, museums, and historical libraries – among them the Archiwum Akt Dawnych (Archive of Ancient Records, 1867) in Warsaw, the Czartoryski Collection in Cracow, and the Kórnik and Raczyński Libraries in Posnania – opened their doors, in each of the Partitions. Work began on historical bibliography, notably under the aegis of Ludwig Finkel (1858–1930) at Lwów, and on all the auxiliary sciences from palaeography and archaeology to genealogy, heraldry, and numismatics. The senior historical journals, the *Kwartalnik Historyczny* (Historical Quarterly, 1887) first edited in Lwów by Ksawery Liske (1838–91) and the *Przegląd Historyczny* (Historical Review) in 1909, began long uninterrupted careers, as did the main series of documentary collections such as the *Monumenta Poloniae Historica,* the *Kodeks Dyplomatyczny Polski,* and the *Scriptores Rerum Polonicarum.* Medieval History flourished in the writings of Stanisław Smolka (1854–1924), Tadeusz Wojciechowski (1838–1919), Karol Potkański (1861–1907), Franciszek Piekosiński (1844–1906), and, of course, of Bobrzyński. Constitutional history attracted the attention not only of Kutrzeba, but also of Oswald Balzer (1858–1933), Adolf Pawiński (1840–96), and Aleksandr Rembowski (1847–1906). Korzon explored the realm of historical demography, statistics, and economy. Smoleński pioneered intellectual history and political ideas.

None of the historians writing before the First World War knew what to make of the nineteenth century. For them, it was contemporary history, and for the censors of the ruling Empires, current affairs. It was at once, dangerously political, and scientifically problematical. Without knowing the outcome of the national struggle which was still in progress, it was impossible to know whether the Partitions had spelt the end of Polish History as a separate subject or not. In the absence of a Polish state, it was difficult to give Polish History any organic structure. Not until the reappearance of the Polish Republic in 1918 could historians regard the period of Partition as a temporary, if somewhat extended, interruption of the thousand-year continuum of the Polish state. In the era of Nationalism, which in Eastern Europe persists to the present day, the permanent existence of the nation, irrespective of political institutions, has never been seriously challenged.

In the interwar period from 1918 to 1939, the surviving mandarins of the Cracovian and Varsovian Schools were joined by a variety of scholars who defy simple classification. Szymon Askenazy (1866–1935) at Lwów, and his younger disciple in diplomatic history at Warsaw, Marceli Handelsman (1882–1945), together with Jan Rutkowski (1886–1949) at Poznań in economic history, commanded influential followings in the profession. But the over-all picture was essentially pluralistic, and by the outbreak of the Second World War no general consensus concerning the interpretation of Polish History had been established, nor indeed attempted. After the war, prominent scholars such as Oscar Halecki (1890–1976), Marian Kukiel (1885–1976), and Władysław Pobóg-

Malinowski (1899–1962) continued their studies in emigration. Halecki's *History of Poland,* written in 1942 from a Catholic and nationalist standpoint, was one of the very few surveys of the subject to be addressed to a foreign readership.[12] Kukiel's *Dzieje Polski porozbiorowej* (History of Post-partition Poland), covers the period from 1795 to 1864.[13] Pobóg-Malinowski's *Najnowsza historia polityczna Polski* (Contemporary Polish Political History, 3 vols. 1959–60), written from a political position close to that of Józef Piłsudski, covers the period since 1864.[14]

With the advent of the People's Republic, historiography in Poland was transformed. In the words of Lenin on a previous occasion, 'Chaos and arbitrariness, which had heretofore dominated people's views on history and politics gave way to an astonishingly uniform and harmonious scientific theory.' The theory in both cases was Lenin's own version of Marx's historical materialism. In 1948, at the First General Congress of Polish Historians, Marxism—Leninism was installed as the sole ideological guide to all investigations into Poland's past. Henceforth, Polish society was to be seen as the object of a dialectical process, which, by the inherent tensions of its contrary elements, propelled itself forward inexorably from one stage of development to the next. At any particular moment, the involuntary struggle of 'progressive' and 'reactionary' forces advanced from crisis to crisis, as the old order was undermined, and replaced by the new: and thus ever upward in the dizzy spiral of progress towards the last blissful Rose of Communism.

Marxism—Leninism offered several substantive attractions to Polish historians. Quite apart from its political convenience, it promised to supply that sense of organic continuity which had hitherto been signally lacking. It promised to interpret the history of the Poles on the same basis as that of neighbouring nations, and thus to soothe their wounded pride. It promised to justify the emergence of the People's Republic as a natural stage on Poland's bumpy road to Communism, and thus to calm the chronic insecurity of the new authorities. It promised to banish the concepts of guilt and of individual responsibility, and to explain the horrors of the recent past as the necessary trials of the nation's progress towards a better future. Above all, it accepted the nation as a permanent and objective reality. In its own special way it combined the Messianism of the Romantics, the Realism of the Stańczyks, the Positivism of the Varsovians, and the Nationalism of them all. For these reasons, it stood to heal and anaesthetize and was readily adopted by a whole generation of scholars who had little ultimate faith in the validity of its precepts.

Yet the Marxification of History in Poland was no easy matter. For one thing, apart from the tiny Association of Marxist Historians founded in 1948 by Arnold, Jabłoński, and Bobińska, there were virtually no native Marxists. A whole generation had to be schooled from scratch by foreign Soviet mentors. For another, the schooling had to proceed in the context of Stalinism, where genuine ideological concern was shamelessly subordinated to immediate political considerations. History was to be used as a blunt political instrument with which the enemies of the regime could be bludgeoned. As Professor Arnold explained at the First Methodological Conference of Polish Historians at Otwock in December 1951, 'the only scientific approach to historical problems is . . . to treat them as a most terrible ideological weapon directed against the rulers of Wall Street.'[15] Worst of all, the specific characteristics of Polish History did not lend themselves easily to existing models of Marxist or Soviet historiography. The weakness of slavery in early Polish society, for example, made it extremely difficult to adopt Engels's scheme of pre-feudal developments. The scarcity of revolutions prior to the seventeenth century made it difficult to be precise about the emergence of Feudalism; whilst the superabundance of violent eruptions in the subsequent period presented an entirely baffling proliferation of socio-economic diversions during the emergence of Capitalism. The absence of a sovereign Polish state between 1795 and 1918 prevented any simple adoption of Russian models, where the role of the state had always received special prominence. From the Marxist point of view it would have been entirely respectable to attribute the Partitions to 'unhistoric forces'. But from the reigning political point of view this was unthinkable, since the expanded territorial base of the Russian Empire, as established by the Partitions and inherited by the USSR, was the principal 'socialist achievement' which the People's Republic and the new Polish History were now required to defend. In consequence, it is not surprising that the Academy of Sciences of the USSR was able to complete a 'History of Poland' long before Polish historians could agree on a synthesis of their own.

The Soviet *Istoriya Pol'shi*, published between 1954 and 1965, is in many ways a remarkable achievement, not least since it confirms that Poland has a continuous historic existence. (Had it been commissioned a few years earlier, there is little doubt it would have proved the opposite.) In general, it applies the standard Five Stage Scheme, identifying Primitive, Feudal, Capitalist, Socialist, and Communist stages of development. But some of its chosen turning-points — at 965, 1795, 1848, 1917, 1944 — are most eccentric. The year 1848, for example, is notable for the fact that the Polish lands were not seriously involved in the excitements besetting almost all the surrounding countries. It is a crucial date in German History, and in the Marxist movement, but not, unfortunately, in Poland. So to make it the starting-point of the Capitalist stage in Polish History is slightly odd. 1917 is equally inappropriate. It is a notorious fact that the Great October Revolution in Russia did not arouse much immediate response in Poland, and that the Polish nation conspicuously resisted the attempts in 1919–20 to impose the Bolshevik system. In Poland, 1918 was an important date, as was 1939 and 1945, but not 1917.[16]

In Poland itself, the argument over periodization has lasted from the 1950s to the present day. The starting-point was Professor Arnold's project presented at Otwock:

1. Epoch of the Primitive Community (to 5th Century AD)
2. Epoch of Feudalism (5th Century AD – 1864)
   A. Period of the emergence of feudal conditions (5th–10th centuries)
   B. Period of early Feudalism (*c*. 1000–1138)
   C. Period of feudal fragmentation (1138–1288/90)
   D. Period of the unification of Polish lands, and of the creation of a national Polish state (1288/1290–1370)
   E. Period of transformation into a multinational state (1370–1492/1505)

    F. Period of the final formation of the feudal serf-owning, multi-national, noble Republic (1492/1505–1572)

    G. Period of the growth of the role of the magnatial oligarchy, and of its decentralizing tendency (1573–1648)

    H. Period of disintegration of the feudal serf-owning Republic (1648–1740)

    I. Period of the beginnings of the capitalist system and of the fall of the noble Republic (1740–95)

    J. Period of national-liberation struggles and of the class struggle of the Polish peasantry in conditions of developing Capitalism (1796–1864)

3. Epoch of Capitalism (1864–1944)

    A. Period of pre-monopolistic Capitalism (1864–1900)

    B. Period of increase of imperialist features (1900–18)

    C. Period of the Great October Socialist Revolution as the source of Polish Independence (1917/18)

    D. Period of the bourgeois-squirearchical Polish Republic (1918–39)

    E. Period of the Second World War (1939–45)

4. Epoch of Socialism (1944–   )[17]

Arnold's project pleased nobody. It displeased the Soviet guests at the conference who, insisting on a closer correlation between the socio-economic 'base' and the constitutional 'superstructure', wanted to place much greater emphasis on the chief dates in the history of the state. But it also displeased his Polish colleagues. They criticized his terminology which preferred 'epoch' and 'period' for the more usual 'period' and 'sub-period'. The criticized his breakdown of the Feudal Period into nine parts, where standard practice favoured a tripartite division into 'emergence', 'stabilization', and 'decline'. Above all, they criticized his neglect of 'regionalization', that is, the problem of adjusting any over-all scheme of Polish History to the experiences of provinces like Silesia or Pomerania which had never formed part of the modern Polish state. Although Arnold was a medievalist, his suggestions for the Feudal Period proved less acceptable than those for the 'Epoch of Capitalism'. Apart from his fatuous inclusion of the Russian Revolution as a separate period of Polish History, his outline for the 'Epoch of Capitalism' is not too dissimilar from the one in use today.

    The genuine Marxists, as distinct from the Stalinist hacks, did not really find their feet until the late 1950s. At the

Historical Congress of 1958, a new generation of historians launched a determined attack against the spurious practices of the recent past. By a decision of the Congress, the Institute of History of the Polish Academy of Sciences was authorized to accelerate publication of its own definitive, multi-volume 'History of Poland'. The main lines of the Academy's *'Historia Polski'* were drawn by an editorial committee council under the late Tadeusz Manteuffel (1902–70). In this version, the 'Epoch of Feudalism' takes over from 'Pre-feudal Society' in AD 965, and lasts to 1864, occupying nine-tenths of recorded history. It is divided into four periods – 'Early Feudalism' to 1200; 'The full bloom of Feudalism' to 1550; 'The entrenchment of the Manorial-Serfdom system' from the mid-fifteenth century to 1764; and 'The Liquidation of the Feudal system' to 1864. 'The Capitalist Epoch' runs for eighty years from 1864 to 1944. This again seems destined for a fourfold division. In the volumes which have so far appeared, 'The Time of Laissez-Faire Capitalism 1850/64–1900' and 'The Stage of Imperialism, 1900–18' have been identified. It is obvious, however, that an agonizing debate is still in progress behind the scenes. In Marxist usage, terms such as *'ugruntowanie'* (entrenchment) or *'rozkwit'* (burgeoning) may aptly convey a correct sense of delight for states of impermanence. At the same time they disclose a definite reluctance to make clear-cut, interpretative decisions. Omissions speak loudest of all. Although twenty years and more have passed since the series was announced, the long-awaited volumes on the contemporary period are constantly delayed. Little has appeared in relation to events in the last forty years. The Polish student has still no authoritative guide to the decades which interest him most. The gestation of just one section of one volume has lasted three times longer than the historical period under discussion. The first editorial meeting to prepare the first section of Volume IV, covering 1918–21, was held on 7 February 1957. This led to the publication in 1966 of an unbound 'dummy' which was later withdrawn. The section was finally brought forth in 1970, after a mountain of revision. At this rate, the chapters dealing with the Second World War can be expected as from AD 2024. Undoubtedly, the labour pains are partly caused by continuing ideological qualms. But they are compounded by extraneous political interference.[18]

Most recently, in 1976, another scholarly synthesis of Polish History has been produced by a team of authors. This 'showpiece of Polish historiography' as one reviewer has called it, represents a very considerable achievement in view of the problems involved. But the high-powered, theoretical introduction of its editor stands in marked contrast to the feeble application of his theories in the body of the work, especially in relation to the contemporary period. Though not an official enterprise, it betrays all the traits and omissions of official ideology and of latter-day Polish Nationalism, and is likely to be viewed in the future as a competent but stereo-typed product of its day.[19]

*   *   *   *   *

In the early 1960s, History was again enjoying wide popularity in Poland. The country was still basking in the afterglow of Gomułka's October. The Stalinist nightmare had passed. The air of gloom and shame which Stalinism had injected into everything connected with Poland's independent past, was quickly dispelled. Pessimism gave way to Optimism, and distant events with the most specious relevance to the present were celebrated on the slightest pretext. Historical anniversaries came into vogue. Everyone knew that the biggest anniversary of all was due in 1966. It was awaited with fervent expectation.

The Roman Catholic Church was particularly well prepared, especially since Polish celebrations would coincide with a Roman Holy Year. Preparations had begun in 1957 with a Great Novena, the nine-year period of prayer and fasting. In 1966 itself, the Cardinal-Primate, Stefan Wyszyński, toured the entire country, province by province. Starting in Gniezno, the cradle of Polish Christianity, on 14 April, he proceeded to Częstochowa on 3 May, to Kraków on 8 May, to Warsaw on 26 June, to Katowice, Gdańsk, Wrocław, Lublin, Białystok, Toruń. Everywhere he was greeted by tens and hundreds of thousands of people, by delegations of miners in uniform, by processions of men, women and children, by girls in regional costume, by crowds upon crowds, standing in the rain or kneeling by the roadside. Never, before or since, has anyone in the People's Republic enjoyed such a massive display of devotion. Every church in Poland displayed the banner 'SACRUM POLONIAE MILLENIUM, 966–1966' (Poland's Sacred Millennium) together with the traditional slogans of 'DEO ET PATRIAE' (For God and Country); 'POLONIA SEMPER FIDELIS' (Poland Always Faithful); or 'NARÓD Z KOŚCIOŁEM' (The Nation is with the Church). In St. Peter's at Rome on 15 May 1966, Pope Paul, assisted by the Cardinal-Primate's Delegate, Bishop Władysław Rubin, celebrated pontifical mass in honour of the Polish Province. In Santa Maria Maggiore, in San Andrea al Quirinale, at Monte Cassino, in Glasgow Cathedral, at Lens in the Pas-de-Calais, in Detroit, anywhere and everywhere which has Polish connections, Polish Catholics gathered to make witness of their Faith. In his sermon at Gniezno, Cardinal Wyszyński made this appeal: 'It is my earnest desire that you take a hard look at the Past and the Present, and, having learned to love the history of this Christian nation, that you will see the (present) reality of its Catholicity with open eyes.'[20] The response was overwhelming.

Not to be outdone, the State-and-Party authorities made preparations of their own. The Sejm of the People's Republic proclaimed the period 1960–6 to be a 'jubilee of Polish statehood and culture'. Archaeological digs were accelerated at Gniezno, Kalisz, Wiślica, and elsewhere, to illuminate the shady state of knowledge on life in Mieszko's realm. Processions were staged to emphasize 'the patriotic and progressive traditions of the Polish people across the ages'. Learned societies held open meetings to discuss the significance of dates and events. Youth organizations launched a huge, voluntary effort to build 'a thousand schools for the thousand years'; and the target was surpassed. Anniversary celebrations proliferated. In 1960, the 550th anniversary of the Battle of Grunwald was celebrated (though not the fortieth anniversary of the Battle of Warsaw). In 1961, the 300th anniversary of the first Polish newspaper, *Merkuriusz Polski,* was acclaimed together with the birth of the Press. In 1962, the 350th anniversary of the Polish occupation of the Kremlin was given a miss. But in 1963, there was the centenary of the January Rising; in 1964 the sexcentenary of the Jagiellonian University, Poland's senior seat of learning, and the Twentieth

Anniversary of the People's Republic; and in 1965 the Twentieth Anniversary of the Liberation. Finally on 1 May 1966 all the state-and-party organs participated in country-wide rallies, receiving the congratulations of fraternal parties and foreign well-wishers, whilst staging colossal processions, marches, reviews, and dancing in the streets.

Amidst the general rejoicing, it would have been churlish to question the exact object of the celebrations too closely. Yet, it was clear all along that no general agreement existed as to what the Millennium (or 'Millenium', as the Poles will have it) really meant. The Church was celebrating a thousand years of Christianity. As the introduction to its anniversary album declared: 'it all began with a christening.' For the Church, the baptism of Mieszko I was all-important. It was a religious, an ecclesiastical occasion. The state-and-party authorities, in contrast, were mounting a purely secular and political demonstration. For them, 'Millenium', with its Romish overtones, was not acceptable. For official purposes the vernacular calque of *Tysiąclecie* was preferred. Whilst the banners on the churches read 'SACRUM POLONIAE MILLENIUM', civic buildings and the streets were festooned with the slogan 'TYSIĄCLECIE PAŃSTWA POLSKIEGO' (A Thousand Years of the Polish State). 'DEO ET PATRIAE' was matched by 'SOCJA-LIZM I OJCZYZNA' (Socialism and Fatherland), 'NARÓD Z KOŚCIOŁEM' by 'PARTIA Z NARODEM' (The Party is with the Nation), 'POLONIA SEMPER FIDELIS' by 'SOCJALIZM GWARAN-CJA POKOJU I GRANIC' (The Communist Regime is the Guarantee of Peace and Frontiers). In the Western Territories gained from Germany in 1945, the banners proclaimed such messages as 'A THOUSAND YEARS OF POLAND ON THE ODRA' or 'A THOUSAND YEARS OF POLAND ON THE BALTIC' — both plain mis-statements of fact.

For the historian, the use to which his subject is put by politicians, both clerical and communist, is not without interest. To the impartial observer, the Roman Catholic identification of Church and Nation in the past is as specious as the communists' habit of identifying Party and People today. Both Church and Party live by dogmas of authority and infallibility, and both conceal the full nature of their complicated relationship with the population as a whole. Once the Millennium was in prospect, both were bound to launch rival, and mutually exclusive, interpretations of its significance.

In the decade since the Millennium, Polish historians have resolved few of their problems. According to the official jargon, the People's Republic is still building Communism in its own Polish way. It is still in the socialist stage of development, but unlike Czechoslovakia or Romania has not cared to raise its status to that of a 'Socialist Republic'. The emphasis on Foreign Trade, the strong military establishment, and, arguably, the mores of Polish youth, are much as they were in the time of Ibrahim-Ibn-Jakub. (The dowry system and sauna baths have disappeared without trace.) The Academy's *Historia Polski* is still incomplete. The official Marxist–Leninist ideology is constantly eroded. A historiographical consensus lies teasingly out of reach. Extraneous interference continues unabated.[21] In this situation, two alternative prospects arise. Either Polish historians will be overtaken by the arrival of Communism before their present task is complete, and, together with the State and the Party, will wither away; or else, more probably, like every other generation of scholars, they will soon be obliged to rewrite Polish History from the beginning, all over again.[22]

CHAPTER TWO
POLSKA:
The Polish Land

Few people have doubted that Poland's geography is the villain of her history. Trapped in the middle of the North European Plain, with no natural frontier to parry the onslaughts of more powerful neighbours, Poland has fought an unequal battle for survival against Germany and Russia. (Poland has been variously described as 'the disputed bride', condemned forever to lie between the rival embraces of two rapacious suitors; or, more cruelly, as 'the gap between two stools'.) An unfortunate geopolitical location is invoked to explain the Partitions of the eighteenth century, the abortive Risings of the nineteenth, and the catastrophe of the Second Republic in the twentieth. As one Polish officer was heard to exclaim in London in 1940, when told that the Allied Governments did not intend to fight both Hitler and Stalin simultaneously, 'Then *we* shall fight Geography!'

Surely, it is argued, the North European Plain, stretching unbroken from the French Atlantic to the Russian Urals, must have affected the states which developed on its seemingly featureless expanses. It offers no protection whatsoever – no obstacles to the movement of peoples or to the progress of armies. It makes for constant insecurity. It encourages raids, invasions, and annexations. It has meant that major territorial changes could be produced by the minor variations in the balance of power, and that states could expand or contract faster and further than anywhere else in Europe. The Polish state was no exception. From a nucleus between the Odra (Oder) and Vistula Rivers, it expanded in moments of strength with great rapidity, reaching the Baltic, the Dnieper, the Black Sea, and the Carpathians. Similarly, in times of weakness, it shrank alarmingly. In 1492, the territory of Poland–Lithuania, not counting the fiefs of Mazovia, Moldavia, or East Prussia, covered 1,115,000 km² or 435,547 square miles. In 1634, at the Treaty of Polanów, with

990,000 km² or 386,719 square miles, it was still the largest territory in Europe, slightly larger than European Muscovy and nearly twice the size of France. With almost 11 million inhabitants, its population was inferior only to France and Muscovy. Yet by 1686 at 733,500 km² (286,524 square miles) it had already fallen to third place; by 1773 to 522,300 km² (204,024 square miles), and by 1793 to 215,000 km² (84,000 square miles),.the size of Great Britain. In 1795, it vanished completely. In various nineteenth-century reincarnations, the Duchy of Warsaw between 1807 and 1813 occupied about 154,000 km² (60,157 square miles), the Congress Kingdom between 1815 and 1874 about 127,000 km² (49,609 square miles). At its first twentieth-century reincarnation, between 1921 and 1938, the Polish Republic occupied 389,720 km² (152,234 square miles) and fifth place in Europe. Since 1945, on a more westerly base, it has occupied 312,677 km² (122,139 square miles) and sixth place in Europe. Unlike the English, who could always retreat behind the Channel and their Navy, unlike the Spaniards or Italians on their self-contained peninsulas, unlike the Swiss amid their Alps or the Dutch behind their dykes, the Poles have had nowhere to hide. Their state has been exposed to every ebb and flow of political power in modern Europe, and the tides have left it alternately stranded and submerged. (See Map 2.)

In view of these violent changes, it is impossible to talk of 'the Polish lands' without regard to the fourth dimension. Despite the Poles' own fervent belief in the *macierz* or 'motherland', it is impossible to identify any fixed territorial base which has been permanently, exclusively, and inalienably, Polish. The Polish *macierz* has not always corresponded to reality, and has often stood in sharp conflict with similar German and Russian fictions concerning the limits and extent of 'the German soil' or of 'our Russian land'. At various times in Eastern Europe, the Polish state has been everywhere and nowhere. Its territory, like the settlement patterns, cultural alignment, and ethnic mix of its population, has been subject to continual transformations. Poland has been a butterfly, gone today but here tomorrow, flitting from one mode of existence to the next. In the terminology of the Prussian historians who first expounded East Central Europe

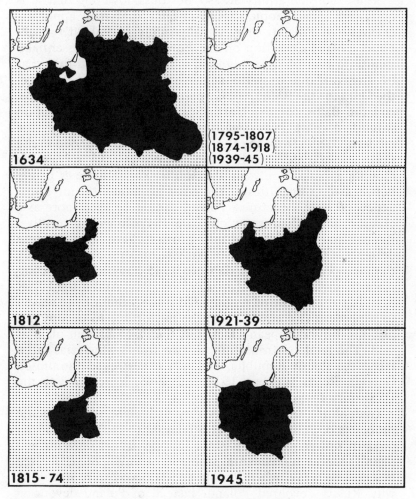

Map 2.   Poland's Changing Territory

to the world at large, Poland was a *Saisonstaat,* a 'seasonal state'.

These considerations are so obvious, however, that it is odd why some people should imagine that they apply exclusively to Poland. They equally apply to Poland's neighbours. Poland's position on the European plain is essentially similar to that of Germany, and is no less exposed than that of Russia. If one were to exchange the Vistula for the Elbe, the Odra for the Rhine, the Carpathians for the Bavarian Alps, and the Baltic for the North Sea, the geopolitical situation would not have been significantly changed. Similarly, the modern USSR, from the Bug to the Ussuri, is bounded in the north by a cold, hostile sea and possesses a serviceable mountain barrier only in the south. So, if there *is* a link between the geopolitics of the great plains and the impermanency of state structures, Poland should be seen more as a classic example than as a unique case. In the longer perspective, the rise and fall of Poland may prove to have been no more dramatic than the history of Prussia or Muscovy. After all, the disappearance of Prussia since 1945 has been more complete than that of Poland in 1795 or 1939. And if the USSR is still at the height of its imperial power, there is no reason to suppose it is eternal. It has the misfortune to occupy not just the tiny European Plain, but the vast Eurasian plain as well. The fatal confrontation on two fronts which has often faced the Polish Republic, and which destroyed the united German Reich between 1914 and 1945, is now facing the USSR on a far grander scale.

Geopolitics, in fact, throws very little light on the specific problems of Polish History. It is relevant to the history of the modern power game in Eastern Europe. But it does not explain the more fundamental problems of why in the first place Poland was weak, when Prussia and Muscovy were strong, or why Russia devoured Poland, instead of Poland devouring Russia. It cannot illuminate the main characteristics of Polish life and institutions.

*　*　*　*　*

When Vidal de la Blanche in his famous 'Tableau de la France' concluded that France was characterized by variety, he was guilty of a Gallicism. For variety can be discerned in the physiognomy of most countries, and especially in those which are constructed from numerous, distinct provinces, each with a life and a past of its own. This was certainly true in the case of historic Poland whose unity proved weaker than the centrifugal tendencies of its many regions. (See Map 1.)

The heartland provinces of predominantly Polish settlement are situated between the Odra and Vistula Rivers. It was here that one branch of the Western Slavs first established itself in the seventh and eighth centuries, and as *Polanie,* (Polanians) or 'people of the open fields', engendered the forebears of the nation who are now known as Poles. Their country, *Polska,* centred on the lakeland region round Gniezno, was later called Wielkopolska or 'Greater Poland' to distinguish it from the southerly extension of their realm into Małopolska or 'Lesser Poland'.

Wielkopolska (Polonia Maior) is drained by the River Warta flowing westwards into the Odra with the water from more than a thousand lakes. It is open country, with broad expanses of meadowland in the valleys separated by rolling tracts of forest. Its soils are fertile, especially on the black earth of its eastern reaches. In early times, both agriculture and communication were easy. Apart from Gniezno, the main cities were Poznań, founded in the tenth century as a riverbank fortress, and ancient Kalisz, mentioned by Ptolemy. The population has a quite undeserved reputation for stolid, humourless efficiency.

Małopolska (Polonia Minor), centred on Cracow, backs against the sub-alpine ridge of the Carpathians. In addition to the high Tatras of Podhale in the south, it carries several upland chains — the Beskidy in the west, the limestone peaks of the Cracovian Jura and the Holy Cross Range in the north, the Roztocza in the east. In between the hills, lie long stretches of fertile lowland among them the Podgórze region, and the valleys of the Vistula and the San. The *górale* (Highlanders) are akin to the Slovaks on the other flank of the mountains, to the former Ukrainian Hutsul and Bojko clans of the Bieszczady, and to the Romanian mountaineers to the east. The hills are rich in minerals, including iron, salt, oil, and now uranium. The lowlands are eminently suitable for cultiva-

tion. The southern valleys produce fruit and wine. The cities
— Cracow, Sandomierz, Lublin, Kielce — are among the most
ancient in Poland. In the countryside, before the recent
advent of modern industry, natural advantages created severe
over-population. In the long period of Austrian domination,
Małopolska formed the western half of Galicia.

Mazowsze (Mazovia) on the middle Vistula has always been
relatively backward. Gravelly soils, morainic deposits, and
poor drainage have inhibited agriculture, leaving wide expanses of heath and scrubland. The province has no natural
resources of note, and its poverty-stricken nobles and peasantry
traditionally provided large numbers of emigrants and
colonists. Its chief city, Warsaw, was raised to distinction for
reasons of convenience, not achievement. Mazovia did not
form an integral part of the Kingdom of Poland until 1529.

Kujawy (Cuiavia), linking Mazowsze with Wielkopolska, is
flat terrain cluttered with glacial remains. Spidery lakes fill
the morainic depressions. Some of the soils, of the so-called
'black marsh' variety, are productive. Poland's oldest town
Kruszwica, huddles on the bank of Gopło, one of its largest
lakes. Bydgoszcz (Bromberg) grew up on the canals and roads
of the east—west throughway.

This Polish heartland is ringed by a circle of provinces
whose associations with the centre have been somewhat elastic.

Śląsk (Silesia, Schlesien), in the valley of the Odra, has a
markedly independent personality. By the early twentieth
century, its ancient connection with Poland, severed in 1339,
had almost been effaced through incorporation in Bohemia
and Austria, and from 1740 in Prussia. Lower Silesia, bounded
in the west by the Sudety mountains, is rural, farming country.
Upper Silesia lies on a high bleak plateau richer in minerals
than in scenic attractions. Until 1945, Wrocław (Breslau) and
the industrial towns round Katowice (Kattowitz) had a strong
German character. In the southern districts, the peasantry,
and in due course the proletariat, were Slavs, who as often as
not considered themselves Silesian rather than Polish.

Pomorze (Pomerania, Pommern) can boast similar Slav
origins, though it, too, has spent most of its career in the
German orbit. The German name of *Pommern,* though derived
from the Slav *Pomorze,* meaning 'By the Sea', does not refer

to exactly the same area.* In Polish usage, all of Western Pomerania lies to the east of the Odra. The area further to the east, centred on Danzig, has been variously called *Pomerellen* (Little Pomerania) and Eastern Pomerania, as well as Royal Prussia, and West Prussia. The damp, inhospitable coastline sheltered small communities of fishermen. The interior, swathed in woods of pine and beech, is pleasant to look at but hard to work. The chief cities, Szczecin (Stettin) and Gdańsk (Danzig), were distinctly German in flavour until their reincorporation into Poland in 1945.

Prusy (Borussia, Prussia, Preussen) was the poorest province of all. A land of dark forests and dark lakes on the bleak Baltic shore, it suffered from every possible disadvantage. (The name of the spruce tree is supposed to derive from the Polish words *z Prus* 'from Prussia'.) The western part astride the delta of the Vistula, including the district of Warmia (Ermeland), overlapped with Pomerania and, as 'Royal Prussia', was joined to the Polish Kingdom from 1466 to 1772. The eastern part, ruled from Koenigsberg, remained in the control of the Teutonic Order until 1525, and as 'Ducal Prussia', was a Polish *fief* until 1657. For much of its existence it was remote, unproductive and undesirable. Under the House of Hohenzollern, it formed one of the two elements of the state of Brandenburg—Prussia, and from 1700 of their 'Kingdom in Prussia'. The population consisted very largely of German colonists and germanized Balts. In modern times, the southern region of Mazury (Mazuria) formed a transitional area adjoining the anciently Polish Mazowsze.

Podlasie (Podlasia), too, is a threshold province. Heavily glaciated and wooded, it includes the vast forest of Białowieża, and divides central Poland from Byelorussia and Lithuania. The southern area, between the Vistula and the Bug, is cattle country. The northern reaches in the Kurpie wilderness were sparsely settled by hunters and fishermen. The urban centres included Białystok, Grodno, Bielsk, and Łuków.

Polesie (Polesia), popularly known as the Pripet Marshes, was a province where time stood still. Swamps mingled with oak groves and lush meadows. Social and economic develop-

---

* German usage prefered the terms *Vorpommern* (Hither Pomerania) to the west of the Odra: and *Hinterpommern* (Farther Pomerania) or *Slavinia* to the east.

ment was as slow as the current of the Pripet, which falls less than 200 feet in over three hundred miles. It is fine duck-shooting country, where primitive people lived for centuries beyond the ken of the outside world. Its one town of note, Pinsk, became almost ninety per cent Jewish.

Wołyń (Volhynia) and Podole (Podolia) were essentially rural provinces. Volhynia is crossed by a great strip of loess, on which wheat and maize grow with alacrity, Podolia by a high plateau reminiscent of the treeless steppes to the east. Towns and hamlets sought shelter from the cold east wind in deeply eroded valleys. The district of Pokucie on the Dniester boasts orchards and vineyards. Traditionally these were areas where the Ruthenian peasantry was dominated by great Polish landowners. They were joined piecemeal to the Kingdom of Poland between 1430 and 1569.

In the south-east, lay Ruś Czerwona (Red Ruthenia), with its city of Lwów (Lviv, Léopol, Lemberg). Incorporated into the Kingdom in 1340, it never lost its marcher character. The fervent loyalism of the Polish element reflected their constant insecurity in face of Tartar raids, Turkish invasions, and a restive Ruthenian peasantry. The gentle landscapes stand in marked contrast to its disturbed history.

Ukraina (Ukraine) straddled the middle Dnieper. As its name suggests, it lay 'on the edge' of Christendom, and of fixed settlement. In the early centuries its phenomenal natural wealth and matchless soil could not be developed for fear of constant wars and incursions. In 1569, when it passed to the Polish Kingdom, it was divided into the palatinates of Kiev, Bracław, and Czernihów, and merged into the virtually unadministered expanses of the *Dzikie Pola* (Wild Plains) and the *Zaporozhe*. It was populated by Cossacks, fugitives, colonists, and in safer areas by free Ruthenian peasants. Its chief city, Kiev, centre of the ancient Ruś, together with the left-bank lands was conquered by Muscovy in 1662. The remainder was annexed by the Russian Empire in the course of the eighteenth century, since when the name of Ukraine has been extended to include all Ruthenian lands south of the Pripet.

Ukraine, in common with neighbouring provinces, was joined to Poland in consequence of its earlier association with the Grand Duchy of Lithuania. In the fifteenth century, in the era of the personal union with Poland, the Grand Duchy had stretched from the Baltic to the Black Sea. It was a curious organism, ruled from Wilno (Vilnius, Vilna) in the north by a Lithuanian aristocracy which was gradually Polonized. Yet the mass of the populace, like the language of administration, was Ruthenian. After the constitutional union with Poland in 1569, it maintained its separate identity on a diminished, territorial base.

The two ethnically Lithuanian territories of Żmudź (Samogitia), the 'low country', and Aukštota, the 'upper country', are dominated by the river network of the Niemen. The land here is often swampy, harsh, and stony, and the population sparse. Even in the twentieth century, one-third of the land was trackless forest. Wilno was culturally Polish by the seventeenth century; all the smaller towns contained a strong Jewish element.

Białoruś (Byelorussia, or more correctly in the historical context, White Ruthenia) stretched from the Dvina in the north to the Pripet in the south and the upper Dnieper in the east. It included the palatinates of Mińsk, Polotsk, Witebsk, and Mścisław. Both in the cultural and the geographical sense, it represented a vast area of transition between Europe and Muscovy, an area of deep, external penetration and of weak local resources and identity. In essence, it was neither Polish nor Russian, but has never in its long career been able to determine its own destiny. Its wide open spaces are neither agriculturally attractive nor militarily defensible. Its Slav population had little sense of belonging except to the 'Christian souls of these parts'.

Czarnoruś (Black Ruthenia), adjoining Białoruś to the south and south-west, lost its separate designation in the eighteenth century. It included the palatinates of Brest, Troki, and Nowogródek.

In the east, beyond Lithuania, Byelorussia, and the Ukraine, lay a further ring of provinces possessing still more tenuous connections with Poland. There was Inflanty (Livonia) on the Gulf of Riga, whose easterly city of Dyneburg (Dvinsk) remained Polish after the Swedish Wars of the seventeenth century; Courland (Kurlandia) which became a joint fief of the united Republic; Smolensk, interminably disputed with Muscovy; Sieviersk on the Desna, captured by Ivan III in 1492, and Moldavia on the Dniester, a Polish fief from 1387 to 1497.

To describe this long catalogue of territories as 'Polish' is no doubt controversial. For the most part, their population has never been dominated by ethnic Poles, and they no longer form part of the Polish People's Republic. But to limit one's understanding of 'Poland' to a presumed ethnic heartland is both unhistorical, and contrary to common sense. In the past, and particularly in the era of the united Polish–Lithuanian Republic between 1569 and 1795, ethnicity counted for little. The united Republic was a multinational state, whose citizens drew their sense of common identity not from the blood in their veins or from their mother tongue but from their common allegiance to the ruler and the law. In the past 'Polish' was not so much an ethnic term, as a political and cultural one. Like 'British' or 'Soviet' today, it referred to all sorts of people and provinces whose origins lay beyond the sphere of the dominant English, Great Russian, or Polish élite. In ethnic terms, Lithuania is no more 'Russian' today than it was 'Polish' in the past, although in respect to specific periods both attributes make exact political sense. Similarly, Silesia, which a hundred years ago could fairly be described as 'German', is now undoubtedly 'Polish'. Despite the clouds of propaganda, ancient and modern, which dim the subject, 'nationality' and 'national identity' cannot be detected in the soil. In so far as the people of Eastern Europe and their outlook have been in constant motion, so too have been the attributes applied to the lands where they live. The reasons why land which once was 'German' and is now called 'Polish' belong to the realm not of law, science, or fundamental rights, but only to that of power and politics. In the twentieth century, Poland is a state of secondary standing, and is not supposed to make territorial claims beyond her ethnic limits. At the same time, many major powers of the day are fully confirmed in their possession of multi-national territories. As usual, what is 'right' for superpowers is 'wrong' for lesser mortals.

The modern concept of frontiers is equally confusing. In

times when land was in superabundant supply and people
alone had political value, there was no point whatsoever in
defining the territory of state or of staking out its boundaries
with a tape-measure. Rulers were less concerned to claim land
as a whole than to dominate the people who could work and
develop the scattered oases of settlement and industry. Political power radiated from a few centres of authority, whose
spheres of influence constantly waxed and waned, and very
frequently overlapped. These centres can best be likened to
magnets, and the people living in between them, to iron filings
pulled hither and thither by fluctuating and conflicting
magnetic fields. In the medieval and early modern periods,
the typical pattern showed small metropolitan areas, where
royal power could be directly enforced, surrounded by huge
intermittent expanses of undefined border territory, where
marcher lords enjoyed far-reaching autonomy. In Eastern
Europe where the distances were so much greater than in the
west, these conditions prevailed to the end of the eighteenth
century. In Poland–Lithuania, no accurate territorial survey
was attempted until after the First Partition, in 1773. In the
greater part of the Polish lands the pull of Cracow's or of
Warsaw's authority was not much stronger than that of rival
political centres in Prague, Vienna, Berlin, Stockholm, or
Moscow. In border areas such as Silesia or the Ukraine, the
local communities were as safe from the enforcement of
central power, as they were exposed to the threats and incursions of foreign powers. At any particular moment, their
loyalties were determined by the delicate balance between
their need for protection and their chances of acting with impunity. Their true predicament could not be described by a
line on a map. The further one retreats from the modern state,
the less the concept of fixed frontiers applies. In relation to the
realms of the medieval princes, it is entirely inappropriate.

A Tableau of Poland, therefore, is bound to be problematical. If one were only to include those provinces which
have been permanently associated in some sort of common
political entity, one would have nothing to describe. Yet
if one includes all the places which at some time or other
have been blessed with the Polish connection, one is sure to
end up with half a continent.

*   *   *   *   *

Despite the superficial appearances of the standard physical
map, the Polish reaches of the European Plain are neither so
flat nor so monotonous as to deny the country any specific
form and character. Nor is it true that Poland has no natural
features suitable for frontier demarcation. In the south, the
mountainous Carpathian chain, extended into the Beskids
and Sudety, forms a barrier as lofty and effective as the
Bavarian Alps or the French Pyrenees. In the north, on the
Baltic coast, the sea is equally effective. In the west, the Odra
(Oder) and Lusatian Nyssa (Western Neisse) present a clear
line of demarcation whose advantages were noticed by geographers such as Pawowski, Romer, or Nakowski long before
politicians dreamed of using them in practice. The Odra–Nyssa
line closes the narrowest gap between the mountains and the
sea, and, with all its tributaries on the Polish side, is unusually
uncomplicated. Only in the east, where the marshes of Polesie
provide only partial cover, is Poland really open to all the
winds that blow. The River Bug does little to shield Poland
from the two great upland pathways out of Russia — the
northerly one along the Minsk Heights as followed by the
Warsaw–Moscow railway, and the more southerly one on the
ancient highway joining Cracow with Lwów and Kiev. Even
so, there are many countries in Europe, from Eire to Hungary
and the two Germanies, which have to make do with boundaries of much greater artificiality.

Within these frontiers, three outstanding physical features
emphasize the latitudinal lines of Poland's structure. Firstly,
the wedge-like shape of the continent at the point where the
Eurasian land mass narrows into the European peninsular
inevitably funnels movement on to the east–west axis. At
longitude 24° E on the Bug, the European Plain is almost
800 miles wide. At 14° E on the Odra, it is only 200 miles
wide. Secondly, the glacial depressions or *pradoliny* — in
particular the Grodno–Warsaw–Berlin Depression and the
Toruń–Eberswalde Depression — provide natural passage ways
parallel to the mountain and coastal barriers. Thirdly, the
great swathe of morainic lakes which stretch from the Valdai
Region all the way to the Odra and beyond, serve to hold

Poland back from the sea, and to shut it into its landlocked heart. The Pomeranian Lakeland, the Mazurian Lakeland, and the Lithuanian Lakeland form belts of sparsely inhabited terrain which interrupt free movement and inhibit settlement. It is interesting to note how the northern frontier of Poland was mainly held on the margin of these lakes from the earliest times to the twentieth century. (See Diagram B.)

In contrast, the river system of Poland emphasizes the longitudinal axis. The basins of the Odra and Vistula both drain from the Carpathians to the Baltic. In Byelorussia, the Berezina, the Upper Dnieper, and the Soz all cut across the overland passageways, just as in Red Ruthenia or Podolia, the numerous tributaries of the Dniester constantly interrupt the sweep of the Podolian plateau. The emergence of the Odra and Vistula from their sources by the Moravian Gate, the one point between the Black Sea and Bavaria where southern Europe can be approached without crossing an alpine pass, underlines the longitudinal axis still further. The Amber Road of ancient times, and the medieval Prussian Road, both traversed Polish territory at this point, whilst countless hordes of barbarians, ancient and modern, have all poured through it on their way to fortune and infamy.

The resultant structure of Poland is one of an irregular grid, a lop-sided frame in which the dominant horizontal warp, is offset by the vertical weave of the rivers. In terms of human activity, it gave every facility for movement and transit, which was matched in early times by favourable opportunities for permanent settlement.

'Life-support capacity' is an ugly but useful piece of jargon invented to express the product of all the factors which encourage or inhibit human settlement in any particular location. In absolute terms, it is highest in the sub-tropical valleys of the Yangtse, the Euphrates, or the Nile where civilization first flourished, and lowest in the middle of Antarctica or the Sahara. On the European scale, it has usually been high on the coastal strips of the Mediterranean islands like Crete or Sicily, or in the northern valleys of the Rhine, the Seine, or the Thames, and low in the taiga and tundra belts of Scandinavia and Muscovy. In Poland, its level is mid-way between that of Western Europe and that of Russia. Taking Warsaw as

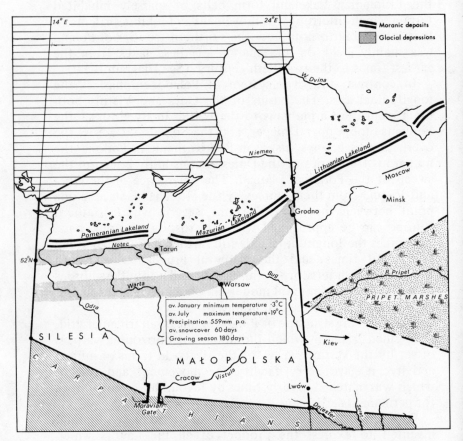

Diagram B.   Poland — Physical Structure

a central point of reference, the latitude of 52° N gives strong summer sunshine, and a hot summer of three months' duration. The climate is continental, with marked seasons, but lacking the worst extremes of summer drought, winter cold, or spring floods which are common further east. Permafrost is unknown and storm-damage is rare. The minimum daily temperature in January averages – 3° C (26° F), the maximum in July 19° C (66° F). Precipitation at 559 mm. or 22 inches is rather low, but rain falls mainly in the agricultural months — 11 inches between May and August. The number of days entirely below freezing-point varies from 30 to 50. Snowcover lasts up to 60 days, river-ice up to 40 days, and the growing season up to 180 days. Wind exposure, especially from the cold easterlies, is considerable, but local wind cover is adequate, especially in the river-valleys and behind high-standing timber. Cloud cover which reaches 150 days per annum, is common in the winter months, and takes the edge off the most extreme climatic conditions. Warsaw, of course, is located in one of the least favourable districts of central Poland, and it would be quite possible to find other areas not too distant, in Lower Silesia or in Małopolska, where the winter is shorter, the sun brighter, the rainfall higher, the soil richer, and where the growing season reaches an impressive 225 days. In the realm of vegetation, central Poland is still within the normal range of the European mainland. The beech-line runs south-eastwards from the Vistula estuary to the Carpathian foothills. The oak-line runs in the same direction but much further east. Warsaw itself lies in an area of rye and potato cultivation, but the limit of wheat production lies much further to the north and east. The stock of natural fauna was once extremely rich, and included tarpan, bears, bison, and wolves as well as the more familiar game animals. It was not seriously diminished until the twentieth century, when distinguished hunters from Archduke Francis-Ferdinand to Air Marshal Hermann Goering did notable damage.

It is difficult to compare this combination of geographical circumstances with that of any other area in the world, although it is not too dissimilar to southern Ontario, where an essentially continental location is ameliorated by the proximity of the Great Lakes, just as Poland's easterly position on

the European peninsula is modified by the continuing influence of the Atlantic and the Baltic. At all events, Poland
lies well within the bounds of both a pastoral and an arable
economy. For the purposes of primitive settlement, Poland,
unlike Muscovy, always lay within the area where a nuclear
peasant family could comfortably support itself by its own
unaided efforts. When Ibrahim-ibn-Jakub stated that the
(Western) Slavs 'inhabited the richest limits of land suitable
for settlement', it seems that he chose his words carefully.

*   *   *   *   *

Archaeological evidence puts the beginnings of human settlement in the valleys of the Odra and the Vistula in the two
hundredth millennium BC. The Old Stone Age left few traces,
although palaeolithic sites do exist in the Ojców Caves near
Cracow and at Świdry near Warsaw. The New Stone Age, in
contrast, left several characteristic cultures from the period
4000 to 1800 BC, each classified by the predominant features
of its pottery. These include the Funnel Beaker Culture, the
Corded Ware Culture, the Bell Beaker Culture, and in the
north-east, the Pit-Comb Culture. The principal sites are
located at Rzucewo near Gdańsk, at Sarnowo near Bydgoszcz,
at Jordanów near Wrocław, and at Krzemionki, Ćmielów, and
Złota near Kielce. The Bronze Age Cultures, each classified
by the location of their initial finds, were still more prolific.
The Uňetice People (c. 1800–1400 BC), first identified in
neighbouring Moravia, were pastoralists who worked both in
bronze and gold. The Trzciniec People (c. 1500–100 BC), first
identified in the area of Lublin, were, like the Iwno People of
the Lower Vistula, patriarchal sun-worshippers who practised
cremation. The Lausitz or Lusatian People (c. 1300–400 BC),
first identified in the Lusatian district of East Germany, lived
from mixed farming and maintained far-flung commercial
contacts with the Danubian Basin and with Scandinavia.
They built wooden fortresses, among them the famous island
stronghold at Biskupin in eastern Posnania, with its elaborate
timber breakwater and high rampart. At nearby Słupca and
Kamieniec, the skeletons of mutilated men, women, and
children, and bone arrow-heads embedded in charred gateposts, vividly evoke the violent end inflicted on the Lusatians

at the dawn of the Iron Age by the first wave of predatory nomads, the Scythians. At Witaszkowo on the Western Neisse, a dead Scythian chieftain was buried with all his treasure. The succeeding Iron Age cultures stretched from the same time right into the medieval period. The Bylany Culture (from *c.* 600 BC) and the Puchov Culture (from *c.* 100 BC) originated in Bohemia and Slovakia respectively. The Zarubinets Culture (*c.* 200 BC–AD 100), which displays close affinities with similar remains in distant Pomerania, and the Chernyakovo Complex (*c.* AD 200–400), which has yielded over one thousand related sites from the Vistula to the Dnieper, are thought to be Gothic in origin. The Przeworsk Culture of Silesia (from 400 to *c.* AD 600) brings Polish archaeology to the dawn of historical times.

Needless to say, the task of matching archaeological cultures to the ethnic groups which have survived in the historical records is very tricky indeed. Polish researchers of the twentieth century have been as eager to prove that the earliest settlers of the present Polish lands were Poles, as their German predecessors were to show that they were Germanic. To the neutral observer, however, the ethnogenetic hunt for the *prasłowianie* or 'protoslavs' smacks of chauvinism no less than the earlier hunt for the *Frühostgermanen*. Given a mass of conflicting evidence, the sceptical enquirer must remain as confused about the origin of the Slavs in general, as of the Poles in particular.

Polish prehistorians of the so-called 'Autochthonous School' have consistently maintained that the ancestral homeland of the Slavs lay in the valleys of the Odra and the Vistula. Starting with J. Kostrzewski writing in 1913, they have included anthropoligists such as J. Czekanowski, philologists such as T. Lehr-Spławinski, and a long line of archaeologists such as L. Kozłowski, T. Sulimirski, and Konrad Jazdżewski. They have presupposed a direct line of Slavonic descent from the Lusatian People of the Bronze Age, through the shadowy Venedii of Roman times, to the known Polish tribes of the tenth century. According to this hypothesis, the modern Polish nation is descended from a uniquely tenacious group of Protoslavs who, whilst their kinfolk migrated to the west, east, or south obstinately remained on their native soil. The

Poles are seen as 'autochtones', as 'permanent residents', and as 'the native population'; all other peoples of the area are relegated to the status of 'aliens', 'transients', or 'invaders'. It is an unusual situation to say the least. At a period when the population was in flux in every other part of Europe, and in every other part of Slavdom, the forefathers of the Poles were planted at a stroke and with extraordinary precision in the one spot of God's earth where they could rest indefinitely. There may be a long prehistory of England before the English, of France before the French, of Bohemia before the Czechs, of Hungary before the Hungarians, even of Russia before the Russians, but not it seems, of Poland before the Poles. Among the foreign scholars of note who have accepted the Polish viewpoint, Father Dvornik has written categorically: 'Only the tribes belonging to the Polish branch (of the Slavs) clung to their original habitat.'[1] (See Map 3a.)

Opponents of the Polish School prefer to place the Slavonic homeland in a more easterly zone, on the forest-steppe which stretches along the northern slopes of the Carpathians between the middle Vistula and the lower Dnieper. This location was first selected in 1902 by one of the pioneers of Slavonic archaeology, Lubor Nederle, and has recently received convincing if not conclusive, confirmation. According to Marija Gimbutas, an American scholar of Lithuanian origin, the elaborate attempt to identify Lusatian Culture with proto-slavic settlement has been quite 'unnecessary'. The so-called Venedian Culture of the Protoslavs must be set aside as yet another red herring. In their place, the supposition of a continuous North Carpathian Culture of Slavonic character, lasting throughout the Bronze Age in its successive Komarov, Bilogrudivka, and Chernoles variants, presents far fewer conflicts of evidence. It allows for the persistence of a similarly stable Baltic Culture to the north, and of the widespread Central European Culture with Uňetice, Urnfield, and Lusatian variants to the west. It agrees with linguistic evidence, which demands firstly that the Slavs did not disperse until relatively recently; and secondly that they should have passed the formative years in contact not only with Germans and Balts but also with Illyrians, Thracians, and Iranians. (See Diagram C.) It also encourages the identification of these early

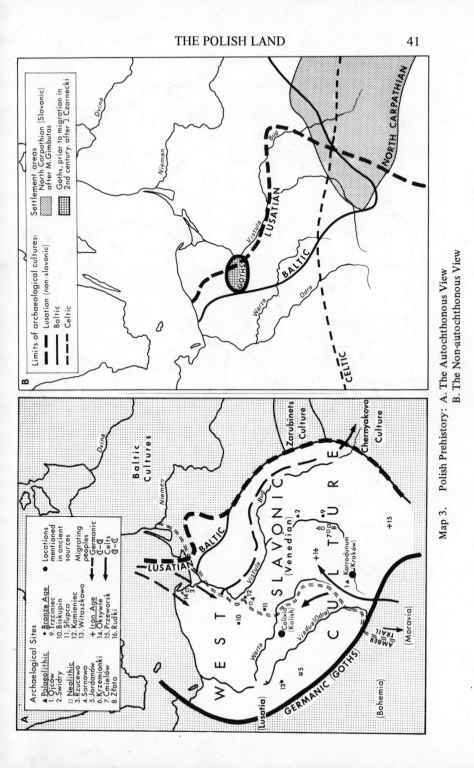

Map 3. Polish Prehistory: A. The Autochthonous View
B. The Non-autochthonous View

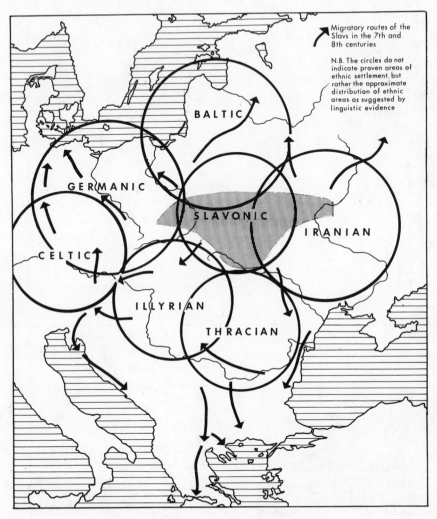

Diagram C.   The Ancestral Homeland of the Slavs

Slavs with the 'Scythian farmers' of the fifth century BC whom Herodotus put at three days' march from the Dnieper. Here the Slavs would have developed their characteristic social institution, the *zadruga* or 'joint family', where all the relatives of the chieftain lived together under fierce patriarchal discipline. Here, subjected first to the Scythians and then from the second century BC to the Sarmatians, they learned their common religious vocabulary, most of which from *Bóg* (God) to *raj* (Paradise) is Sarmato-Iranian by derivation. Here they would have worshiped their numerous deities such as Triglav, the Three-headed One, Svarog the Sun-maker, and Perun, the God of the Thunderclap. Here in the first century of our era, they would have witnessed the slow migration of the Germanic Goths and Gepids whose route from the Baltic Coast to the Black Sea is clearly marked by a trail of characteristic settlement and funeral sites. Here, they would have experienced the successive arrivals of the Huns and the Avars. Their own main expansion, which probably began on the coat-tails of the nomads, grew into a flood with the collapse of Avar supremacy in the seventh century. 'The barriers were down, and the Slavs poured out.' One branch headed north and east into Baltic and Finnish territory to found the East Slav communities – the ancestors of the Great Russians and the Ruthenes. A second branch moved south into the Balkans – the future Serbs, Croats, Slovenes, and Bulgars. The third group turned westward into Germanic, Celtic, and Baltic territory, into lands which ancient authors had known as Bohemia, northern Pannonia, and eastern Germania. These were the forebears of Czechs, the Slovaks, the Sorbs, the Polabians, the Pomeranians, and the Poles. According to this schedule, the 'Protopoles' would have been one of the last of the Slavs to drift away from the North Carpathian homeland, and would have settled in the valleys of the Odra and Vistula in the course of the seventh and eighth centuries. By the end of the prehistoric period, the new wave of Slavonic colonization had obliterated most of the underlying layers of previous settlement.[2]

The main implication of this hypothesis for Polish history is that the Poles would have been but the latest of many Indo-European groups who have settled on the territory of

present-day Poland. Such a conclusion may be unpalatable to
many Polish readers; but it is hard to refute. The first Indo-
Europeans are generally thought to have penetrated into the
North European Plain in the second half of the Fourth Millennium BC, bringing with them the unmistakable trait of bury-
ing their dead in tumuli; but their particular ethnic connections cannot now be determined. From the early Bronze Age,
however, the central and eastern areas of modern Poland
were inhabited by Balts; the north-western areas fell within
the fringe of Germanic settlement, which had stabilized in
southern Scandinavia.[3] South-western areas formed part of
the   Central   European   Culture,   which   possessed   an
Illyrian—Celtic complexion. Only the extreme south-eastern
corner of modern Poland, in the vicinity of Rzeszów and
Przemyśl, would have fallen within the extreme bounds of
Slavonic settlement. In the Roman period, a massive influx of
Celts was provoked by disturbances over the mountains in
Bohemia. The Celts filtered eastwards as far as the River San
and beyond, building an impressive series of hill-forts. At
Rudki in the Holy Cross Mountains they developed the most
extensive iron-mining complex in prehistoric Europe. They
would presumably have provided the dominant cultural element of southern Poland until the arrival of the Slavs. Their
presence may conceivably help to explain the distinctive
characteristics and separate connections of the Vistulanians
in the eighth, ninth, and tenth centuries. Celtic place-names,
such as Tyniec and Soła, have survived to this day in the
environs of Cracow. (See Map 3b, p. 41.)

   Great caution, however, is imperative, not least in the use
of modern labels. If it is unwise to put the Slavonic tag on
any archaeological finds prior to AD 500, it is certainly improper to call anything at all at this juncture 'Polish'. The
cultures of the various branches of the Slavonic family were
as yet largely undifferentiated. The variations within the
group of Western Slavs could not possibly have assumed their
later form. For one thing, the name of Poland derives from
that of just one tribe, the *Polanie* or 'Polanians', who may, or
may not, have been closely related to their immediate neighbours. For another, the Vistulanians to the south, with their
fortress of Cracow, seem to have fostered connections more

with the Danube Basin than with life on the northern plain.
It is an established fact, for example, that in the eighth century they were subjects of the Great Moravian Empire, and
that they first received Christian baptism from the Methodian
mission. At this time, their links with the Polanians, if any,
are completely unknown. It is also known from the writings
of the Byzantine Emperor, Constantine Porphyrogenitus, that
the area round Cracow was once known as 'White Croatia',
and that it served as the spring-board for the Croats on their
long journey to the Adriatic Coast. Etymological clues suggest
that the Croats may have been slavicized Sarmatians (as the
Bulgarians are a slavicized Turkic people). Their lengthy
sojourn in southern Poland in the company of, or in succession to the Celts, may well have inspired the persistent legends
of the Poles' own Sarmatian origins. The plethora of Polish
place-names connected with the root of *Sorb-*, *Sarb-*, and
Serb-, emphasizes the common Slavonic as opposed to any
particularly western Slavonic context of primeval settlement
in the migratory period.

Literary records throw little light on the over-all scene. In
this part of the world, the gap that yawns between the last
writings of the ancients and the earliest chronicles of the
medieval world is all but unbridgeable. Discoveries of Roman
coins and Roman bronzeware as far afield as Prussia and
Mazovia bear witness to the penetration of Roman trade far
beyond the imperial frontiers.[4] Yet the Romans knew little
about the Baltic and the Vistula Basin. Their nearest approach
occurred in AD 178—9 when a company of some 850 men
having completed a punitive campaign against the local
Teutons, bivouacked through the winter in the vicinity of
Trencin in Moravia. Earlier in the same century Tacitus, having described the shore of what he called the Suabian Sea,
admitted that 'at this point our knowledge of the world ends'.[5]
In his review of the tribes of Germania, he mentions the
Lemovii and the Rugii on the coast of Pomerania, and the
Gotones (Goths) on the Vistula. His delphic reference to the
'Venedii' has been variously interpreted as proof of the
existence of Germanic Vandals or else of Slavic Wends. Pliny's
Natural History recalls the exploits of a Roman knight in the
reign of Nero who travelled overland from Carnuntum on the

Danube to the Baltic coast, returning home with a huge quantity of precious amber. But what part of the lands through which the knight travelled were inhabited by Slavs, he fails to mention. And after that, for six hundred years, the records are virtually silent. Throughout this long darkness, there are few glimpses of the settled agricultural population; though from time to time occasional echoes are heard of migrating peoples as they trekked across the darkened stage. Both the Goths and the Vandals lived in the Vistula Basin before migrating to the south and east on the first stage of their complicated wanderings. The Ostrogothic Empire, which flourished right across the Baltic—Black Sea area in the second and third centuries, gave way to the still more ephemeral Empire of the Huns. It is unlikely that Attila himself crossed the Carpathians on his great expedition to Gaul in 451; but there is good reason to believe that in the following decade the retreating Hunnic horde was run to ground somewhere on the Vistula and destroyed by the vengeful Ostrogoths. In this regard, prehistorians are endlessly tantalized by an isolated phrase in a later Anglo-Saxon poem, the *Widsith,* which tells how 'the Hraede with their sharp swords must defend their ancient seat from the people of Aetla by the Wistla wood.'[6] After the Huns came the Avars, whose rise to supremacy in central Europe coincided with the reassertion of the Roman Empire in the East by Justinian. Then, in their turn, following their failure at the gates of Constantinople in 626, the Avars lost control of their tributary lands north of the Carpathians, and their fragile realm disintegrated. From that point onward, the expansion of the Slavonic peoples could proceed without serious hindrance. The nomadic life was losing its appeal. The barbarian incursions were becoming ever more infrequent. With the important intervals of the Magyars in the ninth century and of the Mongols in the thirteenth, the Slavs of the North European Plain could look forward to a long era of consolidation and development.

Inevitably, in the wake of so many human migrations, the ethnic mix of the population was extremely rich. As a result, it is quite impossible to isolate anything resembling an ethnic core, or, at the distance of more than a thousand years, to distinguish Slavonic from non-Slavonic racial elements. In a society that was as yet entirely unlettered, it is impossible to identify a specifically Polish or 'Lechian' culture from within the undifferentiated mass of the western Slavs. People who imagine that the Poles or Polish culture are somehow 'indigenous' to the Polish lands are as mistaken as those who believe that Europe is the original home of the Europeans. They are looking for full-grown, modern blooms in unlabelled packets of prehistoric mixed seeds. To look for Poles in the eighth or ninth centuries, is as anachronistic, and as pointless, as looking for Englishmen in the age of Hengist and Horsa. In the last resort, all our ancestors were alien mongrel immigrants.

The linguistic picture is equally confused. It stands to reason that somewhere there must have been people speaking a language, or group of related languages, from which modern Polish has since developed. Philologists have succeeded in reconstructing the main outlines of protoslavic syntax and vocabulary. But in the total absence of any linguistic records prior to the thirteenth century, any accurate description of the dialects of west Slav speech in earlier times is out of the question. One may suppose that the Polanian, Mazovian, Vistulanian, and Silesian dialects were diverging from common Slav in response to the varying linguistic environment of the areas in which the Slavs settled. But scholars can only speculate about the persistence of common forms and the interrelationships in the Slav group as a whole. (See Diagram D.)

None the less, in the eighth century, at the very start of recorded history in Northern Europe, the main westerly tide of human settlement may be seen to falter, and then to eddy in the opposite direction. The Frankish Kingdom, which stretched right across Germany, held off the Slavs on its eastern borders; whilst the establishment of the Duchy of Bavaria drove the first of several wedges that were to separate the Slavs of the south from their kinsfolk on the northern plain. Before long, the Slavs were to be pressurized both by Scandinavian raiders in the Baltic and by the steady advance of the Saxons on the Elbe and Odra. The return of the Germans across the Elbe in the early tenth century is generally taken to mark the onset of that *Drang nach Osten* which many historians have regarded as the main theme of Central European History over the next thousand years.[7] Yet the easterly

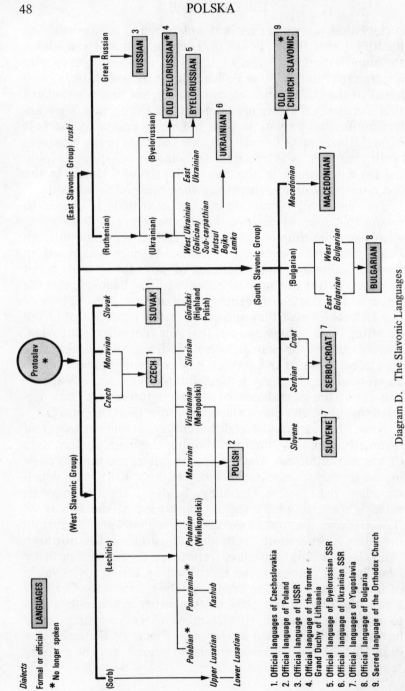

Diagram D. The Slavonic Languages

Dialects

Formal or official LANGUAGES

* No longer spoken

(West Slavonic Group)

Protoslav *

(Sorb)

Upper Lusatian

Lower Lusatian

Polabian *

Pomeranian *

Kashub

(Lechitic)

Polanian (Wielkopolski)

Mazovian

Vistulanian (Małopolski)

Silesian

Góralski (Highland Polish)

POLSKI [2]

Czech

Moravian

CZECH [1]

Slovak

SLOVAK [1]

(East Slavonic Group) *ruski*

Great Russian

RUSSIAN [3]

(Byelorussian)

OLD BYELORUSSIAN* [4]

BYELORUSSIAN [5]

(Ruthenian)

(Ukrainian)

East Ukrainian

West Ukrainian (Galician) Sub-carpathian Hutsul Bojko Lemko

UKRAINIAN [6]

(South Slavonic Group)

Slovene

SLOVENE [7]

Serbian

Croat

SERBO-CROAT [7]

(Bulgarian)

East Bulgarian

West Bulgarian

BULGARIAN [8]

Macedonian

MACEDONIAN [7]

OLD CHURCH SLAVONIC * [9]

1. Official languages of Czechoslovakia
2. Official language of Poland
3. Official language of USSR
4. Official language of the former Grand Duchy of Lithuania
5. Official language of Byelorussian SSR
6. Official language of Ukrainian SSR
7. Official languages of Yugoslavia
8. Official languages of Bulgaria
9. Sacred language of the Orthodox Church

drive has by no means been the sole prerogative of the
Germans. Once the western and central regions of the continent were effectively settled, organized, and defended, the
possibilities for expansion towards the more open marches of
the east proved more attractive for everyone. When the
Germans were trying to recross the Elbe, the French were
beginning to press for the Rhine, just as the Poles were heading for the Dnieper. The area available for colonization has
constantly retreated in an easterly direction. Seen from the
European perspective, therefore, the expansion of the Poles
and Lithuanians into medieval Ruthenia and Ukraine, or the
still more dramatic expansion of the Great Russians from
their base in Muscovy into the steppes of Siberia and Central
Asia, forms a part of the *Drang nach Osten* no less significant
than that of the Germans into Brandenburg, Pomerania,
Prussia, and Livonia.

The history of primitive agriculture in Poland is another
subject where theories are more common than hard facts. It
is clear that conditions have not always been constant. Studies
of variable water-levels suggest that warm periods have alter-
nated with cooler ones throughout the post-glacial epoch.
The water-level at Biskupin rose far enough in the late Bronze
Age to drown the island settlement completely. Later on, in
the seventh century, it subsided to permit the re-establishment
of a flourishing fortress community, which survived for four
hundred years. A number of studies point to the conclusion
that the climate was more favourable in the high medieval
period than at any time before or since. Research in the
Karkonosze Mountains has shown that the tree-line was no
less than 600 feet higher in the fourteenth century than in
the twentieth, and that vines, apricots, and melons were
grown in valleys where they can no longer be produced. In
the Vistula Delta, the accumulation of alluvium has been very
erratic. The main enlargement of the Delta, and the formation
of the spit of Westerplatte, occurred in the seventeenth
century, conceivably indicating an increase of river water and
a lengthy deterioration in the weather.[8] Despite the variations,
however, there is ample archaeological evidence to confirm
that at no point since the Bronze Age was agriculture seriously
interrupted. Sickles and half-scythes, datable to the first

century BC have been unearthed in Nowa Huta near Cracow.
Rotary querns of similar vintage have been recovered at
Wrocław, and at Inowrocław in Kujawy. Ploughshares from
Nowa Huta and from Brzeg in Silesia have been dated to
c. AD 300. Already in the pre-migration period, contacts with
Pannonia across the Carpathians were considerable, and all
four major cereals were in production. The very name 'Polska',
deriving from the Slavonic word *pole* 'field', is sometimes
taken to indicate native prowess in agriculture. Certainly by
the thirteenth century, central Poland was the object of a
major influx of German peasant colonizers, moving into lands
which could sustain a marked increase in the number of its
inhabitants. By the fourteenth century, it was capable not
only of supporting a rapidly growing population but also of
providing a regular surplus for exchange and trade.[9] According
to Haxthausen and others, this situation had not been reached
in the central Muscovite provinces of Russia as late as the
middle decades of the nineteenth century.

The process of Polish settlement defies any precise description therefore; but the resultant pattern can be reasonably
discerned by the beginning of historic times. Given that the
pressure from increasing population and from the westward
movement of peoples out of Asia was equivalent to that elsewhere in Europe, the over-all density of settlement would be
somewhat less in Poland than in Germany or in France, where
conditions were still more favourable. Given also that the
total surface area was far more extensive than the total
cultivable area, it seems reasonable to suppose that only the
very best sites would have been exploited, and that considerable distances would have separated them. Yet once a settlement was founded, the adequate level of 'life-support capacity'
ensured its survival. Harsh winters, inferior communications,
and great distances all combined to isolate neighbouring
communities from each other. Hence the typical Polish pattern
clearly observable in historic times, of deeply-rooted, self-
sufficient but widely scattered localities.

Łowmiański has attempted to put precise figures to the
density of population in the tenth century. Starting from the
basis of a family of six persons working the two-field system,
he calculated that each family required 22 hectares to support

itself. This is equivalent to a density of 13.5 persons per square kilometre of cultivated land, or $4.5/km^2$ of total land surface. It would suppose a total population of 1,125,000 in the nascent Polish kingdom. It compares to a contemporary population density in Bohemia and Moravia of $6/km^2$, in Germany of $10/km^2$, and in Kievan Ruś of $3/km^2$, and with total populations respectively of 450,000, 3,500,000, and 4,500,000.[10]

The strength of the locality was apparent in Poland from earliest times. Though somewhat less prosperous than its French or German counterpart the Polish locality combined the economic self-sufficiency of European settlements with a degree of isolation comparable to that of Russia. Hence, it has been argued, a diametrically different pattern arose from that pertaining in Muscovy, where the localities were isolated but not economically viable, and where the pooling of resources in a strong, communal organization was essential to survival. In Poland, the inhabitants of the localities could well afford to resist the advances of outside authorities as unwarranted interference in their private affairs. Their typical attitudes would be those of individual freedom, allodial land holding, local pride, and regional patriotism. The opportunities for rulers to construct a successful power base was less than in Western Europe, where settlement was denser and connections between localities were closer, and less again than in Muscovy, where the localities readily submitted to the centre in the interests of protection and mutual supply. Thus, on this crucial question of the relationship of the parts to the whole, the pattern of settlement in Poland has been seen to be quite characteristic even in modern times. The traditional term in Polish for the locality was *gniazdo* or 'nest'. It aptly expresses the strong sentimental bond, which tied people to the one small area where most of them would spend their entire lives, and where the peasants on the lord's estate felt greater affinity with their immediate neighbours of all classes, than with anyone from outside. The sociologist, Andrzej Zajączkowski, has argued with some conviction that the political and social life of the pre-Partition Era depended on the interplay of the *'grands voisinages'* and the *'petits voisinages'*, − the former being the political catchment areas of the great magnatial patrons, the latter being the isolated villages and estates within each larger area.[11] In this view, the role of the neighbourhoods set definite limits on the authority of the King and central government, and continued even after the state had been formally destroyed. *Pan Tadeusz,* the epic poem written by Adam Mickiewicz in 1834, can be seen as the greatest of many works of Polish literature which extol the sentimentalities and the individualism of life in a remote rural locality.

The disjunctive pattern of settlement in Poland is well depicted in the surveys of the Crown Estates undertaken from the sixteenth century onwards. These *Lustracje* (Inventories) form a historical source of the first importance, as detailed and as thorough as the Domesday Book of Norman England. Very frequently, they record widely dispersed agglomerations of villages, each clustered round its focal castle, town, or manor, and each separated from the next by an intervening expanse of wilderness. Although they confine themselves to the Crown Estates there is no reason to suppose that the pattern of settlement was any different on land owned by the nobility or by the Church. Any number of examples could be cited. In the *Lustracja* of the Palatinate of Cracow in 1564, for instance, the district of Podhale was held in lease from the Crown by the Pieniążek family. One brother, Jan Pieniążek, chief Magistrate of the Cracow District, held a group of six villages in the upper valley of the Raba. The other, Prokop, Pieniążek, proved his right to a somewhat larger tenancy immediately to the south. He held ten villages in addition to the town of Nowy Targ. Of these, along the headwaters of the Dunajec — by far the most valuable was the manor of Szaflary, which commanded the site of what today is the mountain resort of Zakopane. The detailed descriptions of these isolated rural communities composed in a macaronic jumble of Polish and Latin immortalize those historic moments when the inhabitants of the immemorial countryside first surrendered their anonymity to the agents of the modern state (*see Table pages 54 and 55*). Szaflary was specially remote as a result of the mountainous terrain; but it did not differ significantly from thousands of similar estates across the length and breadth of the land.

*   *   *   *   *

The correlation between the state and the nature of the terrain on which it is situated poses some of the most fascinating problems of political geography. Phrases such as 'river valley despotisms' or 'Gulf Stream democracies' have been coined in attempts to explain why particular locations have spawned particular forms of government. In Western Europe, no one would dispute that the Swiss Alps, the English Channel, the Dutch dykes, or the Venetian lagoon have effectively sheltered the democracies which grew up under their protection. In Eastern Europe, Russia provides the classic example of how extreme conditions of space, climate, and poverty can foster correspondingly extreme traditions of autocracy.

In these general arguments, the Polish—Lithuanian Republic occupies an interesting place. If Muscovy was the home of the 'patrimonial state', where everything and everyone was put to the absolute disposition of the ruler, it is curious that Muscovy's immediate neighbour should have developed precisely the opposite tendency. If Poland—Lithuania occupied a transitional location between Europe and Russia, one might have expected it to have manifested a transitional blend of European and Russian practices. But this is not the case. The Polish—Lithuanian state was as completely de-centralized as the Russian state was centralized. Its ruler was as limited as the Tsar was absolute. Its regions were as way-ward, as the Russian provinces were controlled. Its noble citizens were as free as the subjects of the Tsar were bonded. Its policy was as passive as that of Russia was active; and its failure was as great as Russia's success. The two great states which between them dominated Eastern Europe in the modern period were as different as chalk and cheese.

Like Muscovy, Poland was essentially a land-locked com-munity. Despite modern propaganda, which pays great atten-tion to supposed maritime traditions, Poland's connections with the Baltic were extremely slender. The link with Western Pomerania lasted for only a few years in the tenth and twelfth centuries; whilst the hold over East Prussia between 1525 and 1657 had lost all practical significance long before it was legally terminated. Control of the shoreline of Eastern

The Estate of Szaffliary, with its land and ancient castle

Four witnesses came forward and confirmed under oath that there were eighteen peasants living in the village. They all have small unmeasured plots, dissected by the River Dunajec, for which they pay various rents, calculated together for the year at

	mk./gr./d.		
— Each pays the *obiedni* (meal tax) at 1 gr./6, and *poczty* (fast tax) at 4 gr.:	3	11	15
— Each pays the *robotni* (labour tax) at 25 gr. for they do labour service whenever asked:	2	0	0
— Each pays the *rybny* (fish tax), either at the rate of ten fish, or of 3 gr.:	9	18	0
Sheep tax – with the exception of the Headman, they offered cheeses this year to the value of:	1	6	0
— The Headman, from his cattle and sheep-cheese, paid separately:	16	0	0
	2	6	0
Total	33	41	15

The Manor:

	Seminatio (Seedcorn)	Crescentia (Crop)	Trituratio (Yield)	Victus (Food)	Resta (Remainder) for sale	Taxa (Rate)	mk./gr./d.		
Wheat	2	8	1	3	3	0/10/0	0	30	0
Rye	30	82	1½	50	43	0/ 6/0	5	18	0
Barley	30	230	1	6	194	0/ 5/0	20	10	0
Oats	219	380	2	0	541	0/2½/0	28	8	9
Pisae	½	4	1	6	–	0/ 9/0	–		
Flax	2	6	.	.	.	·	·		
Canapi	2	4	.	.	.	·	·		
Haystacks	–	5	–	1	4	3/ 0/0	12	0	9
	(in bushels)	(in three-score sheaves)	(in bushels of threshed corn per threescore sheaves)	(in bushels)	(in bushels)				
							66	18	9

Total for the cereals of the Estate:

(Two villages belonging to the Monastery of Szczyrzyc, i.e. Ludzimierz and Krauszów, do labour service for this manor, and pay the *osep* (corn-rent).)

mk./gr./d.

Livestock: Milking cows (30) at 2 zl., makes — 37 24 0
sterile cows (2); common cattle (40); calves (8); fattened hogs (8); common sows (60); capons (11); domestic chickens (30).

(Mr Pieniążek maintained that the cattle were his private property, since there were none on the estate when he took over the lease. For the time being, however, the Commission decided to record what they found.)

Domestic Staff: Magierz (peasant foreman) and his wife — 4 mk, plus full maintenance; the cowherd, and the swineherd, — 1 mk/24 gr. each, with full maintenance; two cooks at 36 gr; one maid at 15 gr. for shoes.

Total for domestic salaries: 8 39 0

Total Income from cereals, plus livestock, less salaries: 95 3 9

Freemen (wage-earners, or self-employed)
There are 21 freemen who have settled or are in the process of settling unclaimed land in the wilderness in the following three, new villages, and who exploit the crops there freely according to custom:
— Dunaiecz Biały: There are six peasants living by the river which flows down on the Polish side of the Tatras into the lands of Nowy Targ.
— Bańska: There are ten peasants living on the Polish side of the road by which one reaches the new mines in the Tatras built first by Mr Lubomirski and later by Mr Pieniążek and Kasper Bar.
— Marusina: There is also a village below the Maruszyna Mountain, where three peasants are living, together with the two officials who reside in the customs house.[12]

Pomerania/Western Prussia, with its city of Danzig, prior to 1308 and from 1454 to 1793, gave Poland its one small, but important port-hole on to the northern sea. Expansion towards the distant Black Sea was consistently more practicable than to the near-by Baltic. Poland's long-term partner, Lithuania, had similar experiences. Lithuania's famous boast to stretch 'from sea to shining sea', though technically correct in the fifteenth century, looks considerably less impressive when her dominion on the Baltic was seen to consist of one small town — Palanga (Połąga) — and on the Black Sea of an undeveloped strip of virgin coast between the Dniestr and Dniepr estuaries. At its maximum extent in the late Jagiellonian period, the Kingdom of Poland included only 120 miles of coastline in its 3,800 miles of frontier or about 3 per cent; while the Grand Duchy included some 165 miles out of 2,800, or about 6 per cent. The rest of these immense territories were entirely surrounded by land. In the following period, the efforts of Poland and Lithuania to gain joint control over the seaside territory of Livonia ended largely in failure. In the settlement of 1660, Poland–Lithuania was awarded only a small part of the Livonian interior; whilst its Baltic coastline possessed only the one seaport of Liepaja (Libau, Lipawa). Later Polish states were similarly landbound. Neither the Duchy of Warsaw, nor the Congress Kingdom had any coastline at all; and the Second Republic, even when the extraordinary configuration of the Hel Peninsula is taken into consideration, possessed a mere 45 miles of the Baltic shore. In this light the possession by the present People's Republic of over 300 miles of coastline must be viewed as a radical departure from historical realities. In this perspective, Poland's maritime connections have had only marginal significance. As Sebastian Klonowic wrote in 1596:

> Fair Poland nestles on a fertile sod,
> Content as though within the lap of God.
> What cares the Pole about the ocean's stand?
> He ploughs the land.
> Forsooth, my brother Pole, I know not why
> Thou cravest more? Thy fields supply
> Thy every need. Why seekest thou more betimes
> In far-off climes?[3]

In the modern era, Polish statesmen saw their country's exclusion from the sea as an important cause of political and economic weakness. But they were never able to remedy the situation satisfactorily by their own efforts.

Territorial security was an important consideration, though not a simple one. It can be seen to be the product of several contributory factors, including desirability, accessibility, defensibility, and tenability. (In other words, a given location is only secure when no one potential aggressor either wants it, or can reach it, capture it, or retain it.) Central Poland was certainly a desirable territory, both in itself and as a means of passage to points further afield. To its German neighbours, it offered space and the prospect of land for colonization, the notorious *Lebensraum* (living space) of the twentieth century. To its Russian neighbours, it offered valuable granary provinces, particularly in the south and south-east; a long-desired link with Europe; and a strategic buffer zone. It was also extremely accessible. Armies and people moving westwards out of central Asia, or eastwards out of Europe, were automatically channelled across Polish territory by the configuration of the land mass. Everyone from the Goths, Vandals, Avars, and Magyars, to Batu Khan in 1241–2, Napoleon in 1807–12, and Hitler in 1939–41, not to mention the Crimean Tartars, whose annual incursions lasted for centuries, rode into Poland with the minimum of hindrance. As in Russia, it has always been virtually impossible to deny the enemy an easy initial penetration. Extended lines of defence left unguarded loopholes which could always be swiftly exploited. On the other hand, the country was extremely difficult to hold in subjection. Invading armies melted away into the vast countryside. Insurrectionary forces found easy refuge in remote wildernesses. Almost without exception, the only effective way of controlling Poland for any length of time, once it was overrun, has been by indirect rule and local autonomy. This line has been followed by the Tsarist Government in the eighteenth century and from 1815 to 1830; by the French from 1807 to 1813; by the Germans in 1915–18, and by the USSR since 1944. Numerous attempts to impose direct rule, by the Tsar after 1831, and 1864; by the Bolsheviks in 1919–20; and by the Nazis in 1939–45, have invariably provoked immense local resistance.

From all of this, it should be evident that geopolitics have indeed affected Poland's development, but only in a negative way. The absence of any outstanding geographical features, has served to give added importance to forms of state organization, to the exploitation of resources, and to dynamic psychological factors. The historical geographer is left with questions such as why Poland was unable to organize its considerable human and economic resources as efficiently as its neighbours; why, in the crises of the seventeenth and eighteenth centuries, in terms of soldiers per head of population, Russia was ten and Prussia thirty times more efficient than Poland; or why both Russia and Prussia possessed the demonic drive to expand whilst Poland did not.

One line of approach is provided by relative chronology — by the fact that Poland developed much more quickly than her neighbours. The Polish kingdom as unified in the fourteenth century developed with precocious rapidity, expanded into territories once ruled by the moribund Ruthenian principalities, and associated itself with the overblown Grand Duchy of Lithuania. At this stage, Muscovy was still an insignificant backwater, struggling to shake off the Mongol yoke. Prussia still lay in the grip of the Teutonic Order. In the fifteenth and sixteenth centuries, Poland–Luthuania was the largest, and arguably strongest, state in Eastern Europe. In 1569, when the constitution of the united Polish–Lithuanian Republic was finally sealed by the Union of Lublin, the political link of the Hohenzollern dukes in Prussia with their relations in Brandenburg was confined to the promise of an eventual reversion on the failure of male descent. In Muscovy, Ivan IV, whose barbarous extermination of Novgorod and other Russian countries was matched only by the sensational violence towards his own subjects, had still not crossed the Urals, and was battling to gain a foothold on the Volga at Kazan, and on the Baltic at Narva. Thus the Polish system gelled at a time when internal prosperity was at its height and the external threat was still small. The decentralized traditions of defence, finance, and executive power were perpetuated in line with previous conditions, and not in expectation of increased pressures. It could be argued that Poland developed too soon, or too easily.

A second line of approach is provided by the Lithuanian connection, which complicates any arguments based on the geography of central Poland. For 407 years, from 1385 to 1793, Poland and Lithuania were joined together, first by the personal union of crowns and then by a constitutional union. Their association was longer than the comparable experience of England and Scotland since 1603. The Lithuanian state as founded in the thirteenth century may be seen as the last and most successful of the primitive and usually ephemeral enterprises which emerged in Eastern Europe from the ninth century onwards. Like Kiev Ruś (which has been aptly described as 'a glorified Hudson's Bay Company'), like the Great Moravian 'Empire', or like the primitive Polish Kingdom of Mieszko I, it was created by a team of intrepid warriors whose ability to conquer vast areas of sparsely populated prairie, was far greater than their powers of permanent administration. Its existence was prolonged by the union of 1385 with the Polish monarchy, with whose assistance the rising threat of the Teutonic Order was averted; and its feeble hold on the southern provinces of Volhynia, Podolia, and the Ukraine was ultimately recognized by their transfer to the Polish Kingdom at the time of the constitutional union. Yet Lithuania always remained the more vulnerable and weaker half of the Republic. Its human resources were fewer, its economic base more precarious, its defences more open, its nobility more wayward, its capacity to defend itself was more inadequate. Its position adjacent to Muscovy called for a sterner stance. From the end of the fifteenth century, the Polish army was continually required to bolster the flagging performance of the hard-pressed Lithuanians. As time went on, the Grand Duchy proved to be a burden which weighed ever more heavily on the shoulders of the Kingdom. If one holds therefore that the institutions and traditions of the united Republic grew naturally from the circumstances of Poland, one might equally maintain that their extension into Lithuania was one of the principal causes of their failure. But here again there are serious drawbacks. One has only to remember the role of Lithuania in repeated Polish Risings throughout the nineteenth century, long after the legal link had been broken, to realize that the bond between Poland

and Lithuania was not quite so artificial or burdensome as geography alone might imply.

By this time, the dull sublunary amateur who imagined that Geography could give simple clues to the central problems of Poland's History will be forced to have second thoughts. The once tempting idea that geographical conditions in the Polish lands nurtured Democracy as surely as Muscovy nurtured Autocracy does not find support in detailed research.

At all events, great caution is necessary. It is all too easy, having refined the constituent factors of political geography, to pretend that they represent the elements of a mathematical sum. They do not. They provide the variable constituents of social and economic life which in turn forms no more than the material for the exercise of human will and the making of arbitrary decisions. Political affairs are conducted by men whose perception of the objective realities of their predicament is rarely confident and never exact, and who are free to ignore them or defy them as they choose. In Poland's case at every turning-point, — in 1385, 1569, 1683, 1717, 1794—5, 1918, or 1944 — decisions were taken or avoided which could have been different, and which could have led to different results. The Polish state, like every other political organism, was created not by predetermined forces, but by men. Its collapse in the eighteenth century was no more inevitable than its resurrections in the twentieth. Its future is no more ascertained than that of any other country. Geography, in fact, as 'the science of our revolving earth', describes little more than the potter's wheel. Man is both the Potter, and the Clay; and it is Man, not Geography, that is the villain.

*   *   *   *   *

CHAPTER THREE
PIAST:
The Polanian Dynasty (to 1370)

Reputedly, Piast was a peasant. According to the Anonymous Gaul writing some 250 years later, he ascended the throne in succession to the wicked Popiel who, also reputedly, was eaten by mice in the dungeon of Kruszwica. He is thus a figure which links Poland's legendary past with its recorded history. Before his time, the historian is dealing with the tribal tales of Lech, Czech, and Ruś — the three Slav brothers who founded respectively the Polish, Czech, and Ruthenian peoples — and of King Krak, who killed the dragon of the Vistula. Lech built his 'Eagle's Nest' at Gniezno; Krak built his castle above the dragon's cave on Wawel Hill in Cracow; and Wanda, Krak's daughter, jumped to her death in the river rather than marry a German prince. For his part, Piast was said to be in his garden celebrating the coming-of-age of his son, when two strangers prophesied that the people would choose him to rule over them. From later evidence, it is clear that he must have lived in the middle of the ninth century, and ruled over the Polanians,* the most prominent of the West Slav tribes settled between the Odra and the Vistula. He would have been alive when in the west the Empire of Charlemagne was divided into the three Frankish kingdoms, and, when to the south the Great Moravian Empire was approaching its brief ascendancy. At this period, in France, civil war and Viking raids had reduced the country to helplessness; in England, the young King Alfred of Wessex was preparing to resist the Danish advance; in Russia, Rurik's Varangians were exploring the route from Novgorod to Kiev; in the Mediterranean, Byzantium having weathered the onslaught of Islam, and the convulsions of Iconoclasm, was about to enjoy a new lease of life under the Macedonian dynasty. Christianity, spreading from its twin oracles in Rome and Constantinople, was slowly reaching out toward

* In Polish, *Polanie*: appears in English variously as 'Polanians', or as 'Polians'.

61

the Slavs. Bulgaria was on the point of conversion. The mission of Saints Cyril and Methodius was at work amongst the Moravians and possibly amongst the Vistulanian tribes also.

From his humble beginnings, Piast was to launch a dynasty which lasted for five centuries, and which, after many vicissitudes, was to join the neighbouring tribes into one Polish kingdom. A linguistic theory, which draws on the Polish word *piastować*, meaning 'to cradle in one's arms', and by extension 'to hold office', suggests that like the Carolingians in France or the Stuarts in Scotland, Piast turned the office of major-domo at the princely court into that of hereditary ruler. At all events, his descendants provide the most important thread of continuity over half a millennium. The least unmemorable among them include Mieszko I (*c.* 922–92), the first Christian prince; Bolesław I Chrobry (Boleslaus the Brave, 967–1025), the first crowned King; Bolesław II Szczodry (Boleslaus the Bold, 1039–81); Bolesław III Krzywousty, (Boleslaus the Wry-mouthed, 1085–1138); Konrad Mazowiecki (Conrad of Mazovia, *c.* 1191–1247): and finally Władysław Łokietek, (Ladislaus the Elbow-High, *c.* 1260–1333) and his son Kazimierz III (Casimir the Great, 1310–70), who were the real founders of the Polish monarchy. (See Diagram E.) For practical purposes, their rule can be divided into three distinct periods. The first, to the death of Krzywousty in 1138, embraces the period of primitive monarchy in which the Piast princes succeeded each other in direct line. The second, from 1138 to 1320, was a period of fragmentation, or, as it is presently referred to, of 'regionalization' – where several branches of the dynasty fought for supremacy over the provinces of a divided country. The third, which began with Łokietek's coronation in Cracow in 1320, was followed by the process of reunification and by the growth of permanent institutions.[1]

The emergence of the Piast dynasty from its previous obscurity was provoked in the third quarter of the tenth century by the rise of the neighbouring Saxon Empire. In 955, Otto I, son of Henry the Fowler, gained immense prestige in Central Europe through his momentous victory over the heathen Magyars on the Lechfeld near Augsburg. Seven years later he was crowned Emperor by the Pope in Rome. In the following years he was able to exert considerable pressure over the Slavs on his eastern borders. He had received the homage of the Premyslid prince of Bohemia already in 950; and he now vigorously extended his father's policy of planting German colonies in the Marks of Brandenburg and Lusatia. In 961- 2, he obtained papal support for raising the see of Magdeburg into a missionary diocese over all the Slavonic lands, and sent its prospective bishop on a mission to Kiev Ruś. Such was the context of Mieszko I's alliance with Boleslas of Bohemia — the brother and assassin of St. Wenceslas — and of his Christian baptism. Seeing the inexorable advance of Christendom in general, and of the German Empire in particular, the Polanian prince may well have judged his christening to be the better part of valour. By accepting Christianity from Bohemia, he parried the prospect of forcible conversion, which even then was facing his Wendish and Obodritian neighbours; and he stood to benefit from their distress. At the same time, he stood to put some distance between himself and the Emperor's ambition, and in particular to keep the missionary instincts of the German clergy at bay. In short, the Piast dynasty could hope to preserve a measure of independence. This indeed proved to be the case. Although Mieszko may possibly have made some form of token submission to Otto III in 984, during the infant Emperor's minority, there can be no doubt that Mieszko's heir, Bolesław Chrobry, rose to be one of the Emperor's principal associates. Otto III, whose mother Theophano was a Byzantine princess, was not bounded by the narrow vision of his German ecclesiastical mentors, and his brief dream of a universal western empire undoubtedly held an honourable place for the Slav princes. His visit to Gniezno in AD 1000 and his confirmation of the autonomous Polish See were much resented in Germany. But the marked growth of Polanian power and prestige at this juncture enabled the Piasts to defy later attempts to reassert imperial hegemony.

The territory of Piast Poland cannot be simply described. It is the practice in some quarters to publish a map of 'Poland in the year AD 1000', showing both a clearly marked frontier line and a remarkable resemblance to the territory of the People's Republic since 1945.[2] This map is slightly misleading.

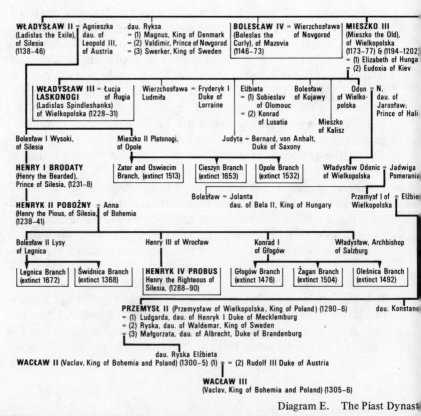

CAPITALS indicate names of Kings/senior Princes providing the line of succession
Dates are regnal dates

WŁADYSŁAW II = Agniezska   dau. Ryksa
(Ladislas the Exile),   dau. of   = (1) Magnus, King of Denmark
of Silesia   Leopold III,   = (2) Valdimir, Prince of Novgorod
(1138–46)   of Austria   = (3) Swerker, King of Sweden

BOLESŁAW IV = Wierzchosława
(Boleslas the   of Novgorod
Curly), of Mazovia
(1146–73)

MIESZKO III
(Mieszko the Old),
of Wielkopolska
(1173–77) & (1194–1202)
= (1) Elizabeth of Hunga
= (2) Eudoxia of Kiev

WŁADYSŁAW III = Łucja   Wierzchosława = Fryderyk I   Elżbieta   Bolesław   Odon = N,
LASKONOGI   of Rugia   Ludmiła   Duke of   = (1) Sobieslav   of Kujawy   of Wielko-   dau. of
(Ladislas Spindleshanks)   Lorraine   of Olomouc   polska   Jarosław;
of Wielkopolska (1228–31)   = (2) Konrad   Prince of Hali
    of Lusatia   Mieszko
    of Kalisz

Bolesław I Wysoki,   Mieszko II Platonogi,   Judyta = Bernard, von Anhalt,   Władysław Odonic = Jadwiga
of Silesia   of Opole   Duke of Saxony   of Wielkopolska   Pomerania

HENRY I BRODATY   Zator and Oswiecim   Cieszyn Branch   Opole Branch
(Henry the Bearded),   Branch, (extinct 1513)   (extinct 1653)   (extinct 1532)
Prince of Silesia, (1231–8)
    Przemysł I of = Elżbie
    Bolesław = Jolanta   Wielkopolska
    dau. of Bela II, King of Hungary

HENRYK II POBOŻNY = Anna
(Henry the Pious, of Silesia, of Bohemia
(1238–41)

Bolesław II Lysy   Henry III of Wrocław   Konrad I   Władysław, Archbishop
of Legnica   of Głogów   of Salzburg

Legnica Branch | Świdnica Branch   **HENRYK IV PROBUS**   Głogów Branch | Żagan Branch | Oleśnica Branch
(extinct 1672) | (extinct 1368)   Henry the Righteous of   (extinct 1476) | (extinct 1504) | (extinct 1492)
    Silesia, (1288–90)

PRZEMYSŁ II (Przemysław of Wielkopolska, King of Poland) (1290–6)   dau. Konstane
= (1) Ludgarda, dau. of Henryk I Duke of Mecklemburg
= (2) Ryska, dau. of Waldemar, King of Sweden
= (3) Małgorzata, dau. of Albrecht, Duke of Brandenburg

    dau. Ryska Elżbieta
WACŁAW II (Vaclav, King of Bohemia and Poland) (1300–5) (1) = = (2) Rudolf III Duke of Austria

WACŁAW III
(Vaclav, King of Bohemia and Poland) (1305–6)

Diagram E.   The Piast Dynast

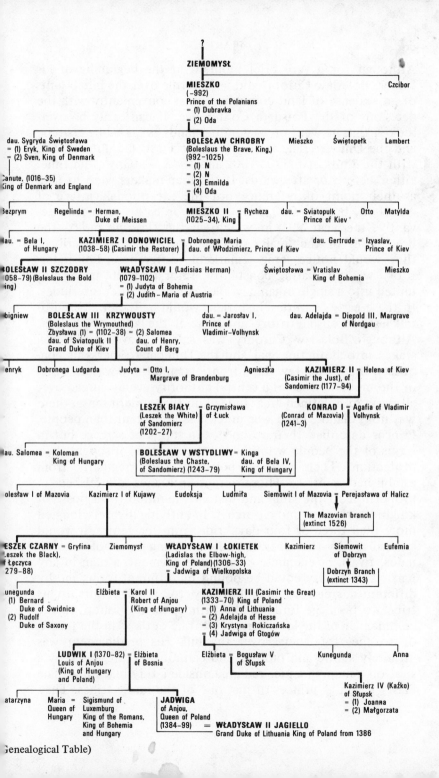

Although for a very brief moment at the beginning of his career, Bolesław Chrobry did indeed rule over the inhabitants of an expanse of land coinciding most conveniently with the decisions of the Potsdam Conference, it can easily be overlooked that he went on to conquer lands as far as the Danube and the Dnieper. The territory of the Piasts did not coincide with the limits of *c.* 990–1002 and 1945 – at any other time, either before or afterwards. If the map-makers were to take as their point of reference not the exceptional vintage of AD 1000, but AD 900, 1100, 1200, or 1300, or, more relevantly, the year 991 in which, in the *Dagome Iudex,* the boundaries of the 'realm of Gniezno' were first described, they would notice some remarkable differences. Polish territory was fluctuating constantly. Prior to 1320, it was not united into a single organic whole, except for brief interludes. In these early centuries, historians would be better advised to talk less of 'Polish territory' and more of 'the Polish obedience'. Although Bolesław Chrobry was said to have driven iron stakes into both the Saal and the Dnieper to mark his conquests, there were few fixed frontiers; and there was no state, in the modern sense of a central authority evenly spread over all parts of a defined area. Indeed, in the modern sense, there was no 'Poland'. Land was much less important than people. Princes described their realm not in terms of acreage but in terms of the people who obeyed their orders, or sought their protection. Their political power pulsed irregularly from established centres, whose direct influence diminished in proportion to the time and distance required for a posse of knights to ride out and enforce it. In outlying districts, located more than three or four days' ride from the centre, it would be reduced by the separate and competing power of subordinates, rivals, or enemies. At any one moment, a man in any particular locality could be bound by different forms and by different degrees of fear and loyalty, to his neighbours, to his tribe, to his liege lord, to the prince, to the bishop, to the commander of the local garrison, to the outlaws in the forest, or to the 'foreigners' over the hill. His predicament was infinitely subtle and mobile, and cannot be represented by a spot on a map, in a nice red area, inside a tidy black line. The Piasts began as princes of just one of the many tribes. They

only assumed control of the Vistulanians and of their town
of Cracow, in 990. Their hold on Pomerania and Silesia was
impermanent, and on Mazovia incomplete. Their conquests in
Red Ruthenia and beyond were not confirmed until the
fourteenth century. Although there is every reason to suppose
that the ruling élite spoke that version of the West Slavonic
language from which modern Polish has developed, they
ruled over people of mixed cultural and ethnic connections.
Their encouragement of a common cultural and political
tradition throughout their far-flung domain can only have
proceeded very slowly. There is no hard evidence for a separate and distinct Polish linguistic community before the
twelfth century. The earliest record of the Polish language is
to be found in the 'Bull of Gniezno' of 1136. (See Map 4.)

In many ways, the history of the ecclesiastical province of
Poland, the See of Gniezno, was more straightforward than
that of the state. Once established in AD 1000, it continued
undisturbed throughout the Middle Ages. In the tenth
century, the baptism of Mieszko I did not lead immediately
to the creation of any formal church hierarchy. There was
just the one apostolic bishopric at Poznań under its missionary
bishop, Jordan. In 991, in the *Dagome Iudex,* preserved in
the papal archives, Mieszko I asked that his realm be placed
under the direct protection of the Pope, presumably to avoid
the closer patronage of one or other of his Christian neighbours. Five years later, his successor received a mission from
Rome headed by Vojtech (Adalbert), the exiled Bishop of
Prague. Vojtech was a devoted missionary, and, after a brief
stay among the Polanians, sailed on from Gdańsk to the land
of the pagan Prussians. There, in 997, he was foully murdered.
His mutilated corpse was redeemed 'for a sack of gold' by
the Polanians, and buried before the altar at Gniezno. He was
speedily canonized, and as the patron 'Saint Wojciech'
became the object of a popular Polish cult. It was the moment
for action. In this year, when the world was supposed to
come to an end, the Emperor, Otto III, was urged by the Pope
to make a pilgrimage to Gniezno, and to create a metropolitan
see. Lavishly entertained by Bolesław Chrobry, he nominated
Vojtech's brother, Radim (Gaudentius), as the first archbishop, and confirmed the request of the *Dagome Iudex.*

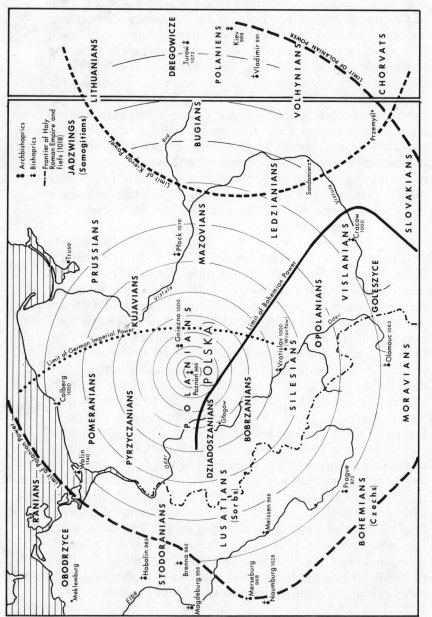

Map 4.   The Realm of the Early Piasts, (10th to 11th Centuries)

Bishoprics were established at Cracow for the Vistulanians; at Vratislav (Wrocław) for the Silesians; and at Kołobrzeg (Kolberg) for the Pomeranians. After Bolesław Chrobry's death, the entire structure of the infant see was crippled in 1035–7 by a vast pagan uprising, which engulfed both State and Church. But it was patiently reconstructed during the next decades; and, with this one interval, began its unbroken career. As fresh provinces came into the Polish orbit, the diocesan structure was expanded. Płock received its bishop in 1050; Włocławek and Lubusz (Lebus) in 1128; Western Pomerania at Wolin in 1140; Red Ruthenia, at Halicz and later at Lwów, in 1367. A parochial network was established in the twelfth century, and steadily consolidated. Monasticism, which made its first appearance with the Benedictines at Międzyrzecz (Meseritz) near Poznań and at Tyniec near Cracow in the early eleventh century, was further strengthened by the arrival of the Cistercians in the twelfth, and of the mendicant orders in the thirteenth century.

The character and connections of the early Christian church in Poland were far from simple, however. Catholic apologists from the Middle Ages onward have always given exclusive attention to the Roman obedience and to the Latin rite. Yet, since the Polanians took their Christianity from Bohemia, it must be remembered that until the end of the eleventh century, the Slavonic liturgy of the Cyrillo–methodian tradition co-existed in the Czech lands alongside the German-sponsored Latin church. Although there is no direct evidence that the baptism of the Vistulanian chieftain by Methodius left any lengthy imprint on religious life north of the Carpathians, there is no doubt that much of the religious vocabulary of the Polish language was adopted from Czech and Slavonic forms, not from German or Latin ones. Words such as *Chrzest* (baptism), *kazanie* (sermon), *kościół* (church), *pacierz* (Paternoster), and *ksiądz* (priest) provide clear examples. Both Wojciech and his half-brother, Gaudentius, were members of the noble Slavnik family which patronized the Slavonic rite, and may be expected to have brought their sympathies with them into Poland.[3]

Relations between the established Church and the nascent state were not easy. In the first stages, the Piast princes badly needed the support of the bishops; but sometimes reacted strongly against them. In 1079, Bishop Stanisław of Cracow, who repeatedly denounced the oppressions of King Bolesław II and who had fomented a baronial rebellion against him, was promptly condemned to be killed and dismembered. The martyrdom of this Polish Becket ensured the success of the rebellion, and the expulsion of the king. Later on, in the period of fragmentation, the clergy increased their landed property, and were able to shed certain princely controls. In 1180, at the Synod of Łęczyca, Casimir the Just, Prince of Cracow and Sandomierz, agreed to limit the jurisdiction of his officials over the population of church estates and to waive his rights to the property of defunct bishops. In the thirteenth century, on the initiative of Archbishop Henry Kietlicz (1150–1219), the agent of the Gregorian Reforms, cathedral chapters assumed the prince's right of appointing bishops. Canon law was extended throughout the ecclesiastical possessions, and the clergy became a privileged, autonomous estate. Divided against themselves, the princes could not resist. Their political power was severely eroded by a united church which readily wielded the threat of excommunication and the promise of coronations. Archbishop Jakub Świnka (d. 1314) was one of several prince-making prelates. In response, the princely families could do little but appeal to the Vatican over the heads of the bishops, and quite incidentally to produce an unprecedented number of saints. There was St. Jadwiga (1179–1243), wife of Henryk the Bearded, Prince of Silesia, canonized in 1267; the Blessed Kinga (1234–92), daughter of Bela IV, King of Hungary, who pursued the virgin life with her husband, Boleslaus the Shameful, Prince of Cracow; and Saint Salomea (d. 1268), daughter of Leszek the White. There were monastic saints – Bronisława, a Premonstratensian nun, and Jacek, a Dominican friar. Even a historian, in the person of the careful Bishop Kadłubek, was raised to the ranks of the Blessed. Undoubtedly, however, the most important canonization was that of St. Stanisław in 1257. His dismembered body was seen as the symbol of a divided country; and its miraculous recomposition was taken as a prophesy of Poland's eventual resurrection.

The status of the monarchy was never clearly defined.

Although for practical purposes the Piasts were undoubtedly masters in their own house, their relationship to the Holy Roman Emperor, and to other neighbouring authorities, was the subject of constant adjustments and accommodations. In the Latin documents of the eleventh and twelfth centuries, the Piasts were most frequently denoted by the dignity of *Dux*. Literally translated as 'Duke', or in German as 'Herzog', the title inaccurately implies a degree of subordination to a feudal superior. By German historians, it was customarily interpreted as a sign of the Piasts' allegiance to the Holy Roman Emperor. In fact, it might better be rendered by 'chief' or 'warleader'. Yet when Krzywousty's Testament divided the realm among his sons in 1138, the title that was chosen for 'the senior prince', who was to hold the province of Cracow and to enjoy precedence over his brothers, was not *Dux*, but *Princeps*. In Polish, the title of *Dux* is generally translated as *Książe* to distinguish the rank of uncrowned prince from that of *król* (*rex*) or 'crowned king' – *król* being a corruption of Karol–Karl–Charlemagne. Coronation, however, was no infallible sign of sovereign status. When Otto III placed his own crown on the head of Bolesław Chrobry during the festivities at Gniezno in 1000, he raised him to the dignity of *patricius*, or 'elder of the Roman nation', and declared him 'brother and aide in the Empire'. Some historians see this as an act of favour between the Emperor and his vassal: others as a gesture of friendship between equals. Otto's agreement to Chrobry's formal coronation was unrealized for a quarter of a century owing to the intransigence of his successor, Henry II. It was put into effect with papal connivance in 1025 during the following interregnum. Thereafter, coronation and recognition of the Polish rulers by no means came automatically. A number of Chrobry's successors admitted the overlordship of the Emperor. In 1033, at the Congress of Merseburg, Mieszko II (990–1034) submitted to the new Salian Emperor, Conrad II, and turned Poland into an imperial fief. In contrast, Kazimierz II Odnowiciel (Casimir the Restorer, 1016–58), who rebuilt the state after the rebellion of 1037, was never crowned. Bolesław II Szczodry (Boleslaus the Bold, 1039–81), imitated his earlier namesake, and in 1076 crowned himself King whilst the Emperor Henry IV was distracted. Władysław

Herman (1043–1102) was not crowned, and submitted to
the Emperor. His elder son, Zbigniew, sought the Emperor's
protection against his younger brother Bolesław III Krzywousty. The latter was a predatory warrior who needed no
one's protection. He did not bother to be crowned, but in 1135
was invested by the Emperor with Pomerania. In the period
of fragmentation, which followed, the interminable struggles
for the Cracovian throne made royal coronations impossible.
On occasion, as with Bolesław Kędzierzawy (Boleslaus the
Curly, 1120–73), Prince of Mazovia, who paid homage to
Frederick Barbarossa in 1157, there were echoes of imperial
suzerainty. After the death of Henryk II Pobożny, (Henry
the Pious, 1191–1241), at the Battle of Legnica (Liegnitz),
the concept of the principate was itself abandoned. Not until
1320, when Łokietek obtained the Pope's approval for his
elevation as monarch of the reunited realm, did the Kingdom,
the *Corona regni Poloniae,* and the royal title of *Rex Poloniae*
(King of Poland) begin their permanent careers. Throughout
these early centuries, the acts of homage and of coronation
were weapons which all princes used in order to reinforce
their precarious authority. In themselves, they were not an
accurate measure of political power. They could be resorted
to by weak rulers in the search for protection and reinforce-
ment, and by strong ones as signs of success and independence,
or as instruments of diplomacy. Equally, they could be
ignored with impunity. Especially in the early period, the
German Emperors naturally preferred to think that the Piasts
owed them allegiance, whether as friends or as allies or as
vassals; and they had several sound precedents to work on.
For their part, the Piasts obviously preferred to consider
themselves rulers of an independent realm, whose alliances
with the Empire were of purely ephemeral significance. They,
too, had their precedents. (See Map 5.)

Royal marriages attested to the eminence of the Piast
blood. Although there are examples of princes who married
beneath their station, dynastic alliances constituted an obvious
source of political power. In the eleventh and twelfth centuries the Piasts could aspire to imperial consorts. Mieszko II
was married to Ryksa of the Rhine (Rycheza), granddaughter
of Otto the Great; Władysław II was married to a sister of

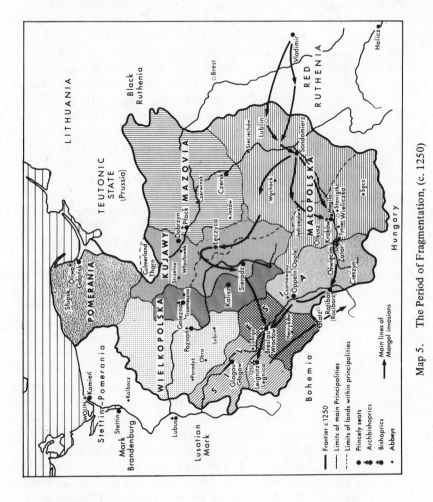

Map 5. The Period of Fragmentation, (c. 1250)

Conrad III of Hohenstaufen. With increasing frequency, however, princely brides were found in the east. As from Kazimierz I, who married Maria Dobronega, daughter of Vladmir, Grand Duke of Kiev and of Anna, sister of Basil II, Emperor of Constantinople, no less than nine of the sixteen claimants to the senior Piast line were married to Ruthenian princesses. From these unions, arose the Piast claim to Red Ruthenia which Casimir the Great successfully pressed in 1340. At various times, marriage contracts were sealed with all the leading dynasties of Central Europe. Świętosława Storrada, the 'Proud', daughter of Mieszko I, was first married to Eric, King of Sweden and then to Sven, King of Denmark, by whom she gave birth to Canute the Great. Of the four wives of Bolesław Chrobry, two were daughters of the Margrave of Meissen, and one the sister of Steven I, King of Hungary; but none, if we are to believe the Anonymous Gaul, were so beloved as his favourite Slavonic bride, Eminilda.

Constitutionally, the realm was regarded as the prince's patrimony, and was ruled by customary laws. The numerous local officials, designated in Latin as *comes* (count), and in Polish first as *pan* (lord) and then as *kasztelan* (castellan), were appointed and removed at the ruler's word. They were responsible for the military and judicial administration of the various districts, each centred on its *gród* or 'fortress'. They also administered the royal estates, and the many forms of customary service and tribute, including the *podwód* (the provision of horses and transport); the *przewód* (the provision of a guard to travellers); the *stan* (the provision of board and lodging); the *narzaz* (tribute paid in cattle); the *sep* (the corn-rent paid by the monasteries); and the *poradlne* (the 'plough-penny') paid by Crown tenants. The princely court did not distinguish between its public and private functions. The chief official, the *Wojewoda* or *Palatinus,* served as the prince's deputy in all matters of war and peace. The Polish title stresses his role as 'warleader', the Latin title his role as 'head of the palace'. He was assisted by the *skarbnik* (*Thesaurius*), or Treasurer; the *kanclerz* (*Cancelarius*) or Chancellor; and by an array of domestic courtiers including the *Komornik* (*Camerarius*) or chamberlain; the *cześnik* (*pincerna*) or cup-bearer; the *stolnik* (*dapifer*) or steward; the *miecznik* (*ensifer*) or sword-bearer; and the *chorąży* (*vexilifer*) or standard-bearer. The princely *Rada* or Council, consisting of some dozen dignitaries, secular and clerical, enjoyed no separate prerogative. In the period of fragmentation, all these offices were multiplied in each of the courts of the provincial princes, and thereafter could not be easily reduced by the recentralized monarchy. Thus the office of *Wojewoda*, originally the object of one single appointment, made its appearance in each of the provinces, and remained as the focus of regional power for centuries to come. It tended to retain the full apparatus of a princely court, even after the regional principalities disappeared, and in many instances could resist the impositions of the king to whom it was theoretically subordinated. To counteract such centrifugal tendencies, Łokietek followed the example of the Bohemian kings by instituting a new and much more dense network of district officers. The function of the new *starosta* (*capitaneus*) inevitably overlapped with those of the old *kasztelan* and the *Wojewoda*, and could not be simply separated from them. Most typically in the political sphere, the *starosta* provided a channel to the king for the aspirations of the provincial nobility against the excessive influence of the *Wojewoda* both in local affairs and the Council. It is also possible that some forms of regional assembly survived the reunification of the kingdom from the previous period. The 'colloquium' of regional dignitaries had assumed extensive judicial functions, and was not challenged by the *'conventiones terrestrae'* of the nobility until the end of the fourteenth century. These conventions could conveniently be regarded as the ancestors of the later *sejmiki*, and hence of the Polish parliamentary system as a whole. But little is known of their workings. In the Piast era, none of these institutions had crystallized into their final form.

Society was organized on a military basis. At the top of the social scale, stood the *Drużyna* or 'Team' of the prince's bodyguards. These seem to have been similar to the *Huscarls* of the Anglo-Saxon kings, and were drawn from a broad class of *heredes* (*dziedzic*) holding land from the prince in return for military service. Among the military class, several strata can be distinguished. The *możnowładstwo* or 'baronial caste' consisted of powerful families, often related to the prince by blood or distinguished service. They dominated the Council, the offices of state, and the political life in general. In the early centuries, they considered themselves to be co-proprietors of the king's realm, and participated in its revenues. They represented a serious limitation on the patri-monial nature of princely power. Although they swore fide-lity to the prince, and formally submitted to his authority, they were the source of most of the rebellions, and of the interminable intrigues of the regional rulers against the senior Piast princes. In due course, their influence was matched by that of the great abbots and bishops who were able to accumulate land and revenues on a similarly extensive scale. As from the early thirteenth century, the warrior caste was headed by the class of *miles* (*rycerz*) or 'knight'. Possessed of sufficient land and manpower to keep himself in horses, armour, and servants, he lived to fight, and to earn the grati-tude of his prince. In Małopolska, there are traces of the semi-knightly class of *włodyka* or 'esquire', which was obliged to work its lands for its living and could only take to the battle-field in the most pressing circumstances. The great mass of *heredes* might only have provided one or two footsoldiers from several families of landholders. All these people might consider themselves members of the *szlachta* or 'fighting class'. But it was not till the very end of the Piast era that they began to develop notions of an exclusive, autonomous estate.

At the bottom of the social scale were the slaves, organized in decades and legions, and designated in the documents as *decimi*. Originating as prisoners of war, they were settled on plots of their own and worked the larger estates. They re-sembled the *servi casati* of the Frankish kingdoms of a century or two earlier, and as such could be bought and sold. Some of the earliest surviving bills of exchange dating from 1226 and 1246 mention transactions involving 'girls and cattle'. Yet by then, slavery was already in retreat. The Church opposed the sale of baptized slaves; and slaves were eager to be baptized. By this time, a numerous sector of free or semi-free peasants had long since been in existence, and represented a growing proportion of the rural labour force. The towns, too, though still small, attracted important concentrations of administrators, merchants, and craftsmen.

In the thirteenth century, fundamental social changes occurred as the result of colonization. The colonists were drawn partly from foreign immigrants, and partly from locals who reorganized existing settlements along new lines. The main stimulus to the movement came from particular areas of western and northern Germany, which had long been able to supply settlers for the eastern marches, and which were racked by the added threats of overpopulation and of intensifying feudal services. Colonization took two different directions — the settlement of rural villages and the establishment of incorporated towns. It was helped by the initiative of Polish princes, whose lands were seriously underpopulated and not infrequently devastated by the ravages of war and of Mongol raids. By offering conditions of tenure superior to those prevailing in Germany, and by appointing a professional *zasadzca* (*lokator*) who could seek out, transport, and organize the newcomers, an energetic prince could transform the strength and economy of his inheritance in the space of a few years. In the case of village settlement, the pace was set by Henryk the Bearded, Prince of Silesia, who in 1205 launched a campaign to attract no less than ten thousand peasant families into some four hundred new villages. Each family was to receive 1 *łan* or 'manse' of arable land; pasture and forest were to be held in common. All services and dues were to be waived during an agreed period of foundation. After that they were to be limited to military service, to rents and tithes, paid partly in cash and partly in kind, and to manorial service and fortress repair occupying 2 to 4 days per year. A detailed agreement signed in 1227 by Henry the Bearded with the Bishop of Wrocław was adopted as the model for most subsequent rural colonies elsewhere in Poland. In the new villages, the colonists enjoyed considerable autonomy. Under their so-called 'German law', they were subject only to the rule of the hereditary *sołtys* (*Schultheiss*) or 'Headman', appointed by the lord, and to the jurisdiction of the 'village bench' over which he presided. They were in a much better position than the rest of the rural population who remained in subjection to the tributes and impositions of the *ius ducale*, or 'Polish law' of the princes. Many of them retained their separate identity until modern times. At

Wilhamowice near Oświęcim in the district of Cracow, a
Frisian settlement established in 1242 has preserved its own
unique dress and dialect until the present day. In the case of
the towns, the ancient 'Law of Magdeburg' was generally
adopted as the model for new corporations. Old Slav towns
such as Wrocław, Poznań, and Kraków, in 1242, 1253, and
1257 respectively, were incorporated as 'German' cities. They
tended to attract citizens of German origin, and gradually
developed a distinct burgher class. Henceforth, they were
known to the outside world by their German names of
'Breslau', 'Posen', and 'Krakau'. Elsewhere, entirely new
cities were founded and populated with German immigrants
from the start. Thorn (Toruń) on the Vistula, was founded
in 1231 by the Teutonic Knights, and Neu Sandez (Nowy
Sącz) in the Carpathians was founded in 1292 by Vaclav of
Bohemia during his dispute with Łokietek. This process,
leisurely enough in the thirteenth century, was destined to
gather pace in the fourteenth, fifteenth, and sixteenth
centuries.

Cultural life in Piast Poland is largely obscured by the
deficiencies of the sources. Secular society was overwhelmingly
illiterate. Popular art forms were either oral or ephemeral.
Such artefacts and writings that have survived are mainly the
products of imported Catholic religious influences. In architecture, the Polish record begins with a number of churches
in the Romanesque style, such as St. Andrew's in Cracow
from the eleventh century, and the cathedral of Płock from
the twelfth. The Gothic begins with the Cistercian abbeys of
Sulejów and Wąchock. The magnificent bronze doors of
Gniezno cathedral, which have been dated to *c.* 1175 and
whose bas-relief panels depict scenes from the martyrdom of
St. Wojciech, were probably of Flemish manufacture. In literature, Latin texts claimed a virtual monopoly until the end
of the thirteenth century. The ancient *Roczniki* (Calendars),
the chronicles of Gallus Anonimus and of Kadłubek, and the
numerous hagiographies, all belong to the universal Latin
tradition. The earliest work of Polish prose, the fragmentary
Kazania świętokrzyskie or 'Holy Cross Sermons', was composed around 1350 by a monk of Częstochowa. Its content is
entirely devotional, and its language contains a strong

admixture of Church Latin. Since Poland did not possess its own university, young men in search of higher education were obliged to travel abroad, especially to France and Italy. The names of several such emigrant scholars, such as Martin the Pole in Paris, a historian, or Nicholas the Pole of Montpellier, a physician, serve to underline the constant cultural intercourse between Poland and the west. Best known of them, however, was Witello or Vitellon (1230–80), a Silesian philosopher active in the second half of the thirteenth century, who was an associate both of William of Moerbecke and of Thomas Aquinas. The son of a German colonist from Thuringia and of a Polish mother, he spent the first part of his career in a Polish monastery before departing for Italy. His fundamental treatise on the science of optics, the *Perspectiva*, was inspired by the belief that an enquiry into the physical properties of light would solve the metaphysical problem of the nature of existence. His study of human sight led him to the distinction between the mechanical operations of the eye and the co-ordinative subconscious functions of the mind. In this way, he is sometimes seen as one of the precursors of modern psychology.[4]

The incorporation of the cities probably provided the immediate cause for the granting in 1264 of a General Charter of Jewish liberties by Boleslaus the Modest, Prince of Cracow. There is little reason to doubt that Jews had lived in Poland from the earliest times, and that Judaism, as preserved by the descendants of the ancient Chazar kingdom in the south-east, had actually antedated Christianity. But no separate legal provisions were necessary until the mid-thirteenth century when the new powers of city corporations might have been used to harass the Jews or to exclude them altogether. As a result, the General Charter specifically listed the right of the Jews to travel round the country without molestation; to engage in trade; to pursue their own religious practices, including worship in their synagogues, Jewish burial, and ritual slaughter; and to be exempted from slavery or serfdom. It could not insist, of course, that the Jews be allowed to reside within the bounds of the city, or that they should enjoy the same rights as those of the autonomous Christian burghers. But it provided the basis of later Jewish prosperity in Poland, and served as the model for all subsequent re-confirmations of Jewish liberties by Polish rulers until the end of the eighteenth century.[5]

In this same era, economic life made rapid advances. The revolution in farm-management, first demonstrated by the Cistercians spread quickly into the secular estates and encouraged the concentration of land holdings in compact units. Bishops, barons, and royal bailiffs, all competed to maximize the output of their lands. All raised their demands on the peasantry. The incorporation of cities in the thirteenth century, was encouraged by the previous functioning of some three hundred chartered markets and by a growing network of roads, horse transport, and storage depots. At the same time, the progress of colonization assisted the growth of a cash economy. Internal trade increased. Mining under royal auspices at Wieliczka for salt, at Ołkusz for lead and tin, and at Kielce for iron, was expanded. The ancient system of coin-age was reformed. The first Polish *denarii* (silver pennies) had been struck in the 980s by Mieszko I. Survivals from the reign of Bolesław Chrobry with inscriptions such as 'PRINCES POLONIE' or 'GNEZDUN CIVITAS' are well known. But the 'thick pennies' of the early Piasts had been repeatedly used to remit more and more 'thin pennies' of the later principalities. In 1337–47, the new coinage was introduced on the monetary scale: 48 *grosze* (grossi) = 24 *skójca* (sesterce) = 4 *wiardunki* (farthings) = 1 *grzywna* (mark) = 197 grams of silver. External trade increased too. The overland trade on the east–west route between Germany and the Black Sea thrived on the exchange of furs, honey, cattle, and slaves, for textiles and implements. In the thirteenth century contacts were established with the Mongol Empire. Cracow also lay on the north–south route from the Baltic to the Balkans. On this ancient 'amber road' in the Middle Ages, Hungarian copper moved north, whilst cloth and salted herrings moved south. The activities of the Hansa, to which both Cracow and Wrocław belonged, affected the interior of Poland no less than the ports of Pomerania and Prussia.

War was the natural condition of medieval society. Apart from the incessant civil wars for control of the monarchy or of the principalities, armed conflict with foreign foe was the

order of the day. In the early period, organized raiding constituted an important sector of the primitive economy — loot,
slaves, and food stores being an essential supplement to the
products of subsistence farming. On the Prussian and Lithuanian frontiers, it continued as the normal way of life until the
end of the fourteenth century, and for the Tartars of the
south—east, well into modern times. Increasingly, however,
wars were fought for the delineation of frontiers, and for the
permanent control of territory. At first, the area of prime
concern lay to the west, with the relentless expansion of
German settlement into the imperial marches of Brandenburg,
Lusatia, and Meissen, and with disputes over Pomerania,
Silesia, and Bohemia. Later, it shifted to the east and to the
north — to Ruthenia, and above all to Prussia. Piast Poland's
one natural barrier stood in the south, where the Carpathian
mountains acted as a lofty, pristine screen.

To sustain constant warfare, a complex military organization was required. In the era of Mieszko I and Bolesław
Chrobry great importance was laid on the royal *gród* or
fortress, garrisoned by a detachment of the guard, and fortified with earthworks, palisades, and moats. Several such garrisons are known — at Gniezno, Poznań, Gdecz, and 'Wladislavia', each with several thousand men. In view of the vast
terrain, it was impossible to deny the enemy access to one's
home territory. To attack, one needed only to exploit the
element of surprise. Defensive tactics depended largely on
channelling the line of the enemy's advance by protective
screens — river patrols and flooded valleys — and on holding
the fortresses with their reserves of food and concentrations
of men. The tribal host must have called on almost every
able-bodied man. From the twelfth century onwards, however, peasants were gradually exempted from regular service,
except when defending their own locality, and were put to
work to support the rising costs of their knightly master's
equipment and training. The proportion of mounted cavalry
in the host grew as the number of spearmen and bowmen
declined. The towns provided their own defence. The reunification of the country after 1320 permitted the mobilization
of much larger forces. Under Casimir the Great, all landholders were legally required to present themselves for war,

complete with arms, armour, horses, and retinue. The *pospolite ruszenie*, the *levée-en-masse* or feudal host, emerged in
the form which was to last for almost five hundred years.
Regiments were organized on the basis of 'clan standards' for
the members of leading families, and of 'district standards'
for the lesser knights, royal officers, and village mayors. Its
strength in 1340 has been estimated at 11 to 12,000 knights,
not counting peasant and town infantry, and was rising
towards 20,000 by the end of the Piast period.

Conflict with the Empire began in the era when the Polish
tribes formed part of a vast swathe of pagan Slavonic settlement stretching from the Dnieper to the Main and the Weser,
and when the repulsion, subjugation, and conversion of the
heathen was regarded as the Christian duty of the neophyte
Germans. In 754 when the Englishman St. Boniface, the
'Apostle of the Germans', was buried at the Abbey of Fulda,
the lands between the Elbe and the Odra had long been an
area where Germanic tribes intermingled with Slavs. In the
tenth century, with the consolidation of the marches under
Otto the Great and the activities of Wichman, Count of
Saxony, and Hodo, Margrave of the Ostmark, the conflict
moved closer to the Polanian heartland. In the decade 963–73,
Mieszko I paid tribute to the Emperor, probably in recognition of Otto I's disclaimer of imperial rights in Pomerania. In
972, at Cedynia (Zehde), he fought and defeated Hodo, and
six or seven years later, having suspended payment of tribute
during the disputed German succession, repulsed the
Emperor's punitive expedition. This was the era during which
Mieszko undertook the conquest of Pomerania, whilst Danish
Vikings established themselves in their fortress of Jomsburg
on the island of Wolin. On the whole, the Piasts enjoyed a
stable relationship with the Ottonians, and shared in their
hospitality towards the pagan slavs of the Marches. Relations
deteriorated after the premature death of Otto III in 1003,
and it seems possible that Bolesław Chrobry, as a partner in
the brief Roman dream of Otto's 'Renovatio Imperii', may
have enjoyed greater sympathy in some parts of Germany
than Otto's successor, Henry II. In 1002–3, 1007–13, and
1015–18, Bolesław Chrobry battled the Saxons for possession of Lusatia and Milzi (Milsko). In these campaigns, he

ravaged the marches as far as the Saal; the Emperor laid siege to Niemcza (Nimtsch) south of Wrocław. At the Treaty of Budziszyn (Bautzen) in 1018, the disputed territories were granted to Bolesław in fief. They were soon lost after his death. Ninety years later, in 1109, the Emperor Henry V again attempted to cross the Odra, but was thwarted by the obstinate resistance of Głogów (Glogau). The royal fortress situated on an island in the river, continued to resist, even, when Polish hostages were suspended from the walls of the siege towers. In the ensuing period of fragmentation, the Emperors were free to intervene in Polish affairs with relative ease. In 1146, Conrad III led an expedition to endorse the claim of his brother-in-law, Władysław II Wygnaniec, (Ladislaus the Exile, 1105–59), Prince of Silesia, to the Piast principate. In 1157, Frederick Barbarossa repeated the exercise with similar lack of success. Thereafter, Silesia was regarded in Germany as an imperial fief. Other Polish principalities were obliged to pay tribute. But the internal weakness of the Empire increasingly left its eastern policy in the hands of its vassals, especially those of the marcher lords of Brandenburg. In 1249, the Brandenburgers seized the territory of Lubusz (Lebus) astride the Odra and turned it into their base for expanding their Neumark into the valleys of the Notec and Warta. In 1308–12, in exploitation of their raid on Gdańsk, they appropriated Słupsk (Stolp), Sławno (Schlawe), and Walce (Walzen), driving a permanent wedge between Wielkopolska and Pomerania.

Pomerania was first settled permanently by West Slav tribes, who like the Sorbs of the Ostmark, were closely related to the Poles. It is generally regarded by Polish historians as a Polish province, and by German historians as a German one. In the course of the Middle Ages, it was much affected by dense German colonization in the western districts and in the lower Vistula valley, and by Polish colonization in between. In the 960s, it was briefly united by Mieszko I, but under his successors was allowed to split into two parts. Eastern Pomerania, known in German as *Pommerellen*, and centred on Gdańsk (Danzig), remained a Polish principality until its conquest by the Teutonic Order in 1308. In the ecclesiastical order, it was subject first to the Bishop of Kolberg, but from

1148 to the Bishop of Kujawy and thus to the Polish See. Western Pomerania centred on Szczecin (Stettin), was ruled by a native Slav dynasty, and was contested in turn by the Poles, Danes, and Brandenburgers, all eager to effect its conversion to Christianity. Bolesław III Krzywousty was particularly active in this area. Having reduced the Pomeranian forts of Białograd (Belgard), Kołobrzeg (Kolberg), Wolin (Wollin), Kamień (Cammin), and Szczecin (Stettin) to submission over a period of years, in 1124 he imported Bishop Otto of Bamberg (1062–1139) to evangelize the heathen on his behalf. At that point, his plans went awry. In 1128 Bishop Otto returned to Pomerania under the auspices of the German King, Lothar of Supplinburg. He subordinated the new bishopric of Wolin to the See of Bamberg thereby propelling the province into the German sphere. After the death of Krzywousty, the Poles lost all direct influence. One of their few memories of the episode, immortalized in a song recorded by the Anonymous Gaul, was that of the taste of fresh sea fish:

> Pisces salsos et foetentes apportabant alii.
> Palpitantes et recentes nunc apportant filii.
> Civitates invadebant patres nostri primitus
> Hii procellas non verentur neque maris sonitus.
> Agitabant patres nostri cervos, apros, capreas,
> Hii venantur monstra maris et opes aequoreas.*

Silesia's fortunes were not dissimilar to those of Pomerania. Lying on the confines of both the Poles and the Czechs, the rich lands of the *Slezanie* were long disputed between them. In the three hundred years between 990 and 1290, lying mainly within the Polish orbit, Silesia played an important part in the construction of the kingdom, and in the politics of its fragmentation. Its native princes traced their origins to the senior line of the Piasts. In the fourteenth century however, it opted in the main for the Bohemian allegiance. Apart from the minor duchies of Cieszyn (Teschen) and Świdnica (Swidnitz) which continued to be contested into the sixteenth century, the whole of the province was renounced by Casimir

---

* Our fathers brought us reeking, salted, fish;/But we, their sons, bring fish that's fresh and wriggling./Our fathers invaded cities in the olden times,/But we, their sons fear neither storms nor thundering waves./Our fathers dealt with deer, and bees, and goats;/Their sons hunt for monsters and for treasures of the deep.[6]

the Great in 1340. Thereafter it passed in 1526 with the rest of the Bohemian kingdom into the hands of Austria, and in 1740 into the clutches of Prussia.

Poland's relationship with Bohemia was of capital importance. As the senior partner of the two leading kingdoms of the West Slavs, Bohemia played an important role in Poland's cultural and political development. Politically united at an early date under the Great Moravian Empire, and familiar with the Latin Christianity and with the German Empire at least a century in advance of the Polanians, the Czechs acted as the principal filter through which knowledge of the Western world reached Poland. It was from Prague, in the persons of Dubravka and Vojtech, that the Poles first adopted the Christian religion. It was from Prague that they learned the subtleties of the German association, Bohemia having become an invested electoral kingdom of the Empire. It was through the Czech language that they received practically the whole of their political, religious, and social vocabulary. Some historians have stressed that at this stage the Poles and Czechs should not be seen as separate nations. In the first half of the eleventh century, there was a real chance that a united West Slavonic state might have been permanently established under Czech or Polish leadership. Yet familiarity did not prevent the usual spate of neighbourly wars. Rather it imparted a rather special flavour to their mutual relations, where each of these Slav brothers would meddle in the most intimate aspects of the other's internal affairs at the least hint of weakness. It was in such a moment of weakness, in the triangular dynastic struggle of Piasts, Premyslids, and Slavniks, that Mieszko I first turned the Silesians and Vistulanians from their Czech allegiance in 990. In 1003, Bolesław Chrobry captured Prague, and was briefly raised to the Bohemian throne. He held the province of Moravia as far as the Danube and Tisza until 1017. Twenty years later, the Czech king replied in kind. Seizing on the opportunity presented by the great pagan rebellion of 1035–7, Bretislav captured Cracow and Gniezno, and carried off the body of St. Wojciech. He held Silesia till 1050. In the wars between the Poles and the Empire, the Bohemian kings often sided with the Empire, raiding deep into Poland and inviting Polish raids in return. In the period of fragmentation, they established their suzerainty at various times over Silesia, Wielkopolska, Małopolska, and even over Mazovia. In 1300, Vaclav II already King of Bohemia and Prince of Małopolska, was crowned King of Poland at Gniezno. He ruled in person till his death five years later. His son, Vaclav III, was murdered on his way to succeed his father in Poland. This brief episode of Czech supremacy attracts little attention from Polish historians. In the eyes of outsiders, however, it is seen as one of the few opportunities where the peoples of Central Europe might have been joined together to face their stronger neighbours. At all events, it gave the final spur to the reunification of the Polish kingdom under Łokietek.

Relations with Ruthenia were less complicated. As an area of Orthodox Christianity and East Slav settlement, Ruś looked mainly towards the Black Sea and to Constantinople. Its horizons rarely overlapped with those of Poland except in the intermediate territory of Red Ruthenia. In 981, in the era of the united Kievan Ruś, Vladimir the Great 'took the forts of Czerwień from the Lachs'. This statement of the Russian Primary Chronicle implies that Red Ruthenia may have originally been settled by West, not East, Slavs. In the next generation, in 1018, Bolesław Chrobry retrieved earlier losses and captured Kiev, striking and denting his sword on the Golden Gate of the capital, and installing his son-in-law, Svatopolk, on the Kievan throne. (A later imitation of the 'notched sword', the *Szczerbiec,* was to be used in the ceremonial of all Polish coronations.) In the 1030s Yaroslav the Wise took his revenge, reoccupied Red Ruthenia, and installed his own son-in-law, Kazimierz I, on the Polish throne. This success was reversed yet again by Bolesław Szczodry, who retook Kiev briefly in 1079. All this was of little moment. But in the subsequent centuries, when Red Ruthenia emerged as one of the independent principalities of Ruś, Polish interest there was of more permanent significance. Close dynastic links between the Houses of Piast and of Rurik provided a constant pretext for quarrels and intervention. In 1205, the intervention of Leszek Biały, Prince of Cracow, and Konrad of Mazovia led to the death of Prince Roman, and to the division of his inheritance into the twin principalities of Halicz and Vladimir.

In 1340, the death of Prince Bolesław-Jerzy Trojdenovitch, the last of his line, gave Casimir the Great the opening to press the long-standing claim, and in competition with the Lithuanians, to launch the final conquest of the province.

The Mongols, the 'scourge of God', who dealt the final *coup de grâce* to Kiev Ruś did not leave Poland unscathed. Advancing from the steppes of central Asia in 1241, the Golden Horde of Batu Khan cut a triple furrow of pillage and destruction right across Central Europe. The ultimate goal was Hungary; but one of their three armies took the northern route along the flank of the Carpathians. Sandomierz, Kraków, and Wrocław were razed, and their inhabitants put to the sword. At Chmielnik, the assembled nobility of Małopolska, perished to a man. At Legnica (Liegnitz) on 9 April 1241 the hosts of Silesia and Wielkopolska were heavily defeated, and their commander, Henry the Pious, killed. Mercifully, the Horde passed on, to Olomouc in Moravia and into the Danube Basin. But its *Baskaks* (Collectors of Tribute) continued to hold sway over all the Ruthenian principalities in the east. Its descendants, known as Tartars, established themselves permanently in the Crimea. Further Mongol incursions occurred in 1259 and 1287. In Cracow, they inspired two local customs which have survived to the present day. One, the *Lajkonik,* is commemorated on the eighth day after Corpus Christi, when a rider in Mongol dress tours the streets on a hobby-horse; the other, the *Hejnał*, or truncated 'trumpet-call' sounded every hour from the tower of St. Mary's Church, commemorates the death of the city watchman who was pierced through the throat by a Mongol arrow as he raised the alarm.

The Teutonic Knights constituted a problem of longer duration. Invited to the country almost casually in 1226 on the private initiative of Konrad of Mazovia, they soon raised the principal threat to the stability and integrity of the Polish lands. They called themselves *Deutschritter,* or German Knights, but were known in Poland, from the black cross on their white mantles, as the *Krzyżacy,* the 'Black Crusaders'. The full name of their organization was 'The Order of the Hospital of the Blessed Virgin Mary of the German House of Jerusalem', and their adventures in Europe were prompted by

the fall of Jerusalem to Saladin in 1187, and by the failure of
the Third Crusade. Reconstituted as a chivalric order in 1198
with headquarters at Acre, and later in Venice, they loaned
their services to any princely ruler who would pay for military
help against the unbeliever. In 1224–5, they made a brief
appearance in Transylvania, and brought themselves to the
notice of the Piast princes. At that very moment, Konrad of
Mazovia was suffering from a serious shortage of manpower.
Already engaged in a major programme of conversion and
subjugation directed against the pagan Prussian tribes to the
north of his borders, he was trying to rule Mazovia, Kujawy,
Sieradź, and Łęczyca, and to bid for the throne of Cracow.
When the Prussians responded to his ministrations with a
salvo of bloody raids and revolts, the minor knightly order,
the Brotherhood of Dobrzyn, which he had settled in 1209
on the Prussian frontier, could not cope. The apostolic see of
Prussia, which he had founded in 1215 with the aid of the
Cistercians of Łękno, was supposedly in danger of collapse.
His expedition of 1222–3, mounted with the combined forces
of Mazovia, Silesia, Małopolska, and Pomerania, failed to
have an effect. The situation was not desperate. But by exag-
gerating the danger of a Prussian invasion, Konrad was able to
justify his appeal to the Teutonic Knights. In 1226 he resolved
to invest them with the District of Chełmno (Kulm), and in
1228, the contract was sealed. Two years later, under their
Landsman, Herman von Balk, the knights arrived and began
their task with a will. For fifty years, they harried the Prussians
with fire and sword, until by 1288 the furthest fastnesses of
the Prussian lands were conquered. By then, the Order had
grown far beyond the control of its original patron; it had
become a power of continental importance and possessed a
state of its own. Konrad of Mazovia was no saint. He practised
all the vices of the medieval warlords. He had murdered his
Wojewoda from jealousy, and he, too, understood his Christian
faith as a licence for murder. Yet even he could not have
dreamed of the monster which grew from the teeth which he
planted in his own garden. (See Map 6.)

The process whereby the Teutonic State was established
betrayed a remarkable fund of energy and unscrupulousness.
From the start, brute force was abetted by diplomacy, by

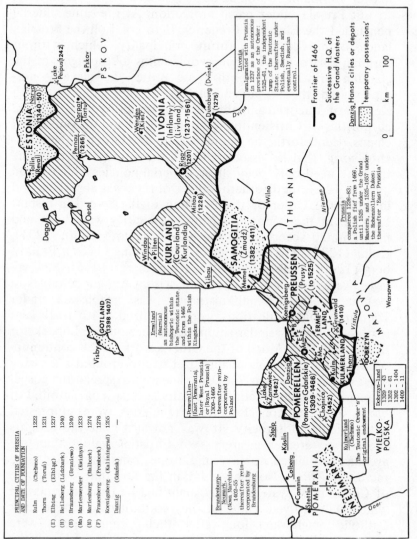

PRINCIPAL CITIES OF PRUSSIA
AND DATE OF FOUNDATION

Kulm	(Chełmno)	1222
Thorn	(Toruń)	1231
(E) Elbing	(Elbląg)	1237
(H) Heilsberg	(Lidzbark)	1240
(B) Braunsberg	(Braniewo)	1240
(Ma) Marienwerder	(Kwidzyn)	1233
(M) Marienburg	(Malbork)	1274
(F) Frauenberg	(Frombork)	1278
Koenigsberg	(Kaliningrad)	1255
Danzig	(Gdańsk)	—

Map 6.   The Teutonic State, (1230–1561)

legalistic wizardry, and by the gift of sound administration. Already in 1226 in the Golden Bull of Rimini, the Grand Master Hermann von Salza had persuaded Pope Gregory IX, to put Prussia under papal protection. At the same time he persuaded the Emperor Frederick II to grant all the Prussian lands to the Order as a future principality, which, without forming part of the Empire, would enjoy all the rights of the German princes. On both these scores, he cleverly misrepresented the scope and nature of the agreement with Konrad of Mazovia, and obtained the sanction of the supreme authorities of Christendom to open-ended and unconditional claims. Henceforth, he could declare the Order to be *reichszugehörig*, that is, 'associated with the Empire'. At the same time, he need only obey those imperial policies which suited him. In 1235, the Brotherhood of Dobrzyń was absorbed, and in 1237 the Order of the Brethren of the Sword in distant Livonia. In the conquered lands, new cities were built and incorporated according to the 'Law of Kulm': Thorn (1231), Kulm (1232), Marienwerder (1233), Elbing (1237), Braunsberg (1240), Heilsberg (1240), Königsberg (1286). New villages were founded, and settled with German colonists; a system of District administration was established under *komturs*. Communications were organized, with roads and castles, and with regular shipping services out of Lübeck for Elbing and Riga. Much of the Order's work struck contemporaries as highly commendable. But it also aroused a growing sense of moral outrage. An Order licensed to spread the gospel of charity was conducting its affairs against a background of blood and coercion. Recurrent rebellions were suppressed with calculated ferocity. It was not just that the Knights showed no greater awareness of Christian values than the average, brutalized nobility of Europe from which they were recruited. The real objection lay in the fact that in the name of Christ they systematically manufactured the violence on which they thrived, and that they continued to plague their Catholic neighbours long after their original goals were achieved. What was worse, they were encouraged by all the vested interests of Christendom — by the Papacy, by the Empire, by the Hansa, by patronizing kings like Ottokar II of Bohemia (after whom Königsberg was named), and by a great array of ambitious clerics, merchants, and princes. Modern Poles, whose understanding of Germanity is equivalent to what the rest of the world thinks of as 'Prussian', may be forgiven for imagining that the Teutonic Order provided the shock troops of a national German enemy. But this was not so. The Order was the manifestation of something more universal. Its membership, though predominantly German in complexion, was swelled by professional recruits from all over Europe, and by the seasonal ranks of crusading package tours. They were the incarnation of the most un-Christian elements of the Christian world and they enjoyed immense worldly success.

The Piasts first came into open conflict with the Knights over the seizure of Gdańsk in 1308. In that year, a Pomeranian rebellion had unseated the Polish rulers. When the rebels invoked the help of Waldemar of Brandenburg, the Polish magistrate invoked the help of the Order. The assistance was forthcoming. Having first bought the legal rights of the Brandenburgers' doubtful claim to Gdańsk – a transaction subsequently confirmed by the Emperor – the Knights drove Waldemar from the city, and calmly slaughtered its inhabitants. Before the Poles could intervene, the whole province was captured. The Grand Master rode in haste from Venice, and in 1309 took up residence in his new castle of Marienburg. For the next 146 years, Pomerania developed in the Teutonic orbit. Gdańsk became 'Danzig', and was resettled with Germans. It grew into the chief emporium of the Teutonic state. Its recovery constituted one of the strategic aims of Polish policy.[7]

In view of these stirring events, it is surprising perhaps that knowledge of Poland to the outside world had hardly increased in half a millennium. In England, for example, Alfred the Great, when translating Orosius, had been able to improve a passage on the lands north of the Danube with a sentence of his own: 'and to the east of Moravia is the land of the Vislani'. Yet the famous *Mappa Mundi* of Hereford cathedral, dating from 1250, has no better information. Its compiler knew only one Polish place-name – Vistula. Apart from 'Praga' in 'Boemia', all his other information on Eastern Europe can be traced to ancient and completely outdated

sources. Obviously, he was not familiar with the work of
Gervase of Tilbury (*c.* 1150–1235) whose *Otia imperialia*
(Imperial Delights) reveals a correct understanding of the
name of Poland – *quasi Campania* – and a detailed knowledge
of what he called 'the land of the Vandals between the
Sarmatian Sea and the Hungarian Alps'. Another author, the
Franciscan, Bartholomew de Glanville, who went to Saxony
in 1230, correctly described Poland's relation to the contingent
countries. Though this was a very meagre tally, it was not
inferior to the information available in France and Germany.
Even the German chroniclers such as Thietmar (975–1018) or
Adam of Bremen (d. 1075), who mention events connected
with Mieszko I and Bolesław Chrobry, have virtually nothing
to say about the Empire's eastern neighbour. Helmut von
Bozow (1125–*c.* 1180), a specialist, who wrote a 'Chronicle of
the Slavs', thought that the Poles lived to the south of Carinthia.
Not until the fourteenth century, in fact, did information
begin to flow in an appreciable quantity, or with reasonable
accuracy. Both the anonymous French 'Description of Eastern
Europe', of 1308, and the Catalonian *Libro del Conoscimiento*
of 1348 show a distinct advance on previous productions.
The French poet Guillaume de Machaut (1300–77), served as
a secretary to John of Luxembourg in Bohemia, visited Poland
on several occasions, and made expert reference to Polish
affairs in many of his works. In England, knowledge about
Poland was mainly garnered by English knights who participated in the crusades of the Teutonic Order. Both John
Gower (1330–1408) and Geoffrey Chaucer (*c.* 1345–1400)
assumed that a spell of fighting in Prussia formed an essential
part of a knight's career:

> There was a knight, a most distinguished Man
> Who from the day on which he first began
> To ride abroad, had followed chivalry,
> Truth, honour, generous thought and courtesy.
> He had done nobly in his sovereign's war
> and ridden into battle, no man more,
> As well in Christian as in heathen places,
> And ever honoured for his noble graces.
> He saw the town of Alexandria fall:
> Often, at feasts, the highest place of all
> Among the nations fell to him in Prussia.
> In Lithuania he had fought, and Russia . . . .[8]

Chaucer's remarks are generally thought to have been inspired by the expedition of Henry Bolingbroke, the future Henry IV, who in 1390–1 took part in the Order's attack on Wilno. Inevitably, English opinions were coloured by the nature of their sources. The inhabitants of Poland were often described as 'Saracens' that is, enemies of the Prussian crusaders. In Sir John Mandeville's *Travels,* which first appeared in 1366, the country is variously described as 'the land of Polayne' and 'the reme of Crako'. The greater interest of this period was undoubtedly stimulated by the reconstruction of the Polish Kingdom which was proceeding at that very time.[9]

The period of fragmentation had lasted for nearly two centuries. It was caused in the first instance by the growing self-sufficiency of the provinces, and by that reaction against central authority which is observable in the second stage of the history of many primitive states. Like the partition of Charlemagne's Empire in 843, Krzywousty's division of the Piast realm in 1138 stood fair to prove permanent. A divided Poland could not resist the incursions of Czechs, Saxons, Prussians, Lithuanians, and Mongols. Yet the nascent Polish community proved surprisingly resilient. Although the Piast princes of Wielkopolska, Małopolska, Mazovia, Kujawy, Pomerania, and Silesia, and of several other minor appanages, warred against each other incessantly, they had the good fortune to live in an era when their neighbours were similarly divided. The German Empire was racked by the contest with the Papacy and by interminable adventures in Italy; Ruthenia was still more fragmented than Poland. By the time that Bohemia had been reconstructed by the Luxembourg dynasty, and Hungary by the Angevins, the last two Piasts, Łokietek and Casimir the Great, had already put their own house in order, and had reunited the Polish kingdom.

Władysław I Łokietek (*c.* 1260–1333) was a warrior, small of stature but great at heart. In his time, as for the past two centuries, the struggle of trying to reunite the Piast principalities resembled a game of primitive pin-ball, where each player sought to roll half a dozen marbles into their numbered sockets whilst his adversaries, as they barged and rocked the table, tried to do the same. He owed his eventual success partly to a charmed life, which outlasted that of all his relations and rivals, and partly to his remarkable single-mindedness. A grandson of Konrad of Mazovia, he inherited the principalities of Kujawy and Łęczyca at the age of seven, and succeeded to that of Sieradz in 1288. But in the long civil war which followed the death of his elder brother, Leszek the Black, in that same year, he failed to press his claim to the succession. He was repeatedly beaten to the Cracovian throne — first by Henryk IV Probus, Prince of Silesia, next by Vaclav II of Bohemia, then by Przemysł II, Prince of Wielkopolska (who was murdered by his would-be kidnappers at Ragazno in February 1296) and finally, for a second time by Vaclav II.

What he lacked in early success, he made up by persistence. During the reign of the Bohemian king, he was exiled, and travelled to Rome to lobby the Pope. It was not difficult to raise a coalition. The Czechs, vassals of the Emperor, had many enemies, not least in Hungary, in the newly elected Angevin king, Charles Robert. By 1306, both Vaclav II and his son Vaclav III, the last of the Przemyslids, were dead. Cracow opened its gates to Łokietek. The war of unification could be organized from the centre. With the exception of Kujawy and Pomorze, Łokietek's successive goals were all achieved. Wielkopolska was secured by 1314. A revolt by the Germans of Cracow, headed by one Albert, and by Bishop Jan Muskata, who thought of returning to their earlier Bohemian allegiance, was suppressed after a year-long siege. In this struggle, the first signs of Polish chauvinism appear. The Czechs were denounced as foreigners, servants of the 'German' Emperor, allies of the 'German' knights in Prussia, and of the 'German' Piasts of Silesia. The Archbishop of Gniezno, Jakub Świnka, brought Bishop Muskata, the 'enemy of the Polish people', before an ecclesiastical court. He excommunicated the princes of Glogau, who 'were turning Silesia into a new Saxony' and had resigned their claim to Pomerania in favour of the Teutonic Order. Investigations into the Cracovian revolt were assisted by a simple language test. Any suspect who could repeat and correctly pronounce *soczewica, koło, miele, młyn* was judged loyal; he who faltered was guilty. The knights who took to the field in Łokietek's cause, and were duly rewarded with grants of land, developed the first hesitant notions of a corporate 'Polish' estate. Łokietek's coronation took place in the cathedral in Cracow on Sunday 20 January 1320. The Pope had agreed on condition that the rate of Peter's Pence was raised from 3d. per family to 1d. per person. Łokietek, wearing a purple cloak, was anointed with holy oil. He took the 'notched sword' of Kiev in his hand, and made the sign of the cross in the air. As the diadem was placed on his head, the Age of Fragmentation ended. The Kingdom was restored.[10]

Łokietek's son, Casimir III (1310–70), the only Polish ruler to be deemed 'Great', added the skills of diplomacy and statesmanship to the warlike prowess of his forebears. His succession was not physically contested. He was young and lusty, with a lifetime before him. The first decade was marked by a long series of diplomatic treaties in which the Polish king painstakingly secured his position at the cost of calculated concessions. In 1333, he made a truce with the Teutonic Order, ending the indecisive war over Pomerania and Kujawy which had occupied his father's last years. His coronation at Wawel on 25 April 1333 was attended by the Grand Master, Luther von Braunschweig. In 1334, he made peace with the Czechs. In the spring of 1335, at the Hungarian castle of Vyshegrad overlooking the Danube, he met with his family's traditional ally, Charles Robert of Anjou, King of Hungary, and their common rival, John of Luxembourg, King of Bohemia. In return for 400,000 silver groats, he persuaded the Bohemian to renounce his claim to Poland and Mazovia, and to accept arbitration over Silesia. In 1339, at the Treaty of Cracow, he formally conceded Bohemian suzerainty over the Silesian princes. In 1343, at the Treaty of Kalisz, after lengthy proceedings both in Rome and in a special judicial enquiry in Warsaw into the misdeeds of the Teuton Knights, he signed a peace with the Order. In return for Kujawy and Dobrzyń, he surrendered the whole of Pomerania with Danzig. By confirming the Order's possession of Chełmno, he lost the point on which all Polish legal proceedings had been based. It was a hard bargain. But thus secured, he could turn to war. Already in 1340, he had entered the lists in the long three-sided contest with the Lithuanians and Hungarians for the inheritance of Red Ruthenia and the coveted title of *Dux Russiae*. In 1343–8, he fought the Luxemburgers for the

Duchy of Świdnica. In 1351, he took the Prince of Mazovia in fief. (See Map 7.)

Meanwhile, almost every aspect of Polish life was brought before the King's reforming and regulating gaze. A distinct caste of royal administrators was created to obviate previous reliance on officials of local significance. In 1347, the whole corpus of existing law was codified, and published in two separate collections − one for Wielkopolska, the other for Małopolska. These original 'Statutes' of Casimir the Great, relating to every sphere of public activity, formed the core round which Polish Law developed over the next four centuries. In the King's lifetime, they were enlarged by the addition of his subsequent decrees and by a body of so-called *preiudicata* or theoretical legal case-studies. The concern for order and permanence was reflected in the new Gothic architecture, everywhere in evidence. Fifty military fortresses were constructed. Trade flourished as never before. Unlike most countries in Europe, Poland escaped the scourge of the Black Death, and economic life was not disrupted. The arrival of numerous Jewish refugees from Germany marked a further stage in the expansion of a community which was destined to attract the largest concentration of Jewry in Europe. The reign saw a further growth of towns, no less than twenty-seven of which were fortified with encircling stone walls. There was a marked improvement in the popular diet, and in the material standard of life for all sections of society. The stage was set for the 'Great Days of Cracow', 1363−4.

Cracow in 1363, thirty years after Casimir's accession, was turning from a wooden town into a city of brick and stone. In the great Market Place, 200 yards square, and laid out after the Mongol invasion, the Gothic Cloth Hall was under construction. The Kościół Mariacki (St. Mary's Church) was in the eighth year of its 53-year remodelling. A site was being prepared for the new *ratusz,* or City Hall. On Wawel Hill, where the third cathedral, redesigned by Łokietek, was within a few months of completion, the stone of the new Royal Castle gleamed white behind the scaffolding. One mile to the east, beyond the walls, stood the new town of Kazimierz, named after the King. On its central square, a synagogue, a *ratusz,* and the Church of St. Catherine were all in the course

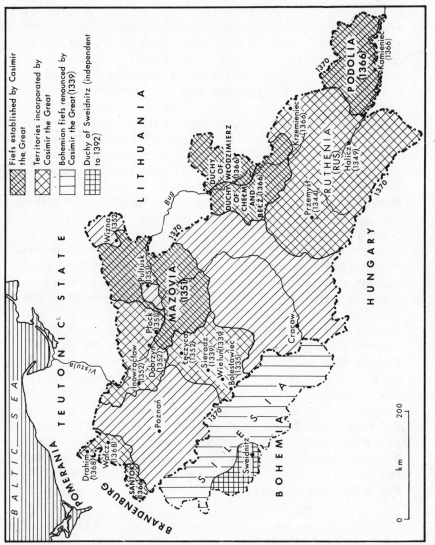

Map 7.   Poland under Casimir the Great, (1330–70)

of construction. In the shadow of this modern magnificence, the wooden houses of the old city behind St. Florian's Gate, with their little chapels and three churches — the Dominican, the Franciscan, and the fortified church of St. Andrew — must have looked woefully small. Here, in the space of a few months, three memorable events were to be celebrated. Casimir the Great, at the height of his fame, presided over the marriage of a future Empress; over the founding of Poland's first university; and over an international congress of kings.

The marriage was that of the King's granddaughter Elizabeth of Słupsk. The bride was a remarkable girl, reputed to be able to break horseshoes in her hand, and to crush suits of armour. The bridegroom was Charles IV of Luxembourg, King of the Romans by election, King of Bohemia in succession to his father. After the wedding, celebrated in the renovated cathedral in May 1363, the happy couple travelled to Prague and then to Rome for their royal and imperial coronations.

The founding of the University of Cracow occurred almost exactly twelve months later. It came at the end of long negotiations in Avignon where Pope Urban had been reluctant to grant Casimir's petition. The royal Charter of Foundation was issued on 12 May 1364. In it the King provided for the creation of one chair in the liberal arts, two chairs in Medicine, three in Canon Law, and five in Roman Law. He endowed them with a guaranteed income payable quarterly from the royal salt monopoly at Wieliczka. Exceptionally, for the practice of the day, he gave control not to the Bishop of Cracow but to the royal Chancellor, Janusz Suchywiłk. On that same day, the city of Cracow issued a charter listing the rights and privileges which it was extending to the University's 'masters, doctors, scholars, clerks, guards, beadles, and their families'. The charter further explained why the University was being founded:

'. . . ut ex congregatione dictorum, magistrorum, doctorum, et scolarium, pro conversione infidelium paganorum et scismaticorum, dicto regno confinancium, maior devocio predicationis et instructio fidei catholicae ad laudem et gloriam omnipotentis dei et genetricis eius gloriosae Virginis Mariae crescat et augeatur.* (*See note opposite.*)

Although the Piast's 'Studium Generale' did not outlive its founder, and did not begin its continuous existence until 1400 when it was refounded by a Jagiellonian monarch, the University of Cracow can fairly claim to take second place only to Prague in the seniority of Central Europe's seats of learning.

The Congress of Cracow, too, was less memorable for what actually happened, than for what it signified for the future. It was occasioned by the visit of Pierre de Lusignan (1329–69), King of Cyprus, who was touring the courts of Europe in efforts to raise a new Crusade. He had attended the coronation of the French King, Charles le Sage at Rheims in May, and had called at Prague to collect the Emperor-elect, Charles of Luxembourg, and bring him along, together with his son, Vaclav of Bohemia, to Cracow. There he was met by the host, Casimir of Poland, and by King Louis of Hungary, King Waldemar of Denmark, and Dukes Otto of Bavaria, Ziemowit of Mazovia, Bolko of Świdnica, Władysław of Opole, and Bogusław of Słupsk. Their time was spent in jousting: in a famous banquet at the house of Nicholas Wierzynek, on the city square: and, incidentally, in discussions about the proposed crusade. Most surprisingly perhaps, the entire proceedings were recorded by one of the leading poets of the age, the Frenchman, Guillaume de Machaut. Having served John of Luxembourg for over thirty years, Machaut was very familiar with Eastern Europe and had visited Cracow with his master in 1335 on his return from Vyshegrad. Although he did not accompany Pierre de Lusignan on this later occasion as is sometimes supposed, he was able to set the scene from first-hand experience:

> Ce fait, de Prague se partirent;
> Or diray quel chemin il firent.
> Parmi Behainge chevauchirent
> Trois journées & plus alèrent
> A Bresselau, à Liguenisse,

---

* '. . . so that, from the assembly of the said masters, doctors, and scholars, and for the conversion of the pagans and schismatics adjoining the said kingdom, a greater love of prayer and a more effective ordering of the Catholic faith may grow and increase, to the praise and glory of Almighty god and of his glorious mother, the Virgin Mary.'[11]

A Nuistat, à Suedenisse.
Costen, Calix, Buton, Glagouve
Passèrent, & par Bassenouve
De la en Cracoe arrivèrent,
Ou les roys dessus dis trouvèrent,
Qui a l'encontre venirent,
Et moult grant joie leur feïrent.
Comment il furent receü,
Honnouré, servi & peü
De pain, de vin & de vitaille
De toute volille et d'aumaille
De poisson et d'autre viande,
Il est moult fols qui le demande,
Qu' on ne le doit pas demander
Pour ce qu'on ni puet amender
Tant furent servi grandement.*

In the discussions on the Crusade, the King of Cyprus had to listen to a procession of pious assurances, first from the Emperor-elect, then from the King of Hungary, and then from Casimir himself:

Après fu le roy de Poulainne
Qui tint Cracouve en sa domaine,
Qu'il promist qu'il y aideroit,
Toutes les fois que poins seroit
Au saint voyage mettre à fin.
Et tuit li prince qui la furent
Li un vouent, li autre jurent
Que volontiers y aideront
Et que leur povoir en feront.**

* Which done, they departed from Prague;/So I shall say which road they took./ They rode through Bohemia/For three days, and then went/To Breslau, to Legnica,/To Neustadt, to Swidnica./Costen, Kalisz, Beuthen, Glogau/Were passed, and then Poznań./They arrived thence in Cracow/Where they found all the aforesaid kings,/Who came out to meet them/And caused them very great joy./How they were received,/Honoured, waited on, and plied/With bread, wine, and victuals,/With all sorts of game and poultry/With fish and other meats,/It would be a very foolish man who asked./Indeed, one should not make demands,/For things which can't be counted:/With such largesse were they entertained.

** Afterwards, it was (the turn) of the King of Poland,/Who holds Cracow in his domain/And who promised that he would help him,/Whenever the conditions were (right)/To put the holy crusade into execution./And of all the princes who were there,/Some avowed, and others swore on oath/That they would willingly assist,/And do everything in their power.

But when it came to jousting, Pierre de Lusignan was unbeatable:

> Mais einsois grans joustes crièrent
> Car il le veulent sestier
> De jouster & de tournier.
> Briefment, il joustèrent ensamble;
> Et l'emperere, ce me semble,
> Jousta avec les autres roys
> Qui estoient en grans arrois.
> Mais l'estrange roy ot le pris,
> Comme des armes li mieus apris.*

After that, having received their gifts and their 'honourable' and 'courteous' wishes, the champion left for Vienna:

> Or chevaucha li roys de Chipre
> Qui n'est pas vestus de drap d'Ipre
> Mais d'un drap d'or fait a Damas.
> Il n'est remes piteus ne mas
> De sa besogne pourchacier.
> Eins ne fait que'aler & tracier
> Les signeurs partout, et querir
> Pour leur aide requerir.
>   Tant a erre par ses journees
> Par froit, par chaut et par jalées
> Qu'a Vienne vint sus la Denoe,
> A x journées de Cracoe.**

There was no question of a general crusade. Pierre de Lusignan returned to Venice and to Cyprus, to the unexpected capture of Alexandria, which was resented no less by the Christian world than by the Turks, and to his death. For the rest of Europe, the Congress of Cracow was an obscure, forgotten episode. For Poland, it was the country's modest début on to the scene of international diplomacy.

---

* But the heralds proclaimed the lists/For they all wished to tarry/To joust and to hold a great tournament./In short, they jousted together;/And the Emperor, as I recall,/Tilted with the other kings,/Who were (there) in great array./But the foreign king took the prize,/Being trained the best in the use of arms.

** Then the King of Cyprus took horse again./He was clad in no (ordinary) cloth of Ypres/But in cloth-of-gold woven in Damascus./Nor was he sorry for himself, nor weary/By the need to pursue (his quest) from place to place/He did nothing but travel, and seek out rulers everywhere, asking/if he could obtain their aid./Day after day he made such speed,/Through cold, and heat, and frosts,/That he came to Vienna on the Danube/In ten days from Cracow.[12]

At the end of his life Casimir had failed in only one respect. As king and ruler, he had been eminently successful; as 'father of his people' he was widely loved, but as dynast he had no acceptable heir. This was surprising, for he had known three legal wives, one bigamous consort, and at least two serious mistresses; he had several daughters and three sons. His first wife, Aldona, a Lithuanian, had died young in 1339. His second wife, Adelaide of Hesse, was only taken after two broken engagements, and soon cast aside for Krystyna Rokičana, a Czech girl from Prague, whom he married against all the rules, in a secret wedding at the Abbey of Tyniec in 1357. His third wife, Jadwiga of Żagań, was taken in 1365 on the strength of a forged papal dispensation. His will mentioned children by a certain Cudna, and there were persistent romantic rumours concerning a Jewess called Esther. The snag about his sons was that he had sired them with a married woman, and could not therefore claim legal paternity. Hence the two immediate candidates for the succession were Louis of Hungary, Casimir's nephew, and Kaźko of Słupsk, his grandson. From the technical point of view, their claims in the female succession were inferior to those either of Władysław Biały of Gniewków, who was a monk in Dijon in Burgundy, or of Ziemowit III, Prince of Mazovia. Casimir had feared a disputed succession all his life. Already at Vyshegrad at the age of 29, he had made provision to be succeeded by Louis of Hungary, or by Louis's brother Jan, in the event of his death without male heir. This arrangement was consolidated by a further, more detailed Treaty signed at Buda in 1355. But later he had second thoughts. In both his wills, he invested Kaźko with the duchies of Sieradź, Łęczyca, Kujawy, and Dobrzyń with the obvious purpose of strengthening Kaźko's position in the event of a dispute with Louis. When he died, on 5 November 1370 early in the morning around sunrise, the matter was still not settled.

Casimir's funeral was on a scale commensurate with his achievement. Within days of the death, Louis of Anjou had arrived from Hungary to prepare his own coronation, and to attend the obsequies:

At the head of the procession, four carriages were pulled by four fine horses. The carriages, the drivers, and the horses were all dressed and covered in black. Forty knights in full armour rode past on chargers decked out with scarlet horsecloths. Twelve of them carried the banners and heraldic shields of the duchies and of the Kingdom. Behind them came a knight, riding in effigy of the late king, dressed in his golden royal robes and mounted on a high-stepping pacer caparisoned in purple. Six pairs of candle-bearers walked in procession with lighted tapers ... Then came the entire clergy of the city and environs, both secular and religious, singing a dirge and leading a line of biers loaded with gifts of samite and other rich materials to be divided among the churches and convents. At the end, King Louis walked between the Archbishop, Bishops, princes, and dignitaries, amongst a great crowd of lords and ladies. More than four hundred courtiers dressed in black mingled among them, groaning and weeping mightily ... In addition, two trusted persons were ordered to carry silver bowls filled with groats, into which some people added their offerings, whilst others were allowed to take as much as they liked. As fast as the bowls were emptied, they were refilled from the money sacks of the attendants ... With such great ceremony, the procession reached the cathedral church, where the Reverend Father, the Bishop, celebrated Holy Mass ... As in all the other churches, the High Altar had been draped with rich purple cloth and with two great streamers of brocade in various colours. One by one, the office-holders of the late king brought the symbols of their respective offices, and laid them before the altar. Thus the Chamberlain and the Treasurer offered up their silver trays, with cloths and towels. The royal Stewards presented four great silver dishes; the Cupbearers presented silver jugs and cups. Then the Marshal led forward the King's favourite steed, whilst his deputy ushered in the knight in effigy, still mounted on his horse ... After these presentations, as is customary, the royal standard was broken in pieces. At this, there arose such a shriek from the congregation in the cathedral, such an outburst of weeping from young and old, from high and low alike, that they could hardly be calmed. And no wonder! The death of the peace-loving king had caused them to fear that the peace to which they had all grown accustomed during his lifetime would now end.[13]

The greatest of the Piasts lay in his grave. But the Piasts were not yet extinct. It was a nice question — by whom, and in what manner, they would be disinherited. Casimir's Vice-Chancellor, Janko of Czarnków, the author of the description of his funeral, was actively intriguing against the Angevin succession. Having stolen the royal insignia from his late master's tomb for future use on behalf of Władysław Biały, his plot was unmasked, and he was banished from the country. Later, having returned to the chapter of Gniezno, he wrote his chronicle in defence of his own actions and of the dynasty which he served.

* * * * *

Having lost their royal dignity, the Piasts played only a fast-declining role in the affairs of the Kingdom. Kaźko of Słupsk died in 1377, in advance of Louis of Anjou whom he was supposed to succeed. Władysław Biały died in 1388 in his Burgundian retreat. Ziemowit III continued to hold Mazovia in fief. His descendants ruled Bełz to 1462; Płock to 1495, and until the death of the last of their line, Prince Janusz III, in 1526, Warsaw. The germanized Piasts of Silesia gradually abandoned their former Polish connections. As vassals of Bohemia, and then of the Habsburgs, they were drawn into the politics of Prague and Vienna, and presided over the division of their domain into ever smaller and more insignificant fragments. They survived in Oels (Oleśnica) to 1492; in Sagan (Żagań) to 1504; in Oppeln (Opole) to 1532; and in Teschen (Cieszyń) to 1625. The final extinction of the ruling Piasts came in 1675 with the death of Prince Georg-Wilhelm von Liegnitz, Brieg, und Wohlau (Legnica, Brzeg, and Wołów). By that time, the name of Piast was little more than an ancient legend in Poland. It was used as a political label at Royal Elections for any candidate who could claim to be a native-born Pole; but it had no other significant connotation. Eventually in the 1780s, it was revived by the historian, Bishop Naruszewicz, to denote that ancient Polanian dynasty which had claimed descent from Piast the peasant but which had never used his name for themselves. It has been used in this way ever since.

* * * * *

In some ways, Piast Poland lacked originality. Like many medieval principalities, it was essentially a replica in miniature of those grander kingdoms of the West which it tried to emulate. Its horizons were largely bounded by the preoccupations of the prelates and princes who sought to impose the values of a Christian society on a remote and backward people. Yet in the long run their mission was well accomplished. The foundations were well laid. After the brief Angevin interlude, the Kingdom of Poland was set fair to found one of the most original civilizations of early modern Europe, which, in union with Lithuania, spread out from sea to sea, and lasted for more than four hundred years.

CHAPTER FOUR

ANJOU:

The Hungarian Connection (1370-1386)

The conduct of the great ruling dynasties of medieval Europe can only be properly compared to that of the modern multi-national corporations. Formed in obscurity in some remote, provincial backwater of France or Germany, the Hautevilles, Hohenstaufen, Luxembourgs, Angevins, Habsburgs, and Bourbons, gradually spread their tentacles into every corner of the continent. By the skilful use of war, diplomacy, marriage, and money, and by the judicious diversification of their interests, they acquired and relinquished lands, thrones, and titles with the same unerring sense of self-aggrandizement that drives the great business empires of today to deal in shares, assets, and companies. Their operations transcended the boundaries of political authority, and could usually override the objections of local rulers or competitors with impunity.

Of all the dynastic enterprises of the age, none was more extensive than that of the House of Anjou. One branch of the family rose to prominence in 1154 through the accession of Henry Plantagenet, Count of Anjou, to the throne of England. As Henry II, he was the father of Richard Cœur-de-Lion and of John Lackland, and the forebear of all the English kings of the next two and a half centuries. But their most spectacular adventures began in 1265, when Charles of Anjou, brother of St. Louis, set out from France for the conquest of Sicily. Thanks to papal support, this second branch of the Angevins contrived not only to occupy the throne of Naples, but also, after the collapse of their Sicilian realm, to be elected as kings of Hungary. From there, through the labyrinthine workings of diplomacy and inheritance, they were only one step removed from the neighbouring Kingdom of Poland. As it happened, the Angevins' connection with Poland lasted for less than twenty years. In the history of the dynasty it represented only a minor episode of temporary importance. But in

106

the history of their Polish and Hungarian subjects, it marked the forging of a link which far outlasted the memory of any dynastic machinations.

The irruption of the Magyars in the tenth century had changed the face of Central Europe. They were the last of the nomadic colonists from the east, and were quite unrelated to any of the peoples among whom they settled. Their recent origins lay in the middle of the Pontic steppes, and their more distant roots in the depths of Central Asia. Their agglutinative language, of the Finno-Ugrian family, was totally incomprehensible to all their neighbours. In the year 907, seven tribes under the warlord Arpad took possession of the plains between the Tisza (Theiss) and Danube rivers. For the next half-century till their defeat at the Lechfeld at the hands of Otto the Great, they lived by annual raids which penetrated deep into the western lands. In 915, 924, and 933, they were in Saxony; in 921 and 947 in Tuscany; in 924 and 951 in Provence and Aquitaine; and in 926 in Burgundy. In 937, their most adventurous sortie took them in a wide arc through Mainz, Orleans, and Rome. After their defeat, however, they turned to more stationary pursuits. Their settlements stretched from the German *Oesterreich* or 'East Mark' on the one side, to the Transylvanian Alps on the other. Their conquests reached from the ridge of the Carpathians in the north to the coast of the Adriatic in the south. Their territory cut right through the middle of the former area of Slavonic settlement, engulfing a number of Slavonic peoples such as the Slovaks and the Croats, and completing the separation of the West and South Slavs.

Despite their different origins, the subsequent history of the Magyars was surprisingly similar to that of the Poles. They accepted Roman Christianity at the same moment and under the same auspices. The coronation of Steven I at Estergom (Gran) in 1001, and the creation of the Hungarian See, coincided almost exactly with the proceedings at Gniezno several weeks earlier. Henceforth, both Hungary and Poland formed the easternmost outposts of the Roman Church, regarding themselves with equal fervour as the twin bastions of the *antemurale Christianitatis*. They both experienced the same ambivalent relationship with the German Emperor —

sometimes overlord, sometimes enemy, sometimes ally. They both grew into multinational kingdoms, where the native cultures of the composite elements were subordinated to the Latin culture of Church and State. Although the Hungarian Crown did not disintegrate into separate principalities to the same degree as the primitive Polish kingdom, it was rent by exactly the same sort of dynastic feuds, heathen revolts, and foreign incursions. The control of the centre was always weak, the centrifugal forces of the regions always strong. In the thirteenth century, German colonization in Slovakia and Transylvania matched parallel movements into Silesia, Pomerania, and Prussia. In 1224, the Saxons of Transylvania, the 'children of the Pied Piper', with their city of Hermannstadt (Kolozsvár), were granted local autonomy. Two years earlier, the Golden Bull of Andreas II had granted far-reaching privileges to the high nobility – the right to voice grievances in their Assembly and to resist a king who breaks the law; freedom from arrest or confiscation without trial by their peers; and freedom from taxation without consent. These were privileges which the nobility of Poland was to emulate in the period of Angevin rule. Most importantly, whilst sharing an undisputed frontier in the Carpathians, Poles and Magyars shared common enemies – the German Empire and Bohemia in the east, the Orthodox Church, Moldavians, and Wallachians, and eventually Turks and Tartars in the east. There were few points of friction, and many sound reasons for close understanding.

Following the crises caused by the cataclysmic Mongol invasion of 1241 and the extinction of the Arpad dynasty in 1301, the fortunes of the Hungarian Kingdom were quickly revived by the Angevins. The route whereby a cadet line of the French Capetians arrived in Buda via the Kingdom of Naples can only be traced by reference to the tortuous decisions of papal politics. But it was no less felicitous for that. Charles Robert (Carobert) of Anjou, son of Charles Martel, King of Naples, was elected to the throne of Húngary in 1308, and reigned for thirty-four years. His son, Louis of Anjou (1326–82), known in Hungarian history as 'Lajos the Great' and in Polish History as 'Ludwik Węgierski' (Louis the Hungarian), enjoyed a reign of still greater length and renown.

Possessed of Europe's most valuable gold mines, and aided by a reformed and efficient administration, he could afford to build an empire. His ambitions were boundless. In 1348, he was styling himself among other things 'King of Jerusalem' and 'King of Sicily'. His expedition to recover Naples from his dissolute second cousin, Joanna, was only prevented by the onset of the Black Death. In a series of wars against the Venetian Republic, he recovered the Dalmatian coast and Ragusa (Dubrovnik). In the east, he asserted his suzerainty over Bosnia, northern Serbia, eastern Bulgaria, Moldavia, and Wallachia. When he took control of Poland in 1370, in succession to Casimir the Great, he reigned over the largest political complex of fourteenth-century Europe.[1] (See Map 8.)

To say that Louis of Anjou was elected King of Poland is rather to miss the point. It would be more realistic to stress that the Polish Kingdom was tacked on to the domain of Louis of Anjou. He was confirmed on the Polish throne for the simple reason that his private dynastic policy accorded well with the interests of the Polish barons. National interest played little part. After his coronation in Cracow, Louis rarely visited Poland. He ruled through regents. The Angevin party centred on the leading families of Małopolska − the Tęczyński, Mełsztyński, Tarnowski, Kurożwęcki. They were happy enough to be left to their own devices to an extent which had not been possible under Casimir. Opposition however collected round the late king's former ministers − Archbishop Jarosław, Chancellor Janusz Suchywiłk, and Vice-Chancellor Janko of Czarnków together with the barons of Wielkopolska and Kujawy. They were ready to intrigue on behalf of the Piasts, and quickly resorted to armed resistance. Intermittent clashes recurred during the reign. The latest of a series of warlords from Wielkopolska, Bartosz of Odolanów, was still in the field in 1382 when Louis died. The regents did not rule comfortably. The first, the King's Polish mother, Elżbieta Łokietówna, resigned in 1376 after a bloody affray in Cracow between her Hungarian guards and the Polish garrison. The second, Władysław of Opole, lasted five years. The third, Zawisza of Kurożwęk, was intended to rule with the aid of a baronial quadrumvirate, but failed to impose his authority. The fourth, the King's daughter, Maria, and her

Map 8.   The Angevin Realm, (c. 1380)

husband Sigismund of Luxembourg, Prince of Brandenburg, were unable to install themselves before the reign ended.

Louis applied the same remedy to the baronial opposition that he had successfully prescribed in Hungary. Having no rooted concern for the kingdom, he bought off the barons with extensive social and legal privileges. In 1351, in Hungary, he had calmed the magnates by confirming the law of entail, which preserved nobles' property from dispersal. Now, in Poland, he prepared still more radical concessions. In the winter of 1373–4, he summoned Polish representatives to his residence in Slovakia; and on 17 September 1374, after much bargaining, issued the famous Statute of Košice (Koszyce). Confirming all previous rights and immunities awarded to the nobility by his Polish Piast predecessors, and in particular the autonomy of the provinces, Louis limited all forms of noble service and obligation to just three heads. Firstly, the nobility were to pay the *poradlne* or land-tax, at a fixed rate of 2 groszy for every łan of private land worked by peasants. Secondly, they were to furnish unpaid military service for defensive operations within the frontiers of the Crown. Thirdly, they were to keep their castles and fortifications in repair. The clergy were to be assessed at 6 groszy and two bushels of rye or oats per łan, but this was later reduced. The towns were to have their liberties extended. Cracow was to enjoy the right of storage enabling local merchants to control all goods brought into the city. In addition, Louis embarked on an extensive programme of 'Restitution', systematically redistributing a vast pool of Crown lands illegally acquired by the nobility and recently seized by Casimir the Great. In the face of such generosity, no baron could afford to resist.

Louis's one lengthy sojourn in Poland, in 1376–7, was occasioned by the disturbances in Red Ruthenia – a province which he regarded as a separate realm, where Hungarian interests were not inferior to those of Poland. At the start of his reign, he had confided the government there to Władysław of Opole, and the experiment prospered. German colonists were established. The liberties of the cities – Lwów, Rzeszów, Jarosław, Krosno, Sanok – were secured; trade with the Black Sea was encouraged. In 1375, a Roman archbishopric was introduced at Halicz, to challenge the Orthodox supremacy. Then, suddenly, in 1376, a Lithuanian army under Kiejstut and Lubart, the sons of Gedymin, appeared from the eastern woods and laid the province waste. Thousands of captives were carried off into slavery. Kiejstut reached the gates of Cracow, before making for home. Louis delivered the retribution in person. In 1377, a Polish–Hungarian force crossed into Lithuania. The territories of Chełm and Bełz were occupied and attached to Red Ruthenia. Władysław of Opole was removed, and transferred to Cracow to govern over all the Polish lands. Red Ruthenia was handed over to the rule of Hungarian governors.

In all his policies, Louis was guided by his main concern for the Angevin succession. He had two surviving daughters, but no son. In 1374, at Košice he had obtained an assurance from the Polish barons that one of his daughters would succeed him in Poland; but in 1382, his unilateral nomination of Maria as regent seemed to pre-empt the issue in no unsubtle manner. It dismayed the majority of Polish lords as much as it angered the Magyars. Even before the King's unexpected death brought the conflict into the open, civil war was brewing. In Wielkopolska, one party urged Maria's husband, the Luxemburger, to take the throne without further ado. A second party, at a gathering of nobles at Sieradz, elected the Piast, Ziemowit of Mazovia. A third party, connected with the barons of Małopolska, sought compromise. After much wrangling, they settled on Maria's younger sister, Hedwig, who was betrothed to Wilhelm von Habsburg, Prince of Austria. At a second gathering at Sieradz at the end of 1383, the spokesman of compromise, Jaśko of Tęczyn, Castellan of Wójnik, persuaded his opponents to relent. Hedwig was to be elected Queen of Poland on condition that the Union with Hungary was abandoned. The pact was sealed; the invitation was sent and accepted. Throughout 1384, the disappointed candidates battled each other's candidacy into oblivion. After much slaughter, the junior Angevin princess, aged 10 years and 7 months, was crowned in Cracow as Queen Jadwiga, on 15 October. In the event, no voice was raised against her.

Historians cannot be prevented from wondering if Louis's efforts were worthwhile. He had certainly mortgaged his daughters' happiness against an uncertain future. His family's precarious hold on their inheritance would obviously depend as much on his daughters' husbands as on them; and one of the two was not yet wed. But such were the unwritten rules of the age. Here was a strong dynast with a weak dynastic hand. No success could redeem the elementary failure to sire a son. In any case, Poland was but one of his many domains, and a touch of confusion there was not the mark of ultimate catastrophe. In the constitutional sphere, it could be argued that the Statute of Košice was merely intended to win time. The growth of a strong executive, and of a robust fiscal and military system on the Hungarian model would undoubtedly have offset those early concessions, and would have put the King in a position to recover his prerogatives. Such may well have been Louis's design. At all events, death intervened before the design could be started. The Crown of St. Stephen in Hungary passed to the House of Luxembourg. The Polish Crown, and the fate of the House of Anjou, rested on the frail brow of Jadwiga.

From Poland's point of view, Louis's short reign was decisive. The privileges which he granted were not rescinded by his death. They put the political initiative into the hands of the nobility at a moment when the cement of social and constitutional structures was starting to set. They obstructed the action of all subsequent monarchs, and formed the foundations of a long tradition. In the sixteenth, seventeenth, and eighteenth centuries, when the Kingdom of Hungary had long since lost its independence, the Hungarian-style liberties of Poland still stood intact.

*   *   *   *   *

In those later centuries, the Polish—Hungarian connection remained close. Under the Jagiellonian kings, the Hungarian alliance formed a corner-stone of foreign policy. In 1440—4, and again in 1490—1516, Polish princes were elected to the Hungarian throne. In 1576—86, a Hungarian prince proved to be the most successful king in Poland's history. Common fears inspired common attitudes. Strong sympathies and personal contacts persisted even when political co-operation was impossible. The Partitions of Poland mirrored the earlier fate of Hungary. The partial revival of Hungary in the Dual

Monarchy in 1867 was accompanied by the partial revival of Poland in Galicia. In the nineteenth century two similar nationalist movements drew on an essentially comparable history to create a common friendship unique among the antagonistic nationalities of the region. In the twentieth century, two independent republics, squeezed between Germany and Russia, followed parallel courses of development. Even in communist Eastern Europe, two fraternal parties show rare signs of genuine fraternity. To this day, almost anyone in Cracow or Budapest can repeat the old jingle in its Polish or Hungarian form:

> Węgier, Polak, dwa bratanki,
> Tak do szabli jak do szklanki.

> Magyar és lengyel jó barát
> Karddal s pohár közt egyránt.

> The Pole and the Magyar like brothers stand
> Whether with sword or with tankard in hand.[2]

CHAPTER FIVE
JOGAILA:
The Lithuanian Union (1386-1572)

The Lithuanians prided themselves on being the last pagan people in Europe. In the thirteenth and fourteenth centuries when all their Baltic neighbours — the Prussians and Sudovians to the south, and the Letts, Finns, and Estonians to the north — had been converted to Christianity, they still resisted. Indeed, under their Grand Prince Gedymin (c. 1275–1341), they forged a state of enormous size and considerable power at the expense of their Christian neighbours. Barred by the Teutonic Knights from access to the Baltic coast, their energies were diverted from the ethnic heartland between the Nieman and Dvina rivers towards the south and east. Here they met with little opposition. The Ruthenian principalities which lay across their lines of expansion were demoralized by the Mongol yoke, and the Mongol Empire itself was contracting. A century of raiding, of castle building, and of exacting tribute, brought startling results. Red Ruthenia was carved up with Poland in 1349. In 1362, at the Battle of the Blue Water, in the bend of the Dnieper, Gedymin's son Olgierd broke the Mongol power for good. Kiev was taken in 1363, Polotsk in 1375, Smolensk in 1403. By the 1370s, when Louis of Anjou reigned in Poland and Hungary, Lithuania already rivalled the Angevin empire. It was ruled from the ancient capital of Vilnius in the north, and dominated by a pagan warrior élite who regarded their lives and estates as the prince's absolute patrimony. Its inhabitants were largely East Slavs, devoted to the Orthodox faith. Its official language was *ruski* or Ruthenian — in a form which is now known as 'Old Byelorussian'. Success on this scale created obvious drawbacks. Like all the primitive states united by conquest — like the empires of Canute the Great, of Rurik, or of Genghis Khan, or indeed of Bolesław Chrobry — there was a very real danger that Lithuania would crumble as quickly as it had been built. It was a cairn of stones thrown together on a bleak plain — with no cement.

It could be undermined by a revolt of its subjects, by dissension amongst its warlords, or by an incursion of its neighbours. Lithuania, proud and confident in the protection of Perkun, the God of the Thunderclap, was none the less lonely and very exposed.[1]

Jogaila (*c.* 1351–1434)* succeeded to the throne of Lithuania at the age of twenty-six, in the prime of life, and lived to be eighty-three. Of all the neighbouring peoples, he had no special love for the Poles, who to his pagan mind were servants of 'the German God'. Right until his elevation to the Polish throne, his raiding parties and rustlers regularly crossed the borders and carried off captives and loot. Yet the Catholic clouds on his western horizon were unmistakable. The consolidation of Poland under Casimir the Great was matched by the relentless advance of the Teutonic State, whose Grand Master, Winrich von Kniprode (1352–1382) was bringing his charge to a peak of condition. Having defeated the Lithuanians at Rudau in 1370, he was now planting colonies in the Samogitian wilderness. He had an open licence to convert the Lithuanians, issued by the Pope in 1339, and made no secret of his intention to subject them to the fate of the Prussians. Jogaila could not hold off two Catholic powers at once. In the long run, he realized that he could only choose the manner of his conversion – and the least agreeable manner was at the point of a Teutonic sword. Christianity was coming, one way or the other. Thus he was driven towards Poland by the coldest and most calculated reasons of state. He was informed no doubt of his grandfather's alliance with Łokietek which had bought some decades of respite in the north. He knew of the marriage of his aunt, Aldona, which at the cost of 26,000 Polish slaves, had been arranged for the same purpose. His duty was clear; and the prospect of a nubile Hungarian princess was an added bonus. In 1385, as soon as Jadwiga arrived in Cracow, the Lithuanian matchmakers made their first approaches. A conjugal and a political union were proposed. It was a decisive moment in the life of two nations. For four long generations spanning 186 years, Jogaila and his heirs drove the Kingdom of Poland and the Grand Duchy of Lithuania in harness, like a coach-and-pair. They

* *Jogaila* in Lithuanian, became *Jagiełło* in Polish, and *Iagiellonus* in Latin.

presided over an era when the Lithuanian élite was polonized, and the Poles acceded to the problems of the east.[2]

In Cracow, the Polish barons, too, had their reasons. After thirteen years of Angevin rule, when they had escaped from the direct supervision of a native king, they were not now disposed to submit to the first man, who by marrying Jadwiga, could impose himself on them. Having rejected Louis's elder daughter, Maria, on the grounds that she was married to Sigismund of Brandenburg, they could hardly accept Jadwiga's present fiancé, Wilhelm von Habsburg, Prince of Austria. For them, the Lithuanian connection was much more interesting. Jadwiga could be told to do her duty. Maidenly and ecclesiastical reticence could be overcome. On 14 August 1385, at Krewo in White Ruthenia, an agreement was signed, in which the Polish barons persuaded Jogaila to concede a number of very advantageous undertakings. In return for the hand of Jadwiga, the Lithuanian prince was ready to accept Christian baptism, to convert all his pagan subjects to Roman Catholicism, to release all Polish prisoners and slaves in his possession, to co-ordinate operations against the Teutonic Knights, and to associate the Grand Duchy of Lithuania with the Kingdom of Poland in a permanent union. On this basis, in February 1386 a great assembly of Polish barons and nobility at Lublin elected Jogaila, whom they knew as 'Jagiełło', as their king.

For Jadwiga, the experience was extremely painful. She was eleven years old, and virtually alone in a foreign country. She was being told to abandon a young man to whom she had been betrothed since infancy and to wed a pagan bachelor more than three times her age, with whom she could not even converse. She was intelligent, pretty, an accomplished musician and scholar, and entirely helpless. After her lonely coronation on Wawel Hill on 15 October 1384, her Habsburg prince had arrived to claim his bride. The German city and corporation of Cracow rejoiced. All the prisoners of the city dungeon were released. But the rejoicing was short-lived. Jadwiga watched as the Castellan of Cracow broke into the royal castle and chased the unhappy Habsburg from the Kingdom. She turned to her mother, who did not want to know, and to the Archbishop, who informed her that her

engagement was annulled. After weeks of agonized prayer,
she bowed to the inevitable. On the 15 February 1386, by
the splash of the baptismal water, Jogaila was transformed
into a Christian prince, christened 'Władysław' (Ladislaus),
and formally known henceforth as Władysław-Jagiełło. Three
days later, the wedding was staged, and in March their joint
coronation. After such treatment, it is not surprising that
Jadwiga turned to a life of charity. She despised the barons,
and loved the poor. The tattered remains of her cloak, with
which she had covered the corpse of a coppersmith drowned
in the river, became the banner of the Coppersmiths' Guild.
The imprint of her shoe, which she had rested on a stone
while tearing off the golden spur to give to a poor mason, was
preserved for posterity in the wall of one of the city's
churches. When she fell gravely ill in 1399, the castle was
besieged by peasants and townsfolk bearing gifts of chickens
and lambs and mushrooms for her recovery, and kneeling on
the cobbles in prayer. In her last days, she thanked God for
the victory of the Tartars on the Vorksla over the Polish and
Lithuanian barons, for the 'humbling of their pride'. She died
on 17 July 1399, at the age of 24 leaving her entire personal
fortune for the refounding of the Cracovian Academy, the
Jagiellonian University. Thus were the fortunes of two
countries served by the tears and humility of an unhappy girl.

The Union of Krewo was abrogated by Jadwiga's death, but
the political arguments which inspired it remained operative
throughout the Jagiellonian era. On every occasion that serious
difficulties arose, they ensured that the Polish—Lithuanian
Union was renewed on terms of increasing intimacy. From
the personal union of 1385—6, the relationship was gradually
strengthened, until in 1569, the prospect of the dynasty's extinction encouraged the creation of a permanent, constitutional union. (The process was essentially comparable to that
observable later in the history of England and Scotland,
where the personal union of crowns under the Stuarts in 1603
led over a bumpy road to the Act of Union of 1707 and the
creation of the United Kingdom in 1801.) The first stage was
effected in 1401. As Jogaila and Jadwiga were childless, it
was necessary to design the machinery of a future succession.
Meeting in their separate camps at Radom and Wilno, the

Polish and Lithuanian barons agreed that nothing should be decided in future without mutual consultation. In the so called 'Wilno–Radom Act', Jogaila's cousin Witold (Vitovt) was to rule Lithuania for life; thereafter, it was to revert to Jogaila and his successors. If Jogaila were to die without natural heirs, the future of his two realms was to be determined by common assent. The second stage was affected in an agreement signed at Horodło in Volhynia on 2 October 1413. Here, in effect, the Polish lords and Lithuanian boyars formed themselves into a joint estate. Among their many provisions it was agreed that matters of concern touching both countries should be settled in joint assemblies of the nobility, and that the Polish lords should participate in the election of the Lithuanian Grand Duke. In this way, the strict monarchical principle, already badly battered by the events of 1370, 1384–6, and 1401, was finally abandoned. Most remarkable, however, was the spirit in which the agreements were reached. It is true that the hearts of the participants of Horodło had been warmed by their recent victory over the Teutonic Knights and that they were all conscious of considerable mutual advantage. The Polish nobility were obtaining a permanent stake in the internal affairs of their partners: the Lithuanians were receiving a guarantee of the separate identity of their state and its ruler. Cynics would say that in such circumstances it is easy to be noble-minded. Even so, noble-minded moments are a rare phenomenon, and the words of the Preamble to the Act of Horodło are worth noting: 'Whoever is unsupported by the mystery of Love', it began, 'shall not achieve the Grace of salvation . . . For by Love, laws are made, kingdoms governed, cities ordered, and the state of the commonweal is brought to its proper goal. Whoever shall cast Love aside, shall lose everything.'[3] In later times, when a weakened Polish–Lithuanian state became the object of derision and the prey of stronger enemies, these words served as a comfort and as a reminder of the high principles on which the Union was first founded. Thus the Polish and Lithuanian nobility looked forward to the future with confidence. To all intents and purposes, they became one nation. Henceforth, to be 'Polish' was to be a citizen of the Polish–Lithuanian state. It was equivalent to being British, as opposed to being English or Scottish. It did not mean that the Poles and the Lithuanians, any more than the English or the Scots, lost their sense of separate identity. Even that large part of the population, who shared neither the political rights of the ruling class nor their Polish culture or language, could take pride in the achievements of the new state. Comparisons with neighbouring countries were not unfavourable.

The strategic security of the state was not seriously threatened. To the north, the three kingdoms of Scandinavia were locked in alternate embraces and quarrels. To the east, the Mongol Empire had dissolved into its component hordes. Novgorod was a peaceable commercial republic. The Russian principalities of Pskov, Tver, Moscow, Ryazan, and Viatka, were small and disunited. To the south, the Luxemburgers in Bohemia nicely offset the ambitions of their relatives in Hungary. The Turks were preoccupied with the Balkans. Even after the fall of Constantinople in 1453, they betrayed no intention of crossing the Dniester. To the west, the Empire was in decline, the prey of its constituent principalities. France and England were fighting the Hundred Years War. Spain was still absorbed with the Reconquest. Italy was flourishing but fragmented. This was an epoch without great powers. Until the rise of Moscow, of the Habsburgs, and of the Ottomans at the end of the fifteenth century, Central Europe lived in constant commotion, but no great danger.

The one persistent nuisance was presented by the Teutonic Order. The disputes were endless — over the right of storage in the Vistula towns, over the legalities of land settlements, over the German colonists in Lithuania. In 1398, the Grand Master seized the island of Götland from its pirate rulers, in 1402, the Neumark of Brandenburg, and in 1404, Samogitia. It was time for a reckoning. After 1386, the conversion of Lithuania had destroyed the Teutonic Knights' original *raison d'être*. But they had no intention of closing their business. Although lacking the resources of the new Polish—Lithuanian combination, they could draw on great reserves of military investment, technical skill, and diplomatic support. They defended their inheritance with steady determination. Two major wars — the Great War of 1409—22, and the Thirteen Years War of 1454—66 — served only to trim the

Order's pride, and to reduce its territory. In between, in the 1430s, the coalition of Polish magnates and Czech Taborites mounted a number of expeditions which penetrated to the Baltic Coast. Finally, in 1519–21, another major war looked set to develop into a life-and-death confrontation, until suddenly in 1525, the Order was secularized and disbanded. The Reformation achieved at a stroke what the combined forces of Poland and Lithuania had failed to achieve over one and a half centuries.

Military problems demanded constant attention. Until the middle of the fifteenth century, the old feudal host performed its tasks with reasonable efficiency. Poland alone, without Lithuania, put 18,000 knights into the field. Fortresses and cities were surrounded by dirt-and-stone walls to meet the challenge of siege artillery. In later decades, however, serious difficulties arose. The old type of army was no longer suited to the open warfare of the south and east. Knights could hardly arrive on the scene of distant action before the season's campaign was ended. Casual finances, which had to be spent before the land tax was collected, no longer sufficed. A standing army was required to supplement the *levée-en-masse*. In the 1490s, the first move in this direction was taken when an *obrona potoczna* or 'current defence force' of some 2,000 men was created to defend Red Ruthenia from Tartar raids. In 1526, it received an established financial grant. Finally in 1563, the institution of the *Kwarta* or 'quarter tax' on the income of the Crown estates, ensured support for a permanent professional force. Even so, numbers were constantly declining. Every campaign necessitated an extraordinary grant from the Sejm. In 1532, the land tax of 12 groszy per łan produced barely enough to keep 3,474 cavalry, paid at 2 zł. a month Field commanders were forced to rely on resourcefulness, and on the quality of their troops. In this regard, Hetman Jan Tarnowski (1488–1561), was an outstanding figure. Like his contemporary in the west, the Chevalier du Bayard, 'the knight without fear or reproach', he was a small man with an immense reputation. It was Tarnowski who modified the Hussite concept of the *Tabor* or 'military train' for use in the east, and turned it into the vehicle of repeated victory against overwhelming odds. The stores of ammunition of his entire

army were carried in huge six-horse wagons, which could keep
on the move over vast distances or which could be chained
together and formed square to make an instant fortress anywhere in the wilderness. A Polish *Tabor* besieged by twenty
or thirty thousand Tartars must have closely resembled the
overland trains of American pioneers attacked by Red Indians
in the West. Tarnowski also developed the headquarters
services of a modern army; horse-artillery; field hospitals provided at royal cost; the corps of *Szancknechte* (sappers); the
Probantmaster's logistical department; the 'Hetman's Articles'
or code of discipline; the system of courts martial; and the
corps of army chaplains. His practical experiences were summarized in a theoretical book, *Consilium Rationis Bellicae*
(An Outline of Military Method), published in 1558. His
watchword was 'Know your adversary'; and he preached the
doctrine of flexibility.

The centrepiece of the struggle with the Teutonic Order
was contested near the village of Grunwald in Prussia, on
15 July 1410. Five days before the end of the previous truce,
Władysław-Jagiełło and his Chief-of-staff, Zyndram z
Maszkowic, had crossed the Vistula near Czerwińsk on a
bridge of pontoons, secretly prepared. They were joined by
Witold with the host of the Grand Duchy, by a Bohemian
detachment under Zyzka, and by a contingent of Polish
knights under Zawisza Czarny z Garbowa, the Black Knight.
The Grand Master, Ulrich von Jungingen, expecting an attack
on the district of Dobrzyń, was taken by surprise and was
forced to ride swiftly to the north to bar the road to the
Marienburg. Some 27,000 knights including many foreign
guests were supported by mortars, and faced a motley collection of some 39,000 Poles, Czechs, Lithuanians, Samogitians,
Ruthenians, Tartars, and Wallachians. By the end of the day,
almost half of the Teutonic Knights were dead. The Grand
Master was slain. Fourteen thousand prisoners were taken for
ransom. The Teutonic camp was captured, and with it a score
of carts loaded with iron shackles intended for the Polish
captives, who had now turned captor. Władysław-Jagiełło,
resplendent in his silver armour on the crest of a hillock,
received the standard of the Prussian Bishop of Pomerania,
and sent it as a trophy to Cracow. With it, he dispatched a

letter to his second wife, Anna of Cilli, describing the events of the day:

Most serene, excellent, Princess, dearest Spouse! On Tuesday, the Feast of the Apostles, the Grand Master with all his power drew close to our forces, and demanded that battle be joined. . . . After we had stood and watched each other for a time, the Grand Master sent two swords over to us with this message: 'Know you, King and Witold, that this very hour we shall do battle with you. For this, we send you these swords for your assistance.' We replied: 'We accept the swords you send us, and in the name of Christ, before whom all stiff-necked pride must bow, we shall do battle.' At which, with the troops standing in full order, we advanced to the fray without delay. Among the numberless dead, we ourselves had few losses. . . . We cut down the Grand Master, and the Marshal, SCHWARTSBURG, and many of the *Komturs,* forcing many others to flee. . . . The pursuit continued for two miles. Many were drowned in the lakes and rivers, and many killed, so that very few escaped. . . .[4]

What actually happened is hard to say. Polish history books attribute the victory to the Polish royal guard, who charged from their station round the King to smash the Teutonic centre after the Lithuanians gave way. Russian sources stress the role of the regiments from Smolensk who moved to the attack when the Poles gave way. Most modern history books treat the Battle as a national, if not a racial, contest between German and Slav – which of course it was not. In German mythology, it was a catastrophe not revenged until the victory at nearby Tannenberg in August 1914. In Soviet mythology, it is a precursor of the Battle of Stalingrad. At all events, the Grand Master did not obtain a favourable result. The headquarters of the Order had to be hurriedly moved to Königsberg, as the Marienburg was besieged. At the Treaty of Thorn, signed on 1 February 1411, existing frontiers were confirmed and free trade on the Vistula assured. The Order made a conditional retreat from Samogitia. It was a very tame treaty for such a famous battle.

In the middle of the century, the Thirteen Years War was fought over eastern Pomerania, or as it had now been rechristened, West Prussia. In 1454, the leading cities of the province – Danzig, Thorn, Elbing – had revolted against the Order, formed the Prussian League, and sought the protection of the Polish King. An 'Act of Incorporation of Royal Prussia' was signed in Cracow on 6 March 1454. After one early disaster at Chojnice, the Polish army recovered, occupied the Marienburg in 1457, and at Żarnowiec in 1462 threw its Knights on to the defensive. The second Treaty of Thorn, signed on 19 October 1466, partitioned the Teutonic State into two halves. The western half was to remain within the Polish Kingdom as the autonomous province of Royal Prussia with its own Diet. The eastern half, now called East Prussia, was to remain in the control of the Order, but as a Polish fief. The Livonian *Land* of the Teutonic State remained independent. In German History, this cruel 'Partition of Prussia' which so affronted Carlyle, was to be used as an explanation of the Partitions of Poland initiated by Frederick the Great in the eighteenth century.

Despite these preoccupations, the Jagiellonian states continued to expand in other directions. The Lithuanians continued to march southwards and eastwards. Despite his defeat on the Vorskla, Witold reached the mouth of the Dnieper. In 1403, he took control of eastern Podolia. For their part, the Poles moved into western Podolia, founding the *Województwo* of Podolia at Kamieniec in 1430. Thus the fifteenth century saw Poland and Lithuania not only gently expanding, but competing to expand into the same regions.

Over this same period, the Jagiellonian state assumed the missionary role of the Teutonic Knights. In 1387, Władysław-Jagiełło went straight to Vilnius from his wedding in Cracow, and decreed the abolition of the pagan gods. The groves of sacred oaks were felled; the statue of Perkun overturned; the eternal fire extinguished. Vilnius became 'Wilno'. The Bishopric of Wilno was founded, with a vast endowment. Those lords who accepted the new faith were offered their personal freedom. The common people were baptized in droves, everyone at each mass ceremony receiving the same white smock and the same Christian name. Pagan practices were Christianized. Polish worship of the Madonna became the Lithuanian festival of St. Mary Perkunatele — the Virgin Mother of Perkun. At the Church Council of Constance in 1415, at which the dispute between Poland and the Teutonic Order over missionary methods was fully aired, the task of converting Lithuania to Catholicism was officially transferred to the Polish See.

At Constance, also, Jan Hus was burned. His movement spread like a bush-fire through the Czech lands and into Silesia. It attracted several important patrons in Polish society from Andrzej Gatka z Dobrzyn, Rector of the Jagiellonian University, to the powerful Spytek of Mełsztyń, Castellan of Bełz. It was condemned by the fierce royal Edict of Wieluń (Wehlungen) of 1424, which introduced the Inquisition. The Hussite Wars which ravaged Bohemia and eastern Germany for several decades spread to the east. In Poland, they were brought to an end on the field of Grotniki in May 1439 when Spytek was killed by the forces of Bishop Oleśnicki of Cracow.

Zbigniew Oleśnicki (1389–1455) incarnated all the ideals of a militant but conservative prelate. He had made his mark at Grunwald where his youthful courage and speed of mind had saved the King's person from the lance of a Teutonic hero. He won his mitre at the age of 34, and a cardinal's hat at 50. He was a lifelong royal secretary, diplomat, and king-maker. In foreign affairs, he nourished the traditional Hungarian connection, and at home the supremacy of the barons. He was eager to extend the power of the Jagiellons in the courts of Central Europe, by their election to the Hungarian throne, but not to encourage it in Poland. At the end of his life, he was the leader of the opposition. He was perhaps the greatest of a long line of great political bishops which included Mikołaj Trąba (1358–1422), Archbishop and Vice-Chancellor; Jan Łaski (1455–1531), Archbishop and Chancellor; and Piotr Tomicki (1469–1535), Bishop of Przemyśl, Poznań, and Cracow, and Vice-Chancellor.

Jagiellonian church affairs were disturbed by continual disputes with the Papacy. The disputes grew out of the struggle with the Teutonic Order, whom the Papacy favoured, and were fuelled by the growing power and confidence of the monarchy. The first exposition of the Polish case had appeared in the work of Pawel Włodkowicz. But the clearest formulation of a consequential political programme was made in the *Monumentum pro Reipublicae ordinatione congestum* (*c.* 1475) of Jan Ostroróg (1436–1501), the fearless Castellan of Poznań. Ostroróg waged a lifelong campaign against papal power, demanding the abolition of annates, of juridical appeals to the Court of Rome, and of clerical exemption from royal taxation. Against this background, all the main religious developments occurred. In 1417, Archbishop Trąba established the title of Primate of Poland, with its associated responsibilities of papal legate and leader of the Synod. In 1463, after a long wrangle, the practice was adopted of appointing all abbots and bishops (of which there were now nineteen) without reference to the Roman Curia. The king's right to do so was confirmed by Leo X in 1513. In 1515 Archbishop Łaski extracted for himself and his successors the title of *Legatus Natus* 'Hereditary Legate' and promptly used it to reject the Vatican's pro-Habsburg plans for a war with Turkey. In 1530 the ageing Primate received a papal *monitorium* or 'warning' which summoned him to appear before a Roman court as a 'traitor' and ally of the Infidel, and which threatened him with excommunication, confiscation, and ruination by a fine of 25,000 ducats. He took no notice, and died. These same ebullient bishops were at once the patrons of the New Humanism and the cause of growing anticlerical feeling. If active Hussitism had been suppressed, demands for the 'Break with Rome' and for control of the wealth and power of the Church, were raised with accelerating insistence. By the time the Reformation appeared in the 1520s, the pitch had been well prepared.

The structures of society were rapidly ossifying. The Jagiellonian period witnessed the emergence of five separate and exclusive estates − the clergy, the nobility, the burghers, the Jews, and the peasantry. Each estate was governed by special rights and rules, its area of competence carefully circumscribed by a body of detailed legislation. Membership of an estate was principally determined by a person's birth, and movement between one estate and another was strewn with obstacles. The process whereby the clergy and the nobility reinforced their privileges in the country as a whole matched by the actions of the Guilds in the cities. It was as difficult for a burgher to become a nobleman, as it was for a Jew to aspire to the rights of a burgher or to buy land, or for a peasant to engage in the activities that occupied the Jews. Constant efforts were made to eliminate independent social groups. As from 1421, the bishops closed the cathedral Chapters to all but noble candidates, thus eliminating that large group of plebeian clerics who by merit and education had risen to occupy an influential position mid-way between the episcopate and the parish clergy. Only two prebendaries, for Doctors of Law or Medicine, were reserved for non-nobles in each Chapter. The nobility attacked the shrinking holdings of the free peasantry and eliminated the special status of the esquires, forcing them to accept the full responsibilities of a nobleman or driving them into the towns or into serfdom. The Guilds attacked the illegal craftsmen's fraternities a *parte,* whose members, known as *partacze* or 'interlopers' contrived to evade established practices of apprenticing and licensing. By doing so, they drove a large part of the urban poor into the service of the noble estates, and fostered the creation of extra-municipal zones within the cities. These zones or *jurydiki,* subject only to the jurisdiction of their noble or ecclesiastical owners, were commonplace by the middle of the sixteenth century. Often located on the outskirts of the ancient city wards, or beyond the walls, they were frequently settled by poor Jews and developed into ghettos. For its part, the Jewish *Kahal* attacked the separate Jewish Guilds which sought to escape from its own rigid control.

In all these social conflicts, the noble estate clearly held the upper hand. It held a monopoly in the running both of the Church and the central legislative organs, and dominated the life of the royal court, army, and administration. In the Jagiellonian period, membership of the szlachta became stabilized. Henceforth, those numerous noble families, whose names first appear in the documents and land grants of the late fourteenth and early fifteenth centuries, have a continuous history into modern times. Among them, a small number of noblemen, begin to accumulate fortunes and influence of disproportionate size. Although the Tęczyński, Tarnowski, Odrowąż, Górka, Firlej, Szamotulski, and Mełsztyński families were small fry compared to the magnates of a later age, their power relative to the rest of society was considerable. If in the Piast period, the cities had stood apart from the landed interest, and were able to act as arbiters or even as princemakers in the internecine feuds of the barons, they were now to be subordinated to the universal pretensions of the szlachta. The new situation was dramatically illustrated by an incident in Cracow in 1462. In that year, Andrzej Tęczyński, brother of the royal Castellan, had given a suit of armour to be repaired by a craftsman called Klemens. When Klemens protested at the payment of 18 *groszy* against the bill of 2 ducats, Tęczynski decided to teach him a lesson by beating him with his stick. During the brawl, a body of townsmen intervened, and the Castellan's noble brother was lynched. Retribution was swift. As the city Corporation could not deliver the unidentified murderers to justice, six of the city aldermen were seized by the Castellan and summarily beheaded. The moral was fairly clear. Even so, the patricians of Cracow, Lwów, and Danzig included some of the most influential men in the land. Figures like Baltazar Behem (1460–1508), the lawyer, whose illuminated codex of Cracovian legislation provides perhaps the richest source of urban history of the period, or Johann Boner (*c.* 1450–1523), an immigrant banker, who founded a noble dynasty, could deal with any nobleman without the least sense of inferiority. Their lofty detachment from the problems of the pullulating urban plebs was even greater than that of a nobleman from the life of his serfs.

Economic progress continued apace both on the land and in the town. The recovery of Danzig, and the unification of the Vistula basin opened up the Polish interior to the grain trade. The steady improvement of agriculture over the preceding period now paid dividends. Large-scale manorial farming and the production of cereals for sale became a very profitable business. What in 1400 was no more than a trickle, by 1500 was turning into a stream, and by 1565 into a flood. But agricultural improvement was no isolated phenomenon. Technical advances and specialization were noted in almost all trades. Water power, known since the thirteenth century, was now harnessed to a multiplicity of enterprises, from flour-milling and wood-cutting to paper- and wire-making. Transport was made more efficient both by the repair of roads, facilitating wheeled traffic instead of pack horses, and by the systematic use of rivers and dykes. Obstructive practices, such as that at Thorn, where, until 1537, all goods on the Vistula could be held up by the local right of storage, were reduced. Mining was markedly intensified. By 1563, salt production at Wieliczka had trebled since the turn of the century. Over one hundred forges, sixty in the Staropolskie Basin alone, were producing iron in quantity. Banking and credit operations proliferated, resulting in the creation of joint-stock companies. In the 1490s, Jan Turzon of Cracow started a company for exploiting the silver mines of the Tatras; in 1525, another Cracovian, Pawel Kaufmann, headed another metallurgical consortium to which all the great noblemen of the day, from Krysztof Szydłowiecki to Jan Tarnowski were persuaded to subscribe. In many of these financial affairs, the House of Boner took a central role. By lending money to kings and cities, they were able to amass lands and offices. In 1514 Jan Boner was knighted, and became burgrave of the Royal Castle, and from 1515, farmer of the Wieliczka salt mine. His nephew and heir, Seweryn Boner (1486–1549), inherited a royal loan of 150,000 ducats, and quickly rose to the high senatorial dignity of Castellan of Cracow. Like his uncle before him, he was in practice, if not in name, controller of the royal finances.

Both export and import flourished. The former was largely run by foreign merchants or by the Jewish entrepreneurs of Cracow, Lwów, and Lublin — among whom were Izaak Brodawka of Brest, Eleazer Abramovitch of Tykocin, and Aron Izraelovitch of Grodno; the latter was handled in the main by native merchants who constantly tried to restrict the activities of German or Scottish dealers specializing in metal-ware or half-finished goods.

This sustained burst of economic activity had four main effects. Firstly, it initiated the beginnings of a countrywide economic 'system' — a Polish market to which all regions of the Jagiellonian realm were connected. This is evidenced not only by the countrywide role of Danzig, but also by the appearance of important overland fairs at Lublin, Gniezno, and Toruń. Secondly, it drew Poland–Lithuania into the orbit of all the continental economic forces of the sixteenth century, including that of the Price Revolution. In Poland–Lithuania, price inflation struck in the 1520s and resulted in a 300 per cent rise in goods prices over the century, as opposed to a 100 per cent rise in wages. Thirdly, it brought

urban life to the peak of its importance. Fourthly, a complete
reform of the monetary system took place. The prevalence at
the end of the fifteenth century of five or six regional cur-
rencies — from Prussia, Lithuania, Danzig, Silesia, and Mazovia,
together with a great variety of debased Polish silver coins
and foreign ducats, bore witness not only to the existence of
a coherent monetary area in which money circulated freely
but also to the inadequacy of existing arrangements. Since
the time of Casimir the Great, the proliferating coinage of the
groszy system had contained an ever-decreasing percentage of
pure silver. In the course of the fifteenth century, the *kwartnik*
(quarter) of 1396 had fallen to one-third of its original value;
the *denarius* or 'bronze penny' was worth twice what it had
been. Thus, in 1526, the Złoty System was introduced into
Poland. The so-called red złoty or 'Polish ducat' was minted
at 3.5 grams of gold; the silver złoty was fixed at 23.1 grams
of silver on a monetary scale where 1 *złoty* = 5 *szostaki* = 10
trojaki = 30 *groszy* = 90 *szelągi* (shillings) = 180 *ternarii* = 540
denarii (pence). Although in many places the old *grzywna* or
'mark' continued to be used as an accounting unit, the new
coinage was extended in 1528 to Prussia, and in 1569 to
Lithuania. Also in 1569, to bridge the gulf between the
separate gold and silver coinages, a silver *talar* (dollar) was
introduced. This was equivalent to one red złoty, or to eight
'silver złoties', and was divided into 5 *orti*. On this scale, one
dollar or ducat was worth 240 *groszy* or 4,320 pence. The
patent simplicity of these details eloquently evokes the
complexity of the preceding chaos.

The growth of towns and trade favoured the further expansion of the Jewish community. The Jagiellonian Kings regularly confirmed the basic Jewish Charter of 1264. As from
1515, Sigismund I encouraged Jewish immigration, especially
from Austria. The large number of exclusionary charters, *De
non tolerandis Judeis,* extended by the King to particular
cities, served only to underline the fact that the Jews were
permitted to settle in all other parts of the realm. The foundations of Jewish autonomy were laid under royal patronage.
Earlier attempts to place the Jews under the care of Chief
Rabbis, appointed separately by the King in Poland and
Lithuania, were abandoned. Instead, the principle was accepted

that the elected Elders of the *kahal* or 'Jewish Commune' should administer their affairs themselves. In each locality, they were to be supervised, and protected, by the royal Wojewoda or Starosta. In 1530, they were granted leave to create a Jewish Tribunal at Lublin. In 1549, they were empowered both to assess and to collect their contribution to the *pogłówne* or 'poll-tax'. In this way, they gradually assumed the attributes of a separate and legal Estate. In financial matters, they established the enviable practice whereby they could bargain freely with the royal officials. As shown by the report of the commissioners who interviewed the Elders of the Cracow *kahal* in 1564, each side adopted an uncompromising negotiating position:

The Jewish Elders, – by name Salmon Krasnik, Joseph Lyblich, Alexander the doctor, and Salmon Landa – stood before the commissioners. Examined under the threat of taking the oath, they declared that ever since the settlement of their forefathers in Cracow, their custom was to pay 200 gold ducats each year directly into the royal Treasury on St. Martin's Day: but that at present they handed the money over in a different way, paying 100 ducats to Mr Grabowieczki, and another 100 to Mr Lukasz.

Asked by the commissioners what in addition they might offer to the Royal Treasury, by way of payments from the income of their abattoirs and other businesses, and from the trade which they pursue on the Market in Cracow, they replied that their exemption from such payments had been confirmed by His Majesty, our present King. But they produced no documents to prove it.

These same Jews declared that in many places they were charged excessive tolls, even for individual persons or for empty carts, which was contrary to custom and to their rights and privileges. They begged that they be freed from these impositions.[5]

At the end of these bargaining sessions, the annual rate of the poll-tax would be agreed, and the Elders would be left to raise it. From the Crown's point of view, the outcome was not entirely satisfactory. As was the case with the nobles' land-tax, which was similarly assessed by the tax-payers themselves, the royal officials could never be sure that they were always receiving their due. As Sigismund-August is reported to have remarked to the Bishop of Cracow: 'Tell me, my Lord Bishop, since you do not believe in sorcery, how is it that only 16,598 Jews pay the poll-tax, whilst two hundred thousand of them apparently live underground?'

Social and economic changes were reflected in the constitutional sphere. The four autonomous estates enjoyed their separate jurisdictions. The fifteenth century saw the definitive stage in the formulation of the privileges of the szlachta, and of their legislative monopoly. The provincial *sejmiki* were regularized; the bicameral Sejm was in place by 1497. The statue of *Nihil Novi* of 1505 ensured the perpetuation of the institutions of the noble democracy into later periods. The towns retained complex liberties of their own. Several distinguished collections of urban law, notably those of M. Jaskier and of B. Groicki, enjoyed widespread application. First the 'Digests' of Polish law printed in 1488, and the new codification of court law for the Kingdom in 1523, and then the publication of First Lithuanian Statute of 1529 for the Grand Duchy, manifested a growing sense of cultural and political cohesion.

The monarchy, nominally hereditary, was limited by the terms of the Lithuanian Union, and was subject to an increasing degree of electoral confirmation by the nobles. At the same time, it retained many of the attributes of earlier kingship. In Poland, as distinct from Lithuania, the King was the executor of a sacred trust, which was not inherited directly from God, but was carefully conferred on him by the clergy, and acclaimed by the people. As shown by the ritual of the Coronation ceremony, the Polish King was explicitly bound by the tenets of the Catholic faith, by the laws of the Church, by the traditions of his predecessors, and by the consent of the people:

Then the Archbishop should ask him in this way:
Will you uphold the holy faith as handed down to you by Catholic men, and observe it with just works?
He replies: Volo [I will].
Q. Will you be the guide and defender of the Holy Church and of her ministers?
A. I will.
Q. Will you defend the kingdom granted you by God, and rule it according to the justice of your fathers?
A. I will. With God's aid, and sustained by the love of all my faithful people, I shall be strong, and I faithfully promise to conduct myself thus in every respect.

Unxerunt salomonem Sadoch sacer
dos et nathan propheta reges in Sion et ambu
lantes leti dixerunt vivat rex in
eternum alleluia

Un — xe-runt Sa — lo-mo-nem Sa — doch sa — cer-dos

et Na -- than pro—phe-ta re-gem in Si — on et am-bu-

lan — tes le — ti di — xe-runt vi — vat rex

in e — ter — num, al — le — lu-ia, al-le-lu — ia.

Then the Lord Metropolitan should address the people with these words:
Will you submit yourselves to such a prince and rector, to confirm his
rule and put your trust in him: will you obey his laws according to the
apostles, and given that his whole mind be subordinated to the higher
powers, will you submit to this excellent king?
Then the surrounding clergy and people should say unanimously:
Fiat, Fiat. [So be it.] Amen.[6]

After that, the plain chant of the choir moved on to another
text: 'And Zadok the priest and Nathan the prophet have
anointed Solomon King in Zion, and the joyful people said,
"May the king live for ever, Alleluia".' Biblical scholars may
have recalled that Solomon was anointed king over Israel on
the orders of his father, King David, *vivente rege*. In Polish
history, however, despite the wording of the coronation
service, numerous attempts to follow this precedent were
blocked by the nobility. Sigismund I in 1530 was the only
Polish king who succeeded in having his son crowned during
his own lifetime. In Lithuania, where a separate grand ducal
coronation took place in Wilno, many of the old patrimonial
practices were retained. Not till 1529, when the First Lithuanian Statute enjoined a broader consultative function for the
Great Council, did the Jagiellonian Grand Dukes care to
reform procedures in the light of their simultaneous experience
as Kings of Poland.

The multifarious political manœuvres of the Jagiellonian
monarchs can be reduced to two main problems. In the
external sphere, they sought to isolate the principal perceived
enemy. Their attentions in the fifteenth century were mainly
directed against the Teutonic Order, and in the sixteenth
century against Muscovy. In the internal sphere, they sought
to reconcile the competing interests of estates, regions, religions, and personalities. On the whole, they were remarkably
successful. In contrast to the confused history of the Piast
era, and the galloping anarchy of the succeeding Republic,
the Jagiellons reigned over a dynamic but stable community.
Their rule was seriously challenged on only one occasion
– in 1429–30. The various oppositions never assumed the
magnitude of an alternative government. The Jagiellonian era
died of natural causes, and was supplanted by a new system
prepared and introduced by its last, heirless representative.

Władysław-Jagiełło lived and ruled for forty-five years after his marriage to Jadwiga. During her lifetime, he was much concerned with preserving the state of the Union, reinforcing the hold on peripheral territories such as Red Ruthenia and suppressing the malcontents, whether of cousin Witold in Lithuania or the former regent, Ladislaus von Oppeln, in Poland. In his middle decades, he dealt with the Teutonic Order, and with related diplomatic problems in Central Europe and in the Church councils. His stand earned him the disgust of the Emperor, the Luxemburgers, and the Vatican, and the respect of the Hussites, who at several points urged him to accept the throne of Bohemia. At the end of his life, he was entirely absorbed with the succession. In spite of four marriages, he did not produce a son and heir until 1425 when he was well into his seventies. Leaving day-to-day business in the capable hands of Bishop Oleśnicki, he made fundamental concessions to the barons to secure his sons' future. In the Statutes of Jedłno (1430) and of Cracow (1433), an old man's fears aroused the very suspicions they were supposed to allay. At the Congress of Łuck in January 1429, Jagiełło's foreign enemies and domestic rivals joined forces. Sigismund of Luxembourg, who held the thrones of Bohemia, Hungary, and Germany proposed that the Union of Horodło should be overturned and Witold crowned King of Lithuania. A rift was opened between the two parts of the Jagiellonian realm. War loomed. But in 1430 Witold died. Jagiełło's longevity was not the least of his talents. (See Diagram F.)

Władysław III Warneńczyk (Ladislaus of Varna, 1425–44) is remembered almost exclusively for the way in which he died. Succeeding at the age of nine, he had no chance to wrest control of Polish affairs from his father's favourite Bishop. The first years of his reign were engulfed by the shock waves from the civil war in Lithuania, where Jagiełło's brother Świdrygiełło was conspiring with the Teutonic Knights to break the union with Poland. The Polish barons took the field in support of Witold's brother, Zygmunt Kiejsztutowicz, whose accession was secured by 1434. In 1435, after the battle of Wiłkomierz (Ukmerge), they had obliged the Order to submit its foreign policy to Polish approval. No sooner were these northern storms calmed,

GIEDYMIN, (Gediminas) Grand Duke of Lithuania (1316–1341)

OLGIERD, (Algirdas) Grand Duke of Lithuania, (1345–77) = (1) Maria of Vitebsk = (2) Juliana of Tversk

YEVNUT IVAN Grand Duke of Lithuania (1341–5)

Monwid

Narymunt Gleb

Vigunt

Kiejstut, Prince of Troki

Koriat, Prince of Novgorod

The Princes of Podolia

Lubart Dymitr, Prince of Vladimir and Słuck.

JOGAILA (WŁADYSŁAW JAGIEŁŁO, Ladislas–Jagiello) Grand Duke of Lithuania (1377–1401) King of Poland (1386–1434) = (1) **JADWIGA** of Anjou = (2) Anna = (3) Elżbieta = (4) Zofia (Sonka)

SVIDRIGAILA (ŚWIDRYGIEŁŁO, Grand Duke of Lithuania, (1430–32)

VITOVT (WITOLD) Grand Duke of Lithuania (1401–30) = (1) Anna = (2) Juliana of Holstein

ZYGMUNT, Grand Duke of Lithuania. (1432–40)

Tovtivil Konrad Prince of Novgorod

Volodimir Prince of Kiev

Skiergiełło, Prince of Troki Polotsk and Kiev (Viceroy of Lithuania)

Korybut Prince of Novgorod– Sieversk

Dymistr, Prince of Bryansk

Andrzej, Prince of Polotsk

Bonifacja

Jadwiga

WŁADYSŁAW III WARNEŃCZYK (Ladislas of Varna) King of Poland, (1434–44) King of Hungary (1440–4)

KAZIMIERZ IV JAGIELLOŃCZYK (Casimir Jagiellon) Grand Duke of Lithuania, (1440–92) King of Poland (1446–92) = Elizabeth of Austria.

ZYGMUNT I STARY, (Sigismund the Elder) Grand Duke of Lithuania King of Poland (1506–48) = (1) Barbara Zapolya of Hungary = (2) Bona Sforza

Zofia–Friedrich von Hohenzollern of Anspach

ALEKSANDER Grand Duke of Lithuania, (1492–1506) King of Poland (1501–1506)

Fryderyk, Bishop of Cracow, Archbishop of Gniezno, Cardinal

Barbara = Georg, Duke of Saxony

Jadwiga = Georg Duke of Bavaria

Kazimierz (saint)

JAN OLBRACHT (John I Albert) King of Poland (1492–1501)

Albrecht von Hohenzollern Grand Master of the Teutonic Order, Duke of Prussia, (1525–68)

Anna = Ferdinand of Habsburg (Holy Roman Emperor, 1556–64)

Władysław II (Ladislas Jagiellon) King of Bohemia (471–1516) King of Hungary (1490–1516) = Anne de Foix

Louis II King of Bohemia and Hungary (1516–26) = Maria of Castile

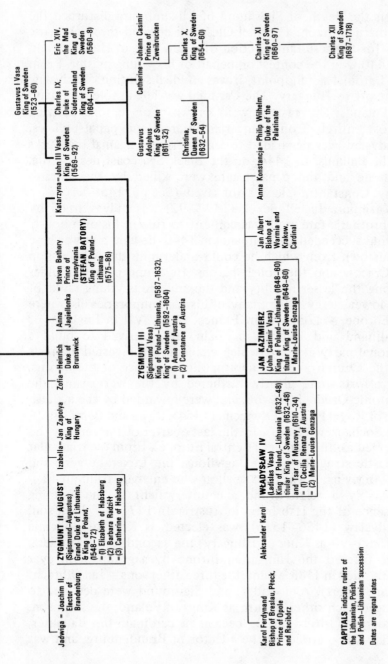

Diagram F.   The Jagiellons and the Vasas, (Genealogical Table)

when the death of Sigismund of Luxembourg disturbed the
southern horizon. Cardinal Oleśnicki entered the diplomatic
lists for the resultant election of a new king of Hungary, and
in 1440 won the contest on behalf of his young master. From
the Cardinal's standpoint, it was an ideal solution. Władysław
went off to Hungary. The Cardinal was left in sole command
in Poland. The rest is well known. For reasons deriving
almost entirely from Hungarian interest and papal policies,
Władysław was persuaded to lead a crusade against the Turks
in the Balkans. In 1444, on the Black Sea coast near Varna,
both he and the papal legate were killed by the Sultan's
army. Constantinople was not saved. (See pp. 145—7.)

Kazimierz Jagiellończyk (1427—92) was duly warned by
his brother's fate, and was content to rule in his own house.
Having succeeded to Lithuania in 1440, he held a power base
of his own from which he could undermine the wily Bishop
of Cracow and the Polish barons. He found plenty of allies
among the lesser nobility and the ambitious young ranks of
the lower clergy. Like many of his contemporaries elsewhere
in Europe — Louis XI in France, Henry VII in England, or
Ferdinand and Isabella in Spain, he contrived to build a
national party at court which challenged the vested interests
of the Church and the habitual disobedience of the barons.
His efforts were greatly furthered by the war against the
Teutonic Order, 1454—66, and were rewarded by the acquisition of Royal Prussia, Oświęcim (1454), Rawa and Bełz (1462),
and Sochaczew (1476). In the last quarter of the century, he
emerged as 'the Father of Central Europe'. From the triangular
dynastic struggles of the Jagiellons, the Luxemburgers, and
the Angevins, it was the Jagiellon who emerged triumphant —
inevitably a relative and a counterweight to the looming
presence of the Habsburgs in Austria. In 1471, his eldest son,
Władysław (1456—1516), was elected as King of Bohemia
and in 1490 as King of Hungary; the second son, Kazimierz,
once offered the Hungarian throne by a group of Magyar
rebels, died in 1483, a saint; the three other sons — Jan Olbracht
(John Albert), Aleksander, and Sigismund were destined to
succeed each other in turn as Kings of Poland; the sixth son,
Fryderyk (1468—1503), became a cardinal; the daughter,
Zofia, was married to the Elector of Brandenburg, and was

mother to Albrecht von Hohenzollern, last Grand Master of the Teutonic Order. The education of this brood was entrusted to the historian, Jan Długosz, formerly secretary to Bishop Oleśnicki and now Canon of Cracow. Together with Ostroróg, Weit Stoss (Wit Stwosz), the painter and sculptor from Nuremburg, Filippo Buonacorsi, the poet and diplomat from San Gimignano, and Archbishop Gregory of Sanok (1407–77), whose palace at Dunajów near Lwów attracted one of the leading humanist circles of Europe, Długosz belonged to a galaxy of intellectual giants who turned the Jagiellonian world into a centre of international importance. As the old King told his sons, 'You have two fathers – myself and Father John.' It was an apt comment on the happy coincidence of political power and cultural prowess. When he died on 6 June 1492, many people had good reason to mourn. (See Map 9.)

Jan Olbracht (1459–1501) occupied an unenviable position. It was not easy in middle age to follow in such a father's footsteps, or to bolster the failing fortunes of his brother Alexander in Lithuania. Both the Muscovites abroad and the magnates at home had waited patiently for the old King's demise before launching their calculated assault on his sons. Jan Olbracht sought refuge in irrecoverable concessions to the nobility, notably at the famous Piotrków Sejm of 1496, and in the vainglorious expedition to Moldavia in 1497. Were it not for the magnificent Barbican built in Cracow as part of the military preparations, this last adventure would have passed deservedly into oblivion.

Aleksander (1461–1506) fared no better. As Grand Duke of Lithuania since 1492, he was the chosen target of Muscovite intrigues. Married to Helena, daughter of Ivan III, as part of his Council's scheme to contain the first Muscovite prince to call himself 'Sovereign of all Russia' he fell victim first to internal subversion and then to external assault. His wife's Orthodox faith provided the pretext for trumped-up charges of religious persecution. His boyars were threatened, bribed, or cajoled from their allegiance. His protestations were interpreted as signs of weakness. In May 1500, the Muscovites marched. On 14 July on the banks of the Vedrosha they destroyed the Lithuanians, and captured the commander Prince Ostrogski. Their Crimean allies raided deep into Poland,

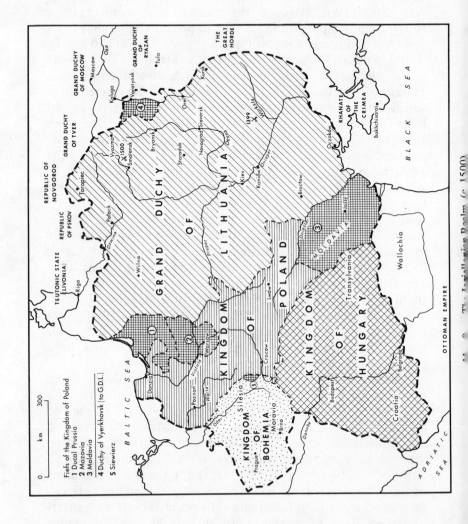

Map 2. The Jagiellonian Realm (c. 1500)

and crossed the Vistula, taking 50,000 captives. Bryansk Sieversk, Vyazma, Toropets, and Dorogobush were annexed. In 1501, another Lithuanian force was annihilated near Mstislav; an auxiliary Teutonic force under Von Plettenberg was crushed at Helmed. In 1502 the once mighty Golden Horde was dispersed for ever. In 1503, in an open letter, Helena Ivanovna publicly defended her husband's conduct, and denounced her father's lies and violences. It made no difference. A truce was signed for six years, leaving all Ivan's conquests intact. The war was to continue at intervals until 1537. In Poland, Aleksander bowed to every wind that blew. On 25 October 1501, in anticipation of his coronation, he signed a document agreed at Mielnik by the Senators of the Kingdom with the lords of the Lithuanian Council, arrogating wide constitutional powers to themselves. It never came into effect. In 1504, the pretensions of the Senate were angrily attacked by Archbishop Łaski at the head of a party of noblemen, who urged that pluralism among the holders of the great offices of state should be curbed. There were demands for the recall of all Crown estates leased to senators, and for the 'execution' of all established laws relating to the privileges of the nobility. This was the start of the so-called 'Executionist Movement' which was to play a prominent role in Polish politics for the next sixty years. In 1505, at the Sejm of Radom, the King withdrew his earlier concessions to the Senate, and accepted the demands of the Lower House. The Statute of *Nihil Novi* established the principle that 'nothing new' should be introduced without the consent of the nobility as a whole.

Sigismund I Stary, the 'Elder' (1467–1548), received his nickname at the end of his life. At the start of his reign, he was not yet forty, and he brought a touch of style and energy to his brother's faltering fortunes. Having ruled in Silesia in the name of his elder brother, Władysław, he was accustomed to govern; and having lived for several years at the court of Buda, he had acquired the taste for artistic patronage at an early age. Long before his second marriage in 1518 to Bona Sforza, he had brought numerous Italians to Cracow, and had developed an expert interest in architecture and music. In political outlook, he was decidedly conservative, preferring to rely on the great magnates of the Senate, and punishing rebels and heretics alike with severity. In foreign affairs, he opted for an enterprising opening towards the Habsburgs. This new departure was sealed at the Congress of Vienna in 1515, where a double marriage contract was signed. Young Louis Jagiellon, King of Hungary and Bohemia, was betrothed to the Emperor's daughter, Maria; the Emperor's son, Ferdinand, took Anna Jagiellonka. The arrangement had obvious advantages for the Jagiellons. It drew the sting of potential conflicts over Hungary and Bohemia, and blocked the feared *rapprochement* between Austria, Muscovy, and the Teutonic Order. It left Sigismund free to fight in the east and north without fear of intervention from the west. At the same time, it represented an obvious gamble. If young Louis should survive, the Jagiellonian inheritance would be preserved; if he should die, it would pass to his Habsburg relatives. At first, all went well. Sigismund held the Muscovites at bay; and he solved the Teutonic problem for the duration. But the real initiative in Central Europe lay beyond his control. The Ottoman Turks of Suleiman the Magnificent were already on the move. In 1521 they took Belgrade; in 1522, Rhodes; in 1526, Buda. In 1529 Vienna itself was besieged. Worst of all, from Sigismund's standpoint, the childless Louis Jagiellon was killed at the Battle of Mohacs. His Bohemian kingdom passed without dispute to Ferdinand of Habsburg; his Hungarian kingdom was turned into a three-cornered battlefield, contested by the Habsburgs, the Turks, and the Magyar lords under John Szapolyai. The whole of Central Europe was thrown into turmoil, whilst the Jagiellonian share of its inheritance was much diminished.

Sigismund's wars were largely conditioned by the circumstances of the day. The Muscovite onslaught, which in its first stage had been solely directed against Lithuania, now engulfed Poland as well. In 1507–8, that same Michał Gliński, who had once distinguished himself in Alexander's service, now headed a rebellion in Wilno. Sigismund rode straight from his coronation in Cracow to drive Gliński into exile, and to repulse the Muscovites who came to his aid. The Tsar responded in 1512, and sustained his attacks with savage tenacity for ten years. The three-year siege of Smolensk cost him ten thousand dead each season; and after one single battle at Orsha, on 8 September 1514, Prince Ostrogski counted 30,000 Muscovite corpses, including 1,500 boyars. But still they came on. As always, their motto was *'U nas mnogo ludei'* (We have a lot of people). Gliński took Smolensk by treachery, and held on to it. The third campaign, of 1534—7, started by Sigismund during the minority of Ivan IV, ended indecisively with a third truce.

This same Muscovite embroilment also lay behind the last Teutonic war. Albrecht von Hohenzollern had been persuaded by the Tsar to demand changes in the Treaty of Thorn of 1466; and in 1519, border skirmishes turned suddenly into war. Königsberg was attacked and the Grand Master only escaped from a humiliating capitulation by the timely arrival of Danish and German mercenaries. Yet the truce of 1521 coincided with the advent of the Reformation. In the space of a few months, the Grand Master saw the ranks of his Catholic crusading Order decimated by mass conversions to Lutheranism. His army melted away. In 1525, to save his livelihood, he begged Sigismund to turn Prussia into a secular fief of the Polish Kingdom, and to accept him as its hereditary duke. The first act of Prussian homage was performed on 10 April 1525 in the Market Square at Cracow. Henceforth, Albrecht von Hohenzollern remained a loyal subject of Poland, and an active participant in Polish affairs.*

* Although it is widely assumed that the Teutonic Order was dissolved after the secularization of Prussia in 1525, and of Livonia in 1561, it has survived to the present day. In 1527, the few remaining Catholic knights who had not left Prussia for Livonia, established themselves at Marienthal (Mergentheim) in Wurttemburg, and proceeded to elect the first of a new and unbroken series of Grand Masters, Walter von Cronberg. Thereafter, as from Archduke Maximilian of Austria, the titular King of Poland, who was Grand Master from 1595 to 1618, the Order gradually fell into the orbit of the Habsburgs; and eventually its headquarters were transferred to Vienna. Commanderies were set up in many parts of Germany and Austria, and impressive architectural evidence of the Order's activities can still be seen, among other places, at Mergentheim, at Marburg, and at Rykhoven in Belgium. The present Grand Master, Dom Ildefons Pauler, resides at Vienna, Singerstrasse 7, in a house once inhabited by Mozart, and rules over three provinces centred on Passau, Freisag, and Lana in Italy. Despite the romantic legend, which in 1813 inspired the foundation of the Order of the Iron Cross in Prussia and later, in the writings of Alfred Rosenberg, some of the grosser fantasies of Nazi ideology, the modern Teutonic Order has confined itself to practical religious and charitable work, and has remained a loyal if obscure instrument of the Vatican in central Europe.

Meanwhile, the south-eastern borders seethed in constant commotion. The preoccupations of the Jagiellons in Muscovy and Prussia were interpreted by the Ottomans' dependants as a licence to plunder the Polish lands. As early as 1412, the Grand Duke Witold had begun to build a chain of forts on the right bank of the Dnieper, and to garrison them with Tartar mercenaries known as *Kazaks* or 'free adventurers'. These frontier communities attracted a growing number of fugitive Slav peasants and outlaws, and formed the core of the later Cossack settlements. But the Cossacks soon adopted the marauding life-style of the Tartars, and by the end of the fifteenth century were capable on their own of raiding deep into Poland. In 1498, they reached Jarosław, west of Lwów, and in 1502 the bend of the Vistula near Sandomierz. This was exactly the kind of threat which the *obrona potoczna* was designed to parry. But neither Cossacks nor Tartars could be persuaded to mend their ways for any length of time. What is more, after more than a century as vassals of the Polish King, the Hospodars of Moldavia transferred their allegiance to the Ottoman Porte. In 1497, Stephen of Moldavia defeated the Polish disciplinary expedition at Kozin in Bukovina, and introduced a further element of uncertainty into the confused politics of the region. In the next thirty years, Moldavian ambitions flourished on the sidelines of the Ottomans' own advance into the Danube Basin, and some headlong collision with the Poles became increasingly likely. In 1529, in the name of the Sultan but without the Sultan's permission, Hospodar Petrylo invaded the frontier district of Pokucie. There, on the banks of the Dniester at Obertyn, on 22 August 1531, he was confronted by Hetman Tarnowski with a small force of some 6,000 men. The furious attacks of 17,000 horsemen repeatedly failed to break the Polish square, until at the end of the day, the garrison sallied forth to sweep the attackers from the field. It was a classic victory – at once the vindication of careful tactics and of the *obrona potoczna.* Ten years later, when the unlucky Hospodar was dethroned at the Sultan's instigation, his removal was declared a fitting punishment for someone 'who had disturbed the Porte's best friend, the King of Poland'.

Sigismund II Augustus (Zygmunt-August, 1520–72), was

schooled for kingship from his gilded cradle. In 1529, he was formally elected to the Polish throne on the wishes of his father, and began to rule under his father's guidance as Grand Duke in Lithuania. Hence for nearly twenty years, there were two King Sigismunds — the 'Elder' one in Cracow, and the 'Young Augustus' in Wilno. The contrast was striking. Despite his regal manner and cosmopolitan education, Sigismund II entirely lacked the assertiveness of the typical Renaissance prince. His temper was mild, and in his later years distinctly melancholy. He was nobody's 'wise fool', but he administered the realm with a grace and ease that bordered on the nonchalant. He was interested in all the progressive movements of the age, from Protestant theology to 'Executionist' politics, and naturally took the part of lesser men who were battling against the privileges of bishops and magnates. Yet he would have nothing of violence and bias; and refused categorically to be drawn into the religious quarrels of the age. His famous statement that he was 'King of the people, not of their consciences' complemented his father's remark to the learned Dr Eck: 'Please permit me, Sir, to be King of both the sheep and the goats.' His personal life was cast before the public eye, and caused him much pain. His mother, Bona Sforza, who had assumed considerable political influence during her husband's dotage, resorted to the most desperate tactics of a Renaissance harpy. In 1545, she poisoned the atmosphere of his first marriage and in due course poisoned the abandoned wife. In 1547, she took offence at his secret marriage with the widowed Barbara Radziwiłł, daughter of the Lithuanian Hetman, and was strongly suspected in due course of poisoning her also. In 1556, she absconded to her native duchies of Bari and Rossano in Southern Italy, taking some 430,000 ducats in cash and jewels from the royal treasury. These 'Neapolitan Sums', which were bequeathed to the King of Spain were still in dispute in the eighteenth century. Yet Sigismund gained little understanding from the Sejm. He was a born parliamentarian, and bore much offence patiently in the hope of reconciliation. He shrugged his shoulders when his own supporters complained bitterly of the way Crown Estates were still being traded for favours and securities: 'I had to mortgage them', he said sheepishly, 'because I had nothing to eat.' But he never forgave his subjects' intrusion into his love for the beautiful Barbara. In the Sejm in 1548, the first of his reign, he submitted to a detailed matrimonial interrogation, and was told by the Senate to arrange a divorce:

Rex: . . . I wish that all people enjoyed true freedom of loving. I cannot break my marriage vows without offence to my conscience . . . There are no genuine grounds for divorce . . .

Archbishop: Your Royal Highness, grounds for divorce could be found . . .

Rex: No doubt they could — if I were a man of ample conscience, but such am I not . . .

Envoy: It diminishes us, Your majesty, that you should have taken as your wife a woman from such a family, and from a nation which received its nobility and its Christian faith from us Poles only one and a half centuries ago . . . [7]

Sigismund bore the insults. Then, after refusing a year's taxes, the Sejm relented. Barbara was crowned. But when she died shortly afterwards, the King was inconsolable. His third, purely political marriage with Catherine of Austria, was disastrous. For the last years of his life, he lived alone and dressed in unrelieved black.

Sigismund's principal foreign preoccupation, the Livonian War, was forced upon him by events beyond his control. Livonia, the northern *Land* of the German Crusaders, had maintained its separate existence. But there, as in Prussia, the Reformation gradually undermined the established political order. In the 1550s, the Livonian state began to crumble. The Lutheran burghers of Riga were at odds with the Catholic Church; and the German nobility were at odds against themselves; the Grand Master of the Knights of the Sword,* von Furtstemberg, was at odds with the Archbishop of Riga, Wilhelm von Hohenzollern. The Swedes were interested in the northern area, adjoining Swedish Finland; the Muscovites were seeking a 'window on the west'. The Danes were interested in obstructing the Swedes. Sigismund was interested

---

* The Order of the Knights of the Sword, founded in 1209 by Albrecht von Buxhovden, Bishop of Riga, had pioneered the conquest of Livonia before being absorbed into the Teutonic Order in 1237. Three centuries later, in consequence of the secularization of Prussia, it was reconstituted under the name of the 'Brethren of Christ's Militia', and operated as a sovereign unit until 1561.

in the fate of his cousin, the Archbishop. In 1557, a Polish army marched towards Riga but halted when the Grand Master and the Archbishop settled their differences. In 1558–9, a Muscovite army seized Dorpat and Narva and carried the Grand Master off as a trophy. It was the signal for a multilateral conflict involving the Swedes, the Danes, the Poles, and the Muscovites, which contested the dominion of the whole Baltic area and was not finally resolved until 1721. The Catholic party, neglected by the Emperor, turned to Poland for protection. In 1561, Furstemberg's successor, Gotthard von Kettler, together with Archbishop Wilhelm and representatives of all the estates of Livonia assembled in Wilno to pay homage to Sigismund I. Kettler was to receive Courland and Semigalia in fief; Riga was to be incorporated into the kingdom with the same privileges and conditions as Danzig. It was a conscious copy of the Prussian submissions of 1466 and 1525. A naval war began for control of the Narva trade. The fifteen ships of Poland's 'Maritime Commission' were licensed for unlimited piracy. An embassy was sent to Denmark to negotiate an alliance. The King's sister, Katarzyna, was sent to Stockholm as a bride for the Swedish Crown Prince. But with Muscovy no *rapprochement* was possible. Sigismund's notification of the Wilno submission was answered by a brusque note from Ivan IV demanding the return of Kiev, Volhynia, and Podolia, 'the patrimony of his forebear, St. Vladimir'. The Lithuanian army was engaged from 1560, the Polish army from 1563. In that year Polotsk was lost, and no means was found of recovering Smolensk or Czernihów or of exploiting Ivan's preoccupations with the Turks and his rebellious boyars. The Polish–Lithuanian Army camped for seven years at Radoszkowice near Wilno, debating the state of the constitution, and waiting in vain for a change in Muscovite attitudes. It was in the long, cold evenings of enforced idleness in this encampment that the nobility of Poland and Lithuania took stock of their mutual predicament. They were faced with a numerous resilient fanatical foe who did not understand the meaning of magnanimity or compromise. They perceived a danger far more acute than that presented by the late Teutonic Order. They foresaw a long, bitter struggle for which their ramshackle political order was poorly designed. They understood that the personal union of the two crowns, agreed in 1386 in face of the Teutonic threat, no longer matched their needs, and that it would have to be replaced by a new, organic, constitutional union. By the end of 1568, when the camp at Radoszkowice disbanded, wide agreement had been reached on the ultimate aim. But the terms were far from settled.

* * * * *

To anyone unfamiliar with the subject, the 'Polish Renaissance' sounds ominously like an oxymoron. It may well seem highly improbable that a northern, Slavonic country, far removed from the influence of the Ancient World or of contemporary Italy, could ever have experienced the Renaissance in any but the most superficial form.

Indeed, in many of the arts Poland did still lie on the periphery of Europe. In architecture, the monuments which remain bear witness to the work of mainly imported talent. The palaces of Baranów and Krasiczyn, or the decorated granaries of Kazimierz Dolny are certainly minor jewels of their kind; but they do not surprise the visitor who has seen Florence or Venice, or the Châteaux of the Loire. In painting, too, the Polish achievement was modest.

In the less tangible world of ideas, however; in science, literature, and learning, the Polish talent was astonishingly rich and profound. Here, in the reigns of the last two Jagiellons one can talk of Poland's *Złoty Wiek*, her 'Golden Age', with no hint of hyperbole.

The flowering of the Renaissance in the sixteenth century was preceded in the fifteenth, by the steady germination of a strong humanist tradition. In the halls of the Jagiellonian University, under a series of outstanding rectors from Paulus Vladimiri to Bishop Tomicki, and in intimate circles forming round the Princes of the Church, from Cardinal Oleśnicki to Archbishop Łaski, the theocratic values of the Middle Ages had long been under attack from wide-ranging philosophical and scientific speculation.

Printing, the technical vehicle of the new ideas, flourished from an early date. The first work printed in Cracow, a Latin almanac, was produced by Piotr Straube in 1473. In 1491,

Swejbold Vehl (Szwajpolt Fiol) printed the first ever book in Cyrillic, an *Oktoich* hymnal, and was fined by an inquisitorial court for his pains. Jan Haller, another Franconian, and Kasper Hochfeld, had the distinction of publishing Poland's first illustrated work, Jan Łaski's legal 'Statutes', in 1506. Florian Ungler (d. 1536) printed the first book in Polish — Biernat of Lublin's *Raj duszny* (The Spiritual Paradise) in 1513; the first Polish grammar — Zaborowski's *Ortografia* in 1516; and Bernard Wapowski's celebrated map of Poland in 1525. Hieronim Wietor (d. 1546), founder of a firm which lasted over a century, produced a work in Greek; the first ever book in Romanian; and in 1519 Maciej Miechowita's *Cronica Polonorum*. This last item is best remembered as the first printed work in Poland to be withdrawn by the ecclesiastical censorship, for naming the lady who, in 1493 on return from a Roman pilgrimage, had first introduced syphilis to Poland. So much for firsts.

Material prosperity contributed greatly. In wealthy cities like Cracow and Danzig, art and commerce thrived in harness. Magnates like Chancellor Krzysztof Szydłowiecki (1467–1532) or Bishop Jan Lubrański of Poznań (1456–1520) gloried in the prestige of patronage. Noblemen could afford to send their sons abroad for an education. The universities of Germany and Italy were flooded with Polish students as never before or since.

The ultimate spark was provided by the Jagiellonian Court. Sigismund I, whose elder brother Ladislas reigned in Bohemia and Hungary from 1490 and whose Queen Bona Sforza inspired an important influx of Italians, presided in Cracow over a brilliant cosmopolitan circle. His son, Sigismund-August, Grand Duke of Lithuania, created an environment where royal servants, to be respected and successful, were themselves required to be poets, philosophers, and scientists. They set an example for the whole of educated society. Poland in the early 1500s was well prepared for the Renaissance, and for two or three generations blazed with its inspiration.

Names in themselves mean little. But the sheer quality of those who contributed to the intellectual and artistic life of the age is truly outstanding, especially in an area where, in later periods, such figures can be very sparse indeed. Among the foreigners, it is necessary to mention Buonacorsi (Calli-machus), Padovano, Berucci, Retyk, Santagucci; among the natives, Janicki, Modrzewski, Iłowski, Goślicki, Rej, Orzechowski, Zaborowski, Wapowski, Górnicki, Copernicus, Kochanowski, Zamoyski.

The greatest name undoubtedly belongs to Nicholas Copernicus (1473–1543). Born in Thorn, in Royal Prussia, he spent the greater part of his career as Canon of the Warmian Chapter at Frauenberg. His mind was universal in the most complete and literal sense. His discovery, of the earth's motion round the sun, caused the most fundamental revolution possible in prevailing concepts of the human predicament.[8]

After Copernicus, Jan Kochanowski (1530–84) holds pride of place. As founder of Polish vernacular poetry, he showed the Poles the beauty of their language. Until at the end of his life he was smitten by personal tragedy, his poems radiate that same joy and freshness which typify his peers — Ronsard and Du Bellay in France, Petrarch in Italy, Spenser in England — and that childlike sense of seeing the beauties of nature and of Man as no one had seen them before. From twenty thousand verses, one is sometimes quoted as his 'Renaissance Manifesto':

Czego Chcesz od nas Panie, za twe hojne dary?
czego za dobrodziejstwa, których nie masz miary?

Kościół Cię nie ogarnie, wszędy pełno Ciebie,
I w otchłaniach, i w morzu, na ziemi, na niebie,

Tyś Pan wszytkiego świata, Tyś niebo zbudował
I złotymi gwiazdami śliznie uhaftował

Tyś fundament założył nieobeszłej ziemi
I przykryleś jej nagość zioły rozlicznemi.

Za Twoim rozkazanim w brzegach morze stoi
A zamierzonych granic przeskoczyć się boi.

Tobie kwoli rozliczne kwiatki Wiosna rodzi
Tobie kwoli w kłosianym wieńcu lato chodzi.

Wino Jesień i jabłka rozmaite dawa;
Potem do gotowego gnuśna Zima wstawa.

Chowaj nas, póki raczysz na tej niskiej ziemi,
Jedno zawsdy niech będziem pod skrzydłami twemi.*

(*See note opposite*)

Last of the Renaissance giants was Jan Zamoyski (1542– 1605). The leading politician of his day, he still found time to reconstruct his native Zamość as a model city of the age. Its physical plan was conceived on the principles of Cicero- nian harmony – with the palace, the *ratusz,* and the collegiate church, each complementing the others. Its intellecual life centred on the famous Academy, or *Hippeum,* which briefly constituted one of the foremost seats of learning in Eastern Europe. In this private microcosm, Zamoyski successfully organized the Renaissance life-style and encouraged the virtues which in the world at large were beyond his grasp.[10]

Despite their different careers, Copernicus, Kochanowski, and Zamoyski had much in common. Firstly, they all received a formal education of very high quality. They were all graduates of Cracow and of Padua, the leading university in Europe, where in 1563 Zamoyski had served as Rector. Secondly, they were all deeply interested in Antiquity, and fully conversant with the classics. As a self-appointed task, Copernicus translated the letters of Theophilactus Simokata (1509). Kochanowski, a pupil of the Hellenist Robortello, specialized in Cicero, and for the first thirty years of his life was a Latin poet in his own right. Zamoyski harangued the Sejm and Senate on the history of the Roman Republic. Thirdly, they all consciously schooled themselves in the full range of accomplishments which their individual abilities permitted. Copernicus, the astronomer, was also a qualified doctor of medicine and of canon law; Kochanowski, the poet, studied politics; Zamoyski, the politician, studied poetry. Fourthly, they were all public figures, with a strong sense of civic duty. Copernicus took an active part in the defence of Royal Prussia against the Teutonic Order, and in 1526 in the

* What wilt thou from us, O Lord, for Thy generous gifts?/What for Thy bless- ings which know no bounds?/The Church will not contain Thee; everywhere is full of Thee/In the pit of Hell, in the sea, the earth, the sky/. . . Thou art Lord of all the world; thou didst build Heaven/And embroider it prettily with golden stars./Thou didst lay the foundation of the unbounded earth/By thy command, the sea stands within its shores,/Fearful to leap beyond its measured limits./. . . For Thee, Spring brings forth various flowers;/For Thee, Summer walks out in a garland of corn;/Autumn gives Wine, and numerous fruits;/Then idle Winter rises for a ready meal./Keep us, as Thou deignest, on the earth below/But let us ever stay beneath Thy wings.[9]

reform of the coinage. As a secular canon, he regularly acted as bailiff, tax-collector, judge, and physician. Both Kochanowski and Zamoyski started their careers as royal secretaries. When the one retired to his estate at Czarnolas the other rose to lifelong tenure of the Republic's highest offices — Grand Chancellor and Grand Hetman of the Crown. Finally, they all professed a high moral tone. They were all striving towards conscious ideals of beauty and harmony. Copernicus was most concerned with the theoretical order of the universe, Kochanowski with the practical ordering of human emotions and belief, Zamoyski with political order.

Humanist learning, reverence for antiquity, individualism and the quest for complete knowledge, an interest in public affairs and in the harmonious purpose of human life — these they shared in full measure. They happen to be the very things which are generally understood to have constituted 'Renaissance Man' — *l'uomo universale.*

*   *   *   *   *

The Sejm which assembled in Lublin three days before Christmas in 1568 had been convoked by the King for the express purpose of forging a constitutional union between the Korona and the Grand Duchy. It was the fourth Sejm in five years to discuss the matter, and was attended both by Lithuanian and Polish representatives. By this time, Sigismund-August was in a hurry. All the old arguments still held good. The growth of a common Polish culture in the ruling class of both states; the common danger from Muscovy; the exposure of the south-eastern provinces; the inadequacy of existing military, financial, and administrative practices — all pointed to the need for fundamental change and rapid agreement. But there was added urgency. The King's third marriage had failed. A divorce was not possible. An heir could not be born. The Jagiellons were sure to die out. The King, tired and sick, roused himself for the last great effort of his life. He alone could break the hesitations of the Lithuanian magnates. In the last decade, he had tried many devices to unite the different traditions which divided the two parts of his realm. In 1559, he had instituted a Sejm for the Grand Duchy, and in 1564 provincial *sejmiki* on the Polish model. At the same time he made great concessions, surrendering all prerogatives of the Grand Duke which limited the property rights of the nobility, and extending full legal privileges to Orthodox gentry. He knew, of course, that habits do not change overnight, and that the representatives of the Lithuanian Sejm and Sejmiki had been selected by the magnates under the threat of the knout. He watched at Lublin how the three leading Lithuanians – Mikołaj Radziwiłł 'The Red', Jan Chodkiewicz, and Ostafi Wołłowicz – simply ordered the rest of their delegation to hold their tongues. After one month of formalities, and a further month of crossed purposes, the King summoned Radziwiłł and Chodkiewicz to appear in person in the Senate and explain themselves. When they fled in the night, he reacted angrily. In the following days, three provinces of the Grand Duchy – Podlasie, Volhynia, and Kiev – were incorporated into the Korona. Two Podlasian officers who refused to swear allegiance to the Polish crown, were promptly stripped of their lands and offices. The implication was clear. If the Lithuanian lords refused to behave like Polish noblemen and debate the issue openly, the King would turn on them with all the fury of a Lithuanian autocrat. In April, the leading lords of the Ukraine reappeared – Ostrogski, Czartoryski, Sanguszko, Wiśniowiecki – and took their places in the Polish Senate. On 17 June, Chodkiewicz himself reappeared, and, in the name of his peers, tearfully implored the King 'not to hand them over to the Polish Crown by hereditary will, to the slavery and shame of their children'. Sigismund-August replied, also in tears: 'God dwells where Love is, for such is his Divine Will. I am not leading Your Lordships to any forced submission. We must all submit to God, and not to earthly rulers.' It was the moment of decision. Chodkiewicz accepted the terms of the proposed Union. The Senate rose to its feet and roared its thanks. Poland and Lithuania were to be joined together, 'freemen with free, equals with equal'. There was to be one *Rzeczpospolita,* one 'Republic' or 'Commonwealth'; one indivisible body politick, one king, elected not born; one Sejm; one currency. The Lithuanians were to keep their own law, their own administration, their own army, and the titles of their princely families. The details were amicably edited.

The King laboured incessantly for hours on end, day after day. 'These are great matters', he said, 'which are to last for centuries; they require long deliberation and good counsel.' Finally, on 1 July 1569, the Act of Union was sealed. Standing at the front, hat in hand and surrounded by the clergy, Sigismund-August received the oaths of loyalty from each of the signatories. Then, he led the entire assembly to the Church of St. Stanisław, kneeling before the altar and singing the *Te Deum* in a strong voice.[11]

Sigismund-August's last years were tinged with remorse. His constant appeals for love and harmony were bred by the fear that love and harmony were in short supply. In 1569, the Sejm promptly returned to a debate on his marital affairs and rose on 12 September without attending to the King's urgent requests. The provisions for drafting electoral procedure, for creating a central treasury, and for preparing judicial reforms were unceremoniously postponed. 'You see that I am a servant of Death', he had told them, 'no less than Your Lordships. If you do not pay heed, then my work and Yours will be turned to nought.' They paid little attention. In Muscovy, Ivan IV was angered by news of the Union of Lublin, and hastened to the crime which more than anything else earned him the name of 'Terrible'. Forged letters were produced to show that the Archbishop and Governor of Novgorod were guilty of treasonable contacts with the Polish King. The Tsar arrived to administer the punishment in person. The inhabitants of Novgorod were systematically seized and tortured, and killed in batches of five hundred and a thousand every day. In five weeks, Russia's most civilized city was depopulated, and reduced to a smouldering heap. Ivan returned to Moscow to prepare the cauldrons of boiling oil and the meat hooks which were to chastise some hundreds of Muscovites suspected of treasonable contacts with Novgorod. What future for 'the Republic of goodwill' with such a neighbour? In 1570, the Sejm debated the problem of tax reform, but passed no taxes; in 1571, it again postponed the King's requests, and in 1572 was dispersed by an outbreak of the plague. Sigismund-August relapsed into despair and insomnia. He locked himself into his favourite castle at Knyszyń near Białystok, and refused to receive his senators. He died on

7 July 1572, surrounded by a motley company of quacks, astrologers, and witches, in a room hung in black in memory of Barbara Radziwiłł. His last will repeated those beautiful lifelong wishes which were so unlikely to come true:

By this our last testament, We give and bequeath to our two realms, to the Polish Crown and to the Grand Duchy of Lithuania, that love, harmony, and unity . . . which our forebears cemented for eternity by strong agreements, mutually confirmed by the citizens of both countries. And to whomsoever of the two nations shall hold firmly to the Union gratefully received from Us, We bequeath Our blessing, that the Lord God in his favour shall grant them honour and power above other peoples, in their wide and common rule, in fame both at home and abroad, in all that is good and needful. But whosoever shall profess ingratitude and follow the paths of separation, may they quake before the wrath of God, who in the words of the prophet, hates and curses them who sow dissension between brother and brother . . .[12]

The last of the Jagiellons, like the last of the Piasts 202 years before, was buried on Wawel Hill. The King's private person was dead. His public person rode in effigy to the burial. The royal standard was broken asunder and, with the royal jewels, cast into the grave. This same act symbolized the transfiguration of the Kingdom of Poland. The late King had ruled as the hereditary monarch of two separate principalities. He was leaving them united in one elective Republic.

Part Two

THE LIFE AND DEATH OF THE POLISH-LITHUANIAN REPUBLIC, 1569-1795

CHAPTER SIX
ANTEMURALE:
The Bulwark of Christendom

At any point between AD 1000 and 1939, quotations can be found to illustrate the conviction that Poland was, is, and always will be, the last outpost of western civilization. In the earliest centuries it was seen to be holding the line against the Prussian and Lithuanian pagans; in the modern period against Islam and the Muscovite schismatics; in the twentieth century, against militant communism. At all times, Poland's 'Place in Europe', like that of neighbouring Hungary, was quite clear; it was the *antemurale*, 'the bulwark'.[1]

The vocabulary has varied, of course. The term *antemurale christianitatis* was generally accepted after the Fall of Constantinople notably in a memorial to Pope Paul II in 1467. Elsewhere, one finds *murus* (wall), *scutum* (shield), *clipeus* (buckler), *praevalidum* (barbican), *propugnaculum* (rampart); in Polish, *przedmurze* (bulwark), *forpoczta* (bastion), and even *płot* (fence), or *straż* (watchtower). In 1573, in Paris, when a Triumphal Arch was raised in honour of Henry Valois's election to the Polish throne, the inscription read: POLONIAE TOTIUS EUROPAE ADVERSUS BARBA- RORUM NATIONUM ... FIRMISSIMO PROPUGNACULO (To Poland, Most Steadfast Fortress for the whole of Europe against the barbarian peoples). Thirty years later, Sully preparing his Grand Design for the regeneration of European unity, described Poland as the 'boulevard et rempart'. In 1623, Wojciech Dembołecki wrote charmingly that 'God has enclosed Christendom with the Polish Crown, as a fence against the pagans'. The Polish kings invariably reminded their foreign correspondents of the Republic's traditional claim. On 11 March 1620, at Whitehall, the Polish Chancellor George Ossoliński, commenced his oration to James I with the words: 'Tandem erupit ottomanorum iam diu celatum pectore virus . . . et publico Barbarorum furore, validissimum christiani orbis antemurale, petitur Polonia.' At the end of the century,

on 25 July 1676, John III Sobieski was writing to Charles II
in almost exactly the same language, informing him how 'vast
Multitudes of Turks and Tartars fell upon this Bulwarke of
Christendome to destroy it.'[2]

The concept of *'Antemurale'* has been specially favoured
by Catholic writers, and in recent times has been adopted by
the Vatican's Institute of Polish History as the title of its
distinguished journal. It is often associated with two other
slogans — that of *'Polonia Semper Fidelis'* (Poland Ever
Faithful) and that of Poland as the 'Haven of Toleration'. In
this way, Roman apologists have created the impression that
Poland was able to hold the barbarians at bay firstly because
it was solidly Catholic, secondly because its marvellous toleration gave no cause for religious strife or for foreign interference. Certainly, the wording and substance of the declaration
of the Confederation of Warsaw of 28 January 1573 were
extraordinary with regard to prevailing conditions elsewhere
in Europe; and they governed the principles of religious life
in the Republic for over two hundred years:

Whereas there is a great dissidence in the affairs of the Christian Religion
in our country, and to prevent any sedition for this reason among the
people such as we clearly perceive in other realms — we swear to each
other, on behalf of ourselves and our descendants, in perpetuity, under
oath and pledging our faith, honour and consciences, that we who
differ in matters of religion will keep the peace among ourselves, and
neither shed blood on account of differences of Faith, or kinds of
church, nor punish one another by confiscation of goods, deprivation
of honour, imprisonment, or exile . . .[3]

Yet the declaration contained the proof of a nice contradic-
tion. If the Catholic Republic were truly the Haven of Toleration, it could only have been so by virtue of the presence
of numerous dissenters; but if the dissenting community was
really so numerous that it had to be tolerated, then the
Republic could not have been solidly Catholic. The exact
measure of Poland's Catholicity, and of her Toleration, is not
easily calculated.[4]

*   *   *   *   *

A short tour of exploration round Poland's religious past is
full of surprises, therefore. On the one hand, there is the

unbroken presence of the Roman Catholic Church, whose establishment reached back to the very beginnings of recorded history, and whose supremacy was only briefly threatened. On the other hand, there is constant evidence for numerous varieties of religious nonconformity, sectarianism, schism, and heterodoxy. (See Diagram G.)

Undoubtedly, fervent Catholicism radiates from the earliest known composition in the Polish language. The hymn of the *Bogurodzica* (Mother of God) was probably composed in the thirteenth century, and survives in a fifteenth-century manuscript. In the Jagiellonian period, it was adopted as the battle-song of the feudal host; and it was sung in chorus by the knights of the Polish—Lithuanian Army before the Battle of Grunwald:

Bogu rodzica dzewica	Virgin, Mother of God,
Bogem slawena maria!	Maria, honoured by God,
Utwego syna gospodzina,	Your son's patroness,
Matko swolena maria,	Maria, chosen Mother!
Sziszci nam,	Assist us.
Kyrieleyson!	Kyrie Eleison![5]

Indeed, the scene at Grunwald, where both armies appealed to the patronage of the Virgin Mary, might suggest that the Poles, no less than the Teutonic Knights, paid court to the crusading tradition. Some historians, such as Lelewel, have chosen to liken Poland's militant role in Eastern Europe to that of Spain in the West with its seven-hundred-year Holy War against the Moors.

In effect, the Poles were never very zealous Crusaders. Their participation in the general crusades to the Holy Land was extremely limited, and the few Polish kings who made Holy War against the Infidel had entirely normal political motives for doing so. On this point, considerable dispute has been aroused by the policy of the young Władysław III Jagiellon, King of Poland and Hungary. In 1443, he heeded the promptings of the Papal Nuncio, Giuliano Cesarini, and led his armies eastwards in an attempt to check the growing power of the Ottomans. In previous years, the Hungarians had contained the Turkish menace with difficulty, and had fought fierce campaigns against the Pasha of Serbia, and against Dracula, Pasha of Wallachia. Now they crossed to the offensive. Passing

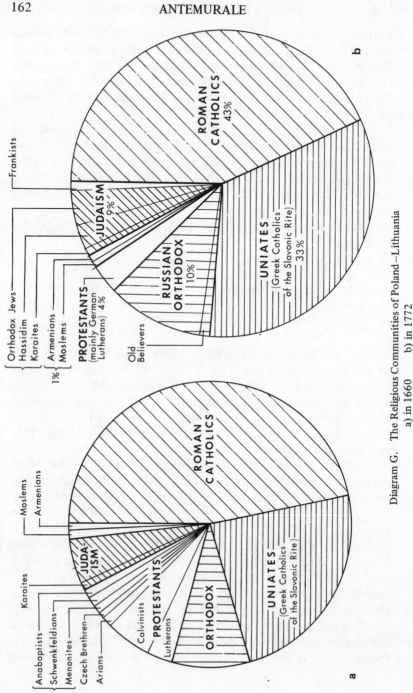

Diagram G.   The Religious Communities of Poland–Lithuania
a) in 1660   b) in 1772

through Belgrade and Sofia, they made for Adrianople. In 1444, the issue hung in the balance. The Ottoman Sultan, Murad II, had forced the Venetian blockade of the Straits, and, landing on the European shore, had brought up much-needed reserves of cavalry. The decisive battle took place on 10 November on the Black Sea coast, not far from modern Varna. The initial success of the Christians was cut short by a foolhardy move to take the Sultan's centre by direct assault. The disaster was complete. The death of the young king was recorded by the Ottoman chronicler, Chodza Efendi (Saad-ed-din):

It was dawn, as the morning star announced the strident call to arms. The archers began the fight, and when the full force of the *sajdaki* had been unleashed, both sides fell on each other sword in hand . . . The enemy was already gaining the advantage, when Karaya, the mighty Beyler-Bey of Anatolia, was struck down by infidel steel. Confused and terrified, the *spahis* broke ranks and fled.

The Sultan, seeing them flee, raised his thoughts to Allah. 'Lord,' he cried, 'By the merit of rulers inspired by thy power . . . by the zeal of the warriors of the Faith . . . by the last and greatest of Thy prophets . . . by the light of his heavenly soul . . . save the army of Islam from the heel of the heretics. Save the defenders of the Faith from the shame of an Infidel victory.' Heaven answered his prayer.

The King of the Infidels, burning with the excitement of victory, heeded the false counsel of one, Janko, to attack the camp of the *padishah* directly. With a handful of soldiers, and brandishing a captured scimitar, he made no attempt to halt his charge as he rode straight towards the Sultan. But Murad, patiently bearing the insult, . . . spoke to the guard about him, 'Cut this accursed madman off from his retinue . . . Give way on both sides as he flies like a wounded boar among you, then suddenly close the gap . . .'

The King careless in his bravery, spurred on his horse far ahead of his followers . . . charging straight for the splendid *bunczuk* of the *padishah*. At first, in accordance with their orders, the soldiers let this soulless dog pass. Then, they surrounded him. A janissary by name of Chodza Kazer threw him to the ground by wounding his horse, then severed the head of this disciple of Hell, and brought it to the *padishah* . . . Those who had followed this crazy youth among our soldiery were chopped to pieces, like rissoles.

Seeing in this event an act of Divine Providence, smiling and full of praise, the Sultan cried aloud, *'Et-hamdu lillahi alazzefer!'* (God be praised for this victory). He then ordered the King's severed head to be impaled on a stake, to terrify the infidels . . . Later, preserved in a pot of honey, it was sent to the capital of the country, to Bursa, to be exhibited to the gaze of the common people . . .

Murad, meanwhile, sent news of this favourable event to all the neighbouring rulers. To Egypt he sent twenty-five of his Christian captives, shackled hand and foot and in full armour . . . When the feeble and faint-hearted Arabs saw the frightening figures of the infidels, as enormous as high fortresses, they cried out in amazement at the prowess of the Turks: *'Allah jensor ibn Osman!'* (The Lord helps the Sons of Osman) . . .

That famous victory, which filled the whole people with joy and strengthened the power of the Ottomans and the fortune of their subjects, was won on Tuesday, the ninth day of the Redzeb Moon, in the 848th year after the flight of the Prophet.[6]

The Polish historians who have implied that Władysław III died the death of a Christian martyr, selflessly laying down his life in defence of the Faith, have provoked a barrage of high-explosive criticism. Their critics maintain that Władysław paid the price of naïve and ill-judged ambition.[7] Certainly, the Varna Expedition would seem to have been inspired much more by Hungarian interests than by Polish ones. It cannot be realistically compared to Poland's relations with the Ottomans, or to the Spanish *Reconquista.*

For Poland, the Ottoman Turks represented less of a menace than the Tartars of the Crimea. The Tartar war-parties made annual incursions along the three great frontier trails of the steppes. They burned, looted, and carried off their *yasir* or 'human booty' to be sold into slavery throughout the Muslim world. It was the Tartars, not the Turks, who inspired the stream of protestations about Poland's single-handed defence of Christendom against the Muslim invasion. Yet these protestations can hardly to taken at their face value. The Tartars were an infernal nuisance; but they posed no threat to European stability. Unlike the Moors or the Ottomans, they entertained no permanent territorial ambitions, and their *czambuls* never ventured beyond the limits of one summer's ride. Polish attempts to control them were accompanied by much pious Christian verbiage; but were more akin to police operations than to religious crusades. After all, the Republic's own Christian Cossacks behaved in much the same fashion; and the Republic's military leaders thought nothing of recruiting Tartar auxiliaries for action against other Christian princes when occasion demanded.

None of the crusading Orders knew much success in Poland. The Knights Hospitallers founded several commanderies at an early date — at Strzygom in Silesia in 1150, at Zagość in Małopolska in 1153, and at Poznań in 1191. But none really flourished. The Silesian commanderies passed under Bohemian control after the secession of the province, and those in the Kingdom of Poland declined after the Mongol invasion of 1241–2. In the fifteenth century, the Hospitallers were associated with the Teutonic Order, and attracted the retribution of the Polish Kings accordingly. By the seventeenth century, there were very few Hospitallers in Poland at all. In this connection, the amazing Bartolomeus Nowodorski (1544–1624) — knight, pedagogue, and philosopher, must be regarded as an exception in every way. In his early years he had served Stefan Batory in the Transylvanian Guard and on embassy to Constantinople, but was exiled in disgrace for duelling. For ten years, he served Henry of Navarre in France, and joined the Order of St. John in 1599. In 1602 he fought in a Venetian galley at the naval battle of Patras and returned to Malta as an invalid. In Malta, he was found by Piotr Kochanowski, who happened to be travelling in the Mediterranean, and was brought back home to Poland. In 1617, in Cracow, he accepted the first chair of secular philosophy at the Jagiellonian University, and founded the city's leading Gymnazium, which still bears his name. In 1618, at the age of 74, he accompanied Chodkiewicz on the expedition to Muscovy, and was wounded in the Battle of Tuszyn. He was put in charge of the one remaining commandery of the Hospitallers in Poland, at Poznań, but died before he could be installed.[8]

Crusading, in fact, could never have been very popular in Poland. The Infidel was too close and too well known to hold much glamour; and there were wars enough as it was. More importantly, throughout the Middle Ages, the Kingdom of Poland had itself been assaulted by western crusaders, who in the pay of the Teutonic Order spent more time fighting their Catholic hosts than converting the heathen. For three hundred years, from 1226 to 1525, the struggle against the 'Knights of the Cross' exerted one of the formative influences on the development of Polish Catholicism. At the Council of Constance in 1414–18 the chief Polish delegate, Pawel Włodkowic, (Paulus Vladimiri 1370–1435), Rector of the Jagiellonian University, systematically condemned crusading as contrary to God's will. His detailed charges against the excesses of the Teutonic Order were supported by arguments from theology and philosophy which provide one of the earliest expositions of a specifically Polish concept of international law.[9]

Moreover, the need for reconciliation as opposed to religious militancy was readily understood in a society where the Roman Church had never enjoyed a monopoly. Unlike the countries of Western Europe, where the ecclesiastical authority of Rome was unchallenged till the end of the Middle Ages, the church in Poland was constantly beset by pagans, dissenters, and schismatics. Paganism thrived long after the formal conversion of Poland to Christianity in AD 966, and continued to provide the official religion of Lithuania till 1386. Traces of ancestor worship were still to be found in remote districts in the nineteenth century; and harmless pagan customs, like the *dożynki* or 'harvest fires', survive in the countryside to this day. Judaism, introduced by Chazars in the ninth century, had a longer history in Poland than Christianity. The eastern lands of the Kingdom were largely inhabited by Orthodox, whilst at the Reformation, Lutherans, Calvinists, and other Protestant sects, founded important congregations. In Lwów and Wilno, Armenian and Tartar minorities established their own churches and mosques. In the united Republic between 1569 and the First Partition in 1772, the Roman Catholics formed the largest single religious group, but accounted for barely half of the total population. (See Diagram G a, p. 162.)

The Catholic Reformation was bound to take these circumstances into consideration. Although the Vatican entertained high hopes of using the Republic as a strategic base for its counter-offensive both against Protestantism and Orthodoxy, the Roman hierarchy in Poland was obliged to act with great discretion. In the critical period, in the sixth, seventh, and eighth decades of the sixteenth century, the militant Bishops did not possess the support of either King or Sejm, and could not use state institutions to enforce their wishes. The Tridentine spirit was first observable in Poland in 1551 at the Synod of Piotrków, where Stanisław Hozjusz (Hosius, 1504–79), Bishop of Warmia, presented the celebrated *Confessio Fidei Catholicae Christiana* (A Christian Confession of the Catholic Faith), which was to propel him towards his Cardinal's hat and to the presidency of the Council of Trent itself. Yet in that same year, when the Bishop of Cracow tried to take action in the ecclesiastical courts against a Calvinist nobleman, it was found that the provincial dietine took to arms in the defendant's defence. In 1552, when the Bishop of Przemyśl tried to prosecute one of his canons, Stanisław Orzechowski (1513–66), who had taken a wife in defiance of the rule of celibacy, it was found that the Sejm of the kingdom sprang to protest. Thus from the outset, inquisitorial methods were avoided. From 1573, when the Confederation of Warsaw was instituted, the principle of toleration was inviolate, and even in the Vasa period when both Court and Sejm were actively Catholic, could only be defied in isolated instances. After 1603, the Index was regularly circumvented, and the prosecution of noblemen who protected condemned heretics made little headway against the prevailing ethos of the noble democracy. Ineluctably, the accent was on persuasion, not coercion, and in particular on education. To this end, Cardinal Hosius introduced the Society of Jesus to Poland in 1565, with their first college at Braunsberg.[10] In the following years, Jesuit colleges were opened at Pultusk (1566), Wilno (1569) and Poznań (1573), and in the east as far afield as Polock, Dorpat, Orsza, Kiev, Perejasław, and Witebsk. The construction of scores of churches, schools, and monasteries in the Baroque period bore witness to their lasting success. Conflict with the Protestants was, at the most, sporadic, and rarely violent. Attacks by Catholic students on a Lutheran funeral or on a Calvinist pastor, or in 1640 the demolition of the Protestant college in Wilno in a Catholic riot, belong to the exceptions. The *Concors discordia* (The Agreement to Disagree) lasted at least till the mid-seventeenth century, and was undermined more by the tensions of wartime than by any deliberate change in policy. Although to the Jesuits' way of thinking, tolerance was generally regarded as a vice, there were loyal

Catholics who thought otherwise. Mikołaj Łęczyca (Nicolaus Lancicius, 1574–1653), the provincial of the Jesuits in Lithuania in the reign of Władysław IV, was the son of a Calvinist printer, a convert to Catholicism, and a noted moderate. Mikołaj Ławrynowicz, a Benedictine author, wrote in 1639 that 'beautiful harmony is born from contrary things, as on a lute made with different strings . . .; the minds of Catholics are actually sharpened and tempered by them, like iron against stone.' Repressive measures, such as the expulsion of the Arians in 1658, were undertaken for political rather than for religious reasons. Poland had its share of Catholic bigots; but the matter was far removed from what Carlyle imagined when he talked of 'savage and sanguinary outbreaks of a type of Jesuit fanaticism as has no fellow'. Carlyle, the British Protestant, had not apparently heard of the Oxford Martyrs, of whom in Poland–Lithuania there was no equivalent.[11] (See Map 10.)

The influence of the Jesuits, though important, must be seen in relation to the parallel expansion of other contemplative, teaching, and mendicant Orders. In the two centuries from their introduction in 1564 to their suspension in 1773, the Jesuits never controlled more than seventy out of the Republic's 1,200 monastic and religious houses. Even in the educational sphere, they never enjoyed anything which resembled a monopoly. A total of 47 Jesuit colleges was complemented from 1642 by the growing network of the schools of the Piarists (Pietists), who specialized in the education of the sons of indigent nobility. In this light, the opinion of Walerian Krasiński that 'the Jesuits and their wretched tool, Sigismund III, were the cause and origin of the ruin of the country', looks somewhat unjustified.[12] The Benedictines, whose earliest Polish foundations dated from the early eleventh century, the Cistercians, whose first house at Jędrzejów was founded in 1140, and the Carthusians, all continued to work and to pray. The Dominicans (Black Friars), to whom the Vatican entrusted its inquisitorial powers, had maintained an unbroken presence since 1222. The Bonifraters, imported from Spain in 1608, were active in the realm of medical and mental care; the Missionary Fathers of St. Vincent de Paul (Lazarists) arrived shortly afterwards from

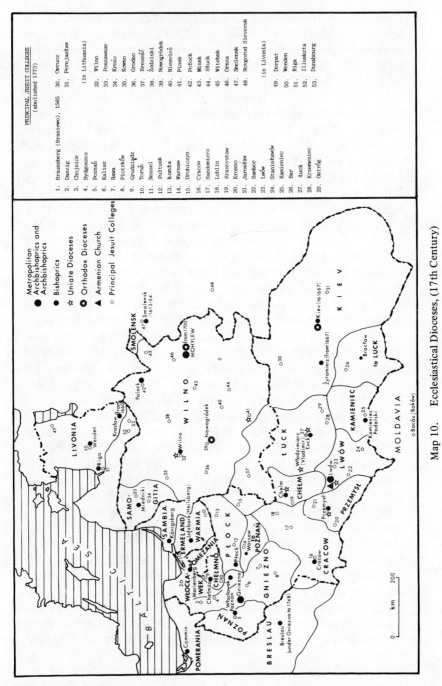

PRINCIPAL JESUIT COLLEGES
(abolished 1773)

1. Braunsberg (Braniewo), 1565
2. Danzig
3. Chojnice
4. Bydgoszcz
5. Poznań
6. Kalisz
7. Rawa
8. Piotrków
9. Grudziądz
10. Toruń
11. Reszel
12. Pułtusk
13. Łomża
14. Warsaw
15. Drohiczyn
16. Cracow
17. Sandomierz
18. Lublin
19. Krasnystaw
20. Krosno
21. Jarosław
22. Sambor
23. Lwów
24. Stanisławów
25. Kamieniec
26. Bar
27. Łuck
28. Krzemieniec
29. Ostróg
30. Owrucz
31. Perejasław
    (in Lithuania)
32. Wilno
33. Poszawsze
34. Kroże
35. Kowno
36. Grodno
37. Brzeŝeŝć
38. Żodziski
39. Nowogródek
40. Nieśwież
41. Pinsk
42. Połock
43. Minsk
44. Stuck
45. Witebsk
46. Orsza
47. Smolensk
48. Nowgorod Sieversk
    (in Livonia)
49. Dorpat
50. Wenden
51. Riga
52. Illuskzta
53. Dunabourg

Metropolitan
Archbishoprics and
Archbishoprics

Bishoprics

☆ Uniate Dioceses

⊙ Orthodox Dioceses

▲ Armenian Church

○ Principal Jesuit Colleges

Map 10.   Ecclesiastical Dioceses, (17th Century)

France, with the original view of converting the Armenians of Lwów; the Marianite Sisters organized a network of convents in the eastern palatinates for the purpose of converting Jewish girls, and of finding them noble husbands. The various branches of the Franciscan Order could be encountered throughout Poland—Lithuania. The Bernardine Friars (Obser-vantists) were specially popular with the nobility, who endowed them with over eighty foundations; the Reformists reached Poland in 1622; the Franciscan Minoresses (Poor Clares) rivalled the Carmelites among the leading female orders; the Capuchins were specially favoured by Jan Sobieski. Taken together, these various Orders far outnumbered the Jesuits, and counterbalanced any exclusive claims which they might have entertained. In the eighteenth century, when the level of learning and missionary zeal declined, the relative status and reputation of the Jesuits declined also.

Polish Catholicism was marked not so much by its external militancy, as by its extreme inward piety. Traditionally in-disposed to forcible conversion, and unsupported by the civil power, the Church could not apply the same ferocious methods as in Spain, Italy, or in neighbouring Bohemia. Rather, it reasserted its position by cultivating all manner of mystic, ascetic, and devotional practices. The seventeenth century saw a revival of interest in reliquaries. Pilgrimages came back into fashion. Complex Calvaries, whose chapels, avenues, and stairways followed the stations of the Cross, were founded by pious noblemen. The elaborate Baroque shrine of Kalwaria Zebrzydowska in the Carpathian foothills of western Małopolska, laid out in 1613 by Michał Zebrzy-dowski, was but one of many, and launched a cult which has lasted to the present day. New ascetic Orders, such as the Cameduli in their enclosed hermitages at Bielany near Cracow, and near Warsaw, struck a new note of unworldliness. Con-fraternities of pious laymen, the *bractwa,* were organized. They were noted for their devotion to the Rosary, for their marathon prayer meetings and processions, and for their public displays of repentance and even of communal flagella-tion. Immense efforts were made to cultivate the lives of the saints, especially of Polish saints, and to press for their canonization. In 1594, St. Jacek, 'Hyacinth of Cracow'

(1185–1257), founder of the Dominican Order in Poland, was canonized. In 1602, St. Casimir of Cracow (1458–84), the second son of King Kazimierz Jagiellończyk, was recognized by the Vatican as the patron saint of the Polish See. In 1622, the canonization of the Spaniard, St. Isidore the Farm-Servant, caused great rejoicing among the *Szlachta,* who propagated his cult as a means of engendering harmony, if not increased productivity, among their serfs. In the course of the seventeenth century, the lengthy process of canonical litigation in Rome was started on behalf of several prospective Polish candidates. The beatification in 1604 of the youthful Jesuit St. Stanisław Kostka (1550–68), prepared the way for his canonization in 1826; the beatification in 1680 of St. Jan Kanty, 'John of Kanti' (1390–1473), born at Kęty near Cracow and sometime Professor of the Jagiellonian University, preceded his canonization in 1767. The Polish Church's martyrs included the Uniate Archbishop Jozefat Kuncewicz of Połock (1580–1623), eventually canonized in 1867, and the priest, Andrzej Bobola S.J. (1591–1657), barbarously murdered by Cossacks near Pinsk and raised to the ranks of the Blessed in 1938. Among the unsuccessful candidates was another Jesuit, Bazyl Narbutt whose case, though officially supported by the Polish Sejm, failed to impress.

As a result of the Catholic Reformation, the Marian Cult reached new heights of intensity. To some extent, the extraordinary veneration awarded to the Virgin Mary in Poland, may be seen as the reassertion of a local 'Old Polish' tradition against the centralizing, Latinizing, Romanizing reforms of the Council of Trent; but it was equally the most obvious expression of Catholic solidarity against the Protestant, Orthodox, and Judaic challenges of the age. In the seventeenth century, more than one thousand Marian shrines were thriving in Poland–Lithuania, each with its miraculous icon of the *Matka Boska,* 'The Virgin Mother of God, Queen of Heaven'. Apart from the Pauline monastery of Jasna Góra at Częstochowa, the principal Marian shrines were at Berdyczów in Ukraine, at Borune in Lithuania, and at Chełm. The exclusively Polish Orders of the Marian Fathers (1673) and of the Sacramentalist Sisters (1683) were founded in honour of the Virgin; whilst many existing monasteries, especially the nunneries of the Polish Benedictines, – the *Norbertanki* (Pre-monstratensians) and *Brygidki* (Bridgettines) – were turned over entirely to the Marian cult. The ceremonial Coronation of the *Matka Boska* at Częstochowa as 'Queen of Poland' in 1717, the year of the Silent Sejm, was a clear sign that the Roman Catholic Church was determined to keep its hold over the masses in spite of the subjection of the country to Russian political interests.

In this same period, devotional literature recovered its role in Polish culture, countermanding the more obviously secular trends of the Renaissance. Polish translations of medieval Latin apochrypha and hagiography, especially concerning the life of St. Adalbert (Wojciech), did much to popularize the vernacular language; whilst Piotr Skarga's *Zywoty świętych* (Lives of the Saints, 1579) competed with Kochanowski's Polish Psalter published in the same year for the accolade of the best known and best loved Polish works of the succeeding centuries.

The predicament of the Orthodox community was particu-larly problematical. In Poland, the Orthodox inhabited the northern flanks of the Carpathians as far west as Sanok and Krosno. In Red Ruthenia, annexed in 1340, and in the Grand Duchy of Lithuania, they represented the dominant element. In the united Republic, they counted for roughly forty per cent of the total population. They belonged to the ancient Orthodox dioceses of Kiev and Nowogródek.

Yet the Orthodox did not live at peace, least of all among themselves. From 1453, when the Patriarchate of Constanti-nople fell into Ottoman hands, they became the constant prey of politically interested parties. On the one side, the Tsars of Muscovy extended claims of universal patronage. On the other side, the Roman hierarchy saw hopes of ending the Schism. The result was constant conflict. In the sixteenth century, after a brief dalliance with Rome under the Cardinal-Metropolitan Isidore and his successors, the Metropolitans of Kiev had returned to their former allegiance to Constantinople. The attempts of the papal legate Antoni Possevini in the years 1581–3 to re-establish Roman control over the eastern church, rebounded to his discomfiture. In 1589, Tsar Feodor, acting in concert with Patriarch Jeremiah of Constantinople, created a separate Patriarchate of Moscow, whose pastoral pretensions spread far beyond the bounds of the Muscovite state. The Republic's Orthodox magnates, accustomed to administer clerical patronage and church property alike, felt their position threatened from all sides. In particular, Prince Konstanty Vazyl Ostrogski (d. 1608), Palatine of Kiev, whose theological academy at Ostroróg was leading an important revival in Orthodox life and had published the first printed Bible in Church Slavonic, was disposed to submit neither to Rome, nor to Constantinople, nor to Moscow. Like most of his co-religionists, he wanted to be left in peace. He was supported by Prince Andre Kurbsky, who had settled in Volhynia in 1567, and applied himself among other things to devotional work. But the issue was forced by the Orthodox bishops. Resentful of the taxes demanded by Constantinople, and of the autonomy granted to the *bratstva* or secular 'brotherhoods', and fearful of the activities of the Patriarch of Moscow, who was systematically undermining their authority, they made common cause with their Roman colleagues. Headed by their Metropolitan, Michal Rahoza, by the exarch Cyril Terlecki, and by Hipation Potij, formerly Castellan and now Bishop of Brest, they addressed a letter to the Pope. It was a request in the name of all the faithful to be admitted to the Church of Rome. On 23 December 1595, in St. Peter's, Clement VIII celebrated the granting of their request with a solemn mass. Meanwhile, at home, resistance mounted. When the joint Synod of the two Orthodox provinces assembled at Brest on 8 October 1596, the bishops were no longer unanimous. Rahoza read the Papal Bull ending the Schism, and led a procession to the Roman church of the Blessed Virgin. He then received a delegation of Roman clergy to the Orthodox church of St. Nicholas, and listened to a joyful sermon from Peter Skarga, the king's Jesuit confessor. The dissentient bishops gathered in a private house elsewhere in the town. Prince Ostrogski arrived with an army of priests, monks, and soldiers, in time to hear the archimandrites of Lavra Piecharskaya, of Pinsk and of Suprasl join the envoys from Constantinople in cursing all those who had 'betrayed Our Mother, the Greek Church'. The day ended with mutual excommunications. From the Roman point of view, the Synod of Brest confirmed the Act of Union. From the point of view of the Orthodox Church in Constantinople and Moscow, it was an act of disunion.[13]

Religious grievances mingled with social and political ones. The Cossacks of the Dnieper did not recognize the Union of Brest. Nalewajko's Rebellion in 1596 was the first of many to justify itself in terms of defending the Orthodox faith against Catholic subversion. Nalewajko, executed in Warsaw as a political traitor, was remembered in the Ukraine as a religious martyr.

Thus, the Orthodox remained divided. That part of the clergy who elected for the Union kept their Slavonic rite, their separate hierarchy, and their right to marry: but they admitted the Roman doctrine of the Eucharist, the supremacy of the Pope, and the discipline of the Vatican's Curia. Members of this 'Greek-Catholic Confession of the Slavonic Rite' were known in the Republic as *unici* or 'uniates'. In the eyes of Constantinople they were schismatics, and of Moscow, traitors. Those who dissociated themselves from the Union were known in Poland as *dysunici* or 'disuniates'. They belonged to the 'Greek Orthodox Confession of the Slavonic Rite' and were counted together with the Protestants among the *dissidentes in religione.* For almost forty years they were denied any form of official recognition.

Turmoil amongst the Orthodox, first provoked by the Union of Brest, continued unabated. Bitter emotions fostered in this period by religious strife undoubtedly sharpened political conflict in succeeding years. Uniates battled disuniates, as both struggled to preserve their independence from the Roman Catholic establishment. Their condition was vividly portrayed in Meletius Smotrycki's contemporary *Lament for the Oriental Church* of 1610. At first, in the south-eastern provinces, a series of regular battles took place, the so-called 'Wars of the Deacons' in which the uniate and disuniate clergy disputed control of the offices and property of the Orthodox Church. In the north-eastern provinces, a similar conflict reached its height when the Uniate Archbishop of Połock, Josaphat Kuncewicz was murdered. Archbishop Kuncewicz was no man of peace, and had been involved in all manner of oppressions, including that most offensive of petty persecutions

— the refusal to allow the Orthodox peasants to bury their dead in consecrated ground. His death was the subject of outrage in Rome, but of some relief in his own diocese. Tempers also flared as a result of the categorical refusal by Sigismund III to approve episcopal appointments made by Muscovite Patriarchs. In 1620, unrest among the Cossacks was sparked off by this very grievance.

With time, however, a more fundamental struggle developed. Both the Uniate and the Orthodox churches, despairing of healing the rift, began to strengthen their own separate identities and to formulate their own doctrines. In this, on the Orthodox side, a prominent role was played by Piotr Mohyla (1596—1647), the Orthodox Metropolitan of Kiev. Mohyla was a member of a princely Moldavian family whose turbulent fortunes had been closely associated with Chancellor Zamoyski's Balkan adventures. His uncle Jarema, his cousin Constantine, his father Simeon, and his elder brother Michael, had all laid claim at various times to the title of Hospodar and to the thrones of either Moldavia or Wallachia. He himself served as a young man in the Polish Army, and in 1621 fought at Chocim under Chodkiewicz. He entered the monastery of Lavra Pecherskaya in Kiev in 1627, and emerged five years later as Metropolitan, and as a lifelong opponent of the Union. Having founded the Mohyla Academy in 1632, he quickly turned it into an outstanding centre of Orthodox theology, a rival of the local Jesuit College and the first seat of higher learning in the East Slav world.[14] His cause was greatly assisted by the Uniates' failure to gain full political rights. Contrary to the provisions of the original agreement, the Uniate bishops were never admitted to the Senate of the Republic. The uniate clergy and nobility were limited to the status of second-class Catholics, which faced them with a permanent crisis of conscience. Their numbers were slowly eroded, both by desertions to mainstream Catholicism and by reversions to Orthodoxy. By the mid-seventeenth century, the success of the Catholic Reformation was being matched by a parallel revival among the Orthodox. In 1633, after thirty-seven years of persecution, the Orthodox hierarchy was officially reinstated.

Yet further upheavals were in view. No sooner had the Orthodox Church reasserted itself against the Uniate challenge, and established its right to be tolerated in Poland—Lithuania, than it began to feel the pulses emanating from Moscow which sought to remodel traditional Orthodox practices and to turn Orthodoxy into a Muscovite state religion. In the mid-seventeenth century, the ancient Greek Orthodox Church of Slavonic Rite was about to be transformed into the Russian Orthodox Church. In 1648, the outbreak of the Cossack Wars severed the easternmost provinces of the Republic from the rest of the country. In 1654, when Chmielnicki's Cossacks accepted the suzerainty of the Tsar and by implication the direct control of the Patriarch of Moscow over the Orthodox population of their vast conquests, the Patriarch Nikon was reforming the liturgy. In 1662, Kiev itself was occupied by the Tsar's Army. Finally in 1667, when the Truce of Andrusovo brought the whole left-bank Ukraine under permanent Muscovite control, the Tsar Alexei was repudiating Nikon, though not his reforms, and subordinating the Orthodox Church to the rule of the state. In this way, the Orthodox faithful were forced to choose between submitting to the new Nikonian liturgy and the new Russian discipline or staying with their old beliefs and being branded by Moscow as schismatics. The result was the great *Raskol* or Schism, which had lasting effects. The Old Believers were naturally drawn to frontier areas where the Tsar's police could not easily reach them. Two early centres of Old Belief, at Starodub and at Wetka to the north of Kiev, were replaced by others further to the west when the new demarcation line of 1667 was created.[15] For their part, those Orthodox communities in the Republic who adopted the reforms and the accompanying Muscovite discipline, gradually moved towards a position where the profession of Orthodoxy was automatically associated with expectations for eventual incorporation into the Russian Empire.

However, despite the growing rift between the Orthodox and the Catholics in Poland—Lithuania, the complexity of their mutual relations cannot be overemphasised. Long after the Union of Brest, there were prominent representatives of the Orthodox faith who strove to remain both loyal subjects of the Republic and ardent advocates of religious harmony. Such a man was Adam Kisiel (1600–53), wojewoda first of Czernihów and then of Kiev. Educated at the Zamość Academy in a spirit of humanism and tolerance, he was the very epitome of moderation. It was Kisiel who persuaded the young King, Władysław IV, to reinstate the Orthodox hier-archy, and Kisiel who acted throughout a long political career as the natural intermediary between Court and Cossacks. The fact that modern Ukrainian historians sometimes choose to belittle him as a renegade to their cause only serves to under-line the many different currents within Ruthenian Orthodoxy which still prevailed in his lifetime.

The fragmentation of the Orthodox Church was reflected in the lives of its leading families, many of whom ceased to hold any fixed religious loyalty. Prince Konstanty Ostrogski himself was married to a Tarnowska, a Catholic. His heir, Prince Janusz, was a Catholic who bequeathed the reversion of the family estates to the Knights Hospitallers. Two of his three sons were Catholic, and one Orthodox; one of his two daughters married Krzysztof 'Thunderbolt' Radziwiłł, the Calvinist Hetman of Lithuania; the other married Jan Kiszka, the richest Arian in the Grand Duchy. The senior lines of the Radziwiłł, Chodkiewicz, Sapieha, Pac, and Wiśniowiecki, all turned Protestant. The Sanguszko, Czartoryski, Czetwertyński, and Ogiński passed from Orthodoxy to Catholicism. In the history of many Orthodox families, the adoption of Calvinism in the sixteenth century acted as a stepping-stone to their Catholic conversion in the seventeenth.[16]

The Protestant community was also fighting on several fronts. Lutheranism was mainly confined to the cities, with their large German populations. Calvinism, in contrast, proved attractive to the nobility. But the Calvinists, too, were divided among themselves. In 1562, a long-standing dispute between the conservatives and the radical wings led to schism. The radicals seceded, and as 'Arians' developed one of Europe's earliest and most thoroughgoing experiments in primitive Christianity. (See Map 11.)

Once the two great rebellions of Danzig were settled, in 1526, and again in 1577–8, the Lutherans were effectively protected from outside interference for more than a century.

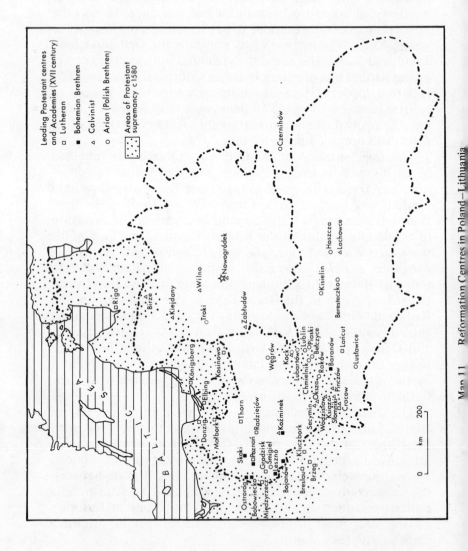

Map 11   Reformation Centres in Poland—Lithuania

Secure in their municipal charters, and in royal promises of toleration first made by Zygmunt-August and repeated by Bathory, the Lutheran burghers enjoyed freedom of worship. Their intellectual activities found a ready focus in the University of Königsberg, founded in 1545 by Abraham Kulwieć (Culvensis, 1510–45), a Lithuanian refugee from Wilno, and in the celebrated Gymnazium at Danzig. They were variously patronized first by Queen Bona Sforza and later by Anna Vasa, the Protestant sister of Sigismund III. Such disputes as arose were directed at the Calvinists no less than at the Catholics. Yet, contrary to impressions created in later times, the ecumenical spirit flourished. In this respect, the history of the city of Thorn serves as a prime example to illustrate the way that protracted harmony passes easily into oblivion, whilst one sensational disaster is meticulously remembered for centuries. In 1595, this largely German city, acted as host to a Protestant Synod convoked to uphold the Confederation of Warsaw. In 1645, it hosted the interconfessional 'Colloquium of Love' proposed by King Władysław IV. For several months, Protestant and Catholic divines discussed their theological and practical differences in an atmosphere of restraint and mutual respect. Although no firm conclusions were reached, they showed that Christian charity could still triumph over sectarian bigotry. In 1674, a Spanish diplomat who visited Thorn on his way to Sobieski's Election, noted the scene with pleasurable surprise:

In this city, as in the rest of the province . . . the free exercise of the two religions, Catholic and Lutheran, is permitted. Those of the latter confession occupy the principal churches of the place, whilst the Catholics have two religious houses, one belonging to the Dominicans and the other to the Company of Jesus, where they celebrate the divine offices with much sumptuousness and magnificence . . . Nevertheless, all live in great harmony with each other, and without disputes or arguments on questions of belief — which is the best way to preserve peace.[17]

No one could have predicted that one single incident fifty years later could brand the name of Thorn forever with the mark of Catholic fanaticism.

Thorn was one of those German cities whose separate privileges had been established by the Act of Incorporation

of Royal Prussia in 1457, and specifically confirmed at the
Treaty of Oliwa in 1660. Its German Lutheran inhabitants
greatly outnumbered the Catholics. On 16 July 1724 the
Catholic Procession of Our Lady was interrupted by a fracas
between the Jesuit students and some Lutheran bystanders.
According to the Jesuits, the trouble started when a Lutheran
burgher, shouting insults and failing to raise his hat when the
procession passed, was forcibly uncovered by one of the
students. According to the Lutherans, the students ordered
the burghers to kneel in the street. On 17 July, a full-scale
riot ensued. The Catholics, having failed to obtain the release
of a comrade arrested by the Burgomaster, began to seize
Lutheran hostages. In retaliation, the city mob descended on
the Jesuit College, demolished its contents and made a bonfire
of them in the market square. For this, according to the
Jesuits, the blame lay chiefly with the city Corporation which
had connived in the mob's excesses. According to the
Lutherans, it lay exclusively with the students, who had gone
on the rampage sword in hand, and had fired from within the
College on guards sent by the Burgomaster to defend it. As
related in Catholic Poland, the event which caused most
offence was the burning of a statue of Our Lady, allegedly to
taunts of: 'Now, Woman, save thyself.' In due course, on a
deposition by the Jesuits, the citizens of Thorn were charged
with sedition in the Crown Tribunal in Warsaw; and on
16 November sentence was passed against them. Burgomaster
Roesner and his deputy, Czernich, were condemned to
decapitation, 'for neglecting to do the Duty of their respective
offices and thereby countenancing the Sedition and Tumult
of the populace'. The burghers Harder, Moab, and thirteen
more, were also to be executed 'as the first aggressors against
the Jesuit College'. Two others, Carwise and Schultz, for pro-
faning the Virgin, were to be mutilated, quartered, and burned.
There followed a long list of fines, banishments, and confisca-
tions. No appeals were allowed. At the end of the month
Prince Lubomirski appeared before Thorn with a regiment of
soldiers, and proceeded to put the sentence into effect. The
condemned men were promised clemency on condition of
conversion to Catholicism. At dawn on 7 December 1724,
Burgomaster Roesner was beheaded. His last words were: 'Be

satisfied with my Body; my Soul is my Saviour's.' Later, the wheel, the whip, and the fire were added to the sufferings of the victims. Two men were saved; one, Heyder, by conversion on the gallows, the other, John-Henry Czernich, the deputy Burgomaster, by a personal pardon from the King of Poland. A Lutheran school, a chapel, and a printing-press were handed over to the Catholic Church. Thus ended the 'Tumult of Thorn', *der Thorner Blutbad.* In Polish history books, it rarely finds mention. In Protestant Europe, and particularly in England, it was the sole event for which the name of Copernicus's birthplace was remembered. (See pp. 374–5, 464.)

In London, the Tumult of Thorn provided a capital sensation. Already on 2 December, before the executions, the King of Prussia had written to George I to arouse English feelings. 'The fury of the Romish clergy is come to such a Height', he wrote, 'that they are now endeavouring not only at the total ruin of the city of Thorn, but likewise at the utter Extirpation of all Dissenters in that Kingdom.' By January, the country was seething with indignation. *The Historical Register,* London's main source of foreign news, carried the most detailed information, carefully supplied by courtesy of Berlin. Its readers were regaled in turn with the text of the Treaty of Oliva; with 'the Council of Thorn's Account of the Tumult that happen'd there last July'; with an 'Abstract of the Affair of Thorn publish'd at Berlin in the German tongue'; with 'the Constitutions of the Diet of Poland and Lithuania in 1724'; and with the entire correspondence of the King of Prussia with their Polish, British, Russian, Danish, Swedish, French, Sardinian, and Imperial Majesties. Most curiously, they were also treated to a number of 'true and faithful Catholick accounts' of the affair, nicely calculated to have the opposite effect than that intended by their supposedly Jesuit authors. To drive the point home, the English editor added his own gloss:

Who can read without indignation, this abominable Account . . . without bringing to mind the impious Doctrines of that Hellish Society . . . ? The Letter of His Prussian Majesty . . . is sufficient of itself to destroy the Credit . . . of the Jesuits, who are justly charged to have fomented the Tumult, in order . . . to blacken the Conduct of the Protestants, and to charge them with Horrid Violences.

Whatever the rights and wrongs of the Tumult itself, there is no doubt that the Prussians systematically exploited it for nefarious purposes of their own. For decades past, the Hohenzollerns had tried to suborn the German cities of Royal Prussia from their allegiance to the Republic. They carefully magnified the grievances of the Lutheran Protestant community, and broadcast them round Europe. They constantly prompted the Russians — if prompting was needed — to take parallel action on behalf of the Orthodox. Their recruiting sergeants were at work in Thorn and elsewhere. For them, the Tumult of 1724 was a heaven-sent opportunity. For the nobility of the Republic, it was the last in a series of provocations which lured them into fatal retaliation. Throughout the Great Northern War (1700–21), they had seen the country torn apart by domestic factions and foreign invaders, all of which competed for the patronage of the 'dissidents'. They had seen the manifest intolerance of all these champions of religious toleration at first hand. In their helplessness, they lashed out in fits of intemperance which rebounded to their own disadvantage. In 1717, the Sejm resolved to limit the rights of the dissidents, and in 1718 expelled the sole remaining non-Catholic envoy, the Calvinist, Andrzej Piotrowski from their midst. In response, they found that the Lutheran Synod of the Republic, calmly debating within the privileged walls of Danzig, was openly calling for the intervention of foreign powers to remedy the 'oppression of the dissidents'. Their exemplary punishment of the Torunians was clearly intended to teach the Lutherans a lesson. By stressing the civil nature of the Burgomaster's offence, it sought to underline the need for civil obedience. Of course, it had the contrary effect. It inflamed the religious passions which it sought to contain, and provided the Republic's neighbours with a pretext for meddling which was never relinquished until the Republic itself was destroyed.[18]

The Calvinist community became a political issue at a much earlier stage. In the *Korona,* it had attracted widespread support from the middling sort of nobleman, who was trying to preserve his independence from the patronage of the great families and who resented the wealth and influence of the Bishops. In the Grand Duchy, it attracted the greatest magnates themselves, as a means of bypassing the influence of Catholic and Orthodox clergy. Soon after its appearance in the mid-sixteenth century, it obtained a number of secure bases on the estates of the Leszczyński at Leszno, of the Oleśnicki at Pinczów, and of the Radziwiłłs at Wilno, Kajdany, and Słuck. As a result, the royal edict against heresy of 12 December 1550 remained a dead letter. Thereafter, Calvinism advanced swiftly. In 1554, the first Calvinist Synod of the Kingdom at Słomniki empowered noblemen to divert the payment of tithes from the Roman Church to their own pockets. In 1555, at the Sejm of Piotrków, Rafał Leszczyński and Hieronim Ossoliński mooted the possibility of creating a national church under Zygmunt-August. In 1556, the first united Synod of Poland and Lithuania met at Pinczów. In 1558, the Calvinists in the Sejm felt strong enough to challenge the right of the Bishops to participate in the Senate. For the next two decades, they constituted one of the most powerful groupings in political life, commanding the allegiance of an estimated 20 per cent of the nobility together with an absolute majority among the lay members of the Senate. They were particularly active in the Executionist Movement. By the inspiration of Jan Łaski (1499–1560), nephew of the late Primate of the same name, the Calvinists actually aimed to win a position of supremacy in the state. Their moments of success came in 1565, when the King formally forbade his Starostas to enforce the decisions of ecclesiastical courts against the nobility in matters of faith, and in 1573, at the Confederation of Warsaw, which was largely of their making. Already, however, they were beginning to moderate their pretensions. Deeply divided among themselves on issues of doctrine and discipline, they resigned themselves, like the Catholic reformers, to defending their established position and to propagating their views through education and publishing.

The divisions in the Calvinist camp were present from the start, and were fuelled by the variegated origins of its members. Repeated attempts to devise a form of Confession acceptable to all, failed repeatedly. In 1555, the declaration of intercommunion with the Czech Brothers displeased as many as it satisfied. In the following year, at Pinczów, Łaski's interim motion to introduce a variation of Melanchthon's

'Augsburg Confession' was clearly designed to reconcile the irreconcilable. In 1562, at the second united Synod of Pinczów, the propositions of the radicals proved repugnant to the majority. The minority then withdrew to found their own separate sects. Formally condemned from Geneva, they never returned to the fold. The solidarity of Polish Calvinism was broken for good.

Calvinist cultural enterprises scored some notable achievements. Although the New Testament had already been translated into both Polish and Lithuanian at Königsberg, the 'Brest Bible' published in 1565 by Mikołaj Radziwiłł marked an important milestone in the progress of the Polish vernacular. In the works of Mikołaj Rej (1505–69) and of Cyprian Bazylik (1535–1592), translator and hymnologist, the Calvinists made important contributions to the literature of the 'Golden Age'. Their printing presses and schools were in no way confined to denominational activities. The original Calvinist Academy at Pinczów, known as the 'Sarmatian Athens', pioneered the teaching of those secular subjects such as mathematics, natural sciences, history, ethics, and modern languages, for which all the Protestant schools were renowned. Calvinist publicists, among whom Francesco Stankar (1501–74), Professor of Hebrew at the Jagiellonian University, and Andrzej Wolan (d. 1610), Secretary to Mikołaj Radziwiłł, deserve mention, maintained a high level of scholarly excellence in the public disputes of their day. Calvinist patrons, among whom the Leszczyński in Poland and the Chodkiewicz, Sapieha, Dorohajski, Zenowicz, and Sokoliński in Lithuania vied with the Radziwiłłs, gave an important stimulus to learning and to all the arts.

The Polish sectarians in contrast made a unique impact on religious life not through the size of their membership, but through the originality of their social experiments and theological doctrines.[19] Variously known as Arians, Antitrinitarians, Unitarians, Polish Brethren, Racovians, Pinchovians, Socinians, Samosatenians, Farnovians, Sabellians, Budneans, Theists, Ditheists, and Tritheists, they professed a multitude of beliefs and associations which explain the baffling variety of their names. They were united only by their rejection of the dogma of the Trinity, and by their claim to the absolute right of free thought. A number of 'anti-trinitarians' came together in Cracow around 1550 in Protestant discussion groups organized by Queen Bona's Corsican Confessor, Francesca Lismanino. They included Adam Pastor, a Dutchman; George Blandrata, Queen Bona's Piedmontese physician; and Lelio Sozzini, a refugee from Venice and Zürich. They were in contact with a group of Moravian Anabaptists who had settled in the Carpathians, and with similar congregations in Transylvania. In the 1550s their ideas were developed by the writings of Piotr z Goniąz (Gonesius, 1530–72) from Podlasia, whose 'Ditheism' expressed in *De Filio Dei* (On the Son of God, 1556), denied the existence of the Holy Spirit; by Grzegorz Pawel z Brzezin (1525–91), whose treatise *O prawdziwej śmierci . . .* (On the reality of Death, 1564) doubted the existence of the Life Hereafter; by Szymon Budny (1530–93), whose 'Non-adorantism' contained in *O przedniejszych artykułech* (On the first principles of the Christian Faith, 1576) has been described as the most daring tract of the century; by Marcin Czechowicz (1532–1613) of Lublin, whose *Rozmowy chrystiańskie* (Christian Conversations, 1575) preached social equality and the wickedness of private property; and above all by Faustio Sozzini (Socinius, 1539–1604), Lelio's nephew, whose treatise *De Jesu Christo Servatore* (On Jesus Christ, God's Servant, 1598) precipitated his expulsion from Cracow. The key moment arrived in 1569–70, when having seceded already from mainstream Calvinism, the sectarians refused to participate in the Compromise of Sandomierz and in the united Protestant front against the Counter-Reformation. Thereafter, some continued on their own lonely path; but many came together in the town of Raków in Małopolska, where, under the protection of Michał Sienicki (1521–82), the 'Polish Brothers' established their celebrated commune. Abolishing the distinctions of rank and estate, they withdrew completely from society at large, denying all allegiance to the state and observing the rules of manual labour, common property, absolute equality, and pacifism. Their renown was propagated by their Academy, which in the early seventeenth century boasted over one thousand pupils from home and abroad; by their tireless printing-presses; and principally by their Catechism, which ran into scores of editions and was translated into almost every European language. Modern scholars pay attention to the Polish Brethren from an interest in the prehistory of modern communism, but contemporaries were mainly concerned with the theological aspect. In the eyes of Christian Europe, whether Catholic, Orthodox, or Protestant, the 'Racovian Catechism' smacked strongly of blasphemy. It must be regarded as a seminal text not merely of Unitarianism in particular but of radical thought in general. In England, for example, the early Latin editions circulated discreetly among theologians (Moscorovius's Edition of 1609 was dedicated to King James I). Yet the popular English edition of 1652, published in Amsterdam, aroused the ire even of Cromwell's Rump Parliament, which ordered the Sheriffs of London and Middlesex to seize all copies and to burn them. The eight chapters were composed in the form of Platonic dialogues, and the passages which seem to have given the greatest offence were those which dealt with the divinity of Christ:

Interrogatio: Quid est Iesus Christus, filius Dei?
Responsio: Est Homo, mediator noster apud Deum. *

and with the Unity, as opposed to the Trinity, of God:

Q. What are the things that pertain to the essence of God, and are simply necessary to salvation?
A. These: that God is; that he is but one; that he is eternal; that he is perfectly just, perfectly wise, and perfectly powerfull.
. . .
Q. And who is this one divine Person?
A. That one God, the Father of our Lord Jesus Christ.
Q. How prove you that?
A. By the most evident testimony of the Scripture. Thus Christ himself, John 17.3, saith 'This is life eternall that they may know Thee (Father), the onely true God . . .
Q. But Christians commonly hold that not onely the Father, but also the Son and the Holy Spirit, are persons in One and the same Deitie.
A. I know it well, but they are grievously mistaken, producing arguments for it out of Scriptures ill understood.[20]

In Poland—Lithuania, the existence of the Polish (Arian) Brethren proved a severe test of the Republic's boast to be

* (Question: What is Jesus Christ, the Son of God? Answer: He is a Man, our mediator before God.)

Europe's 'Haven of Toleration'. As the only sect to be specifically excluded from the terms of the Confederation of Warsaw, it was natural that the Arians should be the champions of religious liberty. It was no accident that the most vehement defence of the principle of Toleration — *Vindiciae pro religionis libertate* (Justifications for the Liberty of Religion, 1639) — should be written by Jan Crell (1590–1633), Rector of the Raków Academy. Even so, persecution of the Arians was extremely desultory. Action against them by the religious authorities led only to their departure to the estates of some sympathetic nobleman. In 1582, when Budny was solemnly anathematized by the Calvinist superintendent of Małopolska, he took refuge with Jan Kiszka at Łuck. In 1618, when the most important Arian centre in Lithuania at Nowogródek was closed by royal decree, its members were taken in by Rafael Kos (1590–1633); and even in 1638, when Raków was closed on order of the Sejm after some of its students had ill-advisedly demolished a wayside cross in the vicinity, the Polish Brethren continued their mission elsewhere in the Republic.

In these circumstances, it was rare indeed that anyone should have paid for their faith with their life. The young Italian, Francus de Franco (1585–1611), executed in Wilno in 1611 on a charge of blasphemy was one exception; and Ivan Tyshkovitch who suffered the same fate in Warsaw in the same year, was another. Tyshkovitch was a citizen of Bielsk in Podlasie, a town belonging at that time to the Queen, Constance of Austria. He was an Arian, a Ruthenian by nationality, and apparently the victim of a local vendetta. He came from a prosperous merchant family, and had recently been appointed municipal tax-collector. The local worthies started an enquiry into his affairs only when they heard that he planned to build an Arian temple in the town; and they found a pretext in the fact that his appointment as tax-collector had been made without the administration of the required oath. According to witnesses present at the interrogation, Tyshkovitch stated that he did not recognize the Trinity, and did not know what it was, since it was not mentioned in Holy Scripture, but that he recognized One God. In the magistrates' record, the clerk reported him as

saying that 'the Trinity is not God' and that 'he did not know
what it was, man or woman'. On appeal to the Crown Tribunal at Lublin, the magistrates' proceedings were declared
improper. But the case was revived by an attack against the
court-house at Bielsk, launched by a band of Tyshkovitch's
armed sympathizers, both Catholics and Arians. This time,
the attack was referred to the Queen's private court, where
the mayor of Bielsk, using blatantly falsified evidence, turned
the verdict against him. In September, the Marshal of the
Sejm in Warsaw gave a personal assurance that Tyshkovitch
would obtain satisfaction. Yet again on 7 October 1611 in
the Assessorial Court in Warsaw, he was condemned to a
500 groszy fine, and to confiscation and banishment. He preferred to fight on. Unfortunately, and despite another unfavourable court action in which he faced the death penalty,
he obstinately remained in the capital. Released on bail, he
was arrested at the gates of the Royal Castle when he came in
person to learn the final verdict. By order of the Queen, the
death sentence was confirmed. On Friday, 16 December 1611,
in the Old Square, Tyshkovitch was executed in public. First
his tongue was excised, as a mark of blasphemy. Then his
body was sawn in two, as a mark of rebellion. Next, his arms
and legs were severed as a mark of desecration. Lastly, for the
good of his everlasting soul, his remains were burned.[21]

The Czech Brethren followed a course which in many ways
paralleled that of their Polish counterparts. Persecuted in the
Habsburg lands from the mid-sixteenth century onwards,
they looked to the Hussite tradition and to the preservation
of Czech culture. Their original settlement established at
Leszno in Wielkopolska in 1550, received an influx of several
hundred families from nearby Moravia on the outbreak there
of the Thirty Years War. In 1628 it gave shelter to the celebrated pedagogue, Jan Amos Komensky (Comenius, 1592–
1671), who, on becoming Rector of the Leszno Academy,
proceeded to raise it to a scholarly centre of continental
excellence. Variously known as the *Unitas Fratrum* or *Polska
Jednota* (Union of Czech Brethren in Poland), and later as
the 'Moravian Church', the Czech Brethren avoided unitarian
doctrines, and in this way were able to enjoy the fruits of
intercommunion not only with the local Calvinists but also

with Prostestant churches abroad, including the Church of
England. At the same time, they shared many of the plebian
and radical social views of the Polish Arians, and in the 1650s
shared their expulsion. In 1656, the citizens of Leszno were
suspected of voluntary collaboration with the Swedes, and
the town was burned by the Polish Army having refused to
surrender its Swedish garrison. Komensky, accompanied by
many of his associates, emigrated to Holland. Even so, the
religious community, survived in straitened circumstances.
The Academy was rebuilt in 1662 by English subscription,
only to be burned for a second time by the Russians in 1707.
Its special Protestant connections were lost when its patron,
Stanisław Leszczyński, was converted to Catholicism, and
sold his estates to the Sułkowski family; but it remained as a
centre of Polish education until 1824.[22]

The British connections of the Polish Reformation have
caused frequent comment, and not a little surprise. The
career of Jan Łaski, in particular, has been the subject of
several learned studies. As 'John O'Lasco', he served as
minister to the Protestant Strangers' Church at the Austin
Friars in London in the reign of Edward VI, and exerted a
definite influence on the formulation of the Book of Common
Prayer. Other contacts are less well publicized. Shortly before
Łaski's departure, in 1553, an unknown Pole in London produced the earliest tract in Polish to be published in England
– *Rzecz Pana Jana Ksyczecia Nortumberskiego*, being a
translation of the recantation on the gallows of John Dudley,
Duke of Northumberland, the father-in-law of Lady Jane
Grey. In addition to the usual stream of incidental travellers,
there were Poles, including Bogusław Leszczyński in 1633
and Daniel Ernest Jabłoński (Figulus, 1660–1741),
Komensky's grandson in 1680–3, who chose to study at
Oxford for religious reasons. Similarly, Poland–Lithuania
sheltered a number of exiles from Great Britain. In the reign
of Queen Elizabeth, Catherine Brandon, Duchess of Suffolk,
and her husband, Richard Bertie, found a home with the
Radziwiłłs at Nieswież. In the early seventeenth century,
large numbers of Scots settled in the Republic. The Catholics
among them gravitated to episcopal cities such as Chełmno,
where their tombstones and memorials can be seen to this

day; the Protestants made either for Danzig or Thorn, or for Calvinist centres such as Słuck or Kajdany in Lithuania. One Scottish immigrant, John Johnstone (1603–75), born at Samter (Samotuly) in Wielkopolska, was educated at Leszno before proceeding to further medical studies at Leyden, St. Andrews, and Cambridge. In that same period, there were English pupils, such as Thomas Segeth, at Raków. In the words of Professor Kot, 'Anglo-Polish cultural relations were neither numerous nor lasting, but they did have their curious and important moments.'[23]

The German cities of the Republic harboured a number of specifically German sects. There were Anabaptists from Münster who settled in Danzig, Elbing, Braunsberg, and Marienwerder; and there was a smattering of Schwenkfeldians — the Quakerish followers of Caspar von Schwenkfeld (1490–1561) of Ossig in Silesia — who took refuge in Wielkopolska.

The Armenians were largely confined to the district of Red Ruthenia, descendants of an ancient commercial community. Their Armenian Catholic cathedral in Lwów dated from the fifteenth century.[24]

The Muslims of the Republic derived mainly from Tartar settlements on the western confines of the Grand Duchy. The first waves of immigration occurred in Jagiellonian times, and another in 1658 after the campaigns against Prussia. Although the Muslims did not attend the Sejm, they enjoyed the full military rights of the szlachta and continued to serve in the ranks of all Polish armies until the Second World War. In 1616, when there were over one hundred mosques in the Republic, an attempt was made by the Catholic bishops to catholicize the children of mixed marriages; but in general they were left to their own devices. In 1939, there were sixteen mosques in Poland. A residual element still lives to this day in the area of Białystok.[25]

Compared to the Orthodox and the Protestants, the Jewish community lived in relative peace and quiet. The Jews were protected by the most ancient charters of religious liberty; and, so long as they observed strict religious segregation, they were not disturbed by attempts to convert them. The Roman authorities were happy enough to receive Jewish converts to Catholicism, of course; but the profession of Judaism was never an offence in itself, except for Christian apostates. One of the very few cases in which a woman, Barbara Weiglowa, in 1539, was burned at the stake in Cracow for heresy, seems to have been occasioned not, as was once supposed, by her attachment to witchcraft or to Lutheranism, but by her return to Judaism in rejection of her earlier conversion to Christianity. There were occasional riots against the Jews, provoked by the time-honoured blood-libel. In the worst such incident, in Cracow in 1637, some eight Jews lost their lives. In 1667, a Jewish pharmacist, R. Matathia, was burned in Cracow for blasphemy. In general, however, the Jews stayed aloof from the squabbles of the Gentiles, having plenty of rich religious arguments, sects, and squabbles of their own.[26]

Of all the Jewish sects of the Republic, the Karaites possessed the longest ancestry. Established in the eighth century among the Jews of the Orient, they were brought to Lithuania from the Crimea in the fifteenth century by Grand Duke Witold, and settled at Troki, which remained their headquarters thereafter. In doctrinal matters, they adopted a fundamentalist position, admitting a literal interpretation of the Old Testament as their sole source of revelation. They derived many of their practices from Islam, and from Islamic attitudes to the Koran. In the Reformation period, they shared their interest in textual criticism of the Bible with the more radical Protestant sects. Interestingly enough, it was the biblical studies of the Polish anti-trinitarians which provided their most famous luminary, Isaac ben Abraham of Troki (1525–86), with his principal inspiration. Troki, in fact, was a natural laboratory for religious cross-fertilization. The Karaite *kenessah* nestled on the shore of the lake alongside a Tartar mosque, a Catholic church, and a Uniate monastery. The anti-trinitarians began to arrive in the 1570s. They included a group, scathingly described as 'uncircumcised Jews', who adopted the ritual practices of Mosaic Law. In 1582, they were joined by Szymon Budny, who has been called 'the best Hebrew scholar of the century', and whose Greek and Hebrew annotations to his translation of the New Testament, published at Nieśwież in 1572, proved a sensation for Jewish and Christian scholars alike. During this period, Isaac ben Abraham followed the disputes between Budny and

Czechowicz on the validity of the Scriptures with intense, professional interest; and painstakingly compiled their arguments for purposes of his own. Whereas the anti-trinitarians were attacking the conventional Christian views in order to show that Jesus Christ was the natural fulfilment of the prophecies of the Old Testament, the Karaite sage now proceeded to draw the opposite conclusions from the same points. His life's work, the *Hizzuq Emunah,* the 'Fortress of Faith', was designed to refute the basic claims of Christianity, and to protect the Karaites from doctrinal contamination. Its historical arguments were based almost entirely on Bielski's Chronicles; its theological arguments were justified by a detailed comparison of the texts of the Brest Bible, of Budny's annotations, and of the Cracow Bible of 1575, which was a Polish Catholic translation of the Latin Vulgate. It was published posthumously, in Italy in 1585, by the author's disciple, Joseph ben Mordecai ha-Qodesh Malinowski. In its own day, this Polish—Hebrew theological cocktail passed virtually unnoticed in the outside world; but with time it fermented into a mixture of explosive proportions. Translated into Latin in 1681, and later into French and English, it provided the very ammunition which later generations of humanist scholars had long needed to blast the bastions of obscurantism of the established Christian churches. It was exploited at length by Voltaire, by the Encyclopedists in France, and by the Deists in England, and can thus be regarded as a seminal text of the European Enlightenment and of Tom Paine's Age of Reason. By that time, the Karaites of Lithuania had amassed a rich literary tradition. Incorporated into the Russian Empire at the Second Partition, they were encouraged by the Tsarist Government as a means of dividing the unity of Judaism, and they continued to flourish into recent times.[27]

In the course of the eighteenth century, however, Jewish sectarianism was proliferating of its own accord. First came the Sabbateists; next the Hassidim; and lastly, the Frankists.

The Sabbateists were followers of the 'pseudo-Messiah', Sabbataj Cebi or Zevi, who had died in Albania in 1676. In the Republic, they won over a number of adherents in the towns of the south-east, on the Turkish frontier.

The Hassidim, in contrast, launched a mass movement

which was destined to capture the allegiance of almost half of Europe's Jews. Their founder, Israel ben Eliezer, 'Baal Shem Tob' (1700–60), commonly known as 'BeShT', started his career as a faith-healer at Międzybóż in Podolia in the 1740s. Having gained widespread celebrity, he then proceeded to denounce not just the doctrines, but in particular the spirit and formalism of orthodox Rabbinism. Like Luther in the Christian world, he stressed the 'omnipresence of God' and showed how ordinary people could commune directly with their maker, bypassing both the mediation of the rabbinate and the necessity for abstruse Talmudic learning. His revivalist fervour struck a note of hope amongst the growing despair of the poverty-stricken and illiterate masses of the Jewish proletariat, and made the pedantry and élitism of the rabbis look ridiculous. In this sense, he may also be compared to his contemporary in England, John Wesley, the founder of Methodism. In due course, his followers broke with orthodox Judaism altogether, and formed their separate congregations, each with its own *zaddik* or 'prayer-leader'. BeShT himself wrote little of importance; but his teachings were preserved and propagated by his two chief apostles, Dob Baer (1710–72), the *Maggid* or 'Great Preacher' of Międzyrzecz (Mezeritz), and Jacob Joseph ha-Cohen (d. 1769) of Polonnoe. Towards the end of the century, when the ecstatic and spiritualist aspects of Hassidism seemed to some to be running out of control, a rational wing of the movement came into being. Known as 'HaBaD' – from the Hebrew acrostic for Wisdom–Understanding–Knowledge – it was launched by Shneor Zalman ben Baruch (1747–1812), who sought to give the Hassidim a stronger intellectual basis. By this step, the fury and resentment of the orthodox rabbinical authorities were raised to new heights. Ever since the suspension of Jewish autonomy in 1764, they had been unable to co-ordinate any policy of defence against the tidal wave of Hassidism. Their arrest and excommunication of Hassidic leaders in Wilno in 1772 had only served to discredit themselves. In 1797, when they denounced Zalman to the Tsarist police, they widened existing divisions still further. Zalman, like many a revolutionary before and after, was cast into the Petropavlovsky Fortress in St. Petersburg, and transformed into a martyr. The stage was set for the long struggle between the Hassidim and their orthodox 'Opponents', the *Mitnaggedim,* which raged in Polish Jewry throughout the nineteenth century.[28]

To modern eyes, the Frankists appear the most exotic of all. Jankiel Lejbowicz (1727–91), later known as Jakub Frank, ran one of the most successful religious frauds in modern history. He was born at Korolówka in Podolia, and spent most of his early life in Turkey, at Salonika and Smyrna, as a travelling merchant-preacher. He seems to have followed the practices of the Sabbateists, complementing the theology of the Talmud with Zoarist jargon and financial wizardry. In 1754, he claimed to have been converted to Islam, thereby imitating his 'Master', Sabbataj Cebi, who ninety years before had appeased the Ottoman authorities by exactly the same step. In the following year he returned to his native Podolia, and soon attracted a host of disciples from the teeming ghettos of the borders. The orthodox Jewish authorities were outraged. One winter's night in 1756, they hastened to the Bishop of Kamieniec having surprised the Frankists *in flagrante.* They had broken into a novices' prayer meeting in the village of Lanckorona, and, in the words of the Bishop's report, had discovered a scene of gross debauchery: 'cantilenas impias, altas ac tripudia devotionibus intermiscentes, carnales commistiones distinctis cum uxuribus, consanguineis, imo et affinibus suis, Mosaicae renuntiando legi publice perpetraverint.'[29] It was the beginning of a scandal which reached the very highest circles of the Republic. Frank, having instructed his followers to proclaim the validity of Catholic teaching on the Trinity and the errors of the Talmud, took refuge across the border. Meanwhile, his supporters were released from arrest by the Bishop, who foresaw the prospect of a sensational conversion. A public disputation between the Frankists and the Talmudists, and a test case in the consistory court, led to open conflict. The public executioner was ordered to burn all the Talmudic books in the diocese. The orthodox Jewish elements replied with violence. The Frankists were attacked in the streets, and were shorn of half their beards as a sign of heresy. Appeals by Baruch Jawan, Jewish aide of the chief Minister, Bruhl, in Warsaw, produced a royal decree to end the disturbances. In January 1759, when Frank recrossed the Dniester into the Republic with twelve apostles, he returned as a conquering Messiah. He staged another disputation against the Talmudists in the Cathedral of Lwów, which he was adjudged to have won six points to nil, with one point drawn. He then requested Christian baptism for himself and all his sect. At one of the mass christenings which followed, his godparents included the Uniate Archbishop of Lwów, the Countess Bruhl, and several eastern magnates. At a second christening in Warsaw, the King-Elector himself agreed to be godfather. Whereupon, a stream of denunciations led to Frank's arrest. Under torture in the Bernardine cloister in Warsaw, he confessed to charges relating to polygamy, embezzlement, and impersonation of the Messiah. In deference to the King, he was incarcerated in the monastery of Częstochowa. But he was far from finished. In 1767, when Russian forces invaded the Republic, Frank offered to turn to Orthodoxy and was released from prison by Suvorov. Fleeing to Austria in 1772, he caused a stir by setting his daughter Eva, his chosen successor, to seduce Joseph II. He finally settled at Oberrad near Frankfurt-am-Main, where he bought a castle, and where, as 'Baron von Frank, Prinz von Polen', he lived in a fairy-tale world of barred gates, spies, and chemical experiments. Surrounded by a guard of one thousand hussars dressed in diamond-studded uniforms, he rode to Mass at the parish church of Burgel in a gilded coach. His funeral, on 12 December 1791, resplendent in eastern splendour and Polish costumes, was the last act of a supreme impresario, the perfect charlatan.

Throughout these thirty years, Frank's followers in the Republic remained unwaveringly faithful. They developed an amazing cult which they called 'Das' (It), and produced the extraordinary 'Bałamutna Bible' — a mystical fantasy filled with animal symbolism, with stories of treasure hidden in mythical caves, and with dreams of a chosen land conquered by their legions to the greater glory of the 'Sennor Santo', 'Der Heiliger Herr', their absolute master. In the 1760s they were baptized into the Catholic Church in large numbers. At the Coronation Sejm of 1764, they established their claim, as converts to Catholicism, to qualify for certificates of

nobility — which they bought at 500 ducats a head. Most amaz-
ingly, they continued to subsidize their master at Oberrad.
It has been calculated, no doubt with some degree of exaggera-
tion, that 24,000 believers, of whom one-quarter lived in
Warsaw, subscribed on average 4.5 million zł. per year. This sum
was larger than the income of the state, and is indicative of the
excesses of sectarianism in a supposedly Catholic country.

In comparison to the troubles caused by religious differences, witchcraft and witch-hunting, gave rise to more human
misery, and more persecution of innocents, than everything
else combined. As elsewhere in Europe, the distinctions
between blasphemy, heresy, sorcery, and necromancy were
not always clear, and their supposed practitioners could
expect no charity. In the Republic, the craze for witch-
hunting reached its height in Mazovia in the first quarter of
the eighteenth century. But isolated incidents occurred over
three hundred years. Suspicions of witchcraft in tiny rural
communities were usually aroused by natural disasters, by
plague, drought, or crop failure, or simply by neighbourly
spite. Charges of sorcery invariably snowballed, as one woman
under investigation would denounce her acquaintances in
desperate attempts to exonerate herself. In the seventeenth
century, there are instances of unscrupulous noblemen
employing teams of witches as instruments of private warfare.
The ducking-stool formed part of the essential equipment of
every village, and torture was a normal ingredient of most
examinations. Naked; shaved above and below; anointed with
holy oil; and suspended from the ceiling, lest by touching the
ground she should summon the Devil to her aid, the miserable
suspect was examined by the magistrates, who fortified themselves with alcohol and urged her to confess. Two such un-
fortunates among thousands were Dorota Siedlikowa and her
'accomplice', interrogated at Kalisz in 1612. Dorota was
suspected of curdling her neighbour's beer, and had been over-
heard by her stepfather to say: 'By the power of the Virgin,
and the help of the Saints, may all such evil people be overturned, and good people take their place, in the name of the
Father, Son, and Holy Ghost.' Her accomplice, who had
claimed that she was not with Dorota on the day in question,
was duly put on the rack:

Ligata nihil voluit fateri jednom chorzi ludzi omywała ziołkami . . .
(Having been bound, she was willing to say nothing except that she had
sometimes bathed sick people with herbs);
Tracta . . . (Having been racked, she said she was not with her, and was
innocent, God knows . . .);
Usta candellis . . . (Burned with the candles, she said nothing, only that
she was innocent);
Spuszczona . . . (Having been lowered, she said that she was innocent to
Almighty God in the Trinity);
Remissa et iterum in terra sedens usta candellis . . . (Replaced, then again
burned with candles as she sat on the ground, '. . . Ach! ach! ach! For
God's sake, she did go with Dorota and the miller's wife to Mrs. Wysocki.')
Thereafter the confessions agreed with those of Dorota.[30]

In the sixteenth century, only 4 per cent of those charged
with witchcraft were actually burned. In the seventeenth
century, this figure rose to 46 per cent, and in 1700–25 to
50 per cent. The total number of victims has been calculated
as 20,000 in Silesia, and 10,000 in the Kingdom of Poland.
Their sufferings did not come to an end until the royal decree
of 1776.

* * * * *

By the end of the eighteenth century, the religious scene in
Poland–Lithuania was considerably altered. In 1569, at the
Union of Lublin, the Roman Catholic establishment had
commanded a dominant minority in a population of multifarious denominational allegiances. In 1791, on the eve
of the final Partitions, it commanded a clear majority. The
Lutherans, Orthodox, and Arians had virtually been eliminated, the Uniates reduced, the Calvinists decimated. Only
the Jews had matched the Catholics in both their absolute
and their relative increase. (See Diagram G b, p. 162.)

This 'Triumph of the Counter-Reformation' in Poland is
sometimes cited as the only instance of a country where the
Roman Catholic Church successfully attacked and reversed
the gains of the Reformation. Yet the Roman Triumph is a
deceptive, not to say an illusory phenomenon; and is largely
attributable to arbitrary or external factors. In the northern
provinces, for example, the Lutherans were never reconverted
to Rome. They dropped out of the reckoning by virtue of the
frontier changes of the Partitions, which left them in the

expanding Kingdom of Prussia. In the East, the Orthodox
were advancing at the expense of the Uniates. They only disappeared from the Polish purview, when they were incorporated into Russia. In both these areas the Roman allegiance
had actually diminished. It had only increased in real terms in
relation to the Calvinists and Arians. Yet in this regard, the
foreign enemies of the Republic achieved drastic results of a
kind which the Jesuits could never emulate. At the time of
the Swedish Wars, by openly championing the Protestant
cause, the Swedes inevitably pushed their Polish co-religionists
under a cloud of political suspicion, and obliged large numbers
of the Calvinist and Arian nobility to turn to Catholicism as
proof of their patriotism. In those same fateful years, the
Muscovite Army systematically attacked the Protestants of
Lithuania with brute force. Chmielnicki's Cossacks treated
Protestants to the same violence that marked their treatment
of noblemen and Jews. In 1648–9, the number of active
Protestant communities in the Grand Duchy was reduced
from 140 to 45. In this way, the work of the Counter-
Reformers was actually performed by its opponents.

Even so, it cannot be denied that the massive solidity of
the Catholic Church far outweighed all ephemeral Protestant
rivals. Polish Calvinism was associated from the start with
feudal privilege, and never penetrated the peasantry. It could
not compete with Lutheranism for the loyalty of the diminutive Christian bourgeoisie. Polish Arianism, too, was an intellectual and a political rather than a popular pursuit, and
could not in its very nature appeal to the illiterate masses. In
the event, the Calvinists and Arians mounted but a light-
weight challenge to the Catholic supremacy. They never
captured the machinery of the state; they never loosened the
grip of the hierarchy on the populace at large; they never
formed a consolidated front with the Orthodox, Uniates,
Lutherans, and Jews. Oddly enough, their initial success was
undermined by that very principle of Toleration which they
themselves had erected. Once the terms of the Confederation
of Warsaw were enshrined in the constitution, the Protestants
had no further cause to protest. They could practise their
religion as they wished, but could extract no significant political or social advantage by so doing. They denied themselves

the likelihood of advancement at Court, and the company of their Catholic neighbours, without any hope of worldly reward. In other words, they lacked the stimulus of persecution. As a result, their numbers were slowly but surely eroded over six or seven decades. The two generations of noblemen who took to the reformed doctrines with such alacrity in the second half of the sixteenth century were dying out by the middle of the seventeenth. As often as not, their sons and grandsons returned unostentatiously to the Catholic fold. The edicts of limitation directed against the Arians in 1658, and against all Protestants in 1718 formally terminated a process which to all intents and purposes was already complete.

Even a cursory survey of the religious life of the Republic, therefore, would seem to prompt some controversial conclusions. In the first place, neither Poland nor Lithuania could fairly claim in this period to be Catholic countries on the monolithic scale of Spain or Italy. The myths of Poland's undivided Catholicity can only have been coined by the apologists of a Church whose supremacy was constantly disturbed, either by internal dissent or by external force.

Secondly, the spirit of tolerance was as rare a virtue as elsewhere. In the Age of Faith, Catholics and Protestants, Orthodox and Uniates, Talmudists and anti-Talmudists, and presumably Armenians and Muslims as well, almost everyone in fact, believed that their own particular doctrine pointed the sole way to eternal salvation. Each of the denominations was as intolerant of its neighbours as it was frightened by deviations among its co-religionists. Fierce punishments for religious offences were generally thought to be right and proper. Kings such as Zygmunt-August and Władysław IV set clear examples of tolerance. Yet the advocates of freedom of conscience were few, whilst the ranks of the devotees were many. For every single reader of Crell or Ławrynowicz, there were thousands who agreed with the Jesuit Skarga in blaming the ills of the Republic on 'the abominable vice of tolerance'.

Lastly, it would seem that Toleration, as distinct from tolerance, *did* prevail. In a state which possessed no strong central executive authority, and where the ecclesiastical courts could not enforce their rulings, religious uniformity could not be imposed. The nobility believed what they wished,

and protected whom they liked. The bourgeoisie and the
Jews were secure within the framework of their autonomous
estates. No one could overturn the Catholic establishment,
and no one could realize its absolute pretensions. The Republic
was indeed a 'land without bonfires'. There were no campaigns
of forced conversion; no religious wars; no *autos-da-fè*; no
St. Bartholomew's Eve; no Thomas or Oliver Cromwell. The
limitations which in time were applied to the Confederation
of Warsaw were trivial in comparison to the horrors which
occurred in most other European countries. The Polish
'Anarchy', and the 'Golden Freedom' of the nobility, proved
an obstruction to efficient government and to religious
fanaticism alike.

CHAPTER SEVEN

SZLACHTA:

The Nobleman's Paradise

By the time of the Union of Lublin, the social order had settled firmly into a system of estates. Four such estates — the Clergy, the Nobility, the Burghers, and the Jews — enjoyed a wide measure of corporate autonomy. Each exercised full jurisdiction over its members in all those matters which did not infringe the privileges of other estates or the prerogatives of the Crown. The fifth estate — the Peasantry — had lost much of its former independence and, with the exception of a small sector of free peasant farmers, was largely subordinated to the control of the Crown, the Church, or the Nobility. Both from the constitutional and from the social point of view, there is a case for regarding the Crown and its dependants as a separate estate on its own. (See Diagram Ha.)

It must be stressed at the outset that the social estates of the early modern period — in Latin *status,* in Polish *Stan* — were based on different criteria from those which characterize the main social groups of later centuries. In particular, they can *not* be equated with the socio-economic classes with which they are so frequently confused. The social estates were defined neither by their relationship to the means of production nor indeed by any other measure of their wealth, income, or economic position, but rather by their intended function within society as expressed in exclusive legal rights and privileges. It is a parody perhaps to hold that medieval social theory intended the Crown to rule, the clergyman to pray, and nobleman to fight, the burgher to trade, the Jew to be a Jew, and the peasant to till the fields; but it is certain that some such assumption lay behind the law-making which had created the estates in the fourteenth, fifteenth, and sixteenth centuries. Economic differences did exist, of course, and exerted a powerful influence on social life; but they existed as much within each of the estates as between them, and they played a much smaller part in the perceptions of

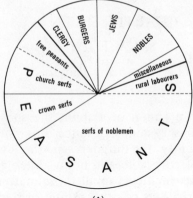

(A)

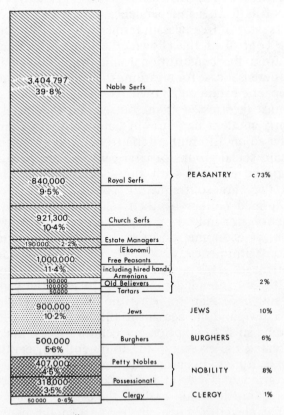

(B)

Diagram H.   The Social Estates of Poland–Lithuania
a) 16th Century   b) in 1791

contemporaries than of present-day ideologists and social scientists. A landless noble family, for example, might well have sustained an existence which by any economic yardstick was indistinguishable from, or even inferior to, that of their peasant neighbours; but their poverty in no way impaired the fiscal, legal, and political privileges to which their inherited noble status entitled them. Similarly, a prosperous Jewish family might easily exceed many of its Gentile neighbours in wealth and affluence; but nothing short of conversion to Christianity could gain them access to the ranks of the Burghers or of the Nobility. Membership of the estates was largely hereditary. Social mobility between the estates was fraught with obstacles. Economics counted for less than the law, heredity, and custom. Indeed, socio-economic classes could not possibly come into being until the legal framework of the former social estates had been dismantled.

Contemporary observers had never heard of class analysis. During the currency of the Republic of Poland–Lithuania, neither 'Feudalism' nor 'Class' had yet been invented. Contemporary descriptions were habitually based on traditional functional or legal criteria. Martin Kromer, the historian, was content to write that people were divided into clergy and laity, and the laity into noble and ignoble. One of the few exercises which required a more detailed breakdown was undertaken by officials of the Royal Treasury for the purpose of assessing the poll-tax. In 1520, for example, the Capitation Register listed forty-nine social categories grouped by estates under the main headings of Crown, Clergy, Nobility, Rural population, City population, and Jews. (See Diagram Ia.) In this, it is interesting to note that the clerical estate was judged to include all academic personnel and students as well as all ecclesiastical serfs and servants; the noble estate was assumed to include most of the inhabitants of the nobility's landed possessions; the burgher estate included all these peasants who lived on municipal land or who otherwise had achieved municipal rights. In this case, therefore, the so-called Rural Population was confined to those few elements of the peasantry, such as village headmen, manorial craftsmen, hired labourers, or the independent farmers who were free from serfdom.[1]

A. According to the assessment of the poll-tax of 1520 (simplified)		
300 fl.	Primate	CLERGY and dependents
150–50 fl.	Bishops and dependents	
25	Abbots	
10–1	Secular clergy	
	Monastic clergy	
	Church officials	
	University scholars	
½ gr.	Students	
60–50 fl.	Senators	CROWN OFFICIALS
	Non-senatorial ministers	
10 fl.	Territorial officers	
30 fl.	Crown monopolists	
	Possessionati	NOBILITY and their dependents
½ fl.		
+ 1 florin for every village		
½ fl.	Soltys (Village headman)	
	Non-possessionati	
	(Petty nobility).	
10 gr.	Hereditary taverners & millers	RURAL POPULATION
3 gr.	Estate officials	
2 gr.	Skilled workmen	
1 gr.	Free peasant households	
5 fl.	Patricians	CITY POPULATION
4 fl.	Magistrates	
30–10 gr.	Merchants	
6 gr.	Guildsmen	
2 gr.	Apprentices	
1 gr.	Domestics & servants	
	Jews 3,000 fl. joint assessment	JEWS

B. According to tax brackets constructed from the poll-tax assessment of 1590 . (after A. Wyczański)		
1	Primate / Bishops	600–200 zł.
2	Senators (Magnates) / Abbots / Ministers ‚Żupnik / Crown monopolists‚ Customs	100–50 zł.
3	Territorial officers / Deans, canons . / Merchants of means	30–10 zł.
4	Middle clergy / Middle noblemen / Lower titular officials / Mastercraftsmen / Middling merchants	8–3 zł.
5	Petty nobles, (zagrodowa) / University personnel / Orthodox clergy / Tradesmen & artisans	2 zł–16 gr.
6	Monastic clergy / Poorest clergy. / Hired workers, / Free peasants.	15–5 gr.
7	Domestics, / Peasants	4–2 gr.
8	Poor labourers / Apprentices / Students.	½ gr.
	Jews (self-assessed)	

Diagram I.   Social Groups in the Sixteenth Century
a) According to the Poll-tax of 1520
b) Tax Brackets, (after A. Wyczański)

Generally speaking, the number of people whose assignment to one of the main social estates could not have been determined, was very small. Members of certain professions such as the doctors and lawyers, or the reformed clergy; of certain specialized communities such as the miners, or of various religious minorities such as the Armenians or Muslim Tartars, could not be easily categorized. If in doubt, contemporary jurists would probably have examined their legal privileges in detail and might well have consigned them to separate, independent estates.

For reasons best known to themselves, modern scholars often reject contemporary practice, and invent new social groupings to meet the requirements of their scientific preconceptions. An analyst intent on reconstructing 'social-property structures', for instance, takes the estate-based categories of the Capitation Registers mentioned above, and rearranges them into eight new tax brackets. In this scheme, the top place in sixteenth-century society is taken by the Archbishop of Gniezno, whose poll-tax assessment stood at 600 zł., and the bottom place by the labourers, students, and apprentices, who, at ½ groszy per head, were required to pay thirty-six thousand times less. (See Diagram Ib.) This sort of exercise is extremely interesting. For analysts who believe economic relationships to be the driving force of social life, it is absolutely vital. It has the disadvantage of being essentially unhistorical.[2]

Among the autonomous estates, the Clergy possessed the longest history. The jurisdiction of the Roman Catholic, Uniate, and Orthodox churches extended over all their members in holy orders as well as over their lands and properties. The numerous and frequently poverty-striken lower clergy were subject to the ecclesiastical hierarchy, and in some cases to the noble patrons of their benefices.

The Burghers traced their origins to the medieval incorporation of cities. Their royal charters guaranteed them control of municipal self-government within the bounds of their jurisdiction. Their commerical activities were governed by the guilds and confraternities. After the sixteenth century, when the cities' former prosperity declined, an urban proletariat devoid of full civic rights multiplied rapidly. (See Chapter 9.)

The foundations of the Jewish estate were laid in the thirteenth and fourteenth centuries, although the institutions of Jewish autonomy were not fully developed until the mid-sixteenth century. Their rivalry with the Burghers, and their alliance with the Nobility, remained constant. (See pp. 409–11.)

The Peasantry, of course, represented by far the most numerous estate, accounting for perhaps 60 per cent of the population in 1569. Given that a considerable proportion of the people enjoying the legal rights of burghers actually lived as peasants, this percentage might be raised accordingly. Although the process of enserfment was far advanced, there always remained both a class of hired labourers, and in certain districts a sturdy class of free peasant farmers. (See pp. 254–61.)

The szlachta or 'nobility',* therefore, whilst inventing the most fanciful legends of its ancient origins, was in fact the most recent estate to emerge. In the sixteenth century, they were still perfecting the laws and institutions which were to characterize their supremacy in the subsequent period. Yet no one could seriously dispute the fact that in the lifetime of the Polish–Lithuanian Republic its members played a preponderant role in political, social, and cultural life. It organized the state in its own interest, and harnessed the other elements of society to its own purposes. If, as a result of religious toleration, Poland–Lithuania was sometimes dubbed 'The Paradise

---

* As usual in social history, terminology presents a serious problem. As often as not, local terms refer to specific local conditions, and are not translatable. In Polish historiography, the term *szlachta* itself is much used, and much abused. Even among those historians who weigh their words with discrimination, usages and translations differ considerably in accordance with varying criteria. Many modern historians insist on the antithesis of *szlachta: magnateria*, whereby the *szlachta* becomes 'the mass of the nobility', as opposed to a 'magnatial oligarchy' distinguished by disproportionate power and wealth. Anglo-Saxon historians, beguiled perhaps by the English distinction between 'gentleman' and 'peer', have tended to concur in this fashion, and *szlachta* is habitually translated as 'gentry'. However, it is important to stress that the Polish Nobility was *not* divided into separate legal sub-categories as in England or Germany, and that the term *szlachta* referred to the whole of the Noble Estate, not just to part of it. It was not characterized by socio-economic criteria, but by its corporate privileges and obligations, and by the body of law and tradition which controlled them. It certainly did not exclude the magnates. For the sake of precision, therefore, it is essential that *szlachta* should be translated as 'Nobility', *szlachcic* as 'nobleman', and *stan szlachecki* as 'the noble estate'.[3]

of the Jews', it might better deserve the label 'The Paradise of the Nobility'. Its critics added that this implied Purgatory for the Burghers, and Hell for the Peasants.

* * * * *

To say that the origins of the Polish Nobility are clouded in mystery is something of an understatement. They are extremely obscure. Scholars infer that some time in the early medieval period the Nobility emerged from preceding forms of social élite. But this is no great discovery, since detailed information on the earlier *rycerstwo* or 'knighthood' is equally meagre, and neither the timetable nor the manner of the emergence can be properly documented. By the thirteenth and fourteenth centuries when some awareness of the exclusive nature of the noble estate was felt, the best that chroniclers could do was to trace its origin to Noah, to Julius Caesar, or to Alexander the Great. Most noblemen in Poland and Lithuania claimed only to belong to the *szlachta odwieczna*, 'the immemorial nobility'. This meant that all certain knowledge of their origins had long since been lost.[4]

The name *szlachta* (pronounced shlákh-ta) has been the subject of considerable dispute. It derives from the Old Low German *slahta*, which is etymologically associated with the modern German words *schlagen* (to strike, fight, cleave, breed) and *Geschlecht* (sex, species, family, race). It came into Polish via the Czech *slehta* (nobility), together with all the basic vocabulary of the medieval polity — *pan* (lord, person with jurisdiction); *król* (King = Karol = Charlemagne); *sejm* (diet, or assembly); *obywatel* (citizen or 'resident'); *herb* (inheritance, heraldic device, coat of arms). However, it is all but impossible to determine either the exact context in which this German–Czech terminology was introduced or the exact point when its later usage was stabilized. Today, many experts would consider that the supremacy of the hereditary principle, or *rodowitość* as Brückner called it, which put the *szlachta* beyond the reach of rulers and princes, and which gave them inviolable, exclusive status for all time, was not finally secured until the reign of Casimir the Great (1310–70). At all events, *szlachta* neatly combines the two senses of 'high birth' and 'military prowess' which together constitute the original ingredients of medieval nobility.[5]

In the absence of definite information, studies on the origins of the Nobility have long been characterized by a number of doubtful hypotheses. One such theory explored the possibility of a prehistoric, alien invasion. Fired by the desire to forge an analogy with the Norman Conquest in England, or with the Varangians in Russia, it found little confirmation in fact.[6] Another related theory, which stressed the role of the 'clans', enjoyed considerable respectability throughout the nineteenth century. It was first developed by scholars whose main interest had been in Germanic folklore, and was later applied to Slav and Polish history. Its basic idea held that both state and society were formed by the amalgamation of numerous related clans hitherto living in natural freedom. It suggested that the early Slav rulers, including the Piast princes, were no more than tribal chiefs (*starosta rodowy*) or overlords of the clans (*nadpatriarch*) and that the nobility was descended from pure ethnic stock whilst the lower estates had intermingled with slaves, prisoners, and aliens. Attempts were made to relate the szlachta not only to a Germanic *'Geschlechtsverband'* and the Balkan 'extended family' or *zadruga,* but even to the Brehon Laws of Ireland and the Highland clans of Scotland.[7]

The theory of clans found considerable support from the specific features of Polish heraldry. In Poland, coats of arms were never provided for individual persons as in England, or for individual families as in Germany, but only for much wider groups of people who shared the same blazon, motto, and device. A Polish nobleman did not possess a coat of arms of his own. The arms he carried were identical to those carried by scores of others to whom he may or may not have been related. This *wspólność herbów* or 'holding of arms in common' was unique in Europe. What is more, the usage of the word *ród* (clan) to describe the heraldic group, inevitably strengthened the mistaken impression that it was originally based on kinship. The Polish nobleman added the name of his clan to his family name. In addition to the adjectival surname ending in *-ski* or *-cki,* the Polish nobleman would customarily write: 'of such and such a clan'. The standard form, which was generally adopted by all noble families between 1350 and

1450, read, for instance: *'Piotr Lubomirski, herbu Śreniawa'*, that is, 'Peter of Lubomierz of the Śreniawa clan'; or *'Jan Zamoyski, herbu Jelita'*, that is, 'John of Zamość, of the Jelita clan'. The adjectival surname replaced an earlier prepositional form of surname equivalent to the German 'von' or the French 'de'. Piotr Lubomirski's grandfather, who died in 1398, still called himself 'Michał z Grabi', that is Michael from Grabie — preferring to base his name on his birthplace rather than on his territorial property.

The names of the clans are marvellously obscure. Boncza (Boniface) was one the many formed from personal names. Śreniawa, Rawa, Leliwa are place-names. Amadej from Hungary, or Rogala from Saxony were foreign importations, as also, presumably, were the founders of Sas (from Saxon Transylvania) and Prus (Prussian). Dąb (Oak) and Poraj (Wild Rose) are plants; Aksak ('Fox' in Tartar), Lewart (Lampart), Raka (Crab), Gryf (Dragon), Łabędź (Swan), Świnka (Boar), and Wąsyk (Snake) are animals; Krzywda (Injustice), Prawda (Truth), Niezgoda (Discord), Mądrostki (Wisdom) are moral qualities; Oksza (Axe) and Łodzia (Boat) are everyday objects. These categories could be extended many times over. Why these names should have been used in the first place is impossible to say, and many are the subject of unlikely legends. Jelita (Bowel) is said to derive from the battlefield of Płowce in 1331, where the Polish King is said to have found one of his knights, Florian Szary, disembowelled by three Teutonic spears. In recognition of his heroism, the Jelita clan was formed with three spears as its device. Writing in the fifteenth century, Jan Długosz listed a total of 139 clans; Bartosz Paprocki in 1584 listed 107; modern genealogies mention several hundred.

The heraldic clan remains something of an enigma. Detailed studies have failed to establish any consistent pattern of membership. The old theory of kinship has been discredited, but not supplanted. Members of the same clan usually fought side by side in battle, forming the basic units of the feudal host. One line of enquiry, which stresses this aspect, is corroborated by clan names like 'Dołęga' or 'Doliwa' which clearly derive from battle-cries. Another line of enquiry has explored the workings of patronage, and has coined the term *ród klientarny* or 'clan of clients'. Sometimes the King would act as sponsor, assigning new knights to clans of his choice. Sometimes prominent noblemen would 'receive' their friends and relations into their clan on their own private initiative. Patronage at all events was not irrelevant. The most convincing hypothesis perhaps is that which relates to the emergence of the heraldic clan to that other unique feature of Polish noble life, the *nagana szlachecka,* or 'Test of Nobility'. In Poland, with no College of Heralds, there was no authoritative institution where records of ennoblement and entitlement were kept for public reference. If a nobleman's title to nobility were challenged, the only place he could prove himself was in the courts. In such cases, which were particularly frequent in the fifteenth century, the defendant was required to present six sworn witnesses who would confirm his noble descent from three generations on both paternal and maternal sides. If successful, he received a certificate of the court's findings. If unsuccessful, he faced the direst penalties. Whatever the result, the experience was extremely troublesome and humiliating. It is entirely plausible to suppose that the heraldic clan was formed to protect its members from the need to face such tests. By attaching himself to a public association of known persons, a nobleman could save himself from malicious insinuations against his rank and status. In the unlikely event of prosecution, he could always count on six of his fellow clansmen to stand witness in his defence. In this light, the 'heraldic clan' constituted a sort of mutual benefit society. It served the interests both of the noble estate as a whole and of its individual members, and it precluded the necessity for a college of heralds, which could have been used by king or royal officials as an instrument of control.[8]

One consequence of the 'holding of arms in common' was that the pictorial aspects of Polish heraldry remained extremely simple. There was no need to follow the labyrinth of inheritance or marriage, or to modify and develop coats of arms in response to changing events. Blazoning, marshalling, quartering, and cadency were unknown. Each clan possessed one simple device, one motto, and one coat of arms, which stayed the same throughout the centuries. All the coats of arms which ever existed can be contained in one relatively slim volume.[9]

* * * * *

If the emergence of the Nobility as a distinct estate was well advanced by the reign of Casimir the Great, the process of reinforcing and codifying their legal privileges continued for at least the next two centuries. Throughout the earlier period, Polish rulers had granted immunities to individual knights or clerics, freeing them from particular taxes or from the obligation to submit their subjects to royal justice. But as from the late fourteenth century similar concessions were exacted for the Nobility not by individuals, but by an estate demanding its corporate rights. In times of crisis, during war or before a succession, the Nobility's bargaining power was high. Concessions obtained were rarely relinquished. In 1374, by the Statute of Košice, Louis of Anjou, anxious to secure the succession of his daughter, Jadwiga, exempted all noble demesnes from the *poradlne* or land-tax, and reduced the rate levied on noble tenants to one-sixth of its previous level. At Horodło, on 2 October 1413, the new terms of the Union of Poland and Lithuania provided for the extension of the privileges of the Polish szlachta to the Lithuanian boyars. Forty-seven heraldic clans opened their ranks to Lithuanian members. At Czerwińsk in 1422, at Jedlno in 1430, and at Cracow in 1433, Władysław Jagiełło's concern for the future of his sons progressively overcame his resistance to *'Neminem Captivabimus'* — the principle, equivalent to the English 'Habeas Corpus', that protected a nobleman's land and person from confiscation and arrest unless sentence had been passed against him in a court. At Nieszawa in 1454, during the second Teutonic War, Kazimierz Jagiellończyk conceded that no new tax would be levied nor army raised without the consent of the new noble dietines. At Piotrków in 1496, in preparation for his ill-fated expedition to Moldavia, Jan Olbracht granted the noble monopoly of land-holding. Five years later, his brother Alexander tried to use the Senate as a brake on the Nobility's pretensions. By the Act of Mielnik, he decreed that the senators were subject only to their peers. But the Sejm soon had its revenge. The constitution of *Nihil Novi* passed at Radom on 14 June 1505, annulled the Act of Mielnik, established the primacy of the Chamber of Envoys over the

Senate, and ruled that no new laws could be introduced without the consent of both chambers. Thereafter, legislation remained firmly in the Nobility's control. The slogan *'Nic o nas bez nas'* ('Nothing concerning us without us') remained the basic concept of their 'Noble Democracy'.

The legislative supremacy of the Nobility was used to wrest further advantages over the rest of society. Not content with their various immunities and with their virtual monopolies in landed property, in government, and administration, and in central political life, they proceeded to bolster their position in the most detailed manner. In 1496, the Sejm which had established the noble monopoly in land, also took pains to restrict the rights of the clergy, the burghers, and the peasants. Henceforth, all the senior appointments in the Church were limited to noble candidates. Except in Royal Prussia, burghers were required to sell the land which they owned. Peasants were not allowed to leave the village for the town. From 1501 onwards, a stream of constitutions tied the peasantry firmly to the land, and to the will of their lord. In 1518, the competence of the royal courts was withdrawn from appeals between lord and peasant. In 1520, the Statute of Thorn fixed labour service at one day per week per łan, initiating a process which legalized the ever harsher conditions of serfdom. In 1550, the Nobility was allowed to purchase houses in the cities, and to enjoy them without paying municipal taxes, notwithstanding all local legislation to the contrary. In 1552, during the Calvinist troubles, the competence of the ecclesiastical courts over the Nobility in matters of religion was withdrawn. In 1563, when the purchase of *solectwa* or 'village jurisdictions' was regularized, the way was open to the absolute control over the population of their estates. In commerce, the Nobility was freed from duty on goods for their own use. In the dietines, they controlled the multifarious systems of weights and measures, and regulated prices. From 1573, the Nobility possessed the exclusive right to exploit the timber, potash and minerals deriving from their land. They had always bought salt at preferential rates. Although they themselves were not expected to engage in commerce — and constitutions of 1633 and 1677 specifically forbade them to do so — the entire economic life of society was organized in their interest.

To this end, the Nobility cultivated a special relationship with the numerous Jewish community. Particularly in the eastern provinces, the Jews proved eminently useful to noblemen who wished to avoid the troublesome regulations surrounding economic life in the towns. They were employed as craftsmen and tradesmen, earning the epithet of *fuszer* or 'bungler' from the guilds whose rights they circumvented. They plied their traditional trades of money-lender, innkeeper, fence, and broker — as evidenced by the constant stream of municipal decrees forbidding them to do so. They obtained favourable rates of interest approved by the dietines, and flourished in the service of the great estates. Although the pullulating masses of the ghetto saw little benefit from the activities of their most prosperous confrères, they all shared in the common opprobrium. In the Ukraine, they were widely denounced as the chosen instrument of 'the Polish lords'. The richer Jews openly aspired to a noble life-style. An edict of Sigismund-August forbade them from wearing swords and gold chains. Despite the law, they often owned land, took out tenancies, or held the deeds in mortgage from the noble owners. Not a few were formally ennobled. They even affected the noble habit of not paying their taxes.

The pretext on which the Nobility's privileges were based is to be found in their obligation to provide unpaid military service. Throughout the Middle Ages, the possession of land was justified by the need to support a military caste, whose expenses were great and whose services were in constant demand. In fifteenth-century Poland and Lithuania, this ancient convention still made good sense, and the Nobility had customarily confirmed or extended their privileges in their armed camp before proceeding to battle with the enemy. In the course of time, however, the noble *pospolite ruszenie* or *levée-en-masse* lost its effectiveness. The commanders and the Noblemen themselves both preferred permanent forces supported by taxation. The *levée-en-masse* remained as a defensive reserve of last resort. It was only called out in desperate situations, and the *okazowanie* or 'annual review', to which the noblemen of each province were required to report, was onerous to no one. The idea that the growth of noble privilege was balanced by a corresponding growth of responsibilities in the military sphere was, by the sixteenth century, quite anachronistic.

There is also the problem of Feudalism. In present-day Poland, it is taken for granted that the Nobility were a 'feudal class' in whose interest the old Kingdom and Republic were organized. Little attention is paid to the fact that the concept of 'Feudalism' was never used in so-called feudal times. Lelewel held that Feudalism was contrary to the Polish tradition, and had never existed in Poland at all. Most later historians would maintain that it only existed for a short time in the fourteenth and fifteenth centuries, and 'as an influence not a system', or *sui generis*. Certainly, there was no simple transference of West European models. Whatever definition of Feudalism one cares to take, and to whatever aspect of social life one applies it, one always finds that historical practices fail to fit the modern theory. In the realm of land law, for instance, the *ius feudale* did exist alongside the *ius`terrestre*. It operated in relation to land held subject to royal assent, and to the normal feudal practices of escheat, wardship, and homage. Yet, after 1450, in the very period when the Nobility were establishing their supremacy, it rapidly declined. In the sixteenth century, a series of Sejm statutes between 1562 and 1588 converted feudal holdings into hereditary, allodial property. In the military sphere, the obligation to serve lay not just on the Nobility but on every free man. It was not channelled through a network of tenants-in-chief and vassals but directly from King to subject. The jurisdictional structure, in contrast, was neatly divided into two. The great offices of state were not tied to the land, and, until the introduction of life-tenure in the seventeenth century, were entirely at the King's disposal. Yet at the local level, jurisdiction *was* tied to the land, and justice was administered by the Nobility. In finance, the King never abandoned his legal right to tax the entire population directly, despite the practical constraints placed on him by the Sejm. Taking into consideration constantly shifting conditions, therefore, and wide geographical divergences, it is not very easy to decide whether Polish Feudalism is myth or reality.[10]

At all events, by 1569 when the united Republic of Poland—Lithuania was formed, the supremacy of the Nobility was secure. By general European standards, they were extremely numerous. Some 25,000 noble families, including at least 500,000 persons, represented 6.6 per cent of the total population of 7.5 million. In the later seventeenth century, this was to rise to about 9 per cent, and in the eighteenth century still further. Not even Spain or Hungary, whose nobility represented up to 5 per cent of the population, could rival them on this score; whilst France with 1 per cent, or England with 2 per cent, stood in marked contrast.[11] The formal privileges of the Nobility protected them from the political pretensions of the king, and from the growth of a modern state. Their relative prosperity was guaranteed by a mass of detailed legislation. They were a closed estate, in control of their own destiny and that of everyone else in their Republic. Their obligations as a military caste were minimal. Their civic duty as a ruling class was governed by their private inclinations. By 1569, they had won their 'Golden Freedom'. It held them all in bondage for as long as their Republic lasted.

*   *   *   *   *

In Lithuania, the Nobility reached a similar destination by a somewhat different route. In the period of the personal union with Poland, from 1386 to 1569, the Lithuanians had gradually adopted Polish laws and customs. But their own highly specific social structures left an enduring mark. In contrast to the Polish szlachta, the Lithuanian nobles had been closely dependent on the ruler, the Grand Duke, and at the same time were split into a number of overlying strata. They had enjoyed no tradition of immunities either as individuals or as an estate, and in return for their land were used to paying personal homage, either to the Grand Duke or to their immediate superior. They served in the army without limit, offered the *dziakel* or 'tribute in kind', and provided a wide range of services from hay-making to fortress repair. At the top of the social scale, a few powerful families like the Ostrogski, the Radziwiłł, or the Sapieha, boasted the title of *Kniaz* or 'Prince'. The greatest of these ruled entire regions in virtual sovereignty, in the style of marcher lords. The lesser families held their baronies in fief from the Grand Duke. At the bottom of the scale, the broad mass of dependent nobles with the title of *boyar* (warrior) varied from families of considerable fortune to domestic servants or petty mercenary nobles. In the middle, lay a group bearing the title of *pan* or 'lord', who benefited from special privileges with respect to military duty. Some of these, such as the Kiezgajłło, rose to positions indistinguishable from those of the princes. Under Grand Duke Witold (1401–30), who sought to centralize the Lithuanian state and even to have himself crowned as king, the waywardness of the greater nobility was sharply pruned. Princely titles were limited either to lifelong tenure, or to strict male descent. New awards were largely confined to Muscovite defectors. At the same time, the corporate sense of a noble estate was being widened and strengthened. In 1387, the boyars were granted the right of property in their family estates, and the personal freedom to marry without their lord's consent. In 1413, at Horodło, the right of property was extended to their feudal holdings. Catholic boyars were invited to join the Polish heraldic clans. From 1434, both the princes and boyars were treated as a common estate for purpose of political privilege bargaining, and in 1447 established their claim to parity with the szlachta.

Even so, the princes contrived to maintain a measure of their supremacy. They took control of the process of 'clan adoption' which, in marked contrast to its egalitarian function in Poland, became an instrument for perpetuating the old practice of homage in a new guise. They took special hold over the Ruthenian nobility, whose Orthodoxy became a definite disability. They preserved their jurisdictional independence right up to the Second Lithuanian Statute of 1566, which they conceded in a vain attempt to stem the boyars' desire to accept the impending constitutional union with Poland. When the Union of Lublin finally established the principle of legal equality not only between the Polish and Lithuanian nobility but also amongst the Lithuanian nobles themselves, the princely families were not seriously shaken. They passed straight to the forefront of the Republic's *magnateria* – equal before the law, but very unequal in political, social, and economic influence.

The career of Prince Mikołaj Radziwiłł the 'Red' (1512–84) amply illustrates the power and wealth to which the magnates aspired. As brother to the ill-starred Barbara Radziwiłł, queen of Sigismund-August, and cousin to Prince Mikołaj Krzysztof Radziwiłł the 'Black' (1515–65), Chancellor of Lithuania and Palatine of Wilno, he was showered with signs of royal favours. As Grand Hetman of the Lithuanian Army, he distinguished himself in the wars against Muscovy, and in 1566 succeeded to his cousin's offices. Yet as a Calvinist he stood aloof from the Roman Catholic establishment, and actively opposed the Union of Lublin until the very last minute. The splendour of his court rivalled that of many a sovereign monarch. It duly impressed the English Ambassador Sir Jerome Horsey, who passed through Lithuania on his way overland to Moscow:

When I came to Villna the chief citie in Lithuania, I presented myself and letters pattents from the Quen, that declared my titells and what I was, unto the great duke viovode Ragaville, a prince of great excelencie, prowes and power, and religious protestant; gave me great respect and good enterteynment; told me, though I had nothing to say to him from the Quen of England, yet, he did so much honnor and admire her excelent vertus and graces, he would also hold me in the reputacion of her majesties ambassador; which was som pollacie that his subjects should think I was to negociate with him. Take me with him to his church; heard divine service psalms, a sermon, and the sacraments ministered according to the reformed churches; whereat his brother cardinal Ragavill, did murmur. His hightness did invite me to dinner, honored with 50 halberdeers thorow the cittie: placed gonners and his guard of 500 gentilmen to bring me to his pallace; himself accompanied with many yonge noblemen, receaved me upon the tarras; brought me into a very large room where organes and singing was, a long table set with pallentins, lordes and ladies, himself under a cloth of estate. I was placed before him in the middest of the table; trompetts sound and kettel droms roared. The first service brought in, ghesters and poets discourse merely, lowed instruments and safft plaied very musically; a set of dwarffes men and women finely attired came in with sweet harmony still and mournfull pieps and songs of art; Davids tymbrils and Arons swett soundinge bells as the termed them. The varietie made the tyme pleasing and short. His hightness drank for the Majesty the angelicall Quen of England her health. Strange portraturs, lyons, unicorns, spread-eagels, swans and other made of suger past, som wines and spicats in their bellies to draw at, and succets of all sorts cutt owt of their bellies to tast of; every one with his sylver forcke. To tell of all the order and particuler services, and rarieties grow tedious; well-feasted, honnored, and much made of, I was conducted to my lodgings in manner as I was brought. Had my letters pattents, and a gentilman to conduct me thorow his countrye; with which I toke my leave. Some pastymes with lyons, bulls and bares, straing to behold, I omytt to recite.[12]

*   *   *   *   *

Although strictly speaking the szlachta is not to be equated with the landowning class, it is undeniable that the possession of land was their main source of wealth. In practice, all landowners were not noble, and all noblemen were not necessarily landowners. But in so far as wealth and nobility were related, the correlation largely depended on the distribution of landed property.

In 1569, noble land accounted for roughly 60 per cent of the total surface of the Republic, as against 25 per cent belonging to the Church and 15 per cent belonging to the Crown. But, since an increasing proportion of the Crown lands were leased to noblemen, and since the bishops, who controlled a large part of Church land, were in effect clerical magnates, the noble sector was in practice still larger. On this noble land, the population had no recourse to the royal courts, and lived almost entirely at the mercy of their noble lords.

The geographical pattern of noble landholding was extremely complicated. In some areas, such as Volhynia or Kiev, a large part of the noble land was concentrated in the hands of just a few magnates. In pre-union Lithuania, about one-quarter of noble land belonged to less than 2 per cent of the nobility, the other three-quarters being divided among more than thirteen thousand families. According to the *Popis Wojska Litewskiego,* or Military List, of 1528, which recorded the assessment of the nobles' estates, 23 families were assessed on average at 261 knights each, a total of 5,993; the remaining 13,060 families could only raise 19,842 knights between them, an average of 1.52 per family.[13] In other areas, like Mazovia, or Podlasie, the magnates played no part whatsoever, and the noble sector was dominated by the plots of the petty nobility. Even within the same province, neighbouring localities showed marked variations. In Royal Prussia of the 1570s, for example, the neighbouring palatinates of Chełmno and

Malbork, differed from each other in several important respects. In Chełmno, the holdings of the nobility were roughly equal to those of the Church and the Crown. In Malbork, they represented only one-sixth of the total, and in the absence of any significant ecclesiastical holdings, were dwarfed by Crown estates and the royal towns. In Chełmno, the average nobleman, possessing 3—10 łan, held strips scattered through several villages. In Malbork, a much smaller number of nobles possessed larger holdings of 10—15 łan. No one, in either palatinate, could rival the Bishop of Chełmno, whose 112 villages, organized in four 'keys' round Lubawa Castle formed the one large latifundium of the region.[14] In the province of Małopolska, too, it is interesting to see that in the sixteenth century the holdings of the Church were still greater than those of any secular magnate. Despite the fact that grants of Crown land to the nobles had been particularly liberal in the vicinity of the ancient capital, no single nobleman could match the wealth of the Bishops of Cracow. In the land-tax assessments of 1564, six of the province's ten wealthiest properties were still shown to belong to the Church. In contrast to the assessment of the Bishop at 457 zł., of the Abbey of Tyniec at 311 zł., and of the Cracovian Chapter at 202 zł., the Castellan of Cracow, Spytek Jordan, was assessed at 383 zł., the Starosta of Biecz at 154 zł., the Starosta of Krzepice at 145 zł., and the *Wielkorządcy* (Royal Governor) of Cracow at 143 zł.[15] Significantly, all the prominent noblemen of this period owed their landed wealth directly to their possession of high public offices. Private landed fortunes in Poland were as yet relatively modest, and were much inferior to those in Lithuania. (See Map 12, pp. 222/223.)

Nevertheless, the economic divisions of the Nobility largely reflected their possession of land. There was no formal economic hierarchy; but by counting a man's estates it was easy to see whether he should be classed as prosperous or poor — whether, in the language of the time, he was *tłusty* (fat) or *chudy* (lean).[16] (See Diagram J.)

At the top of the league, a score of families possessed properties which were numbered in hundreds and thousands. The same families also tended to control the key offices of state, and hence to be strongly represented in the Senate. They

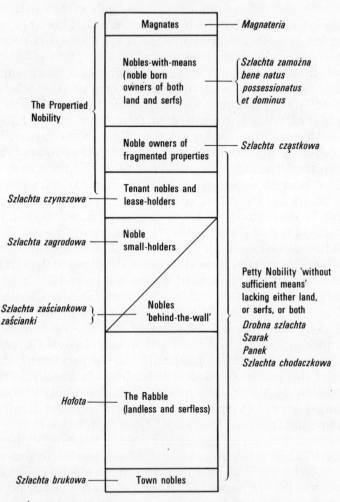

Economic strata within the Noble Estate (Szlachta)

Diagram J.   Economic strata within the Noble Estate (*Szlachta*)

were 'great' both in wealth and in influence. The individual *magnat* or 'magnate' possessed no special rights or privileges. But the group as a whole, the *magnateria,* wielded power and influence on a scale quite disproportionate to their numbers.

In contrast to them, the average nobleman was fortunate if he possessed two or three properties. Yet if his land was his own, and he had the serfs to work it, he owed his living to no one. He was *'possessionatus'* (propertied) and *dominus, Pan Sobie* — a 'lord unto himself'. Contemporaries classed him among the *szlachta zamożna* or 'nobility with means'. Some historians prefer the term 'middle nobility' — which now plays a prominent part in theories about society and politics in the modern period. The lower limit of their holdings has been put at 20 łan. In the era of the Republic, they accounted for between one-third and two-fifths of the noble estate as a whole.

At the bottom of the league, lay the most numerous element of all, the seething mass of petty nobility without means. One such group, the *szlachta cząstkowa* (fragmentary nobles) lived on fragments of larger estates which had been broken up for sale or tenancy. They would generally share the serfs and material resources of the original estate with their neighbours. Many, as *szlachta czynszowa* (rent-paying nobles), were tenants, or leaseholders, of their more prosperous brothers. Another group, the *szlachta zagrodowa* (noble smallholders), possessed land but no serfs, and had to work their own plot or *'zagród'* for themselves. Economically they were indistinguishable from the peasantry. Some of these, the *szlachta zaściankowa* (nobles behind-the-wall), lived in exclusive noble villages, whose perimeter wall protected them from the ignoble world around. But the group which with time became by far the most numerous, the *hołota* or 'rabble', possessed neither land nor serfs. They worked as tenant farmers, as labourers, as domestics, as soldiers; or else, as *szlachta brukowa* (street nobility), were reduced to eking out a penurious living in the towns.

The magnates owed the accumulation of their landed estates to a variety of circumstances. The clerical magnates — 17 bishops, 2 archbishops, and a handful of abbots — stepped, on appointment, into fortunes which had been growing ever

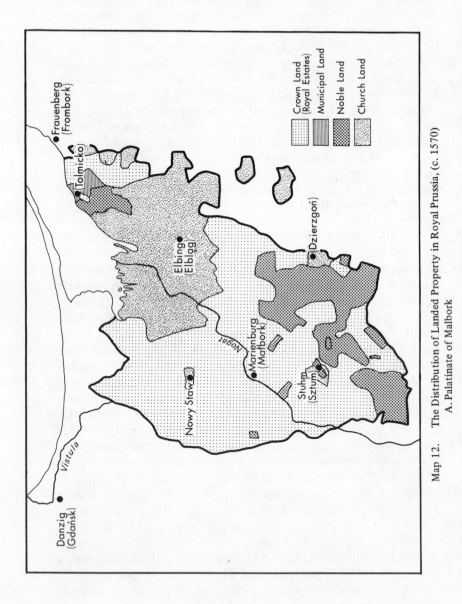

Map 12.   The Distribution of Landed Property in Royal Prussia, (c. 1570)
A. Palatinate of Malbork

Crown Land (Royal Estates)
Municipal Land
Noble Land
Church Land

Frauenberg (Frombork)
Tolmicko
Danzig (Gdańsk)
Vistula
Elbing (Elbląg)
Dzierzgoń
Nowy Staw
Nogat
Marienburg (Malbork)
Stuhm (Sztum)

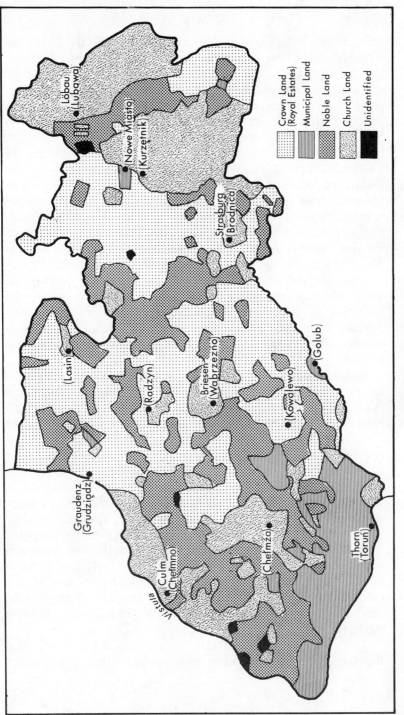

B. Palatinate of Chełmno

Crown Land (Royal Estates)

Municipal Land

Noble Land

Church Land

Unidentified

Löbau (Lubawa)

Nowe Miasto (Kurzętnik)

Strasburg (Brodnica)

Lasin

Radzyn

Briesen (Wąbrzezno)

(Golub)

(Kowalewo)

Graudenz (Grudziądz)

Culm Chełmno

Chełmża

Thorn (Toruń)

Vistula

since the foundation of the Church in AD 1000. By 1512, the
Archbishop of Gniezno possessed 292 villages and 13 towns;
the Bishop of Cracow 230 villages and 13 towns, at a time
when no secular magnate possessed more than 30 such properties. In Lithuania, the Bishopric of Wilno, which was
founded after the conversion of the Grand Duchy in 1387,
had amassed, by the eighteenth century, some 600 villages. A
number of churchmen also possessed secular dignities. In
1443, Bishop Zbigniew Oleśnicki of Cracow bought the
Duchy of Siewierz in Silesia for 6,000 silver groats. He and
his successors enjoyed the title, jurisdiction, and income of
the Duchy until the fall of the Republic in 1795. From 1462,
the Archbishop of Gniezno acquired the title of Duke of
Łowicz, and transferred his residence to the ducal seat at
Skierniewice. In the eighteenth century, the Bishop of Płock
paraded as the Duke of Pułtusk. At the other end of the
scale, there were landless bishops. After 1667 when the
province of Smolensk was finally ceded to Muscovy, the
Roman Bishop of Smolensk lost all his lands, and lived in
Warsaw supported by a government pension of 20,000 zł. per
annum.

Among the secular magnates, most owed their elevation
to the royal service. Others rose by colonizing the Ruthenian
lands of the east. Very typically, however, the greatest
magnatial fortunes were indebted to a combination of factors
— to auspicious marriages, to purchases, exchanges, conquest,
to good management, royal favour, obsessive ambition, long
life, or to dominant male chromosomes. Only a few, like the
Radziwiłł in Lithuania or the Potocki and Tarnowski in
Poland, were preserved over several centuries. Most of them
declined as rapidly as they had flowered. The Kurozwęcki,
Szydłowiecki, and Mełsztyński failed for want of male heirs.
The Lubomirski, whose estates survived division between
three sons in 1642, and confiscation in 1664, had to start
afresh. Many of those who flourished at the end of the
eighteenth century — the Czartoryski, Poniatowski,
Jabłonowski, and the two Branicki lines, were relative
parvenus.

The great magnatial estates were organized as latifundia.
Scattered properties in each area would be linked to a *klucz*

or 'key property' from which the rest were administered. Each 'key' was linked in turn to headquarters in the palace of the magnatial owner. In this way, the latifundium could be run as a single economic unit, where the particular contributions of the parts could be made to benefit the whole. In the case of the latifundium of the Lubomirski, for instance, as recorded in the inventory of 1739, the 1,071 properties were spread over nine southern palatinates of the Republic, from Woła Justowska near Cracow to Tetiev near Kiev. They included cities, towns, villages, and plantations. At Wiśnicz near Cracow, the chief seat of the Lubomirski, there were 29 villages; at Jarosław in Red Ruthenia, there were 18 villages; at Kanczuga, 13. In addition to these family properties, the Lubomirskis by virtue of state appointments and royal favour held a large number of Crown estates on lease. In the days of Alexander Michał Lubomirski, who died in 1677, these had comprised 8 towns and 89 villages. They also held a score of possessions over the southern frontier in Hungary.[17]

The laws of succession caused immense complications. In Poland, the custom was to divide family property among sons and unmarried daughters alike. The division was undertaken piecemeal as the children came of age or married, leaving the home estate in the hands of the youngest son on the death of his parents. In consequence, the larger latifundia frequently disintegrated within two or three generations of their founder's death. Yet disintegration was in the interest neither of the family, nor of the Republic which both stood to gain from the military potential and economic resilience of consolidated holdings. The Law of Entail, known in Poland as *Ordinacja* or *maioratus,* was introduced to guard against it. For the first time in 1589, the Sejm persuaded 'to ordain' the Radziwiłł and Zamoyski estates with legal statutes, which fixed their military contributions to the Republic and at the same time insured them against dispersal. According to the Ordination, a list of named properties could only be inherited by the strict rules of male primogeniture, and could not be disposed of by their owners whether by sale, gift, division, or testament. The *ordinatus* or 'senior male' of the family was required to undertake a number of military duties which included fortress repair, the upkeep of garrisons, the quartering of troops in

winter, and the supply of a fixed quota of regiments in time
of war. In return he was permanently secured in his inheritance. In 1601, similar 'ordinations' were applied to the
Myszkowski estates at Pinczów, and in 1609 to the Ostrogski
estates at Dubno. Later 'ordinations' included those of the
Tarnowski, Chreptowicze, and Sułkowski. Some of them
were preserved intact until 1918 and 1939. Others ran into
trouble as soon as they were formed.

The staff required to maintain and defend a latifundium
was customarily divided into two distinct categories — the
sługa rękodajny, manu stipulatus, or 'noble retinue'; and the
czeladź dworska or 'court personnel'. The former, consisting
entirely of gentlemen clients of noble birth, occupied all
those positions of profit and authority which did not involve
the stigma of a trade or profession. They received regular
salaries, and as signs of their patron's favour, the *suchednie* or
seasonal gifts and bonuses. The latter, consisting of non-noble
employees, provided the servants, specialists, craftsmen, and
mercenaries.

In time, the inflation of magnatial retinues posed an in-
soluble problem for the Republic. The leading families could
command far greater respect and obedience than the state
itself. The growth of large numbers of quarrelsome, peacock-
minded clients, sworn to uphold the honour and interests of
their patron, and dependent for their promotion and livelihood on the successful prosecution of his whims and feuds,
gradually undermined the workings of government at both
the central and the provincial level. In the era of the Partitions,
the 'Alban Band' of Prince Karol Stanisław Radziwiłł of
Nieswież — *Panie Kochanku* or 'the Darling Lord' as he was
known — could field six thousand gentlemen dressed from
head to toe in pure white, and could challenge any state or
private formations of the day with impunity.

The size of magnatial retinues was an obvious measure of
wealth and status. They varied from a handful of tattered old
retainers in the image of Sancho Panza to regiments of trained
officers and administrators rivalling those of a minor principality. In the mid-seventeenth century, Hetman Stanisław
Lubomirski of Wiśnicz, for instance, retained two Marshals,
two chaplains, four secretaries, four sewers, twenty chamber-

lains, and sixty senior clients. In addition, there would have been a swarm of *aplikanty* (candidate clients), *komorniki* (seneschals), *rezydenci* (resident advisers), treasurers, ostlers, masters-of-robes, masters-of-horse, pages, messengers, military captains, and, of course, a similar array of ladies-in-waiting to serve in the female quarters. The non-noble personnel would have included the court physician, the surgeon, the artist, the ballet-master, the pastrycook, the gardener, the engineer, the architect, the director of music, and the *ekonom* or general manager; cooks, turnkeys, carters, carpenters, butlers, ostlers, cellarers, and domestics. There was also an exotic tradition of keeping jesters, foreigners, dwarfs, and historians. It was not exceptional for Polish magnates to have German barons in their retinue. The Tartar custom of carrying off human *yasir* into slavery was matched by the Polish custom of holding Tartar or Negro prisoners as personal slaves.

The scourge of the noble retinues was described by Ignacy Krasicki, Bishop of Warmia, with more than a touch of irony:

> His Grace, the almighty tyrant, the tin-god of his locality
> Maintains a numerous court, as a sign of his splendid quality.
> From this arise higher officials, and a host of lesser creeps;
> The Master-of-Horse who beats, and the stable boy who weeps.
> There's the thieving bursar; and the absentee butler;
> The courtier-footman who expects to be served by a page
> Because his own noble birth entitles him to rant and to rage.
> There's the architect whose plans do not actually work;
> The physician who kills his patients; and the dreaming clerk;
> The steward who shortens his measures; the accountant who fakes
> His figures, like the attorney in court; the agent who takes
> More than he earns, and, whilst cheating the lesser rooks,
> Is himself exploited in the cause of more important crooks;
> The gamekeeper who dines on venison, but never guards the game;
> The 'yes-man' retainer, whose nod to the master is always the same;
> The Captain who fleeces the Jews whenever they come to trade;
> The soldiers who merely act as ushers whenever a banquet's laid;
> The Corporal of dragoons, who pilfers more than his company;
> And the Drum Major who beats the tattoo from his balcony,
> And who, on church parade, as he leads the guests to their places,
> Sounds a ragged drum-roll, not to God's glory, but to His Grace's.[18]

Hence corruption spread from top to bottom. Venality, debt,

and dependence sapped the nobleman's ability to change with the times. Great men exploited their inferiors, and lesser men aped their betters.

The rush of ordinations in the Vasa Period provides clear proof that the magnatial oligarchy was putting down roots. For this reason it was fiercely resented by the Nobility as a whole. There is plenty of evidence, however, which suggests that at least until the mid-seventeenth century the estates of the 'middle nobility' were just as prosperous as those of the magnates. According to Andrej Wyczański, who has reconstructed a theoretical model of these middling estates from the juridical records of the 1560s, the average size was around 130 hectares (321 acres). Upwards of 50 hectares, or roughly 40 per cent of the arable area, was in demesne, and provided 94 per cent of the lord's revenue. The remaining 80 hectares, in peasant holdings, produced virtually no income but served to support the serfs on which the exploitation of the demesne depended. Even so, the serfs rarely sufficed for more than two-thirds of the labour required, and had to be supplemented by salaried personnel and by a hired, seasonal work-force. The average annual revenue worked out at 214 zł. gross, 185.7 zł. net. At contemporary prices on the market in Cracow, 186 zł. would have bought 96 metres of wollen cloth or 385 pairs of shoes or 35 oxen or 900 litres of Malmasian wine. In general, the owner or leaseholder would reside in person, and manage the estate without the help of a numerous staff or retinue.[19]

In contrast to this 'average nobleman', who is no more than a faceless abstraction, the 'petty noblemen' was a very real animal for which several provinces of the Republic were rightly famed. In Mazowsze, over half of the land was owned by the *szlachta zagrodowa*. According to one estimate in 1571 they totalled 32,000 households, working 12,031 out of 23,361 łan or 51.5 per cent of the arable land of the Duchy. Each household contented itself with 0.38 łan (6.65 hectares or 16.43 acres). In Podlasie, similar conditions prevailed. In 1528, the ten parishes of the Ziemia Bielska contained 99 settlements of noble *zaścianki*. In 1775, in the same district, 5,811 out of 6,300 holdings, or 92 per cent, were serfless. In the Republic as a whole, well over half of the

nobility did not possess land. In 1670, 400,000 noblemen, or
57 per cent, were landless, as compared to 300,000 or 43 per
cent, who owned one village or more. These figures are incomparable. Nowhere in Spain, where the tattered *hidalgo*
was a national joke, not even in Navarre, Leon, or Burgos,
where the nobility reached up to 10 per cent of the population, was there anything to match Mazowsze or Podlasie.
What is more, in Spain in the eighteenth century, the petty
nobility was severely pruned. In the Republic, they were
multiplying fast. Their sheer numbers defy any attempt to
regard them as an exceptional element in an essentially landowning class. One has to accept that in the Republic it was
the nobleman with land who was the exception. Numerically
speaking, the petty nobility dominated the noble estate,
providing both its distinctive colour and the material with
which its political and social customs operated. They seem
to have first appeared in the late fourteenth century in
frontier areas threatened by the Teutonic Order. In time they
expanded both by further colonization into Podlasie and Red
Ruthenia, and by cellular division of the original settlements
into constellated villages. In 1699, they joined a memorable
exodus to Podolia, to lands returned to Poland from Turkey
by the Peace of Karlovitz. Their original military role quickly
deteriorated. Although the *levée-en-masse* of Mazowsze might
raise 20,000 knights, their quality was very poor. The fragmentation and pauperization of the original holdings led to a
situation where one village of *zaścianki* with perhaps twenty-
five families could only equip one or two cavalrymen between
them. The fertile birth-rate of Mazowsze together with the
infertile soil led to constant division and increasing impoverish-
ment of the family plots. From the sixteenth century
onwards, the petty nobleman, incapable of equipping himself, none the less perpetuated the military tradition of his
caste by serving either in the professional regiments of the
royal army or in the retinues of the magnates.[20]

In many ways, being both poor and insecure, the position
of the petty nobleman was worse than that of the serfs. In
the eighteenth century, there are many examples of their
voluntary submission to serfdom. Yet even as serfs, or down-
and-outs in the towns, they did not lose their noble status or

their legal rights. A coat of arms hung over the porch of their cottages. They carried wooden swords when they did not own a steel one, and they continued to attend the provincial dietines and to demand a vote at the royal Elections. They attracted a variety of pejorative epithets — as *panek* or 'little master'; as *szarak* or 'grey hare' (who could not afford the nobleman's traditional carmine cloak); as *zagończyk* or 'little ploughman' (who had to work in his own fields); as *chudy pachołek* or 'the lean page', who appears so often in the literature of the period; or as *szlachta chodaczkowa, milites in caligulo,* the 'nobleman in clogs'. They were known to Kadłubek in the thirteenth century, and had parallels elsewhere, like the *Bocskoros Nemes* in Hungary. But they were a Polish phenomenon *par excellence,* at once a cause for amazement and a pillar of the noble estate.

The later condition of the petty nobility was evoked by Adam Mickiewicz:

The hamlet of Dobrzyń has a wide reputation in Lithuania for the bravery of its gentlemen and the beauty of its gentlewomen. It was once powerful and populous, for when King John III Sobieski summoned the general militia, the Ensign of the palatinate brought him six hundred armed gentlemen from Dobrzyń alone. But the family had now grown small and poor. Formerly, at the courts of the magnates or in their regiments at forays, and at the district dietines the Dobrzyńskis used to find an easy living. Now they were forced to work for themselves, like mere serfs, except that they did not wear peasants' russet doublets, but long white coats with black stripes, and on Sunday the *kontusz.* The dress of even the poorest of their women was different from that of the peasants. They usually wore drill or percale, herded their cattle in shoes not of bark but of leather, and reaped and spun with gloves on.

The Dobrzyńskis were distinguished among their Lithuanian brethren by their language, and likewise by their stature and their appearance. They were of pure Polish blood, and all had black hair, high foreheads, black eyes, and aquiline noses. They traced their ancestors to the district of Dobrzyń in Mazovia and, though they had been settled in Lithuania for four hundred years, they preserved their Mazovian speech and customs. Whenever any one of them gave his son a name at baptism, he always chose the name of a saint of the Kingdom, either Bartholomew or Matthias. The women were all christened Kachna or Maryna. In order to distinguish themselves amid such confusion, both men and women took various nicknames. Thus Matthias Dobrzyński, who was the head of the whole family, had been called 'Cock-on-the-Steeple'. Later, after the year seventeen hundred and ninety-four, he changed his nickname and was dubbed 'Hand-on-Hip'; the Dobrzyńskis themselves also called him 'King Bunny'; . . .

As Matthias ruled over the Dobrzyńskis, so his house standing between the tavern and the church dominated the village. To all appearances it was inhabited by mere rabble. At the entrance the gateposts stood without gates, and the garden was neither fenced nor planted. Birches had grown up in the vegetable beds. Yet this old farmhouse seemed the 'Capitol' of the village, for it was handsomer and more spacious than the other cottages, and on the right side, where the living room was placed, it was built of brick. Nearby were a storehouse, a granary, barn, cow shed, and stable, all close together, as is usually the case among the gentry. The whole was uncommonly old and decayed; the house-roofs shone as if made of green tin, because of the moss and grass, which grew as luxuriantly as on a prairie. The thatch of the barns drooped like hanging gardens, and was filled with plants, with nettles and the crimson crocus, with yellow mullen and the bright-coloured tassels of mercury. In them were the nests of various birds. In the lofts were dovecotes; swallows' nests in the windows. White rabbits hopped about on the threshold, and burrowed in the untrodden turf.

But of old it had been fortified! Everywhere there was plenty of evidence of great and frequent attacks. Near the gateway in the grass there still lay an iron cannon ball, a relic of the Swedish invasion, as large as a child's head. In the yard, among the weeds and the wormwood, rose the old stumps of some dozen crosses, on unconsecrated ground, a sign that men lay here who had perished by sudden and unexpected death. When one looked closely at the storehouse, or at the granary, and cottage, one could see that the walls were riddled with holes from top to bottom, as with a swarm of black insects. In the centre of each hole sat a bullet, like a bumble-bee in its earthy burrow. Over the doors could be seen the coat of arms of the Dobrzyńskis; but shelves of cheeses veiled the bearings, and swallows had walled them in thickly with their nests.

The interior of the house, and of the stable and carriage-shed was as full of accoutrements as any old armoury. Under the roof hung four immense helmets, the ornaments of martial brows. Nowadays the birds of Venus, the doves, cooed and fed their young in them. In the stable, a great cuirass was stretched over the manger; a corslet of chain mail served as a chute through which the boy fed clover to the colts below. In the kitchen, a godless cook had spoiled the temper of several swords by sticking them in the oven instead of spits. She dusted her handmill with a Turkish horsetail, captured at Vienna . . .[21]

A specific example of the petty nobility's distress is to be found in the unhappy history of Sieluń in Mazovia, a district to the north of the Vistula, which was dominated by the estates of the Vicar of Płock. These estates, clustered in five keys round the castle of Sieluń, provided one of the richest ecclesiastical livings in Poland and were invariably assigned as a sinecure to a rich, powerful, and absentee cleric. They entirely overshadowed the 29 villages of *zaścianki,* which were scattered among them. After 1526, however, when Mazovia was fully integrated into the Republic, the nobility of Sieluń sought to change the legal conditions on which their land was held, and to resist all further payment of rents and dues. The Vicar, defied by more than 700 families, stood to lose a substantial part of his income. The incumbent of the 1550s, the Revd. Michał Wolski, the future Bishop of Kujawy, was not prepared to concede. His armed gangs toured the villages, raiding houses, burning charters, and arresting anyone who looked to be heading for court. He used his ecclesiastical jurisdiction to prosecute resisters on trumped-up charges, and to hound them from the district. Despite abundant evidence to the contrary, his lawyers argued that the men of Sieluń did not belong to the noble estate and prevented them from appealing to the royal courts. In the space of several years, this galloping cleric, who rode to hounds while the people prayed in church, had established a parochial despotism which lasted for two centuries. In 1598, his successor, the Revd. Jędrzej Opaliński, son of the Grand Marshal of the Crown, assumed the title of 'Prince of Sieluń', and required the local nobles to pay a 'tithe', assessed at the peasant rate of 1 zł. per *włoka.* For 200 years, the phrase *'szlachcic sieluński'* (a nobleman of Sieluń), became a term of derision, known throughout the Republic. Yet from 1750 onwards, litigation proceeded apace. In 1760, at the district court of Rożana, 215 persons from Sieluń obtained a decision in confirmation of their nobility, only to find it referred to the Crown Tribunal (whose President, as it happened, was Bishop Stanisław Miasecki, Vicar of Płock!). In 1767, the case went to the Sejm, in 1776 to the Tribunal once again, in 1791 back to the Sejm, and then to the King. Finally, on 29 November 1791 a Commission of Inquiry annulled all servitudes exacted from the nobility of Sieluń. Yet the victors had only four years to enjoy their success. In 1795, at the Third Partition, Sieluń was assigned to the Prussian Treasury; in 1807–13, to Marshal Ney; and in 1815 to Russia – by which time, all those litigants who set out to prove their noble rights in 1760, were almost certainly dead. So too was the noble Republic whose benefits they had striven so long to enjoy.[22]

*   *   *   *   *

Given the great variety of economic interests within the noble estate, it might be expected that they had few attitudes in common. But this was not so. Throughout the duration of the Republic, the outlook of the Nobility displayed remarkable solidarity, especially on the three cardinal issues of noble status, of equality, and of the 'natural life'.

The nobleman's belief in the exclusive quality of his own estate led to practices which nowadays could only be described as an expression of Racism. Although the myth of blue blood was widespread in Europe, it usually referred to a tiny élite. In the Republic, it referred to perhaps ten per cent of the population, and had to be defended on a much wider front. All the specious arguments of history and religion which were later to be used by nationalist movements to differentiate the development of their own people, culture, and lands from that of 'foreigners', were used in an earlier period to strengthen the identification of the noble estate against the rest of society. Despite the continual process of ennoblement, whereby burghers, peasants, Jews, and foreigners, were added to their ranks, the szlachta continued to pretend that they were biologically unique. There was no strong feeling about bastardy, intermarriage or miscegenation as such – only that the children of irregular unions should not have a claim to nobility. As Walerian Nekanda Trepka, writing in the 1620s put it:

Balsam, when added to tar, ceases to be balsam but turns to tar; and tares, though sown in the finest field, will not become wheat . . . So, if a noblewoman marries a peasant, she will certainly give birth to an ignoble child. For what purity can come from such impurity, what perfume from such a stench! It's a wise proverb: Nightingales are not born from owls.[23]

Mikołaj Rej (*c.* 1505–69), poet and pundit, who had none of Trepka's fanaticism, likened the szlachta to the Cedars of Lebanon, taller and fairer than everyone else.

Trepka (1584–1640), author of the *Liber chamorum* (Book of Hams), devoted a lifetime to defending the purity of the noble estate. He was a cuss and a crank of the most tiresome kind; but his book is a wonderful guide to the social attitudes of his day. In his early days, he had sued a number of acquaintances for ignobility, and was himself involved in various cases of kidnap, assault, horse-stealing, and minting. In 1630, having sold his family lands, he settled in Cracow, where he had nothing to nurse but his grievances. All the while, by examining court records, by travelling round the fairs and assemblies of the province, and by recording every piece of scandal or libel which came his way, he compiled a dossier on all the people he suspected of falsely parading as nobles. (Ham, the ignoble son of Noah, was taken to be the ancestor of all such rascals.) In his introduction, Trepka explains with no small spite how plebeians 'screw their way' into the noble estate. The great magnates helped their clients to noble titles with impunity. The burghers of Cracow were all provided with fraudulent documents. Fathers, whose daughters insisted on marrying a peasant, preferred to adopt the son-in-law into the family clan than to risk a public blot on their escutcheon. Others simply added a -*ski* to their name, and hoped they would not be exposed. There was wide scope for enterprising blackmail. A 'Ham' could count on finding a witness to his nobility, by threatening to bring a case of *nagana* against anyone who refused to oblige. Alternatively, he could arrange a spurious *nagana* against himself, which, when no witnesses came forward, would persuade the court to issue the required certification. It was, as Trepka well knew, a dirty game, and, from Abramowicz to Żyznański, he revelled in it.[24]

The relative value placed on the different estates was nicely calculated in the legal institution of '*Główszczyzna*' or 'Headmoney' (Wergeld), which remained the normal practice for settling cases of assault and murder until the reforms of 1764. In such cases, the family of the aggrieved party was required to bring the body or the corpse to court within twelve weeks, or to demonstrate the nature of the injury (*vulneratus, saucius,*

laesus, or *concussus*). On judging the evidence, the court
would then order a fine against the accused in accordance
with a tariff fixed by statute. These tariffs, like those of a
modern insurance company, were calculated with cold-
blooded precision. In 1347, a statute from Wielkopolska put
the price of a noble life at 30 groats; a noble nose, arm, or
leg at 15; and a noble finger at 3; a dead peasant was costed
at 6 groats, and an injured one at 1½. By this reckoning, one
dead nobleman was worth five peasants. A noseless, legless,
or armless peasant was thought to be worth one-tenth of a
nobleman who had met with similar misfortune. In 1547, a
royal edict of Zygmunt-August increased the differentials. A
noble life was valued at 60 zł., a commoner at 30, a soldier at
15, and a peasant at 10. On the face of it, the nobleman was
now worth six peasants. But a rule which divided compensation for a peasant in the ratio of 6 for the widow, to 4 for the
victim's lord, provokes further considerations. If a nobleman
cared to murder one of his own peasants — and assuming that
his own court would bother to make an award — he only
stood to pay the difference between what he owed the
widow, and what he could claim for himself. At 2 zł. net,
this works out at thirty times less than the 60 zł. involved if
the roles of murderer and victim were reversed. In 1588, the
fines were inflated still further, and prison sentences introduced. For the murder of a nobleman, the offender was to
remain 58 weeks in a closed dungeon, and to pay a fine of
240 groats. If the offence was committed by use of a firearm,
he was to undergo 116 weeks' arrest, and pay 480 groats.
Legs, arms, eyes, and noses were priced at 120 groats each;
blood wounds at 80, fingers at 30, and teeth at 20. By now,
no mention is made of peasant victims. Presumably no one
thought of taking such trifles to court.[25]

Murder, in effect, was considered somewhat less serious
than other types of offence. Noblemen, who always carried
a sword, were expected to fend for themselves. Murder was
considered a fair risk. But rape and false pretences were not.
In 1448, a Mazovian statute provided the death sentence for
the rape of a noblewoman by a commoner, and a fine of
60 groats for the rape of a commoner. (By this score, one
raped noblewoman was worth two dead noblemen at the old

rate; and the hymen of a peasant girl was ten times more valuable than the life of her father.) A person who maliciously initiated a fraudulent *nagana* was punished in Poland with decapitation, in Lithuania by flogging. A corpse, falsely masquerading as the remains of a murder victim, was liable to earn its presenter the same sentence as the murderer.[26]

The Polish belief in nobility caused widespread comment abroad. Daniel Defoe, writing in London in 1728, cited Venice and Poland as being 'the two particular countries where the notions of nobility in blood are at this time carried to the highest and most ridiculous extreme':

In Poland this vanity of birth is carry'd up to such a monstrous extravagance that the name of gentleman and the title of a *Starost*, a *Palatine*, or a *Castollan* gives the man a superiority over all the vassals or common people, infinitely greater than that of King or Emperor, reigning over them with more absolute Power, and making them more miserable than the subjects either of the Grand Seignior or the Cham of Tartary, insomuch that they trample on the poorer people as dogs and frequently murder them: and when they do are accountable to nobody . . .

For take the nobility and gentry of POLAND . . . as they appear in history; in the first place, they are the most haughty, imperious, insulting people in the world. A very valuable historian of our times sayes they are *proud, insolent, obstinate, passionate, furious.* These are indeed the born gentlemen . . .

Yet if you should ask a Polander what he is he would tell you he is a *gentleman of Poland*; and so much so they value themselves upon the name, that they think they are abov being tyed to the rules of honour which are the onely constituting laws of gentlemen. Nay they support themselves in doing the foulest and blackest things . . . and expect allowance even from Heaven itself on account of their birth and quallity: an eminent instance of which we have in an infamous wretch, a Captain Vratz, a Polander, who in cold blood assassinated an English gentlemen, *Thomas Thynne* Esq[re], shooting him into the body in his coach with a musqueteer loaded with 7 bullets; and who, the day before he was to be hanged for it, when he was spoken with by the minister to prepare himself for death, answered that he did not doubt but God would have some respect to him as a gentleman.[27]

To be fair, Defoe added that these 'ill quallityes' were matched by virtues, especially in the field of education. He was specially impressed by the currency of Latin culture in Poland. 'A man who can speak Latin', he reported, 'may travel from one end of Poland to another as familiarly as if he was born in the country. Bless us! What would a gentleman do that was to travel through England and could speak nothing but Latin . . . I must lament his condition.'

Once the szlachta had become a closed, hereditary estate, all means of access to it were jealously guarded. Although during the Republic the King retained the prerogative of ennoblement, the Sejm insisted on ever closer controls. In 1578, it ruled that the King could not create knighthoods except when the Sejm was in session, or when prowess was rewarded on the battlefield. In 1601, it ruled that no ennoblement was valid without the Sejm's ratification, or, in the case of a peasant, without the consent of his lord. In 1641, it extended its competence to grants of nobility to foreigners, in the so-called 'indygenat'; and it revived the semi-noble category of 'scartabellus', whose family could only obtain full political rights in the third generation. In 1775 the possession of land was made a prior condition for all new entrants to the noble estate.

The incidence of ennoblement, in consequence, was not very great. The number of royal creations recorded between 1569 and 1696 did not exceed two thousand — which is far less than the number of families which adopted noble status by illegal means. Only in the eighteenth century, when Saxon clients, magnatial servants, and Jewish converts were received into the nobility en masse, was the Nobility legally enlarged on a substantial scale.

Grants of indygenat or 'naturalization' were equally limited. The candidates were required to submit proof of their service to the Republic, together with a certificate of nobility issued by a foreign court, also to swear an oath of allegiance, and to buy land. Most of them were connected in some way with the Court — as the King's officers, doctors, apothecaries, tutors, architects, secretaries, interpreters, cooks, bastards, or even, in the case of Joachim Pastorius von Hirtenberg, as the King's historian. Under the Jagiellons they were mainly Italian; under Stefan Batory, they included a number of Magyars and Transylvanians; under the Vasas, Swedes and Livonians; under Augustus II and III a wave of Saxons; and under Stanisław-August, a flood of Russians. There were plenty of Germans,

and a steady stream of Irish and Scots. The latter, like Jakub
Butler (1627), 'Henry de Gordon' (1658), 'Hugo O'Kelly'
(1673), Archibald Patrick Middleton (1768), or Joseph
Foresyth (1793), were mainly soldiers. An occasional Englishman appears from time to time, like Mr Corry Frevort,
Consul at Danzig (1773), and a single solitary American,
Stanisław-August's secretary, Littlepage. The ceremonies of
indygenat often took place during the Coronation Sejm at
the beginning of the reign, where one of the candidates
would be chosen as *eques aureatus* or 'Golden Knight' to lead
the band of fortunates. In the eighteenth century, they were
enlivened with the whiff of an auction. In 1764, Pierre
Raucour, a Jewish banker from Paris, long established in
Warsaw, paid 126,666 zł., 20 groszy, for the elevation of himself and his three sons.[28]

The concern of the Nobility for their status *vis-à-vis* the
rest of society was matched by their mania for equality
among themselves. In a land where such extremes of fortune
prevailed, it may seem odd that anyone should even have
talked of equality. In fact, from the psychological point of
view, the pursuit of equality was an essential antidote to the
real state of affairs. It was a defence mechanism, a social
lubricant, which enabled the szlachta to stand together and
face the world outside. It was a beautiful fiction, a cult —
which provided the basic rules of political and social life for
at least three centuries. From the very earliest days of the
Republic, and before, all attempts at differentiating between
the high and the low were fiercely resisted. In 1537, in the
so-called *Wojna Kokosza* or 'War of the Chickens' — so called,
because the soldiery consumed all the poultry of Red Ruthenia
— the mutinous feudal host rejected proposals to create an
upper caste as in neighbouring Bohemia, or in Germany. In
1569, in the Act of Union itself, the titles of the Lithuanian
princes had to be confirmed, for without it the Union would
not have been agreed; but it was ruled that henceforth no·one
should adopt new titles or use a foreign title within the
frontiers of the Republic. In 1638, in view of numerous
contraventions, and again in 1641, 1673, and 1678, the Sejm
banned titulation on pain of infamy. In 1699, when the
noble deputies realized that phrases such as *szlachta mniejsza*

(the lesser nobility) and *szlachta większa* (the greater nobility) had crept into the minutes of the Sejm, they ordered them to be struck from the record as words *contra aequalitatem* (contrary to the principle of equality).[29]

Elaborate social manners were designed to reinforce egalitarian ideas. In public, Polish noblemen were used to address each other as *'Panie Bracie'* ('My Lord Brother'). In the army, everyone was *'Towarzysz'* ('Comrade'). Among acquaintances, people talked in the third person, using *'Wasza Miłość'* or *'Waść'* ('Your Love'), or *'Waćpan'* (*Wasza Miłość, Panie*), in the way that Spaniards use *'Usted'* or the Italians *'Lei'*. Even in the family, parents were accustomed 'to Waszmość' their children, and children their parents. Only at a public execution was a nobleman addressed as *'Ty'* ('Thou'), and that as a sign of equality with the hangman. Noblemen customarily greeted each other with kisses on the cheeks, on the hands, on the shoulder, or even on the belly. This was a sign of mutual respect and submission. Children greeted their parents kneeling, – sons on one knee, daughters on both.

Equality was practised between the sexes. Noblewomen enjoyed the same rights of property and inheritance as noblemen, and did not feel dependent. The *herod-baba* or 'wild woman' has a long record in both history and literature.

The principle of equality may have required that all formal titles be banned. From the practical point of view, however, the ban was frequently circumvented. From the start, all the noblemen who signed the Union of Lublin with a handle to their name were permitted to keep it. This let in all the 'Princes of the Blood' from Lithuania, and a whole host of families who had accepted titles from abroad. Although the Kings were not permitted to grant titles to Polish subjects, they could do so to foreigners. Zygmunt-August conferred lands and titles in Livonia in this way. Stefan Batory continued to make grants in Transylvania, and the Polish Vasas issued putative titles to Scandinavian lands. Augustus II rewarded dozens of his natural sons with earldoms in Poland, whilst Stanisław-August dispensed Polish baronies to his Russian mentors.

In addition to such genuine titles, and a host of more doubtful ones, there were subtler means of underlinings one's status. The magnates drew special prestige from the offices of state. To be called 'Wojewoda', 'Kasztelan', or 'Starosta' – or to bask in the kudos of 'Marshal of the Crown' or 'Grand Hetman of Lithuania' – was no less substantial than to be a prince or a count. There also appeared an informal hierarchy of attributes, used mainly in correspondence. Everyone knew that *nobilis* or *szlachetny* meant 'noble-but-without-significance'. It was used in disparagement of the landless and officeless. *Generosus* was more complimentary, and referred to office-holders. *Magnificus* or even *illustrissimus,* once reserved for royal persons, was applied to magnates whose favours were seriously solicited.

The Nobility's horror of orders of chivalry was more feigned than real. In 1634, Władysław IV's project for launching the 'Order of the Immaculate Conception' with seventy belted knights, was intended as a step towards a permanent Catholic monarchist party. It was opposed by the Sejm and had to be dropped. But the introduction in 1705 by August II of the 'Order of the White Eagle' raised no opposition whatever. By the middle of the century, the Saxon ministers were selling membership at 10,000 zł. a head. In 1765, Stanisław-August introduced the new 'Order of Saint Stanisław' and used it to reward some hundreds of his supporters. By the 1790s his chamberlain was selling tickets for this at 95 ducats each. In effect, the only respectable Order in the Republic's history was the 'Virtuti Militari' of 1792. It was used to honour men who had distinguished themselves in the Russian War of 1791–2, and was predictably suppressed by command of Catherine the Great.

The Nobility's last great obsession was for the land. The pursuit of the 'natural life' was indeed common to all the landowning classes of Europe; but in Poland it formed a specially intense and sentimental trait. In the Republic, the distances were greater than in Western Europe, and the localities still more isolated. Feeling for the local community was strong, and for the national community weak. In conditions of deepening economic regression, the nobleman was inclined to stay at home, to manage his farm, and to count his blessings. Cut off from the outside world, he was deeply convinced that the rest of mankind lived in squalor. Despite their many and obvious faults, the szlachta undoubtedly succeeded in creating a powerful sense of local solidarity, which in the record of literature clearly triumphs over meaner considerations. The natural life was one of the favourite themes of Poland's first great vernacular poet, himself the squire of Czarnolas: What could be more simple, or more sincere, than his ode 'To a Linden Tree'?:

> Dear Guest, sit down beneath my leaves and take your rest.
> The sun will not strike you there, I do insist,
> Though it beat from its noonday height, and its direct rays
> Should pierce such scattered shade as a tree bestows.
> There, a cooling breeze is always blowing from the field;
> There, nightingales and blackbirds their tuneful tales unfold.
> It's from my fragrant blossom that the tireless bees
> Take the honey, which later ennobles your lordly feasts;
> Whilst I, by my soft murmurs, can easily contrive
> That gentle sleep should overtake the unsuspecting fugitive.
> It's true, I bear no fruit; but in my master's eyes
> My worth exceeds the richest scion of the Hesperides.

Or his elegy, to 'The Merry Village'?:

> Sweet village! peace and joy's retreat!
> O who shall tune thy praise to song?
> O who shall make a music, meet
> Thy smiles, thy pleasures to prolong?
> Bliss dwells within thy solitude,
> Which selfish avarice never stains,
> Where thought and habit make us good
> And sweet contentment gilds our gains.[30]

Two hundred years later, Bishop Naruszewicz was expressing the same sentiments exactly:

> I do not care for pomp and ostentation.
> A well-stocked farm is my ambition.
> When doing business with a peasant
> I have the greatest entertainment.
> Better friends I could not know,
> Than my team of oxen yoked to the plough.
> All titles
> Are empty vessels.
> O virtuous countryside! May your name
> Be blessed with burgeoning fame.
> I am yours. You are mine,
> My treasure, my anodyne.[31]

Social harmony was an essential ingredient of the noble-man's idyll. The frequent protestations of *miłość braterska* or 'fraternal love' between members of the nobility were matched by constant appeals for charity and understanding towards the other social groups. The noble toast of 'Kochajmy Się' (Let us love one another!) was raised at innumerable gatherings across the centuries. Not only was it an expression of deep attachment to Christian principles, but it was also a call to alleviate social conflicts. If rank and fortune were determined by God, it was none the less the duty of Man, and of noblemen in particular, to heal social antagonisms and to succour the oppressed. Already in the sixteenth century, Mikolaj Rej, 'the mouthpiece of the middle nobility', had stressed the point in his famous *Krótka rozprawa między panem, wójtem, a plebanem* (A Short Discussion between a Squire, a Village Headman, and a Priest). Nobility, he empha-sized, is a moral quality, whose privileges can only be justified by an exemplary display of honesty, godliness, moderation, and duty. A nobleman's strength lies in the love of his serfs. It may not have been an original thought: *Nobilitas sola est atque unica virtus.* But it was a necessary reminder. Even in the nineteenth century, the ultra-conservative writer, Kajetan Koźmian (1771–1856), was still looking back to these same traditions as the ultimate guide to national salvation. Love for one's neighbour was no less a noble virtue than love of the land and of Nature:

> You, who by innocent taste or blissful destiny
> Are inclined to love the fields and farms of the country,
> Whether you dwell behind some stately gates, or in a lowly tenement
> May you seek the happiness of others, and find your own content.
> There is no need for riches, nor yet for undue exertion.
> The pathway of charity will lead you to its own destination.
> May the deeds of your right hand fulfil what your hearts decree.
> The merry faces of a village are its fairest property.
> Moderation is a supreme good, and a virtue, but the golden chains
> Of unrestrained freedom add little comfort to the prisoner's pains.[32]

In recent years, the szlachta's views on social harmony have been dismissed as humbug. One writer has denounced them as 'a panegyric to vegetation'. 'Love', he writes, 'is an ideological ornamentation of the landed nobility. Its basis is to be found in a class interest threatened by the magnates, by the higher clergy, and by the land-hungry petty nobility.'[33] Certainly, one cannot deny that the gap between the ideal and the reality was enormous. To modern eyes, it may seem monstrous that people who were notoriously cruel to their serfs and openly contemptuous of burghers and Jews, could at the same time profess the tenets of universal love and reconciliation. The incomparable Jan Pasek, for example, when he caught a peasant snaring rabbits without permission, unceremoniously ordered the wretched poacher to eat the wretched rabbit alive. His apparent indifference to the humanity of his serfs stands in marked contrast to the extravagant affection extended to his pet otter.[34] Common cruelty was an established feature of social life. Faced with the congenital idleness, drunkenness, and pilfering of the peasantry, the nobleman frequently replied with ferocious impositions and punishments. The lash and the knout were the accepted symbols of noble authority. The serfs were beaten for leaving the estate without permission, for brawls and misdemeanours, and for non-observance of religious practices. A dungeon, together with chains, shackles, stocks, hooks, and instruments of torture, were part of the regular inventory. In cases of incorrigible theft or insubordination, the death sentence in a variety of forms was readily applied. Although judicial forms were usually observed — Magdeburg Law in some medieval settlements, and customary law in most Polish villages — there was little to prevent the lord from indulging his fantasies. It was all but impossible in a peasant family for the boys to refuse demands for extra labour and for the girls to resist service 'in the House' or the insidious *droit de seigneur.*

In the Nobility's defence, it must be admitted that they were fully aware of their faults. Rej initiated a strong tradition of social satire which took permanent root in Polish literature. His *Krótka rozprawa . . .* is full of exquisite observations on the inconsequentialities of the nobleman's conduct. When the Lord has finished decrying the clergy, and the Rector the nobility, the peasant Headman gives them both an exemplary lesson in fortitude and cheerfulness:

> And yet, in this lowly estate of mine
> I'm no less merry than a palatine.

> For here in our fleeting life on earth
> We've far fewer worries to spoil our mirth.
> Like all honest persons, I keep to my place;
> And other men's matters don't trouble my ease.
> So what, if poverty brings me low?
> I'll bear it while I'm here below;
> And when the order comes to leave
> How shall I then have cause to grieve?
> I won't shed a tear for the sweet hereafter,
> But fly like a sparrow out of the rafter.[35]

A century later, Krzysztof Opaliński savagely condemned the treatment of the serfs, seeing it as the cause of God's wrath so manifestly visited on a sinful Republic:

> As I understand it, God does not punish Poland for nothing,
> But chiefly for the harsh oppression visited on the serfs,
> Which is worse than slavery: as if the peasant
> Were not your neighbour, nor even a person.
> My heart sinks, and I shudder to reflect
> On that oppression, which outweighs pagan bondage.
> For God's sake, have you Poles lost your minds completely?
> Your whole welfare, your supply of food, the wealth you amass,
> All derives from your serfs. It is their hands which feed you;
> And still you treat them with such cruelty.[36]

Even Koźmian, whose opposition to all forms of national and social liberation was complete, did not hesitate to castigate the condition of the nobility's dependants. 'The cattle live like people', he wrote, 'and the common people like cattle.'

The charge against the szlachta therefore is that their social relationships were both sentimental and vicious at one and the same time; that their outlook towards the other estates was characterized by a contradictory mixture of real concern and cruel contempt; that they loved their serfs, and flogged them. It is a nice paradox. Class analysis suggests that whilst the floggings were real, the love was a sham. A glimpse at human nature suggests otherwise. Love and Hate are frequent companions. They represent opposite extremes of the same emotional response to the bonds of mutual dependence. They appear together in the experiences of marriage partners, and of parents and children, and in the life of most known institutions. They are strongest when prevailing circumstances preclude any easy means of escape. It is not at all surprising that they should appear together in the everyday life of a rigid, unchanging society.

Throughout these centuries, the real enemy was apathy. In a system where the Golden Freedom forced no one into civic responsibilities, it was all too easy for noblemen to cultivate their estates and to revel in their petty, private concerns. Social reform was as impossible to introduce as absolute government. The most a sensitive man could do was to reflect on the discrepancy between the world around him and the Christian religion which almost all professed, and to pour cold water on the idyllic fantasies which so many cherished. When remonstrations ran dry, the satirists invited the nobility to chuckle, and by chuckling, to awake to their true condition. The Arian, Wacław Potocki, added a note of truly apocalyptic irony:

> The world sleeps, besotted with wine, and dims its eyes,
> Whilst the Babylonian whore fills up the glass, and the Devil
>   conspires.
> The world, for all its abominations, sleeps like a dead tree,
> Made drunk with wine from the press of God's fury.
> The Devil stands at his post, so that no one awakes,
> Warning with his finger from afar; he even drugs the dogs,
> Having first set drink before them in a great bowl
> To make them sleep; lest any in the temple should howl,
> Even with uncomprehending voice. If one so much
> As turns its greedy snout, he throws it crusts of bread.
> Whoever should shout aloud, like the Hound in the Wood,
> Is a heretic, to be walled up for life in a cloister,
> Or beheaded, or burned at the stake. What? Disturb the world's
> Lovely dream? Let him test his jaws on the executioner!
> Others sing with the Sirens, and sweetly play their harps
> So that the world should sleep more soundly — and he barks![37]

*   *   *   *   *

The life-style of twenty generations cannot be described in a thumb-nail sketch. It is one thing to quote the Memoirs of figures like Jan Chrystostom Pasek or to paint the splendours of a Radziwiłł; it is another to imply that partial glimpses are somehow representative of the whole.[38]

The nobleman's residence was the public advertisement of his rank and fortune. Whether hovel or palace, it was easily

distinguished from the homes of his non-noble neighbours —
by the provision of the obligatory porch, courtyard, and gateway: by the display of ornamentation incorporating the
owner's coat of arms, and by the characteristic luxury of the
internal furnishings. The typical country manor or *dwór*
consisted of a long, one-storied timber construction, with
high, steep roof and low eaves, and was surrounded by
domestic outbuildings of similar profile. The tradition of
building in wood was pursued even by wealthy noblemen
whose magnificent pine or oaken houses, covered in intricate
carving, constituted such notorious fire risks. As the Papal
Nuncio, Malaspina, once remarked, he had never seen 'such
beautiful stacks of fire-wood'. Stone was customarily reserved
for fortifications which often took the form of separate
bastions or enclosures set apart from the regular residence.
Stone castles of medieval vintage were to be found throughout Poland and Lithuania, but especially in western and
northern areas which came under German influence. Examples
still stand at Bolków (Bolkenhain) in Silesia, at Czorstyn on
the Dunajec, and at Czersk and Ciechanów in Mazovia. The
latest, and perhaps the finest castle of all, the fortified pentagon
at Krzyztopor constructed for the Ossolińskis, was never inhabited. Completed in 1644, it was burned by the invading
Swedes eleven years later, and left as an imposing ruin from
that day to this. To the modern eye the happiest blend of styles
occurred in Poland during the Renaissance period when the
strength of turrets, battlements, and crenellations was complemented by the elegance of cupolas, arcades, and roofs, and
by the exquisite details in the architraves of windows and
doors, and sculpted medallions and mouldings. Although
modest in size, the palaces of the Leszczyński at Baranów and
of the Krasicki at Krasiczyn are gems of their kind. In the
eighteenth century, the more grandiose follies of aristocratic
builders, each aspiring to his own Versailles, reflected foreign
rather than native taste. Scattered throughout the broad Polish
countryside, and surrounded by the thatched and wattled
homesteads of their less affluent noble brothers, the Branicki at
Białystok, the Ogiński at Słonim, the Poniatowski at Jabłonna,
and above all the Czartoryski at Puławy, raised lasting monuments to the social supremacy of the magnatial oligarchy.

Internal furnishings were not merely functional. The massive willow table, a few green-painted benches, a cupboard, a chest of drawers, a bed, and the family chest were often the only items of furniture. Windows of green glass, or more frequently of waxed canvas, kept out the weather; a candelabra of brass or horn hung from the carved ceiling; and a huge stove of rough earthenware, or even of porcelain or alabaster, provided warmth in winter. The decorations however, were elaborate. The walls were covered with tapestries, rugs, and gaudy Italian *coltrine*. Persian and Turkish carpets were highly prized. Ancient weapons and hunting trophies hung in places of honour to stress the noble virtues. In rich men's houses, 'sztukwarkowy' furniture imported from Danzig, oil paintings of the ancestors, mosaics, plaster ceilings, *objets d'art*, musical instruments, and materials of superior craftsmanship of every sort — silver, marble, rosewood, velvet, and cloth-of-gold — emphasized the owners' ambitions. In the palaces of magnates, libraries, private chapels, theatres, and even in the case of the Branickis' at Białystok a complete opera-house, proclaimed the master's cultural excellence.

Styles of dress observed similar priorities. It was important that the nobleman and noblewoman should display their quality. For the man, weapons were carried well into the eighteenth century — a sabre when outside, a dagger at his belt indoors. The thigh-length leather boots, so admired by Henry Valois, struck a pose of manliness and chivalry. The ankle-length house-smock, or *żupan*, the sleeveless waistcoat or *delia*, and the huge, flared over-coat or *kontusz*, kept the trousers hidden from view. The close-fitting cap in Poland, and the tall, fur *kolpak* in Lithuania, provided the normal headgear. For the woman, floor-length robes were in fashion across the centuries. All authorities agree that the use of sable fur was a traditional Polish fashion for both sexes. Sable was used for trimmings, for linings, and in the form of *soroki* or bundles of 'forty skins' for winter coats. It was widely remarked, also, that gold and jewels were publicly worn in uncommon quantities, as fastenings, pins, brooches, links, clusters, and as every form of decoration. Poverty-stricken noblemen would rather starve than part with their heirlooms. In common with the nobility elsewhere in Europe, outward splendour contrasted with contempt for underwear. In 1620, the Queen of England, who made a close inspection of the Polish ambassador's infant son, was surprised to find that under the suit of cloth-of-gold he was devoid of linen.

Male hair-styles tended to be exotic. In distinction to Muscovite habits, full-grown beards were rarely cultivated. In the sixteenth century, the clean-shaven, close-cropped, 'Joan of Arc' look was in fashion: in the seventeenth century, 'the Tartar look' which was attained by shaving all the head save one long tuft of hair in the middle. Zygmunt III favoured the Spanish style of close trimmed beard and moustache. Sobieski sported the handlebar whiskers copied by many of his subjects. In the eighteenth century, extravagant powdered wigs on the German model never penetrated far beyond court circles. Pigtails and curls, gradually gave way to Roman styles 'à la Titus', or 'à la Caracalla'. Fashions were largely dictated by the fact that soldiering, private or public, remained one of the szlachta's principal occupations.

Religious observances were strictly kept. In the age of faith, religion was seen as the guardian of the social order and by extension of the ideals and privileges of the nobility. It was the most natural thing in the world for the nobleman to thank God for his good fortune in public, and, as was customary during the recital of the Creed, to stand with upraised sword in defence of the Faith.

The Nobility participated in a great variety of religious celebrations. Special attention was paid in Poland to Lady Day (2 February) with the associated cults of Saints Blaise and Agatha; to Whitsuntide; and to Corpus Christi. On Ascension Day, the figure of Christ would be fastened to the Church steeple whilst an effigy of Satan was cast to the ground below. On Ash Wednesday, girls of marriageable age who had failed to find a husband were harnessed to a log, and, after being paraded in public, were disposed of at a mock auction. At Corpus Christi, it was customary to fire off pistols, or if one was well equipped, a brace of cannon. Whitsuntide, known in Poland as Zielone Świątki (The Green Holiday), was regarded as the festival of farmers and shepherds. On the Wednesday before Easter, Judas was ceremoniously drowned in a sack in every village pond. Maundy Thursday was the day for charitable donations. Easter Monday saw an annual battle of the sexes, at which men and women drenched each other with buckets of cold water. Pre-Christian festivals also survived. At the end of June, the countryside was ablaze with bonfires which were lit in honour of the Sun and of Love. This was one of the few occasions in the year when the szlachta mixed freely with the peasantry, and avoided holding their celebrations apart.

Whilst estate-management inevitably took up most of the nobleman's time, relaxation was most commonly found in hunting. Foxes and hares were coursed with greyhounds; bears were hunted with nets; wolves, which were regarded as vermin, were trapped in pits baited with a goose or a duck; bison were usually attacked by a ring of riders armed with bows and firearms. Martin Kromer, describing an organized bison hunt in Podolia, reveals several features strikingly reminiscent of a Spanish *corrida:*

. . . Meanwhile, one of the hunters, assisted by powerful hounds, approaches and draws the bison round and round the tree, playing it and teasing it until it drops from its wounds or just from sheer exhaustion. Should the hunter falter whilst taking aim, or otherwise be threatened by danger, his colleagues distract the bison by waving large red capes, since red is a colour which drives it to a fury. Thus tormented, the bison releases the first man, and attacks the next one who is then able to finish it off.[39]

Sociability was one of the szlachta's most marked characteristics. The entertaining was of an earthy sort, where carousing and crapulence took their usual toll, and where an evening out was as likely as not to end in an uninhibited brawl:

Once some relations of my wife's mother came to visit us – Pan Stanisław Szembek, the Deputy Starosta of Cracow, and Pan Franciszek Zelecki. They came with a kinsman of theirs called Kardowski, who was a frightful drunkard. I was glad to see them, but was much irritated by that Kardowski, for he was continually insulting the Mazovians, saying that they are born blind, and born under an evil star, and so on. The .others, mightily enjoying it, encouraged him. In fact, they had dragged him there specially in order to tease me. When a calf's head was brought on to the table, he said it was 'the Mazovian Pope', and when he saw the pastry beneath the veal, he said it was made from 'Mazovian communion wafers'. In short, he provoked me greatly . . . After supper, Szembek began to dance, and it wasn't long before they were all dancing the *polonez*. Then, standing in the line of the dance, Kardowski began to croon:

> 'After munching their birdseed porridge, our Mazovians
> Have salty beards, which they dunk in their beer . . .';

and he repeated the ditty several times over until at last I lost patience. As Zelecki was not very big, I was able to pick him up in my arms like a child, and, everyone thought I was doing it out of affection. But just when Kardowski was breaking once more into song, I suddenly pushed past him and butted him hard in the chest with Zelecki. Though apparently as strong as an oak, he was felled at one blow, and, falling backwards, hit his head on a bench and passed out. Zelecki, too, was unable to stand, as I had knocked him against Kardowski with all my might.

And so to sword! Turning to Szembek, I put my blade to his fat belly. 'Stop,' he yells, 'what are you blaming me for?' And the other two are still out cold. 'You need your throats cut,' I say. 'You came here to drink a toast, and have been tickling my nose with that drunkard all day, and I won't stand any more.' Then the ladies jumped up, shouting 'Stop it! Stop it!' And we left each other alone. We picked up Zelecki from the floor, and tried to sober up Kardowski by pouring vodka into his nose and between his teeth. They ran to get the barber—surgeon, since he had cut his head open. Szembek and Zelecki went to bed. After that, I fortified myself with spirit for a laugh, and ordered a round for my servants. My men played some merry pranks on the drunken retainers of our guests, who were lying around the rooms like so much dead wood. They smeared their whiskers with various foul materials, and stuffed lighted matches up their noses. Next morning, we all apologized to each other; and ever since, as often as they have visited me, they have always conducted themselves seriously, and modestly . . . and have treated me with greater respect.[40]

In spite of such minor interruptions, one of the szlachta's favourite proverbs remained: *'Gość w dom, Bóg w dom'* (When a guest enters the house, God enters also).

The earthiness of social life was perfectly compatible with a noticeable taste for bawdy, of which Polish literature could boast a wide repertoire. Among others, Mikołaj Rej, the moralist, the publicist of true nobility, did not omit to compose a collection of rude rhymes for the amusement of his noble readers and as an exercise in the vernacular for himself. His *Figliki* (Little Frolics) of 1562 was written with Chaucerian relish:

There once was a rector, preparing to baptize
A child and to anoint the infant's eyes,
Who asked an old woman, as he mixed the balm,
If she would add some dust to the spittle in his palm.
But as she stooped to gather up the dust,
She let fly a fart propelled with cruel thrust.
Said the priest, 'O Holy Grace!
See what praiseworthy power it doth impart!
A devil has leapt from that lowly place,
Where he tarried so long. I knew it from the start.'
The lady replied, 'Don't look at me,
Dear Prelate; it was the babe.' Said he,
'Yes, I know — it doesn't matter a bit;
You can go in a minute and have a holy shit.'[41]

And there was the girl who believed in dragons:

When news arrived from Hungary that dragons were still alive
And flying around, a certain young maid did contrive
To believe it. She told her friends how the terrible beasts
Had the heads of cats, and the lengthy necks of geese.
A lad explained: 'I've heard much stranger things.
There are plenty of dragons not far from here. They don't have wings:
But their knobs are very cat-like, and goose-like their necks;
They wear baggy trousers which hang down like sacks,
With a groat in each pocket; and they only lie low
And are content, when capped with a sprinkling of snow.'[42]

Dancing was generally acknowledged as one of the Polish graces. In contrast to the jovial romps of the peasantry, where the dancers leap high in the air, the favourite dance of the nobility was undoubtedly the *polonez* (Polonaise), or as it was originally known until exported abroad, the 'Great Dance'. It was danced in a circle, unhurriedly, and with an easy lilting step and demanded precise attention to the rhythm and tempo. Some foreigners, thinking it lacked passion, likened it to a 'strolling conversation', but on closer acquaintance were much impressed by its subtlety and elegance. 'Je n'ai vu jamais rien de plus grave, de plus doux, ni de plus respectueux,' recorded the Frenchman, Laboureur, in 1645.

The szlachta were inordinately fond of ceremony for ceremony's sake. They were specially addicted to processions, where they could dress up in their finery and strut in peacock-displays of their wealth and quality. In 1583, for example, a *'maskarada'* was held in the city square of Cracow to mark the marriage of Jan Zamoyski and Gryzelda Bathory. It depicted the victory of the bride's royal father over Ivan the Terrible:

The procession began when Mikołaj Wolski, the Crown Swordbearer, rode out from the courtyard of the inn 'Pod Baranami'. He and his escort were dressed in Moorish costume. An huge elephant ambled along in the retinue, showering rockets and fireworks from the tower which it carried on its back.

Behind that, Mikołaj Zebrzydowski emerged on a carriage pulled by children representing the hours – twelve in black representing the Night, and twelve in white the Day. They had clocks on their heads, and stars on their backs. A grey-bearded Saturn also rode on the carriage, grasping a scythe. Another figure with a clock on his head in personation of Time, walked behind, and after him a couple more representing the Sun and Moon.

Next the third float appeared, led by Stanisław Miński, driving an azure carriage conveyed on four spheres. This contraption was covered by a 'cloud', masterfully made from a cotton sheet, and drawn by three eagles. It emitted terrifying claps of thunder from all sides, and was surmounted by Jove clutching his flash of lightning. Fortunately, when real fire broke out in the cloud, the 'Thunder-bearer' was able to jump clear, and the fire was extinguished.

After Jove marched a company of knights on foot, dressed in ancient costume. Preceded by resplendent trumpeters, and each accompanied by his personal squire, with banners unfurled, they followed their captains under a mobile triumphal arch.

Next came a 'Victory Car' displaying the effigies of hostile countries, and carrying prisoners of war and captured booty. A woman walked alongside representing the province of Livonia over which the war had been fought. At her feet lay the conquered foe. After that, four white horses pulled a chariot to which the Enemy was shackled, together with his defeated generals, officers and people at large. A placard made fun of the boastful epithets which he had used before the war had started. The whole float was surrounded by white-haired old men, carrying sweet-smelling censers. They represented the decline and lethargy of the Enemy's power.

The fourth group consisted of a hunting-party led by Stanisław Żółkiewski as Diana. This was a sign of our soldiers' relaxation after the toils of war.

The fifth and last group was headed by Joachim Ocieski, *Starosta* of Olsztyn, seated on a wagon in the guise of Cupid among singing choristers.

Venus rode behind, drawn by a pair of whales, whose jaws, nostrils, and eyes emitted clouds of aromatic oil. A bevy of goddesses dressed in gold were dragging a reluctant Paris with them, having bound him with rope. An orchestra went in front, and amidst great merriment, Venus was handing out apples to couples in the crowd, whilst silver thalers were continually scattered among the expectant onlookers . . .[43]

In winter, the *kulig* or 'sleigh-party' provided a suitable outlet for social energies. A train of sleighs, pulled by horses and filled with people bedecked in furs and finery, would set off through the snow on a tour of the district. Led by the bachelors of the party, with music playing from the leading sleigh and bells jingling in the crisp air, they would proceed from house to house. At every stop they drank the health of the host, and pressed the girls of the household to join them. At some point, a longer halt was called, and a ball or banquet improvised. Then in the night, with the revellers holding flaming brands aloft to light their way, the revellers would return home.

As many of these instances show, the extravagance of the szlachta in matters of taste was both material and psychological. Their obvious delight in the possession of valuable objects was matched by their preference for anything which was rich, loud, strange, or new. It inevitably devalued simplicity and usefulness, and led to the eventual substitution of foreign fashions for homespun virtues. Whereas the many Polish noblemen who travelled abroad in the Renaissance period were able to use their Paduan education or the experiences of the Grand Tour for the enrichment of a distinctive native culture, their descendants of the eighteenth century were given to imitating the artistic and intellectual trends of Paris and Berlin in the most blind and superficial way. The deterioration was mirrored in linguistic habits. Whereas Kochanowski and his contemporaries were equally fluent in Polish and Latin, which they used with exact skill on appropriate occasions, subsequent generations lapsed into an inimitable macaronic mixture of the two, or, if they really wanted to impress, into bad French.

Undeniably, therefore, the noble life-style had its negative aspects. In the opinion of historians, and of many contemporaries, it was spoiled by the spirit of excess. It was marked by 'wealth without welfare' and represented in Wacław Potocki's striking phrase, *bogata nędza* — 'rich poverty'. It put ostentation before substance, good form before good deeds. It was maintained by an estate, where some family inventories listed diamonds and pearls by the bucketful and silver plate by the hundredweight, but where the majority of people lived close to the breadline. Indeed, it was perpetuated not so much by the handful of magnates, but in particular by the mass of petty nobility who in defence of their status, were prepared to suffer every exploitation and humiliation. It had many redeeming qualities; but cannot be dissociated entirely from the growth of rigid political conservatism, from economic stagnation, from the misery of the other estates, nor from the consumptive weakness of the noble Republic as a whole.

*   *   *   *   *

Over the nine generations or so which lived through the span of the United Republic, social structures did not remain static. Although no major transformation comparable to that in the nineteenth century occurred, the balance between the various estates and between their component parts shifted considerably. No accurate statistics are available; but the main trends are clear enough. (See Diagram H b, p. 202.) The decline of the Burgher Estate, both in absolute numbers and in relative proportions, was complemented by the parallel advance of the Jews. By 1791, the urban population was showing a definite increase in the Jewish element. As might be expected, the clergy's numbers remained small and stable; but both the peasants and the nobility showed significant increases. The society of Poland—Lithuania was more ruralized than two centuries before. Within the peasantry, the proportion of serfs, and particularly of noble-owned serfs, had been growing steadily, just as within the Noble Estate the number of landless nobles had long since outstripped the dwindling ranks of the *possessionati*. All these features point to a marked degree of social pauperization. Against this background, the merits of a social system managed by a supposedly egalitarian and democratic Nobility were bound to be called into question.

What cannot be questioned, however, is the durability of traditional Polish society. Whereas many characteristic features of the old Republic were destroyed, or were transformed out of all recognition, its social structures and traditions remained essentially intact over several centuries, thereby proving remarkably resistant to political and economic change. In this, they often contrived to transcend the Partitions, and provide one of the few strands of relative permanence and continuity in modern Polish history.

CHAPTER EIGHT
HANDEL:
The Polish Grain Trade

The rise of the Vistula trade can be clearly dated to the middle of the fifteenth century. At the moment when the entire Vistula basin, from source to seaboard, was united under one political rule, external demand for Polish corn was nicely matched by favourable prospects of increased internal supply. Rising prices in Western Europe sent merchants far afield, not least to the Hansa port of Danzig. At the same time, Polish cereal production was approaching the crucial point at which surpluses could be regularly obtained. The influx of the merchants, largely Dutchmen, buying in large quantities coincided with the new-found capacity of Polish landowners to sell. Henceforward, Danzig's trade was to multiply far beyond the modest business established during the century and a half since its capture in 1308 by the Teutonic Order. In 1454 it renounced its allegiance to the Teutonic state, and at the head of the Prussian League, appealed for the protection of Kazimierz Jagiellończyk, King of Poland. The Prussian delegation arrived in Cracow during celebrations of the King's marriage to Elizabeth of Austria, daughter of the Emperor. Among their complaints against the Teutonic Knights, as recorded in the act of incorporation, was one to the effect that a Pomeranian merchant had been condemned to death for sending goods to Cracow in his ships on the Vistula. At the end of the Thirteen Years War in 1466, Danzig became the chief city of the new Polish province of Royal Prussia. From then on, for more than three centuries, it never looked back. It was the natural outlet of a vast Polish hinterland, the natural junction of sea-going traffic with the river-borne trade. Although it never lost its German character, its hostility to Hohenzollern Prussia, and its loyalty to its Polish protectors, rarely wavered. Danzig was a German jewel in the Polish Crown, the chief emporium and shop-window of the multi-national Republic.

The shift in Polish commercial life, which occurred in the 1450s, is well illustrated by the career of the Kopernik family. Until this time, Mikołaj Kopernik had been a burgher of Cracow, the capital in the south. As his name also suggests, he was engaged in the metal trade, having originated from a settlement called Koperniki in Silesia, and worked as a broker in Slovakian copper which passed through Cracow on its way north. In August 1454 he visited Danzig on business and four years later, with the Teutonic War still in progress, decided to settle permanently in nearby Thorn (Toruń), an important entrepôt on the Vistula. In Thorn, he married Barbara Watzenrode, the daughter of a patrician family, and there his fourth child, also Mikołaj or Nikolaus, was born on 19 February 1473. In this way, the early life of the astronomer was closely associated with the Vistula trade. The father's commercial wealth and the mother's ecclesiastical relatives ensured him a cosmopolitan education, in Königsberg, in Cracow, and eventually in Bologna and Padua. From 1510, however, he settled again in his native parts. His scientific research was facilitated by a tranquil life as canon of the Warmian Chapter at Frauenberg and here his revolutionary treatise on the motion of the earth round the sun was conceived, tested, and written.

In the lifetime of Copernicus, the Vistula Trade developed by leaps and bounds. In terms of exported grain measured in *lasts*,* it rose from 5,573 in 1491–2, to 10,000 in 1537, to 66,007 in 1563, and to a peak of 118,000 in 1618. The figure for 1618 was never repeated. But the volume of trade remained substantial. The decline was graceful through the

---

* The Danzig *last* or 'load' was a measure of capacity equivalent to 3,101 litres of rye, or roughly 2.3 tons. (Its exact weight varied according to the commodity, of course. 1 *last* of frothless beer was equivalent to 2,644 litres; to 2,760 litres of frothy beer; or to 2,264 litres of wine.) It was divided into 60 *Scheffel/korczyk* or 'small bushels', of 52 litres. It was approximately 10 per cent smaller than the Polish wholesale '*łaszt*', which, at 3,440 litres of rye, was designed to include an automatic commission for the seller. The Polish *łaszt* was often divided into 30 Varsovian bushels or *korzec,* each of which at 114 litres was twice as large as the Danzig *Scheffel.* In Małopolska, the Cracovian *korczyk* was equivalent to 34 litres. The profusion of Vistula grain measures was standardized in 1850 by the Prussian Customs Service which fixed the *Scheffel/korczyk* at 50 litres of rye.

seventeenth and eighteenth centuries. Like the Vistula itself, the grain continued to flow — erratic and unpredictable; but as time went on, the years of flood grew ever more rare, and the years of ebb ever more frequent. During all this long period, the Grain Trade provided an important stimulus, and was the main index, to the economy of the Republic as a whole.[1] (See Map 13.)

                    *   *   *   *   *

The cycle of the Vistula Trade began with the arrival in Danzig of the foreign entrepreneurs.[2] In the early period, they sailed in for the season, arriving on the Spring tides in March or April and weighing anchor in October before the winter storms. Later on, they settled in Danzig permanently. In the main, they represented Dutch firms, well established in the Baltic *moederhandel* (Mother Trade). By 1650, some fifty Dutch firms maintained resident agents in Danzig, frequently younger sons like Arndt Pilgrom, Helmut von Tweenhuysen, Dirck van der Wolff, Marcus and Pieter Pels, Daniel de Maires, Gilles Thibaut, Jan Voyrknecht, Hans Ghybrechtsen de Veer, or Jacob Jacobsen, whose family businesses were based in Amsterdam. A number of them, like Cornelis Vlaminck or Floris Hackelaer de Jonge, obtained full citizenship in Danzig, just as Danzigers like Wessel Schenck, Hans Schultz, or Ernest Kleinfeldt established permanent family and business connections in Amsterdam. In the same period, there were about twenty British agents, mainly Scots, who formed the core of a flourishing colony. These foreign entrepreneurs, who acted on commission for partners spread throughout Europe, dominated banking and credit operations as well as basic commercial transactions. With greater capital resources, more ships and continental contacts at their command, they gradually squeezed their local competitors until something approaching a foreign monopoly was established. In theory at least they were greatly assisted by the Polish law of 1496 which prevented native merchants from travelling abroad.

The 'Amsterdam Fleet' grew steadily. In 1642, no less than 2,052 vessels called at Danzig.[3] On any one day, but especially during the August Fair which opened on St. Dominic's Day,

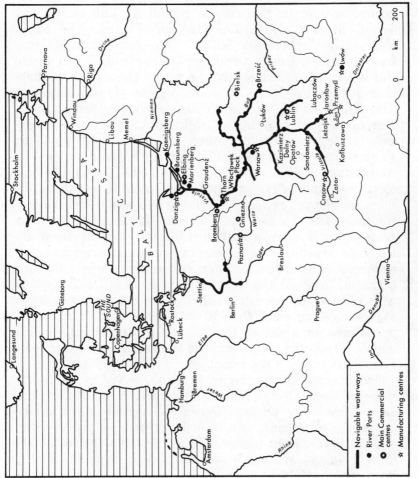

Map 13. The Vistula Trade

four or five hundred ships would have been moored at the quays on the banks of the Mottlau. The size of the vessels grew also. In 1641, although 964 of 1,741 ships had a capacity less than 50 *lasts* (about 115 tons), 103 of them were carrying over 150 *lasts*. Their destinations varied. About half remained within the Baltic itself, bound for Lübeck, Copenhagen, Stockholm, Libau, Riga, or Vyborg. The other half sailed through the Sound. The commonest run was Danzig–Amsterdam–Setubal or Faro in Portugal, where salt and wine were taken on for the grain. The longer Mediterranean runs to Genoa–Leghorn–Venice–Cyprus–Lisbon–Amsterdam; or to the Spanish ports of Huelva–San Lucas de Barrameda–Cadiz–Malaga–Barcelona–Amsterdam, flourished in the late sixteenth century, but thereafter gave way to shorter runs, especially to France or England or just to Amsterdam itself. In the three years 1615–18, one Lisbon merchant, Andres Lopez Pinto, forwarded no less than 200 ships to Danzig, exchanging salt for rye which was thereon transported to Tangier and Ceuta in North Africa. In later years, typical contracts dealt with salt cargoes from La Rochelle or Brouage which were exchanged for grain delivered to Amsterdam. There is some evidence to suggest that on occasion, to avoid the high duties charged at Danzig, goods were transported overland to Stettin. On the direct run, however, with a fair wind, the 850 sea miles to Amsterdam could be covered in a week. The round trip to Portugal took a couple of months and more. The Mediterranean voyages presumably occupied a full season.

The business of the foreign firms was served by the operations of some five hundred local merchants. These were almost invariably German Danzigers, registered in the city and sworn by solemn oath to maintain their corporate rights and privileges. Their names – Ficke, Krumhausen, Schultze, Czirenberg, Gawrock, Strobandt, Hewel, Sieuertt, Kinke, Wichman – could be encountered wherever trade was conducted throughout the Republic. They usually ran small family concerns, where the *patron* employed an accountant, or *buchalter*, one or two apprentices, or *knechte*, and a number of agents, or *faktor*, for travelling the countryside. They made use of a numerous class of brokers, or *makler*, who so lubricated the wheels of trade within the city that in the later seventeenth century they were regularly denounced as parasites. The labour force of porters and stevedores was recruited on the quayside on a piece-rate basis. On occasion, the merchants joined together to form trading companies; but their partnerships were usually no more than ephemeral ventures formed for specific operations too big for one merchant to handle alone.

The relations of the Danzig merchant with the Polish producer depended on an elaborate system of contracting. There were at least four types of contract, the commonest of which, as far as grain was concerned, the *Lieferantzkauf,* provided in advance for deliveries to be made at the producer's risk and expense. In this case, documents were exchanged, usually in Danzig, stating the agreed quantity, price, delivery date, financial advance, and conditions. The regular client, when making delivery one year, could thereby arrange for the disposal of the next year's produce. Alternatively, the merchant's factor, touring the countryside, would contract on similar terms for uncut grain to be delivered later in the season. Less common were contracts where the merchant took the risk and expense of delivery on himself (*kauf auf Abentauer*), or where ready grain was bought on the spot, either 'illegally' outside the city ('*unter dem marckte'*), or else in Danzig itself.

Polish grain producers engaged in the Vistula trade can be divided into three categories. First, there were the great magnates, whose vast estates could produce a large and regular surplus, even in bad conditions or under poor management. Next there were the landowners of lesser standing who depended on efficiency and personal supervision to produce a surplus from lesser holdings of two or three villages. Finally, there were the casual producers – minor nobility, peasants, tenant farmers, who grew corn essentially to feed themselves but who could, on occasion, produce enough to sell. In the sixteenth century, producers of the middling sort dominated the market. Later on, the magnates' share increased significantly.

Magnatial grain production can be illustrated from the latifundium of the Lubomirski family between 1654 and

1750. The latifundium, which in 1739 totalled 1,050 properties, was spread right across the southern lands of the Republic. Some estates like Wiśnicz, Zator, Baranów, Opatów, and Jarosław, specialized in oats. Others, like Niepołomice or Osiek grew both oats and rye in quantity. A few, like Nisko, Ryki, Tuszów, and Lubartów, specialized only in rye. All grew a little barley (*c.* 10–14 per cent of production) and a certain amount of wheat (up to 20 per cent). Some, again, like three in the Sandomierz region – Kołbuszowa, Rzemień, Tuszów – or three others in the Ruthenian palatinate – Kanczuga, Kosina, Łąka – were large, producing on average over 1,000 *kopa** per annum. Most were smaller, averaging 500–1,000 *kopa*; whilst a few produced less than 500 *kopa*. Total production of the four cereals, calculated over the years 1658–62 reached 40,000 *kopa* per annum.[4]

Fluctuations in production were considerable. Hardly a year would pass without some disaster, human or elemental, striking at some part of the latifundium. The Swedish invasion of 1654–60, following Chmielnicki's Rebellion, was exceeded in its destructiveness only by the decade 1700–10 when the Great Northern War ebbed and flowed across Poland. In between times, drought, floods, storms, blight, and the plague did their work. The records of the Lubomirski's estate at Kanczuga, for instance, mention the following incidents:

1654:   Quartering of Crown cavalry and German regiments: looting of Kanczuga town, and Gać village.
1655:   Quartering of Swedish Army.
1656:   Requisitioning by Crown, Swedish, Transylvanian and Cossack forces.
1657:   Transylvanian Requisitioning.
1689:   Drought. Failure of oats, and of sowing.
1708–10:   Military contributions: burning of the barns with all stores: collapse of the town and markets.
1721:   Plague.
1734–5:   Crop failure: passage of troops, requisitioning.

At Opatów, near Sandomierz, the story was similar, though aggravated by the raids of a hostile neighbour, Stanisław Jagniński, whose men, having driven off the inhabitants, would

---

* The *kopa* or 'stack' was equivalent to threescore sheaves.

regularly harvest the Lubomirski's crops for themselves.

In such conditions, trade was bound to be affected. At Kanczuga, in 1654–8, 34 per cent of the rye, 24 per cent of the wheat, 12 per cent of the barley, 15 per cent of the hemp, 3 per cent of the oats, and 2 per cent of the buckwheat was actually sold. In the next five-year period, 1659–63, the percentages rose respectively to 37 (rye), 48 (wheat), 29 (barley), 6 (hemp), 10 (oats), and 1 (buckwheat). On a yearly breakdown for corn sold locally as against corn exported beyond the locality fluctuations are still more marked. In 1654, Kanczuga exported 55.2 per cent of its rye, but nothing else. In 1655 and 1656, barely enough was salvaged for sowing, the only sales being small quantities of rye and oats disposed of locally. In 1657, 56.6 per cent of the rye was exported, but again nothing else. In 1658 and 1659, nothing was exported at all, despite a reasonable harvest. The year 1660 when the war ended, was a bumper one, and 58.5 per cent of the rye and 46.4 per cent of the wheat was exported. In 1661, rye at 44.8 per cent held steady, though such wheat as there was, was sold locally. In 1662 and 1663, rye exports at 9.2 per cent and 3.7 per cent dropped in response to the increased wheat exports, which at 50.6 per cent and 57 per cent were the highest of the decade. Taking the ten years as a whole, therefore, average figures are quite misleading. Of the two major grains, rye seems to have ensured the more reliable surplus. Wheat was only exported when both the harvest and external conditions combined to justify sizeable shipments. From total production, large quantities had always to be held back for sowing, for wages in kind, for feeding livestock, for home consumption, for assisting the serfs, for transfer to other less successful estates of the latifundium, for milling, for military deliveries, for storage, or for local sale; and it was only in favourable years that any one estate produced enough to make export worthwhile. In any given year, an estate would tend either to export upwards of half its rye and wheat, or else to export nothing.

In terms of the total grain exports, the Lubomirski latifundium varied in the period 1663–1750 from a minimum of 13 *lasts,* 11 bushels in 1713 to a maximum of 522 *lasts,* 18 bushels in 1729. The statistical average is around 127 *lasts* per annum for those years in which something was exported. The over-all average would be nearer 50 *lasts.* In themselves, these averages are rather meaningless. But they do contrast very strikingly with the average of 533 *lasts* exported annually in the years 1614—49 before the recession, by the Lubomirski estates from a somewhat different territorial base. And they do give a very rough idea of the scale of magnatial grain operations at that time.

The 'social origin' of grain is a problem which greatly exercises historians in Poland at present, without offering any satisfactory solution. If the calculation of magnatial production, for which there are fairly complete records, is so complicated — how much more imprecise must calculations about the gentry or peasantry be, when one has to work without adequate documentation and without any clear economic criteria for distinguishing one class from another. Nor, in quantitative operations, is it easy to make deductions from the known to the unknown. It does not follow that a 'middle nobleman' owning 3 villages in the vicinity of a magnatial complex of 15 villages, would necessarily have produced grain or grain for sale in proportionate quantities. Economic success responds in geometric progression to the total resources available. Given comparable production methods, unfavourable conditions, which halved the magnate's surplus, could well drive the medium-sized producer from the market altogether and could put the peasant on the breadline. Similarly, favourable conditions which gave the peasant a sack of corn to sell, might give the nobleman a shipload, and might fill the granaries of the magnate for a decade. But again, production methods were not comparable.

Despite these forceful reservations, studies on the production of Polish grain have produced some interesting results, provoking a lively discussion parallel to the debate on the Rise, or Fall, of the Gentry in England.[5] From this, it now seems clear that the magnatial producers enjoyed no special advantage in the grain trade, certainly not before 1650. It is also clear that regional differences were considerable. A detailed study of the Włocławek toll-books between 1537 and 1576 has shown that the heartland of the grain supply lay in Wielkopolska, Kujawy, and Mazowsze, which were all areas where great landed fortunes were signally sparse. Royal Prussia, too, whose grain boom seems to have spanned the years 1570–1620, made a large and regular contribution, whereas Małopólska, Volhynia, and Podolia only contributed in favourable years.

Having grown his corn, however, the producer had still to take it to Danzig, since delivery at the 'Green Bridge' was usually the producer's responsibility under the terms of the contract. In modern times, the only efficient way to transport grain in bulk was by water.

Danzig was connected with the interior by a complex network of rivers. All the main tributaries of the Vistula – the Narew, Pilica, Bug, Wieprz, Wislok, Dunajec, and San were navigable. All possessed river ports, called *pali* – Tarnów, Jarosław, Lubartów, Uściług – where warehouses and boatyards were sited. The farthest reaches in the Beskidy, in the Carpathians, or in Volhynia were over 600 miles from the sea. In the eighteenth century, the Vistula system was linked to the Warta-Brda by the Bydgoszcz Canal (1771), to the Pripet-Dnieper by the Królewski (Royal) Canal (1775–84), and to the Szczara-Niemen by the Ogiński Canal (1765–84).

Riverboats of the period came in six or seven varieties. They were bought, or hired with their crew in the upstream ports, and disposed of in Danzig at the end of the voyage. In 1796, Beneventus von Lessenau, *Kreisingenieur* of Zamość, made a thoroughgoing survey from which costs and prices have been calculated in detail:

A	B	C	D	E	F	G
SZKUTA	Marktschiff	(Raft)	20	1,140	2,500	8
DUBAS	Boot	(Barge)	14	800	1,500	8
BYK	plattesSchiff	(Flatboat)	12	600	500	8
ŁYŻWA	–	(Pontoon)	10	600	1,250	8
KOZA	kleines Marktschiffe	(Raft)	10	500	750	8
GALAR	Galera	(Lighter)	8	400	180	8
BERLINKA	Oder Kahn	(Skiff)	6	300	1,250	8

A, Polish name; B, German name as given by von Lessenau; C, English equivalent; D, Number of Crew; E, Maximum Grain Cargo, in *korcy* (Polish bushels); F, Purchase Price, in Rhenish guilders; G, Average freight cost, in zł. per *last*.[6]

Of these vessels, the *szkuta* was by far the most important for the Grain Trade. The massive, shallow raft, consisting of a floating platform of whole timbers, surmounted by a square silo-container for the grain and a lean-to shelter for the crew, was largely dependent on the current for propulsion, but could be assisted by sailors punting from the sides or sometimes by a huge square sail. It was guided from the stern by a long steering oar, and was frequently linked in chains to form a convoy. On arrival in Danzig, it was broken up, and sold for timber.

The magnates could organize transport themselves. Teams of serfs working as labourers, harvesters, wagoners, boatbuilders and rafters, saw the grain all the way from the fields to the sea.

The public at large had to rely on the professional organizations. The Danzig firms worked closely with specialist shippers who supervised collection, storage, loading, excise and custom payments, and delivery. As distinct from the merchants themselves, the shipper (*szypr*) was usually a Pole. He divided his time between granary management at places like Kazimierz Dolny or Włocławek, and administration of the ship during the river voyage. He would be assisted by a secretary (*pisarz*) and a quartermaster (*szafarz*). The actual sailing of the ship was handled by a guild of boatmen whose members were available for hire at all the river ports. The *rotman* or 'masterboatman' who controlled the crew, and the *sternik* or 'steersman' were skilled craftsmen, who learned their trade after a long period as *'frycz'* or apprentice. Wages depended on the length of the voyage and the time of year, and on varying demand. Those quoted by von Lessenau in 1796 for a *szkuta* on the Zamość-Danzig run were paid in ducats, in addition to full board: shipper 100; secretary 50; quartermaster 20; masterboatman 24; steersman 14; cook 2; 15 sailors at 2–4 ducats: Total, 255.

Timing of the voyage was an important consideration. Grain prices in Danzig fluctuated from season to season, and great efforts were made to effect delivery in the early months of the year when prices were high. Producers from the far south would usually consign their grain to the river in September and October, reaching mid-way points for winter

storage. But the main shipment began in the Spring, as soon
as the ice melted. Hence its name, the *frujor* (Früjahr), when
scores of rafts would race along the swollen waters of the
Vistula to meet the foreign fleet. In June and July, both the
river and the market tended to be low, and traffic slight.

The gentleman-producer lacking his own transport was
faced with three possibilities, therefore. Firstly he could sell
his grain in the local market, where both his costs and his
receipts would be small. Secondly, he could sell it to a neighbour or to a shipper — who would charge him commission to
add it to shipments of their own. Or thirdly, he could take it
to Danzig himself. The last alternative was both risky and
adventurous, but it stood the best chance of making a good
profit, and for personal reasons was often the most attractive.
In 1670, Jan Chrystostom Pasek faced exactly this problem.
Having leased a small property at Smogorzów in Małopolska,
he had succeeded in producing a modest surplus. Some of his
cronies advised him to stay at home, but, like the old soldier
he was, he decided to take his chance. In his Memoirs he
relates how it paid off:

When I lived at Smorgorzów, I went rafting for the first time. As I had
no experience, I asked the advice of the old skippers and was told that
up there (in Danzig) I'd be swindled, being such a novice. By God's
Grace, however, I sold my wheat for a higher price than they did themselves. It happened like this. Two noblemen, Piegłowski, the District
Supervisor of Ujście Solne, and Opacki, the Cup-Bearer of Warsaw, had
quarrelled in Danzig with a group of merchants, who thereupon decided
to buy nothing from them at all. I, being next in line, was paid 150
złoties for my wheat, just to spite those two. I sold it to a Mr Jarlach.
The others (from our convoy) had to plead with the merchants to do
business, and were then paid at only 110 złoties. Thus, they who had
warned that I would be fleeced, were fleeced themselves.[7]

The annual voyage down the Vistula soon became a prominent institution of Polish social life. Together with war, it
provided one of the few occasions when provincial noblemen
could see the world at large, offering excitement and adventure to generations of men whose experience was otherwise
confined by the bounds of their estates. It was a major cultural
stimulus, spawning a rich new vocabulary for the Polish
language, and inspiring numerous works of prose and verse,

not least Sebastian Fabian Klonowic's poem *Flis, to jest spuszczanie statków Wisłą i inszymi rzekami do niej przypadającymi,* published in 1596.[8] *Flis* — whose title may be translated as 'Rafting, or the Descent of Ships on the Vistula and on Other Rivers Flowing into it' — describes a river journey at the end of the sixteenth century. It purports to be a handbook for the traveller setting out for the first time, and is full of detailed explanations and practical hints. Like most works of the time, it affects an air of classical learning; but its charm lies in the feelings of naïve wonder and merry enjoyment which the voyage inspires. Having contrasted the homely, landlocked world of rural Poland with the strange, foreign world of ships and the sea, Klonowic proceeds to tell his reader how to divide his produce for sale and for keeping; how to buy a raft; how to lay in provisions; how to doff his cap to the guildsmen; how to steer; and above all how to deal with the Danzig merchants at his destination. He provides a short glossary of rafting jargon, mainly German in origin, and warns against the dangers of running aground, of hitting one of the sunken logs — which were called *wilki* (wolves) — or fouling the moorings of a floating watermill — which from the characteristic noise of the mill-wheel were called *bździeły* (farters), or most embarrassingly, of colliding with the great wooden boom as one entered the port of Danzig. On the fashionable model of Renaissance topography, he also includes a detailed gazetteer of all the riverside landmarks from the bridge at Warsaw to the Green Bridge in Danzig. One by one, all the towns, settlements, islands, tributaries, boundaries, castles, abbeys, and churches, that can be seen from the river, are mentioned, together with the associated historical anecdotes or legends. There is Czerwińsk, with its convent of Lateran Canons; Płock, with its tall cathedral crowned with two golden crosses; Włocławek, with its toll-house and brewery; Nieszawa, with its long red row of brick silos; and the ruined castle of Zlotoriya; there is ancient Thorn:

> . . . rich in Virtue,
> Where the will of earnest burghers fosters
> Peace and Modesty, where Honesty prospers
> And Justice . . .

Thorn, whose towering walls, spires, and domes 'plough the sky'; there is the River Brda, famous for its salmon; the Hell's Gate Rapids below Fordon; Chełmno — river port for Ducal Prussia, Najburg, where Flemish settlers had constructed an elaborate system of dykes; and the town of Gniewa, whose name comes from the 'anger' of the River Nogat, who, jealous of 'Vanda Vistula, daughter of Krakus the Dragon-King', flounced out of court and found her own way to the sea. There were places to avoid — like the Nieznakowski Island above Płock which harboured a notorious clan of bandits, or another island by the bridge at Thorn inhabited by the city's venereal outlaws. But there were places, too, where every rafter should call — like the Church of St. Barbara, at Sartawice, where the hymn of their patroness 'was sung by the boatmen and learned by the apprentices', or like the 'Ganskrug', 'the Goose Inn', where one took one's last refreshment before crossing the Danzig boom.

Most memorable, perhaps, is Klonowic's picture of the Polish traveller when 'like a true knight', he actually enters Danzig. Gazing in wonder at the granaries, the vast warehouses for timber and potash, the 'artful' elevators and cranes, the sluices, weighbridges, engines, turntables, and not least at the ocean-going ships, with their high castles and crow's-nests — which, as a countryman, he calls *bocianie gniazda* (storks' nests) — confused, elated, and suspicious, he wanders along the quayside to find a buyer for his corn, and a lawyer for his contract:

> Your smart-suited *bosmen* wait here for their clients,
> For gentry from far afield, and for merchants.
> 'For Sale!', 'Buy up!', 'It's a deal!', 'Come off it!'
> Each looks to his profit.
> Smile, if you're selling; wince, when you buy;
> And pick on a dullard, not a bright sort of guy . . .
> Will he pay cash? Insist in advance.
> Your translator's greeting should await his response.
> Or, *sprechen* yourself, if you think you can barter;
> But watch for a sharper.
> In a difficult suit you'll need that translator,
> And a professional agent, a shrewd operator.
> Or else, with those dealers, you'll find yourself pratin'
> In broken Latin:

'Heus, mane, quieso faciesque grautum
Indica nobis, puer, advocautum,
Omnium sub quo dirimuntur omnes
Iudice causae.'
The German's reply is as gross as his grammar
With no sense of shame. 'Pocz my old Mama,'
He cries: 'Kfyd folunt? aut me tomini Poloni
Indice quaerunt?
Hic vere causas adzit adfocatus.
Hiudicat fero dirimitque nostro
More scultetus, focitatque Teuto
Nomine Schultzum.
Ficus est longus, tomus alta toto
Eminet fico; patet illa cuifis
Ista sculteti domus est, in dzilla
Dziura ministrat.'
You ask your friend, 'Hear that Martin!
Does this *Kryksman* speak Latin,
Or is it German? . . .'
Then at the Rathaus, at the Court of Appeal
Your contract is sealed.
As the clocktower's melodies chime on, hour by hour
And you wait at the Prussian Registry, by the door,
A Russian month will pass! How you've been flayed
By this Grain Trade![9]

From an early date, Danzig acquired a reputation for gaiety
and vice. Writing in the first half of the sixteenth century,
Jan Dantiscus, poet laureate of the Empire and later Bishop
of Warmia, likened the sins of his native city to those of
Nineveh in a tirade entitled *Ionas Propheta* (Jonah the
Prophet):

Urbs nova, dives opum, Dantiscum sive Gedanum.
　　Accipe, divina quae tibi mente loquor!
Est breve tempus adhuc: si non peccata relinques
　　Hoc quibus exundas tempore, fracta rues.
Crevisti cito, sic etiam superis male grata
　　Decresces; instant iam tua fata tibi.
Impietas, fastus, luxus, tria monstra, ruinam
　　Iam tibi, ni fuerint prorsus abacta, parant . . .*

(* *see note overleaf*)

Yet time brought little improvement. In 1663, a French tourist called Payen, from Meaux-sur-Marne, described the scene in a Danzig wine-cellar where he was befriended by a Polish nobleman who had just succeeded in selling his corn:

We were on the point of leaving, when a man some six feet tall came in. He had a clean-shaven face, and eyes set in deep folds and wrinkles. It was a Polish nobleman in the company of some fifteen retainers . . . As soon as he saw us, he came over with a declaration of friendship, shaking our hands, and pressing us to accept his expressions of respect and chivalry . . . *We* had to resort to Latin . . . He said he was ill, and that he had been looking for two weeks for someone who might confirm his belief that debauchery was a better cure than dieting . . . After we had consumed some fifteen or sixteen tumblers, my colleague offered him his pipe . . . But *he,* not being familiar with tobacco, thrust the bowl into his mouth, drawing the full draught of burning smoke straight into his stomach. . . . He said that tobacco should be drunk not blown into the air and wasted . . . Suddenly, he rushed from the table and seizing a lighted candelabra started to bang his head on the wall and to writhe on the floor. He was foaming at the mouth like a bull, and looked as if the fury would kill him . . . But then a little vomiting made him more presentable . . . Next he staggered blindly in my direction, smothered me with passionate kisses, and announced that he would give me one of his daughters, together with ten thousand pounds and two hundred serfs . . . In honour of the forthcoming marriage, we drank toast after toast . . . Then I look, and he is stretched out on his back once more, but calling for wine and urging us to drink to the confusion of the Turk and the ruin of the Ottoman Empire . . . By now, he had assured me I was really a Pole, and that I ought to dress like one. Starting with his crimson cloak fastened with sculpted silver pins, he began to strip, and to dress me up from head to foot in his own clothes. Unbuckling his sabre, he ordered me to kiss it and fastened it to my side, declaring that Poland owed all her Freedom to it . . . Meanwhile, I was desperately planning my escape . . .[11]

What a wonderful place Danzig must have appeared to the country visitor! In 1600, with 50,000 inhabitants, it was five times larger than the royal capital in Warsaw and more than

---

* New City, Rich Town, Danzig alias Gedanum,/Accept the prophecy which I am fain to tell you!/The time hereto is brief: if you abandon not the sins/with which at present you abound, you will be dashed in pieces./You have increased quickly, so too/will you decline. Your Fates are at hand./Impiety, Pride, Luxury, Triple Portents, already prove your ruin/unless they be cast aside . . .[10]

three times as large as Cracow or Poznań. It was a republic
within the Republic. Under the privileges initiated by
Kazimierz Jagiellończyk and extended by Batory, it enjoyed
self-government. It raised its own finances, and minted its
own currency. It had its own militia, expert in siege warfare,
and until the 1640s its own warships, which formed the core
of the Royal Fleet. Its society was organized in an elaborate
system of castes and guilds, each with their own exclusive rules
and membership. In the eyes of someone just arrived from a
village of the interior, where the year-long toil of scores of
peasants barely sufficed to produce a few sacks of corn, it
must have looked incredibly rich and prosperous. Its three
thousand workshops turned out all the imaginable luxuries of
the day — velvet, silk, furniture, jewellery, books, paintings.
Above all, it was a shop-window of European life. Its people
were in touch with all the latest news, fashions, and heresies.
They affected Spanish clothes and lived in houses built in the
Flemish style. They travelled abroad, and welcomed all sorts
of refugees from Dutch weavers to French Huguenots. The
patricians, when not talking business, mixed in a high life of
politics, music, libraries, collecting, and of elegant villas surrounded by formal gardens. The artisans and workmen
sweated in an atmosphere of high insecurity and great opportunity, where wages were good but competition fierce, where
privileges were jealously guarded with factions and tumults,
and where municipal charity looked harshly on idleness.
Danzig was an anthill of work, prosperity, and culture,
common enough in Italy or the Netherlands, but unique in
Poland. As such it undoubtedly presented a superlative attrac-
tion, a materialist Mecca to which the Polish nobleman was
drawn and tempted — to buy and sell, to be ruined or to make
his fortune, to load himself with trinkets and luxuries for his
house and family, to hear the news and gaze at the sights, and
at last, relieved and exhausted, to sail against the current of
the Vistula on the long, slow journey home.

To support a high standard of life, the export trade in grain
obviously had to be complemented with a wide variety of
other commodities. Exports were matched by imports. The
ships which took the grain also carried wool, flax, leather,
timber, and metals. On the inward voyage, they brought in

manufactures, colonial products, fish, alcohol, salt, and coal.

The structure of Danzig's trade was in fact very complex. On the inland side, it was connected with all parts of the Republic. To the west, there were connections with Germany, especially Silesia, a source of fine cloth, high-grade metal-work, tools, arms, and implements: to the south, with Cracow and the Danube Basin; to the east, with Łuków, the centre of the cattle and leather trade, with the Ukraine, whence valuable shipments of potash and saltpetre derived; and by extension with Muscovy, whence in 1600 alone some 800,000 fur pelts were delivered to the market at Gniezno. Overseas, there were connections with all the active markets of the world. The over-all picture fluctuated considerably. But the collected statistics for one specimen year, 1641, provide a cross-section of the quantity and variety of the main items:

Foreign Trade of Danzig, 1641

	Exported Goods	Value: in Prussian groats	%
A.	Corn	19,693,862	71.3
B.	Other agricultural produce	2,302,172	8.4
C.	Processed food products	251,290	0.9
D.	Timber etc.	1,022,550	3.8
E.	Metals, minerals	3,184,996	11.4
F.	Manufactures	1,104,118	3.7
G.	Fish (Re-export)	115,319	0.5
		27,674,307	100.0

	Imported Goods		
1.	Manufactures	7,041,870	40.7
2.	Colonial products	3,776,509	21.2
3.	Fish and fish-oil	1,801,813	10.4
4.	Alcohol, Wines and Spirits	1,775,513	10.3
5.	Salt	357,121	2.1
6.	Agricultural produce	171,206	0.9
7.	Fuels, coal, etc.	1,894,012	10.9
8.	Leather, furs, skins	530,165	3.5
		17,348,209	100.0[12]

During this era of prosperity, Danzig handled some three-quarters of the Republic's total foreign trade.

For the eighteenth century, the most minute information on commodities, prices, and the movement of ships has survived in the reports of the French 'Résidents' in Danzig. In the course of the Great Northern War, the government in Paris was seriously disturbed by the growth of Russian power in the Baltic, and by the corresponding decline in French trade. Danzig was adversely affected by the Russian blockade of the Swedish coast, and by severe competition from Königsberg. As a result, the French ministers in Danzig were ordered to keep a detailed record of commercial activities in the port, and to forward their findings to Paris. At the end of each year, lists were compiled to summarize the quantity, value, and destination or provenance of every imaginable commodity, from amber (crude) to marinated sturgeon, exported or imported, during the previous twelve months. Notes were made of fluctuations of prices in Danzig, for comparison with equivalent information in France. Most interestingly perhaps, a special record was kept of every single vessel that entered the habour. A report of 23 October 1717, for example, listed the end-of-season traffic in the five weeks since the end of September. (See Table on p. 275.) It is hard to see that the French Government made much use of these reports, as so few French ships were actually engaged. One suspects that the Résident's commercial interests filled in the long winter evenings between his much more important activities as a military intelligence officer. The French were far more anxious to know the state of the Russian Fleet in Kronstadt than the price of potash in Danzig, although Captains Doring, Kambie, and Rodgers could probably have told them of both.

By this time, foreign merchants other than the French were also feeling the pinch. The campaigns of the Great Northern War and of the civil wars in the Republic had disrupted the commercial life of the interior, whilst the external demand was much reduced. The situation was described in a memorandum prepared by a group of British merchants in Danzig and forwarded to the Commission of Trade in London by George I's ambassador to Poland-Saxony, Richard Vernon:

A State of the British Trade in Dantzig Anno 1715
The British trade to this place has been for 20 years last under a very sensible decay in all its branches. The most obvious causes thereof are

Captain	Home Port	Out of	Cargo	Bound for	Cargo
1. Jakub Doring	Amsterdam	Petersburg	Oxhides	Copenhagen	Plums, Hops
2. Andreas Morrow	Kirkcaldy	Kirkcaldy	—	Scotland	300 Bordillons, Soap, Linen, Dowels
3. Mathew Spake	Newcastle	Gothenburg	Whetstones	Amsterdam	42 l. Rye, 5 l. Potash
4. Alex. Steward	Kirkcaldy	Kirkcaldy	26 herrings	Scotland	Soap, Hemp, Wood, Rope
5. Johann Nordstrom	Lübeck	Lübeck	Ballast	Lübeck	70 l. Rye
6. Hans Hannson	Lübeck	Lübeck	Spices	Lübeck	30 l. Rye, Prunes, Hops
7. Marten Schwerdfeger	Colberg	Colberg	Sealskins	Colberg	45 l. Rye
8. Michel Blank	Colberg	Copenhagen	Herrings	Colberg	13½ l. Rye, 2 l. Barley, Soap
9. Magnus Kehlman	Danzig	Newcastle	Scottish salt	Amsterdam	45 l. Wheat, 105 l. Rye
10. Gerrit Lolling	Amsterdam	Bordeaux	Indigo, Molasses, Turps, 728 barrels of Wine	Amsterdam	95 l. Wheat, 55 l. Rye, Canvas, Hops
11. Herman Tokes	Amsterdam	Scotland	Chalk	Flensburg	30 l. Rye
12. Hertie Jansen	Danzig	France	Salt, Molasses	Amsterdam	60 l. Wheat, 65 l. Rye, Feathers, Canvas
13. Robert Gray	Leith	Scotland	Salted Herring	Lübeck	25 l. Rye
14. Walter Gray	Peterhead	Scotland	Herrings	Scotland	Bordillon, Soap, Linen, Hemp, Hungarian wine
15. Dirk Joppes	Haarlem	Bordeaux	Wine, Vinegar, Molasses	Amsterdam	70 l. Rye
16. Andreas Tenen	Lübeck	Lübeck	Spices	Lübeck	106 l. Rye
17. Jan Glasemeister	Lübeck	Lübeck	Spices	Lübeck	28 l. Rye, Soap, Cloth, Wax, Tar
18. Albrecht Schaff	Amsterdam	Amsterdam	Spices	Amsterdam	72 l. Rye, Feathers, Wool, Canvas
19. Dirk Hannsen	Amsterdam	Amsterdam	Spices	Amsterdam	35 l. Wheat, 81 l. Rye, Potash, Hops
20. Wm. Kambie	Yarmouth	Petersburg	—	London	Potash, Feathers
21. Frank Rodgers	London	Petersburg	—	London	Potash[13]

the long warr and late plague in Poland by which the countrey being extreamly impoverished and in many places depopulated, the consumption of all foreign products is consequently very lessened, But while
trade in general suffers greatly by these calamities, there are other
reasons for the decay of ours in particular in some of its branches as:

1. In that of Northern cloth. Very great quantities of Northern cloths
called dozins have formerly been vended here. The present decrease and
almost loss of that trade is in a great measure occasioned by the manufacture of coarse cloth in Silesia, which . . . being brought hither by
land custom-free is sold in great quantities in the prejudice of our cloth
which being imported by sea pays a very high duty (especially of late
years much higher than at the neighbouring port of Koenigsberg) . . .

2. The finer sorts of mixed and dyed cloth worn in Prussia and Poland
are now imported from Holland, from whence in proportion to the
whole import, the quantity now brought is ten times as great as formerly.
The Hollands cloth is thin and slight, their colours cheap and gaudy,
neither the one nor the other so durable as ours, but suits the humour
of the buyers here who are pleased with what looks fine and costs little.

3. Considerable quantities of crown rash have been formerly imported
hither directly from Britain on British accounts. What is now sold here,
is by foreigners who import it from Holland and Hamburgh, to which
places tis sent white from Britain and (they having dying wares cheaper
than in Britain) is there dyed and fitred for sale. Whereby not only the
advantage of the dying it at home, but the profit upon its sales abroad
is lost to His Majestys subjects.

4. The quantity of tobacco now imported from Britain is so in-
considerable, that we may rackon that amonst the lost branches of
our trade. English rolld tobacco was formerly a most current commodity
here, and very great quantities thereof consumed. But of late years the
Hollanders, affording the growth of their countrey and Germany rolled
up in a Virginia weed at half the price which ours used to be sold for,
do now supply the whole countrey . . . The consumption of Virginia
and Maryland leaf tobacco is likewise extreamly diminished here and
most of the leaf tobacco consumed grows in, and is brought by land
from, Pomerania.

As to herrings, lead, tyn, leather, and groceries, the decay of these
trades is owing to the miserable poverty of the countrey. The grocery
trade is driven chiefly by the Hollanders whose stock being very large
and way of living extream parsimonious, they content themselves with
so small a profit that they have engrossed almost all that part of the
trade from Britain hither to themselves.

Our trade from hence to Britain is chiefly in linnen, wood and pottash.
Since the late imposition on soap made in Britain we have observed the

quantity of pottash exported hence thither less and to Holland greater than before, which we take to proceed from a clandestine importation of soap from Holland to Britain, the high duty tempting people to such indirect practices, whereby His Majesty is not only defrauded of the additional duty on soap imported but of the customs on all the ingredients which would have been used in making it in England, not to mantion the injury such a clandestine trade does us in the imployment of our people and shipping. William Morgan, William Hobman, Jonathan Beaumont, Joshua Kenworthy, Andrew Marjoribanks, Will Miller, James Adies, John Roberts, Henry Culter, Alexander Coutts, John Wightman, Rich. Wilson.[14]

At first sight, the most striking feature of Danzig's Foreign Trade was the extraordinary imbalance of export over import. In 1565, the figures for Danzig and Elbing together reveal an incredible ratio of 6:1. By 1620, the Crown Marshal of Poland, Mikołaj Wolski, was complaining that the ratio had fallen to a mere 5:2. In 1641, judging by Danzig's customs returns, it was down to 2:1. If these figures could be accepted at face value, they would seem to be proof of fairy-tale riches. Yet, taking the Republic as a whole, the Balance of Trade cannot be calculated so easily. The positive balance of Danzig's sea trade was offset on the one hand by leakage of gold and money on the overland trade, especially in the south-east, and on the other hand by the activities of neighbouring ports. Elbing — a staple of the English Eastland Company — was largely concerned with the import of cloth, and had a passive balance. Presumably this would have encouraged a triangular flow of money between Danzig, Elbing, and their common hinterland. Königsberg, in contrast, which dominated the Niemen basin, was a direct competitor for Danzig, exporting the products of Lithuania and East Prussia and importing large quantities of cloth.[15]

Further problems arise in connection with the Baltic Trade in general. From *ad valorem* payments at the Sound, it is clear that in the seventeenth century the English merchants were operating a tidy surplus. But it is far from clear who was funding the deficit. Much work remains to be done on the labyrinthine workings of credit. Specialists are constantly worried by the accuracy of their varying indices of measurement, or by the representativeness of their sample years. No final conclusions have been reached. What can be said with certainty is that the figures for Danzig's balance in the sea trade in the period 1550—1650 accurately reflect neither the over-all balance for the Republic nor the changing situation in later years.

Undoubtedly, profits were there for the making. Until 1650, grain prices in Amsterdam were usually about twice as high as in Danzig, whilst a similar price differential prevailed between Danzig and the Polish provinces. Average profits for the period 1600—50 have been calculated as follows: for Danzig rye-brokers, +29.7 per cent; for Danzig wheat brokers, +28.6 per cent; for Danzig potash brokers, +43.5 per cent; for wheat exported to Spain, +83.4 per cent; for rye exported to Amsterdam, +62.1 per cent. These calculations, especially those for export, are open to severe doubts, notably as a result of variable currency values and of corresponding losses made on various imported commodities. But if the trade was basically unprofitable one cannot imagine why so many ships sailed hopefully to Danzig year after year.[16]

Less can be said for individual voyages, where the prospects were as fickle as the winds that blow. Occasionally, however, records survive to illustrate the minutiae of the sailing of a single ship. Such is the case with a venture of Tewes Gercken, a Dutchman, who in 1621 sent a 40-*last* ship from Danzig to Aberdeen. To spread the risk, he shared the outlay among five other shipowners — Hans Foss, Frantz Flucker, Wilhelm Brun, Hans Grefe, and Hans Schultze. Each held a one-eighth share, except for Schultze and Gercken himself, who both took two shares each. From Danzig, he took a cargo, presumably of grain, which was sold for 533 zł. 10 groszy. From Aberdeen, he carried 27 *lasts* and 4 barrels of coal, bought for 230 zł. and sold for 364 zł. 10 groszy in Danzig. His costs included sums for the wages of four sailors and a cook, for food and lodging, for port and passport dues, for compensation to a vessel which was struck by mistake in the Danish Sound, and for repairs. (See Table on p. 279.) At the end of the voyage, each shareholder received 61 zł. 20 groszy, per share. Given an original outlay which must have been in the order of 432 zł. (or 54 zł. per share) the return represented a return of some 14 per cent over about a month. In other words, in spite of

INCOME:		zł.	gr.	%
Cargo sold in Scotland		533	10	
Cargo sold in Danzig		364	–	
Remaining from previous voyage		46		
	Total	943	10	

EXPENSES:		zł.	gr.	%
Food (including one night's lodging for the captain in a Scottish inn)		63	10	16
Ship's supplies and repairs		7	13	1
Port and Sound dues		55	–	12
Crew's wages		43	20	10
Purchase of coal in Aberdeen		230	–	53
Compensation to damaged ship		35		8
	Total	433	43	(100)

the collision in the Sound, it was a profitable trip.[17]

The return of Gercken to Danzig, and of hundreds of captains like him, formed the last link in the chain of the Vistula Trade. The foreign demand for grain, which attracted the ships in the first place, had been supplied. The Polish grain had been transported down the Vistula by the producer, bought by the Danzig merchant, sold to the Dutch exporter, and delivered to a foreign port. Now the ships had returned with a cargo of goods for import, and lay waiting with empty holds for the next shipment of grain. The cycle was complete.

* * * * *

The social effects of the Vistula Trade form the subject of a continuing controversy, whose contradictory findings can give no clear guidance to the general inquirer. It would be invidious with the present level of research to state unequivocally that Poland–Lithuania witnessed a phenomenon called 'Export-led Serfdom', where the intensification of feudal services was caused exclusively by the economic pressures of the Grain Trade. At the same time it would be foolish to deny that the spectacular growth of the export trade in grain was accompanied by an equally marked rise in the conditions of serfdom, and that in one way or another these twin socio-economic developments of the sixteenth and early seventeenth centuries were closely connected. According to one plausible line of argument, rising prices in Danzig created a sustained demand for grain, which in turn put increasing pressure on the one element of the rural economy, labour, which was capable of more intensive exploitation. In order to meet the demand, the noble landowners exacted more work and harsher conditions from their peasants. As the only enfranchised social estate, they could persuade the King and the Sejm to change the law to their advantage, and could administer existing law at their own convenience. The peasants, unable in general to compete on the open market with the larger producers, gradually found that acquiescence in the new terms of serfdom was preferable to swimming against the tide in the old, free, but insecure and increasingly hungry manner. It is not that the Vistula Trade created serfdom. The *pańszczyzna* or the 'lord's right to unpaid labour services' was known much earlier. What the Grain Trade did was to stimulate tendencies already in evidence. Like the Cotton Trade in America, it drove existing inequalities between landowners and workers to extremes, and as the absolute control of the one over the other was perpetuated by law, turned a casual phenomenon into the basis of social and economic life. Serfdom in Poland—Lithuania was regularized during roughly the same period as slavery in America; and it lasted almost as long. In the wider context, it belongs to that second wave of serfdom which has been identified in various parts of East and Central Europe and which has been given the generic title of 'Neo-serfdom'.[18]

From the peasant's point of view, the key to serfdom lay in the security of possession which it promised to families unable to support themselves in a cash economy. By putting his labour at the disposition of the lord, the peasant was guaranteed possession of the family plot which otherwise he might have been obliged to sell. So long as the conditions of his submission were tolerable, serfdom was seen as an improvement, not to say a progressive development, in the peasant's fortunes. Whilst the lord could discipline the peasant by the threat of eviction, the peasants could easily damage their lord's fortunes by idleness, drunkenness, sabotage, arson, and ultimately by the threat of flight. A nobleman who offended his serfs, or who drove them away, was heading for disaster. It was clearly in the best interests of both lord and serf to work together in an atmosphere of mutual understanding. However, in the course of the sixteenth century, the conditions of serfdom did deteriorate. In 1496, it was enacted that only one peasant could leave each village each year, and only for approved purposes such as education or craft training. By this measure, the mass of the peasantry were effectively tied to the land. In 1521, the royal courts were closed to pleas where a peasant wished to appeal against his lord. From then on the serfs of the nobles' estates lived entirely at the mercy of their masters. They were dependent not only legally but economically and in almost every detail of their daily lives — for permission to marry, for permission to go to market, for permission to go to school. In addition to rising demands for unpaid labour service, they owed their master rent in cash or in kind, tithes for the priest, and taxes for the King.

The stratification of the peasantry was modified, but not destroyed. A small class of prosperous peasants was able to resist the advances of serfdom. By buying their exemption from labour dues, they could keep their personal freedom; and by employing wage-workers, they could share in the benefits of landowning. They were all set for social advancement into the ranks of the commercial bourgeoisie or even of the nobility. In general, however, the former economic viability of the independent peasant farmers, variously known as *kmieć, gbur,* or *włóknik,* declined, and they were inexorably pushed into varying degrees of dependence on their noble neighbours. At the same time, the most numerous class of peasant smallholders — variously known as *zagrodnik* (smallholder), *chałupnik* (cottager), or *ogrodnik* (gardener), provided the main source of recruits for serfdom. Oddly enough, the poorest class of landless peasants, such as the *komornik* (tenant farmer), the *kątnik* (patch-farmer), or the *parobek* (hired hand), possessing no landed assets with which to attract a prospective noble master, had a better chance of escaping the harshest impositions of feudalism.

Important regional differences persisted. In Royal Prussia, tenant farming and cash rents continued to occupy an important sector of the peasantry. In Lithuania, in contrast, where the manorial system was slow to develop, rents were usually paid in kind. In Podolia and Ukraine, on lands opened up by noble colonization, the peasant pioneers were offered ten, twenty, or even thirty years' enjoyment of their land free of labour services.

In the Polish countryside, the principal institution linked with the rise of serfdom was the Folwark — a form of manorial estate specially adapted for the efficient use of serf labour, and, within the technical limitations of the period, for the maximum production of grain. Its name derives from the German *Vorwerk,* meaning originally 'buildings adjacent to the manor' and later 'demesne farm'. Over some 300 years, it became a characteristic feature of the countryside, leaving its mark both on Polish society and on Polish topography. (See Map 14.)

The Folwark developed out of earlier village communities already based on the noble household, and had predecessors in the medieval *praedia militaria* or 'military estate', which had been designed for the upkeep of the knighthood. It took shape gradually, by expanding the lord's holding at the expense of those of the peasants, by land purchase, by agreement, or by the absorption of marginal waste, forest, or unused plots. As it depended on peasant labour, it had nothing to gain from evictions; but it transformed the ancient strip-holdings into large demesne fields, leaving a separate, smaller area for the peasants' individual plots. By 1560–70, its average size in the Kingdom of Poland exclusive of Prussia has been calculated at 3.6 łan, that is, 60 hectares or 148 acres. Although some examples on the great ecclesiastical estates may have reached 20 łan (823 acres), encompassing a dozen settlements or more, others occupied as little as 1 łan (41 acres). Its typical lay-out — with the peasant cottages hugging the fringes of the great house and the enclosed farm buildings — remained unchanged until the nineteenth century. Only then, with the ending of serfdom and labour services, did enclosures and evictions change the pattern once again. Even so, at no time did the folwark system monopolize agrarian land. In the Lustracja of 1564–6 affecting 1,940 royal villages in the Kingdom, only 591, or less than one-third, were run as folwarks. In the review of the Lubomirski latifundium of 1739,

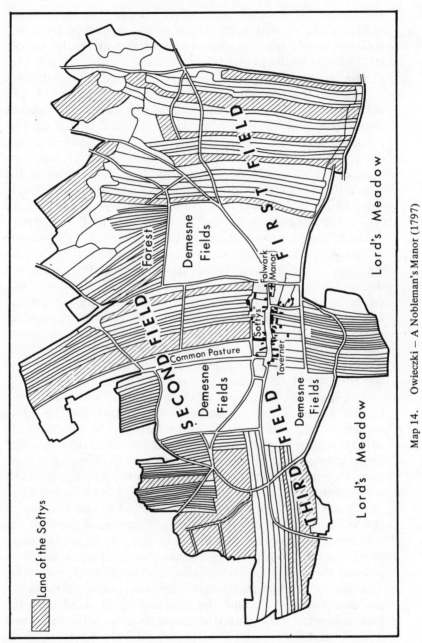

Map 14. Owieczki – A Nobleman's Manor (1797)

FIRST FIELD

SECOND FIELD

THIRD FIELD

Lord's Meadow

Lord's Meadow

Forest

Demesne Fields

Demesne Fields

Demesne Fields

Common Pasture

Folwark Manor

Sołtys

Taverner

Land of the Sołtys

there were 213 folwarks among 940 villages. Among the lesser nobility, the typical pattern was to run the home farm as a folwark, whilst keeping one or two villages under the age-old strip system of the peasant tenants.

The labour-force of the Folwark consisted of two distinct categories, the serf-tenants and the specialist personnel. The serfs, usually 15 to 20 families, held private plots to support themselves and in return provided unpaid labour on the demesne land. In medieval times, labour services had not been very exacting, and took the form either of *jutrzyny*, meaning the cultivation of a specified additional plot in the peasant's own time, or else the rather casual *robocizna*, where the peasant had to work 4, 6, 12, or 20 days in the year, or 'whenever asked', at harvest or threshing. In the sixteenth century, however, the principle of the *pańszczyzna tygodniowa*, or 'weekly service', became general. In the first half of the century, 1 or 2 days' labour from sunrise to sunset was demanded every week in return for every łan of peasant land. In the second half, this was rising to 3 and 4 days per week. In the eighteenth century, 6, 7, or even 8 days were demanded. In practical terms, the husband of the peasant family and possibly one or more of his sons spent most of their time working for the lord, whilst his wife and younger children were left to cultivate the family plot and to beat off starvation.[19]

The specialist personnel of the Folwark, numbering 7 or 8 people, enjoyed less burdensome conditions. In the larger villages, there was the *soltys* (in German, *Schultheiss*), an official who seems to have been more the agent of seigneurial jurisdiction, than, as was once supposed, the head of a communal system of peasant self-government. At all events, he enjoyed possession of a large holding freed from labour dues, plus one-sixth of the rents, and one-third of the revenue of the village court. A *włodarz* acted as foreman of the serfs. He also enjoyed land free of service. In the role of management when the lord was not in personal charge, there would be a salaried *dwornik* (bailiff) and, for the female staff, a *dwórka*. The *woźnic* (carter), *parobek* (ploughman), *pasterz* (cowherd), *owczarz* (shepherd), and the milkmaids, all lived near the manor house, and received clothing, boots, daily meals, and a small annual wage of 36—60 groszy paid at Christmas.

From these details, it must be obvious that the degree of agricultural specialization was very low by modern standards. The manager of the Folwark could only think of producing a grain surplus after self-sufficiency had been achieved in milk, meat, wool, bread, vegetables, leather, beer, and all his immediate requirements. On the noble estates, in 1565 average cash incomes for the typical folwark have been calculated at 239 zł. per annum in Małopolska; 142 in Wielkopolska; 186 zł. per annum overall. On the less efficient, larger estates of the Crown, the Church or the magnates, the folwarks were less remunerative. But there is no comparison between the income obtained from folwarks as a whole – 48 zł. per łan under cultivation – and the meagre 2.5 zł. per łan obtained from peasant holdings. It is true, of course, that the folwark's income hides the valuable item of unpaid labour which would otherwise have contributed to the working of the peasant holdings. Notwithstanding, the discrepancy was enormous. The folwark system worked on the assumption that it gave the serf a minimum of land and security whilst maximizing the noble owner's cash profit.[20]

For reasons which are not entirely clear, the productivity of the folwark reached a point at the end of the sixteenth century beyond which it did not progress. Up to that point, the intensification of serfdom can be seen as part of the response to the prospect of increased prosperity. Thereafter, it must be seen as a means of trying to keep pace with a falling standard of living. Serfdom was thus encouraged both by the rise of the Vistula trade, and also, paradoxically, by its decline.

As it turned out, grain was not the best commodity on which to found the fortunes of state and society. The Grain Trade did not develop many skills, techniques, or forms of organization that did not exist already. It did not require any manufacturing process, except for milling, nor any raw materials whose import would have balanced the export of the fruits of the country's labour. It fostered the massive import of foreign currency which was promptly spent on foreign luxuries. But it did nothing to relieve the immobility of rural agrarian society. On the contrary, it tied the peasantry to the land more firmly than ever before, strangulated the development of towns, and underpinned the mounting supremacy of the landowning interest. In short, at the price of several decades of superficial prosperity, it preserved and strengthened the worst aspects of the medieval economy whilst preventing the growth of that variety and flexibility which enabled stronger economies to ride adversity and to grow. How much more fortunate was England, whose sheep nibbled their way through Feudalism at an early date, or Sweden, whose iron girded a tiny nation with continental pretensions!

The state, in particular, gained very little advantage from the Grain Trade. The producers had contrived to frame the laws of property and taxation to suit themselves. Noblemen paid no excise on their own produce nor on goods for their own use. As taxpayers they were assessed according to the land they held, not according to what they produced or what they earned. This meant that the active prosperous producer paid the same as his idle neighbour. In favourable years, the state benefited little from increased prosperity, and accumulated no funds to offset hard times, when the rate of taxation was necessarily low. In later years, central taxation all but ceased. From 1588, the King took one-half of the port dues raised in Danzig, in addition to the Vistula tolls; and these sums were not negligible. (In 1626–9, when Gustavus Adolphus controlled the Vistula, his income from the tolls is supposed to have covered a quarter of his entire expenses in the German War.) But this was no more than the small change of the Vistula Trade at its height. The really big money sped abroad in the profits of Dutch entrepreneurs, or stayed in Danzig in the coffers of the financiers, manufacturers, and merchants. The Danzig patricians were no less wealthy than the great magnates, many of whom were deeply in debt to them. People in Poland who complained of their usurious lending rates – which at 18 or 20 per cent, were three or four times higher than the rate prevalent in Danzig among themselves – or of their shameless bribery of prominent politicians, found that in practice little could be done. As King Stephen Batory ruefully commented, 'The Danzigers shoot with golden bullets.' In 1637, Władysław IV himself borrowed 1 million zł. from George Hewelka of Danzig. It was symptomatic of deeper ills. Danzig lived well off the

PLATE I
OUTPOST OF LATIN
CHRISTENDOM

(Left) Regina Poloniae (Queen of Poland) – The Black Madonna of Częstochowa

(Below) The Epitaph of Jan z Ujazdu (*c.* 1450)

**PLATE II
THE END OF THE
JAGIELLONS**

(Above) J. Simmler, *The
Death of Barbara Radzi-
wiłł (1551)*

(Right) Anon., *Anna Jagiellonka (1523–96)*

PLATE III
THANKS BE TO GOD

(Above) Anon., *'God and Corn will repay'*, The Vistula Grain Trade

(Left) The Crown of the Law – Jewish Ark Curtain from Przedbórz

PLATE IV. THE UNION OF FREE PEOPLES

J. Matejko, *The Union of Lublin, 1569*

B. Bellotto (Canaletto), *Royal Election at Wola, 1764*

PLATE V. A POWER IN THE EAST

J. Matejko, *Stefan Bathory before Pskov, 1581*

Gniński's Embassy to the Porte, 1677 (miniature)

PLATE VI
THE NOBLES'
PARADISE

(Right) Anon., Sebastian Lubomirski, 1536–1613

(Far right) Anon., Katarzyna Ostrogsska, née Lubomirksa

PLATE VII
MONARCHS OF
THE REPUBLIC

(Right) L. de Silvestre,
Augustus the Strong,
1670–1733

(Far right) M. Bacciarelli,
Stanislas-Augustus in
Coronation Robes, 1764

PLATE VIII. RESISTANCE AND DESPAIR

J. Chełmoński, *'Casimir Pułaski at Częstochowa, 1771'*

J. Matejko, *'Rejtan', 1773*

Republic. In more senses than one, the Vistula Trade was essentially a one-way business.

*   *   *   *   *

The decline of the Vistula Trade after 1648 coincided with the decline of the power and prosperity of the Republic as a whole. Many modern historians would propose that the one was the cause of the other. Others, whilst denying such a close causal relationship between economic and political life, would have to admit that the coincidence is more than a little striking.

Certainly, almost all available indices point to the conclusion that in the mid-seventeenth century the Republic of Poland—Lithuania was beset by an irreversible process of economic regression. By 1750, the Republic's economy was considerably weaker, and its inhabitants considerably poorer, than two centuries earlier. Studies based on the lands of the Archbishop of Gniezno, which were scattered across the *Korona,* show that agricultural methods, no less than agricultural production declined dramatically. Taking the year 1500 as index 100, the figures record steady advance in the sixteenth century, catastrophic collapse in the second half of the seventeenth, and only partial recovery in the eighteenth:

	(1500)	(1600)	(1660)	(1800)
Cultivated area	100	110	65 (1685)	94
Grain Production:				
Peasants	100	100	30	63
Folwark	100	125	45	118
Total	100	104	27	63
Livestock	100	86	60	67
Fallow land	13% (1517)	5%	40% (1685)	26% (1787)

According to this sample, the only sector which recovered at all was that of folwark grain production.[22] Most seriously, the grain yields reverted to medieval levels. Rye yields of 1:3, and wheat yields of 1:3½, which were common around 1750, contrast with 1:3½ or 1:5 respectively in 1600.[23] The mass of the population toiled harder and harder, and earned less and less to eat.

The Grain Trade suffered likewise. Although different researchers use different systems of measurement, the pattern

is the same. Following the peak of 1618–19, the figures never
recover. The war decades of the 1650s, 1700s, and 1730s
witness slumps sinking to one-quarter of the 1618 level. In
between, ever more infrequent peak performances never
surpass two-thirds of their early seventeenth-century equiva-
lents. Mączak's figures for Danzig grain passing through the
Danish Sound are typical:

1618	85,000	*lasts*[24]
1644	59,000	*lasts*
1669	47,000	*lasts*
(1680–90) annual average	48,000	*lasts*
(1700–20) annual average	20,000	*lasts*
1724	54,000	*lasts*
(1731–50) annual average	20,000	*lasts*
1751	50,000	*lasts*

Other sources confirm that in 1751 the Republic crossed the
magical barrier of 100,000 *lasts* of exported grain for the first
and only time since 1619. It was the final success of a dying
trade.

Wars undoubtedly caused immense damage to the Vistula
Trade. In particular, in the years between 1648 and 1660,
when the Republic was submerged by wave after wave of
invaders, losses were inflicted as calamitous as those of the
Thirty Years War in Germany. The Republic as a whole lost
one-quarter of its population, eliminating at a stroke the entire
natural increase of the previous century. In Royal Prussia,
mortality was as high as 60 per cent, in the towns of Mazovia
70 per cent. In 1655, Danzig alone lost 9,000 souls from
plague and siege. At Oświęcim (Auschwitz), the Swedes left
15 houses standing out of 500. In the countryside, estates
were sacked and razed, or ruined by confiscation of all their
stock. Similar horrors recurred during the Great Northern War,
the Wars of the Polish and Austrian Successions, the Seven
Years War, and the Wars of the Three Partitions. At such
moments, sailing down the Vistula with rafts laden with food
was not a viable proposition.

Mere destruction, however, does not explain everything. In
some parts of Europe, in neighbouring Bohemia, for example,
the setbacks of the seventeenth century acted as a spur for
future development. In Poland's case, it is necessary to explain

not just the damage of the war years, but, more importantly, the failure to recover during the years of peace. Present-day Polish historians seek the primary cause within the agrarian system, seeing serfdom and the folwark as crucial elements in a vicious circle of increasing exploitation and diminishing returns. Others pay equal attention to the growing deficiencies of both demand and supply. Already in the 1640s, before the wars, ballast sailings from Danzig, which rose from 5.7 per cent in 1641 to 20.5 per cent in 1648, indicate that foreign entrepreneurs were not finding grain in the required quantity or at the right price.[25] In the 1650s, when Dutch merchants were again offering record prices in Danzig, they could not fill their ships. Thereafter, conditions in Western Europe changed, and demand fell. Large tracts of the Netherlands, of France, and of East Anglia were drained, and turned over to cereal production. The Dutch *moederhandel* was gradually overhauled by the French and English, who had new preferences and new routes. As markets and price differentials shifted, there was no longer the same strong incentive for entrepreneurs to send their ships to Danzig. The break in continuity which occurred in the decade after 1648 was sufficient to interrupt people's habits and to sever contacts built up over the preceding century. Like an engine starved of fuel, the Vistula Trade stalled, and, although restarted, was never able to fire again at more than half power. It fell into a vicious crisis of confidence, where diminished demand increasingly damaged the producer's ability to effect supply. Once the Amsterdam Fleet failed to appear in Danzig in its accustomed numbers, the Polish nobleman felt less willing to risk the long river voyage with his grain, and having omitted to arrange his contract in advance, would be less likely to make provision for a large surplus in the following summer. In this way, he put himself in a position where he could not have met the former demand for grain, even if it had reappeared. Once the trade cycle was broken, it could not be easily restored. The western entrepreneur needed to have confidence in the Polish market before dispatching his fleet to the Baltic, just as the Polish producer needed to have confidence in the foreign demand before he sowed his corn. Once their mutual confidence was shaken, the Vistula Trade could not possibly flourish, even when the wind blew fair and the corn grew tall.

Economic recovery was further hampered by the decentra-lized structure of the Polish–Lithuanian state. In neighbour-ing Prussia, whose independent existence was launched in the midst of the Republic's Swedish War, economic problems of similar magnitude were overcome by state enterprise. The mercantilism of the Hohenzollerns, whose Excise officers ex-celled their grenadiers in determination and ruthlessness, brought the sandy wastes of Brandenburg into bloom, and enabled Königsberg to succeed to Danzig's supremacy on the southern Baltic shore. In the Republic, such methods were simply not permissible. The king possessed neither the means nor the opportunity to take control of economic affairs from the dietines; and the dietines lacked the means of co-ordinating their activities or of initiating anything which resembled a national economic policy.

The withdrawal of the foreign demand, which had stimu-lated the Republic's economy so characteristically in the sixteenth century, inaugurated a social and economic retreat on a wide front. The expansion of the towns came to a halt. The bourgeoisie and the Jews, who had thrived on expanding commerce, fell on hard times, and into increasing dependence on the nobility. The 'middling noblemen', who had figured so prominently in the economic and political life of the preced-ing period, were unable to sustain their position. Having no good reason to exert themselves, they gradually abandoned the spirit of enterprise of their fathers, and, as their income declined, sold off their accumulated assets. In consequence, they became ever more vulnerable to the arrendator and the money-lender, and, in the political sphere, to the blandish-ments of wealthy patrons. The takings fell almost exclusively to the magnates. They bypassed the cities, and bought up the towns; they mobilized the Jews in their own interest, and pressurized the independent gentry. In the land market, they had no serious competitors, and gradually amassed latifundia of unparalleled proportions. Serfdom alone was not put into reverse. Having toiled throughout the sixteenth century to build the prosperity of the Republic's Golden Age, the serfs were now to be driven even harder to mitigate the effects of its misfortunes. Economic life deteriorated both qualitatively and quantitatively. In a world where initiative could not be rewarded, the habits and skills of prosperity were forgotten. The commercial expertise of the sixteenth century found no equivalent in the eighteenth; agricultural techniques degenerated; people were poorer not only in terms of what they earned, but also of what they ate and what they wore. Deprived of their spending power, they could not support the growth of a consumer market, or of industrial manufactures. Possessing little wealth, they could not be effectively taxed, and could not therefore afford to defend themselves. The scene was set for the Sarmatian idyll of the Saxon Era, where prolonged poverty bred ignorance and apathy. When the international vultures began to circle overhead, the impoverished Republic found that it was too weak to resist. In this sense, the decline of the Vistula trade, and the decay of economic life in general, must be seen as a necessary prelude to the Partitions.

*   *   *   *   *

Nowadays, two centuries later, few signs remain of the Vistula's former glory. The river trade never revived, and under Prussian management declined further. The Vistula itself is very quiet, and for long stretches unnavigable. As the dykes have never been extended along the middle reaches, where flooding is endemic, it is quite unsuited to modern traffic of the sort that plies other European rivers such as the Rhine, the Rhône, or the Danube. A few contemporary landmarks have made their appearance, including the petrol refinery at Płock or the chemical works at Puławy. Warsaw, destroyed almost completely in 1944, has been resurrected as a city of glass and concrete. Kazimierz Dolny, in contrast, with its magnificent Renaissance granaries, or Włocławek, with its sleepy old houses on the waterfront, has changed little since Sebastian Klonowic sailed past in 1595, but Danzig has disappeared for ever. As Gdańsk, it is an entirely new and Polish city. In the 152 years of Prussian rule, between 1793 and 1945, it lost all active memory of its erstwhile Polish connections. In the nineteenth century, its German citizens were recruited to German Nationalism. In the 1930s, their wholesale conversion to Nazism played an important part in the pre-war crisis. In 1945–6, those of them that had not fled already were deported to West Germany to make way for Polish immigrants from the USSR. As a result, the city's population is purely Polish for the first time in history. A visitor from Warsaw is no longer obliged to speak in Latin to make himself understood. The ruins of wartime have been cleared away. The historical monuments have been rebuilt, and renamed. The old *Ordensmuehle* constructed by the Teutonic Knights in 1350 is now just the 'Great Mill'; the Protestant *Marienkirche* with its Memling Triptych, is now the Catholic Holy Trinity Church; the former municipal *Artushof,* with its famous ribbed vaulting dating from 1546, is now the *'Dwór Artusa'*; the inimitable *Krantor* overlooking the Mottlau, is now the *'Żuraw'* and overlooks the Motława. The Prussian memorial to the *Leibhusaren Regiments No. 1* is nowhere to be found at all. In view of the horrors of the Second World War and of the Nazi Occupation, it is understandable that the present-day citizen of Gdańsk takes very little interest in his city's German past. Indeed, the authorities go to great lengths to conceal it. They would find it very hard to comprehend the time when German Danzigers were loyal Polish subjects; and for the time being, they simply do not wish to know. The art of rafting has also disappeared. For this, the modern traveller must go to Czorstyn on the Dunajec, 600 miles from the sea, where mountaineers in traditional costume punt groups of expectant tourists through the rapids of the Pieniny Gorge. There, the *flisak* or 'raftsman', who steers their craft through the foaming torrent, wears a hat trimmed with sixteen pairs of sea-shells. He is fond of telling his passengers that each pair of shells represents one of the sixteen journeys to the sea which in time gone by was demanded from every boy before he was allowed to stay at home and find himself a wife. It is a good story; but like so much else in the history of the Vistula, must be counted little more than a watery legend.

CHAPTER NINE

MIASTO:

The Vicissitudes of Urban Life

Cities have never been particularly prominent in Polish civilization. Their origins in the Middle Ages had such strong German connections, that for long historians considered them to be mere colonial excrescences on the essentially rural Polish scene. The moments of prosperity in the sixteenth and early seventeenth centuries passed so quickly that they left few lasting traditions. Their subsequent decay was so complete that there was little to arouse contemporary interest. Yet they present a subject without which the growth of Polish economy and society cannot be properly understood.[1]

It is important to remember that in the medieval tradition, the city – *civitas* in Latin, *miasto* in Polish – was a juridical concept rather than a geographical phenomenon. The city was in no sense equivalent to what today might be called an 'urban area'. Indeed, most of the land within the city limits was devoted to agriculture and was indistinguishable in appearance from the surrounding countryside. Only the cluster of houses, churches, streets, and municipal buildings in the city centre possessed a distinctly urban character, and even there the persistence of gardens, fields, and small-holdings would strike the modern eye as more suited to a village than to a municipality. The city, in fact, was defined in terms of the legal privileges embodied in its charter of incorporation, and in no way depended on the use to which its lands were put. Its bounds were fixed by law, and formed a precise jurisdictional district within which the king or patron had permanently ceded his former rights to the municipal courts. What is more, the gradual proliferation of immunities and private jurisdiction gave rise to a situation where several separate cities co-existed within the same urban conglomeration, together with numerous ill-defined settlements and suburbs. The medieval city of Kraków, for example, did *not* include the separate cities of Kazimierz and Kleparz. Yet it did include many square miles of land beyond the city walls, which has remained essentially rural in character to the present day. Warsaw contained two cities: Stare Miasto (The Old City) founded in 1300, and Nowe Miasto (The New City) founded in 1412. Around these two municipal foci, a multitude of distinct royal, ecclesiastical, or private jurisdictions proliferated, each with its own laws and government. To the casual observer, or to the geographer, the view from the cathedral spire presented a haphazard jumble of scattered groups of buildings. To the jurist, the jumble would have been entirely explicable by the invisible lines of demarcation between the numerous jurisdictions.

It should also be remembered that a considerable number of market towns and prosperous villages, whose outward appearance may closely have resembled that of the smaller cities, did not enjoy municipal status. For want of a patron and a charter, they could not offer their inhabitants the social, political, and economic advantages of self-government, and they remained subject to the owner of the land on which they happened to be located. These charterless towns were joined in due course by the growing ranks of former cities whose charters for one reason or another had fallen into disuse.

The incorporation of cities, first encountered in Poland in the thirteenth century, continued at irregular intervals until the end of the eighteenth. In those six hundred years, almost two thousand acts of incorporation were recorded. In the early centuries, the initiative was usually taken by the King or the ruling prince, or in some cases by the Church. Nysa (Neisse) in Silesia, for instance, received its charter in 1220 from the Bishop of Breslau, twenty-two years before Breslau itself was incorporated. As time went on, however, the incorporation of cities by powerful noble patrons grew increasingly common, until eventually the private city became the commonest variety of all. Most cities were minuscule by modern standards. Most contained less than two thousand inhabitants. Of the 700 chartered cities in the Kingdom of Poland in the late sixteenth century less than twenty — Kraków, Danzig, Elbing, Thorn, Bydgoszcz, Warsaw, Poznań, Lublin, Sandomierz, Lwów, Kamieniec, Korsuń, Kiev, and

Perejasław claimed a population of 10,000 or over. In Lithuania, only Wilno, Polotsk, Kowno, Brześć, Pińsk, Witebsk, and Mohylew; and in Livonia, Riga, could match their larger Polish counterparts.

The pattern of incorporation in Mazovia typified developments in the other central provinces. The first city of Mazovia, Płock, started life as the sprawling faubourg of the castle and cathedral on the banks of the Vistula, and received its charter from the Prince of Mazovia in 1237. Pułtusk in 1257, and Łowicz in 1298 were both ecclesiastical foundations; Warsaw, incorporated about 1300 from an existing market town, was another princely foundation. Mogilnica owed its birth in 1317 to a monastic order. The first noble foundations, Budiszowice and Bolimów, appeared in 1358 and 1370 respectively, at a time when princely and ecclesiastical charters still predominated. The fifteenth century saw the largest number of the province's new cities, forty-three in all. The sixteenth century saw the noble foundations (82 per cent) overtake all the others. The seventeenth and eighteenth centuries saw numerous *jurydyki* (municipal jurisdictions) established by the nobility in the immediate vicinity of Warsaw, but little activity elsewhere. The charters granted in 1670 by the Church to Góra Kalwaria and in 1791 by the King to Myszyniec, were already rarities in their day. All in all, of 156 incorporations enacted in Mazovia between 1237 and 1791, 36 per cent were granted by the Prince or the King, 15 per cent by the Church, 49 per cent by the nobility.[2] (See Map 15.)

The cities of Royal Prussia occupied a special place. Incorporated in the main in the era before 1454, when they had formed part of the Teutonic State, they retained a number of characteristic features. For one thing, in Elbing (Elbląg), Dirschau (Tczew), Frauenberg (Frombork), Konitz (Chojnice), Braunsberg (Braniewo), and Hel, they included the only cities in Poland which adopted the law of Lübeck as opposed to that of Magdeburg. For another, they were solidly German. Most importantly, having been received into the Kingdom *en bloc* as members of the Prussian League, they were able to negotiate far-reaching tax exemptions and autonomous privileges. Between 1454 and 1569, they continued to send their representatives to the provincial Estates

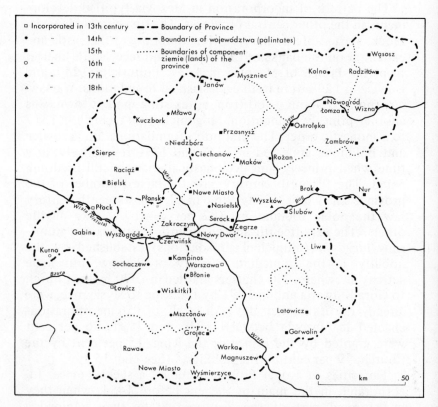

Map 15.　　The Incorporated Cities of Mazovia

of Royal Prussia, and kept a voice in political affairs beyond
their immediate walls. After 1569, together with Cracow and
Wilno they sent 'observers' to the Sejm of the united Republic.
In later years, thanks to the proximity of the Kingdom of
Prussia and to the benefits of Baltic Commerce, they were
less affected by the economic recession than were the cities
of the interior. Royal Prussia was the only province of
Poland—Lithuania where the burgher estate could hold its
own against the encroachments of the nobility.

   Urban society contained several distinct groups and strata.
By tradition membership of the *mieszczaństwo* or Burgher
Estate was confined to Christian tax-payers enjoying full civil
rights, and represented anything between one-third and two-
thirds of a city's inhabitants. It was clearly divided between
the *patrycjat* or 'oligarchy' on the one hand, and the citizens
at large — the commoners who formed the *Pospólstwo,* or
Communitas — on the other hand. In the sixteenth century,
contemporary commentators often talked of the Three
Orders — the 'Senatorial Order' of city Councillors; the
'Second Order' of magistrates; and the 'Third Order' of commoners. The great patrician families of the First and Second
Order in the old royal capital of Cracow, frequently traced
their fortunes to ancestors who had migrated from Germany,
Hungary, or Italy. Their control of the public offices and
commercial enterprises of the cities matched that of the
magnates in the Republic as a whole, whilst their loans and
services to the royal court gave them political influence independent of the nobility. The Turzons, Boners, and the
Montelupi of Jagiellonian Cracow had their later counterparts
in the Blanks and Teppers of seventeenth- and eighteenth-
century Warsaw.[3] The *pospólstwo* in contrast, was drawn
from members of the craft guilds and the merchant confraternities. They saw themselves as the guardians of municipal
democracy, which in their view as threatened no less by the
arrogance of the patricians than by the unregulated activities
of unlicensed craftsmen and artisans. Beyond the burgher
estate, were the so-called plebs, and the Jews. In some cities
the plebs formed an absolute majority of the population.
They were made up from the poor, who were disenfranchised
by their inability to pay their taxes, and from all those

migrants, fugitives, and casual workers whose lack of a permanent residence disqualified them from citizenship. The Jews formed a separate estate of their own, whose own threefold division into patricians, tax-payers, and plebeians closely mirrored that of their Gentile neighbours.

Of Poland's private cities, Zamość, founded in 1580 by Jan Zamoyski was, of course, the obvious showpiece. But it was just one of many. In their way, Tarnów founded by Hetman Jan Tarnowski, or Lewartów founded in 1543 by the Firleys, were equally splendid. Among the smaller foundations were Poniatów (1520) and Siennica (1526) in Mazovia, founded by the Poniatowski and Siennicki respectively; Krasiczyń and Baranów in Małopolska; Żółkiew and Stanisławów in Ruthenia; and Czartorysk and Klewan in Volhynia.

The guilds or *Cechy* made their impact on every sector of urban life. Originally formed to protect the economic interests of particular specialist professions such as the Goldsmiths and the Armourers, they gradually established monopoly control over every craft and trade, and their activites spread into the religious, recreational, educational, military, and eventually the political sphere. In Cracow, the twenty-four guilds of the fifteenth century eventually rose to sixty; in Thorn, in 1650 there were seventy; in Lwów, according to the *Lustracja* of 1661, thirty-eight.* Each guild had its own statute, with its own rules and practices, and exercised control over its own members. Demarcation disputes were legion. The war between the Tailors and Furriers over who should make fur coats ran for centuries. The appearance of artistic sculptors in the Renaissance period led to a long dispute between the Masons and the Painters. Riots and brawls between gangs of apprentices regularly disturbed the peace of the streets. Yet in face of external pressures, the guilds usually closed ranks. They were particularly incensed by infringements of the 'closed shop' principle within the city limits, and were eternally

---

* Butchers, Bakers, Cobblers, Goldsmiths, Furriers, Tailors, Barber–Surgeons, Haberdashers, Swordmakers, Pewterers, Taverners, Locksmiths, Smiths, Boilermakers, Coopers, Carpenters, Jointers, Wheelwrights, Cartwrights, Tanners, Leatherworkers, Weavers, Bellowsmakers, Harnessmakers, Honeymakers, Brewers, Malters, Potters, Ropemakers, Turners, Hatters, Upholsterers, Masons, Needlemakers, Knife-grinders, Armourers, Embroiderers, Saddlers, and Others.[4]

complaining about the Jews, 'bunglers', and interlopers whom they took to be undermining their livelihood. The formation of rival Jewish Guilds in each of the principal trades provided the main grounds for demands to deny the Jews the rights of residence.

Membership of a guild involved a lifelong commitment. The guildsman worshipped in the chapel of his Guild, served in the trained band of his Guild, and frequented the *Dom Bracki* (Guild House) with his family. As an apprentice, he lived and worked for seven years under the roof of a master-craftsman, who was directly responsible for his training and conduct. As a young journeyman, he was sent abroad for one year and six weeks to gain experience in his trade in a distant city, or even in a foreign country. Finally, having completed his *majstersztuk* or 'masterwork' as proof of his competence, he was examined by a committee of the Guild, and admitted to their ranks with all due pomp and ceremony. Once initiated with the title of *Socius, Geselle,* or *Towarzysz* (Comrade) he would then be required to buy a house in the city, to take a wife, to swear an oath of loyalty to the Guild, and to register himself as a full citizen. Not uncommonly, the new member was awarded a descriptive surname, and in this regard the rolls record many examples of coarse humour: 'Moczygęba' (Splash-mug); 'Kłopoczybaba' (Get-Girl-In-Trouble); 'Mokrowstał' (Damp-riser); even 'Pierdzikrzyczywoł' (Farting-shouting-ox). Henceforth, he was entitled to speak at the general assemblies of his Guild, the so-called *morgensprache* or *rozmowa poranna,* and to cast his vote in the elections of Guild Elders.[5] In a sense, the life of the Guilds was highly democratic. All decisions and activities were undertaken communally. In the wider sense, however, the Guilds were often seen to be acting in a sectional spirit, promoting the interests of their members against that of society as a whole. It was in this spirit at the beginning of the sixteenth century that Jan Ostroróg, Chancellor and jurist, sought to check their progress, and recommended their abolition.

The merchants' confraternities or *Gildia* closely resembled the craftsmen's Guilds. In Cracow, they were regarded as a separate order of the burgher estate — the *Ordo Mercatorum* as distinct from the *Ordo Mechanicorum* — and they enjoyed slightly different privileges. Elsewhere they were taken merely as the commercial branch of the guild system. They owed their origins to the much valued Right of Storage which made the fortunes of so many medieval towns; but their cherished monopoly only lost its value when the ancient commercial regulations fell into disuse.[6]

Political life within the cities centred on efforts to check the arbitrary designs of the City Council. In the old days the City Council had itself acted as a democratic check on the powers of the sovereign's representative, the *Wójt*; and Polish cities had passed through that same classical phase, first evident in medieval Italy, where the *Popolo* confronted the *Podestà*. In Poland, however, the supremacy of the *Wójt* was short-lived, and the Council was able to establish its control over the judicial and executive, as well as the legislative, organs of self-government. In Cracow, for example, the royal *Wójt* lost his influence after the revolt of 1320, when Łokietek was happy enough to deprive his representative of the means for further insubordination. Henceforth, the appointment of the *Wójt* passed within the purview of the Council, and the prerogatives of the Magistrates' Bench were merged within those of the Councillors. In consequence, the president of the City Council — the *Burgermeister* or *Burmistrz* (Mayor) — assumed the dominant position formerly wielded by the *Wójt*. What is more, the patrician families who made their fortunes in the Jagiellonian period tended to turn their seats on the City Council into hereditary offices, and to manage all elections and appointments in the City through the devious channels of patronage and nepotism. By the sixteenth century, they had lost all pretence of their democratic origins and formed the core of the élitist, oligarchic establishment. In this situation in each of the cities the Guilds began to agitate against the Council in the name of the people, just as two hundred years earlier the Council had once agitated against the *Wójt*. The resolution of this constitutional struggle differed in every particular case; and in most of the private cities the powers of the patron, whether magnate or Bishop, were destined to reign supreme irrespective of the governmental forms adopted. In the great royal cities, however, the sixteenth century witnessed the evolution of an elaborate system of municipal autonomy that lasted almost until the end of the Republic.

In Cracow, the principal organ of communal control was the *Quadragintaviratus* the 'Group of Forty Men' which first appeared in 1548. Elected by the Guilds and Confraternities from amongst their own Elders, it was the outcome of almost three decades of litigation in the royal courts, where the citizens had complained of the Council's arbitrary proceedings, especially in matters of finance. Henceforth the Forty Men met with the Council to form the joint *Colloquium* or 'City Meeting' at which all new legislation was discussed. Their representatives audited the accounts of the *Lonheria* or 'City Treasury', and their chairman, the *Tribunas Plebis* or 'People's Tribune' signed all important documents in the company of the Mayor. The Council retained considerable powers of discretion in the executive sphere, and supervised the work of all the City Offices. The twenty-four life-tenured councillors controlled the machinery for their perpetual re-election. Every year, the twelve retiring members of the Ruling Council exchanged places with the twelve returning members of the Alternative Council, who could then be counted on to return the compliment twelve months later; and so on, *ad infinitum.* Despite a ruling in the royal courts which prevented the abolition of formal elections, the councillors invariably filled vacancies within their own ranks or on the Magistrates' Bench with candidates of their own choosing. On this score, the Group of Forty was quite powerless. The commoners could not hope to dismantle the oligarchy. Rather, by supervising its legislation and holding its purse-strings, they could only hope to trim its worst excesses.[7]

In Danzig, where there were two distinct cities and corporations, the provisions for communal government were still more elaborate. As in Cracow, the citizen commoners had evolved an organ in the form of the 'Hundred Men' whereby they supervised the conduct of the executive offices. Here, since German was the sole language of government, all Danzig's institutions — from the *Stadtsrat* (City Council) to the *Ratsherrn* (Councillors), the *Schoppenherrn* (Magistrates), and the *Richter* (Judge) — possessed exclusively German names. An account of the government and finances of Danzig is to be found in the papers of John Sanderson, who served as

British consul there in the late seventeenth century:

A short Account of the Present Estate of Dantzig. 1675

Danzig is divided into two parts: viz: the *altStadt* and the *Rechtstadt* or the old and the Right Towne each haveing its distinct magistrates and Senate House. The magistrates of the old towne are; 5 Senators or *Rahts-Herrn*; and 12 *Schoppen-Herrn* alias *Scabini*. One of the Senators is yearely Praesedent, whch they call *wortfuhrender Herr,* or Speaker: and an other is *Richter* or Judge: wch offices are by these 5 executed alternately. The *Schoppen* or Scabinate do iudge all Criminal causes and some civil ones . . .

The magistrates of the Right towne are divided into 3 Orders, viz: the Senate, the *Schoppen,* and the Common councell, called the '100' men. The Senate, consists of 4 burgermasters and 14 *Rahts-herrn* or Senators wch togeth wth one senator from the old towne (who comes alwayes to their Session) is the higheste magistracie, having the Rule of whatsoever concernes the whole Citie in Generall, & the executive power of all their lawes, not onely Civil but alsoe ecclesiasticall, they haveing by a Priveledg from King Casimirus & Stephanus *ius episcopale* over all the churches in their territories: which are 10 within the walls, 3 in the Suburbs & 10 or 11 more in those villadges under the Towne's iurisdiction, onely the Romane Catholicque Churches are excepted, wch are two belonging to the Dominican & Carmelite freijers & one to the Nunns of St. Brigitta's Order, all three being within the walls.

One of the 4 burgomasters is yearely Praesident, et an other Vice-Praesedent, wch offices they all execute by turnes, as for example Buergermaster Krumhausen is now Praesedent, and van Bummeln vice-Praesedent. The next yeare he thats now vice-praesedent must bee Praesedent, &.van Bodecker vice-praesedent who is to bee succeeded by Burgermeister von der Lind. . . .

The Senate doth yearely chuse a *Richter* or Judge wch must bee a Senator, . . . to which belongs all contraversies concerning matters of debt, wch when he hath determined either partie may appeale to the Senate, from whence they may alsoe appeale to the King of Poland, & then the acts are translated into Latin & sent to his Matie. But if the matter in Contraversie does not exceed f. 1000 or 75 lib. sterling, then they will not admit an appeale. . . .

The Salaries allowed them out the Cities Chamber are as follows: to each *burgermeister* yearely 2000 dollers, to each *Rahtsherr* 1000 gilders & to each *schoppenherr* 400 gilders. They are in all 4 burgermasters, 19 *Rahtsherrn,* 24 *Schoppenherrn,* 1 *syndicus,* 1 *sub-syndicus,* 6 secretaries wth severall Clerkes and instigators, wch alsoe receive their salaries out of the Cities Chamber.

The Revenues of the Cities consist in the Lands & houses belonging to it, the accize of Beere, the Costomes upon goods imported & exported, & the Profit of their Great Mill.

The first of these is knowne onely to the senate, wch they keepe very Private, nor will they let the Common-councell knowe what it is though often with much earnestness desired.

The accize of Beere, wch is 3 gilders 16 grosz or 5s 3d sterl. per barrell comes to about 50,000 dollers yearly.

The customes are two fold. The first called *pfahlgeld*, the origin of which was for monnies to buy Piles or long Posts of wood wch are ramd into the river to preserve the Haven from being choaked up with sand or mudd & this comes to about 2½ p Cent whereof one halfe belongs to the King of Poland, the other halfe to this Citie. The other is called *zulag*, wch is an imposition upon all goods & now by this senate made arbetrarie, yet its commonly one halfe more than the pfahlgeld & the King hat no part thereof . . . What these Customes may come to yearely I cannot learne, but I guess them to bee about 70 thousand dollers. Their great Mill wch is within the towne hath 18 wheeles & serves the whole Citie both for brewing & Bakeing. It brings inn yearely about 40 thousand dollers wch comes alsoe into the publicque treasurie. And yet, notwithstanding those large revenues, they are much in Debt, wch they contracted in the last warr with Sweeden, & ended An⁰ 1660. I am assured from a very good hand they pay now yearely above 15 thousand pounds sterling for monnies they have at, & yet they allow but 4½ to 5 p Cent for it.

The Common councell or hundred men have noe iurisdiction, but without them noe law can be made, or nullefied, nor any taxes imposed upon the Burghers.

The Burghers are generally but of indifferent Estates, they living heigh and Splendid. The greatest part of their wealth is in their houses & Granaries for Corne. I do much question if wee can finds 60 burghers in the whole Citie that are worth one with an other tenn thousand pounds sterling.

The ships now belonging to Dantzig are not above 9 or 10 merchant men, & one is a manner built wch will be better than any of the other being above 200 lasts burthen and is to carrie 20 Gunns.[8]

In many Polish cities, the main institutions of municipal self-government were closely reflected in those of the Jewish *kahal* (commune), which usually functioned alongside them. Like their Gentile counterparts on the City Council, the Jewish Elders operated a closed electoral system which was carefully designed to perpetuate the power of its authors. A complicated system of electoral colleges ensured that the *roshion,* (Elders) *tuvim* (Meliores or Betters), and *kahal* (Governors) of the new commune would always be chosen from the circle of the old one. In the Jewish case, the proportion of enfranchised tax-payers and electors to the unenfranchised plebs was even more restricted than in the case of the Christian burghers.[9] (See Diagram H.)

In legal and constitutional matters, the older cities frequently guided the progress of more recent corporations. Just as Breslau imported the 'German Law' from Magdeburg, so Cracow imported it from Breslau, and Lwów from Cracow. The charters of Chełmno (Kulm) in Royal Prussia and of Neumarkt (Środa Śląska) in Silesia served as local models by which later charters were drafted. The judgements of the older, superior courts, known as *urteil* or *ortyle,* served as precedents for the guidance of inferior ones. In the sixteenth century, Cracow's Quadragintavirat system was exported to several other cities, notably in 1577 to Lwów. It reappeared elsewhere in numerous variations such as 'the Twenty', 'the Sixteen', or 'the Eleven', not to mention 'the Hundred' of Danzig's *Rechtstadt.*

The multinational character of the Polish cities in the past is a fact which official Polish historians of today often neglect, if they do not categorically deny. Yet the contention that the main cities of Poland–Lithuania were always predominantly Polish is as absurd as the older prejudice which preferred to see them all as essentially German. In reality, the ethnic composition of urban society in Poland–Lithuania was exceedingly complicated, and was in constant flux. The subject is full of surprises. It is incontestable, of course, that the cities of Silesia and of the Baltic Coast, especially Breslau, Stettin, and Danzig were overwhelmingly German from the thirteenth century onwards. Yet it is curious to find that the cities of medieval Małopolska, too, were largely German in character, whilst the cities of Wielkopolska, which were nearer to Germany, were largely Polish. In the fourteenth century, not only 'Krakau' but equally Bochnia, Tarnów, Wieliczka, Sandez (Sącz), Sandomierz, Lublin, Przemyśl, and even Lwów, were settled by Germans, whilst Poznań and Bydgoszcz stayed more in the hands of Poles. In the sixteenth century, in contrast, when Cracow was turning rapidly towards Polish culture, Poznań was strongly influenced by the Lutheran Reformation and took its first steps towards Germanization. In the 1530s the Sunday services in St. Mary's Church in Cracow were in Polish in the morning and German in the afternoon. German remained the official language of the Cracovian courts until the year 1600. In Wilno at that time, representatives of the four 'nations' − Lithuanians, Poles, Ruthenes, and Germans − took turns as head of the guilds. In Lwów restriction of citizenship to Roman Catholics encouraged assimilation into Polish culture. There, the Armenian community enjoyed the same autonomy as the Jews. In the seventeenth and eighteenth centuries, important changes occurred when Polish noblemen deliberately sought to attract German urban settlers into new textile towns. Cities such as Rawicz (1638), Szlichtingtowo, and Szamocyn (Pfaffendorf) were expressly incorporated for this purpose. As an over-all generalization, it is probably true to say that the German element predominated in the cities of the Republic's western regions (where the rural population was largely Polish), whilst the Polish element predominated in the cities of those eastern and southern regions where the rural population was largely Lithuanian or Ruthenian. Everywhere Jewish communities were well established in all the urban areas.

To most outward appearances the urban life of Poland−Lithuania at the time of the Union of Lublin was heading in the same direction as that of Western Europe. The future must have seemed to hold the prospect of unlimited growth and prosperity. Both the inland and the seaborne trade were flourishing. The spate of new incorporations was still in full flood. Great cities like Poznań and Cracow, and small cities such as Tarnów, and Kazimierz Dolny, were being adorned by architectural wonders commensurate to their new civil pride. Urban society had reached the unprecedented level of 25 per cent of the Republic's total population; and within the urban centres, the Christian burghers still outnumbered the growing Jewish estate. Yet the seeds of decay were already present. In 1565, only four years before the Union, the Polish Sejm had passed a law which forbade native burghers to engage in foreign trade. As a result, thousands of burghers

resigned from the citizenship of their native towns in a desperate effort to preserve their businesses. Henceforth, the more
profitable branches of trade were increasingly taken over
either by agents of the nobility or by foreigners. More seriously,
large numbers of people were already finding the means to
circumvent the regulations of city life, and thus to discredit
it. The nobles ignored the ban on their residence in royal cities,
and broke the city laws with impunity. Their private cities
avoided the tolls, the market dues, the customs and the rights
of storage from which the older cities had lived; and their
jurydyki offered refuge to all the law-breakers and casual
immigrants whom the city courts and guilds sought to control.
Their patronage of the Jews was a major stimulus whereby the
Christian burgher estate came to be physically outnumbered
in their own cities. For the time being, material prosperity
masked the deeper flaws. But the writing was already on the
city walls.

*   *   *   *   *

Like all European capitals, Warsaw is, in its own way unique.
For much of its history, it possessed few of the attributes of
a capital city. For most of the modern period, it was more
distinguished as the resort of intellectuals, burglars, and insur-
rectionists than as the home of a ruling élite. On this score, it
is more akin to Dublin than to London or Washington. It is
less elegant than Budapest or Bucharest, less picturesque than
Belgrade or Sofia, less venerable than Prague, less impressive
than Berlin. Most remarkably, when liberated by the Soviet
Army on 17 January 1945, its ruins sheltered not a single
living soul. In this regard, Warsaw is as ancient as a dozen
European capitals: yet it is the youngest of them all.[10]

Warsaw's rise to pre-eminence among Polish cities owed
less to its inherent attributes than to its commanding strategic
location. Perched on an elevated terrace above the high, left
bank of the middle Vistula, it is peculiarly exposed to the
elements, especially to the east wind in winter. Lying in the
middle of one of Poland's least productive regions, it enjoyed
but modest success in the corn and timber trade. As a minor
provincial fortress of Mazovia, which did not form part of the
Polish Kingdom until 1526, it passed the Middle Ages in the

shadow both of Płock and of Czersk, and could not compare with the royal capital at Cracow. Yet, in time, its central position in the Republic of Poland–Lithuania was seen to offer unequalled advantages. Its position on the Vistula kept its residents in regular contact with Danzig in the north and Cracow in the south, and with the main commercial traffic. Equally, at a time when Poland was consolidating the constitutional union with Lithuania, Warsaw lay astride the main routes from west to east. From 1611, it has been the capital of all the successive states that the Polish lands have produced.

Mazovian Warsaw grew slowly. It was founded in the last quarter of the thirteenth century, in replacement of the nearby fort of Jazdów, destroyed in a Lithuanian raid in July 1262. It was named after some long-forgotten hero or patron called 'Warsza' and around 1300 received its first and long-lost municipal charter according to the Chełmno Law. The Church, later the cathedral of St. John, the princely castle, the Market Square, and the city walls, all date from those early years. By 1321, Warsaw had become the seat of a castellan, and in 1339 hosted the tribunal of inquiry into the conduct of the Teutonic Order, whose advance had recently obliged the Piast Prince of Mazovia to admit the suzerainty of Casimir the Great. In 1350, the Church and monastery of the Augustinians was founded. In the fifteenth century, in the afterglow of the victory at Grunwald, Warsaw outpaced all its local rivals. Prince Janusz the Elder, who ruled from 1374 to 1429 permanently transferred the residence of his line together with the Mazovian archdeaconry from Czersk in 1413. He rebuilt the Castle, the Walls, and City Hall: installed the hereditary *Wójt* in a mansion on the Market Square (nowadays the seat of the Institute of History of the Academy of Sciences), and in 1408 founded Nowe Miasto (The New Town) with a charter and corporation of its own. This last development was intended to check the proliferation of the *freti*, or 'unregulated settlements' beyond the Walls, many of which were swelled by the rapid influx at this time of the Jews. The definitive defeat of the Teutonic Order in the Thirteen Years War made the separate political policies of the Mazovian Princes unnecessary. The last members of the ruling House vainly opposed the steady territorial and administrative encroachments of their Jagiellonian suzerains. The series of sudden deaths by poison, in 1522 of Princess Anna, and in 1524 and 1526 of her two unbalanced sons, Stanisław and Janusz, brought a timely end of the profligate, heirless, and anachronistic rule of the House of Piast. (See Map 16.)

Jagiellonian Warsaw enjoyed royal patronage from the start. The first visit of Zygmunt I in 1526 gave rise to the so-called 'Third Ordinance' for the cities of the Kingdom. Bona Sforza, who inherited her husband's estates in Mazovia, resided by preference in the palace of Jazdów, as did her daughter, Anna Jagiellonka. Zygmunt-August went there regularly on his progresses from Cracow to Wilno, especially in the 1560s when he was constantly drawn to the north by the growing Livonian crisis. In 1568, he supervised the wooden piles as they were driven into the river-bed to carry the first bridge which spanned the Vistula at this point. (Supported across its length of five hundred yards on eighteen arches, the bridge was swept away by the Spring Flood of 1603 and not replaced.) By the time of Zygmunt-August's death, the medieval Castle had been transformed by Giovanni-Battista Quadro into a magnificent Renaissance palace. Most importantly, Warsaw had also assumed an active parliamentary role. Traditionally the home of the dietine of Mazovia which met in St. Martin's Church, the Sejm of the Korona assembled in the Royal Castle for the first time in 1556–7. In 1569, by the Union of Lublin, Warsaw was chosen as the permanent site of royal Elections. Especially under Bathory, it rapidly became the usual place for the biennial sessions of the Sejm of the Republic.

The city's rising political importance was attended by constant municipal strife. The rivalry of the patriciate and the guilds was complicated by the presence of the Jews, whose enterprise in Gentile eyes was largely pursued in defiance of established institutions. The original inhabitants of the ghetto, first mentioned in 1414, were expelled beyond the Walls in 1483, but soon returned. The 'Third Ordinance' of 1526 was accompanied by a decree of *'De non tolerandis Judaeis'*. This, too, had little effect. Henceforth, the ghetto grew and prospered on the fringe of the city centre, in the area bordering the Walls and the New Town. Meanwhile the guilds,

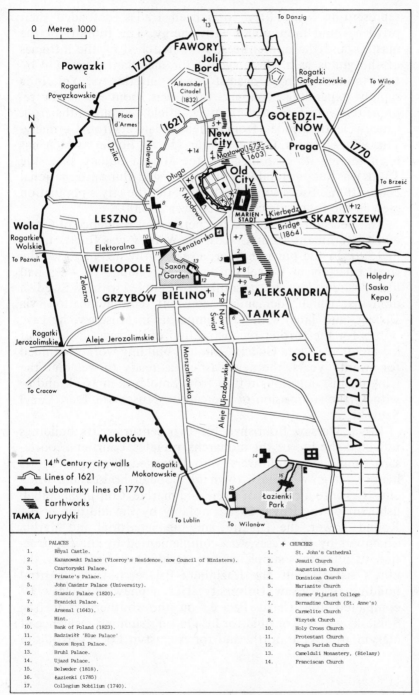

0 Metres 1000

To Danzig

Powazki

Rogatki
Powazkowskie

1770
c

FAWORY
Joli Bord

Alexander
Citadel
(1832)

Place
d'Armes

N

(1621)

Dzika

Nalewki

Długa

5 +

New
City

4 + 14

Mostowa (1573–1603)

+ 6

11

Miodowa

8

LESZNO

9

10

Elektoralna

Senatorska

11

13

WIELOPOLE

Saxon
Garden

12

GRZYBÓW BIELINO + 11

10

Wola
Rogatkie
Wolskie

To Poznań

Żelazna

Rogatki
Gołędziowskie

To Wilno

**GOŁĘDZI-
NÓW**

Praga

1770

To Brześć

+ 12

**Old
City**

2

1

MARIEN-
STADT

Kierbedź

Bridge
(1864)

SKARZYSZEW

+ 7

3

2

+ 8

+ 9

5 E

ALEKSANDRIA

TAMKA

6

Nowy
Świat

Holędry
(Saska
Kępa)

SOLEC

Rogatki
Jerozolimskie

Aleje Jerozolimskie

To Cracow

Marszałkowska

Aleje Ujazdowskie

V I S T U L A

Mokotów

Rogatki
Mokotowskie

14

16

15

Łazienki
Park

To Lublin

To Wilanów

━━━ **14th Century city walls**
◣◢ **Lines of 1621**
━●━ **Lubomirsky lines of 1770**
≡≡≡ **Earthworks**
TAMKA **Jurydyki**

PALACES		+ CHURCHES	
1.	Royal Castle.	1.	St. John's Cathedral
2.	Kazanowski Palace (Viceroy's Residence, now Council of Ministers).	2.	Jesuit Church
3.	Czartoryski Palace.	3.	Augustinian Church
4.	Primate's Palace.	4.	Dominican Church
5.	John Casimir Palace (University).	5.	Marianite Church
6.	Staszic Palace (1820).	6.	former Pijarist College
7.	Branicki Palace.	7.	Bernadine Church (St. Anne's)
8.	Arsenal (1643).	8.	Carmelite Church
9.	Mint.	9.	Wizytek Church
10.	Bank of Poland (1823).	10.	Holy Cross Church
11.	Radziwiłł 'Blue Palace'	11.	Protestant Church
12.	Saxon Royal Palace.	12.	Praga Parish Church
13.	Bruhl Palace.	13.	Camelduli Monastery, (Bielany)
14.	Ujazd Palace.	14.	Franciscan Church
15.	Belweder (1818).		
16.	Łazienki (1785)		
17.	Collegium Nobilium (1740).		

Map 16.   Warsaw – the Growth of the City to 1800

representing some fifty specialized trades, defended their privileges and monopolies with energy. The tumults of the masters and the apprentices, were matched by the intrigues of the guilds as a whole against the merchant clans, and by their common front against Jewish interlopers. Yet, in a rapidly expanding economy, there was room for all. Entrepreneurs were attracted from far afield — goldsmiths from Cracow, leather traders from Bohemia, bankers from Germany. The wine-shop of Georg Fugger (Jerzy Fukier) which has been serving its customers on the Market Square since the 1540s was but one reminder of Warsaw's far-flung international connections. From some 4,500 in 1500, the city's population grew in the following century to over 20,000.

The decision to transfer the permanent residence of Court and Government from Cracow to Warsaw was finally taken in 1596. In the previous year, a serious fire had damaged the royal quarters in Wawel Castle, and Zygmunt III Vasa had little desire to tarry in the south. Preoccupied with his Swedish domains which demanded constant communication via Danzig, and later with the campaigns in Muscovy, he gave orders for the further reconstruction of Warsaw Castle under his architect, Santa Gucci. Although building work continued for twenty years, the new Castle was ready to welcome the King on his victorious return from Smolensk in 1611, and to witness the submission of the captive Muscovite Tsar, Vazyl Szuyski.

Royal Warsaw flourished for two centuries. Its buildings reflected the life of the monarchs, prelates, courtiers, courtesans, and camp followers who thronged the pages of its history. It grew from a town of wooden houses and brick churches into a capital of stone and marble. Continual embellishment of the Royal Castle, notably by the addition of the Round Tower, the Theatre, and the Senatorial and Marble Chambers by the Vasas, was complemented by the construction of numerous supplementary residences. Anna Vasa, the king's sister, built the Kazimierz Palace, now the central building of Warsaw University. Her nephew, Władysaw IV completed the Ujazd Palace, on the southern outskirts. Sobieski was responsible for his Queen's summer residence at Marymont to the north, and for Augustyn Locci's exquisite

'Villa Nova' (Wilanów) to the south; August II for the Saxon
Palace and Garden to the west; and Stanisław-August for the
delightful Łazieńki Palace which he constructed on the site
of Ujazd. Warsaw's first public monument, the Zygmunt
Column raised in 1646 by Władysaw IV in honour of his
father, dominated the Cracow Faubourg until its destruction
in 1939, and has since been rebuilt.

The Counter-Reformation left an indelible mark. In 1602,
St. John's Cathedral received a Baroque façade and a covered
gallery connecting it with the Royal Castle. In 1608, next to
the cathedral, the Jesuits celebrated their rising fortunes with
a magnificent oratory containing twenty marble altars. In
1623, the Reformed Franciscans replaced their wooden
chapel with a stone church, whilst in 1638, the Dominicans
dedicated their new Church of St. Hyacinth. Many other
Baroque churches, initiated in the early seventeenth century
were still awaiting completion long after the Swedish occupation. Such was the church of the Carmelites (1630) on the
Cracow Faubourg, or that of the Piarists on Długa Street
(1681); the Sacramental Convent of St. Kazimierz (1688)
built by Marysieńka in Nowe Miasto; and the Capucin Church,
or the Church of the Holy Cross (1696) by Giovanni Bellotto,
opposite the Kazimierz Palace. Devotional motives inspired
August II's construction in 1724–31, of the Aleje Ujazdowski,
a long straight avenue whose linden trees shaded twenty-eight
calvary chapels. In the reign of Stanisław-August, Catholic
building was outshone by the cylindrical Evangelical Church,
designed in 1777–9 by Simon Zug.

The magnates too were active builders. In the sixteenth
century, the burghers of Warsaw had frequently complained
to the King of the damage inflicted on their gardens, furniture,
wives, and servants by magnatial retinues forcibly quartered
on them by the Crown Marshal during sessions of this Sejm.
Clearly, the courtiers needed town houses of their own. The
early examples, those of the Kazanowski, Koniecpolski,
Krasiński, Ossoliński, Daniłłowicz, and Radziwiłł families
were overshadowed by the magnificent generation of palaces
of Sobieski's reign designed by the Dutch architect, Tylman
van Gameren. Among these, the new Krasiński Palace,
ordered by the Crown referendary, Jan Dobrogost Krasiński

(1640–1717), or the Blue Palace of the Potockis, rivalled the properties of the King himself. In the eighteenth century, new landmarks of elegance were afforded by the horseshoe-form Mniszek Palace (1714); by the remodelled Pod Blachą Palace (1720) adjacent to the Royal Castle, later presented to Prince Poniatowski by his royal uncle; and by Franciszek Bieliński's 'Hotel' with its French rococo interior.

The magnates were largely responsible for the planned development of the city, most characteristically in their *jurydiki* or chartered wards exempted from the Corporation's control. These wards were replicas in miniature of the magnates' private towns in the country at large, and each contained their own and separate administration. The earliest example was given by the *Starosta*, Jan Grzybowski, who obtained a royal grant for the foundation of Grzybów in 1610. This was soon followed by Dziekanka (1617) and Zadzikowska (1638). Nowe Leszno (1648) was the property of the Calvinist Leszczyńskis, and a den of dissident politics. Muranów was named after Sobieski's Venetian architect, Belotti da Murano. Skaryszew (1648) on the right bank, belonging to the Bishop of Płock, was the kernel of the suburb of Praga. Czerniaków to the south belonged to Stanisaw Herakliusz Lubomirski (1642–1702), who founded there a Benardine Monastery, an artificial lake, and the family Mausoleum. Wielopole (1693) to the west was the work of the Crown Chancellor, Jan Wielopolski (d. 1688); Tamka, Alexandria (1670), Kapitulna, Kałeczyn, Bożydar (1702), and Ordynacka extended along the present-day Nowy Świat. The last of these, built by the Palatine of Podolia, Jan Jakub Zamoyski (d. 1790) in 1739, was centred on the remodelled Gniński Palace (now the seat of the Chopin Institute). Bielino (1757) was laid out by the Crown Marshal Franciszek Bieliński (1683–1766) in the region of the present-day Marszałkowska St. 'Marienstadt' (1762) and 'Stanisławów' (1768) on the river bank of Powiśle beneath Nowy Świat were the property of Stanisław-August, who sold them to the city Council in exchange for land adjoining Łazienki. The *jurydyki* reflected the complete individuality of the magnates. Though condemned by the Sejm in 1764, they were not entirely abolished till 1791.

The districts of Joli Bord (later polonized to 'Żolibórz')

and Praga developed more spontaneously. The former, clustered round a Piarist convent and the barracks of the Royal Guard, became the bourgeois suburb, sprinkled with the villas and gardens of high officials. The latter expanded both to the south and to the east. Saska Kępa (Saxon Islet) on the right-bank riverfront, an old Dutch peasant settlement once known as 'Holendry', was graced by the summer pavilion of August III, and attracted an increasing number of wealthy residents. Praga's eastern outskirts on the Radzymin Road were leased by Stanisław-August to a Jewish cattle merchant, Szmul Zbytkower. Their teeming streets, in effect, the right-bank ghetto, were universally known as the 'Szmulowizna'. Each of these new developments devoured large tracts of the City's agricultural land, which had fed the population since medieval times and which lent the City a semi-rural air until the end of the eighteenth century. Except for a makeshift pontoon, installed every summer from 1776 onwards under the management of the infamous Adam Poniński, the two halves of the city remained unjoined by any permanent bridge.

Attempts to contain the City behind fixed limits met with only partial success. The earthworks of 1621–4 were inspired by news of the Turkish victory at Cecora. Joining two points on the river bank north of the New Town and south of the Carmelite Church in a wide arc, they reached as far inland as the Arsenal at the end of Długa Street. They soon fell into disrepair. The earthworks of 1770 were inspired by the threat of plague, and were intended as a basis for police and sanitary controls. They encircled the city on a circumference of some sixteen kilometres on both banks of the river, enclosing Żolibórz in the north, Łazienki in the south, and Praga across the river. In the Rising of 1794 they were impressed into service as the city's last line of defence. In the nineteenth century, they acted as a natural dividing line within which the railway tracks, power stations, gas-works, and cemeteries, were not able to penetrate. Their thirteen Gates or *rogatki* kept the nondescript modern suburbs apart from the historic city centre.

Attempts to regulate the City's administration were constantly obstructed. From 1665, the Economic Offices of the

Old Town and New Town were empowered to levy rates, to present their budget, and to administer municipal enterprises. From 1742, the *Komisja Brukowa* (Street Commission) under Marshal Bieliński addressed itself energetically to the task of paving the streets, laying drains, and building foot-bridges over numerous uncovered streams. But large districts and sectors of the population lay beyond the city's control. Only in the terminal years of the Republic was the old order overturned. Thanks to the labours of the Old Town's Mayor, Jan Dękert (1738–90), the City magistrates joined with representatives of all the cities of Poland, and insisted on radical reform. In 1767, Warsaw was incorporated into a single municipality, within seven wards. On 21 April 1791, a law of the Four Years' Diet extended the liberties of the burgher class.

Schemes for co-ordinating the City's economic activities enjoyed earlier success. In 1691–5, a grandiose Market Hall, modelled on the Palais Royal in Paris, was intended to bring the retail trade of luxury and imported goods under one roof. It was named 'Marieville' (Marywił), like Marymont, after Sobieski's Queen. In 1720, another Trade Hall was founded by two French *émigrés,* Malherbe and Pellison. Their business, which obtained several lucrative monopolies, eventually passed into the hands of the banker, Peter Tepper (d. 1794).

The fortunes of royal Warsaw were not unmixed, however. Natural disasters competed with man-made tragedies. The fires of 1544 and 1607, which consumed the Old Town Square, the plagues of 1624–5, 1652–3, 1707–8, the hurricane of 1602, which destroyed the cathedral tower, all caused grave loss, both human and material. The incessant scandals and tumults of the Court – such as that in 1652 when the royal guards of the King's mistress, Elżbieta Radzie-jowska, the wife of the Vice-Chancellor of the Crown, successfully defended her from the regiments of an irate husband – engendered an atmosphere of violence and insecurity. The royal Elections, which occasioned an influx of fifty thousand or even a hundred thousand armed noblemen with their retinues, were invariably attended by months of intrigue, crime, and violence. Foreign armies occupied the city on repeated occasions – the Swedes in 1655, 1656, 1704, 1705 and 1708; the Transylvanians in 1657; the Saxons in 1704 and 1713; the Russians in 1706, 1717, 1733–5, 1763–4, 1767–73, 1792–3, 1794; the Prussians in 1794–1806; the French in 1807–13.

After each successive disaster, the city's population shrank alarmingly. From 18,000 in 1655, it fell to 6,000 in 1659, and, after the Third Partition, from 150,000 in 1795 to 70,000 in 1806.

Even so, Warsaw's progress contrasted sharply with that of the Republic's other cities. Despite the setbacks, Warsaw was generally growing and expanding throughout an era when most of its competitors experienced a catastrophic decline.

*   *   *   *   *

The ruin of the cities of Poland–Lithuania, like that of the Republic's economy as a whole, can more easily be described than explained. As from 1648, colossal havoc was wreaked by invading armies, particularly in the Swedish Wars of 1655–60, and in the Great Northern War of 1700–21. Those few cities which escaped destruction on the first occasion were invariably visited on the second. The smaller centres, which lacked the means for adequate defence, were specially vulnerable. The *Lustracje* (Surveys of Royal estates) conducted after each of the wars provide a glimpse of deteriorating conditions. In 1661, for just one small example, the city of Jaworów in Ruthenia, at that time in lease to Colonel John Sobieski, could not even produce its records; and the commissioners discovered a very serious deterioration in the city's income since the previous survey in 1627:

Jaworów City
The burghers of Jaworów, called on to present their rights, liberties, and privileges, replied that they had lost them during the recent enemy incursions, and for that reason could not produce the original copies. Instead, they produced a list of such rights drawn up in 1606 . . . and confirmed by our present gracious sovereign, Jan Kazimierz, in Warsaw on 8 October, 1649, together with the signature of the King's Secretary, General Piotr Sławieński, over the great seal of the Chancery of the Korona. In this confirmation, the following is contained:
Firstly, a confirmation on 2 July, 1569 by Sigismund-August, King of Poland, of letters issued on the sixth sunday after the feast of

St. Matthew in 1510 to the noble Łukasz de Gorka, Castellan of Poznań, hitherto the hereditary Lord of Jaworów, . . . by which confirmation, His Majesty also granted the incorporation of the city and its two suburbs, according to the German Law of Magdeburg . . .

Next, a charter issued by King Stephen at Lwów on 22 May, 1578 and confirmed by King Sigismund III in Lublin on 7 November 1588, whereby the petition of several senators for the city of Jaworów to exploit saline deposits commonly called madrepore was conceded . . . :

The first privilege of Władysław IV, dated at Cracow on 15 March 1633, which concerned the construction of the bridge . . :

The second privilege of Władysław IV, dated at Cracow on 13 March 1633, which approved all previous charters granted by his royal predecessors . . . together with the Survey of the city undertaken by the inspectors of the Województwo of Ruthenia in 1629 . . . ;

The burghers also produced a treaty concluded between themselves and the infidel Jews in 1640 . . . and another concluded and confirmed by his excellency the Starosta, Jan Sobieski, in 1655 . . . all of which we have kept and accepted, since nothing therein offends against the law.

The Income from the City of Jaworów with both its suburbs

The burghers pay a rent of 12 gr. for houses on the city square, and 8 gr. for houses on the streets.

— According to the Survey of 1627, rent was paid for 32 houses on the square, apart from those belonging to the Council, the Wójt, and the church organist, i.e.   12 fl. 24 gr.

Now rent is paid for 14 houses: 5 fl. 18 gr.

	(1629) fl.	gr.	(now) fl.	gr.
— For houses on Fara St., formerly 29	7	22		
now 22			5	26
— For houses on Mill St., formerly 15	4	00		
now none			—	
— For houses on Przemysł St., formerly 66	17	18		
now 29			7	22
— For houses on Jarosław St., formerly 10	2	20		
now 5			1	10
— For houses on Lwów St., formerly 40	10	20		
now 18			4	24

— For the city gardens beyond the dyke, formerly	30 26	
now		22 27
— For the city fields . . . formerly	30 12	
now		19 19
— For the city refineries . . . formerly	3 06	
now		1 06
— The Smiths, formerly 10 paid	4 12	
now 4 pay		1 18
— The Cobblers, formerly 16 paid	6 12	
now 24 pay		9 18
— Jewish Taverners, formerly 23 paid	58 08	
now 5 pay		30 00
— Tenant farmers, formerly 33 paid	43 10	
now 12 pay		36 00
— For fodder, nothing is paid, formerly	100 00	—

	fl. gr. d.	fl. gr. d.
— The Greater Suburb of Jaworów, containing 25¼ łan, together with the Orthodox priest and the Tavern used in 1627 to pay rent:	368 07 0	
— 9 bushels of barley @ 10 gr.	3 00	
— 40 hens @ 1½d.	2 00	
and a cash gift	2 00	
Nowadays, since many fields have been abandoned, the residents pay various sums, in rent:		125 01 0
— 13 half bushels of barley @ 1 fl.		13 00
— 20 hens @ 6 gr.		4 00
— Cash gift		2 00
— Honey		16 06 0
— The Orthodox curate (protopop) pays	—	2 00
and the priest of the Nakomiczny Church	—	1 01 0
— The peasants, formerly 15, paid	67 21 0	
now pay		55 12 0

— The Lesser Suburb of Jaworów, containing 3¼ (?) *łan*, used to pay in rent:	58 15 0	
now pay		17 16 9
— The peasants, formerly paid	8 11 0	
now pay		5 03 0
For transport to the River San, both suburbs pay		114 15 0
For cartage, the Nakomiczny Church pays		7 0 0
TOTAL INCOME formerly	842 04 9	
now		508 28 9[11]

The fall of Jaworów's income from 842 to 508 florins over only thirty-four years represented a decrease in money terms of about 40 per cent; but in real terms, owing to rampant price inflation, of at least 80 per cent. The Survey further shows that the city's three churches — the Catholic Dominican Church, the Uniate Bazylian Church, and the Orthodox Church — were exempted from all contributions owing to their dilapidated state. The picture was in no way exceptional. The ravages of the mid-seventeenth century proved permanent. As time went on, the condition of the cities declined still further. Trade dwindled. Artistic patronage vanished. The absolute number of city dwellers constantly diminished, whilst the number of registered citizens, and of skilled craftsmen, decreased in proportion to the plebs, the poor, and the Jews. The urban population sank to a mere 15 per cent of the whole. The great cities assumed the air of small towns; whilst the minor cities were reverting to the state of overgrown, country villages, not to say of ghost towns. By the mid-eighteenth century, in the words of a contemporary description, 'Every street was an open field, every square a desert.' This phenomenon of urban decline was not unknown elsewhere in Central and Eastern Europe at this time; but its manifestations in Poland—Lithuania were unusually severe.

The causes of decline as proposed by historians are many and various. War devastation was obviously important as a precipitating factor, but cannot in itself explain the cities' failure to revive in times of peace. Dwindling trade, too, was bound to affect urban prosperity, but does not explain, why many cities failed to keep their share of such commerce that survived. The growth of mercantilist states on the Republic's borders conceivably provided added competition. The fact that not only Breslau but also Riga after 1621 and Königsberg after 1657 lay beyond foreign customs barriers may have adversely affected the Republic's commercial prospects. Financial historians have stressed the devaluation of the Republic's currency with the associated boost to inflation. The last royal mint in Poland—Lithuania closed in 1688. Social historians have variously pointed both to the exclusiveness of the Jews and to the complacency of the nobility as causes of the distress of the burgher estate. Certainly the noble—Jewish alliance represented an important challenge to the burghers' former supremacy in commercial matters. But none of these points approaches the heart of the problem. Surely, in analysing urban decline, the historian should look less for external scapegoats and more for signs of internal weakness. Here, one is immediately struck by the centrifugal forces within the political life of the cities. There were conflicts between the patricate and the commoners, and between the citizens and the plebs; there were conflicts of a religious and national character between Catholics, Protestants, Uniates, or Orthodox as between Poles, Germans, Ruthenes, and Lithuanians; and there was the fundamental division between the Christian burghers and the Jewish estate. The Guilds were greatly fragmented into official, unofficial, and national sectors. In the political sphere, the cities were defenceless. In their era of prosperity, they had failed to gain adequate representation in the Sejm — the observers from Cracow, Wilno, and Royal Prussia in no way compensating for the absence of a commercial 'Tiers État' in the government of the state. Accordingly in times of adversity, they could neither protect themselves from the nobility, nor seek redress from the King, nor reform themselves. They gradually fell victim to various forms of exploitation and oppression. The waving of an ancient charter did not deter an imperious magnate from subverting the processes of municipal democracy to his own advantage. The possession of a diploma of citizenship did not save the indigent craftsman from the corvée. In the eighteenth century, there were instances where even the mayors of small private towns were driven into serfdom. Only the few great royal cities could resist, and then only in an atrophied mockery of their former splendour. It was a sorry state of affairs, only partially redeemed by the relative strength of urban life in Royal Prussia or in the new textile towns of Wielkopolska.

Attempts at reform had to wait till the second half of the eighteenth century. By that time, the vast majority of the Republic's 1,400 cities were tiny private administrative centres whose average population of 750 persons lived largely from agriculture. From the point of view of modern urban planning most of them were beyond redemption. On the initiative of the Sejm of 1764, a series of *Komisje Boni Ordinis,* or 'Commissions of Good Order', were instituted to investigate the plight of particular cities, and to recommend improvements. At the same time, the central organs of Jewish autonomy, including the Council of Four Lands, were suspended, with a view to reducing Jewish separatism and to creating a unified bourgeoisie. In the following decades, no less than twenty-two commissions were formed, sometimes with important effects. In Warsaw, for example, the separate jurisdictions of the Old City and the New City and of the noble *jurydyki* was abolished in 1767, and replaced by united courts and Council under a new City President. In Cracow, the old corporation was abolished in 1775, and replaced by a new streamlined Council of 12 elected members ruling over the four public departments of Justice, Finance, Welfare, and Police. For a brief period it looked as though the cities of Poland—Lithuania might be restored to economic prosperity and political independence. Intellectual and artistic life revived. Public building started again. The sons of the burghers flocked to the schools of the National Education Commission, and began to take an intelligent interest in their rights and their future. In 1791, following an active campaign by Jan Dękert, President of Warsaw, their admittance to the Sejm, to public office and to landed property was legally affirmed. Yet it was an illusory triumph. The work of the Four Years Sejm was overturned before it could take effect. With the Third Partition of 1795, the cities of Poland—Lithuania were handed over to the mercy of partitioning powers whose own traditions regarding the proper place of the cities within the political order were very different from those of the Republic.

CHAPTER TEN
ANARCHIA:
The Noble Democracy

Throughout the modern period, the history of most European countries is dominated by the growth of the state. The emergence of national states in the fifteenth and sixteenth centuries; the trends to Absolutism in the seventeenth and to Enlightened Despotism in the eighteenth century; and the drive to harness state power to economic, social, and educational programmes in the nineteenth and twentieth centuries, have proceeded with no great regard to expressions of resistance or dissent. Certainly until the First World War, the arguments were mainly concerned with the directions, methods, and priorities of developing state power, and only on rare occasions with fundamental problems as to the desirability or necessity of state power itself. Only after two world wars of unprecedented destructiveness, and the experience of Fascist and communist regimes which have devoured millions of human victims, have the excesses of the state inspired any general discomfort at the political achievements of half a millennium.

In this context, the workings of one of the very few states in which strong traditions consistently opposed the pretensions of central government may prove instructive. In the Republic of Poland—Lithuania as constituted between the union of 1569 and the Third Partition of 1795, political anarchism provided one of the guiding ideals of its noble democracy. Its watchword — *'Nierządem Polska Stoi'* ('It is by unrule that Poland stands') — contains a paradox which Proudhon himself would have admired, and comes close to Bellegarrigue's famous slogan of 1848, *'L'Anarchie, c'est l'ordre'*. Its laws and practices were inspired by deeply rooted beliefs in individual freedom and civil liberty which, for the period, were exceptional. In the sixteenth and seventeenth centuries they seem to have exercised some distant influence on the radical movements of Western Europe, not least

321

through writings of the Polish Brethren. But in the eighteenth century they were completely unfashionable, and widely misunderstood. During the Enlightenment, 'Anarchie' was used as a term of abuse, a synonym for chaos and terror; and in the nineteenth century, the former Republic continued to be the object of retrospective derision. To the Prussian and Russian historians who interpreted its downfall as part of their own rise to fame, it exhibited a degenerate form of government which had been rightly supplanted by the progressive and benevolent rule of their own monarchs. Their opinions largely prevail in existing history textbooks to this day. The Republic of Poland—Lithuania was not a resounding success. For that reason its ideals and institutions have rarely received the attention they deserve.[1]

* * * * *

Appropriately enough, the fundamental constitutional laws which supposedly governed the political life of Poland—Lithuania were nicely contradictory. Indeed the exact nature of the Union was disputed for much of its existence. According to the Union of Lublin, whose provisions were held to be sacrosanct by Polish jurists, the separate sovereignties of the Kingdom of Poland and of the Grand Duchy of Lithuania had been voluntarily dissolved in 1569, and merged for ever into a new sovereign entity, the united *Rzeczpospolita*. All laws contrary to the Act of Union were repealed. According to the Third Lithuanian Statute of 1588, however, the separate sovereignty of the Grand Duchy remained inviolate, and all laws contrary to the Statute, including several clauses of the Union of Lublin, were judged to be invalid.[2] By any stretch of the imagination, the situation was absurd. In Poland, the Third Lithuanian Statute was thought to be unconstitutional. In Lithuania, the 'humiliating' Union of Lublin was seen by the authors of the Statute as an act of duress. Yet no attempt was made to resolve the confusion. Both the Act of Union, and the Third Statute remained in force until the end of the eighteenth century. What the average citizen thought or knew about the problem is difficult to say; but it is clear, whilst most Polish noblemen from the Kingdom held the Union to be binding, a minority of their Lithuanian brethren continued to insist on the Grand Duchy's separate status. In this light, it could be argued that the constitutional union of Poland and Lithuania was not properly consummated until 1791, when the *Rzeczpospolita Obojga Narodów* (The 'Republic of the Two Nations') was solemnly declared as part of the Constitution of 3 May. Yet this latter union hardly left the paper on which it was written. The Grand Duchy of Lithuania was formally abolished by Russian decree after the Second Partition of 1793, just two years before the Polish rump of the Republic was abolished by the Third Partition of 1795. Ineluctably, therefore, in examining political traditions, the historian is obliged to rely less on the theory of the law, and more on the customs and practice of established institutions. (See Diagram K.)

The basic unit of constitutional life in Poland–Lithuania was the *sejmik* or dietine. (Both *Sejm* and *sejmik,* meaning 'assembly' and 'little assembly' derive from the old Czech word *sejmovat,* 'to bring together' or 'to summon'.) It crystallized in the fifteenth century out of earlier forms of meetings organized by the nobility, mainly for military purposes, and became the regular consultative institution in all the provinces of the Kingdom, and later of the Republic. Its decisive moment occurred in 1454, at Nieszawa, at the beginning of the second Teutonic War, when the King conceded the principle that he would neither summon the army nor raise taxes without prior consultation with the nobility. From that point on, the nobles of each province met together at frequent intervals to conduct their own political and legislative business, and to consider the royal policy. When, in course of time, the general Sejm and the Crown Tribunal were established, each of the dietines appointed representatives to pursue its interests in the activities of the central legislature and judiciary. By the sixteenth century, four types of session were held, sometimes successively, sometimes separately. The *sejmik poselski* was called to elect two 'envoys' (*poseł*)* to transmit the 'instructions' of

---

* In Polish, the word *poseł* is used both for 'ambassador' and for a member of the Diet. It cannot be translated into English as 'deputy' because it would clash with the office of 'deputy to the Tribunal', whilst other possibilities such as 'representative', 'congressman', or 'MP', are inappropriate, 'Envoy' seems to be the nearest literal equivalent, but used in the sense of 'delegate'.

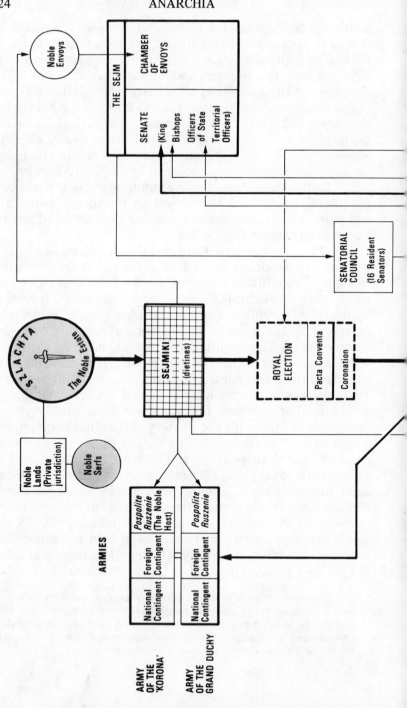

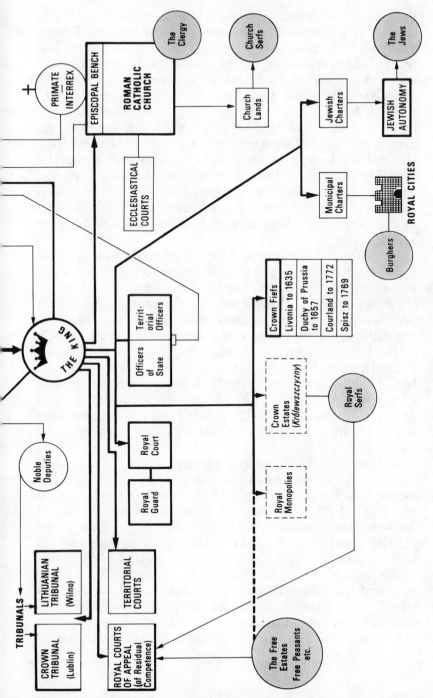

Diagram K. Central Institutions of the *Rzeczpospolita*

the province's nobility to the Sejm; the *sejmik deputacki* elected two 'deputies' (*deputat*) to serve on the Crown Tribunal; the *sejmik relacyjny* met to consider reports and recommendations from the Sejm and to take appropriate action; the *sejmik gospodarski,* or 'economic session', met to administer the trade and finance of the province, and to execute the resolutions of the Sejm in relation to taxes, military service, and land-holding. In this last function, the dietine was assisted by a number of professional administrative officers, headed by the *subdelegat,* whose job was to run everyday business in the intervals between sessions. At the end of its deliberations, the dietine passed its *lauda* or 'resolutions', which carried the full authority of law within the area of its competence. These resolutions did not require the royal assent.

From this, it is important to recognize that the nobility regarded themselves as the supreme authority in the state, and considered the dietines to form the senior branch of the legislative process. The business of the central government occupied only one part of their deliberations, and not necessarily the most important one. They received the proposals of the King, of Sejm, or of the officers-of-state, with strong reservations as to their own competence, and did not feel bound to obey or to conform. Their envoys were expected to stick closely to their instructions and were required on oath to swear 'to Almighty God, Three-in-One, that I shall defend our freedom, and to admit no laws which are contrary to the instructions.'

In November 1585, for example, the nobility of the palatinate of Cracow were summoned to their traditional point of assembly in the parish church of Proszowice, sixteen miles to the east of the old capital. Some six weeks before, a *'uniwersał'* or circular writ had been sent by the King to the Palatine, Andrzej Tęczyński, asking them to assemble on 8 November and to offer their advice on the disturbances which were shaking the country. In the previous year, the forces of the Chancellor of the Crown, Jan Zamoyski, had seized an outlawed nobleman, Samuel Zborowski, and executed him in the market-place at Cracow. Since the victim had openly circulated in the Republic for four years before his capture, and had served as a captain of cavalry in the recent campaigns against Muscovy, his death was widely interpreted as an act of private vengeance. His brothers, Krzysztof and Jan, members of a wild and powerful Protestant clan, were preparing to retaliate. On 7 November Krzysztof Zborowski arrived in Proszowice one day early, and invested the church with a troop of armed retainers. Thus, on the 8th, when the dignitaries of the province arrived to take their places in the 'circle of knights' in front of the altar, they found themselves overborne from the gallery and the organ-loft by rows of pikes and muskets. Before they could proceed, Zborowski had sprung to his feet, and sworn to take revenge 'on the throat of Zamoyski' for the shameful murder of his brother, calling on the assembled nobles to make his cause their own. When the Bishop of Cracow, Piotr Myszkowski, and the Castellan of Biecz, Mikołaj Firlej, suggested recourse to the courts, they were rudely interrupted. The election of the Marshal of the dietine had to be conducted in the grave-yard. On the second and third days, tempers rose still further. Zborowski's adherents sought to get their way by filibuster, or by drowning their opponents' arguments in peals from the belfry. Then, as Stanisław Stadnicki, the Devil of Łańcut rode in and took the Zborowskis' part, a firearm was aimed at Spytek Jordan, the leader of the opposition. Sympathy and force was nicely divided. The one point on which everyone was agreed was that Zamoyski's men had exceeded their rights by trespassing on the estates of the Zborowskis' niece, Katarzyna Włodyk. The fact that the lady was harbouring an outlaw at the time made no difference to the inviolability of her property. According to the law of *Neminem captivabimus,* all nobles were immune from all such invasions until condemned in a court of law. As a lady, and a local land-owner, she attracted great support. On 11 November, the dietine was in a state of schism. Inside the church, the Zborowskis elected two of their own men, headed by Mikołaj Kazimierski, as envoys. Outside the church in the graveyard, the opposition elected another team led by Spytek Jordan. It was with the greatest difficulty that the rival groups were persuaded to pass their common resolutions, and to choose a clerk to write the instructions. In the end, of thirty-seven instructions, only one concerned the Zborowskis. Instruction No. 20 enjoined the envoys to protest in the Sejm against the invasion of the widow Włodyk's estates, and to press for a fair hearing for the Zborowskis.[3]

The detailed, parochial nature of the dietines' instructions is indicative of the nobility's deepest concerns. In 1667, Jan Chryzostom Pasek served as Marshal of the *sejmik* of Rawa in Mazovia, and recorded their instructions in full. Although this was a time of civil commotion caused by Lubomirski's Rebellion, and by the failing powers of the King, Jan Kazimierz, the nobles of the province showed an extraordinary concern for pettifogging detail:

INSTRUCTIONS

To their Lordships, the Honourable envoys of Rawa — *Pan* Adam Nowomiejski, District Judge in Rawa, and *Pan* Anselm Piekarski, Cup-Bearer of Rawa, unanimously elected by the noble *sejmik*:

Inasmuch as everyone can see how our entire country must grieve at the sight of the troubles caused by the exertions of malevolent men, and by the ingratitude of those who disrupt the Diets . . . we, as loyal subjects commend our envoys before all else to express our sympathy to his Royal Majesty, Our Gracious King, and to wish him a long and successful reign . . .

1. As it is through frequent, unfounded, and illegal vetoes that Sessions of the Sejm have been dissolved, to the Republic's detriment, we order our envoys to find a means of limiting such vetoes by law . . .
2. Further, our envoys are to beseech His Majesty to approve the Treaty at Lęgonice . . .
3. Since we cannot afford to raise back-pay for soldiers serving the Republic on credit out of taxes, our envoys will propose these measures:
4. First that the colonels, captains-of-horse, foreign officers etc. postpone their claims, on a surety from the Treasury;
5. Second, that the crown jewels be inventoried, and pawned;
6. that priests, bishops, abbots, and curates prove themselves true sons of the land, and pledge a voluntary subsidy;
7. that Customs and Excise, sales taxes, and the Jewish poll-tax be doubled;
8. that the Army officers surrender their pay for the benefit of the common soldiers;

. . . .

14. that something be done to pay off the debt to his Highness, the Prince of Brandenburg;

15. that the Prince of Kurland retain the city of Piłtyń . . .
16. that the wishes of our brothers from Livonia, whose estates are devastated, be satisfied . . .
17. that the unresolved debt from 1662 be paid to the Orsettis . . . or a suitable security;
18. Our envoys shall press to have the Mint closed, and its dyes destroyed; and . . .
19. press also for the trials of Boratini and Tymff . . .
20. that the administrators of the customs and excise prepare their accounts for inspection . . .
21. that His Majesty fix the prices of cloth and other things, whose insufferable costs burden the Republic . . .
. . . .
25. that the foreign ambassadors who have tarried here so long be dismissed . . .
26. that no private emissaries be sent abroad, without permission . . .
27. Whereas our province has been ravaged more than any other by the movements of the royal and confederate armies, that Our envoys plead for our taxes to be postponed *ad feliciora tempora*;
28. that at least one Hetman be always present in the Army, in the cause of discipline,
29. that absentee officers . . . forfeit their pay . . .
30. that native *szlachta* be permitted to serve in foreign armies;
31. that His Grace, the Bishop of Chełm . . . be awarded a second abbey, regardless of the law against plurality . . .
32. that Alexander Załuski, Chamberlain of Rawa, be suitably compensated for his villages in the Palatinate of Smolensk — Pavlovo, Shapoli, Borodino . . . now overrun by the confounded Muscovites . . .
33. that the devastated city of Rawa . . . be exempt from taxes . . .
34. that the land leased from *Pan* Piotr Sladkowski for a hospital be granted the privilege of ecclesiastical law, as requested by the vicar of Budiszowice . . .

We hereby commend their lordships, our envoys, to seek the *bonum patriae* in faith, honour, and conscience, so that our freedom be embellished . . . and to communicate in all matters with other provincial envoys.

Given at Rawa, in the sejmik of nobles, 7 February, AD 1667,
                    Jan Chryzostom z Gosławic Pasek,
            Deputy chamberlain, Marshal of the Sejmik.[4]

The Sejm, or Diet, was instituted later than the dietines, and in many ways was subordinate to them. It certainly depended on them for the execution of its decisions. It seems to have been inspired by the experience of the Estates of Royal Prussia which had continued to function after the incorporation of that province into Poland in 1466.[5] It first met in 1493 in Cracow, at royal request, as a 'parliament' of the Kingdom, with only forty elected envoys present. After 1569, it was transformed into the joint assembly of the united Republic. It consisted of two chambers – the *Senat* or 'Senate', with 140 members, and the *Izba Poselska* or 'Chamber of Envoys', with 143 – 95 from the Kingdom, and 48 from the Grand Duchy.

The Senate was composed from the chief officers of Church and State – 2 archbishops, 17 Roman bishops, 4 Marshals, 4 Chancellors, 2 Treasurers, 33 Palatines (*Wojewoda*), 77 Castellans (*kasztelan*), and the Starosta of Żmudź.* It was presided over by the Marshal of the Crown, and attended by the king. It had grown out of a medieval Royal Council, and in addition to its function as a chamber of the legislature, it retained its original function as the chief executive authority. In between sessions it appointed sixteen 'resident' senators, who stayed with the king and dealt with the day-to-day business of government. Its 140 members were organized according to an ancient order of seniority. They sat round a rectangular floor with the king on his throne at one end, the bishops on their benches at the other, the state functionaries and Palatines in their armchairs down the sides, and the Castellans packed in round the back.

As a rule, the lower chamber received two envoys from each of the provincial dietines, and two from the City of Cracow. In the seventeenth and eighteenth centuries, when envoys from lands lost to the Republic continued to sit and when some provinces such as Royal Prussia sent as many as eight envoys each, the original 143 members rose to 182 in 1702 and exceptionally, in 1764 to 236. The chair was taken by a 'Marshal of the Sejm', elected by the envoys at the start of each session. According to the Union of Lublin, the Chamber was to meet with the Senate for a six weeks' session at least once in every two years, and to deliberate from 9 a.m.

---

* The four *Hetmans* or Military Chiefs were the only high officers of state without senatorial rank.

to dusk, except on Sundays and Saints' days. From 1702 to
1764, the sessions were fixed well ahead, customarily on the
first Monday after St. Michael's Day, every alternate year. If
these sessions of the full or *'Walny Sejm'* lasted the normal
six weeks and in their regular cadence, they were called
'ordinary' sessions. If they met at urgent request for a shorter
period, they were called 'extraordinary'. On the death of the
king, the Sejm was automatically· convoked by the Primate
acting as *Interrex* or 'Regent', whose task it was to prepare
the election of a successor. This meeting was called the *Sejm
konwokacyjny* or 'convocational assembly'. When the new
king had· been elected, the Sejm met again, first to confirm
the terms of the king's contract in the *Pacta Conventa* at the
Sejm elekcyjny (Electoral Assembly), and then to hear him
swear the coronation oath at the *Sejm koronacyjny* (Coronation Assembly). (The failure of the king-elect to accept the
Pacta Conventa or the oath as they stood would have required
the immediate cancellation of the Coronation, and the calling of a new election.) Ever since 1505, when the constitution of *Nihil Novi* was passed, the Lower Chamber had
enjoyed parity of status with the Senate. Through the *Pacta
Conventa,* it held the ultimate check on the conduct of the
king. As the servant of the dietines, it expressed the will of
the noble citizens of the Republic, and controlled the vital
spheres of military finance and state taxation. It was the
more powerful element in the Sejm, therefore, and, as such,
the highest authority in the state. These arrangements,
completed in time for the accession of the first elected king
in 1573, prevailed until 1791.

During the three centuries of its existence, the Sejm conducted some 230 sessions. 147 of these were held in the
Royal Castle in Warsaw; 38 in Piotrków; 29 in Cracow; 11 in
Grodno (in response to a Lithuanian demand in 1678 to hold
every third session in the Grand Duchy); 4 in Lublin; 3 in
Thorn; 2 in Sandomierz; 2 in Radom; and 1 in each of several
accidental localities. The very last session, assembled in
Grodno to confirm the Second Partition, terminated its
deliberations on 23 November 1793.[6]

A Royal election in Poland was something rather special.
In theory, every nobleman of the Republic was entitled to

attend, and in practice, anything between ten and fifteen thousand usually did. They assembled on horseback on the Wola Field near Warsaw, forming up in serried ranks round the pavilions of their respective provinces. Any Catholic nobleman − citizen or foreigner − was eligible to present himself as a candidate. Each of the provinces discussed the matter beforehand in the dietines, and generally came to Warsaw with some idea of their preferences. Yet the process whereby this horde of armed horsemen reached a unanimous decision from dozens of candidates and viewpoints can only be described as one of collective intuition. At the start of the day, the sponsors of each leading candidate would form a claque to publicize their cause. Deputations would move from pavilion to pavilion, testing the drift of the general mood, canvassing their clients, reporting back to their own provincial pavilion to decide what move to make. All the while the Marshal of the Crown would ride back and forth, urging the doubters to throw in their lot with the front runners, begging the losing parties not to resist unduly, cajoling them all to settle their differences and make their common choice. If he was lucky, by the evening, the name of the expected winner would be raised aloud; one by one the provinces would swell the chanting into a gigantic roar; and at last, swords raised to the sky, the nobility of the Republic would acclaim their King. As often as not, however, the workings of intuition failed to inspire unanimity. Scenes of unutterable confusion, pitched battles, and private fights were commonplace. In 1764, when only thirteen electors were killed, it was said that the Election was unusually quiet. On several occasions − in 1576, 1587, 1697, and 1733 − differences were not resolved on the Field. In this case, a double election ensued, with two 'successful' kings-elect both setting out to enforce their claim in the resulting civil war. The scene in 1669 at the Election of Michał Korybut Wiśniowiecki was described by Pasek:

Announcements went out from the Primate-Archbishop to the provinces urging the estates to make a speedy election . . . But the provinces refused their assent. Indeed, they ordered everyone to horse as if for war. They knew the Archbishop's motives . . . I, having married in the Cracow district, was now serving under the standard of Cracow,

Eustachy Pisarski commanding. We set off for Wysimierzyce, stopping there for more than a week, and set foot in Warsaw in the first days of July. Then the other provincial detachments began to arrive, with large armies, magnatial retinues, and companies of infantry. Bogusław Radziwiłł, for one, was accompanied by 8,000 handsomely equipped men. For the first time in Poland, we heard the so-called Prussian Music, which is played in front of the professional cavalry regiments on bassoons . . .

Having sat through a few sessions and listened to the foreign ambassadors . . . the candidate who appealed to us most was the Prince of Lorraine. He was a soldier and was young, and his ambassador had said these words at the end of his peroration: *'Quotquot sunt inimici vestri, cum omnibus in hac arena certabit.'* . . .

The next day the senators rode out to the Electoral Field, which was covered with armies. Various opinions were being expressed . . . when one nobleman from Łęczyca shouted out, 'If you supporters of Condé do not keep still, you'll see bullets flying.' One of the Senators answered him crudely, and the next minute they began to fire . . . Some squadrons of cavalry charged from the sidelines into the soldiers, trampling them underfoot . . . Finally, the officers collected their men, while the bishops and senators, half-dead, crawled out from under the chairs and carriages . . .

The next day there was no session. The gentlemen were recovering from their fright, drinking hyacinth tea. The provincial delegations stayed in their camp . . .

On 16 June, the provincial envoys sent to the Archbishop, . . . to open further deliberations. He replied that he would not, being unsure of his safety . . . Someone from the throng speaks out: '. . . Since Our Reverend Father is not fulfilling the functions of his office, we'll ask the Castellan of Cracow to preside. After all, it's not a Pope we're electing, and we can dispense with the priest . . .'

As this was going on, the province of Wielkopolska now raises the shout of *'Vivat Rex.'* Several from our delegation dash over to see whom they are cheering for. They returned with the news it was for Charles of Lorraine. In (the pavilion of) Łęczyca and Kujawy, they were saying, 'We don't need a rich man or anyone related to royalty, for that's danger to Liberty. We need a strong, warlike man . . . As God has taken Czarniecki from us, let us elect his disciple, Polanowski.'

Meanwhile, I, out of curiosity, rush across to the delegates of Sandomierz. I find they prefer someone of native blood. Recalling the many merits of the late Prince Wiśniowiecki, they say it would be right to elect his heir, Prince Michał . . . At this, there's a roar from the province of Sandomierz, *'Vivat Piast! Vivat Rex Michael!'* . . . The men from

Kujawy, thinking it's for their Polanowski, started shouting too . . . Our Cracovian officers, having taken a great deal of money from other candidates, say 'Wait! Have we gone mad?' . . . Pisarski asks me what I think of the situation. 'I think what God has put in my heart,' I replied, *'Vivat Rex Michael'.* Whereon, I ride out of our line, charging after Sandomierz; and all our squadrons with their standards follow. . . .

Then we led Wiśniowiecki to the Assembly. There were congratulations for the King, . . . and heartache for the evildoers.[7]

This extreme application of the elective principle to the monarchy of Poland—Lithuania recalls James Bryce's famous judgement on the constitution of the Holy Roman Empire in medieval Germany. Speaking of the formalization of the imperial electoral system by the Emperor Charles IV in 1356, Bryce commented: 'He legalised anarchy, and called it a constitution.'[8] The parallel is an apt one. Many scholars, including Bryce, have held the Polish constitution to be a derivative, if not a copy, of the German system. Certainly, the ultimate supremacy of the Electors over the monarch provided one of the main causes of the monarchy's decline, in Poland—Lithuania, as also in Germany.

Once elected, the king-elect proceeded to the Sejm to hear the nobility's proposals concerning the conditions on which they would agree to his coronation. In 1573, after the first election, nine such articles were drawn up for Henry Valois. In subsequent reigns, these 'Henrican Articles' formed a fixed constitutional contract which never varied. They insisted, among other things, on the nobility's right to elect their king freely in the future, irrespective of the king's plans for his own family; on their right to approve all declarations of war, all impositions of taxes, and all summons of the *levée-en-masse*; on regular meetings of the Sejm according to the Union of Lublin, and on the principle of toleration as enshrined in the act of the Confederation of Warsaw; and on the nomination of the sixteen resident Senators, not by the king, but by the Sejm. A final article enunciated the nobility's right of resistance, indeed their duty to disobey the king if he contravened his oath. In 1576, at the second election, a number of additional articles, called *Pacta Conventa* or 'agreed points', were negotiated with Stefan Bathory. They related to specific promises which he had made at the time of his election regarding the conduct of foreign policy and the management of the royal debt; but they were not renewed. For the rest of the Republic's history, the terms 'Pacta Conventa' and 'Henrician Articles' were used indiscriminately. By these means, the King of the Republic was appointed as a lifelong manager, working on contract to the rules of the firm. From coronation to the grave, he could have no illusions but that he was the servant, and the nobility his master.[9]

Yet parliamentary control over the royal Executive was by no means complete. In the detailed conduct of government, the king retained important powers, and considerable room for political manœuvre. For 98 weeks out of 104, he was the undisputed ruler of the Republic. As the incumbent of the Crown estates, he directly managed one-sixth of the land and population, disposing of economic and military resources greater than those of the greatest of the magnates. As a political patron, he could offer his loyal supporters not merely the rewards of executive office but also lifelong tenancies of rich Crown properties and monopolies. He spoke with a dominant voice in all political appointments. Although he was not permitted to dismiss them unilaterally, he chose the sixteen officers of state – the *Marszałek* (Marshal), the *Hetman* (Commander), the *Kanclerz* (Chancellor), and the *Podskarbi* (Treasurer) of the Korona and of the Grand Duchy, with their duputies; he named the regional officers of *Wojewoda* (Palatine), *Kasztelan* (Castellan), and *Starosta,* and selected judicial officers from lists submitted by the Sejm or by the dietines; and he confirmed all apostolic appointments to abbeys and bishoprics in the Roman, Uniate, and Orthodox churches. In this way, he wielded an influence in the Senate far beyond that which was openly revealed during its formal proceedings. In legislative matters, he continued to issue edicts in all spheres not reserved by privilege to the Sejm; in military matters, he acted as the nominal Commander-in-Chief to whom all soldiers addressed their oath of allegiance; in judicial matters, he retained the right to act with the Sejm as the highest court of appeal; and in political matters, he was the natural protector of the lesser nobles against the magnates, and of the weaker estates – the burghers, Jews, peasants, and clergy – against the nobility as a whole. In foreign affairs, he claimed a leading role in the formulation of policy. In almost all his decisions, he had to carry the resident Senators with him; but he was not necessarily obliged to accept any proposals that were put to him. Even in relation to the Sejm, he could not be said in any sense to be powerless. It was the king who convened the Sejm, and who prorogued and dissolved it. It was the king who directed the programme of debates. It was the king whose signature turned parliamentary resolutions into statutory law. The King may well have been the servant of the noble Republic; but he was no puppet.

The procedures of the 'ordinary' and 'extraordinary' sessions of the Sejm were often as confused, and as complicated as those of the royal elections. In 1585–6, for example, the Sejm which Bathory summoned to Warsaw to settle the Zborowski affair already discussed in the dietines, ended in political stalemate. It was summoned to assemble on 15 January. Three days earlier, the King made his entry into Warsaw from the south, accompanied by Konstanty Ostrogski, Palatine of Kiev, with 1,500 Cossacks and cavalry, and by Chancellor Zamoyski with 1,500 infantrymen. To the west, Krzystof Zborowski was approaching with an army of his own. It was the Chancellor's aim, as the diarist says, to be *'potentior potentia potentissimi'*, to be 'stronger in strength than the strongest'. On the 15th, the Archbishop of Lwów celebrated Mass in the Cathedral of St. John, and the newly elected Marshal of the Sejm, Pękosławski, presented the loyal address. On the 16th, Phase One of the proceedings began with each chamber sitting separately. The Lower House prepared a list of suggested appointees for the vacant offices of state, and debated matters arising from their instructions. When the *rugi* or 'scrutiny of membership' took place, the envoys of the nobles of Volhynia were admitted in place of 'two envoys of the lords of that province' who had held a dietine of their own. The Senate was debating the internal and external problems of the day. Speaking in strict order of seniority, each senator presented his *votum* or 'opinion'. When it came to the turn of the Chancellor, he spoke in detail both about the troubles in Muscovy and the troubles at home. He explained why Samuel Zborowski had been pursued and executed, and insisted on his own good faith. 'I obey the law', he declared, 'and I uphold it.' In subsequent days, it appeared that his ground was well prepared. He had intercepted the correspondence of Krzysztof Zborowski. Letters were produced in which the King was described as 'Baal', 'a graven image', 'a tyrant', and 'a Hungarian hound'. They hinted at a conspiracy to kill him while hunting. A demand was made to charge the culprit with *lèse-majesté*, and to examine him before the Sejm. On 26 January Jan Zborowski, castellan of Gniezno, explained *cum lacrimis* that his brother was quick of tongue and would easily exonerate himself if given a safe-conduct. Following the recess on 2 and 3 February, Zamoyski treated the senators to a discourse on the virtues of the Roman Republic as contrasted with the envy and demagoguery of the present. On the 7th and 8th, the King judged criminal matters, and the Sejm moved on to Muscovite affairs, and interviewed prisoners recently released by the Tsar. By the 18th, when Krzysztof Zborowski had still not appeared, Kazimierski arrived to tell the Senate that his master was not aware of the Sejm's demand, and in any case he was ill, abroad, and unable to attend. At this the King flew into a rage, shouting *'Tace Nebulo'*, 'Be Silent, you lout.' Kazimierski held his ground. 'I am not a slave,' he replied, 'but a Polish gentleman.' None the less Zborowski was called in contempt, and the state prosecutor was ordered to prepare a charge against him in the Crown Tribunal. The next day, the Muscovite ambassadors were received 'with extravagant bows to His Loving Majesty', bringing the news of Ivan the Terrible's death. With this, the Sejm moved into its Second Phase, with both chambers sitting together. Each chamber presented a list of proposals, or 'bills', for their joint consideration, and votes were taken as to whether or not these 'bills' should be passed and be written into the register as 'constitutions' or laws. On 22–3 February, a number of such constitutions were passed, including the charge against Zborowski and several others relating to tolls, the arrears of the Army, and religious intolerance. At the same time, a number of *exorbitancja* or 'injustices' were recorded for the King's attention. These consisted of a list of protests under the standard headings of *incompatibili* (pluralities); *impossessionati* (office-holders without land); *absurda* (nonsensical decisions); *exclusia* (illegal appointments); and *alia* (miscellaneous). They were decidedly sharp in tone, pointing out, for example that Zamoyski's concurrent tenure of the Chancellorship and the Hetmanship was illegal, and that the appointment of the King's brother Andrew Bathory, to a Cardinalcy threatened the Republic with foreign interference. On 28 February, the Sejm was closed. (It was the first Leap-Day in the Republic's history, since the Julian Calendar had just been adopted.) In the closing debate, Kazimierski launched a virulent tirade against Zamoyski, who brought it to an end by snatching away his script. As the members filed out, all except Kazimierski kissed the King's hand. Proceedings were concluded with the singing of a *Te Deum* in the cathedral, the payment of members' expenses by the Treasurer, and the departure of all and sundry to the provinces. With the return of the envoys to the dietines with their 'relations' of what the Sejm had enacted, the legislative process, initiated by the King's manifesto six months before, was now complete.[10]

Lobbying was an established part of political and constitutional life. Sessions of the Sejm provided the only occasion where noblemen from all the Republic's far-flung provinces could meet together informally, and press their affairs on influential courtiers and senators. But the sessions were of special importance to those estates of the realm who were not directly represented in the legislature. The incorporated cities frequently addressed detailed petitions to the Sejm, and municipal records made regular provision for expenses incurred by delegations suitably armed with instructions, gifts, and bribes.[11] The Jewish Council employed a professional *Shtadlan* or 'lobbyist', who resided at the royal court and who was also empowered to intercede with the Sejm on all matters concerning the Jews' welfare. His function mirrored that of similar provincial lobbyists directed by each of the Jewish communes to the local dietines and city councils. Liberal payments behind the scenes, and lavish entertainments, were essential elements in their stock-in-trade.[12]

The Sejm, the dietines, and the Royal elections were all governed by the principle of unanimity. It seems incredible to the modern observer that such an ideal should have been taken seriously. But it was, and it formed the basis of all their proceedings. No proposal could become law, and no decision was binding, unless it received the full assent of all those persons who were competent to consider it. A single voice of dissent was equivalent to total rejection. Majority voting was consciously rejected. There was to be unanimity or nothing; there was to be no middle ground between a state of perfect harmony, and total chaos. Three lines of reasoning can be discerned. One argument, in a state where the executive arm depended on the voluntary support of all its citizens, was purely practical. Laws and decisions which were passed in the face of opposition could not have been properly enforced. The second was based on the consideration that the prospect of chaos might concentrate men's minds on harmony. The third derived from the somewhat naïve belief that institutions which are less than perfect are not worth keeping anyhow. In the hurly-burly of the dietines and the Royal elections, the principle of unanimity could not be applied with finesse. But in the Sejm it was the subject of serious debate, and applied with meticulous insistence. It was responsible for two constitutional practices, the Confederation and the *Liberum Veto,* which made the Republic famous throughout Europe.

The Confederation — *confederatio, konfederacja* — was an institution of ancient lineage in Poland, and an expression of the citizen's fundamental right to resist. It was an armed league, an association of men sworn to pursue their grievance until justice was obtained. It could be formed by any individual or group of individuals. It could be formed by the King, or against him. In 1302, the towns of Wielkopolska formed a confederation to rid themselves of outlaws who were infesting the province. In 1382—4, both burghers and nobles formed a confederation to guard against a suspected plot on the death of King Louis of Anjou. In 1439, a confederation was formed by the magnate, Spitek of Mielsztyn. In the 1560s, the Army went into confederation to ensure payment of its arrears; and in 1573, the whole Sejm joined in the Confederation of Warsaw in order to establish the principle of religious toleration. In the seventeenth century, major confederations were formed in 1656, and again in 1672: and in the eighteenth century, in 1704, 1715, 1733, 1767, 1768, and 1792. By that time, they were almost as frequent as sessions of the Sejm. On all these occasions, the confederates followed a time-honoured procedure. They met together at an appointed time and place, as if to attend their dietine, and drew up an 'act of confederation' which listed their demands and grievances. They would then swear an oath to fight together to the death against all comers. Henceforth, during the life of the Confederation, they kept their common counsel in regular assemblies, and, unlike the Sejm, passed their resolutions on policy and tactics by majority voting. When their ends had been achieved, or when they had been defeated in battle, their association was formally terminated, and they were released from the consequences of their oath. In effect, the Confederation was a legalized form of civil war, and no one thought it unusual.[13]

Confederation, of course, should not be confused with rebellion. To the ideologists of the Republic, the two were entirely different. Confederation was a legal procedure. It was undertaken in the name of the common good, by citizens acting in defence of the law, and conscious of its protection. Rebellion, in contrast, assumed that the aim of the action was illegal, and that legal procedures had not been observed. It is true, of course, that rebels and outlaws would usually try to blur the issue by vaunting their worthy motives and by maintaining that they, too, were acting for the common good. Yet in the greatest rebellion of the Republic's history, the issues were not so blurred. Chmielnicki did not claim that his actions were legal; neither did he attempt to form a Confederation as a cover to his cause. In terms of damage and disturbance, the Rebellion of 1648 was fairly matched by the troubles of the perfectly legal 'Rokosz' of 1606—9 and of 1665—6.

The 'Rokosz' was a particular form of Confederation. In origin, it was a name given to mounted assemblies of the entire nobility as at the royal elections, and derived from the field of Rakos outside Buda, where the Hungarian nobles had customarily met to confirm their privileges in like manner. But in so far as successive monarchs opposed the practice, except for the purpose of royal elections, it came to be associated with movements of resistance against the king. In the reign of Zygmunt III, in the eyes of the Regalist party, it was tantamount to treason; in the eyes of their opponents, it formed the quintessence of the 'Golden Freedom'.

The conflict between King and Nobility came to a head in 1606. The King clearly did not possess either the ambition or the mettle to erect the *absolutum dominium* which his enemies feared. But his narrow, Catholic piety and his blatant indifference to the public affairs of the Republic schooled a large number of malcontents. A Swede by birth and upbringing, he aped the Germanic manners and style of the court of Vienna, and surrounded himself with Jesuits and grandees. The royal court in Warsaw was largely run by German personnel, specially imported from Bavaria. The Regalist party, headed by Piotr Skarga, the King's Confessor; Piotr Myszkowski, Grand Marshal of the Crown; Maciej Pstrokoński, Bishop of Przemysl and Vice-Chancellor; and by Hieronim Gostomski, Palatine of Poznań, certainly dabbled with plans for introducing a hereditary monarchy; for strengthening the executive with extra-parliamentary taxes and a standing army, and for wide-ranging collaboration with the House of Habsburg. In consequence, a conflict developed, not dissimilar to that in Jacobean England, where the loud-mouthed companions of a faint-hearted King, enamoured of the fashionable theories of Divine Right, needlessly disturbed the traditional balance between Crown and Parliament. Already, in the Sejm of 1605, the Chancellor, Jan Zamoyski, had threatened to have the King deported to Sweden if he did not pay more serious attention to the feelings of the country; and Zamoyski's death in the following year removed the last restraint on the frustrations of the opposition. His mantle fell on more excitable men, and in particular on Michał Zebrzydowski (1553–1620), Palatine of Cracow, on Janusz Radziwiłł (1579–1620), and on Cardinal Maciejowski, Bishop of Cracow. The greatest offence was given in December 1605 by the King's marriage by proxy in Gratz to the Archduchess Constance, a marriage arranged unconstitutionally, without the consent of the Sejm. What is more, in the course of the nuptial celebrations in Cracow, the King summarily requisitioned a house belonging to Zebrzydowski and pilfered Maciejowski's papal baldachin from the cathedral. As Zebrzydowski shouted, 'Either I leave my house, or the king leaves his kingdom!' Having registered a protest in vain at the dietine of Cracow, Zebrzydowski proceeded to summon the nobility to a series of armed gatherings, at Stęczyca, at Lublin, and finally at Sandomierz. On this last occasion, the nobility, drawn up on horseback, formally proclaimed the *Rokosz*, and elected Janusz Radziwiłł as their Marshal. Apart from the malcontent magnates, they included a large number of petty nobles fearful of their privileges, of Protestants alarmed by mounting Catholic oppression, and of Orthodox resentful of the recent Church Union. They placed 50,400 signatures to an Act of Confederation which contained sixty-seven points of remonstrance. Their particular grievances, however, were of small account compared with the general feeling, which they all shared, that the ancient traditions of the state were under assault:

> Our ancestors . . . knew that they were born nobles rather than Catholics, that they were not descended from Levi, and that Poland is a political kingdom, not a clerical one; they knew that the Holy Church is the guest of the states of this world, not their hereditary master; and they knew what was due to the Lord God, and what to the country. They did not mix holy religion with politics, and did not submit either to priests or gluttons.[14]

Armed conflict ensued. After the Battle of Janowiec, the confederates announced the king's dethronement, and in the name of all the people withdrew their obedience. The Regalists, having called a Sejm at Wiśnica, made all possible concessions to the stated grievances, but could not calm the mood of outrage. Though heavily outnumbered, they were led by the hardened professionalism of the two Hetmans, Stanisław Żółkiewski, Zebrzydowski's brother-in-law, and Jan Karol Chodkiewicz. At Guzów near Radom on 6 July 1607, the confederates were cut to pieces. The King's cause triumphed. Yet the political result was far from clear. The leaders of the *Rokosz* were not punished. Zebrzydowski, having humbled himself before the King and Senate, was allowed to retain his lands and offices; Radziwiłł kept his forces intact in Lithuania. The Sejm of 1609 granted a general amnesty. It was decided that the nobility's right of *non praestanda obedientia* could only be exercised after the King had been formally warned three times by the Sejm. The King reaffirmed his adherence to the Henrician Articles. The whole affair was treated as an unfortunate misunderstanding. The real issues were ignored. The malcontents were allowed to rouse the entire nobility into a bloody adventure, which divided the state and distracted the government from important foreign engagements in Muscovy and Livonia. And no one was so much as reprimanded. As Korzon remarked, 'this marks the beginning of the Polish anarchy. The nobleman, who inculcated rigour, virtue, and the fear of God, in his family life, hardened his heart in his public life by constant disputes with the king and by refractoriness towards every command.'[15]

Sixty years later, the *Rokosz* of Jerzy Lubomirski revealed complications of a still more dangerous nature. Lubomirski was one of the most popular figures of his day. He had distinguished himself in the Swedish and Muscovite wars, and his campaign to defeat royal plans for an election *vivente rege* was fully in line with the feelings of the mass of the nobility. But in the Sejm of 1664, on evidence of dealings with the Habsburgs in Vienna, he was convicted by his peers on a charge of treason, and sentenced to confiscation and banishment. After that, his followers found themselves in the invidious position of protesting the legality of their actions, whilst promoting the cause of a convicted criminal. Even so, they joined his standard in considerable numbers. In the Sejms of 1665 and 1666, they repeatedly disrupted proceedings, before withdrawing to form their Confederation. In 1667, they confronted the Royal Army in battle in several skirmishes, until, on 13 July, on the shores of Lake Gopło, they won a decisive victory. The confusion of that occasion was observed at first hand by Jan Pasek:

The armies clashed at Montwy, and the distance between them was more than a mile across the ford. The next day, the King ordered us to cross to the other side. The dragoons crossed, and part of the cavalry. The Lithuanians too were about to cross, when suddenly a detachment from Lubomirsky's army arrived at the gallop, not in closed ranks or squadrons, but spread out in Tartar fashion. The first made contact with us, thinking us to be Lithuanians, when suddenly we recognized each other . . . So they lay off, and with their entire force lunge at our right flank, where the dragoons were stood to, together with the Cossacks under Colonel Czop . . . Not an hour and a half passed before they had cut our men down. High-ranking officers perished, including

Czarniecki's commanders, those valiant veterans who in Denmark and
Muscovy . . . had accomplished such marvels . . . And God, on account
of our discords, let it happen. He took away the flower of our brave
cavaliers, who had always withstood the onslaughts of the enemy.

In this battle, everything was in confusion. We had great trouble to
discern who was friend and who was foe. Before attacking anyone, we
first had to ask 'Whose army are you in?' . . . If friend fell upon friend,
they rode off after exchanging a greeting. For it did happen that one
brother might be with Lubomirsky, and the other with the King; the
father here, and the son there, not knowing whether to do battle. To be
sure, they did carry distinguishing marks – kerchiefs tied on the left
arm. But we were slow to spot this. For my part, when they started to
press us rather hard, I tied something on my arm above the elbow . . .
They identify me, and cry, 'Are you ours, or not?' Raising my arm, I
say 'Yours'. But suddenly one of them cries, 'O you sly dog, you're not
ours: clear off, or surrender!'

When the battle was finished, a horseman rode over from Lubomirsky's
army, and ambles up to Colonel Czop, who pays no attention, thinking
him one of his own men. Then he fired into the Colonel's ear with a
pistol, and kills him on the spot. So treacherous was that war. God
grant it may never befall our Poland again.

When I recrossed the ford into our own lines, I found the King in a
state of distress, wringing his hands . . . He sent to Lubomirsky to confront him on the field like a knight in open battle, not furtively like a
wolf. But Lubomirsky answered, 'it is not for me to meet My Lord in
open battle, but simply as an offended citizen to protect myself as best
I can. I am not responsible for this loss of innocent blood, which grieves
me indeed. It is Your Highness himself who is responsible, and those
fine counsellors who have brought us to this sorry pass in order to
destroy our country . . .'[16]

On that day, some two thousand noblemen perished for no
clear purpose. Lubomirski destroyed the King's authority,
without putting anything in its place. After the Treaty of
Łęgonice, he himself retired into exile in Austrian Silesia. The
King resolved to abdicate. The basic constitutional problems
remained unresolved. What was worse, the internal divisions
of the Republic accelerated the progress of external dangers.
Whilst the Royal Army was squaring up to fight Lubomirski
in the west, it abandoned its duty of holding the eastern
borders in the Ukraine against the Muscovites. Lubomirski,
obsessed by the hypothetical threat of the King's electoral
schemes, obstructed all effective defence against the actual

military menace of the Muscovite invasion. In January 1667, faced by the prospect of a further Muscovite offensive into defenceless territory, the King was obliged to sign the Truce of Andrusovo. At the time, the cession of Smolensk, Czernihów, Kiev, and the left-bank Ukraine, was regarded in Poland as a tactical manœuvre, a temporary withdrawal dictated by the Army's preoccupation with the civil war. There was every confidence that it could be reversed. In fact, it proved to be permanent. The ceded territories were never recovered, but served instead to give the Muscovites a preponderance of resources which was felt in all future confrontations. Muscovy received the largest single prize which permitted her transformation into the great Russian Empire. For this, Jerzy Lubomirski, tribune of the Polish nobility, was no less responsible than Bogdan Chmielnicki, the rebel Ataman of the Dnieper Cossacks.[17]

The *Liberum Veto* came into flower rather later than the Confederations, though it too was grown from very ancient roots. It was a device whereby any single member could halt the proceedings of the Sejm by the simple expression of dissent. Such was the strength of feeling about the need for unanimity, that it was considered quite improper to continue when a single voice was raised with the words *Veto* (I deny), or *Nie pozwalam* (I do not allow it). Usually, of course, an interruption of this sort produced nothing more than a temporary delay. Exchanges between the Marshal of the Sejm and would-be objectors were fairly common:

Shouts from the benches: Nie ma zgody. (There is no agreement)
Marshal: Z jakiej raciej? (For what reason?)
A single voice: Nie pozwalam . . .

At this point, the Marshal would call a break in the debate, and inquire more closely as to what the objections were. If a simple misunderstanding was involved, or a call for clarification, the debate would resume quite quickly. If something more serious had arisen, the break might last for several hours or even days, with the Marshal working hard in the corridors to repair the conflict. If the objection occurred during the Second Phase of Sejm, when constitutions were being passed, the particular bill at issue would be dropped, notwithstanding a majority vote in its favour.

After several such difficulties in the early decades of the Republic, including one in 1580 which blocked all taxation for that year, the matter did not really come to a head till the Sejm of 1652. It was the fourth year of Chmielnicki's Rebellion in the Ukraine, with all its attendant horrors. After six weeks in session, the agenda was still full of unfinished business, and the Marshal rose to announce a prolongation. The members were tired, uneasy at the increased taxes which had just been voted, and ready to go home. It was a Saturday afternoon. A single voice was clearly heard: 'Nie pozwalam.' The Marshal called a break, and the chamber emptied. At first, no one seemed to know for certain who had invoked the veto, or what the objection was. On the Sunday, many members started to leave for home, believing the Sejm was complete except for the closing ceremonies. By the Monday, the Marshal learned that a formal statement of veto had been registered with the Crown Secretariat by one Jan Siciński, envoy of Upita in Lithuania. It was an impasse which no one had foreseen. Siciński had apparently gone straight from the Chamber to the secretariat, and had taken horse to the east without a word to a soul. Lengthy consultations with lawyers and colleagues gave the Marshal no solution. He had to admit that Siciński's veto was legal and valid. He could not recall the Sejm, as there were not enough members left in Warsaw to form a quorum. The constitutions could not be written into the Crown Register. All the work of the session was declared null and void. It was a baleful precedent. Henceforth, any member sufficiently determined to destroy the working of the Sejm, had an excellent means of doing so. It is now known that Siciński had acted on the orders of Janusz Radziwiłł, and in future years there were to be many more magnates who were ready to paralyse the central government for their own local advantage.

Oddly enough, the man who served as Marshal of that fateful Sejm in 1652, Andrzej Maksymilian Fredro (1620–79), showed himself to be a fervent advocate of all the libertarian practices of the *szlachta*. His published writings, which included *Przysłowia mów potocznych* (Proverbs of current speech, 1658) and *Monita politico-moralia* (Political and

Moral Admonitions, 1664), consisted largely of collected maxims and aphorisms exuding folksy humour and wisdom, and were soon to be found on every nobleman's bookshelf. His *Scriptorum Fragmenta* (Literary Fragments, 1660) were specifically designed to popularize what he called 'the paradoxical philosophy of anarchy'. An empty treasury, he maintained, prevents a monarch from growing insolent. God keeps Poland poor in order to check the nobles' arrogance. The *Liberum Veto* is a blessing, since it protects the minority of wise men from the dictates of the stupid majority. Fredro firmly believed in the unique advantages of the Polish system. His opinions were shared by generations of noblemen whose prejudices and conceits he so accurately reflected.

Not surprisingly, nothing was done in such an atmosphere to remedy the constitution. In 1666, the *Liberum Veto* was invoked in the middle of the session; and in 1668, for the first time, it was used on the opening day before the debates of the Sejm had begun. In the Saxon Era, the chaos accelerated. In the reign of Augustus II (1697–33), 11 out of 20 sessions of the Sejm were broken. Under Augustus III (1733–63), only one Sejm was able to pass any legislation at all.[18]

In that era, the essential functions of the Sejm in the administrative and financial sphere were adopted, at a very perfunctory level, by the dietines. The Republic's enemies rejoiced. Each of the Powers retained magnates who could break the Sejm at the drop of a ducat. All were intent that none of their rivals should steal a march. The Russians, in particular, were well satisfied. From 1717 onwards they enjoyed a virtual protectorate over the Republic and guarded their western frontier at the cost of a few magnatial pensions. By posing as the champions of 'the Golden Freedom' and of the *Liberum Veto,* they could ensure that the Republic remained incapable of organizing itself or offering resistance to Russian policy. By filling Warsaw with Russian troops on all important occasions, they 'protected the Sejm from outside interference'. By threatening their opponents with arrest and sequestration if they dared to protest, and by obstructing all measures for constitutional reform, they kept the charade in motion for the rest of the century. In 1768, the King's proposal to abolish the *Liberum Veto,* together with other

restrictive practices, was rejected, for fear of the one necessary voice of dissent. In May 1791, the long awaited reforms
were indeed enacted; but only by virtue of the Russians' preoccupations in the Turkish War. At the Sejm of Grodno of
1793, the King was persuaded to retract the offending reforms,
and then to sign the Second Partition. In this way, the 'Golden
Freedom' was perverted from the very ends which it was
originally designed to prevent. The *Liberum Veto,* which was
supposed to check the absolutist designs of the Polish
monarchy, was made to serve the purposes of the Russian
Empire. In theory, it was meant to ensure unity and unanimity;
in practice, in Russian hands, it ensured the perpetuation of
chaos. Behind the façade of the 'Polish Anarchy', the instruments of Russian Autocracy would operate with impunity.

*   *   *   *   *

The assumptions which governed constitutional life in the
Republic were mirrored in the realm of public law. In Polish
eyes, the Law, like the constitution, was too precious a commodity to be left in the hands of the executive authorities. In
the world of perfect freedom, the threat of injustice was
thought to be greater in the long run from the mindless
impetus of organized institutions than from the intemperance
of individuals. Hence, the law was not to be enforced by the
state. Justice was to be exacted by those whose wrong had
been recognized in the courts, and on occasion by the nobility
acting in unison, but never by the magistrates, or by royal
officials. If this meant that the law was frequently defied in
particular cases, the evil was judged to be small, and temporary.
To this way of thinking, those countries which appointed
law-enforcement officers responsible to the state, were trading
the minor advantage of smooth, legal administration, in exchange for a permanent threat to the liberty of their citizens.
For this reason, in Poland—Lithuania, there was never any
Star Chamber; there was no *Oprichnina* on the Muscovite
model, and no one who might have introduced it.[20]

As in all medieval systems, the competence of the various
courts of law was carefully separated. The jurisdiction of the
ecclesiastical courts extended in civil and criminal cases to
the lands, serfs, and clergy of the Church, and in spiritual

matters to the whole population. There, canon law was applied. The jurisdiction of the manorial courts was restricted to the internal affairs of the estates of the nobility, and was ruled by local customary law. The jurisdiction of the municipal courts extended to the territories of the chartered cities, and to the freemen of the city. There, municipal legal codes based on the German Magdeburg Law were in force. The jurisdiction of the Jewish courts applied exclusively to disputes within the Jewish estate, and was administered by the *kahal* according to Hebraic Law. The jurisdiction of the royal courts applied to the lands, serfs, and servants of the Crown; to disputes between noblemen; and to cases involving members of different estates. At the local level, the *sąd ziemski* and *sąd grodzki* were district courts administered respectively by the royal *Starosta* or by the royal Castellan. In addition, in accordance with the principle of legal autonomy, each of the great Officers-of-State maintained a court to try cases affecting his particular domain. Hence, there were Chancellor's courts; Marshal's courts; Hetman's courts; Treasurer's courts; and, for the royal Court, the *sąd dworski,* or 'Court court'. At a higher level, the *Referendaria Koronna* was established in the sixteenth century to hear appeals against decisions involving the bailiffs and tenants of the Crown lands. In theory at least, it gave the royal serfs a measure of justice denied to the serfs of the Church or of the nobility. The *sąd wojewódzki* or 'Palatine's court' dealt with unresolved interjurisdictional disputes. From 1578, the Crown Tribunals at Lublin for Małopolska and at Piotrków for Wielkopolska, Kujawy, and Mazowsze, and the Lithuanian Tribunal at Wilno, for the Grand Duchy, acted as courts of highest instance above the district courts. They were supervised by noble 'deputies' appointed by each of the dietines. At the highest level, the Sejm reserved its right to act as the supreme court of appeal. As the Republic's principal legislative body, it formulated the *constituta/konstytucje* or 'statutes', which governed the work of all the royal courts and Tribunals. On occasion, in the name of the Republic, it tried important cases of treason or of dereliction of duty by the chief Officers-of-State who demanded to be judged by their peers. In such a fragmented system, it was only to be expected that the legal profession prospered mightily. In Warsaw and Lublin especially, the *Palestra* or 'Bar' supported shoals of advocates and attorneys.

Despite these elaborate arrangements the strictures of the law could be easily avoided, especially by the Nobility. They were the absolute masters of their own lands and serfs. They were the corporate employers of the king, and by extension of all the royal officials. They could safely ignore the promptings of the Church, and were specifically protected from prosecution by the ecclesiastical courts in matters of religion. Their peculiar alliance with the Jews derived, among other things, from the defenceless position of the Jewish estate in face of noble coercion. In the cities, they were not subject to the jurisdiction of the municipal courts; and in their numerous *jurydiki* possessed entire wards, where they and their men were safe from interference. As a result, in those few cities which retained an independent existence, they could reside, build houses, amuse themselves, and generally sponge on the community without paying municipal taxes, and without serious fear of disturbance. The action of the city of Poznań, which in 1613 expelled all its noble hooligans and parasites by force, belonged to the rare and enterprising exceptions to the general rule. In the countryside at large, the instances of lawlessness were legion. In Władysław Łoziński's classic study *Prawem i lewem* (By Right or by Might), based on the court records of Lwów and Przemyśl in the first decades of the seventeenth century, a social scene is revealed in which the law was broken more often than it was kept. Rapine, plunder, rape, and private wars were the order of the day. The provincial nobleman defended his inheritance sword in hand, and if possible with cannon and grapeshot. When he could not get his way in the courts, he would take it by any means available. Incorrigible litigiousness was accompanied by wanton violence; perjury and subornation were as commonplace as murder and assault. Conditions resembled those in England during the Wars of the Roses, as described in the Paston Letters, when lesser people lived in fear, and only the barons were safe. Among scores of cases which Łoziński examined are those of Marian Zieliński of Rotów, who complained in 1628 that he had been attacked by the royal Starosta with a hired force of seventy Tartar bowmen; of Walerian Montelupi, the banker's son, who in 1610 returned to the scene of an attempted kidnap, and hung his would-be kidnapper from the gatepost of his own estate; of Mikołaj Ossoliński, Starosta of Nowy Targ, a notorious tyrant and libertine, who fought one war with the Korniakt family for the recapture of his first wife, and another with the Staroleskis for the honour of his second; and of Haras Witoszyński, an Orthodox monk, who in 1639 was killed in a vain attempt to prevent the wholesale enserfment of his illiterate relatives by a local landowner.[21]

The procedures of law-enforcement were extremely haphazard. The royal courts employed only one permanent official for this purpose, the *woźny* or 'usher', whose duties were to serve writs and to give notices of sentence. But he had no means of bringing unwilling defendants to court, or of executing the sentence of the court on fugitive convicts. Although the murder of an usher was one of the few offences in the Republic punishable with death, he made no attempt to coerce refractory noblemen. In many localities, there were condemned criminal noblemen living quite openly on their estates in complete disregard of the courts. Łoziński quotes the case of one Samuel Lasch, a 'pious man', who had been condemned in his absence no less than two hundred times with no effect whatsoever. Of the four punishments to which offenders could be sentenced – decapitation, imprisonment, banishment, and infamy – the death sentence was rare, except in the cities. Nobles would fight rather than submit to judgement on a capital charge, preferring to slash their way out of trouble or to die resisting. Imprisonment *in fundo,* that is, in a closed dungeon with no windows and no comforts, was added in 1588 to the customary fine for the murder of a nobleman. Banishment was common, especially if the convicted man had refused to appear in court. In the event that he returned to the country within the term of his sentence, he could be seized and executed on the spot by anyone who cared to do so. Infamy or 'civil death' was the commonest of all. It deprived the nobleman of his good name and political rights. Yet for the battling nobility of the provinces, who had no good name to lose, it was meaningless. When sentence had been passed, as often as not the offender could not be brought to justice by the court, and the wronged party in the case would set out to execute the sentence in person. In 1660, for example, John Sobieski, the future King, was assigned the Crown lands of Bełz in lease. On trying to take possession, he found that the widow of the late Starosta of Bełz was still in residence, and was refusing to leave. After both Sobieski and the widow had obtained writs in support of their various claims, Sobieski tired of litigation. He descended on the house with 300 hussars, put the widow on the roadside, and marched in. In extreme cases, when public security was at stake, the *Starosta* or Palatine could call out the *motus nobilitate*, or 'posse' of the nobility of the district or palatinate. In 1655, all the noble squadrons of Red Ruthenia were withheld from the campaign against the Swedes because they were still in action against rebellious bands of mercenaries in their own province. In private cases, however, the nobility were most reluctant to act. Once, when the Starosta of Sanok called on his neighbours to apprehend Olbracht Grochowski of Dynów, for tax evasion, only one man reported for service: that man was Jerzy Ossoliński, Chancellor of the Crown.

Private wars persisted right until the end of the Republic. In most cases they were purely local vendettas, caused, as Łoziński puts it, by *amor et demon*. Tartar raids, unpaid soldiery, brigandage, and unloving neighbours were as common as the four seasons, and everyone took precautions against them in his own way. In the unruly south, there was a regular pool of professional mobsters who hired themselves out to needy noblemen. Yet in a few cases, the wars took on the character of major campaigns. The conflict in the early 1700s in Lithuania between the so-called 'Republicans' and the Sapieha, formed an important sideline of the Great Northern War.

In the course of the Middle Ages, the *szlachta* had developed a ritualized procedure for conducting their vendettas. A nobleman who felt aggrieved would write out a challenge in which he detailed the slights he had suffered and his terms for satisfaction. This 'challenge' – in Polish *odpowiedź*; in German, *Absage*; in Latin, *litterae diffidationis* – was equivalent to a declaration of private war. It would usually state its author's intention to execute summary justice on whoever it was that had given offence, to burn down his house and crops, and not to rest until one or the other were dead. It was deposited in the district court, to be delivered by the usher. After that, providing the stated justifications were judged to be genuine, all action taken was perfectly legal. The neighbourhood put up its shutters whilst the contestants and their retainers did battle with fire and sword until a decisive result was obtained. Unfortunately, the nobleman who observed established procedures diminished the chances of success by giving due warning of his intentions. In consequence, the formal challenge was often neglected in favour of a surprise attack or midnight raid. For practical purposes, there was little advantage in having the law on one's side.

When public order was threatened, however, the royal courts were empowered to exact sureties against a citizen's peaceful conduct. The level of the surety, or *vadium regalium,* was fixed in accordance with the status of the prospective disturbers of the peace and with the scale of their suspected operations. Any subsequent transgression led automatically to the forfeiture of all payments made. But it made little difference to established habits and traditions. No one of influence in the Republic was able to promote appropriate legal reforms. The magnates with their large armies were safe enough; the lesser noblemen were either dependent on the magnates' favours, or unwilling to envisage the growth of royal judicial power. All were required to defend themselves as best they could.

Stanisław Stadnicki (*c.* 1560–1616), the 'Devil of Łańcut', was an archetypal figure of the Anarchy, at once a notorious gangster and yet at the same time one of the heroes of the Republic. His career was symptomatic of the social conditions on which he thrived. He was a man of uncommon courage, invention, and energy. But devoured by some inner acid of spite and resentment. His parentage was choicely unrespectable. His father, Stanisław Mateusz Stadnicki, an Arian, had been excommunicated by the Church for heresy. His mother, Barbara Zborowska, belonged to the rumbustious Zborowskis of Niedzica. He was born at Dubiecko in the Carpathians, and on his parents' decease shared his family's fifteen landed properties with his six brothers. He was a member of the heraldic clan of Śreniawa, and adopted the motto: *Aspettate e odiate* (Wait and Hate). His early years were spent soldiering, first in Hungary and then in the Polish service in Muscovy, where in 1581 he was commended for conspicuous gallantry. On his return from the wars, apparently with an incurable grudge over his unpaid salary, he took possession of the estate of Łańcut near Rzeszów, and applied himself systematically to banditry. Turning Łańcut into a fairy-tale robber's castle, he devised elaborate provocations, legal ploys, and even scurrilous verse, by which his intended victims were goaded into action, and then crushed. Soon, the whole area was frothing with indignation. Money was borrowed and not returned; houses were burned down for no apparent reason; a monastery was closed down, and its monks expelled; fairs and markets were terrorized; travellers were harassed, and in some cases purposely mutilated; and trade passed increasingly to Stadnicki's own unlicensed fair at Rzeszów. Every protest brought swift and vicious retaliation. Spies, extortionists, and armed retainers kept the local people in line. The dungeon at Łańcut was equipped with a torture-chamber, where rumour had it that Stadnicki's enemies were buried alive. In 1600, after numerous clashes with his noble neighbours, Stadnicki was sued in the Crown Tribunal at Lublin in connection with his illegal management of the Rzeszów Fair, and he lost his case. His response was to issue a formal challenge to the instigator of the suit, Michał Korniakt, and to lead a punitive expedition against the Korniakts' estate at Sosnica. In 1605–6, he played a prominent part in the noble *Rokosz*. His correspondence at this time, and his public speeches in which he called the King a 'perjurer', a 'sodomite', a 'card-sharper', and an 'alchemist', were vastly treasonable, and can hardly have helped Zebrzydowski to protest the legality of their cause. But he remained at liberty. Eventually, he met his match in Łukasz Opaliński, the victim of a libellous poem entitled *'Słup do gościa'* (A Gallows for my Guest), which had been circulated in broadsides round the entire district. Opaliński, mortally offended by the slight, never forgave him. In 1608, Łańcut was stormed by Opaliński's friends and relations, who slew everyone who fell into their hands. Treasure to the value of 500,000 zł. was taken from the cellar, together with 10,000 zł. in coin, 24,000 gold ducats, and 27,000 thalers.

Stadnicki himself escaped; but his subsequent return to Łańcut and his attempt to restore his reign by an intensified campaign of terror, did not succeed. Betrayed by his own servant, hunted down in the hills, ambushed and wounded by Opaliński's Cossacks, he finally expired as his head was severed by a stroke of his own sword. Yet his wickedness did not impress his contemporaries unduly. On the contrary, he was considered by many to be a champion of liberty. His epitaph, composed by his neighbour Jan Szczęsny Herburt (1567–1616), throbs with outraged virtue:

VIATOR
SI AMICUS ES DOLE, SI INIMICUS SPECTA, SI NEUTRUS MIRARE
RERUM HUMANARUM CASUM ET OCCASUM.
STANISLAS STADNICKI DE ZMIGROD
HAERES IN LANCUT, CAPITANEUS ZYGWULTENSIS,
HIC QUIESCIT
ANIMO INVICTO, GENTE NOBILISSIMA, COGNATIONE PLURIMA
AFFINITATE INFINITA, FORA OPTIMA, IGENIO
PRAESTANTISSIMO,
OPIBUS MAXIMUS,
HIC TALIS AC TANTUS LIBERTANS STUDIOSISSIMUS AMATOR.
O PATRIA, SI TU BELLATOREM HUNC, VIRUM AD RES
GERENDAS
PRO TE ADMISSES, ILLE TIBI ORNAMENTO ET EMOLUMENTO
SI QUIS UNQUAM, DUBITO PROCUL FUISSET.
O NUMEN DIVINUM, VIOLENTIAE IMPIETATIS VINDES,
O SACROSANCTAE PATRIAE LEGES,
O LIBERTAS VIOLATA ET PROSTRATA,
VOS VOCO ET INVOCO
ANNA DE ZIEMACICE CONIUNX ET AMICI POSUERUNT.*

(*see note overleaf*)

The reader must surely wonder whether he is faced with an expression of genuine grief, or of social satire.

*   *   *   *   *

For political theorists, the Republic of Poland–Lithuania provided an inexhaustible fund of curiosities. Its increasingly ineffective practices gave Absolutists ample material for demonstrating the superiority of their arguments; whilst its libertarian ideals gained the admiration of republicans and constitutionalists. Taking the period as a whole, it found as

many admirers as detractors. Nor should it be supposed that
within Poland—Lithuania the Anarchy was suffered in silence.
Political debate was an essential attribute of the 'Golden
Freedom'. Pamphleteers were as common as privateers. Even
before the Union of Lublin, a long-running intellectual debate
had been started as to how the Polish system could be changed
and improved.[23]

The first and most distinguished of Polish critics was
Andrzej Frycz Modrzewski (1503–72), known throughout
Europe as 'Modrevicius'. Born into a family of impoverished
nobility, he rose in the service of Archbishop Łaski, and found
his way by merit into the royal secretariat of Zygmunt-August.
His dominant theme of social justice ran contrary to the
tendency of the age, and assured him an audience both at
home and abroad. He fearlessly condemned the oppression of
the peasants, the exclusion of the bourgeoisie, the ignorance
of the clergy, the luxury of the nobility. He was not in any
sense a democrat, but demanded only that each estate should
contribute to the general good according to its means. 'We
are all as passengers in one boat,' he said, 'when one of us is
sick, the others cannot stay healthy.' His first serious publication, *De Poena Homicidi* (On the Punishment for Murder,
1543), attacked the blatant injustices of the Head-Money
system. His major work, *De Emendanda Republica* (On the

---

*　　　　　　　　　　Traveller!
　　　Grieve if you are a friend; observe, if you are an enemy;
　　　If neither, marvel, at the fall and ruin of human affairs.
　　　　　　　Stanislas Stadnicki of Żmigród,
　　　　Heir to Łańcut, Captain of Zygwult lies here,
　Invincible in spirit, most noble by birth, endowed with numerous
　　　　　　　　　　　kindred
And countless relations; supreme in beauty, outstanding in talent,
　　　　　　　　　Great in deeds,
　　　The incomparable and most diligent lover of liberty.
　　O Fatherland! If you take this warrior, this man of action,
To yourself, he will be an ornament and an advantage for you,
　　　　　As I doubt anyone was before.
　　O Divine will, avenger of violence and treason!
　　　　O sacred laws of the Fatherland!
　　　O Liberty, ravished and overthrown!
　　　　I appeal, and entreat you.
Anna of Ziemacice, his wife, and his friends laid (this stone).[22]

Improvement of the Republic), was composed in the 1550s and published in the first complete edition of five volumes in Basle in 1554. In it he made a whole series of far-reaching proposals — for equality before the law; for a Codex of written law; for the exemption of peasants from direct taxation; for a national church and a scholarly clergy; and for a system of state-sponsored education. In constitutional affairs, he praised the Polish practice where elected kings ruled by consent. 'It is a much better arrangement', he wrote, 'than that where kings impose taxes and initiate wars of their own will, which may easily lead to hideous tyranny.' In religious affairs, he advocated freedom of conscience, but stressed the role of instruction, scholarship, and learning in support of Christian beliefs. In international affairs, he condemned the prevalence of war and the acceptance of territorial aggrandizement. On each of these scores, he attracted the detailed attention of Bodin, of Beza, and of Grotius. Modrzewski's criticisms were of the most detailed, empirical kind, however, and in no sense revolutionary. Even his ideas on education, which seemed so strange to his contemporaries, were advanced in support of the existing order. It was most unfair, therefore, that he should have been attacked in the Sejm for seeking 'not to emend but to destroy.' But he knew how to reply. In 1557 he reminded the Polish nobility that their arrogance and inflexibility would lead to catastrophe. 'No state was ever conquered before being weakened by internal friction;' he warned, 'beware that by your obstinacy you do not hasten your own perdition and that of the Commonwealth.'[24]

Modrzewski was surrounded by a whole generation which shared his critical temper. Mikołaj Rey (1505–69) displayed an acute social conscience. The Polish Brothers had an impact of continental scope in political as well as in religious affairs. Grzegorz Paweł z Brzezin (1525–91), a leveller of the most militant stamp, who condemned the existence of social estates, of private property, and of all state power as the source of wars and conflict, holds an honoured place in the prehistory of the Far Left.

Another voice of warning that was heard and remembered throughout the life of the Republic was that of Piotr Skarga (1536–1612). Skarga, sometime Rector of the Jesuit College and Academy at Wilno, became Chaplain and Prelector at the court of Zygmunt III. In 1597, he preached a series of eight sermons before the Sejm of that year in Warsaw, which as *Kazania sejmowe* or 'Sermons of the Sejm' ran into seven editions, and were constantly read and quoted. Skarga's standpoint was a conservative one. He was counted a pillar of the Regalist party, and favoured the contemporary theories of the Counter-Reformation on the Divine Right of Kings and the prerogatives of the Church. His supposed rejection of Absolutism amounted to little more than a preference for 'Christian Monarchy' of the Spanish type over the 'barbarian tyranny' of Moscow. It is not surprising that Zebrzydowski's rebels considered him the *'praecipius turbator Reipublicae'*, the 'principal troublemaker of the Republic.' Yet the power of his language, the force of his commitment, the detailed nature of his criticism, and his ringing prophecies of the retribution to come, must strike the modern reader as solidly as they shook the senators and envoys in the pews of St. John's Cathedral. 'We are gathered today in the Name of the Lord for the ordering of affairs of state,' he began; 'but everywhere there is discord, treason, and rebellion.' 'Discipline and self-restraint have perished in this kingdom,' he declared; 'No one fears the laws or institutions, no one even thinks of punishment. But there where the Fear of God shall die, and shame decline . . . there, too, the Republic shall die. Everyone defends our noble freedom, whilst honest liberty is turned to disobedience and harlotry. All behave as Sons of Belial, without a yoke, without reins . . .' In the second Sermon, he moved to the subject of Patriotism, the Love of One's Country. Contrary to the later concept of *Ojczyzna* (Fatherland), he talked mainly in biblical and metaphorical terms of 'Our own Jerusalem', and *ta miła Matka,* 'our sweet Mother'. Yet his message was harsh. He quoted the words of Solomon: 'Kingdoms come, and kingdoms go, and nation succeeds unto nation.' The Republic, too, was not eternal; in a state of sin, it, too, would pass away. In the Third, Fourth, Fifth, and Seventh Sermons, he was concerned with the prevalence of Heresy, which he saw as the source of domestic unrest and of unjust laws. He obviously approved of those bishops who in the Senate had condemned toleration as an offence against

God's Majesty; and he called for an end to the 'iniquitous' legislation of the Confederation of Warsaw. There were plenty of Calvinists and oppositionists in the congregation, and one can well imagine how their nostrils quivered. In the Sixth Sermon, he turned to constitutional theory, taking his text from I Samuel 8:5, 'Give us a King to judge us . . . as other nations have.' 'There are', he said, 'two leading members in the human body, the head and the heart'. 'A merry heart and a sane head make for a strong and healthy whole.' It was a classic exposition of the theory of the 'two Swords', of the Division of Powers between Church and State, between God and Caesar. There are three good freedoms, he continued – to refrain from sin; to decline a foreign master; and to resist a tyrant. But the fourth freedom, a 'devilish', a 'hellish', a 'Satanic' freedom, was 'to live without law'. The magnates rode roughshod over common counsels, and a leaderless Sejm was subject to intolerable delays and indecision. Looking no doubt at the rows of envoys before him, he declared: 'What is most pernicious, is that people ascribe such great powers to themselves . . . as if this were a democracy.' To those who were not previously aware, Skarga thought the noble democracy to be a sin. He wanted to prune the privileges and immunities of the nobility, starting with the *Neminem Captivabimus,* to strengthen the Monarchy and Senate against the dietines and the Chamber of Envoys, and to relieve the miseries of the peasantry. In his final, Eighth Sermon, he returned to the theme of the peasants. Having treated his congregation to a rich catalogue of the unpunished sins of the Republic, from blasphemy, sacrilege, murder, usury, adultery, perjury, and treason, to wine, silks, and horses, he suddenly invited them to reflect on the condition of their own subjects. 'Just ask it of yourselves,' he demanded; 'do you have any other state in Christendom where the serfs and ploughmen are so oppressed by an absolute rule as here, where the nobility reigns over them with no legal restraint?' For the szlachta, so fond of their Golden Freedom, and so sensitive to the absolutist pretensions of the King, it was a bitter rebuke indeed. Skarga concluded with a salvo of chilling texts from the Prophets:

Set thine house in order: for soon thou shalt die, and not live:

And the heart of Pharaoh was hardened, neither would he let the children of Israel go; as the Lord had spoken to Moses.

Thus saith the Lord, . . . I shall speak concerning a nation and concerning a King, to pluck up and to pull down, and to destroy it . . . Because my people have forgotten me, . . . I will scatter them as an east wind before the enemy; I will show them my back and not my face, in the day of their calamity.[25]

The conclusion was stark. If the nobility did not repent, their Republic would suffer the fate of Sodom, of Egypt, and of Byzantium.

In the seventeenth century, political critics often turned to satire. Krzyztof Opaliński (1610–56), Wojewoda of Poznań, who led the magnates' opposition against the supposed absolutist design of Władysław IV, and who had the doubtful distinction of submitting to the Swedes at Ujście in 1655, was no flatterer of the 'Golden Freedom':

> 'Nierządem Polska stoi' — nieźle ktoś powiedział.
> Lecz drugi odpowiedział, że nierządem zginie.
> Pan Bóg nas ma jak błaźnów. I to prawdy blisko,
> Że między ludzmi Polak jest Boże igrzysko.*

The trouble with such Jeremiads was that they did not appear to tally with the promptings of practical experience. To the modern observer, the benefits of a centralized state may possibly appear obvious; to the nobleman of the sixteenth and seventeenth centuries, they did not. From the vantage-point of Warsaw or Wilno or Kiev, life in the Republic, despite its discomforts, looked far superior to that in the surrounding countries. To those generations of Poles and Lithuanians who observed the gentilities of Ivan the Terrible at first hand, who watched the subjugation of Hungary by the Ottomans, or the destruction of the Bohemian nobility by the Habsburgs, 'Absolutism' was indistinguishable from tyranny. The Polish nobility had little practical knowledge of conditions in Western Europe. When they talked of the *absolutum dominum* which

---

* *'Poland stands by unrule'* — as someone well remarked.
  Yet someone else replied that by unrule she shall perish.
  The Good Lord takes us for buffoons. It's near the truth
  That of all the human race, the Pole is God's clown.[26]

they so much feared, they were not thinking of France or Spain. For them, the only real models for judgement were the 'clerical' despotism of Austria, the 'oriental' despotism of Turkey, and the 'barbarian' despotism of Muscovy. What is more, Absolutism did not seem to be much of a hedge against civil commotion. The ceaseless alarms in the adjacent Ottoman dependencies of Transylvania and Moldavia; the Time of Troubles in Muscovy; and above all the Thirty Years War in the Holy Roman Empire, all supported the view that political life under Absolutism was no more stable than under the 'Polish Anarchy'. It was all very well for Skarga or Opaliński to denounce the excesses of the 'Golden Freedom'. Their listeners, and their successors, were perfectly aware of that. What they doubted was that the Anarchy could really be exchanged for something better.

Foreign refugees played a definite role in the formation of these attitudes. The Republic was a known haven for political and religious exiles, from Jews and Hussites to the later victims of Absolutism. The arrival of illustrious defectors, like Andre Dudith, Bishop of Pécs, one-time ambassador of the Emperor, of the Mogila factions from Moldavia and Wallachia, or of Prince Kurbsky, counsellor of Ivan IV, could not but confirm the nobility in their entrenched convictions.

Andrei Mikhailovitch Kurbsky (1528–83), in particular, was an active publicist and politician. Born into one of the ancient dynasties of Muscovy, he spent his early career in the service and the company of Tsar Ivan the Terrible. He was a distinguished general in the Kazan and the Livonian campaigns, and a prominent member of the boyar Council. His disaffection began with the abolition of the Council in 1560, and grew amidst the mounting horrors of the *Oprichnina.* In 1564, when commander of Tartu on the Livonian front, he decided to defect, and on the night of 29–30 April, he crossed the lines to the Lithuanian-held fortress of Wolmar. His wife, his son, and his mother, held by Ivan as hostages to his good behaviour, were put to death. Having sworn allegiance to Sigismund-August, Grand Duke of Lithuania, he was rewarded with the castle of Smedyno, and the grant of Crown lands in the *starostwo* of Kowel in Volhynia, and was assessed for a military contribution of 180 knights and 50 soldiers. Once established, he entered into the spirit of the Anarchy with relish. In 1567–73, he regularly appeared as an envoy to the Sejm, associating himself politically with the Orthodox interest centred on Prince Konstanty Ostrogski, Palatine of Kiev. He gained the reputation of a persecutor of the peasants and the Jews. He was twice married, and once divorced, in scandalous circumstances, and his son by his third wife, Michał Dymitr Kurbsky (1582–1645), sometime envoy of Upita, became a notable convert to Catholicism. He constantly feuded with his neighbours, the Wiśniowiecki and the Czartoryski, and at the end of his life he was so burdened by debts incurred in lawsuits that he was obliged to surrender his estates. All the while, he served in the Lithuanian Army. In Batory's wars against Muscovy in 1579–81, he took command at several victorious battles. In Russian history, Kurbsky is mainly remembered as the ideologue of the boyars' opposition to Ivan's autocracy. His famous correspondence with the Tsar over some fifteen years, and his *History of the Grand Duchy of Moscow* (1573?), provide the most detailed and intimate sources of the period. The former, whose authenticity has recently been assailed, is filled with a mixture of rich abuse and high debate on the principles of legitimacy and civil obedience. Kurbsky raged against the 'leprous conscience' of his former master, who 'belches forth his bombastic and learned quotations in untameable wrath.' Ivan called his one-time subject 'a cur', a 'stinking traitor', a 'seducer', a 'Pharisee', a 'perjurer'. The *History* written in similar vein, was inspired by the chilling prospect that on the death of Sigismund-August, Ivan might be elected to the Polish throne. In Polish history, however, Kurbsky is remembered as a prominent recruit to the service of the Republic, and as a living advertisement against the barbarism of Muscovy. Yet it is quite clear from his correspondence that he had little respect for the principles of the noble democracy. 'As for the godless nations,' he said to Ivan in his Second Epistle, 'why mention them? For none of them rule as masters in their own house. They rule as their employees order them to.' The Polish chronicler, Bielski, claimed that Kurbsky fled to Lithuania from fear of the consequences of military failure; and most modern commentators would concede that there was a strong streak of opportunism in his conduct. None the less, the Republic gave him a sanctuary from which to propound his views, and that in itself was a good advertisement.[27]

Foreign comment on Poland–Lithuania had long been delayed by lack of information. But as from the mid-sixteenth century western scholars were well supplied with detailed descriptions. In Italy, the famous account written in 1575 by the Venetian ambassador, Ieronimo Lipomano, supplemented similar reports compiled by each of the Papal Nuncios a decade earlier. Relevant passages in the *Relazioni Universali* (1592) of Giovanni Botero, an official of the Vatican's Office for the Propagation of the Faith, were based on personal and extremely shrewd observation. In France, Poland was little known until the publication of Kromer's Chronicle in Paris in 1566; but great publicity was aroused by the election of Henry Valois in 1573. In Germany, Polish affairs were mainly publicized by German subjects of the Republic who objected to ill-informed attacks on their homeland. The *Encomium Regni Poloniae* (1621) by Jakub Gadebusch of Danzig, and the *De scopo reipublicae Polonicae* (1665) by Johann Sachs of Thorn (Marinius Polonius), were both published from motives of wounded patriotism. In England, a certain limited information was contained in the *Itinerary* (1617) of Fynes Morison. Full-scale treatment had to await the attention of Dr Bernard O'Connor, sometime physician at the court of John Sobieski, who published his two-volume *History of Poland* in 1698. In Sweden, the jurist and historiographer Samuel Pufendorf was able to draw on Swedish involvement in Polish affairs to paint a sceptical, if not pessimistic, assessment. Throughout Europe, however, Polish authors were known and read. Poland–Lithuania belonged to the international 'Republic of (Latin) Letters'. The works of Modrevicuis, Goślicki, Bielski, Kromer, Varsevicius, Opaliński, were accessible to all who cared to inquire.

Western analysts found great difficulty in classifying a constitution, which could not be easily fitted into the traditional Ciceronian categories of monarchy, aristocracy, or democracy. Everyone agreed that the Republic could not be regarded as a 'true monarchy', like most European kingdoms. Botero said it was 'more republican than monarchical'; Bodin

called it a *monarchia libera*, or 'loose monarchy'; Guillaume
Barclay, Professor of Law at Paris, declared: 'The Poles have
neither King nor Kingdom, but a sort of oligarchy concealed
beneath the royal title.' A wide variety of terms were used to
describe the status of the Polish King. Bodin called him
'capitaine en chef'. Others called him 'a first magistrate', 'a
curator', or 'a chairman'. At all events, he was not a sovereign.
Botero added most shrewdly, no doubt with Bathory in mind,
that 'the King has as much power as his skill and understanding can give him.' In so far as Monarchy was generally held to
be a divine institution, instituted by God, there was a widespread acceptance of the myth that Poland's Royal elections
represented the survival of a prehistoric, pagan custom,
variously ascribed to the Goths, the Celts, the Vandals, or the
ancient Sarmatians.

The Republic's detractors were naturally to be found
amongst those who set greatest store on the virtues of
Monarchy; yet their criticisms were usually mild and construc-
tive. Jean Bodin, for one, studied the question with great care
and precision. As orator to the Polish embassy which came to
Paris in 1573, he had debated the issues with the Polish
senators at first hand. His *Six livres de la République* (1576)
revealed a close knowledge of Kallimach, Miechowit, Kromer,
and especially of Modrzewski, whose propositions he reviewed
in detail. Bodin classified the Poles, together with the British
and the Scandinavians, as 'northerners' who are instinctive
haters of tyranny. Whilst criticizing the elective nature of
Polish kingship, he declared that its uncertainties presented a
danger not so much for the king as for the electors themselves,
and recommended that the king's successor should be elected
vivente rege. His harshest comments were reserved not for
constitutional practice, but for the failings of Polish justice,
and for the Head-Money system in particular. At the end of
the next century, Pufendorf, in his *Introduction to the History
of the Main European Countries* (1686) bemoaned the interminable disputes between Sejm and king, and the paralysis
of the legislative machine, but, in the afterglow of Sobieski's
victory at Vienna, gave no indication that the Republic's
internal failings might endanger its international standing.
Bernard O'Connor noted with regret that 'no one in Poland

is willing to be a subject'; and he underlined the harmful effects of the *Liberum Veto,* and of the life-tenure of offices of state. With the insight of a medical practitioner, he expressed astonishment that a body politic with such obvious maladies should have survived so long. He explained the Republic's survival partly to the solidarity of a free people, who postpone their differences in moments of supreme crisis, partly to the disunity of neighbouring states, and partly to military factors. In O'Connor's view, a country which possessed no modern fortresses could neither be defended by its citizens nor suppressed by its invaders. Each of these writers formed their criticisms without malice, and stand in sharp contrast to the unashamed polemicists such as Guillaume Barclay whose *Satyricon* (1614) was composed for the amusement of the French court, or Herman Conring, whose tract *De iustitia armorum Suecorum in Polonos* (On the Justice of Swedish Arms against the Poles, 1655), was written to order for Charles X. Jean Barclay, son of Guillaume, pronounced the Poles to be barbarians — 'a nation born in violence and licence, which they call Freedom, who oblige their King at the point of the sword to uphold the laws of their forefathers, and who, being possessed of self-awarded privileges, are able to injure each other with impunity.' Conring, with a political end in view, went further. The Republic, he wrote, was unloved by its inhabitants, was ruined by noble excess, and was not worth saving.

The admirers of the Republic were first found among theorists of the Right of Resistance. In France, both Catholics and Huguenots were apt to condemn the Republic's reputation for religious toleration: but each, from their opposite points of view, were led to appreciate the Republic's elaborate safeguards against tyranny. Jean Boucher of Paris, whose tract *De justa abdicatione* (On Rightful Abdication, 1589) expressed the views of the Catholic opposition to Henry III, wrote a glowing account of the way that the tyrant had been driven from Poland. Theodore Beza, Calvin's successor at Geneva, praised the institution of the *Pacta Conventa.* Most sensational, however, were the views of the anonymous Huguenot, whose famous *Vindiciae contra tyrannos* (1579), composed under the pseudonym of 'Junius Brutus', is often taken to be the first clear formulation in modern times of the concept of a political contract between rulers and the ruled. According to him, the Polish Republic and the Holy Roman Empire were the only two states of Europe where ancient virtue had withstood the onslaught of tyrannical monarchs. In his description of his ideal of a constitutional monarchy, which would display 'the legitimate power of the prince over the people', he likened the Polish Republic to Venice. Echoes of his opinions were heard throughout the seventeenth century. Sir James Harrington's *Oceana* (1659) invoked the Polish example to embellish his dream of a utopia organized in the interests of propertied gentlemen; Ulryk Huber, the Dutchman, used it in *De iure Civitatis* (1673) to demonstrate the fallacies of Hobbes. In Germany, a tract on Polish politics was composed by the mathematician and philosopher, Gottfied Leibniz when employed as secretary to the ambassador of the Duke of Neuberg at the Royal election of 1669. Masquerading as 'Georgius Ulicovius Lithuanus', he was mainly concerned to further the candidacy of his employer, and took care that his *Specimen demonstrationum politicarum pro elegendo rege Polonorum* (1669) would not offend the Polish electorate. Even so, his arguments for the need to restrain liberty in the interests of external security, and his interesting comparison of the principle of unanimity as conceived in Poland and in the United Provinces, are ample proof of his serious intentions. In Italy, praise for Poland rose from the depths of a Neapolitan dungeon. Tommaso Campanella, a Dominican friar incarcerated for twenty-seven years for heresy, author of the 'City of the Sun', included a long passage on the Republic in his work *De Monarchia Hispanica.* Most surprisingly, perhaps, he composed a sonnet in honour of the Polish electors, urging them to prefer native virtue before foreign princely blood:

> *To Poland*
> High o'er those realms that make blind chance the heir
> Of Empire, Poland dost thou lift thy head:
> For while thou mournest for thy monarch dead
> Thou wilt not let his son the sceptre bear
> Lest he prove weak perchance to do or dare.
> Yet art thou even more by luck misled,
> Choosing a prince of fortune, courtly bred,

Uncertain whether he will spend or spare.
Oh quit this pride! In hut or shepherd's pen
Seek Cato, Minos, Numa! For of such
God still makes kings in plenty: and these men
Will squander little substance and gain much,
Knowing that virtue and not blood shall be
Their titles to true immortality.[28]

In the Saxon Era, the quality of political comment degenerated as surely as the political situation itself. In Poland, intelligent men held their tongues. The realm of political theory was abandoned to the ostrich-like apostles of the 'Golden Freedom'. In a world where would-be reformers recoiled before the overwhelming odds of foreign coercion and internal strife, no challenge was offered to those 'Sarmatists' who pretended that Poland's condition was superior to that of any other country on earth. The prime quotations of Sarmatist opinions are to be found in the amazing encyclopaedia of the Revd. Benedykt Chmielowski (1700–63), whose *Nowe Ateny albo Akademia wszelkiej scjencji pełna* (The New Athens or an Academy full of the sciences, 1746) enjoyed wide popularity. Chmielowski's religious bigotry and political *naïveté* typified the outlook of the dimmer, semi-educated noblemen of his day. 'The first inestimable diamond in the Polish Crown', he wrote, 'is the Golden Freedom. The second bejewelled foundation of our liberty is the *Liberum Regum Electio*. The third is the *Liberum Veto*. Freedom of speech in the Sejm and in the dietines is the mother and soul of freedom; and there can be no sign that the Fatherland is dying so long as they are all still talking.'[29] Having lost all hope of salvation, Polish society turned in on itself, and bewitched by the imaginary idylls of 'Old Sarmatia', began to lose sight of elementary realities.

Abroad, a procession of political writers recounted the obvious ills of the Polish system without caring to examine their causes. As early as 1721, in his *Lettres persanes*, Montesquieu stated 'Poland makes such poor use of her Liberty, and of her Royal elections that she gives thereby no satisfaction but to her neighbours, who have lost both.' In 1740, in his *Anti-Machiavel*, Frederick II noted that in Poland, 'the throne is an object of trade like any other commodity on the public market.' In his *Considérations sur le gouvernement,* the Marquis d'Argenson warned that 'Poland stands open on every side to be taken by anyone who cares to do so. Very soon, her one strength will lie in her very feebleness.' In the article devoted to Poland in the French *Encyclopédie,* the Chevalier de Jaucourt was content to plagiarize the recent work of Abbé Gabriel Coyer on the history of John Sobieski. In it, he mentioned a theme already mooted by Montesquieu to the effect that the decline of the state was due to the 'slavery' of the common people. Similar opinions were repeated by most of the sages of the day – by David Hume, by Adam Smith, by William Paley, and above all, by Voltaire.

Voltaire's numerous, brilliant, and uniformly hostile comments deserve special mention, if only because they were so widely publicized. First in his *History of Charles XII,* then in the drama, *Les Lois de Minos,* and later in his numerous writings on the subject of Toleration, the sage of Ferney missed no opportunity of deriding Poland as the home of 'chaos', 'barbarity', and 'fanaticism'. With no claim to any close acquaintance with Polish affairs, he used the Republic as a cautionary tale to illustrate the fate of all who fell into the clutches of Romish ignorance. 'Braves Polonais! . . . vous n'avez eu depuis longtemps que deux véritables ennemis – les Turcs et la cour de Rome.' Needless to say, he used the Polish leitmotif not as a serious contribution to the study of Poland, but as a polemical weapon with which to humour his readers. Yet in his eagerness to flatter his enlightened correspondents in Berlin and St. Petersburg, he often lapsed into the sort of hyperbole which revealed his true colours. In 1768, for example, he paid a characteristic double-edged compliment to the authors of Poland's 'liberties', congratulating both Stanisław-August and Archbishop Podoski for their fortunate association with the 'Star of the North':

... Not only has the Empress of Russia established universal toleration in her own vast realms, but she has sent an Army into Poland to protect the rights of citizens and to cause fear and trembling among the persecutors. It is the first Army of its kind since the world began – an army of peace! O wise and just King who has presided over this happy reconciliation! O enlightened Primate, prince without pride, priest without superstition, may you be blessed and emulated for ever and ever![30]

In such an atmosphere, it was a bold spirit indeed who dared to say anything favourable of the Polish constitution. Even the apologists of the Leszczyński camp, and the proponents of Reform, from Baudeau to Mably, were given to blackwashing Poland in the hope of provoking change. But Jean-Jacques Rousseau was different. Invited to pen his reflections on the Polish situation by Wielhorski, the agent in Paris of the Confederates of Bar, he expressed a view which was unique in its day. His *Considérations sur le gouvernement de la Pologne,* published in 1772 in the year of the First Partition, mark a triumph at once of independence of mind and of careful scholarship. Rousseau had studied Polish institutions with some care, and was not averse to detailed improvements. But he recognized prevailing conditions as a perversion of worthy ideals, and the general tenor was one of caution. 'Think very carefully', he warned, 'before you disturb that which has made you what you are.' Finally, fully conversant with the intrigues of the Republic's neighbours, he proffered perhaps the most pertinent piece of advice on the Polish condition ever made in modern times. 'If you cannot prevent your enemies from swallowing you whole,' he wrote, 'at least you must do what you can to prevent them from digesting you.' This one sentence was heeded in Poland long after the cumulative wisdom of all the other *philosophes* had been completely forgotten.[31]

*   *   *   *   *

For the political scientist, the *Rzeczpospolita* of Poland–Lithuania displays a number of features which distinguish it from most West European polities of the period. In theoretical terms, the state can better be described as a monarchical republic rather than as a republican monarchy. It was far more republican in structure and spirit than the constitutional monarchies of England or Sweden, and diametrically opposed to the absolutist systems of France, Spain, or Russia. In some respects, it resembled the fragmented and elective structures of the Holy Roman Empire, shorn of the dynastic accretions introduced by the later Habsburg Emperors; and it had much in common with the complicated constitution of the United Provinces. But its authors were specifically inspired by the

Roman Republic of ancient times, from which it took its
name, and by the Republic of Venice, from whose university
at Padua, most of them had graduated. In this light, it would
seem appropriate that in translating the name of the
Rzeczpospolita into English, Anglo-Saxon scholars should
prefer 'the Republic' to the more usual 'Commonwealth'.

The political game as played in Poland–Lithuania was of a
very special type. The absence of chains of command radiat-
ing from the centre, or of a social hierarchy organized in the
interests of the state, permitted individual, local, or provincial
policies to be pursued without fear of restraint from above.
Everything depended on the shifting patterns of patronage,
rank, wealth, merit, and fortune; virtually nothing on *raison
d'état*. The state never pretended to an interest of its own
which was greater than the sum of interests of its individual
citizens. As a result, the external policy of the Republic was
strikingly passive; whilst internal policies were eternally in-
conclusive. In one interesting hypothesis, political life was
compounded from the kaleidoscopic interplay of small-scale,
local interests and of larger, more impermanent, regional
interests: or, as it was put, of 'small neighbourhoods' and of
'large neighbourhoods'.[32] It would take a Lewis Namier –
whose work on the underlying relationships of politics in
Georgian England has a strong scent of his Polish origins – to
test the exactness of this analysis. But it would be well worth
testing, and would make an excellent subject for research.

In fact, the closest parallels to Poland's 'Noble Democracy'
can probably be found outside Europe altogether, in America.
At first sight at least, the outlook of the Polish nobility
would seem to agree with that of the gentry of the English
colonies of the deep South, whose vast plantations and brilliant social life were perpetuated, as in Poland–Lithuania, by
their isolation from central government and by the servitude
of the rural masses. Slave-owning democrats such as Thomas
Jefferson or George Washington, and other founding fathers
of the USA, have much in common with the reforming wing
of magnatial politicians among their contemporaries in
Poland–Lithuania. Further north, in New England, a different
brand of individualism was encouraged by religious beliefs,
and by the colonists' rejection of the spiritual coercion

practised by ecclesiastical authorities in most European countries. The thoughts of Henry Thoreau beside the Walden Pond, or in his 'Essay on the Duty of Civil Disobedience' would have found a greater measure of understanding in the Polish Sejm than in any Court or Parliament in Europe. His famous motto to the effect that 'that government is best that governs least', would have brought a roar of acclaim at any provincial dietine, and encapsulates the opposition of the Polish nobility to the growth of royal power throughout the Republic's existence. Primitive American anarchism, born on the Frontier of a new continent, may well have had a kindred spirit, if not a direct ancestor, in the ideals of that extinct Republic which once roamed the plains of Eastern Europe.

Oddly enough, the ideals of the Polish nobility possess an air of striking modernity. In an age when most Europeans were lauding the benefits of Monarchism, Absolutism, or of state power, the noble citizens of Poland–Lithuania were praising their 'Golden Freedom', the right of resistance, the social contract, the liberty of the individual, the principle of government by consent, the value of self-reliance. These concepts feature widely in the ideologies of modern, liberal democracies. It is inconceivable, of course, that they were cherished by the szlachta from a precocious interest in progressive political theory, rather than from the elemental desire to preserve their ancient privileges. However, there is an obvious connection. By European standards, the Republic provides an instance of grossly retarded development. To observers in the age of Enlightenment, Polish attitudes were reminiscent of those of savage medieval barons. Yet it must not be forgotten that modern Anglo-Saxon democracy has grown from an essentially conservative position, which still sees the medieval traditions of Magna Carta as relevant to the needs of today. The coincidence of view between the Polish nobleman of the seventeenth or eighteenth century with the liberal democrat of the nineteenth and twentieth centuries, is not purely fortuitous. It is caused by their common concern to combat the power of the state. The one opposed the initial manifestations of the phenomenon, the other opposes its modern excesses, but their enemy is the same. For this reason, if for no other, in approaching the history of the Polish–Lithuanian

Republic, the present-day scholar might reasonably be expected to escape from the exclusively negative judgements, whose origins can be surely traced to the exponents of the Enlightenment and to the 'enlightened' apologists of the partitioning powers.

CHAPTER ELEVEN
SERENISSIMA:
Diplomacy in Poland–Lithuania

It may be debatable whether Jan Dantiscus (1485–1548) or 'Dantyszek', was the first Polish diplomat; but he was certainly one of the most entertaining. His eight years and four months as ambassador to the Emperor Charles V between 1524 and 1532, are often cited as the first permanent embassy of the Polish service. In some ways, Dantyszek belonged to the medieval tradition of cosmopolitan clerics who ran international relations as a sideline of ecclesiastical affairs. At the same time, he belonged to a new generation of humanists, for whom artistic patronage, philosophical exploration, and secular curiosity on a wide scale opened up entirely new vistas for their considerable talents. Born in Danzig as Johann von Hoefen, the son of a prosperous brewer, he assumed his Latin *nom de plume* when publishing neo-latin poetry, and his Polish cognomen by serving from the age of fifteen in the royal court at Cracow. He received his church benefices as an adjunct to his diplomatic career, enjoying the Bishopric of Chełmno, and from 1537 the Bishopric of Warmia. In Cracow, he studied under the Hellenist, Paul of Krosno, whilst employing himself as a page in the court retinue, and participating in the disastrous Moldavian expedition of 1502. In 1503 he appears in the secretariat of Archbishop Jan Łaski, and the next year, as a specialist in Prussian affairs, in the royal chancery. In 1505–6, he travelled to Venice and thence to Cyprus, Palestine, and Arabia. In 1512, his action in the royal courts over a disputed family inheritance in Danzig was the immediate cause of the crisis between Poland and the Teutonic Order. He first caught the eye of the Emperor Maximilian at the Vienna Congress in 1515, and when he returned to the imperial court in the following year as the envoy of Sigismund I, he was raised to the rank of *comes palatinus,* and crowned as 'poet-laureate'. In the subsequent period he journeyed incessantly, pressing the causes of his Polish master, and acting as occasion demanded on behalf of the Emperor, or of the cities of Prussia. In 1522–3 he was in England, looking for support against the activities of the Teutonic Order. As he reported back to Sigismund, he was received by Cardinal Wolsey, at Hampton Court, in a darkened room:

When I was brought to him, I found him lying in bed and suffering, so he said, from the colic. But I saw that he had the French pox . . . I greeted him in the name of your Most Serene Majesty, and delivered a short speech on the Turkish and Tartar problems . . . To all this he gave a long answer, for he is quite a learned and a well-spoken man. He said many offensive things about the French, and complained of their perfidy . . . Then I asked and exhorted him to help in the dispute with the Grand Master . . . He answered with a laugh that I came at a good time . . . and concluded, 'The King of Poland is more important to me and my sovereign than those brethren, who are not worth a penny to us'.[1]

Later he met Henry VIII, with Thomas More acting as interpreter, and visited the shrine of Thomas Becket at Canterbury. Still in pilgrim's mood, he set off for Santiago di Compostella, sailing to Corunna from Plymouth in a Portuguese ship, which was storm-driven into Penzance. At which point, the mother of Sigismund's Queen, Bona Sforza, died in Bari, leaving her Polish in-laws with complicated legal claims to her inheritance. Dantyszek left Cracow in search of Charles V on 15 March 1524. It was his third imperial assignment. His instructions made no provisions beyond the immediate issue of the Neapolitan succession. Having met the Doge in Venice, the d'Este duke in Ferrara, the chancellor of the Duchy in Bari, and Francis I at Lyon, he knelt before the Emperor in Madrid on 3 December. Thereafter, the Emperor kept him constantly at his side, for five years in Spain, for one year in 1529 in Italy, and for three more years in Germany. In 1526, Dantyszek's mistress, Izabela del Gada, gave birth to the beautiful Juanita, who was destined to marry the Emperor's secretary, Gratian von Albert. He finally regained Cracow in July 1532, laden with honours, and later retired to his episcopal seat at Heilsberg. He was a personal friend of many notable men of his time, from Cortes to Erasmus and Luther, not to mention Copernicus, who was his immediate client and employee. In his retirement, he was a great correspondent and collector, a true son of the Age of Discovery. As poet, he addressed himself in Latin to a wide world which had still not disintegrated into petty, national cultures. As diplomat, he was prone to celebrate a mission not with a memorandum or a minute but with an epigram:

> Hanc nigram niveamque mihi Iovis alitis alam
> Pro meritis caesar nobile stemma dedit.
> Quod datur ex atavis clarum est, sed clarius omne
> Quod per se virtus propria ferre solet.*

Or a lascivious elegy:

> Quam durae miseri sunt condicionis amantes
> Qui nullas sedes nec loca certa tenent!
> Nil datur aeternum, sed quo rapit impetus, illuc
> Ambigui in dubiis pectora rebus agunt.
> Errant et raro placida statione fruuntur
> Atque alia ex aliis sub iuga amoris eunt . . .**

In Dantyszek's time, Poland was approaching the zenith of its political influence. His master, Sigismund I (1506–48), who sent no less than 148 diplomatic missions abroad, was the most active of all the Polish kings in the international field. In 1569 at the Union of Lublin, the Republic of Poland–Lithuania emerged momentarily as the largest territory in Europe and the leading power of the East. In the diplomatic language of the next two centuries, it was known, like Venice, as '*Serenissima Respublica'*, 'The Most Serene Republic', *'La Sérénissme'*. Throughout the modern period, whether nominatively or accusatively, it was at the heart of European diplomacy.

* * * * *

After the union of 1569, the democratic constitution of the Republic removed diplomacy from direct royal control. According to the *Pacta Conventa* agreed between king and

---

* This black-and-white wingspread of Jupiter's Bird/Was given to me by the Emperor as a noble emblem for my services./That which is inherited from one's ancestors is illustrious; but still more illustrious/Is that which a man achieves by his own merit.

** How hard is the lot of unhappy lovers/Who have no resting place nor fixed abode./ Nothing permanent can be enjoyed; but there, where impulse strikes/ They consume their hearts in guilty affairs./They wander on, rarely enjoying a tranquil sojourn,/but passing from one amorous yoke to another . . .²

nobility at the beginning of each reign, no ambassadors could be appointed without the assent of the Senate. No treaties were valid until ratified by the Sejm. For important negotiations, both chambers of the Sejm would join in appointing parliamentary commissioners, who were considered to possess the highest diplomatic status.

In practice, of course, the king retained considerable executive powers. Although foreign policy was not conducted on his behalf but in the name of 'the Senate and Republic', his influence was far greater than that of any other individual. His was the most powerful voice in the periodic formal sessions of the full Senate, which established the main principles of policy, as it was among the sixteen resident senators, or in the *senatus consilium* (Senate Committee) which directed everyday business in the long intervals between sessions. In normal times, the king exercised close control over the four chancelleries — two for the Kingdom and two for the Grand Duchy — and in particular over the lesser Chancellery of the Kingdom, which customarily attended him on his progresses and which was able to establish a dominant role in diplomatic affairs. There were moments, as in 1609 under Sigismund Vasa, when the Sejm was prepared to allow the King to decide on war and peace at his own discretion; and there were others, as in 1656 under Jan Kazimierz, when the absence of the Sejm left the king in sole command. It is true that some Polish kings may well have looked with envy at the powers of their confrères elsewhere in Europe, who largely contrived, even in the constitutional monarchies, to keep foreign affairs within the royal prerogative. But given skill, and a reasonable standing in the eyes of the chief officers of state, they were far from helpless.

In accordance with the far-reaching dispersion of authority within the Republic, the state did not claim a monopoly in diplomatic affairs. If the Sejm or the Senate could prevent the king from making commitments of which they did not approve, so equally there was no objection to the king persuing a private policy of his own so long as the interests and resources of the state were not thereby compromised. During the Vasa era, royal diplomacy undertaken by courtiers as opposed to state officials, pressed the king's dynastic claims to the Swedish throne through channels quite separate from those of the state. In the Saxon Era, a very clear distinction was drawn between the undertakings of the king and those of the Republic. It was quite possible for the Wettin, as Elector of Saxony, to be at war with Sweden for example, whilst the same man, as King of Poland—Lithuania, was at peace. The Hetmans, or army commanders, were empowered from the early sixteenth century to enter diplomatic relations as an adjunct to their military duties. Especially in the south and east, whence communication with Warsaw was excessively slow, a Hetman would fight a campaign or sign a truce with the Muscovites or Tartars on his own lawful initiative. In the process, he regularly sent envoys to Moscow or to the Crimea, and received embassies in return. The great magnates claimed similar licence, although in their case the line between con-stitutional and treasonable conduct was harder to define. Certainly the Radziwiłł who signed his private treaty with the invading Swedes in 1655 was a traitor, and was universally condemned as such. But earlier in the seventeenth century, when Chancellor Zamoyski used his personal army and his private diplomacy to make and to unmake the Hospodars of Moldavia, he did so with impunity. In Muscovy's 'Time of Troubles', it was the private adventures of George Mniszek and his fellow-conspirators who, contrary to the wishes of the Sejm, dragged Poland into the internecine struggles of Russia. Increasingly, the Polish magnates acted much like the princes of Germany — as virtually independent rulers whose overlord was too distant and too preoccupied to care. In times of Confederation, when the nobility convoked armed leagues for the pursuit of legal political objectives, the Confederate leaders were fully entitled to use diplomatic means in support of their campaign. During the Great Northern War these con-federations lasted for decades, and diplomacy was fragmented to a degree far beyond the control of any central authority. At various times, both the city of Danzig and the Cossacks of the Dnieper maintained their own diplomatic services with the full consent of the state authorities. During the frequent interregna, conduct of foreign affairs traditionally fell to the Primate, the Archbishop of Gniezno, who as *interrex* was empowered to pursue yet another category of 'primatial diplomacy'.

The division of administrative responsibility was no less complicated than that of executive authority. In each of the separate administrations of the Kingdom and the Grand Duchy, the care and supervision of foreign diplomats, and the co-ordination of different sections of the Republic's diplomatic service was ascribed to the Marshal. The diplomatic secretariats were the responsibility of the Chancellors, but were usually managed by one of the vice-chancellors, or *podkanclerz*. As time went on, the administration of the Kingdom was by far the more important, although the Lithuanians for long emphasized their right to supervise relations with Muscovy. In the Kingdom, a Chief Secretary or *secretarius supremus* co-ordinated the work of the secretariat, whilst four chief notaries or *pronotarii* acted as heads of department. The latter specialized in relations with particular countries or regions, and were authorized to observe the proceedings of the Senate and of the Senate committee. In addition there were refe-rendaries, copyists, interpreters, and archivists – some twenty persons in all. In the early years of the Union, the personnel of this Polish secretariat was quite outstanding. Its list of employees included names like Jan Kochanowski, Łukasz Górnicki, Andrzej Frycz-Modrzewski, Jan Zamoyski, Marcin Kromer, Stanisław Hosius – and claimed a high proportion of the leading intellects and artists of the day. In addition to its main task of foreign correspondence, the secretariat had to compose reports, to prepare ambassadors' instructions, to issue their twofold letters of credence from King and Senate, and to keep the records. Zygmunt-August was particularly interested in their work, and personally inspected the inventories. From 1503 onwards, ambassadorial reports were kept in the *Libri Legationum,* and the general diplomatic correspondence in the *Metryka Koronna,* or 'Crown Register.'

The languages of Polish diplomacy were many and varied. In the sixteenth and seventeenth century, the primary language was Latin, used both for official documents within the Polish service itself and also for communication with most foreign countries. All of Western Europe and Scandinavia, together with Prussia and Courland, lay within the Latin sphere. The first attempt in Warsaw to use French occurred in 1636, when Richelieu's envoy, de Rorte, dared to put the opening sentences of his oration to the Senate into his native tongue. Thereafter French made headway for the purposes of informal conversation, especially in the Francophile court of Jan Sobieski, but not as an official language. Sobieski wrote to Charles II of England either in French or in Latin, addressing him as 'Très Affectionné Frère', and signing himself as 'Bonus Frater'. Polish was common enough in ambassadors' instructions and in reports for internal circulation, and in the time of the Great Elector was still understood by the Prussian diplomats. Italian, too, was in current use, having been strongly implanted into the Polish service by the Court of Queen Bona Sforza, and by a long line of Paduan graduates. Both Zygmunt-August in the sixteenth century and Jan Kazimierz Vasa in the seventeenth habitually used Italian in their everyday speech and correspondence. Zygmunt III used German.

Communication with the East was more difficult. In dealings with Muscovy, it was standard practice for the representatives of the Republic to use Polish when acting on behalf of the Kingdom or of the joint Sejm, and to use Ruthenian (Old Byelorussian) when acting specifically on behalf of the Grand Duchy. The Tsar and his representatives replied in Russian. In dealings with the Tartars, a similar convention existed where each side expressed itself in its own tongue. In formal documents, such as the Treaty of Cecora of 1595, one copy would be drawn up in Polish, and another in Tartar, the latter written in Serbian or Cyrillic letters. In dealings with the Turks, Latin, Polish, Italian, or Turkish would be used in accordance with the varying abilities of available interpreters and secretaries. In 1568, the Porte appointed an islamized Pole as envoy to Poland — one Ibrahim Bey, whose name prior to his capture in a Tartar raid, had been Joachim Strasz. The Poles frequently employed Armenians. In 1602, a Polish envoy to Persia, one Sefer Muratowicz, surprised the Shah by speaking in Persian. Under Zygmunt-August, whose secretary, Krzystof Dzierżek, was sent to study in Istambul at royal expense, a permanent tradition of oriental expertise was established. Under Zygmunt III, Tomasz Zamoyski, who was a scholar of some distinction, filled the same function.[4] Under Stanisław-August, the King's oriental interpreter was one Antoni Crutta, an Albanian formerly in the Venetian service.

The spread of diplomatic activity provided the stimulus for regular postal services. The first step seems to have been taken in 1515 at the Congress of Vienna when the Emperor Maximilian met his two Jagiellonian relatives, Sigismund of Poland and Władysław of Bohemia and Hungary. 'Postae celerrimae' were instituted to link the royal capital of Cracow with the imperial post at Breslau in Silesia. In 1558, the death of Bona Sforza inevitably multiplied correspondence with the Empire and with Italy, and a permanent weekly courier service was established in both directions between Cracow, Vienna, and Venice, managed by one Prosper Provana. In 1568, this service was contracted out to the Florentine Montelupi family, who thereupon settled in Cracow and, changing their name to 'Wilczogórski', ran the Polish posts for the next century and more. In due course, the posts were extended to Warsaw, and from Warsaw to Danzig and Wilno, and in 1667 to Moscow. On other routes, the ancient arrangement continued whereby diplomatic mail was consigned to bankers, merchants, or even to casual strollers. It is interesting to note that the efficiency of the post did not improve with time. In Provana's day, in 1558, a rider left Cracow at daybreak on Sundays, reached Vienna on the Wednesday evening, and delivered the mail in Venice on the following Tuesday, after 10 days on the road. The 625 miles (1,125 kilometres) were covered at an average of 62 miles a day. This is close to the 'amazing speed' of the messenger who in 1526 brought news of Mohacs to Cracow within 8 days of the fateful battle. But the timetable of the Venice run soon deteriorated to 15 days. In 1583, when the Montelupi redirected their couriers through Slovenia, they cut it back for a time to 11 days. A full run from Wilno to Rome took up to eight weeks. Amsterdam and London, which could be reached out of Danzig in two or three weeks, were somewhat closer. Spain, which could be contacted either via Danzig or Naples was at least three months distant. Later on, during the Great Northern War, the post disintegrated almost completely. Diplomatic mail was carried by foot instead of on horseback, and replies were not expected soon.

To protect the diplomatic mail, a number of ruses were practised. Several copies of a letter would normally be sent to their destination by different routes, to ensure that one at least was safely delivered. Ciphers, however, introduced into Poland by Kallimach in the fifteenth century, were not employed on all occasions. Pope Gregory XIII, who in 1585 was using the Republic as a staging post for his advances to Muscovy, was said to be concerned lest his secrets be revealed in unciphered Polish correspondence. He was not amused by the Polish ambassador's remark about ciphers being unnecessary 'because *we* have nothing to hide'. A century later, in 1683, the interception of the French Ambassador's correspondence and the successful cracking of his code revealed a conspiracy with the King's political enemies. It occasioned both the recall of the ambassador, the Marquis de Vitry, and the momentous transfer of Sobieski's support from France to Austria. In 1758, another Frenchman, the Comte de Broglie, was still more unlucky. During his absence in Paris for consultation over the 'Diplomatic Revolution', his embassy in Warsaw was burgled by the Prussian ambassador in person and his correspondence read directly.

The modern system of permanent embassies did not emerge until the late sixteenth century, and even after that date, the former practice of sending envoys abroad on specific missions of short duration was by no means abandoned. At the time of the Union of 1569, there were permanent Polish missions in Madrid, Vienna, Naples, and Rome. In the seventeenth century, Polish agents resided in most European capitals, maintaining some continuity of relations between the intermittent visits of senior representatives. In the 1630s, in Copenhagen, Vienna, and Naples, there appeared the first stirrings of a Polish consular service.

The status of embassies was equally uncertain, since it depended as much on the rank of the individual ambassador as on his destination or on the nature of his mission. The highest rank of *Orator* was equivalent to that of *'Wielki poseł'* (Grand Envoy), reserved for missions to Moscow. It was followed by *nuntius* (envoy), *internuntius* (sub-envoy), *agens* (agent), and at the bottom of the scale, the *missilis* (messenger). All, however, were inferior in authority to the parliamentary commissioners, who headed Polish delegations to the most important diplomatic conferences. About half of the embassies were entrusted to senators, both clerical and secular. In the sixteenth century, the royal secretaries also featured prominently, but not without a touch of friction. In 1554, at Vienna, the chief Polish delegate, Mikołaj Myszkowski, Castellan of Radom, so objected to the inclusion in his embassy of Marcin Kromer, a mere historian, that he tried to occupy both of the chairs provided for them at their audience. Yet the humblest commoners could be employed on embassy when required. Armenian merchants played a prominent role in relations with the Crimea, just as in the 1520s Queen Bona's Neapolitan cook, Cola Maria de Charis, was chosen to represent the King in Italy. In embassies to Moscow and the Porte, the question of status gained added meaning, since the hosts were apt to gauge the Republic's sincerity by the eminence of the envoy's rank and the splendour of his retinue. The dispatch of an ambassador of inferior standing or of modest means was received as a calculated insult, which could abort the mission from the start.

Within the Republic, foreign missions were expected to observe strict procedures. On reaching the frontier, they reported to the Starosta of the nearest town, who was charged with escorting them to the capital and with discouraging them from conversing with local people. In the Grand Duchy, the same function was filled by a special official, the *przystawa,* as in Muscovy. On arrival in Warsaw, missions were welcomed by the Marshal, to underline the supremacy of the state over the Court. Papal Nuncios and monarchical ambassadors were expected to make a ceremonial entry, riding in the king's personal carriage. At the Royal Castle, they were received in audience by the king, who in the company of his senators remained both standing and covered. The formal reading of letters of credence took place before the full Senate, where the ambassador's oration was answered in Latin by the Chancellor. This was followed by courtesy visits to each of officers of state, starting with the Marshal, the Hetman, the Chancellor, and the Treasurer. At the time of royal Elections, the entire diplomatic corps was dismissed from the capital, each mission being assigned a country palace in which to reside for the duration. By this ingenuous rule, formalized in 1683, the Sejm sought to limit foreign interference. In practice, the ambassadors were able to contact their partisans from outside Warsaw as easily as from within, and, with gold to spare, their nefarious activities were impossible to control. On the day of the Election, the ambassadors were permitted to enter the Wola Field and to speak on behalf of their candidates. Afterwards, they proceeded to St. John's Cathedral to assist in the official *Te Deum,* and thence to Cracow for the coronation. On taking their leave at the end of a mission, they were required to quit the territory of the Republic within three weeks of submitting their letters of recredence.

Diplomatic immunity was a fragile privilege in early modern Europe. In Muscovy or in Turkey, where physical violence and deliberate humiliations were an accepted instrument of negotiation, it was unknown. In the Republic it was recognized, but was subject to several signal lapses. French ambassadors figure prominently among the victims, perhaps because under Louis XIV their activities were particularly blatant and deeply resented. In 1683, the Marquis de Vitry was expelled from the Republic not just for his private intrigues but equally to save him from the Sejm which was clamouring to have him publicly birched and castrated. In 1702, M du Heron was summarily arrested at Thorn on suspicion of conspiring with the Swedes. In response, Louis XIV ordered all Polish citizens in France to be interned as hostages against his ambassador's safety. In 1733–6, the Marquis de Monti, whose zeal for the cause of Stanisław Leszczyński had led to the burning of Saxon books in the market place at Warsaw and the purchase of all the city's printing-presses to prevent their use by his rivals, spent some three years in prison after his seizure in Danzig by his victorious opponents. The worst fate of all, however, awaited Jan Rheinhold Patkul, the Russian ambassador to Augustus II during the Great Northern War. As a native of Swedish Livonia, Patkul was regarded by the Swedes as a deserter and a traitor, and a clause for his extradition to Charles XII was specifically included in the Treaty of Altranstadt. In 1706, the unhappy ambassador was broken on the wheel, and quartered.

At all official functions, protocol demanded meticulous attention to precedence. As a Catholic country, Poland gave automatic priority to the Papal Nuncio, and observed the traditional order of seniority, as drawn up in the papal bull of 1516. The imperial ambassador claimed precedence over the representatives of other crowned heads, who in turn preceded the representatives of electors, princes, dukes, and republics. The Republic, as successor to the Kingdom of Poland, retained its monarchical status, but had to be content with the thirteenth, penultimate, place in order of seniority, between Bohemia and Denmark. In 1574 at Henry Valois's coronation banquet in Cracow, the Nuncio sat at the King's right hand in the company of the monarchical ambassadors, whilst a lower table was occupied by the envoys of the Venetian Republic, the Elector of Brandenburg, the Dukes of Ferrara and Brunswick, the Prince of Transylvania, the Duke of Prussia, and the Duke of Pomerania.

Disputes over precedence were legion. In the seventeenth century, French ambassadors at Warsaw customarily withdrew rather than cede to their imperial colleagues. On 21 November 1648, when news of the Treaty of Westphalia inspired the Vicomte d'Arpagon to raise his hat to the Marquis de Grana in public, it was the first time such a gesture of Franco-Imperial politeness had been made within living memory.

For sheer wrangling in matters of protocol, however, no one could match the Prussians or the Muscovites. Both these powers were immediate neighbours of the Republic. Both in their different ways made good in the world at Poland's expense, the one by renouncing its ties of dependency, the other by annexing vast expanses of the Republic's territory. Both in the early days were denied full diplomatic rights, the Prussians as vassals, the Muscovites as 'schismatics and barbarians'. Both harboured colossal resentments, and both in time found fertile ground in the Polish Court for cultivating their ever-mounting claims. The persistence with which they clawed their way up the ladder of diplomatic respectability nicely illustrates their rise to power and influence in Europe as a whole. Both set off in the sixteenth century with elaborate displays of servility. Both ended up two centuries later by behaving with insolence.

The rise of the Hohenzollerns was perhaps the more astonishing. As Electors of Brandenburg and Dukes of Prussia, they were simultaneously subjects of the Empire and vassals of the Republic. To exploit their unique predicament, they perfected the art of tergiversation, always contriving to protect an act of blatant treachery in one direction by a specious gesture of loyalty in the other. In Poland, when it suited their purpose, they were model citizens, urging their rights as 'native princes' and noblemen to play an active role in Polish affairs. At other times, they acted the part of foreign princelings, demanding to be treated as sovereign and equal rulers. It was exactly the reverse of the game that they played with the Emperor. In 1525, Albrecht von Hohenzollern, the last Grand Master of the Teutonic Order rode into the Market Square in Cracow to kneel before the King of Poland and receive the Duchy of Prussia in fief. On 5 October 1641, the same ceremony of investiture was enacted in Warsaw by the 'Great Elector' Frederick-William. On both occasions, as the King placed the Prussian standard into the hands of the new duke, a second prince of the House of Hohenzollern stepped forward to touch it, signifying the family's claim to the right of reversion. At the same moment, two Polish senators stepped forward to shout a ritual protest, as a device for invalidating the investiture if the terms of acceptance were avoided. In 1641, the Grand Elector was contesting the title of 'First Prince of Poland' customarily reserved for the Primate – a claim not enhanced by his appearance at the investiture ball wearing mud-spattered riding boots. In 1648, however, he succeeded where his predecessors had failed, and obtained a vote at the royal Election. Having used his vote in favour of Jan Kazimierz and having sworn allegiance to the new monarch, he then proceeded to conspire in the Swedish invasion of the Republic and to participate in the occupation of Warsaw. In 1657, he insisted on recognition of his claim to sovereignty in the Duchy of Prussia, as his price for abandoning the Swedes. Only three years later, he was pressing Jan Kazimierz again to address him as 'Brother', having exacted the same doubtful favour from Louis XIV. Jan Kazimierz, whose vassal he remained for Bytau and Lauenberg if not for Prussia as a whole, categorically refused, and no official of the Republic was to concede anything further for the next century. In 1698, the Grand Elector's grandson, Frederick-William II laid claim to a royal title. Augustus II, careless of the distinction between his powers as Elector of Saxony and those as King of Poland, readily agreed to the wording 'Koenig *in* Preussen'. Nor did he object when at that same Johanisburg meeting, the Hohenzollern contrived to sit beside him in an identical armchair. It was a sign that the two men had accepted the equal standing of their respective domains. As Stepney, the British Ambassador, remarked, 'It is true the Elector hath gained this point, and has his arm'd chair, which "triomphe de fauteuil" you may expect will be placed among the trophies of the Family.'[5] The grant of the Prussian title was not ratified by the Sejm until 1764, and then only under duress. The wording 'Koenig *von* Preussen' was not approved until after the First Partition in 1773. Throughout the period from 1657 to 1764, Polish officials confined their address of the Hohenzollerns to 'le Règnant de Berlin' or 'Sérénissme Souverain'.

As sticklers for form the Muscovites were equally intractable. Until the time of Peter I, when their ambassadors suddenly appeared in wigs and gaiters in the European style, they had always been regarded as savage exotics living beyond the pale of Christendom. In Warsaw, their embassies were received with a mixture of awe and amusement. On the one hand, the luxury of their following – their retinue of hundreds of horsemen and merchants, their pearl-encrusted furs provided at the Tsar's expense, their elaborate gifts of jewels and wild animals, their long beards, pointed hats, and caftans, and the chanted tones in which they affected to speak, were all designed to create a strong impression. On the other hand, many of their habits and demands were so extreme that western ambassadors were invited to watch their performance in court from behind a curtain. For one thing, they had a justified reputation for violence. The story was told how in 1570 Ivan IV had ordered Zygmunt-August's gift of a stud of stallions to be served up as mincemeat when he suspected that his own gift to the Polish King was not fully appreciated. More than a century later, the experiences of the English ambassador to Ivan were still being retailed – Sir Jeremy Bowes was entertained first by the killing of a boyar who had dared to precede him up the stairs of the antechamber, and then by the suicide of another boyar who as proof of his loyalty was

asked by the Tsar to jump through the window.[6] The plea of
Zygmunt III to Queen Elizabeth I of England to desist from
sending arms to 'these barbarians', 'because we know what
they are like,' was based on hard experience.[7] For one thing,
they were excessively suspicious, especially of their own
people. In 1635, Alexis Jaroslavsky, Governor of Suzdal,
caused an uproar in Warsaw by demanding the surrender of
those members of his embassy who had defected; and in 1646
a scandal arose when the Queen's Confessor, Monsigneur de
Fleury, was unceremoniously frisked during a fur-buying spree
at the Muscovite embassy. They were also excessively sensitive of criticism. In 1650, Gregory Gavrilovítch Pushkin,
Governor of Nizhny Novgorod, arriving to congratulate Jan
Kazimierz on his election, demanded the execution of all those
Polish authors whose books contained uncomplimentary
comments about the Tsar. After much remonstration, he
finally settled for a private bonfire of a selection of the
offending volumes arranged in the courtyard of his residence
by the Crown Marshal. Finally, they were famed for their
drunkenness. At all official banquets they insisted on total
inebriation as a mark of appreciation to the hosts, and special
requests were made to the diplomatic corps not to take
advantage of their Russian colleagues when they had fallen
beneath the table.

Yet it was in matters of titulation that the Muscovites
really excelled. As Grand Dukes of Moscow, Ivan IV and his
successors had no acknowledged right to the battery of titles
which they habitually professed. In the accepted European
order of seniority, they were placed among the Italian princes,
below the Electors of the Empire but above the dependent
dukes and republics. 'Tsar' (Caesar), 'Samodzierzhava' (Autocrat), and even 'Rossiya' (Russia) itself were all terms which
they had invented for themselves, and no one in Europe for
long took them seriously. For the Poles their pretensions
were particularly galling, since a large part of the territorial
dignities of the Tsar actually belonged to the Republic and
had never belonged to Muscovy. The claim that the Tsar
was ruler of 'all the Russias' was quaint indeed when 'White
Russia' and 'Black Russia' were in Lithuania, 'Red Russia'
was in Poland, and 'Great Russia' alone was in Muscovy.

Such is the stuff of which empires are made. Muscovite ambassadors, living under the threat of their sovereign's wrath, habitually recited the Tsar's titles aloud and in full as a prelude to every public occasion, and regularly protested whenever they caught wind of ancient Polish titles, such as that of 'Dux Russiae', of which they disapproved. In 1635, Jaroslavsky staged a notable demonstration by attending his audience with Władysław IV wearing two hats — one to be raised in greeting as required by protocol, the other to be kept on his head as the Tsar had commanded. In the eighteenth century, Peter I instructed his ambassadors that his new style of 'Emperor-Autocrat of All-the-Russias' entitled them, as servants of 'the New Rome', to take precedence over the Holy Roman Empire. For many years, the Republic resisted these pretensions without admitting them to documents or treaties. But the first sign of change came in 1671 when a Muscovite envoy made his entry into Warsaw in the King's carriage. In 1677, the papal Nuncio, looking for Muscovite support against the Turks, asked John Sobieski to recognize the title of 'Tsar'. It was, he explained, 'a barbarian name' like that of 'Sheriff' among the Arabs, or of 'Sophie' in Persia. Yet the officials of the Republic were still keeping to the formula of 'Très Puissante Souveraine Tsarine, Grande Duchesse de Moscou' in the mid-eighteenth century. They finally capitulated in 1764 to the combined bullying of Catherine and Frederick of Prussia, who imposed their respective titles on a helpless Sejm as a symbol of political defeat.

Diplomacy, of course, costs money. In the Republic it was paid for from state taxation. The costs were shared out in the ratio of roughly two-thirds from the Kingdom and one-third from the Grand Duchy. The decline of the central treasury was an obvious cause of waning diplomatic energy. Contrary to some accounts, however, Polish diplomats were not starved of their expenses, and it was not for financial reasons alone that diplomacy fell into the hands of the magnates. It is true that the cumbersome machinery of the Sejm often caused delay, but recent studies show that even during the Swedish wars expenses did get paid, and paid in full. An ambassador's expenses could be enormous, and methods of payment were often tortuous. Dantyszek's expenses for his stay in Madrid between 1524 and 1530 were paid partly via the Treasurer of the Queen's Duchy of Bari, partly through a loan from the Fuggers in Venice. They included 100 ducats a month from Bari for his upkeep, plus 500 florins for the journey. Although he spent 318 ducats on the way from Cracow to Madrid, he was soon deep in debt, having paid 1,000 ducats as an inducement to the imperial chancellor, Gatinara, to fix the Neapolitan succession in Poland's favour. In the seventeenth century, sums like this would have looked paltry. In 1672, for example, the Sejm reimbursed 53,000 zł. to Gniński for his recent mission to Moscow, and 134,000 zł. to Radziejowski for his embassy to the Porte. (In the same session, 13,800 zł. were awarded to Sobieski for his outlay as Grand Hetman of the Crown in the war against Turkey.) Personal expenses, however, represented only a small part of the diplomatic budget. In dealings with the East, gifts and subsidies were an essential ingredient of negotiations. If the Republic did not choose to fight its enemies, it had to buy them off — in effect to compensate them for loss of earnings from loot and pillage. In the case of relations with the Tartars, it has been calculated that in the eighteen years between 1654 and 1672, almost 2½ million zł. were spent on 'diplomacy', of which 2 millions and more were attributed to gifts.

Gifts and appeasements	2,122,930 zł. 18 gr. 2d.
Embassies to the Crimea	87,402 zł.
Maintenance of Tartar envoys	199,074 zł. 44 gr.
Miscellaneous: including ransoms	83,506 zł.
Total	2,492,912 zł. 62 gr. 2d. [8]

In view of the facts that the Tartar alliance was part of the Republic's defence against Moscow, and that in 1654 alone no less than 13 million zł. were spent on military measures to contain the Muscovite invasion, those 2½ millions lavished on the Crimea represented good value for money. Overall, the cost of sending embassies abroad was roughly matched by that of maintaining foreign embassies in Warsaw. Together they constituted about one-fifth of the state's expenditure.

*   *   *   *   *

If the Polish school of diplomacy produced its most distinguished practitioners in the early years of the Republic's existence, its outlook and traditions were not analysed and expounded until the end of the sixteenth century. Christopher Warszewicki (1543–1603), or 'Varsevicius', had the distinction of publicizing them throughout Europe.

Christopher Warszewicki belonged to that most brilliant of Polish generations, raised in the cosmopolitan circles of 'the Golden Age', where Renaissance ideals mingled with the highest affairs of state. He was almost the exact contemporary of Chancellor Jan Zamoyski. His elder brother, Stanisław, a convert to Catholicism, was a prominent Jesuit, founder and rector of the Jesuit Colleges at Wilno and Lublin. Both brothers studied in Wittenberg, but whereas Stanisław returned to Poland as a royal secretary, Christopher served as a page in the Viennese court of Ferdinand, King of the Romans. In 1554 he witnessed the marriage in Winchester of Mary Tudor and Philip II of Spain. In the 1560s, he was Secretary of the Bishop of Poznań, and in the reign of Stefan Batory (1576–86), a regular envoy of the King to Muscovy and Scandinavia. In between times, he was variously in the service of the Papal Nuncio to Poland, of Henry III in France, and of the Emperor in Prague. Owing to political activities on behalf of the Habsburgs at election times, he repeatedly fell from grace, and died in Cracow in 1603 after the last of a long series of exiles. As an author, he published a wide variety of serious works – from a guidebook to Venice (1572), to *Turcicae Quatuordecim* (Fourteen Orations on Turkey, 1595), *De optimo statu libertatis* (On the best form of Liberty, 1598), and *De Cognitione* (On Knowledge, 1600). His reflections on diplomacy appeared as *De Legato et Legatione* (On Ambassadors and Embassies), published in Cracow in 1595, and thereafter many times reprinted, in Rostock in 1597, in Lübeck in 1604, and in particular in George Forster's pocket edition in Danzig in 1646.

In the practice of diplomacy, Warszewicki advocated a straightforward policy of honour, piety, prudence, and magnanimity. In his view, the ambassador is a Christian missionary as well as a servant of the prince. In the long run, virtue and honesty pays. 'God does not will protracted success to those who deal in impiety and fraud', he wrote. Or again,

'To behave like a King, is to attract many men by one's bounties, even when one knows that few are really faithful . . . to direct one's wrath more against things than against persons, and not to be moved by the ingratitude of others.' Whilst drawing the distinction between prudent reserve (*dissimulatio*) and deliberate deceit, and excusing a certain measure of pre-varication, (*mendacia quae dicuntur officiosa*) he none the less insists that a diplomat's word is his bond, and that treaties are made to be respected. He puts loyalty, handsomeness, honesty, and education, above noble birth as qualities expected in an ambassador, quoting Virgil, Tacitus, Aristotle, and a host of contemporary examples in support of his view. Dantyszek is praised repeatedly, as is Martin Kromer, the historian. Andreas Dudith, one-time imperial agent in Poland, is censured for 'levity', and Jean Monluc, Ambassador of Charles IX of France, for his 'vanity'. The Muscovites, for their 'ridiculous arrogance' and 'perfidy' are not to be counted among civilized negotiators. In summarizing the characteristics required of ambassadors destined for particular countries, he makes the following observations:

To Turkey, it is necessary to send steadfast and generous envoys (*fortes et liberales*), men who are also honest. There is no point in sending cowards or misers, since these might weaken under the browbeatings to which the Turks habitually subject them. And they must know how to dispense largesse. The position in Moscow is suited to wary men (*cautos in Moscoviam*), for there 'The Greek faith' is practised, and nothing can be obtained without lengthy disputes. For Rome, pious men must be appointed, men noted for their devotion to religion (*pii et religionis observantia noti*), but laymen in preference to clerics, since the latter tend to bow to the authority of the Holy Father. To Spain, individuals of a calm temperament should be sent, men devoid of adventure, since in that country one has to lead an ascetic sort of life whether one wants to or not. In Italy, in contrast, it is right that the state be represented by civilized and courteous men (*humanes et officiosi*) since questions of manners and etiquette cause continual problems there. France is a place for versatile men of speedy intellect (*ingenuo celeri aut potius versatili*), who can adapt themselves quickly and grasp the point of an argument. In England, handsome, high-born envoys are best suited (*formosi et proceres*), for the English have great respect for that sort of person, telling them apparently that it is a pity they are not Englishmen themselves. In Germany, diplomats need to keep to their promises (*promes-*

sorum tenaces), the Germans being famed from time immemorial for their constancy and perseverance. Everywhere, diplomats must be temperate and abstinent (*continentes et abstinentes . . .*)[9]

These remarks, made nearly four hundred years ago, are not entirely obsolete.

All in all, Warszewicki's political attitudes are sensible and high-minded, but somewhat naïve. They are markedly different both from the Jesuitical improvements on Machiavelli which were appearing elsewhere in Catholic Europe, and from the oriental mysticism which prevailed at points east. Judging from the frequent reprints, they were widely respected beyond the Republic, providing a refreshing change from the cynicism and fanaticism of the age.

The extent to which individual Polish diplomats conformed to Warszewicki's standards is impossible to say; but one at least provides an object lesson in how an ambassador should never behave. Paweł Działyński, Castellan of Dobrzyń and a secretary to Zygmunt III, who left Poland on a mission to England in May 1597, must surely have been familiar with Warszewicki's recently published handbook. But first at The Hague and then at Greenwich, he provoked a couple of incidents which reverberated to his discredit throughout the courts of Europe. At that juncture, England and Holland were both at war with Spain, and were seizing all the Spanish ships which tried to trade with Danzig. Działyński's task was to persuade the Protestant powers to desist. But his methods were all too direct. At The Hague, he threatened to close Danzig completely, and to 'starve' the Dutch into submission. His Dutch hosts listened in stony silence. At Greenwich, on 25 July 1597, he repeated his threats and treated Queen Elizabeth to a pompous oration whose contents were 'prolix, thin, and promiscuous'. Apparently, before leaving Poland, the city council of Danzig had urged him to take a strong line, and he used their advice as a pretext for exceeding his terms of reference. When the Queen realized what had happened, she turned on him with all the force of her famous temperament. As an English witness observed, 'lion-like rising, she daunted the malapert orator . . . with the tartness of her princely checks':

Expectavi legationem. In vero querelam mihi adduxisti. Per litteras accepi te esse Legatum, inveni vero Heraldum. Nunquam in vita mea audivi talem Orationem. Miror sane, miror tantam et tam insolitam in publico audaciam. Neque possum credere, si Rex tuus adesset, quod ipse talia verba protulisset, sin vero tale aliquid tibi fortasse in mandatis commisit, quod quidem valde dubito, eo tribuendum est, quod cum Rex sit Iuvenis, et non tam iure sanguinis quam iure electionis ac noviter electus, non tam perfecte intelligat rationem tractandi istiusmodi negotia cum aliis Principibus, quam vel majores illius nobiscum observarunt, vel fortasse observarunt alii, qui Locum eius posthac tenebunt.

Quod ad te attinet tu mihi virderis libros multos perlegisse, libros tamen Principum ne attigisse, sed prorsus ignorare quid inter Reges conveniat. Nam quod Juris Naturae et Gentium tantopere mentionem facis, hoc scito esse Juris Naturae Gentiumque, ut cum bellum inter reges intercedit, liceat alteri alterius bellica subsida, undicunque allata, intercipere, et ne in damnum suum convertantur precavere . . .

Intera vero valeas, et quiescas.*

In the margin of the official copy of this outburst, an obviously feminine hand has added the words: 'O quam decepta fui' (Oh, how I was deceived!). Działyński's mission was an outright failure. But his troubles continued. On returning to Poland, he found Zygmunt III preparing to cross the Baltic to Sweden in a fleet of ships impressed from the English merchants of Elbing. He was all set to join the expedition, and, on coming aboard was greeted by a broadside salute.

---

* 'I expected an Embassy. But in fact you have levelled an accusation at me. From your credentials, I took you to be an ambassador. But in truth all I have found is a page-boy. Never in my life have I heard such an oration. I am exceedingly amazed and astonished at such great uncommon effrontery in public. Nor can I believe that your King, had he been present himself, would have spouted such words. If, however, he did commend something of the sort to you in his instructions, which I very much doubt, one can only attribute it to the fact that your King, as a young man and one newly chosen not by right of blood but only by right of election, does not properly understand the rules for negotiating such matters with other princes – rules which greater than he observe with us, and which others no doubt observe who hereafter will take his place. As for you, you seem to me to have perused a great many books irrelevant to the matter in hand and to be quite unaware of prevailing conventions between monarchs. For, although you repeatedly talk of the *ius naturale et gentium*, I know this much of the law of nature and of peoples that when war occurs between monarchs each side *is* entitled to intercept the war supplies of the other, wherever they come from, and to prevent them being used for hostile purposes . . . Meanwhile, I bid you be well, and be silent.'[10]

Unfortunately, 'the Gunner did it in such haste, as one of the peaces fyred two barrels of powder, and those blew upp those partes of the shippe where Dzialynskes plate and stuffe was, and scattred it in the sea . . .'. As George Carew, the English ‧ Ambassador, noted, Działyński 'remaineth still discontent with our nation'.[11]

Działyński's error was not repeated, but something of his native blandness characterized a number of other memorable Polish embassies of the period. No doubt his compatriots interpreted the grand style as a suitable reflection of their country's honour and integrity. All too often it was interpreted abroad as empty show, or mere oriental opulence. Certainly, it was not particularly effective. In 1633, when Jerzy Ossoliński entered Rome with an entourage of 300 gentlemen and a retinue of stunning sumptuosity, it is hard to see what good purpose the vast expense was intended to serve. Quite apart from Ossoliński's private and voluntary contribution, the Republic had been forced to borrow large sums from Jewish money-lenders in Lwów and to mortgage Crown estates in Lithuania in order to support the mission. Yet no known political advantage accrued. Ossoliński, who enjoyed the confidence of Władysław IV and rose to be Chancellor between 1643 and 1650, did not have general support within the Republic for his dream of an ultra-Catholic monarchy; and by parading his feathers and his princely title in Rome and in Regensburg, he did not improve his chances. Similar scenes were repeated in Paris in October 1645, when the Polish ambassadors, Krzysztof Opaliński, Palatine of Poznań, and Wacław Leszczyński, Bishop of Warmia, arrived with a splendid retinue to collect Marie-Louise Gonzaga before her marriage to Władysław IV.[12]

Vanity however, was not the dominant note. In the second half of the century, Polish diplomacy was beset by indecision and resignation. Possibly in reaction against former assertiveness, the Republic's diplomats now tended to the other extreme. Despite the background of military prowess, Sobieski's ambassadors became unnecessarily concessive. This is certainly true of two crucial missions, of Jan Gniński to the Porte in 1677, and of Krzystof Grzymułtowski to Moscow in 1686.

Gniński, Wojewoda of Chełmno, was a life-long committeeman. As a youth he had accompanied Opaliński to Paris. Thereafter, he served as envoy to practically every Sejm of the next three decades. He was repeatedly appointed as Marshal of the Sejm, Marshal of the Crown Tribunal, and as Parliamentary Commissioner. He signed the treaties of Oliwa and Andrusovo, and travelled as ambassador to almost every country of Northern Europe. He was loyal to his original French connections, and, from an early date, to the Sobieski camp. In 1677, he was chosen by the Sejm to seek a final peace with Turkey, after the five recent campaigns in Podolia for possession of Kamieniec Podolski. The mission was a costly failure. A large retinue of 450 men and 650 horses was essential to any entry to Istambul. But Gniński spent most of his eighteen months in Turkey idle, waiting for an audience with the Grand Vizier, Kara Mustafa, and eventually with the Sultan. He found that the Turks would not lower their demand for the cession of all Podolia and all the Ukraine. Except for confirmation of the truce of Żurawno of November 1676, he returned home at the end of 1678 virtually empty-handed. He had spent large sums redeeming prisoners of war, and pandering to the cupidity of the Grand Vizier. He had failed to press the Republic's interests or to stage any demonstration of serious purpose. But he was not held responsible, and in 1683 he was able to accompany Sobieski to Vienna, and, with his own regiment of hussars, to join in the charge which shattered the Turkish siege. To that extent, he had his revenge. He died in 1685.[13]

Grzymułtowski (1620—87), Wojewoda of Poznań, despite a different temperament, did not obtain a better result. He was related on the maternal side, and also by marriage, to the Leszczyński family, and educated in France by the Jesuits of Dôle. He was known as a zealot of noble privileges, and was no politic servant of royal authority. In 1657, he was created Senator for rallying the levée-en-masse of Wielkopolska after Opaliński's capitulation. Yet he was frequently involved in French and Prussian intrigues. In 1664—5, he refused to act against Lubomirski's Rebellion, and in 1670 was charged with treason by the Sejm for conducting a ciphered correspondence with Versailles. In 1676, he became marshal of the Queen's Household. In 1681 he was responsible for breaking

the Sejm against Sobieski's wishes, and he opposed the
Austrian alliance. His appointment in 1683–6 as Chief Commissioner to the peace negotiations with Moscow was occasioned no doubt by his reputation as a man above fear or
favour. Once in Moscow, however, his independence of mind
proved too much for his parliamentary colleagues. The Treaty
of 3 May 1686, which ceded Kiev and all the Republic's
Dnieper lands, was not acceptable in Warsaw. Grzymułtowski
was judged to have exceeded his instructions, and was
suspected of submitting to Muscovite bribes. His death in
May 1687 removed him from a serious predicament. It is difficult to say what truth lay in the allegations against him. But
the Sejm clearly had neglected Warszewicki's advice of
'cautos in Moscoviam'.[14]

*   *   *   *   *

Of all the many foreign diplomats who served in the Republic,
none was more extraordinary than Andreas Dudith, Bishop
of Pécs, (1533–89) sometimes and most inappropriately
referred to as the 'Hungarian Erasmus'. Born in Buda of an
Italian mother, he had numerous clerical relations, and was
educated at Breslau and in Italy. In Padua, where he was
outstanding among an outstanding generation of students, he
translated Dionysius of Halicarnassus. He attracted the attention of Cardinal Pole who took him on his mission to recover
England for Catholicism. His experiences in England, however,
and still more his contacts across the Channel with French
Protestants, drove him into a radical position on the religious
issues of the day. On return to Hungary in 1560, he occupied
the post of secretary to the Primate, and quickly climbed the
episcopal ladder as Bishop successively of Tina (Dalmatia), of
Csanad in the Banat, and of Pécs. In 1563 he was the star of
the Hungarian delegation to the third session of the Council
of Trent. His speeches on subjects such as the Trinity and on
the elevation of the Host, published in Venice in book form,
put him in the forefront of theological debate. His friendship
with prominent Cardinals like Hosius and Moroni, soon earned
him the rank of imperial councillor.

Dudith's arrival in Cracow in 1565 as imperial ambassador
was followed by a grand sensation. His task was to extricate

the Queen, Catherine of Austria, from the disgrace of her separation from Sigismund-August, and, failing a reconciliation, to arrange the succession in a way advantageous to the Habsburgs. The Jagiellonian dynasty was heirless; Arians and Calvinists were pontificating in the Sejm; and Union with predominantly Orthodox Lithuania was imminent. There was concern lest Poland should slip from the Catholic orbit altogether. Yet the King was intractable. His reply to Dudith's suggestion of renewing conjugal life with the Queen was 'Più tosto la morte'; and he was quite unwilling to override the elective principle by monarchist intrigue. At this point, in 1567, Dudith suddenly renounced his clerical vows, and married a girl, Regina Straszowna, whom he had wooed in the Queen's suite. It was notorious enough that the reverend ambassador of his Most Catholic and Imperial Majesty had habitually consorted with heretics and astronomers. But now as an apostate and a seducer, he was excommunicated from the Church, deprived of his benefices, and banished from the Empire. Yet he did not lose the Emperor's personal favour. Maximilian, who composed an *Excusatio* on Dudith's behalf, could not save him from the Vatican's wrath; but he did retain him as a confidential agent. Dudith was soon married for a second time, into the Protestant Zborowski family, and involved with them in the anti-Habsburg rebellion in Hungary. He stayed in Poland, received the *indygenat,* and set to work as the imperial party manager during the ensuing interregna. In 1574, it was Dudith who first learned of the death of Charles IX of France and whispered the news into Henry Valois's ear. It was Dudith who, following the Election of 1576, advised the Emperor to make war against the successful candidate, Stefan Bathory; and for his pains, was banished once again, this time by his fellow Hungarian and student companion. He died in Breslau in 1589, having written a treatise on comets. His son, Andrzej Dudycz, the love-child of his apostasy, died in Moscow in 1606 as chancellor of the first False Dmitry.[15]

Dudith's adventures in Poland were symptomatic of the Habsburgs' difficulties there over a much longer period. Despite many obvious advantages, the Habsburgs regularly failed to realize their considerable ambitions. As the leaders of the Catholic world, they were in full alignment on religious and ideological issues, especially when Polish Catholicism assumed an increasingly devout and political character in the course of the seventeenth century. As neighbours along a secure and undisputed frontier in Silesia and the Carpathians, they had no territorial anxieties. Facing the Turks in the east, and the Swedes and Prussians in the north and west, they shared a certain strategic interest with the Republic; and as chief stable for the supply of royal brides, they were constantly in close liaison with the Polish monarchy. Habsburg brides set up house in Poland on no less than nine occasions between 1548 and 1795, supplying wifely comforts to seven of the eleven kings of the Republic. Yet no Habsburg candidate ever contested a Polish election successfully. On only one occasion did Habsburg treaties succeed in raising Polish military support for the Empire. In this, as in so many ways, Sobieski's expedition to Vienna in 1683 was exceptional, and from the Polish point of view, prejudicial. It seems that the Habsburgs were too obviously associated with the Court and the high clergy to win the confidence of the electors in general, or to build up a broad-based party among the nobility.[16]

The Habsburgs' position in the Republic was bolstered by their Spanish relatives. The Spanish trade with Danzig was of the first importance, and a constant stream of ambassadors out of the Spanish Netherlands maintained close relations. In 1596, Don Francisco de Mendoza arrived in Warsaw to combat the Anglo-Dutch blockade of Spanish ships at Danzig. (He was the source of Działyński's counter-mission to London in the following year.) In 1633, the Baron d'Auchy made one of several attempts to draw the Republic into the Thirty Years War on the imperial side. In 1670, Spanish contacts briefly increased in response to Michał Korybut Wiśniowiecki's marriage to Eleonora of Austria, sister of the Queen of Spain; as it did eighty years later when Charles III of Spain was married to one of the daughters of Augustus III. In the 1760s, Charles III's ambassador, Don Pedro Pablo Abarca de Bolea, Count of Aranda, was the life and soul of a Varsovian generation which danced out in the Saxon Era in endless nights of opera, masquerade, and carnival.[17]

In contrast to the steady mediocrity of relations with the Habsburgs, Polish relations with France were wildly erratic. France had few direct military or territorial interests in Poland. But close connections at various times with Sweden, Brandenburg, and Turkey inevitably plunged her into the political combinations of Eastern Europe. Her sporadic triumphs in Poland were separated by long periods of disenchantment. In 1573, the success of Henry Valois at the first Election of the united Republic augured an era of Franco-Polish collaboration; but his flight in 1574, and his dethronement by the Sejm, proved such a disgrace that relations were completely severed for nearly thirty years. In the seventeenth century, French hopes sprang eternal that their Habsburg rivals could be finally outflanked by a combination of Sweden, the Republic, and Turkey. But there was always one piece out of place, and the French never progressed beyond the middle game. In 1648 and 1674, French Queens reversed the Habsburg tendencies of preceding reigns. In the case of Sobieski's Queen, Marysieńka, the connection proved negative when, in the cause of her son's succession, she showed increasing hostility to her French compatriots. Polish—Swedish rivalry proved the greatest stumbling block. In 1625—9, the mission to the Republic of M. de Charnacé, Richelieu's envoy, was ruined by Gustavus Adolfus's invasion of Polish Pomerania. In 1635, the Comte d'Avaux was entirely preoccupied with the Peace of Stumsdorf, just as twenty years later Antoine de Lumbres spent his energies regulating the effects of Charles X's invasion. In 1675, however, all looked set for a major breakthrough. Sobieski had weathered the first storm of the Turkish campaigns, and at Jaworów on 11 June signed a treaty with the French ambassador, the Marquis de Béthune, his own brother-in-law. But in 1683, De Vitry's exposure caused a total rupture, and Sobieski marched to the aid of Vienna. In the 1690s, the genial abbé, Melchior de Polignac, one of Sobieski's favourite house guests during his later years, did much to restore French fortunes. In the 1697 election, the French candidate, Conti, succeeded in being elected, only to find himself chased from the country by Russian and Saxon forces. In the eighteenth century, similar misfortunes were repeated in connection with Stanisław

Leszczyński. French gold was persuasive, and Leszczyński's supporters numerous; but they could not compete on an equal footing with Russian armies.[18]

In terms of concrete achievement, the embassy of Antoine de Lumbres, Seigneur d'Herbinghem, was one of the very few occasions when French influence might be said to have been really decisive. In July 1656 he had been instructed by Louis XIV to proceed from Königsberg to Warsaw, and to mediate between the Swedes and the Republic in the war which was ruining French designs in Northern Europe. At first, the Polish Senators were suspicious of a Frenchman coming from Prussia, and of his meeting with Queen Marie-Louise. His credentials were only accepted when he had signally refused to accompany Charles X on his occupation of the Polish capital. He was finally received by Jan Kazimierz in Danzig, but could not yet persuade him to submit to mediation. As the King explained, 'Ils ne doutaient point de la grandeur de la France, mais, comme elle était fort éloignée. . .'. After 1656, his chances improved in proportion to the Swedes' discomfiture. The remarkable military resurgence of the Republic, the Polish treaty with Denmark, and the unreliability of the Prussians, all combined to cool Swedish enthusiasm. In 1659, de Lumbres met with Eric Oxenstierna, in the presence of Colbert Jr., and a peace conference was agreed. On 4 January 1660, the delegates assembled at the Abbey of Oliwa in Pomerania, and began five months of nervous bargaining. The Poles resided in Danzig, six miles to the east, the Swedes at Sopot, three miles to the west; and de Lumbres scuttled between the two in the style of an erstwhile Henry Kissinger. At the very last moment on 30 April, when Jan Kazimierz shied away from the loss of his lawful claim to the Swedish throne and suddenly departed, de Lumbres had to ride after him at high speed, and haul him back for signature. At midnight on 2 May the great organ of the Abbey proclaimed the Peace, and Abbot Kęsowski intoned the *Te Deum*. After Oliwa, de Lumbres stayed on in Poland for five more years, scheming with the childless royal couple to arrange a French-sponsored succession. In July 1663 he signed with Jan Kazimierz the abortive, and in the eyes of the Republic, the unconstitutional project whereby the Duke d'Enghien, son of Condé, was to be raised to the throne. In 1665, embarrassed by the Lubomirski Rebellion and criticized in the Sejm, but laden with honours, he left for home and well-deserved retirement. Throughout the nine years of his mission, he had maintained a weekly correspondence with Louis XIV and de Lionne. His *'Relations'* are a model of punctilious observation and human insight.[19]

In a situation where Polish politics were dominated by Franco-Austrian rivalry, the Vatican represented one of the few authorities capable of holding the ring. Rightly or wrongly, the Republic was counted as one of the major gains of the Counter-Reformation, and at the end of the sixteenth century figured prominently in the Vatican's plans for consolidating its position in Eastern Europe. But in the course of the seventeenth century, local politics constantly impinged, and a long line of Papal Nuncios battled on against problems increasingly beyond their control. During the Wars of the 1650s, Monsignor Vedoni did much to inspire Polish resistance with Catholic fervour, and in 1657, the miraculous preservation of the monastery of Częstochowa from Swedish cannonballs under the patronage of its Black Madonna raised the Marian cult into a national religion. When Vedoni first intoned *'Regina Poloniae Ora Pro Nobis'* in the cathedral of Lwów, he was starting a Catholic tradition which still regards the 'Queen of Heaven' as 'Queen of Poland'. But in the 1660s, Monsignor Pignatelli, the future Innocent XII, watched helplessly as Lubomirski's Rebellion led to Civil War and then to the fragmentation of the Roman Party. Pignatelli's successor, Galeazzo Marescotti, arrived in Warsaw in mid-1668 at the time when Jan Kazimierz was sinking towards abdication. After his welcome by the Bishop of Kiev and his formal entry into the capital, he attended regular audiences with the King on Sunday afternoons. But he could do nothing to shake the King's determination to resign the burdens of office. During the ensuing election, in July 1669, he remained in Warsaw in defiance of the law, and canvassed the candidature of the Prince of Lorraine, the Emperor's choice. But on the day, at the Wola Field, he confined his address to the electors to remarks about the Republic's need for a God-fearing and Catholic King. Marescotti attended the ceremony of the *Pacta*

Conventa in the Cathedral of St. John, and travelled to Cracow for King Michał's Coronation in September. On 16 February 1670 at Częstochowa, he married the King to the Archduchess Eleonora of Austria. At which point he was promoted to the nunciatura in Madrid.

In Sobieski's early years, papal designs were complicated by the French connection, but in 1679–88, Monsignor Pallavicini succeeded for a time in overcoming past difficulties and in co-ordinating the Republic into the operations of the Holy League. At the election of 1697, papal plans misfired once again, and the Republic slipped for ever beyond the close orbit of the Catholic-Imperial Camp. In general, the expectations of the nuncios in Warsaw were high, their influence slight, and their task thankless.[20]

The limitations of diplomacy are underlined still more by the experiences of the Englishman Lawrence Hyde, who journeyed to Poland in 1676. In pursuit of the *rapproachement* with France, and of his plans to recover Prussia, Sobieski sought to exploit Louis XIV's recent patronage of Charles II and to deflect England from its traditional Protestant, Prussophile alignment. On 29 October 1675, he wrote to Charles II inviting him to act as godfather at his daughter's christening. Lawrence Hyde was chosen as ambassador and proxy for the King. As son of the late Earl of Clarendon, architect and historian of the Restoration, he was well suited to dabble in French-sponsored intrigues. He was just 35 years old, Member of Parliament for Oxford University, and Master of the Robes. He left Portsmouth on *The Tyger* on 11 July 1676, arriving at Danzig on 8 August. Having presented his credentials to the syndics of the city – 'Our trusty and well-beloved Lawrence Hide, Esqr, Our Master of Our Roabes, being to passe into Poland as our Amb^r, . . .' – and settling a dispute over the rights of inheritance of English and Scottish citizens resident in Danzig, he met up with the Marquis de Béthune, Ambassador of France. This latter, brother of Queen Marysieńka, was the prime mover of Hyde's mission. They decided to journey together in search of Sobieski who was campaigning against the Turks and Tartars in the far south-east. As Hyde reported to the Secretary of State, Sir Joseph Williamson, 'it is a pretty step'; and 'I have no minde to ramble up and down very much in Russia.' Moreover, the Tartars were raiding deep into central Poland, and to run the gauntlet, the two ambassadors had to travel under escort in very undiplomatic conditions: 'M. de Béthune and I came hither in one coach and lay together in one barne. I hope that you will not be apprehensive that I could lose any dignity . . . I am confident it will never be prejudiciall to the precedency of an English Ambassador.'[21] At Lwów, Hyde learned that Sobieski was under siege in his camp at Żurawno on the Dniester, and incommunicado. Motivated no doubt by the lateness of the season and his desire to see Sobieski after so much effort, he made a mistake which was literally fatal. He tried to mediate. He composed three letters, one to the King of Poland, one to the Turkish Commander, and one to the 'Prince of the Tartars':

Your Highness is not ignorant what a strict and antient friendship hath been between the Most Serene and Most August Ottoman Port and His Sacred Majesty the King of great Britaine, France and Ireland, my most gracious master; by whom being sent great Ambassador to the Most Serene King of Poland and Lithuania, where I understand there was a treaty of Peace begun . . . and thought it part of my care and duty . . . to prevent as much as in me lyes . . . the further effusion of blood, I judged it best to give your Highness notice of my arrivall here, and at the same time signify that if the intercession and mediation of the aforesaid Most Serene King of great Britaine, France and Ireland . . . may promote so becoming, so noble, so great an act of love and respect, I wil endeavour to my utmost that such a mediation be interposed by his sacred Royal Majesty. And for as much as by a singular good fortune I have upon my coming hither lighted upon the most mighty King of France and Navarre's . . . wee have both of us thought fit jointly to offer our endeavours and entreaties by the same messenger, a servant of the Most Serene King, my master . . . In the meanwhile, I hope your Highness wil take this in good part: in confidence whereof I wil commend myself to the favour of your Highness. Leopol, 15 Oct New Style 1676.[22]

The sorry end of the proposed mediation was related in his next report five days later:

I have occasion before my departure from hence to make you this sad relation of the trumpetter I had sent with the Letters to those Princes I mentioned in my last to you, who was mett ye very day he left this place, about 3 leagues offe, by 40 or 50 Tartars, and miserably cutt in pieces, he, his interpreter and his guide, and onely the guides boy who was also left for dead upon the place too gott away in the night and brought me the sad news, which hath infinitely afflicted me, as it ought to do, having all the reflections which were obvious having exposed a fellow servant and fellow subject to so untimely an end without more authority than I had for it . . . The man's name was Christmasse, a mightly honest fellow that went as willingly on this errand as he made the rest of the journey; I know he hath left a wife and children, which to me is another sensible addition of greife, for whom I take myself in conscience bound, to doe what God shall enable me, but in the meantime if you can prevaile with the D. of Monmouth . . . that . . . till my returne . . . pay may be continued, I hope it is not an unreasonable proposition . . .[23]

So much for the view that the truce of Żurawno between Poland and Turkey was arranged by the ambassadors of France and England. Shortly afterwards, Hyde toured the King's camp and battlefields, marvelling at the 'great wonders' which had preserved the Polish army against overwhelming odds. On Sunday 2 November, he was received by the royal couple at Żółkiew, the modest house near Lwów where Sobieski was born. He had nothing much to say, since the one remaining royal daughter had been christened long since. He made the usual English representations on behalf of the Protestant subjects of a Catholic monarch, and was pleased by Sobieski's promise to press the Tartar Khan for satisfaction about Christmas's murderers. On Sobieski's request, he penned a letter of introduction to the English ambassador at Constantinople for Gniński, who was preparing to leave for Istambul. Then he left. He travelled home via Cracow and Vienna, and was in time to attend the Congress of Nymuegen. His subsequent career as Earl of Rochester, and one of the mandarins of the High Tory Party, spanned four reigns. When he died in 1711, the Polish—Lithuanian Republic was already in dire trouble, Sobieski's glories had long since faded, and the idea that England might entertain a *rapproachement* in that direction was completely forgotten. England, in fact, was too distant from the Republic, both in terms of geography and of emotional commitment. Anglo-Polish diplomacy never rose above the level of sporadic courtesies.[24]

A later British ambassador, Sir Edward Finch, MP for Cambridge University, sent in 1725—6 to intervene on behalf of the Protestants of Thorn, met troubles of a different kind.

His presence in Warsaw was not very welcome, and he was aware that his contacts with the dissidents and with his Prussian colleague were viewed with great suspicion. Knowing furthermore that the interception of his correspondence could have fatal consequences for his protégés, he disguised the more delicate passages of his letters in code. On 21 August 1725 (Old Style), he told London how an agent of the city of Thorn had been threatened by one of the Polish Ministers:

. . . The same Minister added that he
167 416 339 790 997   488 884 & 25   652 289
232 439 548 955 612   17   1047, for if   548   569
23 562 195   351 241 & 548   807 294   870 172 32 18
184 52 724 59 should follow 548 704 985 814 548 219
After this compliment, Your Lordship may be sure
241 497 9   25   40   26 407 508   814 862
552   813 hearing that   548 865   911 98 997 488
295 699 782 323 724 and at the Prussian Minister's . . .
But I managed 54 707 138 7   330   118   195 &
782 179   419 8 349 488   8   488   844
I sent Your Lordship an abstract last Post, but
984 25 548   6   298   15   525   375 for fear they should
914 47 782 326 . . .[25]

As translated by the cipher clerk in London, the passage read as follows:

. . . The same minister added that he should be on his guard/and not tamper with the Protestant Ministers here./for if/they caught him at that/he and the present President of Thorn/should follow/the example of the last./After this compliment, Your Lordship may be sure/he has not been very fond of coming right now,/hearing that/they have a constant Guard at my door/and at the Prussian Minister's . . . But I managed/an interview between him and my secretary in a third place . . ./'I sent Your Lordship an abstract last Post, but/dared not send the piece itself/for fear they should/open my letter . . .'[26]

Even in Hyde's time, the only foreign powers which had permanent influence in the Republic were her immediate neighbours – Muscovy and Prussia. The rapid decline of Sweden and Austria, as well as that of the Republic, provided a happy hunting-ground for Muscovite and Prussian ambitions. The reluctance of diplomats to adjust to changed conditions could not alter the profound shift in the balance of power which was then taking place.

From the formal point of view, for example, the embassy in 1686 of Boris Petrovich Sheremetiev was undoubtedly a failure. He was sent to the Republic by Peter I to receive ratification of the 'eternal peace' recently agreed by Grzymułtowski in Moscow. Young and confident, aged 35, and destined to a brilliant career as manager of Peter's reforms, he arrived in Lwów surrounded by sixty boyars and a thousand-strong retinue. Yet the Poles refused to be impressed. Sheremetiev was politely, but pointedly snubbed. Although Sobieski had already ceded the Muscovite claim to the title of 'Tsar', at least in conversational exchanges, Sheremetiev was not permitted to dine at the King's table. It was a clear sign that Muscovy whatever her military prowess, was still not counted among the civilized nations. What was worse, the Sejm declined to ratify the Treaty. It was hard for the Poles to believe that the loss of the Dnieper lands was other than temporary or that the Muscovites' imperial pretensions were serious. From the Russian point of view, it looked very much like an act of bad faith – an early instance of the *folie de grandeur* which has entered so firmly into the Russian stereotype of the Polish character. In 1710, when the Grzymułtowski Treaty was finally ratified by the Sejm, the Russians had learned to obtain recognition of their demands not by polite request but by brutal commands.[27]

Prussian diplomacy experienced similar difficulties. When Jan von Hoverbeck first came to Warsaw in 1632, in the Prussian delegation to the enthronement of Władysław IV, he saw how their request to be presented to the Senate was refused on the grounds that they were envoys of a vassal. Yet when he died in Warsaw fifty years later, in 1682, not only was he ambassador of a sovereign state, he was one of the most influential men in Poland. This Flemish refugee, whose parents came to the Republic from the Spanish Netherlands for reasons of religion, served the Hohenzollerns for half a century, speaking Polish and establishing unrivalled connections in political circles. He survived numerous turns of fortune. In 1641, he assisted at the last Prussian investiture. In 1648 he placed the Grand Elector's vote in favour of Jan Kazimierz; in 1669, in favour of the Duke of Neuburg. In 1649, he was proxy to the Great-Elector's oath of allegiance to Jan Kazimierz, in 1670 to the act of homage for Bytau and Lauenberg. During the Swedish War, he opposed the Great-Elector's submission to Charles X, and was denounced in Berlin as a *polnischer Hund*. In 1657 he was instrumental in the Prussian reconciliation with the Republic in the Treaty of Wehlau. In 1660, his contribution to the Peace of Oliwa was honoured by the title of Baron of the Empire. He was not personally involved in the Kalkstein affair of 1670, although the task of repairing relations with Sobieski inevitably fell to him. During the same period, he fought to save Prussia from Polish reprisals, promising to cede Riga to the Republic in exchange for Polish neutrality. After Fehrbellin, the danger was much relieved. In 1681, Hoverbeck's brokerage in the marriage of Charlotte Radziwiłł and Ludwig von Hohenzollern — which was arranged in spite of the bride's betrothal to Jakub Sobieski, the King's son and heir — expressed the nonchalant attitude which the Prussians could now afford to take towards Polish sensitivities. Like Sheremetiev, Hoverbeck still occupied a modest position in the formal world of diplomacy and protocol. But in the real world of power and influence, the looming status of the Prussians could no longer be ignored. Hoverbeck's son, Johann Dietrich, Prussian resident in Warsaw from 1690 to 1697, may still have been objecting to the lowly place awarded to him in the processions of ambassadors. But by then, the Prussians were building a new state without regard to the Republic on whose distress their own fortunes were in part founded.[28]

The balance of power in Eastern Europe shifted unobtrusively but irrevocably in the last quarter of the seventeenth century. John Sobieski came to the throne in 1674 with every hope and intention of reversing the recent Prussian and Muscovite advances. The Treaty of Wehlau (1657), which released the Hohenzollerns from their Polish fealty, was seen as a concession of doubtful validity exacted under duress. The Truce of Andrusovo, which left Smolensk, Kiev, and the left-bank Ukraine in Muscovite hands, was supposedly a temporary measure. (See p. 425.) Such, indeed, was Sobieski's complacency on these two issues that he felt quite free to pursue his Turkish campaigns to the end. (See pp. 451—2.) In that era, the Ottomans posed a more direct and appreciable

threat than did Muscovy, just as the invincible Swedes seemed
infinitely more dangerous than the Prussians. Sobieski can
hardly be blamed for lacking prescience of the future. Even
so, as a direct result of Poland's preoccupations in the Danube
Basin, the Hohenzollerns were both given licence to consoli-
date their gains, and to steal a decisive march on their rivals.
By the time that Sobieski died, Frederick III was posed to
found a kingdom, and Peter III an empire. The idea that
Poland–Lithuania might somehow challenge these developments was already judged unrealistic. The Ottomans had been
humbled, and Sweden under Charles XII stood on the brink
of disaster. The way lay open for the full emergence of the
two powers, Prussia and Russia, whose growth and competition were to dominate Eastern Europe for the next 250 years.
The Republic's place in the international order slipped away
almost by default.

In the eighteenth century, the international standing of the
Polish–Lithuanian Republic slumped alarmingly. In the wars
of the Holy League (1683–99), John Sobieski had played a
prominent if not a decisive role. But the price was high. To
fight the war, the Republic had to turn its back on the French
connection, to resign its plans for recovering Prussia, and to
abandon the Ukraine to Muscovy. In 1686, the 'Grzymułtowski
Peace' confirmed Moscow's possession of Kiev, the left-bank
Dnieper lands, Czernihów, Sieviersk, Smolensk, and Krasny
Gorodok, providing the new territorial base which transformed
old Muscovy into Peter I's new Russia. Sobieski's campaigns
specially benefited the three neighbouring powers which
eighty years later were destined to partition the Republic
between them. In 1697, Sobieski's successor, Augustus II of
Saxony (1697–1733), was elected by Russian connivance in
a disputed election which divided the country into rival
camps for the rest of his long reign, paralysing any resistance
which might have been offered to the depredations of foreign
armies during the Great Northern War. After Poltava in 1709,
when Russian supremacy was assured, the Russians in particular were able to behave with impunity, terrorizing the
constitutional institutions of the Republic, and encouraging
the disruptive elements. As the French consul in Danzig
observed in 1717, 'the Muscovites claim to be in command

wherever they happen to be, pretending that everything they find belongs to them, and that they can behave as they like.'[29] In the succeeding reign of Augustus III (1733–63), almost as protracted as his father's, the slough of Polish despond deepened. Wars, depredations, magnatial factions, a rival election, a Pretender, the collapse of the central legislation and treasury – all combined to obstruct reform.

Under such conditions, the Polish diplomatic service inevitably declined. Augustus II, as King of Poland, sent only 38 missions abroad in 36 years. Under Augustus III, only one of thirteen missions was directed to the West. The King entrusted foreign affairs increasingly to his Saxon ministers, ignoring the dwindling protests of the Republic's officers. Foreign ambassadors resided in Dresden, visiting Warsaw ever less frequently. The only diplomatic activity which enjoyed any sense of continuity was that of the Hetmans, who during the Great Northern War had often been left to their own devices and who kept control thereafter of relations with the Turks and Tartars. In the absence of central policy, each interest within the country developed its own diplomacy. The Protestant churches, for example, had their own contacts with the Protestant powers. The Jews of the Republic sent their own representatives abroad. Above all, the great magnates established private policies. In 1758, when Stanisław-August Poniatowski reported in St. Petersburg as Ambassador of Poland–Lithuania, it was no secret that he was appointed to pursue the designs of his Czartoryski relations in conjunction with their Russian patrons. By the time Augustus III died in 1763, there was little scope left for foreign intrigues. The pantomimes of previous elections were not repeated. The French ambassador, the Marquis de Paulmy, embarrassed by disasters during the Seven Years War, could not emulate the Marquis de Monti who in pursuit of 'le secret du Roi' had turned the electoral contest of 1733 into an auction.[30] In 1764, Russian bayonets lined the electoral field; the opposition candidates withdrew; and all unseemly disturbances were avoided.

Stanisław-August had returned to Poland from his Russian embassy as the Empress's, king-designate. His subsequent reign (1764–95) witnessed a long, but in the end, vain struggle to escape from Russian tutelage. In 1766, the Sejm approved a budget for diplomatic expenses, which in 1768 rose to a grant of 1 million zł. Polish ambassadors reappeared in the capitals of Europe. During the wars of the Confederation of Bar, they sought assistance for both sides in the conflict. In London, Tadeusz Burzyński, Marshal of the Lithuanian Tribunal, acting on behalf of the King, tried to persuade the British Government to mediate. In Paris, Michał Wielhorski courted French support for the Confederates, establishing contacts in French intellectual circles with figures like Mably and Rousseau, who were to furnish the main flow of information and opinion about Poland during the Enlightenment. In effect, divided counsels obstructed any concerted resistance to Russian intervention or to the First Partition of 1772. In 1775, however, the germ of a Foreign Ministry was planted as the 'Departament Interesów Cudzoziemskich' (Department of Foreign Affairs), attached to the Permanent Council. Like all institutions created during this period, it had to contend with the taint of Russian ingerence, but it represented a definite step in the direction of an independent stance in foreign affairs. In 1789, after the death of Frederick the Great, it achieved the alliance with Prussia, which, complementing the internal constitutional reforms of 3 May 1791, was intended to act as an instrument of liberation. In the event, the Prussians' loyalty to this alliance proved weaker than their fear of Russian retribution. In 1793 and in 1795, the Second and Third Partitions proceeded without significant diplomatic opposition.

Throughout the century, in fact, Russian ambassadors in Warsaw made no secret of their view that diplomacy was an adjunct to force. Almost invariably, they kept a Russian army in the Republic, at the Republic's expense, and regularly used it to suppress opposition. As Prince Gregory Dolgoruky, Peter I's long-term resident in Warsaw, told the Lithuanian Hetman who had protested at the abduction of Polish citizens, 'If my sovereign orders me to abduct you, I shall do *that* too.' Prince Repnin, Catherine's first ambassador in 1763–9, behaved with similar licence. Demanding to reside in a palace protected by a regiment of the guard — whilst his opposite number in St. Petersburg received expenses for one room — he dictated the politics of the decade with cynical brutality. His deportation of the Bishop of Cracow, together with other offending dignitaries, was but the most celebrated of numerous arbitrary acts.[31] Baron Staekelburg, who ruled in Warsaw from 1773—90, was only marginally more sympathetic, having succeeded his one colleague, Gaspar de Saldern, who had dared to criticize the Empress's policy. On receiving Saldern's demand for recall in protest against the First Partition, Catherine remarked that he had 'gone mad'. In January 1794, Baron Sievers, who had the difficult task of controlling Warsaw after the War of the Second Partition, was brusquely dismissed for permitting Polish officers to wear their decorations in public. Incidents such as these, notable for their pettiness and violence, crowd the annals of Russian conduct in the Republic throughout the century, amply supporting the view that the conditions on which Russia intended to tolerate the Republic's independence were a charade from the start.

Over the two centuries of the Republic's existence, the passive character of its foreign policy had become increasingly evident. Unlike its neighbours, it made no territorial aspirations, served no dynasty, and professed no religious or political ideology. Whilst Russia ruthlessly pursued the 'gathering of the lands'; whilst Prussia toiled for the greater glory of the Hohenzollerns, or Austria shouldered the burdens of Christendom, the Republic boasted nothing beyond the welfare of its citizens. In the world of militant and militarist modern states, it was an anachronism. The Republic happened to be formed in 1569 with a vast territory which already exceeded its needs and with a defensive constitution designed to preserve the existing order. No Polish king could hope to entertain foreign ambitions, but 100,000 noblemen would ask the reason why. Thus, self-preservation was the main consideration from the start. At the end of the eighteenth century, even this had become something of a forlorn hope.

* * * * *

The 'Serene Republic' of Poland—Lithuania was finally extinguished in 1795 within a couple of years of the extinction by Napoleon of its Venetian namesake. What is more, since

Poland and Venice also held other things in common, including the tradition of democratic government and the fear of modern militarist empires, it is fitting that an obituary written for the one, should be read in memory of the other:

> And what if she had seen those glories fade,
>   Those titles vanish, and that strength decay:
> Yet shall some tribute of regret be paid
>   When her long life hath reached its final day.
> Men are we, and must grieve when even the shade
>   Of that which once was great is pass'd away.[32]

CHAPTER TWELVE

VALOIS:

The French Experiment (1572-1575)

Seven weeks after the death of Sigismund-August, there occurred in France one of the most sanguinary outrages of the sixteenth century. On 24 August 1572, the Eve of St. Bartholomew, twenty thousand Huguenots were slaughtered in cold blood by their Catholic royalist enemies. At the time, the two events in Poland and in France had no apparent connection. Yet within a year, one of the perpetrators of the massacre was elected to the Polish throne in succession to the last of the Jagiellons. Henry de Valois, Duke of Anjou, the third son of Henri II and Catherine de Médici, brother and heir of Charles IX, one time brother-in-law to Mary, Queen of Scots, Lieutenant-General of France, was just twenty-two years old.[1]

Henry left France for Poland on 3 December 1573. Accompanied by 1,200 gentlemen, he crossed the frontier of the Empire from Metz, and proceeded through Saarburg, Mainz, and Frankfurt-am-Main. He spent Christmas at the Abbey of Fulda, and the New Year at Torgau in Saxony. He crossed the Oder at Frankfurt on 17 January, and the Polish frontier at Międzyrzecz (Medzeritz) near Poznań ten days later. On the long wintry stages of his journey, he was entertained by the verses of the court poet, Philippe Desportes, and by readings from Aristotle's *Politics* recited by his secretary, Guy du Faur de Pibrac. He stood before the gates of Cracow on 18 February 1574, after three-and-a-half months on the road.

In Paris, Henry's departure was the cause of considerable rejoicing. The Huguenots were no doubt relieved to see the back of the victor of Jarnac. The royalists and Catholics were pleased to see their influence extending to distant parts. On 13 September 1573, the eleven ambassadors of the Polish–Lithuanian Republic, headed by Adam Konarski, Bishop of Kujawy, had been received in the Palais de Justice by the King and Queen, in the presence of Catherine de Médici and the royal pair of Navarre. The Electoral Decree, signed by one hundred and seven senators and hung with one hundred and twenty-one seals, was read aloud, and laid on the altar of the Sainte-Chapelle, as Henry solemnly undertook to preserve the constitution of the Republic. The guests were banqueted at the Louvre. Henry's personal triumph was shared by the whole of France. It seemed that the national enemy, the House of Habsburg, had at last been outflanked. France, in conjunction with Poland, could straddle the Empire's ambitions. As Charles IX said to his brother before he left, 'Nous tenons les deux bouts de la courroie.' (We now hold both ends of the bridle.)

In Cracow, Henry's arrival was awaited with impatience and high expectations. In the eighteen months of the interregnum much had been achieved. Under the guidance of Jan Zamoyski, the convocational Sejm had successfully concluded the constitutional debate which had dragged on ever since the Union of Lublin was signed. The details of electoral procedure and of the *Pacta Conventa* had been agreed without demur. On 28 January 1573, in the Confederation of Warsaw, the entire Sejm had resolved to maintain freedom of conscience and religious toleration as a cardinal principle of public life. The election itself had passed off in May with exemplary speed and harmony. Held for the first time at the Wola Field near Warsaw with the active participation of 40,000 noble electors, it caused no major disturbance. The eloquent promises of the French ambassador, Jean de Monluc, Bishop of Valence, gave the Valois an early lead from the start. The supporters of the rival candidates − of Archduke Ernest of Austria and John III, Vasa King of Sweden − were persuaded to relent. As a sign of reconciliation, Henry Valois was proclaimed King on 12 May 1573 by the leading opponent of his candidature, the Protestant Marshal of the Crown and Palatine of Cracow, Jan Firlej.

Yet the air of harmony was deceptive. Trouble began at the Coronation on 21 February. The king had already taken communion and sworn the oath, when Firlej advanced to the altar with his hat firmly on his head. He was not content with the traditional wording of the oath and insisted that Henry swear specifically to the terms of the Confederation of Warsaw.

He said, *'Jurabis aut non regnabis'* (You shall swear or you shall not reign). He was not going to leave room for a Polish St. Bartelémy. Henry replied cautiously, *'Conservare curabo'* (I shall take care to uphold it). The Bishop of Kujawy exclaimed *'Salvis iuribus nostris'* (Our laws are saved); and Henry rejoined, *'Salvis iuribus vestris'* (Your laws are saved). It was a tense moment.

Two days later, murder was committed. The Zborowski clan were among the foremost supporters of the French party. Of the five brothers, Andrzej, and Jan, Castellan of Gniezno, were Catholics; Piotr, Krzysztof, and Samuel were Calvinists. Between them, they carried great weight. They were flushed with success and not to be crossed. At the tourney held in honour of Henry's coronation, the youngest brother, Samuel Zborowski had ridden into the arena and thrown down a gauntlet which no one of substance accepted. Challenged by a common soldier in the service of the Tęczyński family, he took it as a mortal insult and raised an affray. In front of the Castle Gate at Wawel, and in full view of the King, he tried to assault Tęczyński in person, and struck with his mace at a courtier who had tried to keep them apart. The man, Wapowski, died. The penalty for murder committed during a session of the Sejm was death. Wapowski's widow brought the corpse and laid it out beneath the King's window. Her relations were baying for revenge. The Zborowskis were pleading for lenience. Henry resolved on compromise. His first judgement in Polish justice condemned Samuel Zborowski to perpetual banishment. It displeased everyone. It was too harsh for the Zborowskis, and too indulgent for the nobility as a whole. It started a series of feuds and vendettas which persisted for a generation.

The Sejm could not be ruled. At their first meeting with the monarch, the senators had presented him with rich gifts of camels and Tartar slaves. But before long, they were quarrelling. At one of their sessions, a participant shouted to the Primate above the hubbub that the 'house was on fire'. Having gained the desired effect, he then explained that he was referring not to the senatorial chamber but to the entire Republic 'which has been too long without a king and without law'. Henry threatened to go on hunger strike unless agreement was reached. The opposition were still pressing for more explicit guarantees of the Confederation of Warsaw.

Foreign policy offered no easy success. The French had been hoping to mount a grand anti-Habsburg coalition, of which the Poles and the Turks would form the eastern pillars. Before leaving France, Henry had attended the conference at Bramont in Lorraine where proposals to this end were seriously discussed. In effect, the incessant embroilments of the Republic on its eastern borders, with the Muscovites in Livonia, with the Tartars, and at that juncture with the Turks over the disputed suzerainty of Moldavia, made any early co-ordination impossible.

There was also the problem of Anna Jagiellonka. Among the many promises made in Paris, or at the Election, there was an undertaking that Henry would marry the late king's sister, the last of the Jagiellons. At their first personal encounter, on the day of his entry into Cracow, Henry had behaved graciously. The middle-aged spinster dressed in plain grey twill missed a heartbeat at the prospect of a lusty French husband, twenty-six years her junior. She set her ladies to embroidering the fleur-de-lys on all her dresses. In reality, Henry had no honourable intentions. With no serious hope of procreation, the marriage was entirely unsuitable for the Valois heir; and Henry's passionate thoughts flew elsewhere.

Henry's anxiety increased on many scores. According to Zamoyski, he was disappointed by the poverty of the Polish countryside: by the wooden houses and grey fields which looked their worst in the damp spring. He disliked the Italian furnishings of the Royal Castle, and ordered a complete refit. He was bored by the constant debates in Polish and Latin which he could not follow, and was affronted by the argumentative demeanour of the senators and envoys. He was offended by the extravagant drinking habits of the Polish court, and, if Desportes is to be believed, depressed by his enforced separation from the beautiful Marie de Clèves:

> De pleurs en pleurs, de complaints en complaints,
> je passe, helas, mes languissantes nuits
> Sans m'alleger d'un seul de ces ennuis
> Dont loing de vous ma vie est si contrainte.
> Belle princesse, ardeur de mon courage,

Mon cher desir, ma peine et mon tourment
Que mon destin, las! trop soudainement
Par votre absence a change de visage . . .*

He took to taking pills and potions, to diplomatic absences
from court, and to long week-ends at the royal hunting-lodge
at Niepołomice. Above all, he was worried by the alarming
news of his brother's illness.

In all the negotiations surrounding Henry's Election, the
possibility of him succeeding to the throne of France had not
been seriously considered. At the time, his brother, Charles
IX, was only twenty-four years of age, a man of great physical
energy, and a young husband with every prospect of fathering
a son and heir. Yet within a month of Henry's coronation in
Poland, it was known that Charles was gravely ill. At the end
of March, two prominent figures from the French retinue in
Cracow, the Marshal de Retz and the Duke of Nevers, left for
home on different pretexts. Cheverny, the head of the
Catholic faction in Paris, wrote to say that in the event of
Charles's death it was Henry's duty to ride post-haste for
France, to secure the Catholic succession, and to forestall the
partisans of his reformist younger brother, François d'Alençon.

Charles IX died on 30 May 1574. The news reached his
successor in Wawel Castle at 11 a.m. exactly two weeks later,
from the lips of the Imperial ambassador. It was confirmed at
midday by a messenger from Catherine de Médici. To all outward appearances, Henry was undecided what steps to take.
On 15 June he met the Senate, and asked their advice in a
long Latin address. He dispatched letters of regency to his
mother in Paris. On the 18th, he joked and danced with his
Polish lords. Declining an invitation to call on the Jagiellonka,
he retired early to bed. It was not unusual. There was a guard
on the door of his suite. Tęczyński was at hand, on behalf of
the Senate, to watch developments. Yet unbeknown to all
but a handful of French advisers, the King was preparing to
depart. Fearing no doubt that an open departure might invite

* With tears upon tears, and lament upon lament,/I spend, alas, my nights of
  yearning/With no relief in any way from the troubles/Which, far from you,
  crowd my life./Oh fair princess, the inspiration of my valour,/My dear desire,
  my sorrow, my torment!/How suddenly, alas, through your absence/My fate
  has changed its countenance![2]

delays, either from the Poles or from the Imperial authorities across whose territory he had to pass, he was preparing to escape in secret.

It was Saturday night. Wawel Castle was locked and bolted. The King changed into some nondescript riding clothes, and crept from his room through a backstairs entrance concealed by a tapestry on the rear wall. Two pages, standing to attention beside the screens of his bed, were unaware that he had gone. An accomplice obtained the keys of the gate on the pretext of a gallant escapade, and passed off his muffled companion as a 'Capitain Lamotte'. They walked out through the Jewish Quarter of Kazimierz, and across the Vistula bridge to an abandoned chapel where horses were waiting. By dawn, they had covered the twenty miles to Zator, and were riding hard for the frontier.

But they knew they were followed. On leaving Wawel, 'Capitain Lamotte' had been unlucky enough to pass the castle chef who was returning from the town. Nothing was said, but suspicions were aroused. Tęczyński was alerted. After much shouting and confusion the King's suite was searched, and his absence discovered. When Tęczyński set off in pursuit, with 200 horsemen and a troop of Tartar archers, he was three hours behind. Yet he was crossing his own estates and was gaining with every stride. Taking the shorter, more northerly road through Liszki and Babice, he reached Oświęcim (Auschwitz) in time to alert the Starosta. By this time, the King was in full view, galloping across the meadows of the frontier bridge at Harmeze. As he crossed the old dilapidated bridge, his last glimpse of his Polish kingdom was of the loyal Starosta of Oświęcim, manfully swimming towards him in the middle of the Vistula and shouting at the top of his voice: '*Serenissima Maiestas, cur fugis?*' (Serene Majesty, why do you flee?).

Henry de Valois left Poland for France on 19 June, after a reign of 118 days. He clearly intended to retain both his thrones. At the town of Pszczyna (Pless), where· he was caught and surrounded by his pursuers, he assured Tęczyński of his good intentions: 'Comte, mon ami, en prenant ce que Dieu me donne par succession je ne quitte pas ce qu'il m'a acquis par élection. Quand j'aurai fait ce que j'espère, je vous reverrai, car, Dieu Merci, j'ai les épaules assez fortes pour soutenir l'une et l'autre couronne.' In effect, it was the parting of the ways. Tęczyński returned to Cracow. Henry pressed on in to Moravia. On that first day, he rode 72 miles without rest. But that was the end of his haste. In Vienna, he tarried three days with the Emperor, Maximilian II. In Venice, he stayed on to have his portrait painted by Tintoretto, and to be treated to a display at the Arsenal where a galley was launched in his honour in the morning, and fully fitted out by sunset. He visited the d'Este Duke in Ferrara, the saintly Carlo Borromeo, Cardinal Archbishop of Milan, and his aunt, Margaret of Savoy in Turin. He did not cross Mont Cenis in a glass-covered litter till the end of August. He met his mother at Bourgoin near Lyon on 5 September. It was on this return journey that Desportes was to compose the bitter lines which so exactly express the Frenchmen's disillusionment with the entire venture:

> Adieux Pologne, adieux plaines desertes,
> Toujours de neige et de glaces couvertes . . .
> Barbare peuple, arrogant et volage,
> Vanteur, causeur, n'ayant rien que language,
> Qui jour et nuict dans un poisle enfermé
> Pour tout plaisir se joue avec un verre,
> Ronfle a la table et s'endort sur la terre,
> Puis comme un Mars veut estre renommé.
> Ce ne sont pas vos grand lances creusées,
> Vos peaux de loups, vos armes deguisées
> Ou maint plumage et maint aile s'estend,
> Vos bras charnus, ny vos traints redoubtables,
> Lourds Polonais, qui vous font indomptagles:
> La pauvreté seulement vous défend . . .*

From start to finish, the French experiment in Poland had lasted less than two years.

* Farewell Poland! Farewell deserted plains/Eternally covered with snow and ice . . ./Oh Savage people, arrogant and thieving,/Boastful, verbose, and full of words,/Who, wrapped night and day in shaggy furs, takes its only pleasure by playing with a wineglass./By snoring at table and falling to sleep on the floor/And who then, like Mars, wishes to be famous./It is not your great, grooved lances,/Your wolf's clothing, your misleading coats-of-arms/Spread all over with wings and feathers,/Your muscular limbs, nor your redoubtable deeds, Dull-witted Poles, that have saved you from defeat:/Your miserable condition alone protects you . . .[3]

In retrospect, it is easy to identify the flaws which rendered the Valois candidacy unworkable. It is hard to see how the untried, republican constitution of Poland–Lithuania could ever have been smoothly operated by a youthful prince whose meagre experience was confined to an absolutist court and to sectarian warfare. It is difficult to believe that the infinitely devious Catherine de Médici could really have expected her son to graft French interests and designs onto a distant, proud, and quarrelsome country. Yet both sides had wished fervently for a mutually advantageous arrangement. Wishful thinking and fair words won the day, and paved the way to rapid disillusionment. It must be remembered, however, that the negotiations of 1573 had been undertaken with a view to a reign of forty or fifty years, and with the aim of founding a new branch of the Valois dynasty. The premature death of Charles IX − the blow which brought the experiment to a sudden end − was foreseen by no one.

Henry never relinquished his claim to the Polish throne. He kept the Polish title in his royal style till the end of his life. But he never tried to renew the Polish alliance, and never returned to Poland. Nor did he bring much profit to France. The religious wars continued amidst mounting blood and intrigue. Surrounded by his *mignons,* his 'pretty young men', Henry earned from the common people the epithet of the 'New Herod', and from his mother 'le Roi de Rien' (The King of Nothing). Having murdered his main Catholic rivals, Duke Henry and Cardinal Henry de Guise, he was himself knifed to death at St. Cloud on the 2 August 1589 by the stiletto of a Dominican monk, Jacques Clément. By that time, Poland–Lithuania had already completed one of the most brilliant decades of its history, and was again wrestling with the effects of a royal election no less unfortunate than that of 1573.

CHAPTER THIRTEEN
BATHORY:
The Transylvanian Victor (1576-1586)

If in the case of Henry de Valois, a catastrophic reign was preceded by a model election, the elevation of Poland's most successful king was preceded by an interregnum of indescribable chaos.

The confusion caused by Henry's flight provided ideal conditions for political adventures both internal and international. It lasted for nearly two years. At first, the headless Republic could make no decision about its absent monarch. At a meeting of the Sejm held in August 1574, Henry was given nine months' grace in which to return. At the end of this period, in May 1575, in a huge wooden rotunda on the banks of Vistula at Stęczyc, the throne was formally declared forfeit by the assembled nobility. On both occasions, a serious rift appeared between the Senators and the noble envoys. At Stęczyc, the Lithuanians, fully prepared in chain-mail, disputed the legality of the proceedings, whilst the royal artillery fixed its sights on a private army drawn up by Adalbert Łaski, Patatine of Sieradź. Meanwhile, candidates had been offering themselves for the throne whether it was officially vacant or not. The electoral Sejm, which finally met at Warsaw in November 1575, resembled a battleground. There were more Cossacks than voters, and every voter carried an arquebus, mace, or lance. There were at least half a dozen serious candidates and twice as many sponsors prepared to spend words and ducats. There was Alfonso II d'Este, Duke of Ferrara, sponsored in spite of himself by no less than Dr Solomon Askenazi, a Jewish physician from Constantinople.[1] He was announced by the poet Guarini, who described his master's 'incredible love for the Polish Nation'. There was Ivan the Terrible, whose troops happened to be ravaging the eastern provinces at the time. At the previous election, he had suggested that he would willingly rule over Lithuania, and Poland as well if so invited, and would multiply their

liberties, but that he would like Livonia and the Ukraine to
be given to Moscow. 'It is good to enlarge one's state,' he said,
'not to diminish it'. Then there was the Archduke Ernest
again, and John of Sweden, and another Habsburg, the Archduke Ferdinand. Finally, there was Stefan Bathory, the
Prince of Transylvania. After extraordinary contortions, in
which the Nuncio offered to give Ivan the title of 'Emperor
of Constantinople' if he withdrew in favour of Ernest, whilst
the dotty old Primate, Jakub Uchański, proposed that Ivan,
John Vasa, and the Emperor should rule simultaneously, a clear
contest emerged between the Habsburgs and the Transylvanian.

Unlike most of the other competitors, Stefan Bathory was
admirably qualified for the task.[2] He had not sought election
for himself, but had been approached by a constellation of
interests who were determined to exclude the Habsburgs. At
the electoral Sejm, his ambassador, Bishop George Blandrata,
had confined himself to a promise of personal rule, and
assurances for 'the defence of Christendom'. Bathory at 42
was a hardened campaigner. Born at Somlyó, the youngest
son of the Palatine of Transylvania, a partisan of Szapolyai,
he had received an impressive education. He had toured
Western Europe, studied in Padua, and served at the imperial
court in Vienna. For fifteen years he had fought as commanding general in the long struggle of his native province for
independence. In 1562 he had been wounded at the siege of
Hadad, and for three years from 1565 to 1567, had been held
prisoner in Prague. In 1571, following the Treaty of Speier
with Austria, he had been elected Prince of Transylvania. He
was a fervent Catholic, who had made his career in resistance
to the Most Catholic Emperor. He ruled over a state where all
four religions enjoyed autonomy. He was familiar both with
forceful action and with government by consent.*

Bathory's further progress in Poland was taken in hand by
Zamoyski, who, in conjunction with former supporters of the
Valois like Tęczyński and with the Arian, Michał Sienicki, the

---

* The Transylvanian syndrome, usually associated with the earlier Count
  Dracula, also emerged in Stefan Bathory's niece, Elizabeth of Nàdasdy, who in
  1610 was found to have murdered 650 young girls in order to bathe in their
  warm blood and thereby restore her youth. See S. Baring-Gould, *Book of
  Werewolves*, London 1865.

tribune of the lesser szlachta, had decided to force the pace. The condition of the Republic was critical. The electoral Sejm was dallying to the accompaniment of internal strife and external attack. Danzig was in revolt. The Muscovites were in Livonia. The Tartars launched the biggest raid in Polish history. In the autumn of 1575, the Khan of the Crimea, Davlet Girej, led a horde of 100,000 men into Ruthenia. When they returned, their numbers had been doubled by droves of captives. Some 35,340 noblemen alone were carried off into slavery. It was no time for legalities. Although the Primate had unilaterally declared the Emperor Ferdinand II to have been elected, a group of noblemen assembled in the Old Town Square of Warsaw on 14 December resolved to offer the crown to Bathory. Their condition was that he should take Anna Jagiellonka to wife. Bathory did not delay. He would wear the Polish diadem, he said, 'if only for three days'. He was helped by the Ottoman Sultan who ordered his army to march against the Empire as a means of frustrating the Habsburg candidacy. He hastened over the Carpathians, and entered Cracow on 23 March 1576, the very day on which the Emperor was finally undertaking to do the same. He rode a Turkish charger, and wore a heron plume in his tall fur *kolpak*. He was attended by 500 Transylvanian knights, with leopard skins slung over their golden breast-plates, and by 1,000 veteran *hejduks*. He was welcomed by 8,000 Polish noblemen drawn up by Tęczyński. On 1 May, he married the Jagiellonka, and, contrary to all the rules, was anointed king by Bishop Karnkowski. At that, all resistance ceased. Zamoyski was rewarded with the seal of the Vice-Chancellor of the Crown, and a famous partnership began. The Republic was to be swept clean by a new broom of decisiveness, energy, and high ambition.

Bathory's personality was dutifully described by Reinhold Heidenstein (1556–1620), a German from the Rhineland who worked in the royal chancery and was able to observe the King from close quarters. Heidenstein's writings, *Rerum polonicarum libri duodecim* and *De bello moscovico* (On the Muscovite War, 1584), form a prime source for the politics and wars of the reign. He was an unashamed admirer:

Nature endowed King Stefan with the best attributes of body and mind. One might say that she sought to create in him a model of rare perfection. In his bearing, in his face and in his speech, he was the incarnation of majesty. At the same time he was possessed of a strange sensitivity and simplicity, together with great humanity. Notwithstanding the regal dignity and high seriousness which he affected toward everyone, he would enter into spirited discussions even on matters of the greatest confidence, and repeatedly enjoined the reticent members of his entourage to speak their mind more openly. It is impossible to say whether people loved him more than they feared him. He was a Catholic of the most devout kind. In his testament, addressed to his son-in-law, Prince Sigismund of Transylvania, he instructed him in burning words to protect the Catholic religion and the Jesuit College which he had founded in order to convert the Arians. Yet he maintained that all sectarians should be tolerated, and should be left to God and to Time rather than to persecution. His knowledge was enormous. It derived partly from his familiarity with the practical affairs of the Hungarians, Turks, Germans, and Italians, but above all from his reading of History. His favourite author was Caesar, whom he read and re-read constantly. He was extremely eloquent, conversing customarily in Latin with everyone. His every word was so weighed that often he would assume an oracular quality. When he knew that the right was on his side, he would refuse absolutely to compromise. As a lover of the truth, he never avoided it on his own behalf, and easily recognized it in others. In many people's eyes, he was unduly given to anger and to cruelty . . . but I can confirm that there was no person who forgave and forgot more readily. Apart from that, he had a long memory for services which had benefited him. On several occasions, men who had long forgotten that they had ever rendered a service and who expected no reward, were overwhelmed with largess. On the whole, when it came to increasing the estates of his mighty subjects, he was thought to be excessively thrifty. And thrifty he was, though when necessary he knew well enough how to be both generous and magnanimous . . .

At the Sejm of Thorn in 1576, when some of the members kept pestering him to explain his intentions . . . he flew into a rage . . . 'I was not born in a pig-sty', he said. 'I was born a free man . . . I love my freedom, and intend to guard it. By God's will, it was you who elected me King. It was at your request that I came here. It was you who placed the crown on my brow. So I am your King. But I will not be a fashioned or a painted one (*non fictus neque pictus*). I wish to rule, and will not let anyone pick my nose. It is agreed that you be guardians of your own freedom. But I will not allow you to act like schoolmasters over me and my senators. Watch for your freedom, but lay off any pranks.[3]

Danzig was the first to be disciplined. Having defied the recommendations of the Commission of 1570 which had regulated relations between the Republic and its chief city, it had thrown its weight behind the Habsburg candidate. In September 1576, it was placed under ban by Bathory, who announced a commercial blockade and the transfer of all Polish trade to Elbing. When resistance continued and the Abbey of Oliwa was burned by rioters, Danzig was attacked by force. On 17 April 1577 at Lubieszów (Liebischau), the royal army of Jan Zborowski killed nearly twice their own number when challenged by the Danzigers under Johann Winkelbruch von Köln. But it was unable to storm the city, or to take the Lantern Fortress which guarded the port. At the Treaty of Malborg, Bathory withdrew the terms of the Commission in exchange for a hefty subsidy, and agreed to further negotiations. A new convention was finally agreed in 1585.[4]

Bathory turned next to judicial reform. Seeing that the business of the higher courts of royal justice had been suspended for half a decade, he abandoned the monarch's prerogative to hear appeals in civil and criminal cases. Instead, he directed Zamoyski, now raised to the Crown Chancellorship, to devise a system whereby judicial affairs could be directly controlled by the nobility. The institution of the Crown Tribunal in 1578 and of a similar Lithuanian Tribunal in 1581, removed any possible fears of impending royal tyranny, and ensured the co-operation of the Sejm and the nobility for the king's more pressing interests.[5]

The royal army was also transformed. In 1578, the Sejm was persuaded to approve the formation of the *piechota wybraniecka* or 'selected infantry'. They were drawn from the peasants of the Crown estates, in the ratio of one man for every twenty holdings. Each soldier was to be clothed and supported by the nineteen neighbouring families who did not serve. They were armed with muskets. At the same time, the old *jazda kopijnicza* or 'mounted spearmen' was gradually replaced by the winged *Husaria*, one of the legendary formations of European battlefields over the next century.[6]

After the army, it was the turn of the Dnieper Cossacks. Settled on the outer fringes of organized government, they had

defied all previous attempts to control them. They lived in
Tartar style from loot and pillage. In years when they re-
frained from devastating Poland or Lithuania, they were
devastating the Republic's neighbours. Yet in 1578, they
approached Bathory with a proposition of service and
obedience, and it was accepted with alacrity. A named register
of Cossack volunteers was established, who, in return for taking the oath of allegiance, were to receive an annual fee equal
to that of the Hussars. They were to serve under their own
Ataman who was to take his orders from the royal *starosta*
at Czerkask. It was no secret that they were expected to direct
their talents against Muscovy. Cossacks who persisted with
adventures of their own invention received no mercy. In 1584,
Bathory did not wait for senatorial approval before executing,
in the presence of the Sultan's ambassador, thirty Zaporozhians
who had crossed into the Turkish lands without permission.[7]

The magnates, too, were brought to heel. Although feuding
in the provinces continued to be endemic, the King would not
tolerate disruption on a major scale. To this end, he permitted
the Chancellor to make an example of Samuel Zborowski.
Banished in 1574 by Henry de Valois, Zborowski had taken
refuge in Transylvania and had backed Bathory's cause. But
this did not save him when he abused the King's disregard of
his illegal return to Poland by feuding with his neighbours. In
1584, he was seized by Zamoyski, and peremptorily executed.
In the same way, Bathory executed one Ivan Podkova in Lwów,
who had thought fit to lead a private expedition into Wallachia;
the Lithuanian Ośćik who had dared to have treasonable
communications with Muscovy; and the Castellan of Iłgów
for criminal offences. In contrast, he rewarded his loyal supporters most liberally. Zamoyski enjoyed the two chief offices
of the Crown as well as five or six starostwa; in Lithuania,
the Radziwiłł family were granted all the chief offices of state
both civil and ecclesiastical. The King's friends lived well,
while his enemies trembled.

Bathory displayed considerable skill in the art of finance.
At the accession, both the royal and the public treasuries
were sadly depleted. The mint had ceased to strike coin. Over
ten years, almost all items of royal revenue were increased,
and the total nearly doubled:

ROYAL REVENUE (Zł.)	*1576–7*	*1585–6*
1. Crown estates: rent	70,000	74,000
2. *podwodny* tax ⎫	2,500	2,500
3. *stacyjny* tax ⎬ on Crown land	3,000	3,000
4. Coronation tax ⎭	9,000	–
5. Customs and excise: inland	50,500	65,000
maritime	–	44,000
6. Salt mines (Wieliczka)	28,000	66,000
7. Ruthenian saltpans	14,000	20,000
8. Lead mines (Olkusz)	1,400	4,000
9. Royal Mint	–	4,000
10. Grand Ducal Revenue (Lithuania)	53,000	130,000
Total	231,400	412,500

In view of the fact that there were magnates in the Republic who took more than a million złoties per year from their estates, or who gave 100,000 zł. for their daughters' dowries, the royal revenue was extremely modest. Yet it was conserved by austerity at court and by careful management. In addition to the *kwarta* tax permanently earmarked for the standing army, it contributed a grand total of 577,679 zł. to the defence of the realm during the reign.[8]

Public finances were nursed accordingly. The land-tax raised by the Sejm was notoriously hard to realize. The nobility constantly demanded the surrender of Crown leaseholds from the magnates before voting supplies, and the *sejmiki* were not averse to ignoring the votes of the Sejm. Even so, Bathory contrived to extract much blood from the noble stone. In 1577, he was assured revenue from the land-tax for two years in advance, in return for lowering the rate from 20 to 15 groszy per łan. In that year, public revenue was approximately three times the royal revenue.

PUBLIC REVENUE (1577) (Zł.)

pobór (land-tax) ⎫		
szoz (town-tax on property) ⎬ Direct Taxes...		318,000
pogłówka (poll-tax) ⎭		
Income from Alcohol.................		180,000
Prussian excise		40,000
Excise .·............................		38,000
Grand Duchy of Lithuania		103,000
Total........		679,000

The real problem was to match expenditure to revenue. Given the fact that an army of 20,000 mercenaries cost 1.3 million zł. per annum, or twice the income of the state, it would seem that extended military campaigns were out of the question. Yet Bathory contrived to bridge the gap. He did so partly by special funding, and partly by trading political concessions for hard cash. In his first year alone, he took 200,000 ducats from the city of Danzig, and another 20,000 from the Brandenburg Hohenzollerns for granting the right of reversion to the Duchy of Prussia. He cajoled the clergy into a 'voluntary payment' of 33,000 zł., and raised a cool 150,000 at 5 per cent interest from a consortium of German princes.[9] As usual, everything flowed from confidence. A ruler who was trusted by his subjects was able to mobilize unseen resources. When the private contributions of nobility and magnates had been added to the forces paid for by king and state, Bathory briefly achieved the impossible. He transformed a budgetless Republic, barely capable of its own defence, into a major power.

The prime object of Bathory's concern was the Republic's eastern neighbour — the Grand Duchy of Moscow and its Grand Duke, Ivan IV, called the 'Terrible'. Muscovy was no ordinary state, and Ivan was no normal neighbour. It was not just that Muscovy had been in conflict with Lithuania over Smolensk throughout the century; nor that Ivan had renewed the war in Livonia during the late interregnum. Such things were commonplace. Nor did it matter unduly that the Muscovite's cruelty and ambition was unmatched in a cruel and ambitious age. Bathory's concern centred on the demonic quality of Moscow, which was visibly consuming not just the lands of its neighbours but the best citizens and traditions of Russia itself. It enabled Ivan to pursue claims to lands and honours in Russia far beyond any which he, or his forebears, or his remote principality, had ever possessed. The 'gathering of the Russian lands' by this 'Third Rome' had as much rationale in Eastern Europe as might have been professed in Western Europe by some Irish prince who thought to gather the Celtic lands of France, Spain, and Britain under the aegis of Dublin, or by some Duke of Franconia who sought to restore the Frankish Empire of Charlemagne. Entirely devoid of any taint of the Renaissance or Reformation, Ivan's Moscow lived by its own pathological values in its own closed world. Yet forty years of unbridled barbarity had failed to arouse the retribution which elsewhere would have flowed as a matter of course. What is more, Ivan enjoyed a certain cachet in the eyes of people not directly affected. It was all very well for Elizabeth of England to foster trading contracts round the North Cape or for the Emperor in distant Vienna to engineer diplomatic alliances. But for Poland–Lithuania, it was different. Resistance to Muscovy at this time was a matter both of principle and of survival. When at his election Stefan Bathory had promised action 'for the defence of Christendom', he was not calling for a crusade against the Turks, whose culture he admired and whose suzerainty over Transylvania he had long accepted. He was calling for war against Muscovy.[10]

The war lasted for seven seasons from 1576 to 1582. At first, the Republic was unable to respond to Ivan's initial aggression. But in 1577 the Lithuanian Hetman, Nicholas Radziwiłł the Red, captured Duneburg (Dvinsk); and in 1578 the Polish cavalry took Wenden by storm in a nocturnal charge. In 1579, Bathory determined to carry the fight into enemy territory. An army of 22,000 knights, drawing rations for at least 100,000 men — Poles, Lithuanians, Prussians, and Magyars — reduced Polotsk by siege. In the south, Prince Ostrogski raided deep into Polesie. The next year Bathory struck north to Vielikie Luki, driving a wedge between Moscow and Livonia. Zamoyski cut his way through trackless forest for three weeks, before destroying the fortress with mines and fire-balls. Hungarian engineers built a firm road all the way back to Polotsk. In 1581, the campaign moved north-wards again, in the direction of the ruins of Novgorod. The Sejm had voted more than 2 million zł. over two years, on condition that the war was now brought to a close. A clear result had to be obtained while funds lasted. Bathory had recruited an expert force of foreign mercenaries. He had several German and Scottish regiments, and a number of Italian, French, and Spanish captains. Ivan complained that he was being attacked 'by the whole of Italy'. The principal

obstacle lay in the embattled city of Pskov. It was protected
by walls some eight miles in circumference, defended by
7,000 cavalry and 50,000 infantry, and commanded by
Prince Ivan Petrovich Shuyski. The siege was laid in August.
Meanwhile, Radziwiłł dared to approach the Tsar's residence
at Staristsa on the Volga, and Polish detachments roamed as
far as Lake Ladoga. By now, Muscovy had lost some 300,000
people in the war. Some 40,000 prisoners were in Polish
hands. Livonia was isolated from the east, and the Swedes,
having taken Narva, were advancing from the north. On
1 December Ivan sued for peace.

In the middle of the war, the religious factor was suddenly
underlined when Ivan sent an envoy to the Pope. He complained that the unity of Christendom was being disturbed by
the activities of a 'Turkish employee'. The Vatican responded.
Mindful of the long-held project of union between the Catholic
and Orthodox faiths, agreed in 1439 but never implemented,
it dispatched a Jesuit diplomat, Antoni Possevini, to see what
could be arranged. In 1581, Possevini met Bathory in Wilno,
and later proceeded to Moscow. Ivan showed interest in his
shaven face and in the Pope's good fortune in being carried
around in a litter. He refused to discuss religion. The unity of
Christ was not enhanced.[11]

The siege of Pskov assumed legendary proportions. Outside
the walls the attacking force numbered some 170,000 knights
and servants. As the Russian winter advanced they built
themselves an entire town of wooden houses, complete with
regular streets and a market-place. An early breach was not
to be exploited. Inside the city, a local gunsmith called
Dorofei was visited by the Virgin Mary, who told him where
the cannon should be placed and assured him that the town
would not fall. Elsewhere, an anonymous chronicler was relating the course of events for posterity:

The siege of Pskov began in the year 7089, in the month of August and
the 18th day, on the feast of the holy martyrs Frol and Laurel. Then it
was that the Lithuanian people started to cross the river and to appear
before the city with their regiments . . . The King himself came before
Pskov. In that same month of August on the 26th day, on the feast of the
holy martyrs Adrian and Natalya, this man, the Lithuanian king, drew
close with all his many forces, like a wild boar from the wilderness . . .[12]

In due course, the 'much-proud Lithuanian King Stepan' left the 'evil-hearted and greatly-proud Chancellor—Pole', Zamoyski, in charge.

The Peace of Yam Zapolski was signed in the presence of Possevini on 15 January 1582, whilst the siege continued. Muscovy abandoned the whole of Livonia with Polotsk, Velizh, and Ushviata. At Pskov, a fierce winter froze cavalrymen dead in their saddles; but Zamoyski remained in place until the Tsar's commissioners arrived to surrender the keys of the Livonian castles. He moved off on 4 February for Dorpat, where he relieved the Muscovite garrison after twenty-four years of occupation. To the Poles it appeared a famous victory. To the chronicler of Pskov, it looked like an act of divine intervention:

And so, by the great and ineffable grace of the Holy Trinity, of our helpers and suppliants from the whole family of Christ, and of the most holy, heavenly powers; by the prayers and intercessions of the great miracle-workers, including the miracle-worker Nikolai, pre-eminent in miracles, whose saintly vision thrice manifested the Holy Trinity at sunrise; by the founders and defenders of the God-preserved city of Pskov, by the leaders in Christ of the True Faith of the whole Russian land, and by the Orthodox Tsar and Grand Duke of noble root; by the prayers of the true-believing and God-loving Grand Duchess Olga, baptized by Helen, of her saintly grandson, the true-believing Grand Duke Gabriel Vsevolod, of our reverend father Efrosin, of the miracle-workers of Pskov, and of all the saints; by our Lord the Tsar, the true-believing Grand Duke, Ivan Vasil'evitch, beloved of Christ, who holds all Russia in his patrimony; indeed, by all the wonders which God performed, the city of God with all its people was saved from the Lithuanian King, and from all his host.

Then, on the fourth day of February, the Polish Hetman and Lord Chancellor moved off from Pskov with all his array to the Lithuanian land. In the city of Pskov, the gates were opened. And I, having completed this story in all its fullness, have brought it to its end.[13]

Thus did the Muscovites celebrate a severe defeat.

Bathory's triumph soon cooled. Having made his reckoning with Muscovy, he began to dream of grandiose alliances on a continental scale. In 1583, he made a bid to win the Tsar for a joint crusade against the Crimea. In 1584, he was thinking in terms of an expedition against Constantinople, and then, after the death of Ivan, of a federation of Poland, Lithuania,

Hungary, and Muscovy. The Sejm was not impressed. Its last meeting in 1585 broke up amidst the endless Zborowski quarrel, and no taxes were voted. The King fell into a deep depression. On 15 May 1585, at Niepołomice, where he was shunning the company of his wife and court, he composed his will, berating the Poles for their ingratitude and confining his largess to the interests of his native Transylvania. He languished in this mood for more than a year, and died suddenly at Grodno on 12 December 1586, unshriven. There were fears of poison.

Bathory's reputation was not entirely unblemished, therefore. If he was largely remembered as the hammer of Ivan the Terrible, there were voices at the end which called him, too, a tyrant. His success was largely personal. By sheer force of character, he had imposed his will on the Republic, and drove the creaking governmental machine into motion. But little of his achievement was durable. By the time that the protracted autopsy was complete, and his body interred in its elegant tomb in Cracow, the Republic was floundering once more in the same quagmire of chaos with which the reign began.

CHAPTER FOURTEEN

VASA:

The Swedish Connection (1587-1668)

Sweden, which faced the Polish—Lithuanian Republic across the Baltic Sea, resembled its southern neighbour in several important ways. It was a dual state whose two main elements, Sweden and Finland, had been joined first in a personal and then in a constitutional union. Its society was dominated by a powerful class of noble families strongly based both economically and politically on their extensive estates. Its monarchy was relatively weak, and had been subjected during the Middle Ages to a variety of dynastic alliances and constitutional experiments. The Union of Kalmar with Denmark and Norway had been terminated in 1523, when Gustav Eriksson I of the House of Vasa established a purely Swedish monarchy. Thereafter the constitutional position was unstable, with the noble Diet holding very strong sanctions of election and consent over the growth of royal power. Protestantism made rapid progress, especially among the nobility, and a national church was established, as in England, by royal initiative. In the 1570s the Roman Church was working for a revival. The Jesuits held high hopes, as in Poland—Lithuania, for turning the flank of Protestantism in the north. In 1580, when Possevini was appointed Legate to Poland and Muscovy, he had just returned from three years at the head of the *Missio Suetica* in Stockholm.

At the same time, there were serious grounds for potential conflict. The relationship between Poland and Sweden was sufficiently close to provoke competition and rivalry. The structure of power in the Baltic was changing rapidly. Sweden was entering an era of dynamic expansion. She was destined to raise one of the great armies of history, and already possessed a fleet of one hundred battleships. In due course, she was to aspire to the *Dominium Maris Balticae* – a policy for turning the sea into a Swedish lake. Poland—Lithuania, in contrast, adopted an essentially passive posture, being thoroughly preoccupied with existing possessions. The Republic held the richest Baltic port, Danzig, and a long stretch of the southern shore which would have to serve as the base for any Swedish involvement in continental affairs. The strategic implications were obvious. In the Duchy of Prussia, the Protestant Hohenzollerns could exploit their key location for leverage against Polish suzerainty. In Livonia, the polygonal war which pitted the numerous local factions against their patrons — Denmark, Poland, Muscovy, and Sweden — inevitably led to armed clashes, in which both Swedes and Poles were involved. Religion, too raised its head. In 1585, the citizens of Riga, incensed by Polish rule in general and by the introduction of the Catholic Gregorian Calendar in particular, rose in revolt and turned to the Swedish King for protection. As Catholic fortunes ebbed in Sweden but flowed in Poland–Lithuania, tensions mounted. Most immediate however, were the problems of the Swedish royal House of Vasa, closely linked since 1562 with the Polish Jagiellons.

The House of Vasa was divided against itself. The four sons of Gustav I were each moved by contrasting temperaments and by warring supporters. Eric XIV was a homicidal maniac, who was deposed in 1568 and eventually poisoned. John, Duke of Finland, was a scholar and theologian. Charles, Duke of Södermanland and master of Stockholm, was the champion of the Protestant nobility. Magnus, Duke of Ostergotland, was killed with Eric. The Duke of Finland, who was elected in Eric's place in 1569 as John III, was quickly adopted by the Catholic Party. His Queen, Katarzyna Jagiellonka, sister of Zygmunt-August of Poland, was a fervent Catholic. Her dowry consisted of her mother's Sforza fortune, frozen in Naples but — it was hoped — to be realized by Catholic influence with the Pope and the King of Spain. On Eric's orders, she had spent the first four years of her marriage with her husband in the dungeon of Gripsholm, where their son Sigismund was born in 1566. Her influence on religious developments was considerable. In 1576, at her instigation, John introduced a new ecumenical liturgy, blending elements from both the Tridentine Catholic and Swedish Lutheran models; in 1578, he was secretly received into the Roman faith by Possevini. In his delicate predicament at home, it was only natural that he should strengthen his hand by exploiting his Polish contacts. In two Polish elections, in 1573 and 1575, he was unsuccessful; but in 1587, at the third attempt, he engineered a victory on behalf of his son and heir, Sigismund. Although the descendants of John III Vasa were to lose control of Sweden, they remained on the throne of Poland–Lithuania for the next eighty-one years. Sigismund was succeeded in turn by his two sons Władysław (Ladislas) IV (1632–48), and Jan Kazimierz (John Casimir, 1648–68).[1]

The Polish election of 1587 combined the worst manifestations of the two preceding occasions – a double election, and a successful candidate who was more concerned with his homeland than with the affairs of the Republic. It led to ceaseless strife: to civil wars first in Poland and then in Sweden, and to repeated and prolonged wars between the two countries.[2] In Poland, Sigismund's cause was championed by the 'Black' Faction, so-called from the mourning clothes which they wore in memory of Bathory. Headed by Zamoyski, and by Bishop Karnkowski, now Primate, they determined once again to exclude the Habsburg candidate at all costs. Yet the Habsburg court was confident. Backed by the blessing of the Pope and by the gold of the Spanish ambassador, Guillen de San Clemente, it was counting on the Archduke Maximilian, brother of the Emperor Rudolf II. When the electoral Sejm broke up in disorder, the Habsburgs took to arms. But Zamoyski was ready. Repulsing the Austrians from the gates of Cracow, he rushed to Danzig to escort the bewildered Sigismund towards his coronation, as Zygmunt III, which took place on 27 December. In the following year at Byczyna (Pitschen) in Silesia, he took Maximilian prisoner, and did not release him until Vienna had undertaken to abandon all pretensions to the Polish throne. From the practical point of view, Zamoyski's campaign was completely successful. He soon regretted it.

Zygmunt III was the victim of complications beyond his control. As a Swede by birth, and as grandson of the great Gustav Eriksson, he naturally laid greatest store on his Swedish inheritance. As a fervent Catholic and pupil of Polish Jesuits, he understood that Poland could play an important part in the recovery of Northern Europe for Rome. As the dutiful son of his late Jagiellonian mother, he listened to the pleas of his aunt Anna, Bathory's widow, who begged him to accept the Polish throne for her sake. These interests proved quite irreconcilable. In Sweden, before sailing for Danzig, he was obliged to sign the Statutes of Kalmar, which protected the Protestant Church and the Diet from any changes resulting from the union of crowns. On arrival in Poland, and in spite of his vocal protests during the ceremony in the Abbey of Oliwa, he was obliged to swear to the *Pacta Conventa* and to the terms of the Confederation of Warsaw. At the Coronation Sejm, he watched with anger while the nobles introduced a new definition of *lèse-majesté* which expressly excepted all forms of verbal abuse. Henceforth, he could be, and was, slandered with impunity. He specially resented the tone of Zamoyski, who had called him 'our dumb phantom imported from Sweden'. Zamoyski's posturing against the Habsburgs, and his plans for hedging the monarchy with even stricter limitations, appeared to be motivated increasingly by private interest. In 1588 in Lithuania, Zygmunt was obliged to sign the Third Lithuanian Statute, in direct contravention to the Union of Lublin, but as the necessary price for his acceptance by the magnates of the Grand Duchy. It is not surprising perhaps that he thought of abdicating on the spot. In 1589, he bargained with Vienna, seeking to sell his Polish crown to the Archduke Ernest for 400,000 guilders. He met his father at Reval, and announced his impending return to Sweden. Yet he could not escape. The Swedish nobility made it clear that they could well do without him, especially when he took the Habsburg Archduchess, Anna, for his wife. When John III died in 1593, Zygmunt was to encounter the same humiliations in Sweden that he had already borne in Poland.

The disputed Swedish succession produced a ten-year crisis. When Zygmunt arrived in Stockholm attended by Jesuits and confessors, and by the Nuncio, Germanico Malaspina, he found that the opposition had stolen a march on him. The Convocation of the Church of Sweden had already decided in advance to establish the Augsburg Confession and the Lutheran catechism, and to banish Calvinism and Zwinglism as heresy. There was no room for a Roman proselyte. At the Coronation itself, performed by the Protestant Bishop of Stregnas in the cathedral of Uppsala, there were scenes reminiscent of Henry de Valois's ordeal in Cracow twenty years before. Zygmunt's uncle, Duke Charles, intervened during the ceremony, insisting that the King keep all three fingers exactly erect during the swearing of the oath. He refused to kneel before the new monarch, and rolled his coronet at the King's feet as a sign of defiance. After five months of fruitless argument, and a number of incidents between the Polish and Transylvanian guard and the Stockholm mob, Zygmunt fled, leaving Duke Charles and the aristocratic Council as joint-regents.[3] When he arrived in Cracow, he forestalled a movement to hold a new election. Whichever way he turned, it seemed, he was bound to lose. In 1598, he returned to Sweden with an army, but to no effect. At the first confrontation, at Stangebro, he ordered his victorious troops to refrain from fratricidal slaughter. At the second, at Linköping, his cavalry refused to charge. He left Sweden for ever. In 1599, he was formally deposed. Duke Charles gradually eliminated those nobles who had remained loyal to their rightful king; and in 1604 with the aid of the Diet was able to arrange for his own election. As Charles IX, he was thus the founder of the line of Protestant Vasas who made such an impression on seventeenth-century Europe. (See Diagram F.) This long struggle had inevitably alienated many of Zygmunt's Polish subjects. Whatever policies he pursued in the future, he was sure to be seen as a ruler who had shown more concern for Sweden than for Poland. For this reason, if for no other, his reputation has always suffered in Polish eyes. (See Map 17.)

In effect, both Zygmunt and his sons proved to be competent managers. They were not allowed to be innovators. But neither were they fanatics, nor latent despots. Of course, they made mistakes. But most of the troubles which shook the Republic in their time can be attributed less to poor leadership than to the inflexibility of a system whose arteries were visibly hardening. What is more, in the three or four decades which preceded the shattering rebellion of Chmielnicki in 1648, in an era when the rest of Central Europe was rent by disasters of every sort, the Republic of Poland–Lithuania reached its greatest territorial extent and enjoyed prosperity and security to a degree which was never repeated.

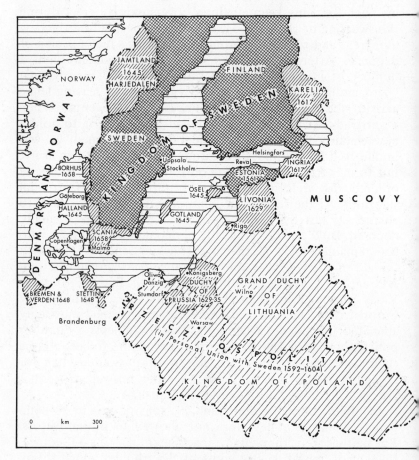

Map 17.   The Vasa Realm, (c. 1600)

In matters of religion, fashionable excess was largely avoided. Like Bathory, Zygmunt III was a devout Catholic, and a firm adherent of the aims of the Counter-Reformation. Jan Kazimierz actually served for a time in the ranks of the Society of Jesus, and became a cardinal. Catholics were preferred at court, and in state appointments. Large numbers of nobles returned to the Roman faith. The predominant tone, set by Skarga, was one of enthusiasm but not of coercion. Sectarians of all shades flourished, although a certain intolerance was seen in specific acts of the Sejm in the 1630s. Calvinists, Lutherans, and Jews maintained their privileges. At the Union of Brest in 1596, the Orthodox community entered a period of strife which was brought under control, if not solved, by the compromise of 1632.

In social affairs, a decisive stage was reached in the growth of magnatial fortunes. Zamoyski, who started his career as a tribune of the noble democracy, emerged as an overmighty subject of the most embarrassing kind. Radziwiłł was equally powerful in Lithuania. Their power was perpetuated by the rush of 'Ordinations' which began in 1589. The pattern was repeated through almost all the provinces of the Republic. After the death of Zamoyski in 1605, and the Zebrzydowski *Rokosz* of 1606—9 which the Great Chancellor's intrigues had so helped to foment, the internal political scene settled down. But the Sejm, the dietines, and the lawcourts were increasingly controlled by magnatial patronage. The voices of the independent nobleman and of the burgher were choked; and the groans of the peasantry were suppressed. Social legislation, which had been so lively in the sixteenth century, virtually disappeared.

Economic prosperity was accompanied by several incurable disorders. Although the first half of the seventeenth century witnessed the zenith of the Baltic Trade, and of urban and commercial life in general, the rewards of affluence were spread ever more unevenly. The luxury of the nobles contrasted with the deepening miseries of the peasants. The wealth of individual cities, especially of Danzig, underlined the growing chaos of royal and state finances. The currency was depreciating with every year that passed. Price inflation continued to soar. In 1576, the average price of an ox was 4 zł.; in 1660,

30 zł. Taxation yields diminished, both in the real value of the money collected, and in the efficiency of its collection. In the later years of Zygmunt III, almost half of the state's taxes failed to arrive in time to be spent on the purposes for which they were raised. In 1629, the abolition of the old method of assessing the land-tax, 'by the łan', caused real hardship. The new *podymny* rate, fixed at 15 groszy 'per chimney' in the countryside and at 1−3 zł. in the towns, fell with equal force on every household, irrespective of the size of its property or of its ability to pay. The contributions of rich landowners diminished; those of the poor rose sharply. Revenue jumped briefly by 60 per cent; but soon failed to meet mounting costs. Over the next three decades, the Sejm was obliged to raise the rate almost fifty times. By 1661 the basic annual 15 groszy rate had risen to 25 zł.

The Jewish community consolidated its position in the Republic, reaching a high plateau of affluence and security which was not to be repeated. The principles, and the institutions, of Jewish autonomy were assured. (See Diagram L.) In 1580, the Jewish Tribunal at Lublin was superseded by the 'Council of the Four Lands' − a supreme legislative and judicial body which survived for nearly two hundred years. Slightly later, a 'Council of the Provinces' served the united communities of the Grand Duchy. In 1592, Zygmunt III restated the General Charter of Jewish privileges in full. Immigration and natural increase brought numbers to an estimated 450,000 by 1648, equivalent to 4.5 per cent of the total population. Jews expanded their traditional range of activities, from banking and money-lending, to every form of trade, commerce, and industry. They established the right to form craft guilds of their own, in defiance of the monopoly of the hitherto exclusively Gentile organizations. Most importantly, they left their traditional urban refuges, and penetrated into every nook and cranny of the rural areas. In the service of the nobility, they played an important pioneering role in the development of the south-eastern lands, especially in the Ukraine. Their success, however, was attended by severe defects. The sheer weight of numbers in specific localities caused acute overcrowding. Constant immigration caused immense resentment among established communities who felt their identity threatened. The resentment was no less prevalent among Jews than among non-Jews. As shown by an ordinance of the Jewish commune of Cracow in 1595, the Elders did everything in their power to restrict immigration and to keep the newcomers out:

He who, without having the right of sojourn (hazaqah), shall try to settle here without the permission of the Elders and the Kahal and shall establish himself either in the Jewish quarter or elsewhere in Kazimierz, Cracow, Kleparz or Stradom, or in the district belonging to these localities, be it man or woman, widow or widower (notwithstanding the rights of his or her deceased spouse) shall be excommunicated from all the holiness of Israel, shall be set aside both from this world and from the life hereafter, shall have no child circumcised, and shall not be buried in a Jewish graveyard. Nevertheless, should such a person deliberately attempt to settle here in the Jewish quarter, no houseowner shall venture to admit him, under the same penalty, together with the payment of 30 florins to the governor, and 15 florins to Charity, and the confiscation of the house by the community.[4]

More seriously, in the provinces of the south and east, Jewish entrepreneurs associated themselves to their lasting detriment with the *arenda* system, whereby landed estates were leased out to agents and managers. It was a system which suited the purposes of the great magnates, of absentee landlords, and of all impoverished noblemen who did not care to manage their estates in person. By putting their affairs into the hands of a leaseholder, the landowners could raise a loan, assure themselves of a steady income to make the repayments, and divert the animosities of their peasants. For his part, the leaseholder took possession not merely of the economic management of the estate but also of all the feudal rights, dues, and jurisdictions attached to it. A typical agreement of 1594 listed the items in detail:

[Prince Piotr Zabrzeski hereby leases all his possessions] . . . in the district of Krzemieniec, including the old and new city of Krzemieniec, New Zbaraż and Kolsec with all the settlements appertaining to these estates, together with the noble boyars, the burghers, and the serfs of those cities and villages . . . all their debts, obligations and privileges, with the arendas, taverns, tolls, ponds, the mills and their revenues, the manors, the various tithes paid by the boyars, burghers and serfs of those districts, together with all the other revenues, to Mr Mikołaj Wransowicz and to Efraim the Jew of Międzybóż, for the amount of 9,000 złoties of the Polish currency, for three years.[5]

(A)

N.B. All delegates to the Councils from inferior bodies carried 'instructions' drawn up by their constituents

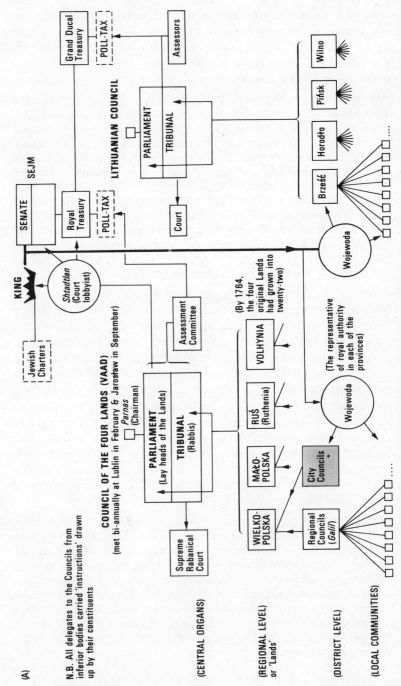

COUNCIL OF THE FOUR LANDS (VAAD)
(met bi-annually at Lublin in February & Jarosław in September)

LITHUANIAN COUNCIL

KING

Shtadtlan (Court lobbyist)

Jewish Charters

SEJM

SENATE

Royal Treasury

POLL-TAX

Grand Ducal Treasury

POLL-TAX

Assessors

PARLIAMENT

TRIBUNAL

Court

Wilno

Pińsk

Horodło

Brześć

Wojewoda

Parnas (Chairman)

PARLIAMENT (Lay heads of the Lands)

TRIBUNAL (Rabbis)

Assessment Committee

Supreme Rabanical Court

WIELKO-POLSKA

MAŁO-POLSKA

RUŚ (Ruthenia)

VOLHYNIA

(By 1764, the four original Lands had grown into twenty-two)

Wojewoda

(The representative of royal authority in each of the provinces)

City Councils

Regional Councils (*Galil*)

(CENTRAL ORGANS)

(REGIONAL LEVEL) or 'Lands'

(DISTRICT LEVEL)

(LOCAL COMMUNITIES)

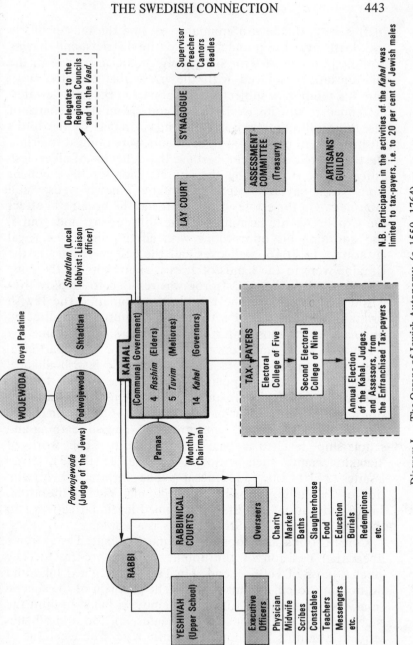

Diagram L.   The Organs of Jewish Autonomy, (c. 1550–1764)

In this way, the Jewish arendator became the master of life and death over the population of entire districts, and, having nothing but a short-term and purely financial interest in the relationship, was faced with the irresistible temptation to pare his temporary subjects to the bone. On the noble estates, he tended to put his relatives and co-religionists in charge of the flour-mill, the brewery, and in particular of the lord's taverns, where by custom the peasants were obliged to drink. On the church estates, he became the collector of all ecclesiastical dues, standing by the church door for his payment from tithe-payers, baptized infants, newly-weds, and mourners. On the estates of the starostas, he became in effect the Crown Agent, farming out the tolls, taxes, and courts, and adorning his oppressions with all the dignity of royal authority. In 1616, well over half the Crown Estates in the Ukraine were in the hands of Jewish arendators. In the same era, Prince Konstanty Ostroróg was reputed to employ over 4,000 Jewish agents. The result was axiomatic. The Jewish community as a whole attracted the opprobrium directed originally at its most enterprising members, and became the symbol of social and economic exploitation. Their participation in 'the oppressive practices of the noble-Jewish alliance' provided the most important single cause of the terrible retribution which was to descend on them on several occasions in the future, particularly in 1648–55, and in 1768. Yet for the time being, calm prevailed. Jewish learning and scholarship reached a peak of profundity. The work of 'halakhic giants' such as Solomon Luria (1510–73), Moses Isserles (1510–72), or Mordecai Yaphe, inspired a rich tradition of Talmudic, cabbalistic, and popular Yiddish literature. Jewish education and literacy attained levels far superior to those of the noble and urban classes as a whole.

Constitutional development ground to a halt. The extreme libertarian position of the nobility was not redressed. The great *Rokosz* of 1606–9 ended in a stalemate. The King could do nothing to enlarge his powers. The problem of the succession was not resolved. Although Zamoyski failed to limit the succession to certain named candidates, so, too, did all subsequent attempts to arrange it *vivente rege*. The elections of 1632 and 1648 were unmemorable. The great officers of state were awarded lifelong tenure. Finance remained firmly in the purview of the nobility.

Some changes were made in military organization. Although the traditional use of massed cavalry brought some success, particularly at Kirchholm in 1605 and at Klushino in 1610, the prestige of the Swedish example led to important modifications designed to increase the army's fire-power. In 1618, the *kwarta* tax was doubled in order to support improved gunnery, which in 1637 was organized in a separate Corps of Artillery with its own General. The army was divided into two separate formations. One, the so-called 'National Contingent', included regiments of Hussars, Cossacks, and Tartars, and was drawn from private retinues and from the noble 'comrades-in-arms'. The other, the Foreign Contingent, included the regiments of infantry, dragoons, and rajtars, and was freely recruited 'by the drum', that is, by colonels who paid and equipped the men themselves. The over-all size of the infantry was much increased, the traditional 'Hungarian-style' regiments armed with muskets and halberds being supplemented with new and larger 'German' regiments of musketeers and pikemen. In peacetime, the standing army made up of the Royal Guard, the Registered Cossacks, and the *Kwarciane* numbered some 12,000 men. In wartime, it could be quadrupled without difficulty. Much work was done on fortresses especially at Zamość in the Italian style, at Danzig, Brody, and Wiśnicz in the Dutch style, and at Kudak on the Dnieper by the French engineer, Beauplan. A school of theoretical writing flourished, associated with the names dell'Aqua, Freytag, and Siemienowicz. In Stanisław Żółkiewski (1547–1620), Crown Hetman from 1613, Jan Karol Chodkiewicz (1560–1621), Lithuanian Hetman from 1605, and Stanisław Koniecpolski (1593–1646), Field Hetman of the Crown from 1618 and Grand Hetman from 1632, and Stefan Czarniecki (1599–1665), the Republic saw its most brilliant generation of field commanders.[6] The Royal Fleet, never of much significance, was liquidated in 1641.[7]

The Dnieper Cossacks were not tamed. On the contrary, they grew and multiplied. Despite Bathory's establishment of the Register, they continued to live off the land, not only in the Ukraine but also deep into the Balkans and the Danube valley. In 1589, they crossed the Black Sea in their boats, and looted a number of Turkish towns. In 1590, on the initiative of the Sejm, they were obliged to accept noble captains from the regular Polish army and were forbidden to recruit fugitive serfs or *swowolniki* (hooligans). As a result, they quickly converted their Polish officers to their own ways, and added a touch of born leadership and professional training to their frequent rebellions. In 1591–3, Ataman Kosiński, a Polish nobleman from Podlasie, led a force of some 5,000 men against the Ostrogski and Wiśniowiecki estates in Podolia, and triggered off widespread peasant disturbances throughout the Ukraine. In 1595–6, Seweryn Nalewajko undertook a similar venture until he was caught and viciously executed in Warsaw. From these events, it was known that the colonizing activities of the great magnatial families were causing resentment on the steppes, and that the peasants of the Ukraine, recruited in the first instance by promises of *'sloboda'* (freedom) and land, were not taking easily to the fashion for enserfment. But no cure was at hand. The size of the Cossack Register could never be agreed. The authorities wanted to indenture as many Cossacks as possible, to keep them out of trouble and available for service, whilst the Cossacks insisted that the Register be kept to a minimum. The forays continued. In 1614, under Ataman Sahajdaczny, Trebizond and Sinope in Asia Minor were looted, and Istambul itself made to tremble. In 1629, the much-sung Stefan Chmielecki rounded up 80,000 Tartars at Monasteryszcze and captured the brother of the Khan. In 1635, the royal fortress at Kudak was razed. In 1637–8, when the Sejm had threatened 'to put idle Cossacks to the plough', the peasant Pawluk and the Ataman Hunia sett off in imitation of Kosiński and Nalewajko. They ended their careers in a similar gory fashion. Severe repression gained respite, but offered no final solution. Proposals to integrate the Cossacks into the political life of the Republic by offering them the status of nobles met with constant opposition in the Sejm. As one noble spokesman put it, 'the Cossacks are the finger-nails of our body politic. They tend to grow too long, and need frequent cutting.'[8]

The unrest of the Cossacks was symptomatic of much deeper disease in the whole of the south-eastern lands. In the period of their attachment to the Grand Duchy, the palatinates of Ukraine lay beyond the easy reach of central government; after 1569, in the *Korona,* they were still left in large measure to the private administration of a few powerful families — the Koniecpolski, Wiśniowiecki, Potocki, Kalinowski, Ostrogski. The population was still chronically insecure. The isolation of tiny oases of settlement along the scattered trails of the prairie, in lonely townships and monasteries, the constant raids of Cossacks and Tartars, the feuds of the lords, the great social and economic contrasts dividing rancher-lords from runaway serfs and free peasant colonists, the rich ethnic mix of Ruthenians, Poles, and 'Romans', and not least, the growing religious differences of Orthodox, Uniate, Catholic, and Jew, all combined to foster a life of violence and turmoil. This was the last frontier of Europe, and no less rough or ready than its later counterpart in North America. Unlike the American West, however, the Polish East was open to outside intervention. The people of the Ukraine were fiercely independent, and resentful of interference from the government. But if they so insisted on their independence that all means of common defence were destroyed, there were powers at hand which would interfere in a much more painful way. In this respect, the tragic fate of Ukraine in the seventeenth century provided a foretaste of the fate of the whole Republic in the eighteenth.[9]

*   *   *   *   *

The Swedish connection obviously had its greatest impact on the conduct of foreign policy. Here it turned the Republic in directions which might otherwise have been avoided. Despite his dethronement in 1599, Zygmunt III maintained his title to the Swedish throne. The claim was pursued until 1660. In a monarchical age, it provided the legal pretext for the wars with Sweden. These automatically revived the old rivalry with Muscovy. The Muscovite wars in their turn were closely related to further campaigns against the Turks and Tartars.

In Livonia, till Bathory's time, the principal contest had been that between the Poles and the Muscovites. After the expulsion of the Muscovites in 1582, it turned into a struggle between the Poles and the Swedes. Firmly established in the north of the province, in Estonia, and welcomed by the Protestant burghers and German nobility, the Swedes quickly tightened their grip. When the internal crisis in Sweden was finally resolved, Charles IX decided to use Polish Livonia as a means of rewarding his supporters with lands and offices. Open warfare began in 1601, and continued intermittently for nearly thirty years. In 1605, at Kirchholm near Riga, a Swedish force was cut to pieces by Chodkiewicz's Lithuanian hussars, and driven into the sea. But it soon returned in strength. The Republic was unable to spare the men to garrison this outlying territory, and every time its attention was distracted, the Swedes made progress. The decisive campaigns were fought by Gustavus Adolphus in 1617—22 — where the centre-piece was formed by the fall of Riga, on 26 September 1621 — and in 1625–6, when the conquest of Livonia was completed.[10] (See Map 18.)

With Gustavus Adolphus (1611–32), the Lion of the North, Swedish ambitions were greatly magnified.[11] Having through his Articles of War organized an army twice as numerous as the forces of the Republic from a population only one-fifth its size, he needed to fight to keep them fed and diverted. Having decided to intervene in the Thirty Years War in Germany, he first needed to secure a mainland base. In 1626, he shipped his army from Livonia to Prussia, and proceeded to seize the Baltic ports and to tap the Vistula trade for customs duties. Pilau (Piława), Braunsberg (Braniewo), Frauenberg (Frombork), Elbing (Elbląg), and Oliwa were quickly reduced and their treasures sent to Sweden; but Danzig contrived to resist for the duration. For three years, a series of Polish counter-attacks made little impression on the splendidly fortified Swedish bases. The naval encounters were indecisive, although off Oliwa on 28 November 1627, a Polish flotilla managed to drive off a Swedish squadron and sink two of its ships. Fortunately for them, the Swedish flagship, the *Vasa,* was overturned by a squall in Stockholm harbour on her maiden voyage on 10 August 1628. She never reached her intended destination in the Southern Baltic. Built by a Dutch shipwright, Henryk Hybertsson, she would have been one of the great vessels of the age, and was certainly superior to anything in the British, not to mention Polish, service at

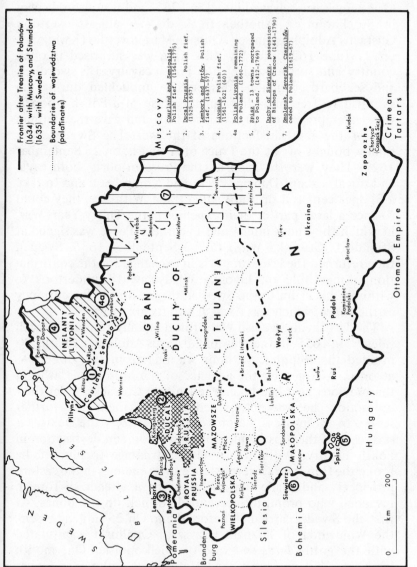

Map 18. Poland–Lithuania at its greatest extent, (1634–5)

the time. Her displacement weight was 1,300 tons, and she carried sixty-four 24-pounder cannons on two gun decks. (The wreck was salvaged intact in 1961, and is now on display in Stockholm.)[12] Another freak disaster almost overtook Gustavus Adolphus himself. Outside Marienwerder (Kwidzyń), on 27 June 1629, the Swedish King was surprised in open country and surrounded by the Polish cavalry. His swordbelt and scabbard, which he desperately unbuckled during the skirmish to free himself from the grasp of a Polish trooper, were later presented to Koniecpolski, and gave the Hetman one of the few satisfactions of the war. The Swedes were finally bought off at the Truce of Altmark, on 26 September 1629. They were to keep all the Prussian ports, both royal and ducal, except Danzig, Puck, and Königsberg, and to take a 3½ per cent toll on the Vistula trade. With this, they could finance a large part of their expenses in the Thirty Years War, in which they now intervened in earnest. Peace was signed at Stumdorf (Stumska Wieś) on 12 September 1635. Sweden then returned the Prussian ports in exchange for the confirmation of her hold on Livonia. Władysław IV undertook to withhold his claim to the Swedish throne during the currency of the Peace, which was fixed at twenty-six years.

The last great Swedish War proved equally ruinous to both sides.[13] In 1655, the nephew of Gustavus Adolphus, Charles X, invaded the Republic without warning from two directions at once. Alarmed by the advance of the Muscovites, who in the previous year had taken the Dnieper Cossacks under their protection, he was determined to deny them any further scope. In the process, he provoked the *Potop*, 'the Deluge' — six years of the most deplorable confusion and destruction in Polish history. Without any clear advantage to himself, he broke the Republic's last resistance to its enemies in the eastern provinces, and made her the prey of a stream of foreign invaders, who promptly descended to pick up the bones. At first the Swedes carried all before them. On 25 July, at Ujście, the Wojewoda of Poznań, Krzysztof Opaliński, capitulated with the entire *levée-en-masse* of Wielkopolska. One month later, at Kajdany, the Grand Hetman of Lithuania, Janusz Radziwiłł, accepted a Swedish protectorate over the Grand Duchy. The Polish Vasa, Jan Kazimierz, took refuge in imperial

Silesia. The greater part of his army entered the Swedish service. Warsaw was occupied; Cracow was taken by siege; a large number of smaller towns and estates were burned and plundered. Resistance was reduced to the unco-ordinated activities of peasant bands and to the miraculous defence of the fortified Pauline monastery of Jasna Góra, on the 'Bright Hill' of Częstochowa. At this, the Polish chronicles waxed very eloquent:

General Müller, who had directed his forces against the monastery of Częstochowa, was now faced with a more severe task, for he was defying the Almighty . . . The monastery of Jasna Góra is consecrated to the Immaculate Virgin Mary, whose famous and miraculous icon is to be found there, painted on a board of cypress wood by Saint Luke the Evangelist himself. It was this icon, a source of great veneration and of immense treasure amassed from the offerings of three centuries, that inspired the enemy to lay the siege and to offset his war costs by plunder. The initiator of the enterprise was apparently a Czech, Jan Weihard, Count Vresovic, whom Müller sent ahead with four thousand troops to frighten the monks by a demonstration of strength. Vresovic approached the monastery to a peal of trumpets, and rudely ordered that the gates be opened . . . But having met with a refusal based on religious arguments, the Swedes decided to apply force.

After Vresovic . . . Müller arrived from Wieluń at the head of nine thousand infantrymen, and with a train of artillery. It was a formidable force, originally destined for the campaign in Prussia . . . But the fathers of Jasna Góra, called on again to admit a Swedish garrison, replied boldly that they were bound to God's service by their vows and that to surrender the ancient place of pilgrimage would be sacrilege.

When negotiations brought no result, the Swedes began a violent bombardment of the walls. Then, in order to spread fear among the defenders, they started to hurl in blazing firebrands, setting the monastery's barn alight together with a great quantity of corn. Next, all around the monastery, they set up a camp with wooden palisades and gun emplacements. Müller took the northern side, from which he tried to rush the defences. The southern side was held by the Landgraf of Hesse and Colonel Sądowski. But their attacks had little effect. The walls were banked with earth on the inside, and only a few bricks were displaced by the cannon. Before long, the defenders opened fire in reply. The aim of their gunners was so accurate, that after three hours the Swedes were obliged to pull back with great loss. Meanwhile, the inhabitants of houses adjacent to the monastery, where the enemy had found shelter, set their homes on fire, not counting the cost, and reduced them to dust . . .

The Swedes renewed their attack on the 19th November, the Day of the Transfiguration of the Virgin. They had received six explosive mortars from Cracow, and a great store of ammunition. Their soldiers, fresh from nearby billets, went into battle with enthusiasm . . . The *Gigantomachie,* the official printed description of this siege, records that the bullets and missiles fell so thick on the church and tower that they seemed to be in flames. But the use of unnatural means did not succeed. The cannon-balls bounced off the walls and tiles or flew over the church roof, causing no damage. The artillerymen and pyrotechnicians could not cope . . . Since many of them died horrible deaths, the enemy ascribed their failure to the work of evil spirits . . . But Müller was most angered by the monks, who would climb to the top of the tower and in full choir pour down pious hymns on his soldiers. They made him a laughing-stock . . .

Among the defenders were Stefan Zamoyski of the Róża clan, the Sword-bearer of Sieradz, and Piotr Czarniecki, cousin of [Stefan Czarniecki] . . . Over-all command was taken by the Prior of the monastery, Augustyn Kordecki, who also took great care of the artillery. Zamoyski commanded the infantry . . .

Once when the Swedes had postponed their attacks on account of poor light, Czarniecki determined to deal them a nocturnal surprise. Sallying from the walls at the break of dawn at the head of sixty soldiers he crept right into the General's encampment, where he fell on the weary and somnolent Swedes with a sudden shout and a hail of bullets . . . He caused immense slaughter, killing Count Horn, a notable military engineer, with his own hand . . .

Yet Jasna Góra was not saved by men. The holy place was preserved by God, and more by miracles than by the sword. A thick mist screened the monastery from attack . . . Müller himself saw a Lady in a shining robe on the walls, priming the cannon and tossing shells back in the direction from which they came . . . There were Swedes who froze stiff whenever they put their eye to the sights of their musket, and others whose cheeks stuck to the gunbarrel till the surgeon could cut them free . . . In the monastery, a grenade which landed and exploded in a baby's cradle did not hurt him, whilst in the Swedish camp six gunners were blinded by one single explosion . . .

Before the siege began, the monks had hidden their silver in a nearby lake, thinking that it would be safe under the ice. But a lad from one of the Polish regiments serving with the Swedes, angling for fish through a hole, hauled up a catch of silver chalices. When Müller ordered everything to be handed over, the Poles refused . . . In this way, dissension was sown between the commander and his Command . . .

Meanwhile, the winter set in, making siege operations most difficult.

Müller was furious when he saw that an unsuccessful siege was ruining his reputation . . . His fine career, established in the long wars in Germany, now fell shamefully to pieces . . . He launched his last attack on Christmas Day, firing off all his guns in one salvo, and sending his entire army to storm the walls . . . But at that very moment, he suffered a fatal accident. He was eating breakfast in a fairly distant house, and cursing Jasna Góra with blasphemies, when suddenly an iron shot penetrated the wall, knocked all the plates, bottles, and glasses from the table, scattered the guests, and struck him in the arm . . . Müller sent the defenders the following letter:

'Reverend, Mighty and Noble Sirs! . . . What more can we do when you continue to confront my Gracious King with faces harder than stone? We magnanimously offer you two alternative means of salvation: either you surrender yourselves and your fortress to the protection of His Majesty, the King of Sweden . . . or else, after taking the oath of allegiance to Him, the monks and the nobility each pay a fine of 40,000 thalers, to cover the costs and damage which this long siege has brought to the whole kingdom. If you should accept neither of these propositions, then we will measure your punishment to the extent of your obstinacy, which deserves the Stake of Buzyrod or the Bull of Perillus.

Given in our camp, on 25 December, in the Year of Our Lord, 1655 . . .'

At last, in the night before St. Stephen's Day, the Swedes started to drag the guns from their emplacements, to collect their equipment together, and to direct their wagons in the direction of Klobuck. The infantry and cavalry were the last to leave, at nine o'clock in the morning. Müller was making for Piotrków . . . Sądowski for Kalisz, Vresovic for Wieluń, and the Duke of Hesse for Cracow. Having missed their expected morsel, they ground their teeth in anger, and were consumed with shame.

Of course, no heretic will believe that cannon-balls were repulsed from the walls of Jasna Góra by supernatural means . . . But all that I have described is true, though Swedish chroniclers are silent about these events, suppressing at once their shame and . . . the need to praise God for the successful defence . . .[14]

Thereafter, the Republic was resuscitated. The army returned to its duty. The tireless energy of Stefan Czarniecki began to turn the tide. The Swedes were driven from Warsaw. Their Prussian allies were persuaded to defect, and their Transylvanian imitators routed. In 1658–9, Czarniecki was free to attack Sweden from the Danish bases in Jutland. In that year

Charles X died. On 3 May 1660, at the Treaty of Oliwa, peace
was concluded. In return for Elbling in Prussia and Dunebourg
in Semigalia, Sweden kept the whole of Livonia. The Swedes
abandoned all further claims on the Republic. Jan Kazimierz
abandoned the traditional claim of his family to the throne
of the Vasas. At this point the Republic's link with Sweden
was formally severed. (See pp. 370–1.)

Thus, after a century of struggle, Semigalia and the Duchy
of Courland were the only two parts of the former Teutonic
state of Livonia which remained under Polish control. The
former, known henceforward as 'Polish Livonia', was tacked
on to the three coastal enclaves of the territory of Piłtyń
(Ventspils), and administered as an integral part of the
Republic. The latter was left in the capable hands of its
Kettler dukes, as a joint fief of Poland and Lithuania. Its
capital city of Mitau (Jelgava) and the port of Windau
(Windawa) developed into important centres of trade and
culture. The greatest of its dukes, Jakub Kettler (1638–82),
was a prominent figure in Baltic politics, with important
connections in Holland, and, as godson of James I, with
England. He even branched out into colonial enterprises. In
1645 he bought the island of Tobago from the Dutch, and in
1651 established a trading-post on Fort James Island in
Gambia, in West Africa. His activities were interrupted
between 1655 and 1660 during the Swedish occupation of
Courland, when he himself was held as a prisoner-of-war.
His descendants held the Duchy until 1737, when, with the
Biren dynasty in power, it passed into the Russian orbit.[15]

Throughout the long era of Swedish wars, the conduct of
Muscovy was of constant importance. As shown both by the
Livonian struggle and by the policy of Charles X, Moscow
played a part in all calculations relating to the Polish–Swedish
conflict. The Baltic power struggle was not just 'bi-polar'. It
was triangular. Muscovy, Sweden, and Poland–Lithuania
were all locked in the same three-sided arena. Each of the
contestants had to shift its position continually, to accom-
modate the changes occurring in the postures of the other
two. When one of the powers was strong, the others had to
consider combining to resist. When one was weak, both the
others would compete to exploit it. This situation lasted from

the start of the Livonian war in 1558 until the Treaty of Oliwa in 1660. After that, when the Polish side of the triangle had collapsed, Sweden was left facing Muscovy alone, and did so until the defeat of Charles XII by Peter the Great at Poltava in 1709. The introduction of the Republic into this complex involvement was one of the principal effects of the Vasa connection; and the only beneficiary in the end was Moscow.

Hence in accordance with the laws of the triangle, the Republic's wars with Sweden were interlaced with related campaigns which each of them fought against Muscovy. In the case of the Republic, following Bathory's victories in 1579–81, there were Muscovite wars in 1609–12 and 1617–19 during Moscow's 'Time of Troubles'; in 1632–4 over Smoleńsk; and in 1654–67 in the Ukraine. The final round was fought in 1700–21 in the Great Northern War.

Unfortunately, the Time of Troubles in Muscovy is best known to the outside world in caricatures deriving from Russian folk-history or from the stage of the nineteenth-century opera:

Second Act: Throne room of King Sigismund. The King is celebrating his victory. The Polish lords dream of occupying the rich Russian land . . . Carousing and confusion. Sigismund directs a posse of his knights to bar Minin from the road to Moscow, to take him prisoner, to destroy the villages and burn the towns – in short, to subjugate Russia.[16]

In reality, matters were somewhat different. The idea that the Republic of Poland–Lithuania, with its modest military resources and creaking finances, could ever have contemplated 'occupying' or 'subjugating' the vastnesses of Russia is preposterous. The Polish commanders, and especially Żółkiewski, were consistently opposed to intervention; the Sejm was hostile towards intervention; and the King only gave way to intervention on two brief occasions.[17] The Poles were only able to intervene at all because powerful factions among the Muscovite boyars were pressing them to do so. And they had no clear plans about the future. Whatever modern Poles may care to believe to bolster their self-respect, there was never any war of conquest comparable to Napoleon's campaign of 1812. Polish operations amounted to nothing more than a series of minor adventures in a vast civil war.

In the early stages of the Troubles, the Republic as such played no part whatsoever. The first False Dmitri was privately managed by Jerzy Mniszek of Sambor, Wojewoda of Sandomierz. He was schooled by Polish Jesuits, who persuaded the King to receive him at court and to smile on their devious schemes for the sake of Faith. When, in 1605, like some latter-day Lambert Simnel, he had actually been crowned in Moscow as the long-lost son of Ivan IV, his marriage to Mniszek's daughter, Maryna (1588–1614), took place by proxy in Cracow. In Zamoyski's opinion, it was 'a comedy worthy of Plautus or Terence'. It ended when the remains of the murdered pretender, trampled to pulp by the Muscovite mob, were fired to the four winds from a cannon on Red Square.

Thereafter, the Second False Dmitri, the 'thief of Tushino', the Perkin Warbeck of the story, was adopted by yet another private consortium of Polish and Lithuanian adventurers including Alexander Lisowski, Prince Roman Rożyński, and Jan Sapieha, Starosta of Uświat. It was they who recruited the dowager Maryna to the altar once more, and whose unruly retainers laid siege to Moscow from their camp at Tushino. It was they who inspired the memorable memorial tablet at the Troitsko–Sergievskiy monastery at Zagorsk: 'THREE PLAGUES – TYPHUS, TARTARS, POLES.' Meanwhile, the Tsardom had been assumed by Prince Vasili Shuyski. Only at this point did the Polish Court begin to take an official interest. In the coup of 1606, at Shuyski's instigation, some five hundred Poles from Mniszek's entourage had been massacred in Moscow. Worse still, Shuyski was putting out feelers for an alliance with Charles IX of Sweden. Zygmunt III spurned the constitutional niceties and the advice of the Sejm and decided to march — 'for the glory of the Republic'. An expedition moved off in the autumn of 1609 under the command of the reluctant Żółkiewski. Its one precise aim was to recover the fortress of Smoleńsk. The siege was laid. But in the following July, after Żółkiewski's startling victory at Klushino, in which the combined Tsarist and Swedish armies were destroyed, unexpected developments occurred. Szujski was removed by a court rebellion. The Poles advanced to Moscow unopposed, and the assembled boyars invited Żółkiewski to protect them from the unbridled anarchy of the warring factions. In a treaty signed on 27 August, the boyars were to receive the rights and privileges of the Polish szlachta, whilst the King's son, Prince Władysław, was to be proclaimed Tsar. A Polish garrison under Alexander Gosiewski, Starosta of Wieliż, was installed in the Kremlin. All went by improvisation. With no precise instructions to hand, Żółkiewski was not to know that the King disapproved of his dispositions. Szujski was sent to Warsaw, to be paraded with his brothers in front of the Sejm before dying in detention at the castle of Gostyń. Both King and Żółkiewski returned to Poland. The predicament of the Polish garrison in the Kremlin deteriorated sharply. Isolated by the defection of their previous Russian sponsors, their efforts to defend themselves against the intrigues of one Lepunov, caused the Great Fire of 1611. The situation was described by Żółkiewski, whose *Beginnings and Progress of the Muscovite War* was written to justify his own conduct:

Anxious to execute his scheme for clearing our men out of the city . . . and in league with people in Moscow who were favourable to his enterprise, Lepunov called out the *Streltsy* quietly at night, and concealed them in the houses of accomplices. There were also many Muscovites friendly to us who gave warning . . . for Lepunov himself was approaching the city . . . and a strong force of boyars had been assembled. They were a mile or two from the capital when our men caught sight of them. Thereon, our men resolved among themselves to set fire to the wooden-town and to the district inside the White Wall: to shut themselves inside the Kremlin and in Kitaygorod: and to attack the *streltsy* and anyone else they met. On the Wednesday before Easter they did so. Having been drawn up and marched out by regiments, they set fire to the wooden-houses. The Starosta of Wieliż himself went out by the gate on the right side, onto the ice of the river: Pan Alexander Zborowski with his regiment was in the centre: Colonel Marian Kazanowski on the left toward the White Wall: Pan Samuel Dunikowski next to him. The first to be killed was Prince Andrew Galitzin, who up to that point had been under guard . . .

Although the Muscovites were shaken by our men's quick resolve and by the Fire, many of them sprang to arms, occupying the Gate and a great part of the White Wall. But Kazanowski attacked and drove them off . . . There was great slaughter among the press of human beings, and much weeping, with the cries of women and children, as at the Day of Judgement. Moreover, many men threw themselves into the flames together with their families, and were burned. Others decided to flee to the armies which they knew to be in the vicinity . . .

On Holy Thursday, there was a report that Prince Dimitr Trubetskoi and Prince Vasili Massalsky were approaching with the other boyars . . . The Starosta of Chmielnik, and Zborowski, having selected part of their regiments, went out to meet them. Our men joined battle with the Muscovites only one mile from the city, and routed the entire force.

So Moscow burned, with much bloodshed and incalculable loss, for it was a large and rich city of great circumference. Indeed those who have been in foreign lands say that neither Rome nor Paris nor Lisbon was so large. The Kremlin stood intact through everything; but Kitaygorod was robbed and plundered by the mob . . . The churches were not spared. The Church of the Blessed Trinity, which is held *in summa veneratione* by the Muscovites, and stands very marvellously constructed in the square almost in front of the Kremlin Gate, was stripped and plundered . . .[18]

After that, the die was cast. The boyars abandoned their thoughts of Polish protection, and widespread popular resistance began. Smoleńsk surrendered to the Poles after a two-year siege in June 1611. But in Moscow, the Polish garrison could not be saved, even by the approach of Chodkiewicz. Reduced to selling the Tsarist crown jewels for bread, they capitulated on 22 October 1612. Half of them were butchered on the spot. Four months later, the fifteen-year-old Michal Fyodorovitch Romanov, founder of the greatest Russian dynasty, was proclaimed Tsar. In Poland, the confederated army was demanding its back pay, and did not disperse till in 1614 it received a sixfold levy of the land-tax. A minor expedition, mounted in 1617–18 on Prince Władysław's personal initiative, achieved nothing. The Truce of Dyvilino, signed on 3 January 1619 for fourteen and a half years, left Smoleńsk, Siewiersk, and Czernihów to the Republic; Władysław undertook not to press his claim to the Tsarist throne. In terms of men killed and of money squandered, the Time of Troubles was almost as troublesome for the Republic as for Muscovy.

War with Muscovy was resumed in 1632, when a large Muscovite force attacked Smoleńsk. Inspired by the call of the *Ziemsky Sobor* for vengeance, it was led by Michal Borisovitch Sheyn — the same general who had defended the city so bravely twenty years before. On this occasion when he failed to get results, he was hanged as a traitor. The Eternal Treaty, signed on 14 June 1634 on the banks of the Polanovka River near Smoleńsk, repeated the territorial provisions agreed at Dyvilino. Władysław IV, now confirmed by election in his Polish inheritance, was pleased to accept 200,000 roubles for relinquishing his claim to Tsardom.

'Eternity' lasted only twenty years, however. In 1654, Moscow made its decisive bid for revenge. Tempted by the constant upheavals of the Ukraine, Tsar Alexi Mikhailovitch prepared his path by taking the Dnieper Cossacks under his protection. Then he attacked, and he kept attacking for the next twelve seasons. In this war, the Muscovites displayed that marvellous stamina which is one of the marks of their history. Despite a short break in 1657−8 occasioned by the activities of the Swedes, they kept their double-handed stranglehold on the Republic in place, both in Lithuania and in the Ukraine. At the Truce of Andrusovo, on 3 January 1667, they reversed the provisions of 1634 and took Kiev and the entire left-bank Ukraine under their control. These new terms were not confirmed till the next 'Eternal Treaty' of 1686, and were not ratified by the Republic until 1710. But for practical purposes, left-bank Ukraine became a dependency of Muscovy. The ancient Muscovite pretensions to view their Grand Duchy as an 'Empire of Russia' were rapidly gaining real substance.

Concurrent to the workings of the 'northern triangle', a 'southern triangle' was created by the presence of the Turks on the Black Sea coast. Here, the three sides of the arena were formed by the contiguous territories of the Republic, Muscovy, and the Ottoman Empire. In effect, the danger from this quarter rarely materialized. Preoccupied with their campaigns in the Danube valley and in Asia, the Turks usually left the fighting north of the Carpathians to their Crimean vassals. Year by year, throughout the Vasa period and beyond, the Crimean Tartars tried all the possible permutations in turn. They launched raids in the service of Muscovy against the Republic; raids in the service of the Republic against Muscovy; raids with the Cossacks or against the Cossacks; and raids on their own.[19]

The short Turkish War of 1620–1 was the only occasion between 1498 and 1672 when the Poles came into conflict with the main Ottoman Army directly, and that in consequence not of a Muscovite intrigue, but of a Transylvanian one. In 1618, Zygmunt III had sent some cavalry detachments to Vienna, to help his brother-in-law the Emperor against the attacks of Bethlen Gabor, Prince of Transylvania. It was Bethlen who intrigued with the Porte to stage a suitable response. In September 1620, Iskender-Pasha advanced against the Republic, and at Cecora on the Pruth inflicted a crushing defeat on the Poles, taking Hetman Koniecpolski into captivity and receiving the severed head of Żółkiewski on a pike. A year later, the fortunes of war were dramatically reversed. Sixty-five thousand Poles and Cossacks under Hetman Chodkiewicz and Ataman Sahajdaczny were surrounded in their camp at Chocim on the Dniester by an Ottoman army three times their number under the personal command of Sultan Osman II. Their fate appeared to be sealed. The scene, and the later action, was recorded in the Latin memoirs of Jakub Sobieski (1588–1646), Wojewoda of Ruthenia, which in due course served to inspire Wacław Potocki's, *Wojna chocimska* (The War of Chocim), perhaps the most celebrated epic poem in Polish literature:

> White gleamed the hills by the banks of the Dniester
> (Like land all covered with fresh-fallen snow),
> As the Turk drew close, and with marvellous speed
> Arranged his pavilions in endless array . . .
> When Osman looked down and viewed our lines,
> Like a ravenous lion baring his claws,
> With bristling mane and quivering tail,
> Hungry for gore, he eyed his prey
> Which lay like a bison stricken on the plain . . .
> In their midst, the *Janchar-aga* in peacock plumes
> Sent his fiery regiments to the fore;
> Astride his white Arabian steed,
> In cloak of gold beneath a canopy of feathers,
> Under the Ottoman *bunchuk* with its crescent moon,
> He blazed like a comet between the stars . . .
> Beside the janissaries, to left and right,
> We looked on wonders strange to our eyes,
> On fearsome elephants with trunks and pointed ivories:

Each bore thirty archers in lofty towers . . .
There stood the wondrous Moors, ranged in gloomy clouds.
Out of their swollen lips and faces black as pitch
Shined pearly tusks, as bright as ice,
Like the sparks that glitter on a charrèd log.
Here stood the Mamelukes in broad, white robes,
Scattered across the field like a flight of swans
Beside the ravens . . .
And as for ordnance, they had surrounded their camp
With cannon, which crowded the ditch and breastworks,
Thundering beyond belief. Chodkiewicz himself,
Our old commander, since he joined the trade of Mars
Had never seen such mortars, that shook the very ground
As they belched forth shot of wellnigh sixty pound.[20]

The pride of the Turks preceded a great fall. Incessant attacks
and bombardments throughout the month of September failed
to dislodge the defenders, who were said to have fought to
their last barrel of gunpowder. In October, like Tarnowski's
men at Obertyn, the Polish cavalry rode out to the counter-
attack and broke the will of the besiegers. The Sultan sued
for peace. Both sides realized that there was no real basis for
hostility. The Sejm, which had paid out a record eightfold
land-tax for the emergency, was persuaded to treat the Turks
with greater circumspection. The King and his adventurous
son were warned to avoid unnecessary military commitments.
Henceforth, having made peace with the Turks, they also
steered clear of the Thirty Years War, and left their Habsburg
relatives to their own devices.

Oddly enough, one of the most serious losses to the Republic
in Vasa times was inflicted not by enemy action but by the
diplomatic manœuvres of a slippery vassal. Ever since 1525,
the successors of Albrecht von Hohenzollern had sworn fealty
to the Polish Crown for their Duchy of (East) Prussia, and
had made annual contributions to the Crown Treasury and
Army. At the same time, they had pursued a policy of dynastic
aggrandizement of unrelenting single-mindedness. In 1563,
five years before his death, Duke Albrecht had arranged for
his co-enfeoffment together with Joachim II Hohenzollern of
Brandenburg-Anspach, thereby securing the reversion of the
fief within the family. In 1577, the Brandenburgers had bought

the wardship over Duke Albrecht's grandson from King Stefan Bathory, thereby establishing a regime which continued during their ward's long illness and insanity. This was the state of affairs inherited by the Vasas. Finally in 1614, Johann Sigismund of Brandenburg, who was married to the heiress of the Prussian line, succeeded in uniting both parts of the family's inheritance in his own person. Yet it was not until two generations later that Friedrich Wilhelm (1620–88), the Great Elector, could rise above mere provincial distinction. Thrust into responsibility as a youth of twenty, and swept from Berlin by the tides of the Thirty Years War, he cultivated his Polish connections and swore allegiance both to Władysław IV and to Jan Kazimierz. But in 1648 at the Treaty of Westphalia, he was emboldened by the grant of numerous small territories, including a sliver of Eastern Pomerania, and was encouraged to take an active part in the subsequent Northern War. In 1656 at the Treaty of Labiau, he persuaded the Swedes to recognize his claim to independent status as the price for deserting his Polish suzerain. A few months later, he persuaded the Polish negotiators to confirm his independence as the price for deserting the Swedes. Having obtained formal release from his feudal obligations to Poland at the Treaty of Wehlau (Welawa) on 19 October 1657, he then withheld his vote in the imperial election until the prospective candidate, Leopold of Austria, had released Brandenburg from its jurisdictional subordination to the Empire. Every step was immaculately timed so as to leave the new principality of Brandenburg–Prussia as one of the principal beneficiaries of the Peace of Oliwa. Two hundred years after the partition of the Teutonic State, the Great Elector restored Prussian sovereignty, largely at the expense of the Vasas' Polish kingdom.

* * * * *

In the last two decades of the Vasa Era, in the sorry reign of Jan Kazimierz, all the existing strands of internal and external conflict were suddenly twisted together into a web of strangulating complexity. Cossacks, Tartars, Muscovites, Swedes, Prussians, and Transylvanians were drawn one by one into a tightening mesh involving traitorous magnates, rebellious soldiers, religious dissenters, and international plotters. Jan Kazimierz himself was hardly to blame. He was a serious and dutiful monarch who succeeded his elder brother at the age of thirty-nine. Having served as a volunteer in the Habsburg Army, he was experienced in military affairs; and, as a Jesuit novice and aspirant cardinal, he was no stranger to the religious politics of the age. As a prisoner and hostage of the French, he knew the perils of international relations at first hand. Yet he had been personally associated with his brother's *rapprochement* with the French court, and was destined to accept his brother's French widow, Marie-Louise de Gonzagues, in marriage.[21] On the surface, all was set fair for a prosperous reign. Underneath, an eruption of volcanic proportions was brewing. It all began with the last and greatest of the Cossack rebellions, launched in the winter of 1647–8 by Bogdan Chmielnicki (1595–1657).[22] (See Map 19.)

The horrors and the pointless waste of the next twenty years were underlined by the fact that they followed one of the most temperate decades in the Republic's history. The shock was magnified by the preceding calm. Władysław IV, ruling since 1632, had contrived to stay aloof from most of Europe's troubles. The Peace of Polanów (1634) with Muscovy, and the Peace of Stumsdorf (1635) with Sweden, settled the main outstanding conflicts. The Vistula Trade flourished. Religious discord was soothed, and in 1635 the King invited the various denominations to reconcile themselves in a public 'conversation of love'. In the Ukraine after the pacification of 1638, there followed a golden decade of quiet. Such was the illusion of well-being that in his address to the Sejm in 1646 the Chancellor, Jerzy Ossoliński, could boast how 'the Poles have planted on our open plains a free kingdom which is bounded only by the wall of love and common trust between the estates.'

By this time, however, it was also known through Koniec-polski's spies that the Cossacks were treating with the Khan of Crimea. It was not considered unduly dangerous. Indeed, the King took it as a splendid opportunity for a final reckoning with the Tartars and with the preoccupied Turks. He called a delegation of Cossack leaders to Warsaw, among them Chmielnicki, drew them into his confidence, confirmed their

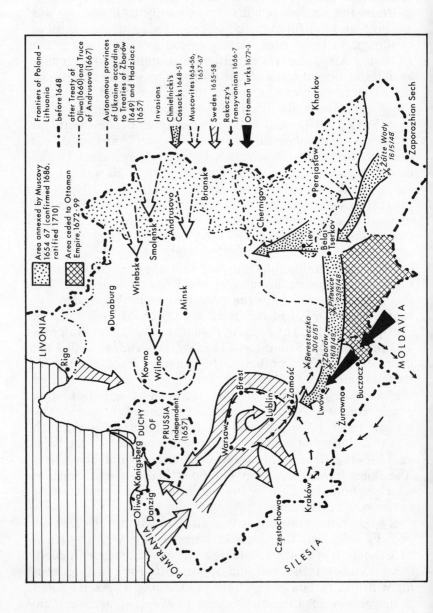

Frontiers of Poland –
Lithuania
before 1648
after 1648
after Treaty of
Oliwa (1660) and Truce
of Andrusovo (1667)
Autonomous provinces
of Ukraine according
to Treaties of Zborów
(1649) and Hadziacz
(1657)

Invasions
Chmielnicki's
Cossacks 1648-51
Muscovites 1654-56,
1657-67
Swedes 1655-58
Rakoczy's
Transylvanians 1656-7
Ottoman Turks 1672-3

Area annexed by Muscovy
1654-67 (confirmed 1686,
ratified 1710)
Area ceded to Ottoman
Empire, 1672-99

Kharkov

Zaporozhian Sech

Żólte Wody
16/5/48

Perejasław

Chernigov

Andrusovo

Smolensk

Brjansk

Kiev

Belai
Tserkov

Witebsk

Dunaburg

Minsk

Pilawce
23/9/48

LIVONIA

Riga

Kowno
Wilno

Bereszteczko
30/6/51

Zborów
16/8/49

MOLDAVIA

Zamość

Lwów

Buczacz

PRUSSIA
independent
(1657)

Brest

Żurawno

DUCHY
OF

Lublin

Warsaw

Königsberg

Oliwa
Danzig

Kraków

POMERANIA

Częstochowa

SILESIA

ancient privileges, and prepared them for a joint expedition against the infidels. What went wrong thereafter is not entirely clear. The King's Turkish expedition was opposed in the Sejm. Koniecpolski, the one man who might have led it with success, died. Jarema Wiśniowiecki, Wojewoda of Ruthenia, decided to lead it himself. In 1647, in defiance of both King and Sejm, and at the head of 26,000 men raised from his own plantations, he marched towards the Crimea. Chmielnicki was outraged, deeply betrayed by the abrogation of his agreement with the King. So, instead of joining the expedition to the Crimea, he attacked it. Instead of fighting the Tartars, he called them to his aid, and set off in search of justice.

The rebellion of Bogdan Chmielnicki produced effects far exceeding its original aims. Marching westward from the Cossack *sich* (their main camp or settlement) on the Dnieper, he won two signal engagements against the armies of the Republic, at Żółte Wody and at Korsuń, and approached the Vistula. He seems to have had no clear intention except that of pressing his grievances and those of the Cossacks on the King in person. In all his early correspondence, he signed himself under the title of 'Hetman of His Gracious Majesty's Zaporozhian Host'. But the sudden death of the King in May 1648 left him stranded, and his failure to reach agreement with Jan Kazimierz, whose election he had supported, obliged him to fight on. Meanwhile, the ungoverned Ukrainian provinces were ravaged by rampant peasant bands and by the savage reprisals of the magnates headed by Wiśniowiecki. These killings closed the door to compromise. On 29–30 June 1651 at Beresteczko, Chmielnicki was routed. Driven back towards the Dnieper, he looked round for assistance. Inevitably, his plight alerted the Muscovites, and in January 1654, at Perejasław, he swore an oath of allegiance to Tsar Alexei Michailovitch. That same Spring, the armies of the Tsar invaded the Republic on two fronts. In turn, the Muscovite invasion alarmed the Swedes. In 1655, the Swedish King, Charles X, descended on the Republic from Pomerania and Livonia. His operations provoked the intervention in 1656 of the Great Elector of Brandenburg–Prussia, followed in 1657 by George Rakocsi, Prince of Transylvania. These were the years of The Deluge. Towards the end of the decade, Poland's military fortunes revived. In May 1660 all fighting in the West was stopped by the Peace of Oliva, although in the east the Tsar continued to campaign.

The strains of incessant war caused internal inflammations. Attempts by the King to remedy constitutional and financial defects led first to conflict with the Sejm, and then to civil war. The nobility rejected proposals for majority voting, for an election *vivente rege* and for a central Treasury. Their leader Jerzy Lubomirski, Marshal of the Crown, was pushed into treasonable contacts with Austria, and eventually to open mutiny. From 1661–7, the King vainly confronted first the military leagues and then the armies of the *Rokosz*. At Mątwy, on the borders of Silesia, on 13 July 1666 he met defeat. The Crown forces were fought to a standstill. Jan Kazimierz resigned from his political plans, and received Lubomirski's submission. In 1667, Lubomirski left for voluntary exile in Breslau. In the east, at the Truce of Andrusovo, the Muscovites were able to strike a hard bargain. In 1668, Jan Casimir abdicated, and retired to France. What Chmielnicki had started, Lubomirski and the Tsar completed.

In this light, it may seem odd that historians have tried to connect Chmielnicki's Rebellion with contemporary events in England, France, and Spain.[23] Some maintain that he formed part of a vast international conspiracy. For that, beyond the fact that he is supposed to have visited Paris and to have corresponded with Cromwell, there is no evidence. Others relate him to some general 'European crisis'. Yet none of the suggested hypotheses can be made to fit all the events in question. The concept of a 'national rising' is apt enough for Portugal and Catalonia. It is largely irrelevant to the English Civil War and to the 'Fronde' in France. In the Republic, it is less convincing as an explanation of Chmielnicki's activities, than of widespread resistance in central and western parts to the Swedes. The concept of a 'social revolution', too, is problematical. In the case of the Republic it cannot be ignored completely. The peasantry of the Ukraine certainly did participate in the Rebellion whilst elsewhere they acted on their own accord in repelling the foreign invaders. Yet it seems they were inspired by Chmielniecki *malgré lui*. Neither the

Cossacks, nor the Tartars, nor the King, nor least of all the Tsar of Muscovy, had any intention of emancipating the serfs. It can be argued, of course, that the peasants rose in desperation against the inexorable advance of serfdom. If so, it must be admitted that their 'revolution' was a total failure. Despite the secession of the Ukraine, the progress of enserfment in Eastern Europe continued unabated. Perhaps in the concept of some generalized 'constitutional crisis of the modern state', one might find some threads of over-all relevance. As elsewhere, the relationship in the Republic between the central government and the peripheral regions was put to a severe test. The ancient representative institutions were incapable of resolving the torrent of new social and political problems. In the Republic, it was an obvious source of tension that the Cossacks were denied ennoblement, and that the Orthodox and Uniate bishops were excluded from the Senate. But here, if one accepts the constitutional theory, one is bound to relegate Chmielnicki's role to that of an angry passer-by who happened to blunder into the already tottering structure of the state by accident.

The destructive effects of the Rebellion are undeniable. For the Republic as a whole, it precipitated a process of decline which was never successfully reversed. For all the Republic's citizens, it provoked an orgy of destruction of life and property commensurate to that of the Thirty Years War in Germany. For the Jews and Protestants it brought bloodshed and persecution on an unprecedented scale. The scattered and defenceless Jewish settlements attracted the wrath not only of Chmielnicki's Cossacks and of the peasant bands, but also of the Tsar's army. The entry of the Muscovite soldiery into Wilno on 28 July 1655 was attended by the indiscriminate slaughter of its remaining inhabitants. The death-toll of some twenty thousand persons included a large proportion of Jews. The total number of Jewish casualties in the period 1648—56 has been put at 56,000; the over-all decrease in the Jewish community through death, flight, and destitution approached 100,000.

Chmielnicki's reputation largely derives from the scale of these catastrophes, rather than from any practical achievement. He is claimed by a number of competing interests. In

Ukrainian history, as 'Khmel'nyts'kyy', he appears as a pioneer of national liberation. In Soviet Russia, as 'Khmyel'nitskiy', he is remembered as a Moses who led his people's exodus from Polish bondage towards the great Russian homeland. In the Valhalla of Marxist and sociological heroes, he is presented as a champion of social conscience and protest. He was none of these things. He was a deserter from the army of the Republic where he had obtained the rank of *pisarz* or 'scribe', and the son of an officer who had fought at Chocim in 1621. He barboured a deep, personal, and understandable grudge against Jarema Wiśniowiecki, whose men had assaulted his property; and he gravitated to the *Sich* as the natural haven for all such fugitives and malcontents. Then, having failed to obtain redress by his initial resort to force, he had no alternative but to fight to the end. Otherwise, he would have been hanged as a traitor. The sparks of his resistance fired a conflagration whose spread he could not possibly have foreseen. Soon, in the Ukraine, his Cossacks would be fighting for their own survival against their Muscovite protectors. In 1657, by the Treaty of Hadziacz, their leaders sought to reincorporate the Ukraine into the Republic as an autonomous duchy. But it was too late. Their rebellion had so encumbered the Republic with other, more pressing problems, that it was unable to help. The Cossack horse, having thrown its Polish rider, was now to be bridled by a far more demanding master. And by that time, Chmielnicki himself was dead. Like the Polish insurrectionaries of the nineteenth century, Chmielnicki's main achievement was to have brought the problems of his homeland to the attention of the world at a time when they were largely ignored and neglected.

Ten years later in 1667, that other great rebel, Jerzy Lubomirski lay dying. He complained of a headache. 'Those that live by the head', he sighed, 'must die by the head.' It was a fitting comment on the state of the Republic to whose discomfiture he had so conspicuously contributed. This Republic, with its fine ideals of unanimity and personal freedom, was run on the most delicate understanding between king and citizens. If it was to work at all, it had to be led by intelligent men. It had no reserves of power, no means of coercing the unreasonable rebel. When intelligence gave way to brute force, it threatened to collapse. As with Lubomirski, a 'headache' could prove fatal.

In 1672, Jan Kazimierz died a lonely death in exile, in a monastery at Nevers-sur-Loire in Central France. His heart was preserved in a casket in St. Germain-des-Prés in Paris. His body was brought back to Cracow for burial. One of the few lasting reminders of his sorry reign were the coins minted in the 1660s by Boratini and Tymff. Each of these Masters-of-the-Mint had produced wonderful schemes for curing the Republic's ills at a stroke. Both turned out to be incompetents, if not plain swindlers, whose debased productions plagued everyday life for the next hundred years. Boratini obtained a royal licence to mint copper shillings worth one-third of a *grosz*. In 1660–6, he produced over 900 million of them, flooding the market and causing untold chaos. In succeeding years, the value of these *'boratynki'* slumped from 90 to the złoty, to 800. Tymff's scheme was to mint silver złoties, whose value was to be arbitrarily equated with that of the gold ducat. His coins contained only 13 of the stated 30 groszy's worth of pure silver. On the reverse side, they carried the King's monogram, I.C.R. – Iohannes Casimirus Rex. When people learned what their coins were really worth, the name of the last of the Vasas was taken as a symbol of corruption and debasement. Henceforth his initials were universally known in a new interpretation – I.C.R. – INITIUM CALAMI-TATIS REGNI: 'The Start of the Kingdom's Calamity.'[24]

CHAPTER FIFTEEN
MICHAŁ:
The Austrian Candidate (1669-1673)

The Wiśniowiecki (Vyshnyevyetskyy), the 'Lords of Cherry Village', possessed one of the most redoubted names of the Ukraine. The protoplast of the clan, Dymitr Wiśniowiecki (d. 1563), half Ruthenian, half Romanian, had founded the first Cossack *sich* at Chortyca on the Dnieper. He died on the hook in Istambul, having been captured by the Turks for piracy. His son signed the Union of Lublin. His grandson led the notorious expedition to Moldavia in 1616. His great-grandson, Prince Jarema Wiśniowiecki (1612−51), Wojewoda of Ruthenia, the chief enemy of Bohdan Chmielnicki, was one of the most colourful and controversial figures of Polish history. In that most popular of all Polish historical novels, *Ogniem i mieczemi* (By Fire and Sword) of Henryk Sienkiewicz, he appears as a rumbustious nobleman, fighting for the Republic and punishing the Cossacks and the Tartars with calculated severity. In the eyes of other commentators, he was a common bandit, a despoiler of widows, a turncoat, a traitor. Wherever the full truth may lie, one cannot deny that he was involved in some acts of sensational cruelty, and also that he was popular enough among his peers.[1] Over the previous century, the Wiśniowiecki family had amassed one of the great fortunes of the Republic, wrested from the virgin lands beyond the Dnieper, worked by some 230,000 serfs, and defended by one of the fiercest of private armies. In the prevailing circumstances, one might well have expected them to produce a challenger for the throne. No one would have expected them to produce a nonentity like Michał Korybut Wiśniowiecki (1640−73), Prince Jarema's son, the reserve candidate of an Austrian electoral intrigue, the un-witting pawn of ambitious supporters. This mountain of a family brought forth a royal mouse.

The reign of Michał Korybut lasted barely four years. In this time, a few salient events occurred in the Republic. First, in July 1669, the King was elected, virtually by mistake. Second, in July 1670 in celebration of the French party's defeat, he married the Archduchess Eleonora of Habsburg. Having greeted his bride on the Silesian frontier, he led the bridal party to the ancient cloister of Jasna Góra, where the wedding took place in the company of the Nuncio, the Empress, and the Senate. The wedding breakfast was recorded for posterity by the Nuncio with obvious relish:

After the singing of the *Te Deum* before the miraculous icon of Our Lady and to the strains of an orchestra, the young couple made their way with their retinues to a magnificently decorated suite of rooms in the monastery . . . At the banquet on the following day, the dishes were served in such abundance that it is hard to say whether they caused greater hardship for the servants who had to carry them than for the guests who had to contemplate eating them. The menu called for three hundred pheasants, five thousand brace of partridge, six thousand brace of turkeys, six thousand calves, four hundred oxen, four thousand sheep and at least as many lambs, one hundred stags, five salmon, two thousand hares, and several dozen wild boars. Afterwards, a great quantity of fruit and preserves was handed round, and at the end, tables were set out carrying sweets constructed into pyramids and colossi. Then, with the banquet finished, the King at the head of six Senators, and the Queen at the head of her ladies, launched into a Polonaise, making two complete circuits of the room . . .[2]

Third, later that year, the Prussian ambassador organized a raid in Warsaw to recapture a fugitive citizen of Königsberg called Kalkstein. Fourth, in 1672 the second Turkish war began with the invasion of Podolia by Sultan Muhammad IV. The fortress of Kamieniec Podolsk was captured, and its cathedral turned into a mosque. Fifth, on 16 October 1672, at Buczacz near Tarnopol, the royal envoys signed a treaty of capitulation. All districts of the Ukraine still left to Poland by the Truce of Andrusovo were signed away to the Turks. An annual tribute of 22,000 gold ducats was to be paid. Sixth, both meetings of the Sejm in this shameful year were cut short – once by the *Liberum Veto* and once by the voice of a determined lady. A certain Kunicka, who claimed to have been wronged by a Senator, entered the senatorial chamber of the Royal Palace in Warsaw to seek redress in person, and to demand execution of a court order providing for the surrender of her fugitive serfs. Angered by a long debate as to whether the king should be allowed to wear a French perruque in public, she launched into a tirade from the gallery:

Marshal of the Sejm: Don't interrupt, Dear Madam: we are taking counsel on the defence of the frontiers . . .
Pani Kunicka: What's the defence of the frontiers to me, when the conduct of Your Palatine there is worse than the Tartar Horde . . .?[3]

The offending Palatine was exposed, and paid 2,000 zł. *ex nunc* and surrendered one serf.[3] Seventh, the Austrian and the French factions among the nobility formed armed confederations to press their rival policies against the vacillating King.[4]

On all these occasions, the textbooks underline what the King did not do. He exercised no control over the magnates, the Army, the Turks, his wife, or the Nuncio. It is very difficult to learn how exactly he occupied his mind. He died on 10 November 1673 from a surfeit of gherkins, presumably in his prime.

CHAPTER SIXTEEN
SOBIESKI:
Terror of the Turk (1674-1696)

'Sobieski' is one of the very few names from Polish History to be widely known in the world at large. He has been eulogized by contemporaries and by historians alike. According to John Milton, he was 'the first of the Polanians to show that the terrible, main Battalion of the Turk might be broken at one stroke.' His military skill was specially praised by Clausewitz. A household word in Poland, he has been remembered throughout Europe as a king who saved the Empire and Christendom from the Infidel. For this very reason, it is not easy to discuss the face behind the mask of glory, or, more importantly, to describe the problems of a kingdom overshadowed by the feats of its king.[1]

* * * * *

Jan III Sobieski (1629–96) was born at Olesko, near Lwów, the second son of Jakub Sobieski, Wojewoda of Ruthenia, and of Maria Daniłłowicz. He received his Latin education at the Nowodworski Gymnazium in Cracow and at the Jagiellonian University, and in 1646–8 departed on a Grand Tour which took him to Paris, London, and Amsterdam. In 1652, on the death of his elder brother, he stepped into the combined inheritance of three great families – the Sobieski, the Żółkiewski, and the Daniłłowicz. But from early manhood he chose a military career; whilst his wealth and connections gave easy access to court, diplomacy, patronage, and politics. He first joined the army in 1648, and fought throughout the dozen years of Chmielnicki's Rebellion and the Swedish 'Deluge' under the orders of Jerzy Lubomirski and of Stefan Czarniecki. For seven months between August 1655 and March 1656, together with many deserted royal officers, he accepted a colonel's commission under Charles X. He first joined an embassy, to Constantinople, in 1654; was first presented at court in 1655; and was first elected as an envoy to the Sejm

473

in 1659. Thereafter his promotions succeeded each other in steady procession. In 1665 he received the wand of the Grand Marshal, in 1666 the dignity of the Field Hetman, and in 1668 the supreme military honour, the baton of the Grand Hetman of the Crown. In the reign of Michał Korybut, he spent his time warring against the Turks. His astonishing annihilation of an entire Ottoman Army under Hussein Pasha, on the site of Chodkiewicz's earlier victory at Chocim on the Dniester, occurred on the day following the King's death. Three months later, he entered Warsaw in triumph in the middle of the electoral Sejm, and was acclaimed King with very little opposition. With the exceptions of the battles of Batoh in 1652, where his brother Marek was killed, and of Mątwy in 1666, where he had faced his old patron and commander, Lubomirski, he had rarely known defeat. Few monarchs, and certainly no hereditary monarch, have ever acceded to the throne with so many advantages or such wide experience.

As with Bathory almost one hundred years before, the King's personality dominated political life to a remarkable degree. It was observed, admired, and described by the English divine, the Revd Robert South, who visited Poland in person:

The king is a very well spoken prince, very easy of access, and extreme civil, having most of the qualities requisite to form a complete gentleman. He is not only well versed in all military affairs, but likewise, through the means of a French education, very opulently stored with all polite and scholastic learning. Besides his own tongue, the Sclavonian, he understands the Latin, French, Italian, German and Turkish languages; he delights much in natural history, and in all the parts of physic. He is wont to reprimand the clergy for not admitting the modern philosophy, such as Le Grand's and Cartesius's, into the universities and schools.

As to what relates to his Majesty's person, he is a tall and corpulent prince, large-faced, and full eyes, and goes always in the same dress with his subjects, with his hair cut round about his ears like a monk, and wears a fur cap, but extraordinary rich with diamonds and jewels, large whiskers (i.e. moustaches) and no neck-cloth. A long robe hangs down to his heels in the fashion of a coat, and a waistcoat under that of the same length, tied close about the waist with a girdle. He never wears any gloves, and this long coat is of strong scarlet cloth, lined in the winter with rich fur, but in summer only with silk. Instead of shoes he always wears both abroad and at home Turkey leather boots with very thin soles, and hollow deep heels made of a blade of silver bent hoop-wise into the form of a half-moon. He carries always a large scimitar by his side, the sheath equally flat and broad from the handle to the bottom, and curiously set with diamonds.[2]

Sobieski's confidence was undoubtedly heightened by the rewards of an intense, unusually successful, and sometimes stormy marriage. For from 1665, he was married to the most sensational woman at Court — Marie-Casimire de la Grange d'Arquien, universally known in Poland as 'Marysieńka'. Their remarkable partnership can only be compared to that of their younger contemporaries, and equals in love, war, and politics — John Churchill, Duke of Marlborough, and Sarah Jennings.

In its own way, the personality of Marysieńka (1641—1716) was equally remarkable, and equally active at the centre of the web of politics. She had come to Poland at the age of four, in the suite of the French Queen, Marie-Louise. She was the daughter of a Captain in the French Guard and of the Queen's former governess (although rumour hinted that she was really the Queen's bastard by one of her former lovers, Gaston d'Orleans or the unlucky Cinq-Mars). Throughout their married life, she was Sobieski's intimate companion, the confidante of his deepest thoughts, the inspiration of his prowess. Yet to the end, she exercised the right of feminine caprice, and an intriguing mind of her own. She had known Sobieski since her girlhood, but she did not betray any personal interest in him until she was married at the age of twenty to the ageing Jan Zamoyski, grandson of the former Chancellor. Thereafter, their relationship developed into a 'grande affaire' within the 'Grande Affaire' of Jan Kazimierz's French court. They were secretly married in May 1665 before the body of her late husband was buried, on the painful condition that Sobieski accept the office of Marshal from the deposed Lubomirski. They had several children; both sons and daughters, whose interests were invariably interpreted by the Queen in an opposite manner from the King. Most inte-restingly from the historian's viewpoint, whenever public affairs kept them apart they conducted a lengthy cor-respondence. Sobieski's marvellous *Listy do Marysieńki* (Letters to Marysieńka) constitute a prime source for his career. Through the welter of Gallicisms, and of conspiratorial pseudonyms — among which for 'Celadon' read Sobieski, and for 'Astrée' read Marysieńka — it is possible to enter into the King's innermost feelings:

c. 14 VII 1665

Mon cœur, mon âme et mon tout!

Having ridden throughout the night we halted at the very dawn, just a third of a mile now from His Majesty the King and the army. *M. Palatin de Cracovie* will probably join us tomorrow for he is just four miles from His Majesty [the King]. There are very few mounted regiments with the King and [there is] no sign of the newly hired mercenaries. All my troops, graceful God, were here and they have already sworn their allegiance to the King. There was news that Lubomirski has already passed Szczebrzeszyn; I think then that all this will not now go on for long. We shall soon see God's design.

We have suffered unbelievable *incommodité* on the way without any provisions whatsoever. Such barrenness it is impossible to imagine. I do not know for the life of me nor can I imagine what we can possibly eat here in the camp. I hope to see His Highness the King in three hours and derive fresh information.

My servants have forgotten my black travelling chest without which I am as a man without an arm. Seek out an occasion and send it on to me as soon as possible, by the Duke of Leipzig unless he has already left. I have the keys.

I remain as I have been throughout the journey in great melancholy sustained by those words of Astrée on our separation when she promised to reward that unslept night with love, which I entreat you to bear in your memory. Celadon has well merited that he be loved and endowed with *complaisance* from time to time. He, if God grants his health improve, will strive with every means to seek no greater or more loved beauty than that of his Aurore to whom, kissing a millionfold, he bids farewell and swears that while there is life in his body he will be her most faithful servant and that which God has wished him to be.

Thank the Master of the Royal Hunt for the horses and for all his favours without which I should have been severely *mal accomodé*. I undertake to repay his every convenience.[3]

In Sobieski's style, which impressed itself so firmly on the conduct of public affairs, the 'oriental tradition' held pride of place. Sobieski belonged to a fraternity of magnates from the south-eastern provinces whose interests, training, and attitudes were quite distinct. Especially in the seventeenth century, these easterners were preoccupied with the problems of the adjacent Ottoman world to a degree which in Warsaw, Cracow, or Danzig would have appeared obsessive. What is more, by virtue of their exceptional landed fortunes, unrivalled in any other part of the Republic, and of their vast private military establishments, they were able to impose their own concerns on the political life of the state as a whole. Perhaps the best example of this class was Tomasz Zamoyski (1594–1638), Wojewoda of Kiev, and briefly, like his more illustrious father, Crown Chancellor. Having acquired vast estates in the region of Bracław, he was trained from childhood in oriental affairs. A friend of the Crimean Khan, Izlam Girej, who had spent a period of captivity at Zamość, he had a fluent command of Turkish, Tartar, Arabic, and Persian. He turned his father's Academy into a centre of oriental studies under its learned rector, Jan Iwaszowicz, and Zamość itself, with its Armenian and Jewish colonies and its Persian carpet manufactory, into a hub of the eastern trade. He was the father of Marysieńka's first husband.[4] Sobieski grew up in similar surroundings. He was born in a thunderstorm during a Tartar raid. His maternal grandfather, Hetman Żółkiewski, and his brother, were both beheaded on the battlefield by Tartars; and his uncle, Stanisław Daniłłowicz, died in Tartar captivity. He could not but be profoundly affected by the family vault at Żółkiew, and its tombs of heroes, and its inscription: *O quam dulce et decorum est pro patria mori.* In 1653, he voluntarily submitted himself as a hostage in Bakhchisaray; in 1654, he was in Istanbul; in 1657, he commanded the Republic's Tartar auxiliaries. No one was more experienced in, or fascinated by the ways of the East than he. The oriental tradition manifested itself in many forms. It inspired an exaggerated awareness of the Republic's Catholicity, justifying anything and everything in terms of the defence of Christendom. It inspired the fashionable dress and manners of the day, making Turkish saddles, Tartar haircuts, and Persian rugs part of the equipment of any self-respecting nobleman. It encouraged a conservative outlook on social problems, stressing the individual's necessary submissiveness to Divine Will and to an unchanging social order. It confused the direction of foreign affairs by neglecting developments in Muscovy, Scandinavia, and Prussia, and by interpreting the Republic's interest exclusively in terms of the Muslim menace. Most significantly, it assumed that war prosecuted habitually and unremittingly, was the chief and proper means of asserting the integrity and honour of the state.

Military affairs loomed large, therefore, partly from the King's natural inclinations and partly from the pressure of external events. As from 1676, both the organization and the equipment of the army were reformed. In the infantry, the number of pikemen was drastically reduced; the musketeers were rearmed with short axes, which served simultaneously as musket stands. In the cavalry, the dragoons were enlarged; the Cossack regiments were issued with chain mail, being classified thereafter as 'armoured cavalry'; the light Tartar Horse was issued with short lances. Special attention was paid to the mobility of the artillery. All these changes were intended to provide fuller support for the strike-force of heavy Hussars — Sobieski's favourite department, and the agent of all his greatest victories. The defensive arms — of engineers, sappers, and siege-layers — tended to be neglected. The army establishment had been fixed since the reign of Jan Kazimierz at 12,000 men for the Crown and 6,000 for the Grand Duchy. It was now raised to 36,000 and 18,000 respectively, within the framework of the permanent cadres. Great emphasis was laid on the contributions of the magnates' private armies. In this, Sobieski led by his own example, dispensing his personal fortune in the service of the state without hesitation. He belonged to a class who mistrusted the growth of state power and counted more on the loyalty and generosity of wealthy noblemen. As a result, little was done to improve the system of military finance. Expenses were assigned to the provinces in proportion to their capacity to pay. Taxes were often collected with considerable delay. Responsibility for detailed supervision fell to the dietines. By virtue of his personality, Sobieski was able to inspire the Republic to unparalleled efforts, in short bursts. But he left the outdated machine virtually exhausted. In due course, after two decades of overuse, it failed to respond. At the end of the reign, unpaid soldiery constituted a generalized plague in many provinces.[5]

In origin, the Turkish War was not of Sobieski's making, although he was closely involved from the start. It had been launched by the Turks as part of their strategic encirclement of the Habsburgs, and in response to Wiśniowiecki's Habsburg marriage. After Chocim, when Sobieski's victory redeemed the shame of Buczacz, fortunes were evenly balanced. In 1674–5, the King was hardly seen in Warsaw, and the royal coronation was repeatedly postponed. The Turkish siege of Lwów was broken. The fortress of Trembowla was saved by the courage of the commander's wife who threatened to kill herself if he proceeded with his intention of surrendering. So long as these dangerous operations were in progress, Sobieski's policy was paralysed. Yet in 1676, both sides showed signs of exhaustion. The Polish army was locked in its armed camp at Żórawno on the Dniester by the overwhelming forces of Ibrahim Sheytan, who none the less, was unable to break their skilful resistance. On 24 September, a truce was signed, leaving most of the Turkish gains intact. A Polish embassy under Jan Gniński was dispatched to the Porte in the hope of securing lasting peace. (See pp. 364–5.)

Once the initial Turkish invasion was under control, however, Sobieski turned to France. Ever since his marriage, he had been closely associated with the French party at Court. In 1666, he had been offered the baton of a Marshal of France by Louis XIV, and in 1672 at the head of the French-backed Confederation of Szczebrzeszyn he had prepared to do battle against the pro-Habsburg Confederates of Gołębie. So, in many ways, a French alliance was the natural step for him to take. It meant that the Republic would be tied to the anti-Habsburg combination of France–Sweden–Turkey–Hungary; but it offered many advantages. It put the French diplomatic service at Poland's disposal in the search for a Turkish peace, and in the lingering negotiations with Moscow; it promised to offset the manœuvres of the Habsburg faction in the Republic's internal affairs; and it opened the way for an expedition to re-establish Polish suzerainty over Prussia. For their part, the French would be delighted to establish an eastern base from which they could direct operations in Hungary, and against Vienna. The Treaty was signed at Jaworów on 11 July 1675. Sobieski was to receive a French subsidy of 200,000 thalers to mount an expedition against Brandenburg–Prussia as soon as the Turkish campaign was terminated. A *rapprochement* was to be arranged with Sweden.

The French were to be allowed to establish contacts with the Hungarians from the Republic's territory. Sobieski had brought the Republic into the main tangle of European politics. He seemed to have made a firm choice on the position to be adopted in the Franco-Imperial struggle. He was immediately regarded as the Sun King's chief lieutenant in the east, and established contacts with Francophile parties all over Europe. He wrote to Charles II in England and invited him to be godfather to his newly born daughter. (See pp. 372–4.) In 1677, he signed a convention with the Swedes at Danzig.[6]

The calculations of 1675 soon proved to be ill-founded. Many of the pieces required for the proposed French gambit were shown to be seriously out of place. To start with, the invincible Swedish Army which had advanced southwards out of Livonia, was soundly trounced by the Prussians at Fehrbellin, and was chased back to Riga. This made the chances of success for the prospective Polish expedition against Prussia very bleak indeed. Secondly, the Porte refused to make peace. Gniński's embassy was a failure. Thirdly, Moscow succeeded where Gniński failed. A Turko-Muscovite treaty was signed in 1677. Any Polish involvement in Prussia, or against Austria would run the risk of a stab in the back from Muscovy. Fourthly, the excesses of the French party in Poland threatened to revive the armed confederations in 1672. The new Grand Hetman, Dymitr Wiśniowiecki, was hatching a plot with Vienna to remove Sobieski. Fifthly, the Sejm refused to ratify the Treaty of Jaworów. Hence the King's policy was already seriously undermined before it collapsed completely. In 1679, Louis XIV made his peace with the Emperor at Nyjmegen, and signed a treaty with Prussia without reference to Poland. At Kurfurst, the Prussians defeated the Swedes for a second time. Sobieski was humiliated, isolated, and furious. From this point on, he smiled on the Imperialist camp in Poland, as French influence waned. The Turks under their new Grand Vizier, Kara Mustafa, were known to be yearning for a new round of the Holy War. In 1683, after four years of wavering, the die was cast. As the Turkish horde prepared to move swiftly out of Belgrade on the shortest road to Vienna, the French ambassador in Warsaw was discovered in treasonable correspondence, and had to be expelled. When the Emperor

Leopold II appealed for urgent help, Sobieski was well disposed. On 1 April an agreement of mutual assistance was signed with the Imperial ambassador, Count Waldstein. Sobieski was to receive a subsidy of 1,200,000 ducats to send a relief expedition to Vienna, and was promised the appointment of Commander-in-Chief of the allied forces if he attended the siege in person. The official document was antedated to 31 March to avoid the stigma of April Fool's Day.[7]

Vienna's plight in the summer of 1683 rapidly grew desperate. The Turks came on much faster than the allies, and laid siege in the middle of July with a force of some 140,000 men. The defenders under Rudigen von Starhemberg were obliged to lock themselves inside an encircled city. The Emperor withdrew his Court to Linz. For Sobieski the prospect was invigorating. It was a situation he had faced before on many occasions, against an enemy whose every move he knew by heart. An autumn canter across the Carpathians, expenses paid, to relieve the capital of Christendom was irresistible.

The Polish expeditionary force began to assemble at Cracow in mid-summer. The royal camp gradually filled with 26,000 men and 29,000 horses — 25 regiments of Hussars; 77 troops of Cossacks; 31 of Light Horse; 2 of arquebusiers; 37 regiments of infantry, and 10 of dragoons; and the Corps of Artillery. A much smaller force of 10,000 men was dispatched to Podolia to create a diversion on the Turkish flank. The Lithuanians with a further ten thousand were ordered to make for a rendezvous in Moravia. The main army moved off on 29 July in two columns. One under Hetman Jabłonowski marched on a northerly route to Silesia through Tarnowitz (Tarnowskie Góry), Ratibor (Raciborz), and Troppau (Opava); the other under the Field Hetman Michał Sieniawski went through Bielsko (Bielitz) and Teschen (Cieszyn). Joining together at Olomütz, they made for Nikolsburg, and for Tulln on the Danube, where they were due to meet the German princes under Charles of Lorraine. Eight thousand wagons with food for six months rumbled on at fifteen miles a day. From Brno, Sobieski wrote to Marysieńka:

A mile Beyond Brno, in the village of Modric,
29 VIII 1683, Before midnight.

There have been no remarkable occurrences since my last from Olomouc. We hear no more of Tokoly; and the Tartars have disappeared without a trace. Once we have crossed the bridge, those who are to follow must exercise caution, and make a wide detour from the direct road to Vienna. I urge this particularly upon the Palatine of Pomerania who bears about him my monies from the Prince-Bishop of Warmia. From there it is only thirteen miles to Vienna. The Marshal of the Court intercepted me with the post the other side of Brno. There, too, I encountered the former Princess of Holstein, who had attended Queen Eleanore, and several other ladies-in-waiting. She is married to the Duke of Lichtenstein, whose boorishness is among his lesser vices. I confess that she is so altered that we who knew her formerly can scarce persuade ourselves that it is indeed she, — so fat and tall, just like Mme. l'Etreux.

I heard Holy Mass at the Franciscan church in Brno. It was a time of Indulgence, and the establishment of the feast of St John the Baptist, whose martyrdom is celebrated today. The town is beautiful and well-walled; the castle on its high hill is particularly notable — a great fortress. As for the country, there is nothing to equal it in the world: — the soil surpassing that of the Ukraine: the hill-sides strewn with grape vines that cover the houses like peach-blossom: more hayricks in the fields than one might ever hope to see. Tomorrow, God willing, I shall join with the Palatine of Volhynia, and, the following day, with the Duke of Lorraine, whom the Marshal of the Court describes as short, *gros, sans mine,* melancholic, humourless and pock-marked. He dresses like a pauper in a torn and shabby gown, and a hat with neither feather nor ribbon, which is battered and greasy — in other words a good natured fellow, of some intelligence, but taciturn, shy, and quite evidently afraid of transgressing court protocol. I lunched today in Brno with one Kolowrat, Governor of the province, who once represented the emperor at the Treaty of Oliwa. He entertained us with style — quite in the French manner. I have told the Palatine of Ruthenia to follow me with the Hussars and the rest of the army, keeping the infantry in the rear.

As I write the Duke of Lorraine's ensign has hurried in with letters. He sends me a message from Starhemberg, the commandant of Vienna, written on the 27th. They request assistance urgently, for the enemy already occupies the same ravelin with them, and is digging tunnels beneath the bulwark called *Burgbastei.* Our own sappers can feel it as they dig their counter-mines. He adds that the Vizir has pushed almost his entire army into the siege trenches in preparation for some major action; and we have still not put up a bridge. Almost all the armies of the Princes and Electors will have gathered by tomorrow; but those of

Brandenburg will not arrive in time. We do not know why the Turks are trying so insistently to repair the bridges which the Duke of Lorraine burned down near Vienna, together with the entrenchments which he had destroyed there. He tells us that he has again sent in a thousand infantry to that area.

Tomorrow, God willing, we expect to hear Vienna's guns, and the day after that to drink the Danube's waters. If Dumont has arrived, please send on to me what he has brought at the earliest opportunity. Let me know what news there is of the Cossacks, and hurry them on after me, having taken Mężyński to task for his dalliance. Tell me also what has happened to the Lithuanians, who are my greatest problem, for they do not need them here at all and constantly plague me about it. Everyone wants them to go into Hungary, and at least to create some kind of diversion for the enemy in recognition of the money that has been paid them.

Since our parting I have not had the slightest indication of your health, my Love. Although many people arrive from those parts, my ill-fortune is such that none has travelled along the road where he might have met you. I kiss you, embracing with my whole heart and soul all the beauties of your sweetest body. *Mes baisemains a M. Le Marquis et a ma sœur.* I kiss and embrace the children, and send them my love.[8]

Next day, Sobieski took command of the combined relief force of 74,000 men. The Poles distinguished themselves in building a pontoon bridge across the racing waters of the Danube, and in hauling their artillery into position over the slopes and dense vegetation of the Vienna Woods. The day of reckoning was fixed for 12 September.[9] As always, accounts differ as to who was really responsible for the victory. German historians used to draw attention to the role of Charles of Lorraine and his successful action on the left wing beneath the peak of the Kahlenberg; Polish historians stress the role of the Polish artillery which repulsed a Turkish counter-attack in the middle of the afternoon. At all events, it fell to Sobieski and his winged Hussars to mount the spectacular charge in a small valley on the right flank, and to drive the Infidel from Central Europe for good. He called the attention of his Captain of Hussars, Zbierzchowski, to the huge white expanse of the Grand Vizier's tent, and ordered him to ride straight for that. At half-past five, with Zbierzochowski at his side, he was galloping through the Sultan's camp amid scenes of panic, confusion, and slaughter. The following night, from the Grand Vizier's tent which he now used as his headquarters, he wrote again to Marysieńka:

In the Grand Vizir's Camp
13 IX (1683) at night
Only solace of my heart and soul, my fairest, most beloved Marysieńka!

Our Lord and God, Blessed of all Ages, has brought unheard of victory and glory to our nation. All the guns, the whole camp, untold spoils have fallen into our hands. Having covered the trenches, the fields, and the camp with corpses, the enemy now flees in confusion. The camels, mules, cattle and sheep, which he kept nearby are only today being rounded up by our troops, who also drive herds of Turks before them. Others, particularly *des renégats,* flee to our camp of their own accord, mounted on fine horses and in beautiful dress. Such is the unbelievable nature of events that there was alarm today both among the townspeople and here in our camp, no-one being able to think or believe that the enemy would not return. There is enough powder and ammunition alone for a million men. This past night I saw also what I had always longed to see. Our marauding bands put light to the powder in several places; it seemed as if Judgement Day was upon us but no harm was caused. We watched the smoke forming clouds in the sky. Yet it is most unfortunate that there should have been such wasteful destruction.

The Vizir took such hurried flight that he only had time to escape with one horse, and in the clothes he wore. I have indeed succeeded him, for the greater part of his riches have fallen to me. Chance would have it that being first in the camp and close on the Vizir's heels, one of his servants betrayed his allegiance and pointed out his tents. They are as extensive as the cities of Warsaw or of Lwów within their walls. I have all his personal insignia which were borne before him, and the Mahometan banner which his Emperor gave him for the war, and which even today I sent in the care of Talenti to the Holy Father in Rome. I have all the tents, cars *et mille d'autres galanteries fort jolies et fort riches, mais fort riches* and a vast array of other things still unseen. *Il n'y a point de comparaison avec ceux de Chocim.* Several quivers, studded with rubies and sapphires, are alone worth several thousand gold zloties. You will not be able to say to me as the Tatar women do to their husbands when they return empty-handed: 'You are no warrior to return without booty', because he who captures booty must be at the front. I have the Vizir's horse with all its caparison. He himself was hotly pursued but managed nonetheless to escape. His *kihaj*, that is, his second-in-command, was killed, and no small number of his pashas. Gold swords and other military equipment lie in abundance. The night prevented a conclusion. Furthermore, in retreating they put up a fierce opposition *et font la plus belle retirade du monde.* They abandoned their janissaries in the trenches, who were put to the sword during the night because such was their arrogance and pride that whilst some of them were fighting us in the fields, the others were storming the town, as indeed they had the equipment to do.

I estimate their numbers, excluding the Tatars, at some three hundred thousand: others put the numbers of their tents alone at three hundred thousand and take an average of three to one tent, which would make an unheard of total. However, I reckon there to be no more than one hundred thousand tents, distributed in several camps. For a day and two nights anyone who cares has been dismantling them, but I warrant they will not pull them down in a week. They left behind them a mass of innocent local Austrian people, particularly women; but they butchered as many as they could. Bodies of dead women lie in great numbers; but there are also many wounded, and those who might yet live. Yesterday I saw a three-year old child, a most pretty little boy, whose face and head had been savagely slashed by an infidel.

The Vizir had captured a marvellously beautiful ostrich from one of the Emperor's palaces here; but this too he had killed so that it would not fall into our hands. What luxuries he had surrounding his tents it is impossible to imagine. He had baths; he had a garden and fountains; rabbits; cats; and a parrot which kept on flying about so that we could not catch it.

Today I was in the city, which could have held out five more days, no more. Eyes have never seen things such as the mines have done there; the fortified towers, enormous and high, stand like craggy skeletons and are so damaged that they could survive little longer. The Emperor's palace is completely ruined by shot.

All the armies which gave such good account of themselves give praise to God and ourselves for this victory. When the enemy began to retreat and allowed himself to be broken – the Vizir, with whom it fell to me to do battle, turned his entire forces against my right wing, leaving our middle, or mainguard, and the left wing with nothing to do. As a result, they sent me all their German reinforcements. The Princes, such as the Elector of Bavaria and Prince Waldeck, rushed up to me clasping me around the neck and kissing me on the mouth. The generals did like-wise on my hands and feet. What then the soldiers! The officers and all the cavalry and infantry regiments cried out: '*Ach, unzer brawe Kenik!*' They listened to me as our soldiers never do. I dare not speak of the delight of the Princes of Lorraine and Saxony this morning (I did not have occasion to see them yesterday, since they were on the extreme of my left wing where I had sent the Marshal of the Court several squadrons of Hussars) nor of Stahremberg, who is commandant here. They all embraced me, congratulated me, called me their saviour. Afterwards, I went to two churches. All the common people kissed my hands, feet, clothes; others only touched me saying: 'Ach, let us kiss so valiant a hand!' They all wished to cry *'Vivat'*, but it was plain that they feared their officers and superiors. One group could not refrain from doing so, however, and I saw that it was looked on disapprovingly. Therefore, having dined with the commandant, I left the city to return to camp. The people, waving all the time, accompanied me to the very gates . . . It is said that when the Vizier realised he could not hold out against us, he called his two sons to him, and having embraced them, exclaimed in tears to the Tartar Khan, 'Save me if you can'. But the Khan replied, 'We know the King of Poland well. He is irresistible. Let us consider rather how best to escape.' . . .

I am preparing to ride into Hungary, and hope, as I said when I left you, that we will meet at Stryc . . . The princes of Bavaria and Saxony are ready to accompany me to the end of the world. We shall have to quicken our pace for the first couple of miles on account of the unbearable stench of dead men, horses and camels. I have written to the King of France. I told him that it was he, the Most Catholic Monarch, who should receive my report on the battle won for the safety of Christendom. Our son, *notre Fanfan,* is brave in the highest degree.[10]

When Sobieski posted the green standard of the Prophet to the Pope, he appended a suitably terse message: VENI, VIDI, DEUS VINXIT. (I came, I saw, God conquered.) Then he rode off in pursuit. On 7–9 October at Parkany, near Estergöm, the Turkish rearguard was destroyed. Hungary lay open to reconquest. The memories of Varna and Mohaćs were expunged. Europe was saved.

It would be wrong to say that the taste of victory soon turned sour. Such is the nature of victory that its aftermath always comes as an anticlimax. Yet it is undeniable that Sobieski's exploitation of his victory was markedly inferior to his performance on the battlefield. In one view, his great mistake was not, as some historians maintain, to have joined the relief of Vienna in the first place. It was hardly in the Republic's interest to see any further extension of the Turks' empire, when already, as one envoy in the Sejm put it, 'the Pasha of Buda could easily spy out Cracow from his perch in the mountains'. At its nearest point, the boundary of Ottoman power had reached to within forty miles of the old Polish capital. The deflation of the Ottoman bubble, and the tremendous psychological uplift which ensued, were obviously to the Republic's advantage. Sobieski's great mistake, having achieved his triumph, was to commit himself in 1684 to the subsequent wars of the Holy League. The cost was enormous; and the dividend accrued almost exclusively to the Republic's neighbours and enemies. Seventeen years of campaigning exhausted the Republic almost beyond repair, and prevented any serious attention to internal reform. Not just the Prussian expedition, but the whole question of the Republic's standing in the Baltic area, was forgotten. The crucial problem of the eastern frontier, and of the Republic's relations with Muscovy, was trivialized. In 1686, at the whim of one wayward ambassador, the entire Ukraine, provisionally assigned to Muscovy since the truce of 1667, was needlessly abandoned. This one step, which more than any other marked the transformation of little Muscovy into 'great Russia' and tipped the scales of power in Eastern Europe in Moscow's favour, was taken casually, and accepted apathetically. How the Kremlin must have rocked with amazement at this free gift! How much saner was their own policy of joining the ranks of the Holy League only when their possession of the Ukraine had been confirmed. From 1686, the Muscovites were fighting the Turks to some real purpose; the Poles were fighting for nothing. The eventual recovery of Podolia at the Treaty of Karlovitz in 1699 was small compensation. By that same treaty, an enlarged Russia and a resurgent Austria emerged as major powers; Prussia was poised to declare itself a Kingdom. The framework of eighteenth-century politics in this part of the world was already constructed. The Republic of Poland–Lithuania and the Ottoman Empire were clearly recognizable as the two invalids of Europe. The prospect of the Partitions came suddenly into view. All was not yet lost. But it would need a new Sobieski, and a new Murad the Conqueror, to retrieve the game. (See pp. 364–6, 376, 377–8).

Sobieski's powerlessness was reflected in the sorry condition of Lithuania. In the 1670s, the Grand Duchy had been overrun by magnates of the Habsburg faction, and in the 1680s fell under a regime of terror instituted by the all-powerful Sapieha clan. Nothing that happened thereafter could reconcile them to the King or reintegrate them into the political life of the Republic. In 1683, Kazimierz Jan Sapieha deliberately delayed the march of the Lithuanian army, and arrived in Austria after Vienna was relieved. He sent his troops on a merciless devastation of Slovakia, which obstructed Sobieski's efforts to reach an understanding with the Hungarians. The Lithuanian troubles spilled over into the Republic as a whole. The Sejm was repeatedly broken by the *Liberum Veto*. The provincial dietines usurped the rights of taxation and recruitment, and under the rod of local magnates raised regiments and taxes of their own. The Hetmen used royal troops for their private purposes. In the 1690s, hordes of unpaid soldiery took the law into their own hands. The spread of anarchy was unmistakable, providing a foretaste of things to come.

Deprived of any firm control of the state, the King, too, immersed himself in his private business. The 'gentleman monarch' became an avid dynast. His participation in the later campaigns against Turkey, and in particular in the Moldavian expeditions of 1687 and 1691, was mainly motivated by a desire to ensure a royal future for his son, Jakub. Inevitably, perhaps, he stirred up ancient factions at the court, and precipitated fierce rows with Marysieńka. Jakub's marriage caused endless difficulties. In 1681, a major uproar was caused when Jakub's fiancée, Charlotte Radziwiłł, suddenly opted to marry Ludwig von Hohenzollern, Prince of Prussia. In 1683–4, negotiations were well advanced for a betrothal with a Transylvanian princess, when the Habsburgs took offence and threatened an open breach. So, by a process of elimination, it seemed that a Habsburg bride would .be the best solution. But this so offended Marysieńka, that she opposed all plans for her son's accession to the Polish throne. The King's physical deterioration mirrored the state of public affairs. His muscular body turned to fat, assuming gross proportions. A series of severe heart attacks from 1691 onwards pointed to a constant convalescence and the likelihood of sudden disaster. Life at Wilanów was well suited to Sobieski's circumstances. Built in 1681–6 by Locci, as a summer residence on the southern outskirts of Warsaw, the palace was elegant and practical. Significantly, it was much smaller in Sobieski's time than in the eighteenth century when remodelled to magnatial taste by the Sieniawski and Potocki families. It served as a base for the King's hunting parties, and as a refuge from court and politics. It was surrounded by an Italian baroque garden, and adorned with sculptures and paintings by Schlüter, Siemiginowski, Callot, and Palloni. Its library was stocked with books, especially the King's favourite subjects of law, astronomy, militaria, and mathematics, and was used as a writing room for his correspondence with scientists such as Hevelius and Leibniz. One glimpse at Wilanów reveals a great deal about Sobieski and his kingdom.[11] He lived to the end of his days in the style of a wealthy nobleman, of a private citizen rather than a monarch. He had none of the ambition of a Louis XIV, none of the vision which inspired other contemporaries and neighbours like Peter the Great or Frederick William the Great Elector. He was a warrior, with all the instincts and limitations of his trade. He did his duty with a touch of bravado, and left it at that. He died a disillusioned old man. When Bishop Załuski urged him to draw up his will, he replied indifferently: 'They don't want to listen to me when I'm alive, so why should they obey my wishes when I'm dead?' A final heart attack put an end to the old champion on 17 April 1696.

*   *   *   *   *

Although Sobieski's dynastic schemes misfired, his descendants did not escape the royal touch completely. His son, Jakub Sobieski, was not elected; but his grandchild, Clementina Sobieska (1702–35), Jakub's daughter, helped found an extraordinary line of British pretenders, the Sobieski–Stuarts. The acquaintance of the two ex-royal families, Polish and Scottish, began in Rome where Marysieńka and her children had retired, and later at the Château of Blois, where they lived as pensioners of Louis XIV. In 1718, Clementina was betrothed to James Edward Stuart, the Chevalier de St. George, the 'Old Pretender', James III. On passing through Innsbruck later that year on the way to her wedding in Italy, she was kidnapped by imperial agents acting on behalf of the Emperor's Hanoverian allies, but was released by an Irish rescue party under one Charles Wogan, who contrived to substitute a female accomplice for the imprisoned princess. In May 1719, in Bologna, she married her Stuart, and on 31 December 1720 gave birth in Rome to Charles Edward

Louis Philip Casimir, the 'Young Pretender', 'Bonny Prince Charlie', and from 1766, Charles III. Her second son, Henry Benedict Maria Clement, titular Duke of York and from 1788 Henry IX, joined the Church and died in 1807 with the title of Cardinal-Bishop of Frascati. Thereafter, the line of Stuart pretenders descended into bastardy and charlatanry. One branch was headed by General Charles Edward Stuart, Baron Rohenstart, *soi-disant* grandson of Bonnie Prince Charlie's Scottish mistress, Clementina Walkinshaw. His death in a coach accident at Dunkeld in 1854 left the field clear for his rivals, the Sobieski—Stolberg—Stuarts. The members of this branch traced their descent from Bonnie Prince Charlie's deserted second wife, Louisa von Stolberg, Countess of Albany, who was supposed to have handed her infant son to a Captain Allen (alias O'Halleran) RN, to avoid a squad of Hanoverian assassins. According to the *Dictionary of National Biography*, their story is 'demonstrably false'; but it was freely accepted in many courts of Europe. It provided a living for two enterprising brothers, John Sobieski-Stolberg-Stuart (1795–1872) and Charles Edward (1799–1880), who successively assumed the title of 'Comte d'Albanie' on the undisprovable grounds that their father, Lt. Thomas Allen RN was the son of the rescued Stuart heir. Their uncle, and their grandfather, John Carter Allen (d. 1800), were both Admirals of the Royal Navy, whilst they themselves chose to live first in Napoleonic France, then in Prague and Vienna, and at various times on an island in Eskadale. In their Scottish period, John Sobieski-Stolberg-Stuart became a prolific poet, very conscious of his supposed Polish ancestry. In a modest reference to his own role in the Battle of the Nations at Leipzig, he composed the immortal line: 'Stuart swam the wave where Poniatowski sank.' In their Austrian period, Charles Edward married well. His son, also Charles Edward Stuart (1824–82), and his grandson, Alfred Edward Charles von Platt, became high-ranking officers in the Royal-Imperial cavalry. His granddaughter, Clementina Sobieska von Platt died as a Passionist nun at a convent in Bolton, Lancashire, in 1894.[12] It was a far cry from the boy-child born in a Tartar raid at Olesko in Red Ruthenia in 1629.

* * * * *

In later days, the memory of Sobieski's victories gradually effaced all recollection of his political failures. In the dark decades of defeat and national humiliation of the nineteenth and twentieth centuries, all Poles have looked with pride to a Polish King whose deeds reverberated to their credit throughout Europe. Anyone who has seen the glittering Turkish trophies from Vienna still exhibited in Cracow is bound to reflect with wonderment at the man who dared to humble an enemy possessed of such wealth and power. As a result, historical judgements have been lenient. It is true that Sobieski did not possess much freedom of manœuvre. He was constrained by the egoism of the magnates, whose stranglehold on political life could not have been easily released, and by the obstinacy of the Porte, which in this one period insisted on regarding the Republic as its enemy. But that is merely to enunciate the central political dilemma of Sobieski's career. It does not excuse seventeen years of ruinous warfare which banished all chance of repairing the Republic's structural weaknesses. Sobieski entered the Holy League from his own free will. He must be held responsible for the consequences. Almost two hundred years after Sobieski's birth, in 1828, Tsar Nicholas I of Russia came to Warsaw for his coronation as King of Poland, and was taken to see Sobieski's statue in Łazienki Park. Thinking of his own costly Turkish wars, he looked up at Sobieski and said, 'There is the other fool who wasted his time fighting the Turks.'[13] The Tsar of Russia was in a position to know. He was one of the few beneficiaries.

CHAPTER SEVENTEEN
WETTIN:
The Saxon Era (1697-1763)

The sixty-six years which separate the reign of John Sobieski from that of Stanisław-August Poniatowski are often regarded as the most wretched and the most humiliating in the whole of Polish history. Poland's miseries during this period are usually explained by her subjection to the alien interests of foreign kings. When Thomas Carlyle described Poland as a 'beautifully phosphorescent rot-heap', it was this period that he had in mind.[1]

The Saxon House of Wettin acceded to the Polish throne against all reasonable expectations. At the Royal election of June 1697, the Austrian candidate, Jakub Sobieski, son of the late King, was forced to withdraw for want of cash. The Frenchman, the Prince de Conti, although acclaimed by the Primate and supported by the majority, was unable to benefit from a technical victory; and in the end Friedrich-August, Elector of Saxony, a last-minute entry, walked off with the prize. The result was achieved by bribery, by threats, and by skilful timing. When the supporters of the favourites were locked in combat, the Saxon agent, Count Fleming, had made the timely promise of his master's conversion to Catholicism, and, having pawned the Wettin's jewels in Vienna, distributed the proceeds among the electors. In collusion with Nikitin, the Russian resident, who delivered an appealing peroration in Polish, he succeeded in splitting the electoral field in two, and persuaded the Bishop of Kujawy to declare the Saxon elected. It was a double election, reminiscent of 1576 or 1587. In the brief civil war which followed, the invading Saxons and Russians enjoyed every advantage over the French party. By September, when Friedrich-August had already been installed and crowned in Cracow as Augustus II, the Prince de Conti was still at sea on his way to Danzig.[2]

Once the election was decided, however, the personal union of Poland—Lithuania and Saxony offered favourable prospects for both partners. Both felt threatened by their common neighbour, Prussia, whose obvious territorial ambitions could now be neatly outflanked. Both felt the need for mutual assistance in the dangerous world of Northern Europe where the Prussian, Swedish, and Russian armies were far more formidable than their own. Both may well have foreseen, as proved to be the case, that both might 'hang separately', if they did not 'hang together'. In so far as Poland–Lithuania was the larger of the two, the nobility of the Republic had every reason to suppose that they could maintain their separate interests. As constitutionalists, they could hope to control a foreign monarch better than a native one, expecting him to arbitrate with impartiality, or at least with indifference, over the internecine feuds of domestic politics. For this very reason, in this same era, the English Parliament invited a Dutchman, and later the Hanoverians, to rule over them in preference to the native Stuarts. Ramshackle dynastic states were commonplace in eighteenth-century Europe, and there is no *a priori* factor which explains why some of them, such as 'England-and-Wales/Ireland/Scotland/Hanover' should have thrived, whilst others like 'Poland–Lithuania/Courland/Saxony' should have floundered. (See Map 20.)

Apart from that, Augustus the Strong was an interesting prospect in himself. As Duke of Saxony, Meissen, and Lusatia, he possessed the means to live of his own. As an Elector of the Holy Roman Empire, he wielded influence in the world, but not unlimited power. As commander of imperial armies in the campaigns of the Holy League he had a distinguished military reputation. As the father of some three hundred children, including the famous Maurice de Saxe, Marshal of France (1696–1750), his personal prowess was beyond reproach. He looked a fitting successor to the great Sobieski.[3]

Augustus the Strong's amours formed one of the wonders of the age, attesting no less to his catholic and cosmopolitan taste than to his phenomenal stamina. After a series of youthful adventures in Madrid and Venice, where he had variously disguised himself as a matador and a monk, he returned to Dresden in 1693 to the charms of his bride, Eberdine, Princess of Bayreuth, to the labours of the Electoral Office, and to the cultivation of a covey of concubines — official,

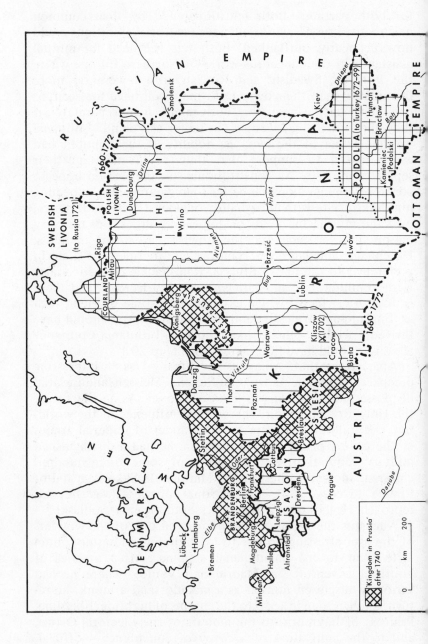

Kingdom in Prussia
after 1740

confidential, and top secret. Maurice de Saxe was the Elector's son by his one-time Swedish favourite — Aurora, Countess of Königsmark. He received his name, it was said, in memory of the famous victory that was gained over his mother at the royal hunting-lodge at Mauritzburg. His half-brother, Count Rotowski, was the son of Fatima, a Turkish girl captured at Buda in 1684. His half-sister, Countess Orzelska, Princess of Holstein, was the child of Henriette Duval, daughter of a Warsaw wine-merchant. In Poland, the new King left no stern unturned. When the Countess d'Esterle, who had journeyed with him to Cracow to witness his coronation, was surprised *in flagrante* with Prince Wiśniowiecki, she lost her place to Princess Lubomirska, wife of the royal Chamberlain and niece of a cardinal. The latter, having changed her name to Mme Teschen, soon yielded to the businesslike Mme Hoym, who negotiated a legal contract and a salary of 100,000 RM per annum. This professionalism was copied by most of her successors, not least by Mme Cosel, who insisted on the erection of a suitable palace for herself in Dresden, and by Maria, Countess of Denhoff, daughter of the Polish Crown Marshal, whose interests were astutely managed by a mother-in-law intent on recovering her family's insolvent fortunes. The most extraordinary story of all concerned the abandoned mistress of the British ambassador to Saxony, who, having turned for comfort to the Elector-King, scored the only known non-event in fifty years of gallantry.[4]

Yet, unlike his spermatozoa, most of the political ventures of Augustus the Strong failed to reach their target. In the foreign field, his private alliance with Russia, first discussed during Peter I's visit to the Republic in 1698 and sealed in 1699 at the Preobrazhenskiy Treaty, proved disastrous. In 1704, he was faced in the Republic by a rival king raised and crowned by his opponents, and in 1706 was chased from Dresden. He recovered his fortunes almost exclusively by favour of his Russian patron, in whose interests he had squandered his inheritance and on whom thereafter, he was totally dependent. Meanwhile he had presented the Hohenzollern with the golden opportunity of founding a 'Kingdom in Prussia' and of shifting the balance of power in Germany unmistakably in the direction of Berlin. In the internal sphere, he met with constant trouble. His running fight with the Saxon Diet over some sixteen years ended in uneasy compromise. Although in 1710, he grandly declared an end to his traditional *condominium* with the Estates, he was never able to circumvent them completely. His introduction of an excise system on the Prussian model in 1705 did not give him independence of means. His army was constantly below strength, never rising above 30,000 men; his debts reached the equivalent of some thirty-five years' revenue; his expenditure — on his castle of Zwingler in Dresden, on his art collection, and on entertainment — was prodigious. Most importantly, perhaps, his insensitivity to religion deeply shocked a religious age. His conversion to Catholicism caused great resentment in Lutheran Saxony. His acceptance of discriminatory legislation against the Catholics of the Electorate set the tone for similar measures in the Polish Diet directed against the Protestants of the Republic. In Saxony, as in Poland–Lithuania, the interests of the ruler consistently diverged from those of his subjects.

The Great Northern War (1700–21), which marked Russia's decisive bid for power against Sweden, was launched for reasons quite incidental to Polish–Lithuanian affairs. Augustus's treaty with Russia, negotiated exclusively in his capacity as Elector of Saxony, did not involve the Republic. His attack on Swedish Livonia in 1700 was largely motivated by considerations of personal gain. Yet the Republic was implicated in spite of itself, and became one of the principal victims.[5] It is true, of course, that the presence of a victorious Saxon army in Riga would have done much towards restoring royal authority in Lithuania, which had virtually seceded from Poland by virtue of decades of magnatial feuding. For this reason, the predominant Sapieha faction in Lithuania hastened to support the Swedes against the Saxon–Russian combination. But Augustus never achieved a position where he could have enforced any consistent policy; and the potential threat of his Saxon guard was systematically exaggerated by his enemies in the Republic in order to justify their resistance. As events worked out, Augustus's initial failure before Riga began an interminable game of cat-and-dog, in which the Elector-King was chased from pillar to post throughout the length and breadth of his Saxon and Polish dominions for nearly twenty years. (See Map 21.) In 1700, having saved Riga, Charles XII of Sweden occupied the Republic's Duchy of Courland. In 1702, he marched right across the Republic from north to south, occupying Wilno, Warsaw, and Cracow. After breaking the Polish cavalry in the one set battle, fought at Kliszów on 19 June 1702, he found that Augustus had doubled back on a roundabout route to Pomerania. In 1703, the Sejm made provision for expanding the Republic's forces; but their expectations were dashed by a second Swedish victory at Pułtusk, and by the outbreak of Palej's rebellion in Ukraine. In 1704, Augustus was faced in the Republic by the Swedish-sponsored Confederation of Warsaw which produced its own claimant to the throne in the person of a nobleman of Wielkopolska, Stanisław Leszczyński (1677–1766). The pro-Saxon Confederation of Sandomierz relied heavily on Russian auxiliaries. Augustus took evasive action against the Swedes by retreating to Lwów, before advancing once more to Warsaw. In 1706, Charles XII determined to put an end to the comedy by marching into the heart of Saxony. At the Treaty of Altranstadt he obliged Augustus among other things to renounce the Polish throne in favour of Leszczyński; but then learned that the Russians and the Confederates of Sandomierz had succeeded in redressing the balance by defeating a secondary Swedish army at Kalisz.

After seven campaigns, it was clear that no satisfactory verdict would be obtained without an invasion of Russia. After a year's preparations, Charles XII set off eastwards from Grodno in January 1708, leaving Leszczyński with General Krassau to hold his bases in the Republic. In the campaign of 1708–9, which led to the epoch-making Russian triumph at Poltava, a conspicuous part was played both by Polish peasants who harassed the Swedish columns and by the Confederates of Sandomierz, who prevented any reinforcements reaching the beleaguered Swedes. Poltava put an end to the Swedish party in the Republic. Leszczyński and Krassau were pursued to Stettin. The Confederation of Warsaw was disbanded. In 1710, Augustus returned in triumph. The Saxon monarchy was restored.

Yet the Republic's troubles continued. The reintroduction of the Saxon Guard and their brutal impositions rekindled

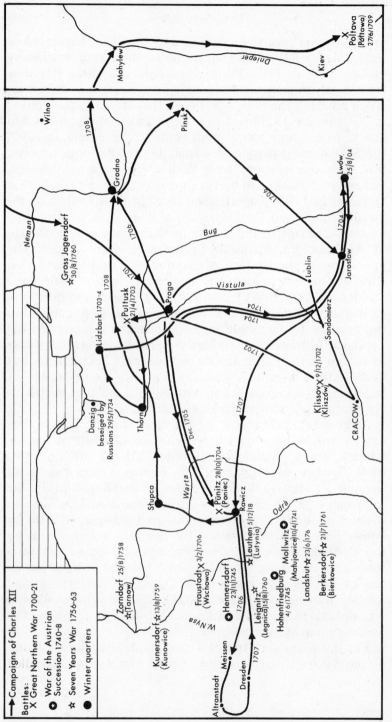

Map 21. International Wars in the Eighteenth Century

the animosity of a people who had been schooled to think of all foreign troops as the instruments of royal tyranny. In November 1715, the Polish nobility found common cause once more in the General Confederation of Tarnogród which swore to expel the Saxons lock, stock, and barrel. For a time, it looked as though they would succeed. Augustus, having lost Poznań, was being pushed back towards Saxony, when a sense of cold reality was suddenly injected into the situation by the appearance of a Russian Army. The Tsar, irritated by the squabbles of his Saxon and Polish clients, was threatening in no uncertain terms to knock their heads together. By offering to arbitrate in their dispute, he stood to gain a permanent grip on Polish affairs. After seventeen years of punishing warfare, the battered Republic was exhausted, and divided against itself. Such was the setting of the notorious Silent Sejm of 1717.

Peter the Great's policy to Poland–Lithuania had matured over the two decades of the Northern War. The first stage, of putting his Saxon client into a position of dependence, had been completed within five or six years of his original election. The second stage, of turning Russia's military supremacy into a durable political system, took rather longer. In 1706–7, when Augustus had deserted his throne, Peter passed many months in Poland looking for a 'head' to put on the body of the decapitated Republic. Residing in Sobieski's favourite castles of Żółkiew, Jaworów, and Wilanów, and selecting vast quantities of plundered treasures for removal to Russia, he conducted lengthy negotiations with the Confederates of Sandomierz. He was shocked by what he learned. The Polish 'republicans' expected to treat with the Tsar as with an equal. They were men who would take neither orders nor bribes. One magnate refused an offer of the Crown on the grounds that he was not going to be 'any Tsar's fool'. Others responded to the Tsar's expensive gifts by sending still more expensive gifts in return. After that experience, Peter knew what he was dealing with. (The term 'Polish Anarchy' appeared in Russian documents for the first time in this period.) The Tsar had either to hold Poland–Lithuania by force, which was beyond even Russia's capacity, or he had to chain the Wettins to their task in such a way that neither they, nor the Polish nobility, could challenge the arrangements. His opportunity came with the war of the Confederation of Tarnogród. At negotiations held in Warsaw in 1716, his diplomats were able to persuade the King to a permanent withdrawal of the Saxon Army from the Republic's territory. At the same time, the representatives of the Sejm undertook to place a permanent limit on the size of the Republic's finances and armies. The Tsar undertook to guarantee the agreement in the form of a written constitution. In this way, both King and nobility were deprived by the means of threatening each other. By no mere coincidence, they were also deprived of the means of resisting the encroachments of the Russian Tsar who henceforth could legally intervene in Polish affairs at will. The terms, agreed in advance, were to be put before a meeting of the Sejm sworn to accept them without debate or protest. The operation was completed on 30 January 1717, in less than one day. The Silent Sejm, surrounded by Russian soldiers, signed away Poland's freedom for the duration; and no voice was raised against it.[6]

The troubles of the Great Northern War thus mark the beginning of the modern political history of Poland. Russian supremacy, first instituted in 1717, has persisted in one form or another to the present day. The Russian protectorate has sometimes been exercised by manipulating the activities of an autonomous, but dependent Polish state — as was the case for most of the eighteenth century — and sometimes by incorporating large parts of the Polish lands into the Russian Empire. It has sometimes been exercised by Russia alone, and sometimes in conjunction with Russia's German or Austrian associates. But in two hundred and sixty years, it has only been interrupted for brief periods, notably for the twenty-four years between 1915 and 1939. What is more, whilst Poland's other 'protectors' have come and gone, the Russians do not go away. In this situation, political life quickly assumed a different tone. Political attitudes were formed less in relation to Polish needs, but increasingly in response to Russian demands. Political factions rose or fell not merely in relation to popular support in Poland, but principally in response to the favour, or disfavour, of St. Petersburg. The Polish political classes, appalled by the realization of their subjugation, flitted easily from abject indifference to desperate rebellion, defending their remaining privileges with a truculence that always seemed to invite the impending disaster. In the short term, indeed for the rest of the Saxon period, the establishment of the Russian protectorate reduced Polish politics to unplumbed depths of corruption and paralysis. In the long term, it provided an unwavering stimulus to the growth of modern national consciousness.

The effects on the Republic were immediate and profound. The campaigns of the Great Northern War, which were largely contested on the territory of Poland and Lithuania, had devastated the countryside and divided the nobility into armed camps. The economy was shattered. The restoration of Augustus II in 1710 was achieved at the price of ratifying the Grzymułtowski Treaty with Russia, resisted since 1686. The eastern lands were lost forever. The King's constitutional manœuvres in Saxony excited exaggerated fears in Warsaw. Ridiculous as it seems, the szlachta genuinely suspected him of 'absolutism'. Religious passions were revived. Seeing the restrictions placed on Catholics in Saxony, the Sejm answered by restricting the civil liberties of 'dissidents' in the Republic. The Tumult of Thorn of 1724, with all its sorry consequences, was characteristic of a situation where foreign meddling and home-grown suspicions fed on a diet of basic mistrust. The Sejm was repeatedly broken; government was interrupted; the Republic was defenceless. In return for the cancellation of the King's non-existent plans of subversion, and for the guarantee of their dubious privileges, the nobility watched as massive limitations were placed on the organization of their finances and their army. Henceforth, it was illegal for the citizens of the Republic to reform their state without the Tsar's permission. By venting their spleen on their harmless Saxon King, the Poles saddled themselves with a protector whose absolute pretensions were clear for all to see. Such was the disillusionment of August II with his Polish realm that twice, in 1721 and again in 1732, he openly talked of auctioning it off.[7]

The Saxon connection was not in itself prejudicial to Poland, therefore. The fault with the Wettins was that they themselves had fallen into the hands of Russia at an early stage. As a result, far from strengthening Poland's position in the European arena, they served only to lead the Polish Republic into the Russian camp by the nose, and thus to initiate that political bondage from which the Poles have never fully escaped.

The powerlessness of the King, and the collapse of the Sejm, left the government of the country in the hands of the magnates. The management of the dietines, of the Tribunals, of the Army, and of the Church hierarchy, fell by default to a narrow oligarchy of magnatial patrons, who monopolized all the great offices of state and treated with the Saxon Resident as with an equal. Each member of the oligarchy ruled in his own domains like a princeling in his own *panstewko,* his own 'state within the state'. He maintained his own clientele of nobles who defended his interests in the dietines or the courts, and who staffed his own private army. He conceived his own alliances both domestic and foreign, following one of several alternate 'orientations' — Russian, French, Prussian, or Austrian — according to the dictates of his own finances and inclinations. From the early eighteenth century onwards, the power of the magnates burgeoned. Political life was reduced to the feuds, fortunes, and the follies of a few families — some, like the Radziwiłłs, Lubomirski, Sapieha, Potocki, Wiśniowiecki, or Czetwertyński clans were families of ancient distinction; others like the Sułkowski, Jabłonowski, Poniatowski, Tarło, Czartoryski, Sieniawski, Ogiński, Denhoff, or Branicki broods, were relative parvenus.[8]

The emasculation of the Republic was best reflected in the catastrophic decline of its armed forces. As from 1717, the Komput was indefinitely fixed at 24,000 men — 18,000 for the Korona, and 6,000 for the Grand Duchy. Owing to the inclusion in these estimates of top-heavy administrative staff, the nominal establishment was effectively reduced to less than twenty thousand fighting men. What is more, the Army was deprived of central financial support, and was expected to support itself by 'exactions' levied on Crown Estates specifically earmarked for the purpose. Henceforth, each regiment was responsible for collecting its own supplies, and was loath to leave the vicinity of the particular starostwo on which its survival depended. The Hetmanship was retained; but the unscrupulous conduct during the Great Northern War of

Hetman Adam M. Sieniawski (1666–1726) in Poland, and especially of Hetman Adam Pociej (1641–1713) in Lithuania, had greatly diminished the prestige of the office. Neither the King, nor the Sejm, nor indeed the Army was prepared to entrust itself to the Hetmans, whose positions rapidly assumed the character of lucrative sinecures, well-greased channels for Russian influence and corruption in the heart of the Republic's affairs. In such circumstances, the Army's effectiveness as a fighting force virtually disappeared. Morale and technical proficiency collapsed in almost every branch of the service. In the National Contingent, noble cavalry troopers commonly absented themselves by offering a couple of *sowity* or 'substitutes', usually serfs, in their place. In the Foreign Contingent, commissions were bought and sold, mainly by Germans from Saxony. Only the Artillery, for whose maintenance the *Kwarta* tax was now exclusively reserved, managed to keep itself in some sort of order. At all levels, the soldiers were overwhelmed by a profusion of self-seeking officers, bureaucrats, and camp-followers. As the saying went: *Dwa dragany, cztery kapitany* (For every two dragoons, we need four captains). In any emergency, the Army's instinct was to retreat to its permanent quarters in the countryside, and to dig in. It was incapable of controlling the proliferating gangs of bandits, not to mention the private armies of the magnates. It had no intention whatsoever of challenging the professional armies of foreign powers.[9]

The gravity of the situation was magnified by the fact that the military collapse of Poland–Lithuania coincided with the massive militarization of the neighbouring states. At the accession of the Wettins, the Army of the Republic was roughly equivalent to those of its potential adversaries. Its 36,000 regulars had outnumbered the standing armies of both Prussia and Sweden, and were not far exceeded by those of Russia or Austria. At Kliszów in 1702, and again at Warsaw in 1705, it was twice defeated by a numerically inferior enemy. Thereafter, its strength was dissipated by the warring Confederations, and was permanently hobbled by the provisions of the Silent Sejm. Within twenty years, it was completely outmatched in every department. In the course of the Saxon Era, the disparity in the ratio of the Republic's armed forces in relation to Prussia was to rise to 1:11; in relation to Austria to 1:17; and in relation to Russia to 1:28.[10] The huge quantities of indigent petty nobles, who formed a pool of military manpower unequalled in Europe, preferred to serve in the retinues of the magnates than in the regiments of the state. The first attempts to create an armaments industry, and to provide military training commensurate with the technical developments of the age, were undertaken not by the Republic as such, but by the private enterprise of the Radziwiłł or the Branicki. Poland—Lithuania was not short of soldiers. It was a curious paradox; but the most militarized society in Europe was unable to defend itself. This sorry state of affairs was first brought to the attention of the world by the War of the Polish Succession.

In 1733 the death of August II led to a repetition of the conflicts which had divided the Wettin realm during his early career. In Saxony itself, he was succeeded by one of his few legitimate sons, also Friedrich-August, without dissent. But in the Republic, there were difficulties. At an election held in Warsaw on 12 September 1733, the French candidate, Stanisław Leszczyński, was again successful. His success sparked off another international war.[11] Russia and Austria had declared in favour of the Wettin succession, and a Russian Army marched in to enforce it. In almost three years of fighting, all opposition was crushed. French intervention was confined to indirect action against Austria in Lorraine and Savoy. The election was re-run in October under the safety of Russian bayonets, and a hand-picked electorate acclaimed the Saxon as August III. The confederated Royal Army was obliged to retire from Warsaw. A coronation was staged in Cracow in January 1734. The city of Danzig, which had refused to surrender, was besieged, and fell to the Russians in May. The Confederation of Dzików, which under Adam Tarło had raised its standard in the cause of national independence in October 1734 was defeated by Prussian and Russian troops, after a bold attempt to cross the Oder and carry the war into Saxony. Its end came in May 1735.[12] In the Ukrainian palatinates, especially in Bracław, and in the Kurpie region of Royal Prussia, the anti-Russian movement assumed the form of peasant risings, and persisted into 1736. By that time this

War of the Polish Succession had been officially terminated long since at Vienna by agreement of the powers.

The accession of Augustus III brought general relief. Despite the sordid and violent operations by which it was achieved, no other solution was possible in prevailing political circumstances. The Republic resigned itself to an extended association with Saxony. Saxony rejoiced in the fact that its ruler's fortunes in the Republic had been reprieved. In January 1734, for the royal Coronation in Cracow, the Saxon Music-Master at Leipzig hurriedly set an existing composition to new words: 'Blast Lärmen ihr Feinde' (Raise your alarms, oh enemies). In October, he was taken by surprise when the impending arrival of the Court was announced on the anniversary of the Polish accession. In three days, he produced an entire *Cantata Gratulatoria in adventum Regis* in nine parts:

1. *Chorsatz*   *Preise dein Glücke, gesegnetes Sachsen,*
                (Praise thy good fortune, blessed Saxony)

2. *Rezitativ*   *Wie Können wir, grossmächtigster August . . .*
                (How can we, most mighty Augustus, lay at thy feet the unfeigned impulse of our Respect, Faithfulness and Love)

3. *Arie*   *Freilich trotz Augustus' Name . . .*
                (Augustus's Name, such a noble seed of God, certainly defies all mortal might)

4. *Rezitativ*   *Was hat dich sonst, Sarmatien, bewogen . . .*
                (What has stirred thee, Sarmatia, that thou hast preferred the Saxon Piast, great Augustus's worthy son?)

5. *Arie*   *Rase nur verwegner Schwarm . . .*
                (Bluster now, presumptuous swarm, in thine own bowels! Steep thy insolent arm, full of fury, in innocent fraternal blood, to our abhorrence and thine own hurt. For the venom and the fierceness of thy envy strikes More at thee than at August.)

6. *Rezitativ*   *Ja, ja! Gott ist uns nach mit seine*
                (Yea, yea! God is nigh, with his succour to protect Augustus's throne. He ensures that the whole North has been contented by the royal election . . . and does he not allow that city which so long opposed him to feel his favour more than his anger?)

7. *Arie*   *Durch die von Eifer entlammeten Waffen . . .*
                (To punish one's enemies with weapons inflamed by zeal brings honour and renown to many men; but to requite

> Evil with good deeds is only for heroes, and is Augustus's prerogative.)

8. *Rezitativ*   *Lass doch, o teurer Landesvater, zu*
(Grant then, o Father of our country, that the Muses may sing and honour the Day when Sarmatia elected Thee as King . . .)

9. *Chorsatz*   *Stifter der Reiche, Beherrscher der Kronen, . . .*
(Founder of empires, Lord of Crowns, support the throne which Augustus occupies. Adorn his House with imperishable prosperity . . . May his lands dwell in peace . . .[13]

The full-blooded words of No. 5 refer to the defeat of the French party in Poland; those of No. 6 to the recent fall of Danzig. For them, the librettist Johann Christian Clauder, received 12 thalers, as compared with the composer's 50, and the total cost of production of 229 thalers 22 grosz. The chronicler of Leipzig, Salomon Reimer, recorded the first performance on 5 October 1734, beneath the Elector-King's open window on the city square:

Towards nine o'clock in the evening, their Majesties were presented by their subjects with an *Abend-Muzik* with trumpets and drums. It was composed by Music-Master, Mr Joh. Sebastian Bach, cantor at St. Thomas's. Whereat, six hundred students carried wax torches whilst four Counts acted as marshals. The procession emerged and . . . passed along the Ritter, Brühl, and Catherine Streets to the King's lodging. As the orchestra arrived at the *Wage,* the trumpets and drums opened up, whilst a choir broke into song from the City Hall. After handing over the libretto, the four Counts were left behind to kiss the sovereign's hand.

Then His Majesty, with his royal consort, and the royal princes, stayed by the window as long as the music lasted, listening most graciously and heartily enjoying it.[14]

Two days later, on the Elector-King's birthday, another Cantata was produced on the text 'Schleicht spielende Wellen und murmelt gelinde! Nein rauschet geschwinde!' (Glide along, ye waves in play and murmur gently. No, rush along swiftly!) It formed a symbolic play on the rivers of Poland—Saxony, where the Elbe was sung by the tenor, and the Vistula, *der beglückter Weichselstrom,* by the bass. Over the next two centuries, the occasions which prompted these Cantatas have passed into oblivion. But the music is immortal. The bass aria, No. 7 from Bach's gratulatory Cantata BMV 215 can more usually be found as No. 47 in the 'Christmas Oratorio'; the opening chorus, *Preise dein Glücke,* now forms the 'Hosannah' of the B Minor Mass:

For the next thirty years, the reign of Augustus III passed almost without incident. The outlook of the second Elector-King has been likened to that of a pudding – soft, sweet, and inert. He had no real power, and no intention of finding out whether he had or not. He owed his position in the Republic to the Russian Army, which he made no effort thereafter to dismiss. The Russians came and went as they pleased. He surrendered all active participation in Polish business to his ministers, especially to Count Heinrich Brühl (1700–63), who established a position in Warsaw approaching that of a personal dictator. In 1740–2, he made no move to obstruct the Prussian conquest of Austrian Silesia which drove a lengthy wedge between his Saxon and Polish dominions. In the subsequent War of the Austrian Succession (1742–8) and the Seven Years War (1756–63), he followed a policy conceived exclusively in the name and interest of Saxony, seeking to use the Republic as a milch-cow for his domestic luxuries and his military expenses. He was powerless to prevent the excesses of the Russian forces which tramped across the Republic towards Prussia and Pomerania, or those of Frederick the Great who in 1762–3 imposed forced contributions on the northern provinces of Poland as a means of restocking a bankrupt Prussian treasury. To facilitate their depredations, the Prussians flooded the Republic with forged and worthless imitations of the Polish coinage. During these decades, most central government of the Republic was suspended. The work of the Sejm was referred to the local dietines. The magnates, notably the Russian-backed Czartoryski and the French-connected Potocki, ruled supreme in their private empires, and paralysed all attempts at forging a common purpose. The Tribunals were terrorized. The tiny royal Army stayed in its barracks, for fear of action. The economy stagnated. The towns shrank. The bourgeoisie all but disappeared. The peasantry toiled with no hope of amelioration. Ignorance and poverty multiplied, whilst Warsaw danced to an endless succession of aristocratic balls, where all that mattered was the size of one's partner's latifundium. The opera and theatre flourished. The parks, the architecture, and the music were superb. All the arts found ample patronage. Some commentators thought that the 'Polish disease' was less harmful than the wars and violence which consumed neighbouring countries; others likened it to Sodom and Gomorrah. In the words of a popular refrain:

> *Za króla Sasa*
> *Jedz, pij, i popuszczaj pasa!*
> (Under the Saxon King, eat, drink, and loosen your belt!)

In these circumstances, the Saxons' leading rival for the throne of the Republic, Stanisław Leszczyński (1677–1766), can hardly have regretted his repeated failures. This refined and jovial nobleman, a magnate of Wielkopolska, and scion of an ancient Protestant family, was the lifelong candidate of the Franco-Swedish party. He had been crowned King of Poland twice, once in 1704 and again in 1733. On the first occasion his reign lasted for five years until the Swedish defeat at Poltava; on the second occasion, it was cut short after five months. Trapped in Danzig by the Russian siege, he fled to Prussia in peasant's clothes. Exiled in Versailles, he married his daughter to the King of France; and in 1735 was himself rewarded with the Duchy of Lorraine and Bar in fief. His court at Lunéville was a model of the Enlightenment, the resort of *philosophes* and of *bons viveurs* alike. He kept in close contact with Poland, and welcomed large numbers of his countrymen to the schools and enterprises of his Duchy. He was the author of *Głos wolny wolność ubezpieczący* (A Free Voice insuring Freedom, 1749), the most influential reforming tract of the age.[15]

The spirit of improvement was by no means totally absent. Many magnates, like Leszczyński, were acutely aware of the Republic's plight, and within their considerable private means sought to develop the country's resources and to raise its morale. In Lithuania, the Radziwiłłs had been building manufactories since the 1740s. Michał Ogiński, author of an article on 'The Harp' in Diderot's *Encyclopédie,* was building his canals. As from 1760, Andrzej Zamoyski (1716–92), a future Chancellor, abolished serfdom on all his estates, setting an example which he was to promote in public policy. Stanisław Konarski (1700–73), pedagogue and publicist, founder of the 'Collegium Nobilium', which opened its doors to pupils in 1740, was equally concerned with political reform. His tract *O skutecznym rad sposobie* (Concerning an Efficient Method of Government), published in the year that Augustus III died, voiced the doubts of a generation. Here lay the seeds of future change. Most remarkable perhaps was the work of the Załuski brothers, Andrzej Stanisław Kostka (1695–1758) and Józef Andrzej (1702–74), Catholic Bishops of Cracow and Kiev respectively. Bishop Stanisław, who rose to the dignity of Crown Chancellor, pioneered the development of iron mining, metallurgy, and the science of mineralogy. Bishop Józef Andrzej, who with Konarski had spent a period of exile at Lunéville, founded a collection of books, which was opened in Warsaw in 1748 as the first public library in Europe. It was housed in the 'Blue Palace' by the Saxon Garden, built for one of the late king's natural daughters, Maria Orzelska. In time it contained some 400,000 volumes, all magnificently catalogued in rhyming Latin verse. Its treasures were the object of learned pilgrimages, and were described by the French scientist, Jean Bernouilli:

The Palace is a veritable labyrinth of rooms, all crammed with books. The most remarkable room, and indeed the only one to be tastefully decorated, is devoted to showpiece volumes, many of them French, outstanding for their engravings and bindings. It is long and high, and adorned by numerous statues in honour of the most famous men of the country. It is adjoined by Bishop Załuski's own bedroom.

The Latin collection occupies another large hall on the third floor . . . I was shown a couple of beautiful manuscripts of Longinus and Macrobius, and a very ancient copy of Ovid's *Letters* and *Metamorphoses,* and then several exceptionally fine ecclesiastical works. One of these was a folio Codex, entitled *Pontificalis ordinis liber,* written and illuminated on parchment, and dating from around 1500 . . . I also saw a ninth-century Burgundian Missal and the *Decretalia* of Pope Gregory IX, written in gold letters on vellum, and illustrated with more than a thousand miniatures . . .

As for Polish documents, they attach great importance here to the enormous legal collection of Acts of the Republic in twenty-seven volumes, twelve of which are not originals but copied from the Jagiellonian Library in Cracow . . .[16]

In his will, Bishop Załuski bequeathed his library to the Republic. But he could not control its fate. In 1795 it was plundered by the Russian Army, and sent in packing cases to St. Petersburg where in due course it was joined by half a million more volumes taken from other Polish libraries. Modern diplomacy has failed to recover any significant part of the spoils. Modern visitors to the Soviet state libraries in Leningrad are not usually told of their true origins.[17]

The death of Augustus III on 5 October 1763 brought the Saxon Era in the Republic to its natural term. There was no question of electing his son, Friedrich-Christian. This time the Russians had plans of their own. Catherine II was intent on reforming her Polish protectorate in her own image. In this, she was bound to compete with the Polish reformers, and in the end, if she persisted, to provoke conflict. Thus, after thirty years of somnolent sclerosis, the body politic of the Republic was about to be thrown into violent convulsions. To many who lived through the era of the Partitions, the 'good old Saxon days' must surely have been remembered with a touch of regret.

CHAPTER EIGHTEEN
AGONIA:
The End of the Russian Protectorate (1764-1795)

The partitioning of Poland, effected in three stages in 1773, 1793, and 1795, was without precedent in modern European History. Although victorious powers habitually stripped their defeated rivals of territorial possessions and were not averse to dividing the spoils of India, America, or Africa, there is no other instance when they deliberately annihilated one of Europe's historic states in cold blood. Poland was the victim of political vivisection — by mutilation, amputation, and in the end total dismemberment; and the only excuse given was that the patient had not been feeling well. The death-throes of the Republic coincided exactly with the reign of its last King, Stanisław-August Poniatowski (1732–98), from 1764 to 1795.[1] (See Map 22.)

The wags of the Enlightenment sharpened their wits on Poland's misfortunes. Frederick II of Prussia, a Protestant prince and one of the principal meddlers, boasted that he 'partook eucharistically of Poland's body'. Voltaire uttered his famous wisecrack: 'One Pole — a charmer, two Poles — a brawl; three Poles — ah, that's the Polish Question.' Their audience tittered elegantly, believing that Poland had somehow deserved her fate. As Vorontsov, the Russian Chancellor, declared in 1763, 'Poland is constantly plunged in disorder; as long as she keeps her present constitution, she does not deserve to be considered among the European powers.'

It is undeniable, of course, that Poland's label as 'The Republic of Anarchy' did not entirely lack foundation. For nearly fifty years since the silent Sejm of 1717, the politicians had been powerless to repair a number of grave weaknesses. The state was still a dual Republic in which the conflicting interests of the two constituent parts, the Kingdom of Poland and the Grand Duchy of Lithuania, nicely obstructed all attempts of reform. The monarchy was still elective, and a plaything of international diplomacy. The Sejm was still

511

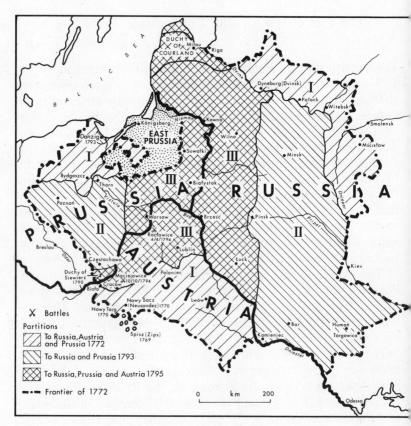

Map 22.   The Partitions of Poland, (1773–95)

hamstrung by the *Liberum Veto*. The unreformed constitution still permitted the formation of Confederations. Despite a population of 11 million and a territory of 282,000 square miles — which was larger than either France or Spain — there was still no central treasury, and in practice a royal army of only 12,000 men. The 'Golden Freedom' which most of the noble citizens were taught to regard as the glory of their Republic, had lost its meaning in a land where nine-tenths of the population lived in poverty and servitude, and where all was customarily arranged by the promise of French gold or by the threat of Russian coercion. For nearly fifty years, Poland—Lithuania had been ruled as a Russian Protectorate, by methods which in civilian life would have been described as a protection-racket. Everything was quiet so long as the Russian gangsters received their dues, and the Polish mugs and gulls accepted their protection. As soon as the protected tried to shake off their unwanted protectors, trouble was bound to occur.

The confusing developments of the Partition period can never be properly understood unless it is realized that Poland's internal troubles were systematically promoted by her more powerful neighbours. Russia had been interfering in the internal affairs of state for over a century. It was Peter I who had insisted on appointing himself as the 'patron' of the Orthodox minority; who had successfully schemed to put the House of Wettin on the Polish throne; and who had forced a silent Sejm to pass the strictures on finance, army, and reform which blighted public life thereafter. Not only Russia, but Sweden, Prussia, France, and Austria, used Poland as a battleground on which to settle their quarrels inexpensively. It is the simple truth that Poland's weakness suited the purposes of her neighbours most conveniently. In a tag of the day, Poland was *Karczma Europy* — 'Europe's Staging Inn'. What is more, whenever the Poles took steps to put their house in order, both Russia and Prussia took counter-steps to see that nothing changed. In 1764, when the convocational Sejm appointed a Commission of Finance to create a general customs system in line with other modern states, Frederick of Prussia set up a fort at Marienwerder, on his side of the river Vistula, to bombard and terrorize Polish shipping until the new proposals were dropped. In the same year, the Russians dispatched the latest of their military expeditions to see that the coming Royal election was enacted as planned. If in the subsequent period the Poles are judged to have contributed to the catastrophe themselves, it was more by their desperate efforts to escape from Anarchy than from their supposed desire to wallow in it. It should have been clear to all that the despots of St. Petersburg and Berlin, who denied most civil liberties to their own subjects, could never be the genuine champions of any genuine 'Golden Freedom' in Poland.

The same sort of hypocrisy was current in matters of religion. It is true that the Roman Catholic establishment of the Republic, despite the long tradition of toleration and freedom of worship, had denied the religious minorities, Orthodox and Protestant, full political rights since 1718. In this, Polish practice resembled that of Great Britain or Holland, and, until the bishops were goaded into retaliation in the 1770s, had been far more tolerant than that of Russia, whose visiting armies had invariably inflicted forcible conversion on the Republic's Uniates. But this did not prevent the Russian court from posing as the defender of oppressed minorities. On this issue, Frederick the Great had no illusions. 'What would (the Russian Minister) say if France were to invade Holland in order to force the Estates-General to admit papists to public charges?' he asked, '. . . would he not say that France had been the aggressor? But apply this to the present situation in Poland . . . It's the Russians who are the aggressors.'² Frederick knew his collaborators well, but did not flinch in joining them in their pious demands for religious rights in Poland. If the Republic had been strong, there is no doubt that the diplomats would have praised her tradition of religious enlightenment instead of cultivating the grievances of the 'dissidents'.

Russia's expansionist policy towards Eastern Europe, and to Poland in particular, came in two variations. On the one hand, the military party were openly in favour of direct annexations. They believed that Russia's interests could best be served by seizing the territory of her neighbours on every possible occasion. Chernyshev, the Vice-President of the War College, expressed this view when, at the new Empress

Catherine's council called to discuss the death of the King of Poland, he proposed an invasion of Polish Livonia and of the palatinates of Polotsk, Witebsk, and Mscisław. He commanded the support no doubt of those who in the previous years, with the Russian Army in Berlin, had urged the late Empress Elizabeth to dismantle the upstart Kingdom of Prussia. The politicians, on the other hand, were more cautious. Panin, Catherine's principal adviser on foreign affairs, held to the older and deeper Russian game whereby rivals were disarmed by promises of protection, and where the victim was not gobbled suddenly but chewed at leisure. Panin had hopes of a Northern System, where alliances with Prussia, Sweden, and England could be used to confound the Southern System of Louis XV's Minister, Choiseul. In Panin's scheme, the Republic was to continue as Russia's advance post in Europe, a vassal protectorate whose dependence could be perpetuated by endless manipulation and at minimal expense. Catherine undoubtedly shared his intentions at the outset; and one vital strand of the politics of the Partitions can be traced in her progressive abandonment of the policy of leisurely rumination for that of instant consumption.[3]

Prussia's outlook was somewhat different. In comparison to Russia, it was a tiny state, whose marvellous efficiency could not always preserve it from the consequences of insatiable ambition. The seizure of Silesia in 1740 had provoked two decades of wars which all but overwhelmed their instigator. In 1762 with the treasury empty and Berlin occupied, Prussia had only been saved by the sudden death of the Empress Elizabeth and by the timely accession of Peter III, Frederick's most fervent admirer. Prussia was in fact a cheerful international parasite. On three occasions, in 1656, 1720, and 1733 it had been party to abortive plans for dismembering the Republic. In 1752, Frederick's *Political Testament* had likened his Polish neighbour to 'an artichoke, ready to be consumed leaf by leaf'.[4] For the 'Kingdom in Prussia' did not yet possess a consolidated territorial base. The possessions of the Hohenzollerns were scattered across Northern Europe in unconnected clutches. The two largest elements, Brandenburg and Ducal (East) Prussia, were still separated by the broad Polish province of Royal (West) Prussia, which Frederick saw as the first leaf of the artichoke. After the crisis of 1762, his policy was no more repentant than before, but more circumspect. Lone banditry had proved too risky. He was now intent on forming a gang.

The Republic's other neighbour, Austria, lacked both Prussia's dynamism and Russia's resources. Exhausted by the Seven Years War, the Austrians possessed more than enough territory to keep their creaking administration busy. They had no plans of expansion. Their mountain frontier in the Carpathians, dividing them from Poland, and from Northern Europe in general, was complete except for the one minor gap at Spisz (Zips). In any case they were Catholics like the Poles, and still remembered the legendary occasion in 1683 when Sobieski had broken the Siege of Vienna. They hated the Prussians, and feared Russia. It seemed unthinkable that they might make common cause with Poland's assailants. But they did.[5]

Ruling personalities also played a part. Frederick of Prussia, brilliant, cynical, and unscrupulous, knew exactly where he was going. He was dealing with a couple of Empresses whose weaknesses he exploited with consummate skill, flattering the one, and teasing the other. Catherine II, recently elevated to the throne of All-the-Russias after the murder of her husband, Peter III, was the daughter of a Prussian Field Marshal. She was as heavy handed with her allies as with her countless lovers. Maria Theresa, 'widow Queen of Hungary and Empress of Austria', was devout and anxious. When the First Partition was eventually complete, Frederick remarked: 'Catherine and I are simply brigands; but I wonder how the Queen-Empress managed to square her confessor! . . . *Elle pleurait quand elle prenait; et plus elle pleurait, plus elle prenait.*' Finally, there was Stanisław-August Poniatowski, the polished, pliable, cosmopolitan nephew of the Russian-backed Czartoryski faction. When Polish plenipotentiary in St. Petersburg in 1755–8, he had been Catherine's most passionate lover – 'poor, foolish Poniatowski', in Carlyle's unkind words, 'an empty, windy creature, redolent of macassar'. He was the obvious instrument for displacing the somnolent Saxons from the throne of Poland. To everyone's surprise, he turned out to be an ardent patriot, and a convinced reformer.[6]

The prospect of a Royal election in Poland accelerated existing intrigues. Both Frederick and Catherine had anticipated the event, the one in 1762, by co-ordinating his plans with the ill-fated Peter III, the other in January 1763 by imposing a new ruler by armed force on the Duchy of Courland. Now they conspired more closely. On 11 April 1764 a treaty was signed in which Frederick succeeded in winning Catherine to the points agreed earlier with Peter: namely, that both would support a 'Piast' candidate, for the Polish throne, and that both would act together in defence of the 'Golden Freedom' and of the rights of religious dissidents. Frederick's main motive was to unseat the Saxons, his rivals in Germany. Catherine's motive was to smooth the way for Poniatowski. At the outset of this exercise, she was sufficiently ingenuous to issue a declaration to all the courts in Europe, disclaiming the rumour that a Partition was being prepared. 'If ever malice in concert with falsehood', she wrote indignantly, 'has been able to contrive a completely baseless rumour, it is assuredly the one which dares to imply that we have resolved to support a Piast for one purpose only, namely that, with his help, we could then easily invade several provinces of the Realm of Poland, dismember them, and appropriate them forthwith to Ourselves and Our Empire.'[7] Seeing the anaesthetic effect of this disclaimer on the European powers, the Prussian and Austrian Ministers in Warsaw made similar statements of their own.

As it happened, Poniatowski's road was smooth enough. The Electoral Field was lined with Russian soldiers and with retainers of the Czartoryski. On 6 September 1764, those nobles of the Republic who had not already left in disgust acclaimed their new King with a unanimous shout. As the victor himself remarked, it was the least troublesome election in the Republic's history.

Stanisław-August's position was far from comfortable, however. In the first four years of his reign, he only succeeded in offending all those who had regarded him as the servant of their interest. He promoted the Whiggish Andrzej Zamoyski as Crown Chancellor; but he soon fell out with his Czartoryski relations, who resented his plans for constitutional reform. In 1766, he successfully instituted the Corps of Cadets under

Adam Kazimierz Czartoryski, as the kernel of military education and expansion. But he had a difficult relationship with
Catherine's agent, Repnin, whose threats and violence made a
mockery of the monarch's prerogative. He angered Frederick
by the customs proposals, and disappointed the 'dissidents'
who had been led to regard him as their ally. He particularly
incensed the established Church by failing to make his position
clear on the religious issue. The first Sejm of the reign, in 1766,
turned into a fiasco. The King's proposals for ending the
Liberum Veto were rejected, whilst the efforts of the Bishop of
Cracow, Kajetan Sołtyk, to obtain a declaration about the
'Security of the Faith' led to repeated uproar. By the end of the
year, the country was dividing up into several armed camps.

The year 1767 marks the nadir of the 'Polish Anarchy', in
which the baleful provocations of the Russians were plainly
revealed. At first, two armed confederations of dissidents
emerged, one at Thorn for the Protestants, the other at Słupsk
for the Orthodox. The element of genuine religious motivation in these developments may be judged from events at
Thorn where the confederation was organized by a Russian
officer, who began by arresting everyone, including the
city corporation, who opposed the will of the Empress. There
then emerged at Radom a more serious movement, which
gradually spread into a countrywide 'General Confederation'.
Some of these confederates, like the Radziwiłłs in Lithuania,
were aiming to dethrone the King. Some were merely trying
to block his programme of reform. Others thought they were
saving the Church. All were being manipulated. On this occasion, Repnin not only succeeded in stage-managing the
conduct of both the Opposition and the King; he actually
persuaded the King to join the Confederates. In October, he
showed his hand. Having arranged an extraordinary meeting
of the Sejm, he promptly arrested the four leading oppositionists and sent them in chains to Kaluga. He announced his
action in a brief note to the House:

The troops of Her Imperial Majesty, my Sovereign, and the friend and ally
of the Republic, have arrested the Bishop of Cracow, the Bishop of Kiev,
the Palatine of Cracow and the starosta of Dolin, whose behaviour, by
impugning the purity of Her salutary, disinterested, and loving intentions
towards the Republic, has insulted the dignity of Her Imperial Majesty.[8]

Thereupon, Repnin's appointees suspended the Sejm in favour of a special Commission, which proceeded to pass the so-called 'cardinal laws' perpetuating the reign of Anarchy. The nobility were confirmed in their monopoly of political rights. The *Liberum Veto* was retained. Royal elections were to be 'free'. In short, the 'Golden Freedom' was clearly exposed as a hollow sham. The only person legally empowered to change it was the Empress of Russia. The system of 1717 was restored.[9]

At this point, Catherine must have been well pleased. The Republic lay prostrate before her in an agony of self-induced paralysis. The Russian party was in control. She had no further demands. In fact, unbeknown to herself, she was cornered. Her moment of satisfaction soon passed. She had not counted on the Poles, or the Turks, or on Frederick of Prussia. She was soon obliged to rethink her policy.

In 1768, the repercussions of Russian brutalities in the Republic made rapid progress. On 29 February, at Bar in Podolia, a new Confederation was constituted by a consortium of disillusioned nobles headed by Jan Michał Pac (1730–80), together with members of the Potocki, Sapieha, and Krasiński clans. They started a war which the Russians were unable to stamp out for nearly four years. They generated an idealism, a questioning of fundamental principles, which had not occurred for decades, and which was to form the starting-point of modern Polish nationalism. At the same time, they provoked violent side-effects which were completely beyond their control. In the Ukraine, their forces were taken in the rear by the so-called 'Kolivshchyzna', a peasant and Cossack rising which left a horrifying trail of butchered noblemen, Jews, and priests. The rising briefly diverted the attentions of the Russian and Royal armies who were advancing together against the Confederates. At Uman (Humań), it led to a massacre of legendary proportions. Some twenty thousand Catholics and Jews, herded respectively into their churches and synagogues, were murdered in cold blood. The rebels produced the slogan: 'Pole-Jew-Dog: all of one Faith', and in three weeks of unbridled violence killed almost two hundred thousand people. Thereafter, they were suppressed with matching severity. Their leader Maksym Zelezniak, was taken into custody by the Russians, and deported to Siberia. His chief lieutenant, Ivan Gonta, was handed over to the Poles, to be flayed and quartered alive.[10] In the following months, the Russians under Krechetnikov aided Hetman Branicki in his pursuit of the Confederates. But in October, they sparked off a further reaction from Turkey. Exasperated by Catherine's broken promises to withdraw her forces from Poland, the Porte ordered the arrest of the Russian Minister in Constantinople. It was a declaration of war. Catherine was caught by the 'fork' of her simultaneous commitments in Poland and in Turkey.

Catherine's troubles multiplied fast. Fighting a war against the Turks, she could not spare the troops to crush the risings which sprang up in Cracow, in Wielkopolska, and in Lithuania. In 1769 she found that the Confederates of Bar had set up a 'Generality' at Biała on the Austrian frontier, and that French officers were assisting in their activities. In 1771, open war flared again. The young Suvorov was hard pressed to contain the brilliant improvisation of Casimir Pułaski in Poland, and of Hetman Ogiński in Lithuania. The last centre of resistance at the monastery of Jasna Góra, at Częstochowa, was not suppressed till 18 August 1772.[11]

Frederick of Prussia was delighted with the turn of events. He waited until the Polish pot was nicely on the boil, before giving it a stir himself. In September 1768, he produced a plan of Partition, supposedly worked out by one Count Lynar. On finding that Catherine was not yet ready, he bided his time, hinting all the while that the Empress's indulgent treatment of the ungrateful Poles was more than they deserved. Had she not guaranteed their 'Golden Freedom'? Had she not championed the cause of religious toleration? Had she not suffered enough insults from dangerous Republicans and upstart bishops? Catherine, flattered by the neatness of Frederick's solution, but still humiliated by the failure of her original scheme, gradually surrendered to his prompting. If she did not yield to Frederick's proposals, she had to face the prospect of Prussia joining Austria and Turkey in a grand coalition against her.

Surprisingly enough, the blows which finally broke down Catherine's reluctance were struck by the Austrians, and in particular by Maria Theresa's astute adviser, Kaunitz, who showed remarkable ability in serving his mistress's advantage. In 1769, profiting by the Republic's preoccupations, Austrian troops marched into Spisz and annexed it, *'ad damnum evitandum'*. In 1770 they marched on to Nowy Targ and Nowy Sącz, which were also annexed. Noises were made in protest against Russian activities in Poland, and in 1771 Austria joined her traditional Turkish enemy in a secret alliance against Russia. It was just what Frederick needed. He was now able to argue that the Republic's weakness had reached the point where it was threatening international stability, and where a legal Partition was necessary to put an end to arbitrary annexations. His brother, Prince Henry of Prussia, had visited St. Petersburg in the autumn of 1770 and pressed these arguments. They proved conclusive. In June 1771, a Partition of Poland was agreed in principle between Prussia and Russia. In February, 1772, after a decent hesitation, Maria Theresa accepted the invitation to partake. All was settled bar the details.

The sharing of the spoils exercised the minds of the diplomats for barely five months. Frederick, as instigator of the exercise, modestly helped himself to Royal Prussia, Kujawy, and Chełmno. His abstinence from Danzig was proof of his moderation. Catherine, confined herself to Polish Livonia, and to the counties of Polotsk, Witebsk, Mscisław, and Homel. She confirmed her control over Courland. But Maria Theresa, having dallied the longest, could afford to raise her price the highest. Kaunitz insisted on the larger part of southern Małopolska, from Biała on the Silesian border in the west to the Turkish frontier on the Dniester in the east. In the final reckoning, Prussia took 5 per cent of the Republic's territory and a mere 580,000 of its citizens; Russia took 12.7 per cent of the territory and 1,300,000 people; Austria, received only 11.8 per cent of the territory, but no less than 2,130,000 souls. (See Diagram M.) The bad consciences of the partitioners had been nicely measured. The Treaty of Partition was signed in St. Petersburg on 25 July/5 August (Julian/Gregorian calendar) 1772.[12] Its preamble stated the reasons:

In the Name of the Most Holy Trinity! The spirit of faction, the troubles and intestine war which had shaken the Kingdom of Poland for so many years, and the Anarchy which acquires new strength every day . . . give

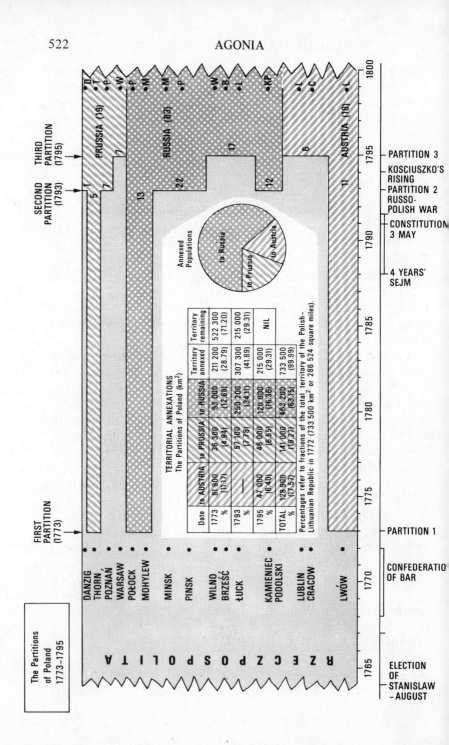

The Partitions of Poland 1773–1795

TERRITORIAL ANNEXATIONS
The Partitions of Poland (km²)

Date	to AUSTRIA	to PRUSSIA	to RUSSIA	Territory annexed	Territory remaining
1773 %	81 900 (11.17)	36 300 (4.94)	93 000 (12.68)	211 200 (28.79)	522 300 (71.20)
1793 %	—	57 100 (7.78)	250 200 (34.31)	307 300 (41.89)	215 000 (29.31)
1795 %	47 000 (6.40)	48 000 (6.55)	120 000 (16.36)	215 000 (29.31)	NIL
TOTAL %	128 900 (17.57)	141 000 (19.27)	463 200 (63.15)	733 500 (99.99)	

Percentages refer to fractions of the total territory of the Polish–Lithuanian Republic in 1772 (733 500 km² or 286 524 square miles).

Annexed Populations

to Russia
to Prussia
to Austria

Timeline labels (right side):
PARTITION 3
KOSCIUSZKO'S RISING
PARTITION 2
RUSSO-POLISH WAR
CONSTITUTION 3 MAY
4 YEARS' SEJM
PARTITION 1
CONFEDERATION OF BAR
ELECTION OF STANISLAW–AUGUST

Timeline labels (left side):
THIRD PARTITION (1795)
SECOND PARTITION (1793)
FIRST PARTITION (1773)

PRUSSIA (19)
RUSSIA (83)
AUSTRIA (18)

RZECZPOSPOLITA

DANZIG
THORN
POZNAŃ
WARSAW
POŁOCK
MOHYLEW
MINSK
PINSK
WILNO
BRZEŚĆ
ŁUCK
KAMIENIEC PODOLSKI
LUBLIN
CRACOW
LWÓW

just apprehension for expecting the total decomposition of the state . . .
at the same time, the Powers neighbouring on the Republic are burdened
with rights and claims which are as ancient as they are legitimate . . .

The Poles were required to submit to their treatment in
the most proper way possible. On the initiative of the new
Russian ambassador, Staeckelberg, a Sejm was called. For a
salary of 3,000 ducats a month, the Marshal of the Sejm,
Adam Poniński, was raised to the dignity of Treasurer in
return for managing the confirmation of the treaties. As part
of the process, yet another Confederation was formed, and
after that yet another Commission. The King was persuaded
to join, and in the summer of 1773 signed the necessary
documents. The three treaties of cession between the Republic
and each of the partitioning powers were completed on 7/18
September 1773. Legal niceties were observed to the end. The
air was full of compliments to the gracious Kings and
Empresses and of homage to the 'Golden Freedom'. In effect,
the victim not only gave his assent for the operation; he was
persuaded to wield the knife himself. The one sovereign to
protest was the King of Spain.

In a world careless of the Republic's fate, the mechanics of
Partition passed almost unnoticed. The platitudes were widely
believed. The faults of the Poles were universally recognized.
Court apologists from Berlin, St. Petersburg, and Vienna
stressed the difficulties in which their sovereigns had been
placed. In due course, court and state historians from Karamzin
to Treitschke, expatiated on the Poles' good fortune in receiving the blessings of foreign rule.[13] No one seemed to notice
the sleight of hand which concealed a sophisticated form of
international violence. Carlyle came near the mark when he
called the Partitions an act of 'decisive surgery'. He only
forgot to mention that the purpose of genuine surgery is to
cure and to heal, not to maim or to kill. For Frederick had
designed an operation whose avowed purpose was to weaken
the Republic, and to destroy its powers of resistance. Dis-
satisfied with the side-effects of his earlier, direct acts of
aggression, he was now perfecting a technique which cost less
and looked better. The demon-surgeon picks his victim well
in advance, and locates its weaknesses. Posing as a well-wisher
disturbed by the symptoms, he pokes the affected area until

convulsions are produced, and the victim is writhing in agony. Next he advises preventive surgery, to which the desperate patient is easily persuaded to submit. During the operation he takes care to leave enough of the diseased tissue untouched so as to ensure future inflammation, and invites his assistants to amputate an arm or a leg by way of surgical practice. Afterwards, when the greatly weakened patient suffers further convulsions, another operation can be prescribed, and then another, and another. If, at the end, the patient is dead, and his property is in the surgeon's pocket, the world can be told, with regret, that his illness was malignant from the start, and that costly and elaborate efforts were made to save him. After all, it is the surgeon who makes out the death certificate. Who will know that the patient's disease was not really fatal? Who will suspect that he has been foully murdered? As Frederick well knew, his new technique of 'decisive surgery' gave all the appearances of legality and respectability. It was much safer and much more efficient than assaulting one's victim in the street. Indeed, as it involved minimum of overt violence, it earned the skilful practitioner the admiration of the civilized world. It is a marvellous technique which Catherine II was destined to master in her own right, and which aspiring tyrants of later ages have been only too willing to imitate.

To the modern observer, the perspicacity no less than the cynicism of European statesmen regarding the consequences of the First Partition may seem surprising. In a world where diplomacy was uncomplicated by moral scruples, and where Frederick could cheerfully compare his Polish victims to defenceless Iroquois Indians, the deeper effects of the Partition were observed and recorded with cold precision. In reference to his fateful alliance with Russia, Frederick freely admitted: 'How blind and insane is Europe to contribute to the rise of a people which may someday become her own doom.' 'The Empress of Russia has breakfasted', wrote Edmund Burke, 'Where will she dine?' Elsewhere, in reference to the inability of the western powers to intervene in Eastern Europe. Burke commented that 'Poland must be regarded as being situated on the Moon.'[14]

The more serious implications of the First Partition were apparent within a few years of its completion. Writing in

1788, in his *History of the Prussian Monarchy,* the Comte de Mirabeau, stated that it would be 'both impossible and reprehensible' to justify the treaties of Partition, 'which have given Europe but a servile peace'. 'In the future', he wrote, 'the destiny of Liberty, of Property, and of Human Life itself will be determined by the whims of despots . . .' In the following fateful year, speculating on *The Peril of the Political Balance in Europe,* the Swiss journalist Jacques Mallet-du-Pin, predicted that the Partitions would become 'the horror of our age'. By the mid-nineteenth century, such comments were commonplace. In an era when repeated Polish Risings drew attention to the iniquities of the European System, it did not need a genius to see that the much-vaunted principle of 'Legitimacy', and the 'Holy' Alliances of the Empires had been built on international pillage. Macaulay was but one of many who condemned the Partition as 'a shameful crime'.[15]

In the last resort, of course, all such moral protests were distinctly double-edged. As Bismarck was wont to point out, the partitions of Poland were no more reprehensible, and no less, than the Polish partitions of Ruthenia in the fourteenth century, or of Prussia in the fifteenth. They were no worse, or better, than the colonial Partitions of Asia, Africa, and America, which all the European powers were about to undertake. All states are created by force, and all come into being by cannibalizing their predecessors. The special sense of outrage which attended the fate of the Polish Republic was partly due to the fact that European princes had eaten a fellow European. But it was also due to the particular moment. Poland was partitioned on the eve of the birth of Nationalism and Liberalism, and thus became a symbol of all those people for whom self-determination and the consent of the governed provide the guiding principles of political life.

For the Republic, the most demoralizing aspect of the whole business was seen in the spectacle of a large number of Poles who willingly served the interests of the partitioning powers. After fifty years of factional politics and Russian 'protection', there was no shortage of citizens who made their careers by working in the Sejm, in the dietines, or in the Confederations on behalf of foreign paymasters. Indeed, many were sufficiently confused by the corruption and double-talk of the time to have sincerely accepted the Russians as the genuine protectors of traditional Polish values. In the period of the Partitions, these 'collaborators' were drawn from the highest circles of the land. One of the most scandalous, the dissolute priest Gabriel Podoski (d. 1793), was raised by Catherine to the rank of Archbishop and Primate. Two others, Józef Kossakowski (1738–94) and Ignacy Massalski (1729–94), were Roman Catholic bishops. The former, like Poniński, lived from a hefty Russian pension; the latter was dismissed from the National Education Commission for embezzlement. Many, like Seweryn Rzewuski (1743–1811), Franciszek-Ksavery Branicki (1730–1819), Stanisław-Szczęsny Potocki (1751–1805), Piotr Ożarowski (1741–94), or Bishop Kossakowski's brother, Szymon Kossakowski (1741–94), monopolized the leading military commands in the Republic, and belonged to the most wealthy magnatial families. During the revolutionary years, many were destined to meet with retribution. Yet such as these were legion. Men who dared to risk their lives and careers by protesting against the prevailing violence were few and far between. In the Sejm of 1773, at the First Partition, only two honest men could be found. Senator Sołtyk resigned his office. 'I would rather sit in a dungeon and cut off my hand than sign the sentence passed on my fatherland;' he wrote to Staeckelberg, 'a Pole who permits the partition of his country would be sinning against God. And we senators . . . would become perjurers.' Tadeusz Rejtan (1746–80), envoy of Nowogródek, went further. Having begged the members in vain to reject the Partition, he rent his clothes and threw himself on to the floor of the chamber: 'On the blood of Christ, I adjure you, do not play the part of Judas; kill me, stamp on me, but do not kill the Fatherland.' Seven years later, driven to distraction, he committed suicide.

The eventual consequence of the First Partition was, of course, the Second Partition; and of the Second, the Third. Violence bred violence. The tensions provoked on the first occasion were not resolved, and were ready to break surface again as soon as Russian vigilance wavered. Their reappearance would provide the justification for yet another intervention. Between 1773 and 1793 and again in 1794–5, the entire scenario was re-enacted with only minor variations. On each occasion, a pattern was clearly observable. The Polish reformers, obstructed in their plans to remedy their country's ills by legal means, turned to an illegal adventure which had to be forcibly suppressed by Russian arms. On each occasion, in order to avoid the risk of a wider conflagration, and prior to her punishment of the rebellious Poles, the Empress of Russia was obliged to seek the consent and the assistance of her Prussian or Austrian rivals. On each occasion, as the price of their consent and assistance, Berlin or Vienna demanded a slice of Polish territory. In this way, each Partition was the logical consequence of an attempt to launch a programme of reform. Once this mechanism is understood, it is clear that the Partitions were not merely unfortunate accidents of foreign policy whose chance occurrence interrupted the progress of internal reform. The Partitions were a necessary part of the process whereby reform had to be obstructed if Russian supremacy was to be maintained. The Republic of Poland– Lithuania was not destroyed because of its internal anarchy. It was destroyed because it repeatedly tried to reform itself.

The lines of conflict were clearly drawn. The main protagonists were on the one hand, the Empress of Russia, who sought to defend the status quo, and on the other hand, the Polish reformers, who demanded change. The Empress could count on the constant support of the leading Polish magnates, whose privileges she had sworn to uphold; on the religious dissidents, whose indignation she kept inflamed; of the Polish Army, which was under the magnates' command; of the Polish Church, whose bishops were in Russian pay; and of the majority of the Polish Sejm, which was packed with magnatial pensioners and Russian agents. The reformers in contrast could only count on the intermittent support of a vacillating King, on a handful of noblemen who opposed the main magnatial Opposition; on the sporadic interest of Russia's foreign adversaries, such as France, Sweden, and Turkey; on a minority of the Sejm; and on the incipient patriotism of the country at large. The contest was heavily weighted from the start. The Russian Party, though lacking in popular support, enjoyed the advantages of the Law, of superior numbers, of the professional armies, and of a unified policy

directed from St. Petersburg. The Reformers had little but
their wits, their powers of improvisation, and their sense of
superior moral purpose.

For more than a decade after the First Partition, the rival
parties observed an uneasy truce. The Russian Party had
proved the strength of its hand, and could afford to make a
number of concessions. The Reformers, conscious of the
limits within which they had to work, were content with
piecemeal innovations. The King, grateful for an end to the
preceding turbulence, managed the country amicably enough
in conjunction with a new series of Russian ambassadors
hand-picked for their tact and restraint. Limited reforms,
which did not contravene the principles of the protectorate,
were positively encouraged. In 1773, the Commission of
National Education was created by the very Sejm which had
just passed the Partition. In 1775, the establishment of a
Permanent Council greatly strengthened the executive government, whose five departments formed the core of a modern
administrative system. In the 1780s, Stanisław-August began
to edge his way towards an independent foreign policy.
Catherine preoccupied by her disputes with Sweden and
Turkey, was losing the sympathy of Prussia and Austria. After
the death of Frederick the Great in 1786, there were distinct
signs that his successor, Frederick-William III, might be willing
to support the Polish reformers as a way of embarrassing
Catherine.

Yet the utter helplessness of Poland—Lithuania in this
period could not be easily disguised. The King and his circle
could not escape from the web of external coercion and
internal disloyalty in which they were trapped. Indeed, their
renewed efforts to extricate themselves were the direct cause
of their downfall. In 1787, learning of Russia's international
troubles, Stanisław-August tried to exploit the situation to
Poland's advantage. Having invited the Empress Catherine
and Prince Potemkin to the royal palace at Kaniów on the
Dnieper, he proposed a straightforward political bargain. In
return for a Russo-Polish Alliance against the Turks, he
pressed the Empress to allow him to expand the Polish Army
and to share in the expected profits of the Black Sea Trade.
In the expectation of a positive response, the Polish Sejm was

ordered to assemble in October 1788. The Empress's response, however, was negative. Assured that the Republic's disaffected Hetmans, Branicki, Rzewuski, and Potocki, would support her Turkish campaigns unconditionally, the Empress saw no reason to bother herself with the King's proposals. As always, Russia had nothing to gain by condoning Polish reforms, and Poland had nothing to offer by way of inducements. 'It is necessary to dismiss the personal concerns of the King and his Ministers', Catherine wrote in a private letter, 'and to keep the constitution as it is now. For truth to tell, there is no need or benefit for Russia in Poland becoming more active.[16] A clearer appreciation of the political realities could not be imagined. The British Minister in Warsaw, writing on 7 July 1788, reached the same conclusions:

Since the Partition till this very day, Poland possesses neither her own history nor politically independent existence. Deprived of trade, having not a single external ally, possessing neither sufficient internal strength nor revenues enabling emancipation from foreign rule, squeezed by three powerful monarchies on all sides, she seems to be waiting in silence for a sentence that will bring about her emptiness . . . This is the fate of a country which, under clever government, could easily rank among the first powers of Europe . . .[17]

The ultimate consequences of the King's *démarche,* though entirely logical, were not foreseen at the time. The Polish Sejm, originally convoked to approve the projected Russo-Polish Alliance, turned instead to the associated proposals of Reform. An assembly which had served for decades as the conveyor-belt of Russian policies seized its chance to act as the launching-pad of political liberation. Whilst the Russian cat was away at the Turkish War, the Polish mice began to play with fire. In the four years 1788–91, the reformers of the Sejm abolished all those constraints, which had per-petuated the Republic's bondage. By so doing, they under-mined the foundations of the Russian protectorate in Poland, and overturned the system which had prevailed ever since the baleful settlement of 1717. It was inevitable that the Russian Government, and the Russians' Polish clients, would intervene at the earliest opportunity – as they surely did. Thus, the King's ingenuous attempt to organize a genuine alliance with Russia gave rise to the Four Years' Sejm: the Sejm to the

Constitution of 3 May; the Constitution to the Confederation of Targowica; the Confederation of the Russo-Polish War of 1791–2; the War to the Second Partition of 1793; the Partition to Kościuszko's National Rising of 1794; the Rising to the Third Partition and the destruction of the state. In circumstances where the least movement could provoke incalculable consequences, the Republic's only chance of survival had been to stand absolutely motionless. Instead, by taking one small innocent step, the King precipitated an avalanche whose accelerating momentum engulfed the entire country in total disaster.

In those same years, the appearance of the French Revolution heightened existing tensions in Eastern Europe. The Empires felt threatened by the forces of Universal Revolution. Europe was dividing into armed camps. The mild-tempered reformers in Warsaw could be denounced as disciples of the Jacobins of Paris.[18] Not for the last time, Poland could be crushed in order that Europeans everywhere might sleep more peacefully.

Internal developments in Poland at this time raise two peculiar historical problems. One concerns the relationship of political ideas to political action. The generation of leaders which came to prominence in the course of Stanisław-August's reign was exceptionally well-versed in contemporary progressive thought; yet they failed to put their ideas to good effect. For twenty years, the journal *Monitor* (1765–85) had faithfully relayed all the debates and developments of Western Europe, regularly translating and republishing the cardinal texts of the French *Encyclopédie*. From 1782, the *Pamiętnik Historyczno-Polityczno-Ekonomiczny* (Historico-Politico-Economic Record) had systematically discussed programmes for reviving the country's fortunes. A bevy of politically conscious writers flourished. Franciszek Bohomolec (1720–84), an editor of *Monitor,* did not live to see the revolution. A former Jesuit, he devoted his later life to the theatre, to the Polish language, and to social criticism. Ignacy Krasicki (1735–1801), poet, satirist, translator, and Prince-Bishop of Warmia, inimitably fostered both patriotism and anticlericalism. At once the King's chaplain in Warsaw and a frequent companion of Frederick II in Berlin, he made his début in 1774 with his *Hymn do miłości ojczyzny* (Hymn to the Love of one's Country), and his reputation in *Myszeis* (The War of the Mice), *Monachomachia* (The War of the Monks), *Satyry* (Satires), and *Bajki i przypowieści* (Tales and Stories). The Revd Hugo Kołłątaj (1750–1812), Rector and reformer of the Jagiellonian University, was one of the ideological leaders of the Four Years Sejm and one of the authors of the Constitution of 3 May. His 'Kuźnica' (Smithy), a group of progressive, reformist politicians, actively propagated increasingly radical ideas. The Revd Stanisław Staszic (1755–1826), philosopher, geologist, and translator of the *Iliad,* belonged in contrast to the bourgeois tradition, pioneering the field of economic and scientific development. A physiocrat in origin, and a lapsed priest, he became one of the most eloquent patriots and republicans of his day:

O great Nation! How long are you going to dwell in such insensitivity? Or perhaps you intend to perish, leaving nothing behind but infamy. There is no example where a people counting nearly twenty million, settled on the most fruitful land and endowed by Nature with all resources, should await slavery with such complacency and frigidity . . .[19]

In his *Przestrogi dla Polski* (Warnings for Poland, 1790) and in his *Ród ludzki* (The Human Race, 1792), he fervently described and denounced the social, economic, and political evils of his day. Julian Ursyn Niemcewicz (1757–1841), dramatist and novelist, started his literary career as a French translator. His comedy *Powrót posła* (The Return of the Envoy), first staged in 1791, mercilessly mocking the selfishness of the magnates, significantly sharpened the political atmosphere. In it, he penned the lines which so aptly summarize one of the basic defects of the whole period: 'For we ourselves are to blame for our own misfortunes . . . We thought of ourselves and never of our country!'[20] Elsewhere, in the *Fragment Biblie targowickiej* (Fragment of the Bible of Targowica, 1792), written in pseudo-Old Testament style, and in his *Obrona wojska moskiewskiego* (Defence of the Muscovite Army, 1793), he perfected the art of political travesty. All these men were in close touch with the King, who shared an interest in their ideas. They frequented the King's philosophical lunches which were held every Thursday at the Royal

Palace. They were all familiar with conditions abroad, having
travelled widely or studied in France or Italy. They had a
ready clientele in Warsaw in the graduates of the Collegium
Nobilium, and in the Corps of Cadets. As the ideals of the
Enlightenment and later the slogan of 'Liberté, Egalité,
Fraternité', made their impact, they knew perfectly well
what was involved. The trouble was that they had no freedom
to put their ideas to the test. They had to count on the
certainty that any attempt to remove political reform from
the stage, the newspaper column, or the debating chamber
into the realm of concrete action would immediately arouse
the protest of the Russian ambassador and the eventual intervention of Russian troops. They were advanced political
gastronomists, highly skilled in the theory of *haute cuisine.*
They knew their French recipes by heart, but had no hope of
feeding the nation on any sort of diet until they took control
of their own kitchen.

The second related problem concerns the significance of
lost causes. In all the volumes expended by Polish historians
on the period 1788–94, very few words are wasted to explain
that none of the splendid constitutional and social projects of
the reformers were ever put into effect. Neither the Constitution of 3 May, nor Kościuszko's Manifesto of Połaniec, was
ever implemented. The future of the inhabitants of Poland—
Lithuania was decided not by the reformers and revolu-
tionaries, but by the despots of St. Petersburg, Vienna, and
Berlin. It is in this period that the historian first meets with
that Polish tradition where the 'Word' has precedence over the
'Fact': where more attention is paid to what people would
have liked to happen than to what actually occurred. In Polish
eyes, the refusal to accept the political situation as the reality
has formed an essential spur to national consciousness; but it
has tended to cloud the vision of the past. At the same time,
one cannot deny that idealism is itself real enough. In the
revolutionary era, as in the nineteenth century, there were
many Poles who were not content to dream. They worked
and fought and bled for their ideals in the most real and
practical way. The problem is whether they should be brought
to the centre of the historical stage, or left in the wings. Does
it not matter that their sacrifices brought no tangible result?

It is regrettable no doubt; but it is hard to conclude that Tadeusz Kościuszko influenced the course of Polish history as effectively as Catherine the Great or the Confederates of Targowica.

Tadeusz Andrzej Bonawentura Kościuszko (1746–1817) combined the idealism of intellectual circles with the practical skills of a soldier. He was one of those providential figures who in ordinary times might well have lived in obscurity but who was thrown into prominence in spite of himself. He was born into a military family, the son of the 'Sword-bearer' of Brześć, and educated in a Piarist school near Pinsk, and later in the Cadet School. For five years between 1769 and 1775, he was trained on a royal bursary in France, at Versailles, Paris, and Brest, in the Corps du Génie. On his return to Poland, he was unable to afford the 18,000 zł. required for a commission, and left almost immediately for North America with a group of French volunteers. As an officer-engineer in the United States' service, he distinguished himself in the War of Independence at Saratoga and West Point, building fortifications, directing river-crossings, and rising to the rank of Brigadier-General. At the end, he was invested with the Order of Cincinnati, whom he promptly imitated by returning home to the plough and to his native village of Siechnowice. In 1789, at the age of 43, he was finally recruited to the Polish service on the orders of the Four Years Sejm, which realized that a strong army was the only safe guarantee for its political deliberations. This 'hero of two continents', 'the Polish Lafayette', together with the King's nephew, General Józef Poniatowski, who had been retrieved from the Austrian Service, was set to work on the painstaking task of Army Reform.[21]

To anyone with a sense of reality, it was clear that the work of the Four Years Sejm initiated in October 1788, ran a serious risk of Russian intervention. Unlike all its predecessors, it refused to recess after the usual six weeks, but constituted itself into a legal Confederation, determined to stay the course until meaningful legislation had been passed. Under its energetic Marshal, Stanisław Małachowski (1736–1809), it launched a large number of projects and commissions aimed at the recovery of national sovereignty and the growth of the economy. Benefiting from Russian preoccupation with the French crisis and with the Turkish War, it was able to push its demands much further than normal times would have permitted. In December 1789, it received a demonstration by representatives of 141 towns, who paraded in black in protest against their exclusion from the constitutional life of the country. In 1790, it divided itself into two chambers, to speed up business. Finally, on 3 May 1791, it was the scene of a carefully planned *coup d'état*. Kołłataj's 'Patriotic Party', acting in collusion with Małachowski and with the knowledge of the King, picked a day when two-thirds of the deputies were absent on holiday. A bill, secretly prepared, was read to a half-empty House:

Freed from the shameful coercion of foreign orders, and cognizant of the ancient faults of our system of government, and valuing national independence and freedom over life itself . . . We pass the following statute in recognition that the fate of us all depends exclusively on the foundation and perfection of a national constitution . . .[22]

Queries about a quorum were quashed. The King was persuaded to sign. The soldiers and the crowd in the Castle Square greeted the news with cries of *'Vivat Rex! Vivat Konstitucja!'* It all seemed deceptively simple. The harmful practices of the old Republic — the *Liberum Veto,* the right of resistance, the Confederations, the 'free' elections — were to be abolished. Although the King was a confirmed bachelor, the monarchy was to be hereditary. The 'Committee of Two Nations' was to replace the separate offices of State of the Crown and Grand Duchy. The *Straż Praw* (Guardians of the Laws), consisting of king, Primate, and five ministers were to act as the supreme executive Cabinet. The citizens of the towns were to enjoy the same rights and privileges as the noble citizens of the Republic. The peasantry were to enjoy 'the protection of the law and government of the country'. The Army was to receive its long-awaited establishment of 100,000 men. The various local commissions of Law and Order, and of Civil and Military Affairs, were to provide the basis for the territorial organs of a centralized administration. Discussions on the details proceeded in the Sejm for a further twelve months.

To later generations, this Constitution of the Third of May assumed a symbolic importance out of all proportion to its practical significance. It was the Bill of Rights of the Polish tradition, the embodiment of all that was enlightened and progressive in Poland's past, a monument to the nation's will to live in freedom, a permanent reproach to the tyranny of the partitioning powers. Like many liberals of the nineteenth century, Karl Marx expressed his fulsome admiration. 'With all its shortcomings', Marx wrote, 'this constitution appears against the background of Russo-Prusso-Austrian barbarity as the only work of freedom which Central Europe has ever produced of its own accord. Moreover, it was created by a privileged class, the gentry. The history of the world knows no other example of such generosity by the gentry.'[23] In 1918, when the Polish Republic was restored, 3 May was adopted as the national holiday.

Needless to say, in the eyes of Tsarist officialdom, the Sejm had compromised itself beyond repair. Its contacts with the French Assembly were taken as proof of an international revolutionary conspiracy. It had to be suppressed, with all its works. In this, the lead was taken by the Empress's principal Polish pensioners – Stanisław-Szczęsny Potocki, the two unemployed Hetmans, F. K. Branicki, and Seweryn Rzewuski, and the two Kossakowski brothers. These men assembled in St. Petersburg over the winter, and, having synchronized their plans with their Russian patrons, on 27 April 1792 signed an Act of Confederation designed to overthrow the Polish Sejm and the Polish Constitution. For the sake of good form, they concealed the existence of the Act until they had time to make their way on to Polish territory at Targowica in the Ukraine. There, on 14 May, they formally raised their standard, and were joined by a Russian Army only four days later. The trial of strength, for which Kościuszko and Poniatowski were preparing, had arrived.

The Russo-Polish War of 1792–3, or the War of the Second Partition as it was later called, lasted more than a year. Yet its outcome was decided by a couple of unexpected political reversals within the first three months. The Russian victory owed less to the brilliance of Suvorov than to the pusillanimity of Stanisław-August and the treachery of Frederick-William.

On 18 June at Zieleńce, the Polish forces repulsed the Russians with heavy losses. The leading officers were decorated by the King with medals, and inducted into his new Order of *Virtuti Militari.* But then the King lost heart. He watched in dismay as two Russian armies advanced in a wide pincer movement, forcing Kościuszko's defence of the Bug at Dubienka on 18 July, and threatening to encircle Warsaw. In August, almost without warning, he announced his adherence to the Confederation of Targowica, and ordered his troops to hold their fire. It was a shocking betrayal, executed for the most humane of motives. Faced by the Russians' threefold numerical superiority − 96,000 men to 36,000 on the Polish side − he wanted to save his country unnecessary suffering. The Army dispersed. The commanding officers and the reforming politicians left hurriedly for exile. Warsaw was occupied without opposition. Further resistance was scattered, prolonged, and pointless.[24]

On the diplomatic front, the Russian success was ensured by means of a bilateral pact with Prussia. In the preceding years, when the Russians and Austrians were still engaged against the Turks, Frederick-William II had encouraged their adversaries, including the reformers in the Polish Sejm. In January 1790, he had made overtures to the Porte, and in March his ambassador in Warsaw, Luchesini, had negotiated a formal treaty of friendship with the Republic. In the event of an attack on Poland−Lithuania, Prussia was to supply an army of 18,000 men for Poland's defence. Prussia was to be rewarded with the cession of Danzig and Thorn, whilst Poland could be compensated by the restoration of Austrian Galicia. But there Prussian intrigues ended. At the Congress of Reichenbach (Dzierżoniów) in Silesia, convoked in June 1790 at Austrian insistence, Frederick-William's representatives were persuaded to abandon their anti-Austrian schemes. The Polish representative, Jabłonowski, flatly denied that the Republic would ever cede Danzig or Thorn to anyone. The news from Paris was driving the monarchies together. In August 1791, at the Congress of Pilsnitz (Piłczyce), attended by the French King's brothers (the future Louis XVIII and Charles X), Frederick-William met the Emperor Leopold in person, and agreed to support the principle of Monarchy wherever it was threatened. In February 1792, in anticipation of the first Revolutionary War, Prussia and Austria entered an anti-Revolutionary alliance. In this situation, Catherine could dispose of Poland as she thought fit. The Poles could be crushed as dangerous Jacobins without fear of outside interference. The Prussians, already engaged in France, could be invited to approve Russian action in Poland or to answer for the consequences if they refused. Frederick-William could not hesitate. At a convention signed on 7 August 1792, he agreed to the Russian plan on condition that he was paid off with a suitable share of the proceeds. By a simple act of treachery, he enlarged his kingdom, and abandoned the Poles to their fate. Thus, when the Russian Army was completing its conquest, the Republic discovered that its precious Prussian ally had gone over to the enemy. In the autumn of 1792 a Prussian Army appeared in Poland to complete the Russian conquest. A Treaty of Partition signed on 4 January 1793, gave Prussia not only Danzig and Thorn but the whole of Wielkopolska – the cradle of the Polish kingdom. Russia took 100,000 square miles of the eastern provinces, thereby annexing the remainder of the Grand Duchy of Lithuania. Austria, which was demanding its share after avoiding the dirty work, was given nothing.[25]

As in 1773, the defeated Poles were obliged to submit in a legal and orderly manner. From June to October 1793, the last Sejm of the Republic's history was assembled at Grodno in order to reverse the legislation of the previous five years. Its membership was carefully screened. Its deliberations, conducted under the sights of Russian guns, were a charade. The Constitution of 3 May was formally rescinded. The 'Golden Freedom' was restored. The Second Partition was approved. The King was persuaded to sign. The nobility, threatened with the wholesale sequestration of their estates, were obliged to assent. Here was another brilliant operation of decisive surgery. The treaties of cession were completed with Russia on 11/22 July 1793, and with Prussia on 25 September 1793.[26]

Matters could not rest there, however. Having first encouraged the people to resist, the King could not now command them to desist. The reformers had not been finally defeated. In the winter of 1793–4, the Russians failed to bring the Republic to heel. Ministers deserted their posts. Officers refused orders. Local dietines passed resolutions of protest. Government business ground to a halt. News from France, where Louis XVI had been guillotined, spelled danger for the despots. This was the hey-day of Robespierre. The partitioning powers were thoroughly frightened, and involved with the revolutionary war. Moderate men, deprived of their Sejm but not yet of their hopes, grew more radical. The exiles were planning a counter-coup from their refuges in Leipzig and Dresden. Conspiratorial cells were formed, and oaths sworn. In Warsaw, the nervous authorities took offence at the libretto of Bogusławski's comic opera *Krakowiacy i górale* (Cracovians and Highlanders). The spectacle of a tenor in popular costume singing 'the sharper are the thistles, the sweeter is the victory' was judged altogether too suggestive.[27] The theatre was closed after three days. When, on 12 March, General Madaliński categorically refused to disband the cavalry garrison at Ostrołęka, but set out instead for Cracow, the conditions for an insurrection were already very ripe. Kościuszko's return was imminent.

In essence, therefore, the National Rising of 1794 was the natural culmination of the reformist movement. Its Jacobinist overtones were rather academic, and at most a sign of the times. Its desperate methods were the reflection less of a guiding philosophy than of the brute repression with which it was faced. The aim, as in the debating chamber of 1791, was independence. The unprecedented appeals for social revolution were motivated by the realization that nothing short of the entire nation in arms could match the overwhelming numbers of the enemy. The rendezvous was arranged in Cracow. On 24 March 1794, on the western side of the Market Square, Kościuszko read the 'Act of Insurrection of the Citizens and Inhabitants of the Palatinate of Cracow'. Dressed in national costume, with a feather in his four-cornered hat, surrounded by the blue and silver of the infantry and the green, black, and gold of the artillery men, by the banners of the guilds and by placards proclaiming 'Equality and Freedom' and 'For Cracow and the Fatherland', he swore the solemn oath:

I, Tadeusz Kościuszko, swear before God and to the whole Polish nation, that I shall employ the authority vested in me for the integrity of the frontiers, for gaining national self-rule and for the foundation of general liberty, and not for private benefit. So help me, Lord God, and the innocent suffering of Thy Son![28]

Next, the assembled citizenry swore 'to free the country from the shameful oppression and the foreign yoke, or to perish and be buried in the ruins'. A Supreme National Council was to direct the government. Its seals were to bear the inscription 'Liberty, Integrity, Independence'. All men from 18 to 28 regardless of rank were to be conscripted. This form of proceeding was adopted in all the cities and provinces to which the insurrection spread. Ten days later, on the field of Racławice, battle was joined with the Russians of General Tormasov. The issue was decided by the brave charge of Kościuszko's peasant scythe-men, who captured the enemy's guns. Tormasov withdrew. Amid the popular rejoicing, Kościuszko conducted the last ceremonial ennoblement of the Republic's history. Wojciech Bartos, a peasant, who was first to reach the guns and had placed his cap on the barrel of a cannon to the amazement of the Muscovite gunner, was dubbed with the noble name of 'Głowacki', received into Kościuszko's own clan of Korczak, given possession of his land, and offered an officer's commission. In the same spirit, on 7 May Kościuszko issued the 'Manifesto of Połaniec', freeing the peasantry as a whole from servitude, halving their dues, and promising the help of the insurrectionary authorities against the wrath of the landowners.[29]

Meanwhile, both Warsaw and Wilno had been liberated. In the Polish capital, in Easter Week, rumour spread that the Russians would try to disarm the Polish garrison when the people were at prayer in the churches. On Easter Thursday, 17 April, therefore, the Polish troops and the city mob took the Russians by surprise. Good Friday turned into an orgy of killing. Isolated Russian patrols were hounded through the streets and cut to pieces. The pace was set by the revolutionary tailor Jan Kiliński (1760–1819), and by the Guild of Slaughterers under their President, Sierakowski, whose spikes and axes added a professional touch to the business in hand. The Jacobin Club came into the open. The prisons were opened.[30]

The Russian ambassador fled. The remnants of his guard struggled out of the city across the Vistula bridges. Bishop Kossakowski, and Hetman Ożarowski, together with Jozef Zabiełło (d. 1794), Marshal of the Permanent Council and of the Confederation of Targowica, and Jozef Ankwicz (1750–94), leader of the Russian Party at the Grodno Sejm, were dragged before an Insurrectionary Court, summarily sentenced, and on 9 May publicly hanged. In June, the mob took justice into its own hands. Bishop Massalski together with Prince Adam Czetwertyński, Ambassador Karol Boscamp-Lasopolski, and an assortment of other policemen, priests, lawyers, courtiers, and suspected spies were dragged from their cells and lynched in the streets. Archbishop Michał Poniatowski (1736–94), the Primate and King's brother, committed suicide. In the Lithuanian capital, similar scenes occurred. The Polish garrison under Colonel Jakob Jasiński (1761–94) struck one hour after midnight, and by dawn the city was in their control. Hetman Kossakowski was caught trying to escape in a boat, and was hanged under the inscription, 'He who swings will not drown.' An Act of Insurrection of the Lithuanian Nation was produced, and duly signed. For a few brief months through the summer, the two parts of the old Republic were reunited. An Insurrectionary Government obtained the blessing of the King, took control of Warsaw from the local Jacobins, and ruled in the name of the whole country from 28 May to 4 November. Tadeusz Kościuszko, the *Naczelnik* (Commander), in the company of his adjutant, Julian Niemcewicz, busied himself for the coming showdown with the Russians. His orders called for 'a war to the death against Muscovite tyranny'. News came from France of the fate of Archbishop Podoski, whom death could not save from his deserts. Having fled to France, and having died in exile in Marseilles, he still did not escape retribution. His body was disinterred, torn to pieces, and cast into the sea.

The suppression of the Rising was taken in hand by the Empress Catherine in conjuction with the Prussians under the personal command of Frederick-William III. In the summer, the situation remained extremely fluid. The defeat of Zajączek at Chełm on 8 June, the recapture by the Russians of Cracow on 15 June and of Wilno on 12 August, were offset by the breakout of Polish forces in Prussian Poznania under General Dąbrowski. The siege of Warsaw had to be abandoned on 9 September. But by the end of the month, it was renewed. The Prussians to the west and north were faced by Poniatowski and Jasiński. The Russians to the south under Fersen were waiting to be joined by Suvorov marching out of the Ukraine with a new army. The Poles' last chance was to strike at the point of junction before the ring was completely sealed. Accordingly, on 10 October, Kościuszko attacked Fersen at Maciejowice, forty miles to the south-east of Warsaw on the right bank of the Vistula. For some hours, it seemed that he would win the day. But the Russians, counting on a fourfold numerical superiority, re-formed ranks, and, regardless of their terrible losses, advanced to a complete victory. Kościuszko, wounded in three places and unhorsed, was taken into captivity, together with Niemcewicz and most of his surviving staff. Suvorov's road was open. He joined with Fersen at Mińsk Mazowiecki, and on 26 October broke the Polish rearguard at Kobyłka. On 4 November, his Cossacks stormed the defences of the capital's eastern suburb, Praga, enlivened by the promise of unlimited plunder. The defenders were overwhelmed. Jasiński was killed. The population was put to the sword. Warsaw capitulated. All resistance was broken.[31]

The end of the Rising produced a number of lapidary and apochryphal remarks. On completing his task, Suvorov sent a three-word report to the Empress: 'Hurrah–Praga–Suvorov'. He received the reply: 'Bravo–Feldmarschal–Catherine'. On falling from his horse at Maciejowice, at the moment when Freedom is said to have 'shrieked', Kościuszko was wrongly reported to have uttered the words 'FINIS POLONIAE' (This is the end of Poland').

But it *was* the end of Poland. On this occasion the legalities were slightly curtailed. Once the Russian Army had suppressed the Insurrectionary Government, and deported the King, there was no Polish authority with whom the Third Partition might have been negotiated. In any case, there was no point in seeking Polish approval for an act which was to abolish the Polish state completely. Everything proceeded on the understanding that the Poles and their Republic no longer existed and that no expression of consent was necessary. In 1795,

eager to forestall their exclusion from the spoils two years
earlier, the Austrians occupied a huge area round Cracow and
named it 'New Galicia'. The Prussians replaced the Russians
in Warsaw, and named their acquisition 'New South Prussia'.
The Russians contented themselves with a slice of the eastern
borders greater than the Austrian and Prussian gains put
together (see Diagram M). On 25 November 1795, in his exile
in Grodno, Stanisław-August abdicated. The final Treaty of
Partition, signed in St. Petersburg by Russia, Prussia, and
Austria on 15/26 January 1797, appeared as a simple act of
territorial delimitation. A secret and separate article provided
for the permanent suppression of the name of Poland:

In view of the necessity to abolish everything which could revive the
memory of the existence of the Kingdom of Poland, now that the
annulment of this body politic has been effected . . . the high contracting parties are agreed and undertake never to include in their titles . . .
the name or designation of the Kingdom of Poland, which shall remain
suppressed as from the present and forever . . .[32]

*   *   *   *   *

The death-throes of Poland—Lithuania caused little comment
on the international scene. The eyes of Europe's statesmen
were fixed on France. At a time when the revolutionary
armies had overrun Belgium, Holland, and the Rhineland, and
were advancing into Piedmont, Catalonia, and Spanish Galicia,
no thought could be spared for a country whose extinction
was a foregone conclusion. Only a handful of foreign representatives stayed in Warsaw to observe the last rites, for by
1794 the Most Serene Republic had passed beyond the
ministration of diplomacy.

Sensing their predicament, the diplomats left Warsaw one
by one, like the players of Haydn's 'Farewell' Symphony —
gathering up their scores, snuffing out their candles, and tip-
toeing off the stage. The last ambassador of the King of
France, M. d'Escorches, had already gone. On 25 August 1792,
this Jacobin, *ci-devant* Marquis, had celebrated the Saint-Louis
for the last time, commending his King and country to the
Supreme Being. He was expelled that same October, by the
Confederates of Targowica, who also prevented him from publishing his account of the Revolution in French. His secretary,

Bonneau, was arrested by the Russians and spent three years under arrest in the Schlüsselberg. His replacement, Citoyen Parandier, dispatched by the Committee of Public Safety, never arrived. Baron Osip Andreivich von Ingelstrom, who took over the Russian Embassy from Sievers in January 1794, barely had time to commence work before the outbreak of Kościuszko's Rising on the night of 17 April forced him to escape, having burned his ciphers. But one of his colleagues, Baron von Asch, was captured, and imprisoned as a hostage. The entire diplomatic corps signed a petition to the King, protesting at the assault on their immunity. But neither they nor the King could influence the contest developing between Kościuszko and the Russians. In June, Ludwig von Buchholtz, the Prussian, fearing the Varsovians' wrath, packed his bags and departed briskly. In July, Benedict de Cache, the Austrian, made an excuse to leave for Carlsbad on vacation, but never returned. In August, the Swedish ambassador, General Toll was arrested as a result of a conspiracy among his own staff, one of whom, Samuel Casstrom, took his place. In November, the Russian Army under Suvorov appeared on the east bank of the Vistula. The storming of Praga, and the horrendous massacre of its population, ended the Rising. Colonel William Gardner, the British Minister, and the Papal Nuncio, Mgr Lorenzo Litta, crossed the river to plead for the lives of the capital's inhabitants. Suvorov relented. On 7 January 1795, the King, surrounded by 120 Russian dragoons, was escorted on to the road to exile with all due pomp and ceremony. The following day, the counsellor of the Russian mission, Divov, informed the remaining ambassadors that the King's departure had ended their missions, 'since the court to which you are accredited has ceased to exist!' He ordered them to inform their governments of the changed situation and to remove the armorials from the gates of their residences. On 8 February, Stanisław-August, writing from Grodno, bade them adieu in separate letters, requesting them to stop all communication with his former ministers, as this could only serve to intensify Russian suspicions. This prompted the departure of Don Dominic d'Yriarte, Secretary and envoy of the King of Spain, who had come to Warsaw out of curiosity when the execution of Louis XVI had cut short his mission to Paris. Colonel Griesheim, the Dutchman, left when he learned that Holland was invaded by the French revolutionary armies. Thereafter, the diplomats were left to their own devices. On 22 November 1795, Johann Jakub Patz, the Saxon Minister, died at his post. He was buried in the evangelical cemetery, on the same afternoon that the Nuncio was offering a *vin de congé* to Suvorov, who was bound for his new assignment in Germany. On 2 December, according to the terms of the Third Partition, the Prussian Army replaced the Russians in Warsaw. Casstrom, the Swede, and the other chargés d'affaires closed their embassies for good. Only the Nuncio and Gardner, the Englishman, remained – the one to protect the Catholic Church, the other to settle his debts. Throughout 1796, the Nuncio refused to leave. The armorials of St. Peter which defiantly hung on the gates of the Nonciatura were the last public evidence of condolence for the deceased Republic. He finally left on 15 February 1797, instructed by the Vatican to proceed to St. Petersburg. As his cortège turned the corner of the street, the police removed the offending armorials, and placed them as trophies in a museum. It was the last diplomatic incident in Warsaw for 121 years. Gardner alone stayed on, as a bankrupt private citizen.

Gardner's dispatches during the death agony of the Republic make pathetic reading indeed. On 12 November 1794, he wrote to the British Secretary of State about the storming of Praga:

It is with regret I inform your Lordship that the day of the forcing the lines of Prag was attended by the most horrid and unnecessary barbarities – Houses burnt, women massacred, infants at the breast pierced with the pikes of cosaques and universal plunder, and we now know the same fate was prepared for Warsaw . . .[33]

After the massacre, it was obvious even to the most sanguine observer that the Russians were determined to put an end to a state which repaid the benevolence of their Empress with such fierce ingratitude. But no inkling of their immediate intentions was available in Warsaw. Suvorov was as much in the dark as the foreign ambassadors. Instructions arrived from St. Petersburg, and had to be executed without query or explanation. Gardiner had nothing to tell the government at home and confined his comments to vague speculations, and to observations on the Russians' extraordinarily conspiratorial behaviour. In December 1794, he had suspected that Stanisław-August was about to be deported, and wondered whether his own possession of two sets of letters of credence, one for the Republic as well as that for the King, meant that his mission to the Republic could continue after his mission to the King had ended. He watched the King's departure. 'It is impossible', he wrote, 'for any person really attached to royalty, not to feel most sensibly on such an occasion. I hope, however, that the King of Poland, even divested of his sovereignty, has yet some happy days before Him.'[34] When Divov called on him, he had no idea whether the Russian's interpretation of the situation was correct or not. But it made no difference, since there was no one who would have listened to his representations one way or another. On 13 February 1795 he received the King's last official letter, painfully written in French, and sent a copy to London:

Dear Gardiner, Comme mon rôle, et le vôtre auprès de moi paroissent finir très prochainement, et comme je n'espère plus de vous voir, il m'importè au moins de vous dire Adieu, et celà du fond de mon cœur. Vous y garderez votre place jusqu'à ma mort, et j'espère bien qu'on nous rejoindra au moins là où des âmes honnêtes et des cœurs bons devraient je crois se trouver ensemble à jamais . . . Toujours il restera vrai que j'aime et j'honore votre roi et votre Nation, et vous le leur direz. Toujours, il restera vrai que je désire que vous conserviez souvenir et affection pour votre Ami,

Stanislas Auguste Roi. *

Meanwhile, Gardner constantly begged London for an advance to pay off his creditors. He had been feeding three hundred refugees in the embassy, and had never received the

---

* Dear Gardiner, As my function, and your own at my side appear to be finishing very shortly, and as I no longer hope to see you, I am obliged at least to say Adieu, and that from the depth of my heart. I shall always keep a place for you there until I die, and I hope indeed that we shall at least be reunited where, I believe, honest souls and good hearts should be together for ever . . . It will always be true that I love and honour your King and your Nation, and you will tell them so. It will always be true that I would wish you to preserve in memory and affection your Friend,

Stanislas-August, King. [35]

salary for his previous post as Governor of Hurst Castle in 1789. It was three years before Canning at the Treasury relented, and a payment of £2,000 was approved. Gardiner's final communication from Warsaw is dated 11 December 1797. In 1798, he proceeded to Berlin where he deposited the archives of the Warsaw Legation with the British ambassador to Prussia. At that point, the last mission of a diplomat accredited to the 'Most Serene Republic' finally closed. The Republic had been dead and indecently buried for three years past.

Notes

PREFACE

1. W. Reddaway, ed. *The Cambridge History of Poland* (Cambridge, 1941–50): vol. 1, to 1696; vol. 2, 1696–1935.
2. A. Gieysztor, S. Kieniewicz (editor-in-chief), *et al.*, eds., *History of Poland* (Warsaw, 1968); second revised edition (Warsaw, 1979).
3. e.g. W. Allison Phillips, *Poland* (London, 1915); Lord Eversley, *The Partitions of Poland* (London, 1915: republished, 1973); Major F. E. Whitton, *The History of Poland: from the earliest times to the present day* (London, 1917); W. J. Rose, *The Rise of Polish Democracy* (London, 1944); S. Sharpe, *White Eagle on a Red Field* (Cambridge, Mass., 1935) etc.
4. W. R. Morfill, *Poland* (London, 1893; reprinted, 1972).
5. See J. Michelet, *La Pologne Martyre* (Paris, 1863).
6. Jan Kochanowski, 'Człowiek boże igrzysko', *Fraszki*, III, No. 76.
7. Stańczyk (1480–1560), the court jester of King Zygmunt I: Franciszek Zabłocki (1752–1821), satirist and dramatist, translator of Molière and Fielding; Stanisław Kostka Potocki (1755–1821). See J. Krzyżanowski, 'Blazen starego króla: Stańczyk w dziejach kultury polskiej', in *W wieku Reja i Stańczycka* (Warsaw, 1958).

CHAPTER 1. MILLENIUM

1. Monumenta Poloniae Historica (New Series) i. *Relacja Ibrahim Ibn Jakuba z podróży do krajow słowiańskich w przekładzie Al Bekriego*, ed. T. Kowalski (Cracow, 1946), contains both the original Arabic text and a later Latin version, *De Slavis* (Concerning the Slavs). See G. Labuda, 'Najstarsza relacja o Polsce w nowym wydaniu', *Roczniki Historyczne*, xvi (1947), 100–83.
2. Pierre David, *Les Sources de l'histoire de la Pologne à l'époque des Piasts (963–1386)* (Paris, 1934). The principal texts are in *Monumenta Poloniae Historica. Pomniki Dziejowe Polski* (Lwów, 1864–93), 6 vols., reprinted Warsaw 1960–1. See also: *By czas nie zaćmił i niepamieć: Wybór kronik średniowiecznych*, ed. Antonina Jelicz (Warsaw, 1975).
3. M. Bobrzyński, S. Smołka, *Jan Długosz: jego życie i stanowisko w piśmiennictwie* (Cracow, 1893). The Latin chronicles, first published as *Joannis Dlugossii Senioris Canonici Cracoviensis Opera Omnia* (Cracow, 1863–87), 15 vols., are available in Polish translation: Jan Długosz, *Roczniki czyli kroniki sławnego Królestwa Polskiego*, ed. J. Dąbrowski (Warsaw 1960).
4. N. Rutkowska, *Bishop A. Naruszewicz and his History of the Polish Nation: a Critical Study* (Washington D.C., 1941).
5. W. J. Rose, 'Lelewel as historian', *Slavonic and East European Review*, xv

(1936–7), 649–62; M. H. Serejski, 'Joachim Lelewel, 1786–1861', *Acta Poloniae Historica*, vi (1962), 35–54. See also M. H. Serejski, *Koncepcja historii powszechnej Joachima Lelewela* (Warsaw, 1958); S. Kieniewicz, *Samotnik brukselski* (Warsaw, 1964).

6. M. H. Serejski, 'L'école historique de Cracovie et l'historiographie européenne', *Acta Poloniae Historica*, xxvi (1972), 127–52.

7. M. Bobrzyński, *Dzieje Polski w zarysie*, 4th Edition, with continuation (Warsaw, 1927), 3 vols,; 'O podziale historyi polskiej na okresy', *Szkice i studja historyczne* (Cracow, 1922), i, 36–62.

8. Stanisław Kutrzeba, *Historia ustroju Polski w zarysie* (Warsaw–Lwów, 1920), 4 vols.

9. A. F. Grabski, 'The Warsaw School of History', *Acta Poloniae Historica*, xxvi (1972), 153–70.

10. T. Korzon, *Historya nowożytna* (Warsaw, 1903–12), 2 vols. There is a valuable collection of Korzon's writings recently republished as Tadeusz Korzon, *Odrodzenie w upadku: wybór pism historycznych* (Warsaw, 1975).

11. W. J. Rose, 'Polish Historical Writing', *Journal of Modern History*, ii (1930), 569–85; 'Realism in Polish History', *Journal of Central European Affairs*, ii (1942–3), 235–49; O. Halecki, 'Problems of Polish Historiography', *Slavonic and East European Review*, xxi (1943), 223–39; Claude Backvis, 'Polish Tradition and the Concept of History', *Polish Review*, vi (1961), 125–58.

12. Oscar Halecki, *History of Poland*, Revised edition, with continuation by A. Polonsky (London, 1978).

13. M. Kukiel, *Dzieje Polski porozbiorowej, 1795–1921* (London, 1961).

14. W. Pobóg-Malinowski, *Najnowsza historia polityczna Polski*, 2 vols. (London, 1965–7).

15. *Pierwsza Konferencja Metodologiczna Historyków Polskich: Przemówienia, Referaty, Dyskusja* (Some Problems in the Periodization of Polish History) (Warsaw, 1953), i 157. See also E. Valkenier, 'The Soviet impact on Polish post-war historiography', *Journal of Central European Affairs*, xi (1950–2), 372–96.

16. *Istoriya Pol'shi*, USSR Academy of Sciences (Moscow, 1954–65), 3 vols.

17. Stanisław Arnold, 'Niektóre problemy periodizacji dziejów Polski', *Pierwsza Konferencja Metodologiczna*, op. cit. 155–85.

18. *Historia Polski*, Polish Academy of Sciences (Warsaw, 1957–   ), 4 vols. in 10 parts (incomplete). See W. Drzewieniecki, 'The new Historia Polski of the Polish Academy of Sciences', in D. Wandycz, ed., *Studies in Polish Civilisation* (New York, 1966), 176–96; also E. Valkenier, 'Sovietisation and Liberalism in Polish post-war historiography', *Journal of Central European Affairs*, xix (1959–60), 149–73.

19. Jerzy Topolski *et al.*, *Dzieje Polski* (Poznań, 1976). A similar survey in paperback displaying the same traits, has recently been written in Cracow, viz. J. Nierozumski, J. A. Gierowski, J. Buszko, *Historia Polski*, 3 vols. (Warsaw, 1978).

20. *Millenium Poloniae Christianae, 966–1966* (Centralny Ośrodek Duszpasterstwa Emigracji) (Rome, 1966), 335.

21. For recent views, see A. F. Grabski, 'Interpreting History', *Polish Perspectives*,

xiv, 12 (1971), 18–28; A. Mączak, 'The Style and Method of History', *Polish Perspectives*, xvi, 7/8 (1973), 12–17.

22. The fullest survey of Polish historiography is the compendium edited by M. H. Serejski, *Historycy o historii* (Warsaw, 1966), vol. I, 1775–1918; vol. II, 1918–39.

CHAPTER 2. POLSKA

1. F. Dvornik, *The Making of Central and Eastern Europe* (London, 1949), 14. Konrad Jazdżewski, *Ancient Peoples and Places: Poland* (London, 1965), summarizes the Polish hypothesis, which is preceded by an interesting survey of the development of Polish archaeology.

2. Marija Gimbutas, *Bronze Age Cultures in Central and Eastern Europe* (The Hague, 1965). This author's other study *The Slavs* (London, 1971), Ancient Peoples and Places, vol. 74, although included in the same series as Jazdżewski's volume, contradicts him on many essential points.

3. Jan Czarnecki, *The Goths in Ancient Poland: a study in the historical geography of the Oder-Vistula region during the first two centuries of our era* (Miami, 1975).

4. Mortimer Wheeler, *Rome beyond the Imperial Frontiers* (London, 1955). The richest find of Roman imports in 'Free Germany' was made at the burial site of five barbarian chieftains near Lübsow (Lubowo) in Pomerania.

5. Tacitus, 'Germania' in *Tacitus on Britain and Germany*, translated by H. Mattingly (Penguin Books, London, 1948), 101–40.

6. J. Otto Maenchen-Helfen, *The World of the Huns* (Berkeley, 1973). See Gerard Labuda, *Źródła, Sagi i Legendy do najdawniejszych dziejów Polski* (Warsaw, 1961), contains studies of Alfred the Great, the Gotho-Hunnic wars, the *Widsith*, and the *Chanson de Roland*.

7. F. Dvornik, 'The first wave of the Drang nach Osten', *Cambridge Historical Journal*, vii (1943), 129–45.

8. See Karol Buczek, *Polska przed 1000 lat*, PAN – Prace Historyczne no. 5 (Warsaw, 1960).

9. J. Wielowiejski, 'The Development of agriculture in the Polish territories during the period of contacts with Celtic and Roman culture', *Ergon*, ii (1960), 284–99.

10. H. Łowmiański, 'Economic problems of the early feudal Polish state', *Acta Poloniae Historica*, iii (1960), 7–32; also *Podstawy gospodarcze formowania się państw słowiańskich* (Warsaw, 1953).

11. Andrzej Zajączkowski, *Główne elementy kultury szlacheckiej w Polsce* (Wrocław, 1961), 113; in German translation, *Hauptelemente der Adelskultur in Polen* (Marburg/Lahn, 1967).

12. *Lustracja Województwa Krakowskiego, 1564*, Part I, ed. J. Małecki, Polish Academy of Sciences, Institute of History (Warsaw, 1962), 148–9. Local weights and measures and monetary units cause endless complications in understanding these texts. The exact volume of the bushel in Nowy Targ at this time is not known. In neighbouring Nowy Sącz, the *korzec* (bushel) was the same as in Cracow, i.e. about half of the Danzig measure. Within thirty miles, at Czchów, it was equivalent to 1½ Cracovian bushels, and at Biecz 2.

The monetary units in use were: 1 mark (*marca/grzywna*) = 48 groschen (*grossi/groszy*); 1 florin (*florenus/złoty*) = 32 groschen; 1 *grossus/grosz* = 3 shillings (*solidi/szelągi*) = 18 pence (*denarii*). Total sums were calculated in terms of marks, grossi, and pence: mc/gr/d.

13. Sebastian Fabian Klonowic, *Flis* (Rafting . . .) lines 181–4. ed. S. Hrabec (Wrocław, 1950) (Translated by J. P. Wachowski.) Quoted by M. Haiman, *The Polish Past in America* (Chicago, 1974), 4.

CHAPTER 3. PIAST

1. Among many introductions to Piast Poland, Bobrzyński's *Dzieje Polski w zarysie* (Warsaw, 1879), i, was the standard work before the last war. The *Historia Polska* i, Part 1, to 1454, ed. H. Łowmiański (Warsaw, 1957), is the main textbook for present-day students. There are two attractive volumes in the 'Historical Confrontations' series of the Academy of Sciences' Institute of History, i.e. *Polska pierwszych Piastów*, ed. T. Manteuffel (Warsaw, 1970); and *Polska dzielnicowa i zjednoczona*, ed. A. Gieysztor (Warsaw, 1972).

2. e.g. *Słownik Historii Polski*, 6th Edition (Warsaw, 1973), frontispiece; and in almost every current textbook in Poland, and abroad; see Oscar Halecki, *A History of Poland*, with additional material by A. Polonsky (London, 1978), frontispiece.

3. See A. P. Vlasto, *The Entry of the Slavs into Christendom* (Cambridge, 1970): 'The Western Slavs', 86–154; also H. Łowmiański, 'The Slavic Rite in Poland and St. Adalbert', *Acta Poloniae Historica*, xxiv (1972), 5–21; and K. Lańckorońska, 'Studies in the Roman–Slavonic rite in Poland', *Orientalia Christiana Analecta* (Rome, 1961), 196. On the early history of the Roman Catholic Church in Poland, see J. Dowiat, *Historia Kościoła Katolickiego w Polsce do połowy XV wieku* (Warsaw, 1968).

4. Władysław Tatarkiewicz, *Historia Filozofii*, 7th Edition (Warsaw, 1970), 'Filozofia Scholastyczna w Polsce', 297 ff.

5. Adam Vetulani, 'The Jews in Mediaeval Poland', *Jewish Journal of Sociology*, iv (1962), 274–94; Isaac Lewin, 'The Protection of Jewish Religious Rights by Royal Edicts in Ancient Poland', *Bulletin of the Polish Institute of Arts and Sciences in America* i (1942–3), 556–77; also 'The Historical Background to the Statute of Kalisz, 1264', *Studies in Polish Civilisation*, ed. D. Wandycz (New York, 1966), 38–53; R. Grodecki, 'Dzieje Żydów w Polsce do końca XIV w.', in *Polska Piastowska* (Warsaw, 1969), 595–702.

6. 'De expeditione in urbem Coloberg facta', Galla Kronika Xięga II, 28, *Monumenta Poloniae Historica* (Warsaw, 1968), i, 447.

7. The history of the Teutonic Order was one of the prime concerns of the old Prussian School, exemplified in Treitschke's *Das Deutsche Ordensland Preussen* (Leipzig, 1903). The huge bibliography is collected in E. Wermke, *Bibliografie zur Geschichte von Ostund Westpreussen* (Aalen, 1962); and K. H. Lampe, *Bibliografie des Deutschen Ordens bis 1959*, Bd. I (Bad Godesberg, 1975). The doyen of Polish scholars in this field is Professor Karol Górski, of Toruń, whose recent monograph *Zakon krzyżacki a powstanie państwa pruskiego* (Wrocław, 1977), which is also published in Italian, summarizes over forty earlier studies. The same author's article, 'The Teutonic

Order', *Mediaevalia et Humanistica,* fasc. 17 (Boulder, Colorado, 1966), 20–37, reviews the differences between German and Polish interpretations. See also Marian Biskup, 'Polish Research Work on the History of the Teutonic State Organisation in Prussia', *Acta Poloniae Historica,* iii (1960), and 'Rola Zakonu Krzyżackiego w XIII–XVI w.', in *Stosunki polsko-niemieckie w historiografii* (Poznań, 1974).

8. Geoffrey Chaucer, *The Canterbury Tales,* translated by Nevill Coghill (London, 1951), 26.

9. Henryk Zins, *Polska w oczach Anglików, XIV–XVI w* (Warsaw, 1974), 374; see also A. F. Grabski, *Polska w opiniach zachodniej Europy XIV–XV w* (Warsaw, 1968).

10. Paul W. Knoll, *The Rise of the Polish Monarchy: Piast Poland in East Central Europe, 1320–70* (Chicago, 1972), 276, presents an admirably clear and reliable survey of mid-fourteenth-century developments. See also J. Baszkiewicz, *Polska czasów Łokietka* (Warsaw, 1968); J. Dąbrowski, *Kazimierz Wielki: twórca Korony Królestwa Polskiego* (Wrocław, 1954); Z. Kaczmarczyk, *Polska czasów Kazimierza Wielkiego* (Cracow, 1964).

11. See S. Krzyżanowski, 'Poselstwo Kazimierza Wielkiego do Avinionu: pierwsze uniwersyteckie przywileje', *Rocznik Krakowski* (Cracow, 1900). Quoted by Paul W. Knoll, 'Casimir the Great and the University of Cracow', in *Jahrbucher für Geschichte Osteuropas* (Munich), New Series, xvi, nr. 2 (June 1968), 232–49. The literature inspired by the sexcentenary of the Jagiellonian University is vast. See *Dzieje Uniwersytetu Jagiellońskiego w latach 1364–1763,* i, ed. K. Lepszy (Cracow, 1964); also Janusz J. Tomiak, 'The University of Cracow in the period of its greatness', *Polish Review* (New York), xvi (1971), No. 2, 25–44; No. 3, 29–44.

12. Guillaume de Machaut, *La Prise d'Alexandrie – ou Chronique de Roi Pierre I de Lusignan,* ed. M. L. de Mas Latrie (Geneva, 1877), lines 1268–88, 1327–34, 1357–65, 1402–13.

13. Janko z Czarnkowa, *Kronika Polska:* cited in Polish translation by Antonina Jelicz, *By Czas nie zaćmił i niepamięć: wybór kronik średniowiecznych* (Warsaw, 1975), 129–30.

CHAPTER 4. ANJOU

1. General histories of Hungary include C. A. Macartney, *Hungary: a short history,* Revised edition (Edinburgh, 1962); and in Polish, Wacław Felczak, *Historia Węgier* (Wrocław, 1966). On the brief Angevin union of Hungary with Poland, see J. Dąbrowski, *Ostatnie lata Ludwika Wielkiego, 1370–82* (Cracow, 1918).

2. B. Toth, *Szajrul Szajra* (Budapest, 1901), 188. The Hungarian version is taken from an anthem composed in 1880 in honour of General Bem, the Polish General of the Hungarian revolutionary army in Transylvania in 1849.

CHAPTER 5. JOGAILA

1. See C. R. Jurgela, *History of the Lithuanian Nation* (New York, 1948); ed. A. Gerutis, *Lithuania – 700 years* (New York, 1969).

2. The standard studies of the Jagiellonian period are: O. Halecki, *Dzieje Unii Jagiellońskiej* (Cracow, 1919–20); and J. Kolankowski, *Dzieje Wielkiego Księstwa Jagiellonów* (Warsaw, 1930). See also Henryk Samsonowicz, *Złota jesień polskiego średniowiecza* (Warsaw, 1971).

3. J. Żerbiłło Łabunski, *Unia Litwy z Polską, (1385–1569)* (Warsaw, n.d.), 179 ff. This volume contains all the texts of the Polish–Lithuanian Union, in the original Latin with Polish translations. See also S. Kutrzeba, 'Unia Polski z Litwą', in *Polska i Litwa w dziejowym stosunku,* ed. W. Baranowski (Warsaw, 1914), 447–657.

4. On Grunwald see S. M. Kuczyński, *Wielka wojna z zakonem krzyżackim 1409–11* (Warsaw, 1966), 311 ff., with exhaustive bibliography; Jagiełło's letter is in Micler, *Zbiór Dziejopisów,* iii, 83 ff. See also J. Długosz, *Banderia prutenorum,* ed. K. Górski (Warsaw, 1958); and in English, Geoffrey Evans, *Tannenberg 1410–1914* (London, 1970).

5. *Lustracja Województwa Krakowskiego, 1564,* Part I, ed. J. Małecki (Warsaw, 1962), 26.

6. S. Kutrzeba, 'Ordo Coronandi Regis Poloniae', *Archiwum Komisji Historycznej,* x (Cracow, 1916), 133–210. This particular text, which survives as Codex 17 in Połkowski's Catalogue to the MSS, of Cracow cathedral, was drawn up for the coronation of Władysław III in 1434, and was used as the basis for all subsequent coronation oaths during the Jagiellonian period. It was also used for the coronations of the elected kings of the Polish–Lithuanian Republic from 1574 to 1764, except that the original phrase *'regnum tibi a deo concessum'* (the kingdom granted to you by God) was amended to read *'regnum tibi a deo commisum vel concessum'* (the kingdom entrusted or granted to you by God). As befitted the constitutional era, the ambiguous phrasing of the amended text left the King in some doubt about God's real intentions.

7. Halecki op. cit. ii, 114–18; Karol Szajnocha, 'Barbara Radziwiłłówna', *Szkice Historyczne* (Lwów, 1854), 111–74.

8. On Copernicus, see *Bibliografia kopernikowska 1509–1955,* ed. H. Baranowski (Warsaw, 1958); Nicholas Copernicus, *Complete Works* (Facsimile) (London–Warsaw, 1972); A. Armitage, *The World of Copernicus* (East Ardsley, 1971); Maria Bogucka, *Nicolas Copernicus: The Country and the Times* (Wrocław, 1973), F. Kaulbachet *et al., Nicolaus Copernicus zum 500 Geburtstag* (Köln, 1973).

9. Wiktor Weintraub, 'Kochanowski's Renaissance Manifesto', *Slavonic and East European Review,* xxx (1952), 412–24. See also David Welsh, *Jan Kochanowski* (New York, 1974).

10. W. Sobieski, 'Żałobny Hetman', in *Szkice historyczne* (Warsaw, 1904), 4–45; *Trybun ludu szlacheckiego* (Warsaw, 1905); Artur Sliwiński, *Jan Zamoyski: Kanclerz i Hetman Wielki Koronny* (Warsaw, 1947); S. Herbst, *Zamość* (Warsaw, 1955).

11. Łabuński, op. cit. 229 ff. Halecki, op cit. ii, cz V, 'Unia Lubelska', 248–353.

CHAPTER 6. ANTEMURALE

1. See J. Tazbir, 'Przedmurze jako miejsce Polski w Europie', in *Rzeczpospolita*

i Swiat: studia z dziejów kultury XVII w (Wrocław etc., 1971), 63–78; also, a more general discussion, W. J. Rose, *Poland's Place in Europe* (London, 1945).

2. 'A true copy of the Latine oration of the excellent Lord George Ossolinski ... as it was pronounced to his Majestie at White-hall by the said Embassadour ... with a Translation of the same into English ... London, 1621.' Printed in *Anglo-Polish Renaissance Texts,* ed. W. Chwalewik (Warsaw, 1968), 247–62. John III Sobieski to Charles II 25 July 1676: Latin original and English translation, in PRO SP/88/14, 181–5.

3. M. Kridl, J. Wittlin, and W. Malinowski, eds., *The Democratic Heritage of Poland: 'For Your Freedom and Ours'*, preface by Bertrand Russell (London, 1944); also published under the title: *For Your Freedom and Ours: The Polish Progressive Spirit through the Ages* (New York, 1943). This volume contains a unique anthology of Polish historical texts in translation.

4. There is no over-all synthesis of Polish religious history in the modern period, although there are many excellent monographs on particular aspects such as Roman Catholicism, Toleration, Judaism, or the Reformation. Recent introductions to church history include J. Tazbir, *Historia Kościoła Katolickiego w Polsce* (Warsaw, 1966); and F. Manthey, *Polonische Kirchengeschichte* (Hildesheim, 1965). See also, W. Ręczlerski, *The Protestant Churches in Poland* (London, 1944).

5. *Bogurodzica,* ed. J. Woronczak (Wrocław, 1962).

6. *Cudzoziemcy o Polsce: relacje i opinie,* ed. J. Gintel (Cracow, 1971), 89–97.

7. See Oscar Halecki, *The Crusade of Varna: a discussion of controversial problems* (New York, 1943); and the retort by F. Babinger, 'Von Amurath zu Amurath: Vor – und Nachspiel der Schlacht bei Varna (1444)', *Oriens,* iii (1950), 229–65.

8. B. B. Szcześniak, *The Knights Hospitallers in Poland* (The Hague, 1969).

9. The Revd Stanisław Bełch, *Paulus Vladimiri and his doctrine concerning International Law and Politics* (The Hague, 1965), 2 vols.

10. A. F. Pollard, *The Jesuits in Poland* (Oxford, 1892; republished in New York, 1971); see also S. Załęski, *Jezuici w Polsce* (Cracow, 1905), 4 vols.

11. Wiktor Weintraub, 'Tolerance and Intolerance in Old Poland', *Canadian Slavonic Papers,* xiii (1971), 21–43, also in Polish translation in *Twórczość* (Warsaw, 1972), nr. 12. See also J. Tazbir, *Dzieje polskiej tolerancji* (Warsaw, 1973); W. Czapliński, 'Parę uwag o tolerancji w Polsce w okresie kontrreformacji', *O Polsce siedemnastowiecznej* (Warsaw, 1966), 101–29.

12. Walerjan Krasiński, *A Historical Sketch of the Rise, Progress and Decline of the Reformation in Poland* (London, 1838), 2 vols; for long the only available study of Polish religious history in England, and the source of many partisan opinions.

13. See J. Woliński, *Polska a kościół prawosławny* (Lwów, 1936); O. Halecki, *From Florence to Brest, 1439–1596* (Rome, 1958); and Ks. E. Likowski, *Unia brzeska* (Warsaw, 1907).

14. H. F. Graham, 'Peter Mogila, Metropolitan of Kiev', *Russian Review,* xiv, 4 (1955), 345–56.

15. See K. Chodynicki, *Kościół prawosławny a Rzeczpospolita Polska: Zarys historyczny, 1370–1632* (Warsaw, 1934); J. Woliński, *Rzeczpospolita i Kościół prawosławny* (Warsaw, 1936).

16. See Stanisław Kot, *La Réforme dans le Grand-Duché de Lithuanie*, (Bruxelles, 1953).

17. F. A. Navarro, Relacion . . . de Senor Don Pedro Ronguillo: quoted by P. Skwarczyński, C. Scott, 'A Spanish Diplomat's View of Poland (1674)', *Slavonic and East European Review*, xl (1961–2), 497–517.

18. 'A faithful and true Catholick Account of the horrid Tumult and most barbarous Prophanation of the Chapels and sacred Oratories, together with the overthrowing of the Altars . . . and sacrilegiously burning in the open street of the images of our Saviour, the most Blessed Virgin and other Saints, accompany'd with infinite blasphemies and mockeries; and lastly of the pillaging of the whole College of the Jesuits of Thorn, committed by the Hereticks of the same city, on the 27th July 1724.' *Historical Register . . . for the Year 1725*, x, No. 37 (London, 1725) 31 ff; x, No. 38, 106 ff. contained 'The Speach of Advocate for the Jesuits at Thorn in Assessorial Tribunal in Warsaw . . .': 'The Speach of His Britannick Majesty's Ambassador . . . at Ratisbon': 'The Defence of the Court of Saxony': 'Constitutions of the Diet of Poland and Lithuania 1724': and letters of Louis XV of France to the Kings of Sweden and Prussia.

19. See S. Kot, *Socinianism in Poland: the Social and Political Ideas of the Polish Anti-trinitarians in the sixteenth and seventeenth centuries* (Boston, 1957); J. Tazbir, *Arianie i katolicy* (Warsaw, 1971).

20. *Catechisis et Confessio Fidei Coetus per Poloniani congregati in nomine Iesu Christi, Domini Nostri crucifixi et resuscitati* (Cracow, Typis Alexandri Turobini, 1574), Bodleian Library Mason A.A.8, and *The Racovian Catechisme wherein you have the substance of the Confession of those churches which in the Kingdom of Poland and Great Dukedom of Lithuania that . . . do affirme that no other save the Father of our Lord Jesus Christ is that One God of Israel . . .* (Amsterdam, 1652).

21. J. Tazbir, 'Sprawa Iwana Tyszkiewicza', in *Rzeczpospolita i Swiat*, 147–69.

22. See N. Hans, 'The Polish Protestants and their connections in England and Holland in the seventeenth and eighteenth centuries', *Slavonic and East European Review*, xxxvii (1958–9), 196–220.

23. S. Kot, 'Anglo-Polonica', in *Nauka Polska*, xx (1935). See also Jan Dąbrowski, *Polacy w Anglii i o Anglii* (Cracow, 1962).

24. H. Zavrian, 'The Polish Armenian Colony', *Armenian Review* (1951), 13 ff.; also G. Petrowicz, *L'Unione degli Armeni di Polonia con la Santa Sede, 1626–86* (Rome, 1952); M. Zakrzewska-Dubasowa, 'Z badań nad osadnictwem ormańskim . . .', in *Polska w Europie*, ed. H. Zins (Lublin, 1968), 161–74; C. Lechicki, *Kościół ormański w Polsce – Zarys historyczny* (Lwów, 1928).

25. L. Bohdanowicz, 'The Muslims in Poland', *Journal of the Royal Asiatic Society* (1942), 163–80.

26. The standard work, S. M. Dubnow, *The History of the Jews in Russia and Poland* (Philadelphia, 1916–20), 3 vols., is somewhat tendentious. The best introduction to Jewish problems is in the copious articles of the English language *Encyclopaedia Judaica* (Jerusalem, 1971–). See also Gershon Hundert, 'Recent Studies relating to the Jews in Poland from the earliest times to the Partition period', *Polish Review*, xviii, No. 4 (1973), 34–51.

27. *Encyclopaedia Judaica,* op. cit. x, 761 ff. See also S. Assaf, *The Rise of the Karaite Sect* (New York, 1937); ed. P. Birnbaum, *Karaite Studies* (New York, 1971); G. Scholem, *Sabbatai Sevi: the mystical Messiah, 1626–76* (London, 1973).
28. Martin Buber, *The Origin and Meaning of Hasidism* (New York, 1960); H. M. Rabinowicz, *The World of Hasidism* (London, 1970).
29. Quoted by Z. L. Sulima, *Historya Franka i Frankistów* (Cracow, 1893), Ch. 8. See also A. Kraushar, *Frank i frankiści polscy* (Warsaw, 1895), 2 vols.
30. *Księgi Miejskie Kaliskie* (1612), A Dekret 1/k 180, quoted by B. Baranowski, *Procesy czarownic w Polsce w XVII i XVIII wiekach* (Łódź, 1952).

CHAPTER 7. SZLACHTA

1. A. Wyczański, *Uwarstwienie społeczne w Polsce w XVI-ym wieku* (Wrocław etc., 1977), Part III, 'Grupy społeczno-zawodowe', 202–24.
2. Ibid. Part I, 'Struktura społeczno-majątkowa szlachty'.
3. The usage of *Szlachta* in the limited sense of 'the gentry' is not confined to Marxists, although it accords very conveniently with Marxist criteria. Dictionary definitions offer no solution, since they record the various usages which occur, but without making judgements on them. The *Kościuszko Foundation Dictionary* (The Hague, 1965), ii, gives *Szlachta* = noblemen, nobles, nobility, gentlefolk(s), gentry; the *Wielki Słownik Polsko-angielski* (Warsaw, 1969), gives *szlachta* = nobility.
4. On the origins of the Szlachta, see Władysław Smoleński, 'Szlachta w świetle własnych opinii', *Pisma historyczne,* i (Cracow, 1901), 1–30. On the growth of the *szlachta's* legal privileges, see J. Bardach, ed., *Historia państwa i prawa Polski do 1795 r* (Warsaw, 1964), and more specifically S. Kutrzeba, *Przywilej jedleński 1430* (Cracow, 1911); M. Bobrzyński, *O ustawodawstwie nieszawskim Kazimierza Jagiellończyka* (Cracow, 1911); A. Vetulani, 'Geneza statutu warckiego o wykupie solectw', *Kwartalnik Historyczny* (1969), nr. 3, 557–81.
5. See Karol Szajnocha, 'Nastanie szlachty i herbów w Polsce', *Dzieła,* ii (Warsaw, 1876), 215–56.
6. Z. J. Gąsiorowski, 'The Conquest Theory of the Genesis of the Polish State', *Speculum,* xxx (1955), 550–60.
7. See J. Adamus, *Polska Teoria Rodowa* (Łódzkie Towarzystwo Naukowe: Publications nr. 23) (Łódź, 1958), contains an extensive survey of the historiography.
8. See O. Halecki, 'O początkach szlachty i heraldyki na Litwie', *Kwartalnik Historyczny,* xxix (1915), 177–207.
9. Franciszek Piękosiński, *Heraldyka polska wieków średnich* (Cracow, 1899). See also S. Konarski, *Armorial de la noblesse polonaise titrée* (Paris, 1958); A. Boniecki, *Herbarz polski,* Part I (Warsaw, 1899–1913), 17 vols.; W. Dworaczek, *Genealogia* (Warsaw, 1959).
10. P. Skwarczyński, 'The Problem of Feudalism in Poland up to the beginning of the sixteenth century', *Slavonic and East European Review,* xxxiv (1956), 292–310; see also O. Backus, 'The Problem of Feudalism in Lithuania, 1506–48', *Slavic Review,* xxi (1962), 639–59; and T. Manteuffel, 'On

Polish Feudalism', *Mediaevalia et Humanistica* (Boulder, Colorado, 1964), fasc. 16, 94–104.

11. The specific characteristics of the Nobility in particular societies are well revealed by comparative studies of different countries. See Jean Meyer, *Noblesses et pouvoirs dans l'Europe d'Ancien Régime* (Paris, 1973), especially the chapter 'Le Croissant Nobiliaire: Pologne–Espagne'.

12. Quoted by W. R. Morfill, *Poland – the story of the nations*, No. 33 (London, 1893), 84–6. On the rise of the magnates, see Chapter XVII, note 8.

13. See J. Ochmański, *Powstanie i Rozwój latyfundium Biskupstwa Wileńskiego, 1387–1550* (Poznań, 1963), *passim*.

14. Marian Biskup, 'Rozmieszczenie własności ziemskiej województw chełmińskiego i malborskiego w drugiej połowie XVI w', *Roczniki Towarzystwa Naukowego w Toruniu*, Vol. 60, (for 1955), nr. 2 (Toruń, 1957).

15. Wyczański, op. cit. (see note 1), 57–9.

16. Despite the apparent simplicity of the exercise, scholars have not established any generally accepted analysis of the internal structures of the *Szlachta*. See Karol Górski, 'Les structures sociales de la noblesse polonaise au Moyen-Âge', *Le Moyen Âge* (Paris), lxxiii (1967), 73–85; Andrzej Zajączkowski, 'En Pologne: cadres structurales de la noblesse', *Annales* (Paris) xviii (1963), 88–102.

17. Adam Hornecki, *Produkcja i handel zbożowy w latyfundium Lubomirskich, c.* 1650–1750, PAN-w Krakowie: Prace Komisjii Nauk Historycznych, nr. 27 (Wrocław, 1970).

18. Ignacy Krasicki, Satyra X, 'Pan niewart sługi' (A Lord unfit for his servants), lines 75–96, *Pisma Wybrane* (Warsaw, 1954), ii, 50–1.

19. Andrzej Wyczański, 'L'économie du domaine nobiliaire moyen en Pologne, 1500–80,' *Annales* (Paris), xviii (1963), 81–7.

20. Maria Biernacka, *Wsie Drobnoszlacheckie na Mazowszu i Podlesiu*, Polish Academy of Sciences: Institute of the History of Material Culture (Wrocław, etc., 1966).

21. Adam Mickiewicz, *Pan Tadeusz*, Book VI; adapted from the prose translation by G. R. Noyes, Everyman's Library No. 842 (London, 1930), 167–70.

22. W. Smoleński, 'Mazowiecka szlachta w poddaństwie proboszczów płockich', *Pisma historyczne*, i (Cracow, 1901), 111–72.

23. W. N. Trepka, *Liber Generationis vel Plebeanorum* (Liber Chamorum), ed. W. Dworaczek (Wrocław, 1963): 'Proemium'.

24. Abramowicz, an ex-carter from Biecz who obtained the leasehold of the manor of Kwiatonowice, admitted his ignobility in court in 1622 after failing to attend the annual review of the *pospolite ruszenie*. Zyznański, a former cobbler from Chęcin, masqueraded as a nobleman after obtaining the office of secretary in the District Court. *Liber Chamorum*, Nos. 1 and 2534.

25. See W. Łoziński, *Prawem i Lewem: Obyczaje na Czerwonej Rusi* (Lwów, 1913), 2 vols.; Chapter 1, 'Niedostatki Prawa'.

26. Ibid.

27. Daniel Defoe, *The Compleat English Gentleman*, ed. K. D. Bulbring (London, 1890), 21, 29–31, 114.

28. See *Materiały do Biografii, Genealogii, i Heraldyki Polskiej*, ed. S. Konarski (Paris–Buenos Aires, 1963–7), 5 vols.

29. Cited by E. Starczewski, *Możnowładztwo polskie na tle dziejów* (Kiev, 1916), 2 vols, Chapter II.

30. Jan Kochanowski, *Na Lipę* (To the Linden Tree), *Fraszki*, Bk. II, translated by Norman Davies; *Wsi wesoła, Wsi spokojna*, translated by John Bowring, *Specimens of the Polish Poets* (London, 1827), 63–6.

31. From Adam Naruszewicz, *Nic Nad To* (Nothing More Than That), in *Liryki Wybrane* (Warsaw, 1964), 46–8.

32. From Kajetan Koźmian, *Ziemiaństwo Polskie* (The Polish Gentry), 'pieśń IV' (1839) in *Zbiór poetów polskich XIX w.* (Warsaw, 1975), i, 332 ff.

33. Andrzej Zajączkowski, *Główne elementy kultury szlacheckiej w Polsce* (Wrocław, 1961), 69.

34. W. Czapliński, 'Pamiętniki Paska: stan badań i postulaty badawcze', *O Polsce siedemnastowiecznej* (Warsaw, 1966), 201–17. All references which follow are to the recent English translation by Catherine Leach, *Memoirs of the Polish Baroque: the writings of Jan Chryzostom Pasek, a squire of the commonwealth of Poland and Lithuania*, foreword by Wiktor Weintraub (Berkeley, 1976).

35. Mikołaj Rej, *Krótka rozprawa między trzemi osobami panem, wójtem, a plebanem*, ed. K. Górski, W. Taszycki (Wrocław, 1953), lines 963–74.

36. Krzysztof Opaliński, *Satyry*, Bk I, No. III, lines 1–10, ed. L. Eustachiewicz (Wrocław, 1953), 23.

37. Wacław Potocki, 'Niechaj śpi pijany – na tóż trzeci raz' in *Moralia (1688)*, iii (Cracow, 1918), 246.

38. See J. Bystroń, *Dzieje obyczajów w dawnej Polsce* (Warsaw, 1960), 2 vols.; W. Łoziński, *Życie polskie w dawnych wiekach* (Cracow, 1964); A. Brückner, *Dzieje kultury polskiej* (Cracow, 1931). The first two works are republications of classic studies of everyday life in the early modern period.

39. M. Kromer, *Polonia, sive de situ, moribus, magistratibus et republica R.P* (1577) in K. Hartleb, *Kultura Polski . . . wypisy źródłowe* (Lwów, 1938), 31.

40. Pasek, op. cit. (anno 1669), 209–10.

41. Mikołaj Rej, *Figliki* (Warsaw, 1970), No. 181.

42. Ibid. No. 52.

43. Marcin Bielski, 'Maskarada', from *Kronika Polska* (1551), quoted in K. Hartleb, *Kultura Polski* (Hanover, 1945), 52–3.

CHAPTER 8. HANDEL

1. The economic history of pre-Partition Poland is surveyed in J. Rutkowski, *Histoire économique de la Pologne avant les partages* (Paris, 1927), 268; and more recently in B. Zientara, A. Mączak, I. Ihnatowicz, Z. Landau, *Dzieje Gospodarcze Polski do 1939 r.* (Warsaw, 1965); and Antoni Mączak, *Polska Rzeczpospolitą szlachecką* (Warsaw, 1965).

2. The modern literature on the Baltic Trade is colossal, and is recorded in the annual *Hansische Geschichtsblätter* of the Hanseatic History Society in Leipzig. For Polish aspects of the subject, the seminal work of Marian Małowist is most easily accessible in 'The economic and social development of the Baltic countries from the fifteenth to the seventeenth centuries', *Economic History Review* (Second Series), xii (1959–60), 177–89: 'The

problem of the inequality of economic development in Europe in the later middle ages', ibid xix (1966), 15–26: and *Wschód a Zachód Europy w XIII–XVI wieku* (Warsaw, 1973). See also Antoni Mączak, *Między Gdańskiem a Sundem* (Warsaw, 1972), 183; and 'La Zone Baltique . . .', *Acta poloniae historica,* xi (1965), 71–99.

3. See Maria Bogucka, *Handel Zagraniczny Gdańska,* Polish Academy of Sciences: Institute of History (Warsaw, 1970); also S. Hoszowski, 'Handel Gdańska w okresie XV–XVIII wieku', *Zeszyty naukowe Wyższej Szkoły Ekonomicznej w Krakowie,* nr. 11 (Cracow, 1960).

4. Adam Homecki, *Produkcja i Handel zbożowy w latyfundium Lubomirskich w drugiej połowie XVII i pierwszej XVIII wieku,* Polish Academy of Sciences: Prace Nauk Historycznych No. 27 (Cracow, 1970), 136.

5. The study of the production and distribution of Grain forms a necessary basis for the present-day Marxist theory of the 'Manorial-Serf System' and hence for the prevailing interpretation of the 'Feudal Period' in Polish History as a whole. See the Academy of Sciences' *Historia Polski,* i, Pt. 2 (1454–1764), 'Epoka feudalizmu: gospodarka folwarczno-pańszczyźniana – Wiadomości wstępne', 5–77.

6. See J. Burszta, 'Materiały do techniki spławu rzecznego na Sanie i średniej Wiśle w XVII i XVIII wieku', *Kwartalnik Historii Kultury Materialnej* (Warsaw), iii (1955), 752–82.

7. Pasek, *Memoirs,* op. cit. (anno 1670), 217.

8. Sebastian Fabian Klonowic, *Flis: to jest spuszczanie statków Wisłą i inszymi rzekami do niej przypadającymi,* ed. S. Hrabec (Wrocław, 1950).

9. *Flis,* op. cit. lines 1660 ff.

10. Ioannis Dantisci, *Carmina* (Wrocław, 1952).

11. *Cudzoziemcy o Polsce,* ed. J. Gintel (Cracow, 1971), i, 275–83.

12. After Maria Bogucka, op. cit. 36, 47: Table V, 'Struktura Eksportu', and Table XIV, 'Struktura Importu', whose figures are based on the Danzig port custom records.

13. Edmund Cieślak, *Les Rapports des Résidents français à Gdańsk au XVIIIᵉ siècle'* (Warsaw, 1965–9), 2 vols., i. 77–9.

14. Public Record Office (London), State Papers Foreign, January 1716, PRO – SP/88/23; published by Józef A. Gierowski, 'Z Dziejów stosunku Anglii do Gdańska w początkach XVIII wieku', *Sobótka* (Wrocław), nr. 2 (1975), 333–42. Studies on Anglo-Polish commerce in the earlier period include H. Zins, *England and the Baltic in the Elizabethan Era* (Manchester, 1972); and A. Mączak, 'The Sound Toll Accounts and the Balance of English Trade with the Baltic Zone, 1565–1646', *Studia Historiae Oeconomicae* (Poznań), iii (1968), 93–113.

15. See A. Mączak, 'The Export of Grain and the problem of the distribution of natural income in Poland, 1550–1650', *Acta Poloniae Historica,* xviii (1968); 'The Balance of the Polish Sea Trade with the West, 1565–1646', *Scandinavian Economic History Review,* xviii (1970); and 'Eksport zbożowy i problem bilansu polskiego w XVI i XVII w', in *X Zjazd Historyków Polskich w Lublinie: Referaty* (Warsaw, 1968).

16. Bogucka, op. cit. Chapter VI, 'Ceny i Zyski' (Prices and Profits).

17. Ibid. 113–15.

18. 'Neo-serfdom: a symposium', *Slavic Review,* xxxiv (1975), especially Andrzej Kaminski, 'Neo-serfdom in Poland–Lithuania', ibid. 253–68. See also B. Zientara, 'Z zagadnień spornych tzw. wtórnego poddaństwa w Europie Środkowej', *Przegląd Historyczny,* xlvii (1956).

19. Andrzej Wyczański, *Wieś polskiego odrodzenia* (Warsaw, 1969), 190; *Studia nad folwarkiem szlacheckim w Polsce w latach 1500–1800* (Warsaw, 1960); *Studia nad gospodarką starostwa korczyńskiego 1500–1660* (Warsaw, 1964); 'L'économie du domaine nobiliaire moyen en Pologne, 1500–80', *Annales* (Paris), xvii (1963), 81–7.

20. See Wyczański, *Wieś polskiego odrodzenia,* 107–13.

21. See J. Topolski, 'La régression économique en Pologne', *Acta Poloniae Historica,* vii (1962), 28–49; W. Kula, 'L'histoire économique de la Pologne du XVIIIeme siècle', *Acta Poloniae Historica,* iv (1961), 113–46; and 'Sur les transformations économiques de la Pologne au XVIIIeme siècle', *Annales Historiques de la Révolution Française,* xxxvi (1964), 261–77.

22. J. Topolski, *Gospodarstwo wiejskie w dobrach arcybiskupa gnieźnieńskiego od XVI do XVIII wieku* (Poznań, 1958).

23. Leonid Żytkowicz, 'Grain yields in Poland, Bohemia, Hungary and Slovakia in the XVIth to XVIIIth Centuries', *Acta Poloniae Historica,* xxiv (1972), 51–73.

24. Antoni Mączak, *Między Gdańskiem a Sundem: Studia nad handlem bałtyckim od połowy XVII do połowy XVII wieku* (Warsaw, 1972), provides the most comprehensive analyses and statistical tables to date.

25. Bogucka, op. cit. 31.

CHAPTER 9. MIASTO

1. The standard introduction to the history of Polish cities in the modern period is J. Ptaśnik, *Miasta i mieszczaństwo w dawnej Polsce* (Cracow, 1934). See also A. Gieysztor, 'Les recherches sur l'histoire urbaine en Pologne', *Acta Poloniae Historica,* viii (1963), 79–90.

2. St. Pazyra, *Geneza i rozwój miast mazowieckich* (Warsaw, 1959).

3. See I. Ihnatowicz, *Burżuazja warszawska* (Warsaw, 1972).

4. *Lustracja województwa ruskiego, 1661–5,* Part II, Ziemia Lwowska, (PAN, Warsaw, 1974), 8.

5. Ptaśnik, op. cit. Chapter V, 'Cechy'.

6. Ibid. Chapter VI, 'Kupcy'.

7. Ibid. Chapter IV, 'Pospólstwo'.

8. Public Record Office (London), SP/88/14.

9. See Mayer Bałaban, *Historia Żydów w Krakowie i na Kazimierzu* (Cracow, 1931–6), 2 vols.

10. S. Dziewulski, *Rozwój terytorialny miasta Warszawy w ciągu wieków, 1230–1930* (Warsaw, 1930); Adam Kersten, *Warszawa kazimierzowska 1648–68: Miasto, Ludzie, Polityka* (Warsaw, 1971).

11. *Lustracja województwa ruskiego, 1661–5,* Part II, Ziemia Lwowska, ed. E. and K. Artomowscy, (PAN, Wrocław, 1974), 127–30.

12. Ptaśnik, op. cit. Chapter XIII, 'Upadek'.

CHAPTER 10. ANARCHIA

1. On political ideas in Poland–Lithuania, see C. Backvis, 'Les thèmes majeures de la pensée politique polonaise au XVIe siècle', *Annuaire de l'Institut de Philologie et d'Histoire Orientales et Slaves* (Brussels), xiv (1954–7), 309 ff.; K. Grzybowski, *Teoria reprezentacji w Polsce epoki odrodzenia* (Warsaw, 1959); S. Kutrzeba, *Historia ustroju Polski w zarysie* (Warsaw, 1907); J. Bardach ed., *Historia państwa i prawa Polski* (Warsaw, 1964); and most recently, T. Wyrwa, *La Pensée politique polonaise à l'époque de l'humanisme et de la renaissance* (Paris, 1978).

2. See Juliusz Bardach, 'Les status lituaniens: codifications de l'époque de la Renaissance', in *Poland at the 14th International Congress of Historical Sciences in San Francisco* (Wrocław, 1975); also L. Okirshevich, *The Law of the Grand Duchy of Lithuania* (New York, 1953); Jonas Žmuidzinas, *Commonwealth polono–lithuanien ou l'Union de Lublin* (1569) (Mouton, The Hague, 1978).

3. Marek Bogucki, *Sejmy i sejmiki szlacheckie* (Warsaw, 1972). The classic study, recently republished, is A. Pawiński, *Sejmiki ziemskie: początek i rozwój* (Warsaw, 1895).

4. Pasek, *Memoirs*, op. cit. (anno 1667), 189–95.

5. Karol Górski, 'The Origins of the Polish Sejm', *Slavonic and East European Review*, xliv (1966), 122–38; 'The Royal Prussian Estates and their relation to the Crown of Poland', *Acta Poloniae Historica*, x (1964), 49–64; 'La ligue des états et les origines du régime représentatif en Prusse', in *Album Helen Maud Cam: Études Présentées* . . . (Paris–Louvain, 1960), i, 173–86. See also A. Prochaska, *Geneza i rozwój parlamentaryzmu za pierwszych Jagiellonów,* (Cracow, 1899).

6. See W. Czapliński, 'The Polish Sejm', *Acta Poloniae Historica*, xxii (1970), 180–92.

7. Pasek, op. cit. (anno 1669), 210–15.

8. James Bryce, *The Holy Roman Empire* (London, 1875), 238.

9. Paul Skwarczyński, 'The origin of the name Pacta Conventa in 1573', *Slavonic and East European Review*, xxxvii (1958–9), 469–76; and 'Les tractations autour de l'élection de Henri de Valois comme Roi de Pologne 1573', *Revue Internationale d'Histoire Politique et Constitutionnelle* (Paris), v (1955), 173–317. W. Sobociński, *Pakta konwenta* (Cracow, 1939).

10. *Dyarusze sejmowe r 1585:* Scriptores rerum polonicarum No. 18, ed. A. Czuczyński (Cracow, 1889).

11. Daniel Stone, 'The End of Mediaeval Particularism: Polish cities and the Diet, 1764–89', *Canadian Slavonic Papers*, xx (1978) nr. 2, 194–207.

12. Bogucki, op. cit. quotes the saying: 'Kto o żydach dobrze mówi jest przekupiony, kto na nich wygaduje chce nim zostać.' (Whoever speaks well of the Jews has been bribed and whoever criticizes them wants to be.)

13. On the rise of confederation, see R. Grodecki, 'Konfederacje w Polsce XV w', *Sprawozdania PAN,* lii (1951). There is a detailed study of a Confederation and the text of the Act of Confederation in *Diariusz kotowania i konfederacji pod Golębiem i Lublin w 1672 r.,* ed. A. and K. Przyboś (Wrocław, 1972).

14. Quoted by Tadeusz Korzon, *Historiya Nowożytna* (Cracow, 1889), i, 489.

There is a very rich literature from the *Rokosz*, notably *Pisma polityczne z czasów rokoszu Zebrzydowskiego 1606—8* (Cracow, 1916), 3 vols., ed. W. Czubek.

15. Korzon, ibid. 483.
16. Pasek, op. cit. (anno 1666), 185—7.
17. Wiktor Czermak, *Z czasów Jana Kazimierza. Studya historyczne* (Lwów, 1893).
18. W. Konopczyński, *Liberum Veto: studyum porównawczo-historyczne* (Cracow, 1918); W. Czapliński, *Dwa sejmy w roku 1652: Studium z dziejów rozkładu Rzeczypospolitej Szlacheckiej* (Wrocław, 1955), Chapter VIII, 'Pierwsze Liberum Veto', 115—30, 9 March 1652.
19. J. Michalski, 'Les diétines polonaises au XVIIIème siècle', *Acta Poloniae Historica*, xii (1964—5), 87—107.
20. W. J. Wagner, *Polish Law Throughout the Ages* (Stanford, 1970).
21. Władysław Łoziński, *Prawem i lewem* (Lwów, 1913).
22. Quoted by Łoziński, ibid. 451—4. The epitaph was never inscribed on any known gravestone, and might conceivably be a squib. Stadnicki features frequently in the ditties and political songs of the Rokosz of 1605—7 — 'Stadnicki diabel wcielony/Puscił głosy na wse strony/. Że pana z królestwa zrzuci,/Krążąc, ryczy bałamuci . . .' See *Pisma polityczne* . . . ed. Czubek. op. cit. i, 125 ff.
23. Stanisław Kot, *Rzeczpospolita polska w literaturze politycznej Zachodu* (Cracow, 1919).
24. A. B. Ulam, 'A. F. Modrevius, Polish political scientist of the sixteenth century', *American Political Science Review*, xl (1946), 485—94.
25. Piotr Skarga, *Kazania Sejmowe,* ed. J. Tazbir (Wrocław, 1972). See also A. Berga, *Un prédicateur de la Cour de la Pologne sous Sigismond III: Pierre Skarga,* (Paris, 1916); and Jan Tazbir, *Piotr Skarga, szermierz kontrreformacji* (Warsaw, 1978).
26. Krzysztof Opaliński, *Satyry,* Bk. III, no. 6, 1—4.
27. Oswald P. Backus, 'A. M. Kurbsky in the Polish—Lithuanian state, 1564—83', *Acta Balto-Slavica* (Białystok), vi (1969), 29—50; also *The Correspondence between Prince A. M. Kurbsky and Tsar Ivan IV of Russia, 1564—79,* ed. J. L. I. Fennell (Cambridge, 1955); E. L. Keenan, *The Kurbski—Groznyi Apochrypha* (Cambridge, Mass., 1972).
28. 'Sopra i regna', *The Sonnets of Michelangelo Buonarotti and Tommaso Campanello now for the first time translated into rhymed English by John Addington Symonds* (London, 1878), 149.
29. B. Chmielowski, *Nowe Ateny albo Akademiya wszelkich scyjencyj pełna, na różne tytuły jak na classes podzielona, mądrym dla memoryjału, idiotom dla nauki, politykom dla nauki, melanholikom dla rozrywki erygowana,* quoted by I. Chrzanowski, *Historia Literatury niepodległej Polski* (London, 1942), 384—6. See S. Cynarski, 'The Shape of Sarmatian Ideology', *Acta Poloniae Historica,* xix (1968), 5—17.
30. *Œuvres complètes de Voltaire* (Paris, 1879), xxvi, 582; quoted by Emanuel Rostworowski, in *Polska w świecie: szkice z dziejów kultury polskiej* (Warsaw, 1972), 299. See also, E. Rostworowski, 'Voltaire et la Pologne', *Studies on Voltaire and the Eighteenth Century* (Geneva), lxii (1968), 101—21.

31. J. M. Fabre, *Jean-Jacques Rousseau et le destin polonais* (Paris, 1961); *Stanislaus-Auguste Poniatowski et l'Europe des lumières* (Paris, 1952), 746.
32. Zajączkowski (see above, Chapter 2, note 11).

CHAPTER 11. SERENISSIMA

1. H. Swiderska, 'J. Dantyszek: a Polish diplomat in England in 1522', *Oxford Slavonic Papers*, x (1962), 38–45.
2. Ioannis Dantisci, *Carmina* (Wrocław, 1951), Nos. 20, 21.
3. See Renaud Przezdziecki, *Diplomatie à la Cour de Pologne* (Paris, 1934); Alfred Poniński, 'Les traditions de la diplomatie polonaise', *Revue de l'Histoire Diplomatique*, xxix (1925), 366 ff.; *Polska służba dyplomatyczna, od XVI do XVIII w.*, ed. Zbigniew Wójcik (Warsaw, 1966); Stanisław E. Nahlik, *Narodziny nowożytnej dyplomacji* (Wrocław, 1971).
4. Adam A. Witusik, 'Tomasz Zamoyski a świat turecko-tatarski', in *Polska w Europie: studia historyczne*, ed. H. Zins (Lüblin, 1968).
5. Przezdziecki, op. cit. Chapter 3.
6. 'And among other discourse, there was some of Sir Jerom Bowes, Embassador from Queene Elizabeth to the Emperor of Russia, who, because some of the noblemen there would go up-stairs before him he would not go up till the Emperor had ordered those two men to be dragged downstairs with their heads knocking against every stair till they were killed. And when he was come up, they demanded his sword of him before he entered the room. He told them, if they would have his sword, they should have his boots too. And so caused his boots to be pulled off, and his night-gown and night-cap and slippers to be called for . . . And lastly, when the Emperor in contempt to show his command of his subjects did command one to leap from the window and break his neck in the sight of our Embassador, he replied that his mistress . . . did make better use of the necks of her subjects . . .', *Pepys's Diary*, 5 September 1662.
7. It would appear that the Tudors relished their dealings with Ivan the Terrible — which may explain their reluctance to heed Polish warnings about the nature and designs of the Muscovite state. (See note 10 below.)
8. B. Baranowski, *Polska a Tatarszczyzna w latach 1624–9.* (Łódź, 1948); see also Zbigniew Wójcik, 'Financial aspects of the Polish-Tatar alliance, 1654–66', *Acta Poloniae Historica*, xiii (1966), 87–102.
9. Christophori Varsevicii, Equitis Poloni, *De Legato et Legatione Liber, Illustrissimo Domino Achatio Przyłęcki, Castellano Oswiecimensis*, Jan 1646, (Georg Förster, Bibliopola Dantiscanus); see also Angelo Tamborra, 'Cristoforo Warszewickie la Diplomazia del Rinascimento in Polonia', in *Italia, Venezia e Polonia*, ed. M. Brahmer (Wrocław, 1967), 159–205.
10. *Calendar of State Papers Foreign* (London, 1916), xix, also in *Elementa ad Fontium Editionés*, iv (Rome, 1961), No. 137, 192. This latter series, produced by the Polish Historical Institute in Rome, aims to publish all the Polish papers in the diplomatic archives of Western Europe.
11. George Carew to Robert Cecil, Danzig, 12 Aug. 1598, *Elementa*, No. 143, 220.
12. See P. D. Massar, *Presenting Stefano Della Bella: Seventeenth Century Printmaker* (New York, 1971).

13. Adam Przyboś, 'Ian h.Trach Gniński', *Polski Słownik Biograficzny* (Cracow, 1959–60), viii, 149–51. See W. Czapliński, *Polska a Turcja, 1683–1792* (Warsaw, 1935).

14. K. Lepszy, 'Krzystof h.Nieczuja Grzymułtowski (1620–87)', *Polski Słownik Biograficzny* (Cracow, 1960–1), ix, 124–6. A Jabłonowski, ed., *Listy i mowy Krzystofa Grzymułtowskiego* (Warsaw, 1876).

15. H. Barycz, 'Dudith (Dudycz), Sbardellat Andrzej (1533–89)', *Polski Słownik Biograficzny*, v, 445–8.

16. K. Koczy, 'The Holy Roman Empire and Poland', *Antemurale*, ii (1955), 50–66.

17. On Polish–Spanish relations, see E. C. Brody, 'Spain and Poland in the age of the Renaissance: a comparative study', *Polish Review*, xv (1970), 86–105; V. Meysztowicz, ed., *Documenta Polonica Archivo Generali Hispaniae in Simancas*, Parto I–VI (1514–1791), Rome.

18. W. Gąsiorowski, ed., *La France et Pologne à travers les siècles* (Paris–Lausanne, 1917); L. Franges, ed., *Recueil des instructions données aux ambassadeurs et ministres de France depuis les traitées de Westphalie jusqu'à la Révolution Française: Pologne* (Paris, 1888), 2 vols.

19. *Les Relations de Antoine de Lumbres* (Paris, 1912), 3 vols.

20. Przezdziecki, op. cit. Chapter I, 'La Nonciature Apostolique'.

21. PRO – SP 88/14. The originals of this correspondence are in Latin. The English translations are attached to copies which Hyde sent back to London.

22. Ibid.

23. Ibid.

24. R. Przezdziecki, *Diplomatic Ventures and Adventures: some experiences of British envoys at the Court of Poland* (London, 1953).

25. PRO – SP 88/30. The numbered sections were transmitted in a simple random substitution cypher.

26. Ibid.

27. R. Przezdziecki, 'Les ambassades moscovites en Pologne au XVIème et XVIIème siècles', *Revue de l'Histoire Diplomatique*, xliii (1929), 312–49. See also R. N. Bain, *Slavonic Europe: a political history of Poland and Russia from 1447 to 1796* (Cambridge, 1908); O. Halecki, 'Polish-Russian Relations Past and Present', *Review of Politics*, v (1943), 322–38; S. Konovalev, *Russo-Polish Relations, an historical survey* (London, 1945).

28. Max Hein, *Johann von Hoverbeck. Ein Diplomatenleben aus der Zeit des Crossen Kurfürsten* (Königsberg, 1925).

29. 30 June 1717, To Louis Alexandre de Bourbon. Comte de Toulouse, in Edmund Cieślak, ed., *Les Rapports des résidents français à Gdańsk, au XVIIIème siècle* (Warsaw, 1965–9), i, no. 27, 67.

30. See E. Rostworowski, *O Polską Koronę: Polityka Francji w latach 1725–33* (Wrocław, 1958): also L. Oliva, 'France, Russia and the abandonment of Poland: the Seven Years' War', *Polish Review*, vii, No. 2 (1962), 65–79.

31. See Stanisław Lubomirsky, *Pod władzą księcia Repnina*, (Memoirs of the period 1764–8) (Warsaw, 1971), translated with introduction by Jerzy Łojek; A. Kraushar, *Książę Repnin a Polska* (Warsaw, 1900), 2 vols.

32. William Wordsworth, 'On the extinction of the Venetian Republic', in *Poetical Works of William Wordsworth* (London, 1865), 219.

CHAPTER 12. VALOIS

1. P. Champion, *Henri III, Roi de Pologne* (Paris, 1944), 2 vols. See also P. Skwarczyński, 'The Decretum Electionis of Henry Valois', *Slavonic and East European Review*, xxxvii (1958–9), 113–30; Maciej Serwański, *Henryk III Walezy w Polsce: stosunki polsko-francuskie 1566–76* (Cracow, 1976).

2. Philippe Desportes, *Œuvres*, 'Complainte pour luy mesme estant en Pologne' (Paris, 1855), 411.

3. Desportes, ibid. 'Adieu à la Pologne' (Farewell to Poland). This verse, rarely quoted in Poland, was seen as a slur on the national honour, and evoked a number of patriotic responses: 'We chose a king and he deserted us./He spun us tales about his rich gifts./You Frenchmen, you came in the night,/And you left in the night without honour./We have things in Poland which you don't have./We have Liberty, the Supreme Good,/whilst in your stone palaces, what servitude!' Czubek, *Odpowiedźprzez polaka wselecznemu francuzowi*, quoted in Champion, op. cit., ii, 31.

CHAPTER 13. BATHORY

1. R. Nisbet Bain, 'The Polish Interregnum of 1575', *English Historical Review*, iv (1889), 645–66; C. Roth, 'Dr Solomon Aszkanazi and the Polish Election 1574–5,' *Oxford Slavonic Papers*, ix (1960), 8–20.

2. J. Dąbrowski, ed., *Étienne Batory, Roi de Pologne, Prince de Transylvanie* (Cracow, 1935); also E. Niederhauser, 'Bathori dans l'historiographie polonaise et hongroise', *Publicationes Institutionis Philologicae et Slavicae Universitatis Debrecenienis*, xlvii (1964).

3. Reinhold Heidenstein, *De bello moscovico*, quoted by Ignacy Chrzanowski in *Historiya Literatury Niepodległej Polski 965–1795* (London, 1943), 196–7. See B. Kocowski, *Trzej padewczycy: wpływ Batorego i Zamoyskiego na działalność R. Heidensteina* (Lwów, 1939).

4. C. Lepszy, 'Gdańsk et la Pologne', in Dąbrowski, op. cit. 212–41. See also W. Odyniec, *Dzieje Prus Krolewskich 1454–1772* (Warsaw, 1972), 103–40.

5. S. Kutrzeba, 'La Réforme judiciaire', in Dąbrowski op. cit. 292–304.

6. M. Kukiel, *Zarys Historii Wojskowości w Polsce* (Cracow, 1929; London, 1949), Chapter II. See also Henryk Kotarski, 'Wojsko polsko-litewskie podczas wojny inflanckiej, 1576–82', *Studia i Materiały do Historii Wojskowości*, xvi (1971), xvii (1972); and J. Cichowski, A. Szulczyński, *Husaria* (Warsaw, 1977).

7. On the Cossacks, see Zbigniew Wójcik, *Dzikie Pola w ogniu: o Kozaczyźnie w dawnej Rzeczypospolitej* (Warsaw, 1968); also W. Tomkiewicz, *Kozaczyzna ukrainna* (Lwów, 1939); and L. Podhorodecki, *Sicz Zaporoska* (Warsaw, 1960). The classic work is M. Hrushevsky, *Istoriya Ukrainy-Rusy* (Kiev, 1909–31).

8. J. Rutkowski, 'Questions économiques et financières sous le règne de Étienne Bathory', in Dąbrowski, op. cit., 305–34. The classic work is A. Pawiński, *Skarbowość w Polsce i jej dzieje za Stefana Batorego* (Warsaw, 1881).

9. Ibid. 330 ff.

10. Otto Laskowski, 'Les campagnes de Bathory contre la Moscovie', Dąbrowski, op. cit. 375–403.

11. P. Pierling, *Un arbitrage pontifical au XVIème siècle entre la Pologne et la Russie: la mission diplomatique du Père Possevino, 1581–2* (Brussels, 1890); *Le Saint-siège, la Pologne et Moscou, 1582–7* (Paris, 1885).

12. *Povyest 'o prikhozhenii Stefana Batoriya na grad Pskov*, ed. V. I. Malyshev (Moscow–Leningrad, 1952), 59 ff.

13. Ibid. 98 ff.

CHAPTER 14. VASA

1. On the early years of Zygmunt III, see K. Lepszy, *Rzeczpospolita Polska w dobie Sejmu Inkwizycyjnego 1589–92* (Cracow, 1939); also his 'The union of Crowns between Poland and Sweden in 1587', *Poland at the XIth International Congress of Historical Sciences in Stockholm* (Warsaw, 1960), 155–78. For the Vasa period, the works of Władysław Czapliński are of prime importance, among them *O Polsce siedemnastowiecznej* (Warsaw, 1966) and *Władysław IV i jego czasy* (Warsaw, 1972).

2. Henry Biaudet, *Les Origines de la candidature de Sigismond Vasa au trône de Pologne en 1587* (Helsinki, 1911); *Sixte Quinte et la candidature de Sigismond Vasa* (Helsinki, 1910).

3. J. A. Pärnänen, *Le Premier Séjour de Sigismond Vasa en Suède, 1593–4* (Helsinki, 1935).

4. Salo Wittmayer Baron, *A Social and Religious History of the Jews, Vol. XVI: Poland–Lithuania 1500–1650* (New York, 1976), 11–12.

5. Ibid. 272. See Maurycy Horn, *Żydzi na Rusi Czerwonej w XVI i pierwszej połowie XVII w: działalność gospodarcza na tle rozwoju demograficznego*, Żydowski Instytut Historyczny w Polsce (Warsaw, 1975) (English summary).

6. See Jan Wimmer, 'Wojsko i skarb Rzeczypospolitej u schyłku XVI i w pierwszej połowie XVII w', *Studia i Materiały do Historii Wojskowości*, xiv (Warsaw, 1968).

7. See K. Lepszy, *Dzieje floty polskiej* (Gdańsk, 1947); also W. Czapliński, *Polska a Bałtyk w latach 1632–48: Dzieje floty i polityki morskiej* (Wrocław, 1952).

8. See above, Chapter 13, note 7. See other works by W. Tomkiewicz, especially *Powstanie kozackie w roku 1638* (Cracow, 1930); H. Havelock, 'The Cossacks in the early seventeenth century', *English Historical Review*, xiii (1898), 242–60.

9. Polish views on this subject continue to be strongly coloured by the universally popular but strongly prejudiced novels of Henryk Sienkiewicz. See Olgierd Górka, 'Ogniem i Mieczem a Rzeczywistość Historyczna (Warsaw, 1934). On this sore point, the conclusions of Professor Wójcik deserve to be quoted. 'One of many harmful historical myths is the one that describes Poland's role in Ukraine in the period of the Rzeczpospolita's supremacy, as exclusively positive. Another harmful myth is that which puts virtually all the blame for bad Polish–Ukrainian relations on to the Ukrainians. Things were not like that . . . However, the author will have fulfilled his task if History . . . enables the reader to understand many of our contemporary problems'. Wójcik, *Dzikie Pola*, 236.

10. On Poland's conflict with Sweden over Livonia, see *Sveriges Krig, 1611–32*.

Part 2, 'Polska Kriget' (Stockholm, 1936); also A. Szelągowski, *O ujście Wisły: Wielka Wojna Pruska* (Warsaw, 1905).

11. Michael Roberts, *Gustavus Adolphus: A History of Sweden 1611–32* (London, 1953–8), 2 vols.; *Gustavus Adolphus and the Rise of Sweden* (London, 1973); *Essays in Swedish History* (London, 1967).

12. Anders Franzen, *The Warship Vasa: Deep Diving and Marine Archaeology in Stockholm* (Stockholm, 1961).

13. On the Polish War of Charles X, see K. Lepszy, ed., *Polska w okresie Drugiej Wojny Północnej, 1655–60* (Warsaw, 1957), 4 vols.; also the military study, Jan Wimmer, ed., *Wojna polsko–szwedzka, 1655–60* (Warsaw, 1973); also E. Haumant, *La Guerre du Nord et la paix d'Oliva (1655–60)* (Paris, 1894), and K. Marcinkowski, *The Crisis of the Polish–Swedish War 1655–60.* (Wilberforce, Ohio, 1952).

14. Wespazjan Kochowski, *Annalium Poloniae Climacter Secundus,* Cracow (1688): published in Polish translation as *Lata Potopu 1655–7,* ed. L. Kukulski *et al.* (Warsaw, 1966), 92–105. See also O. Górka, *Legenda a rzeczywistość obrony Częstochowy w r. 1655* (Warsaw, 1957).

15. Walter Eckert, *Kurland unter dem Einfluss des Merkantilismus: ein Beitrag zur Staats- und Wirtschaftspolitik Herzog Jakubs von Kurland, 1642–82* (Riga, 1927).

16. Programme Notes to Glinka's *Ivan Susanin,* Bolshoi Theatre, Moscow, 1963. This opera, one of the great works of the Russian Romantic school, was originally called *A Life for the Tsar.*

17. Jarema Maciszewski, *Polska a Moskwa 1603–1618* (Warsaw, 1968); also 'La noblesse polonaise et la guerre contre Moscou, 1604–18', *Acta Poloniae Historica,* xvii (1968), 23–48.

18. *Expedition to Moscow: a Memoir by Hetman Stanislas Żółkiewski* (London, 1959), 123–5. Preface by Sir R. Bruce Lockhart, ed., Jędrzej Giertych; Wacław Sobieski, *Żółkiewski na Kremlu* (Cracow, 1920).

19. See Bohdan Baranowski, *Polska a tatarszczyzna w latach 1624–29* (Łódź, 1949).

20. From Wacław Potocki, *Transakcja Wojny Chocimskiej,* Part IV, in *Poeci polskiego baroku,* ed. J. Sokołowski, K. Zukowska (Warsaw, 1965), ii, 11–14.

21. W. T. Kane, 'Poland's Jesuit King', *Thought,* xviii (June 1943), 257–63.

22. The immense literature on the Chmielnicki Rising was vastly inflated by academic festivities surrounding the 300th Anniversary of the Perejasław Treaty in 1954: e.g. *Sesja naukowa w trzechsetną rocznicę zjednoczenia Ukrainy z Rosją 1654–1954: Materiały* (Warsaw, 1956), 420. Important items from Polish historiography include K. Szajnocha, *Dwa lata dziejów naszych, 1646–8* (Lwów, 1869); K. Tomkiewicz, *Jeremi Wiśniowiecki, (1612–51)* (Warsaw, 1933); F. Gawroński, *Bohdan Chmielnicki,* ii (Lwów, 1909); L. Kubala, *Szkice historyczne* (Warsaw, 1923–4), 2 vols.

23. Discussions on Poland's place, if any, in the Seventeenth-Century Crisis can be followed in A. Wyczański, 'W sprawie kryzysu XVII stulecia', *Kwartalnik Historyczny,* lxix (1962), 656–72, and in W. Czapliński, 'Wiek siedemnasty w Polsce: próba charakterystyki', in *O Polsce siedemnastowiecznej* (Warsaw, 1966), 7–62.

24. See Wiktor Czermak, *Ostatnie lata Jana Kazimierza* (republished Warsaw, 1972).

CHAPTER 15. MICHAŁ

1. W. Tomkiewicz, *Jeremi Wiśniowiecki (1612–51)* (Warsaw, 1933); also 'Historyczne wartości Ogniem i Mieczem', *Przegląd Powszechny* (Warsaw, 1934); text in O. Górka, op. cit. (see above, Chapter 14, note 9).
2. Galeazzi Marescotti, (1627–1726) 'Relazioni', in *Relacye Nuncyuszów*, ed. E. Rykaszewski (Berlin, 1864), ii, 387.
3. Quoted in *Illustrowana Kronika Polakow* (Warsaw, 1967), 84. The entire proceedings of the Sejm in 1672–3 were published by F. Kluczycki, *Diariusz Sejmu Warszawskiego w styczniu roku 1672* (PAU, Cracow, 1880), et seq.
4. A. and K. Przyboś, ed., *Diariusz kotowania i konfederacji pod Gołębiem i Lublinem w 1672 roku wraz z Aktem Konfederacji* (Wrocław, 1972).

CHAPTER 16. SOBIESKI

1. See J. B. Morton, *Sobieski King of Poland* (London, 1932); O. Laskowski, *Sobieski, King of Poland*, translated by F. C. Anstruther (Glasgow, 1944); L. R. Lewitter, 'John III Sobieski, Saviour of Vienna', *History Today*, xii (1962), 168–76, 242–52; K. Waliszewski, *Marysieńka: Marie de la Grange d'Arquien, reine de Pologne, femme de Sobieski, 1641–1716* (Paris, 1904). The historical novel by Tadeusz Boy-Żeleński. *Marysieńka Sobieska*, foreward by W. Czapliński, contains much fascinating material.
2. Robt. South, quoted by W. Morfill, *Poland*, The Story of the Nations, no. 33 (London, 1893), 175–6.
3. *c.* 14 July 1665, Jan Sobieski, *Listy do Marysieńki*, ed. L. Kukulski (Warsaw, 1973), i, 41–3.
4. See above, Chapter XI, note 4.
5. M. Kukiel, *Zarys Historii Wojskowości w Polsce* (Cracow, 1929; London, 1949), Chapter 3. See also Jan Wimmer, *Wojsko polskie w drugiej połowie XVII wieku* (Warsaw, 1965).
6. On Franco-Polish Relations, under Sobieski, see Toussaint de Fourbin, in *Revue d'Histoire Diplomatique*, xxiii (1909), xxv (1911), and xxvii (1913); also S. Rubinstein, *Les Relations entre la France et la Pologne de 1680 à 1683* (Paris 1913); and K. Piwarski, 'Polska a Francja po roku 1683', *Przegląd Powszechny*, i (1933), 71–92, 236–51.
7. On the shift in diplomatic relations under Sobieski, see Z. Wójcik, 'Zmiana w układzie sił politycznych . . . w drugiej połowej XVII w', *Kwartalnik Historyczny*, lxvii (1960), 25–57.
8. *Listy do Marysieńki*, ii, 29 Aug. 1683, 194–6. (Translated by Bolesław Mazur.)
9. John Stoye, *The Siege of Vienna* (London, 1965). See also Jan Wimmer, *Wyprawa wiedeńska* (Warsaw, 1957).
10. *Listy do Marysieńki*, ii, 13 Sept. 1683, 214–19. (Translated by Bolesław Mazur). A different translation of this same letter appears in Morfill, op. cit. 165–70. Pasek has his own description of the siege and booty, *Memoirs* (anno 1683), 262–9.
11. Juliusz Starzyński, 'Wilanów: Dzieje budowy pałacu za Jana III', *Studia do Dziejów Sztuki w Polsce*, v (1933). After its tasteful post-war reconstruction, Wilanów is one of Poland's favourite tourist attractions, and houses the

national collection of Polish portraiture. See W. Fijałkowski, *Wilanów* (PWN – Zabytki Warszawy), Warsaw 1973.

12. 'John Sobieski Stolberg Stuart, 1795?–1872' and 'Charles Edward Stuart, 1799?–1880', *Dictionary of National Biography*, xix, 104 ff.

13. Probably apocryphal.

CHAPTER 17. WETTIN

1. Thomas Carlyle, *History of Frederick II of Prussia, called Frederick the Great* (London, 1858–65), 6 vols. Carlyle protested against those who like Lord Macaulay, had denounced the Partitions of Poland as a 'crime': 'Poland was now dead or moribund, and well deserved to die. Anarchies are not permitted in this world. Under fine names they are grateful to the populaces and to the editors of newspapers, but to the Maker of this Universe they are eternally abhorrent . . . To this condition of a beautifully phosphorescent rot-heap had Poland ripened in the helpless reigns of those poor Augustuses.' vi, 404–10.

2. C. Sass, 'The Election Campaign in Poland, 1696–7', *Journal of Central European Affairs,* xii (1952), 111–27; L. R. Lewitter, 'Peter the Great and the Polish Election of 1697', *Cambridge History Journal,* xii (1956), 126–43. See also Michał Komaszyński, *Księcia Contiego niefortunna wyprawa po koronę Sobieskiego* (Warsaw, 1971).

3. F. L. Carsten, *Princes and Parliaments in Germany,* Part III, 'Saxony' (Oxford, 1959).

4. Karl Ludwig von Pollnitz, *La Saxe Galante or the Amorous Adventures of Augustus of Saxony . . . together with diverting remarks on the ladies of the severall countries thro' which he travelled, translated from the French by a gentleman of Oxford* (London, 1750). See H. Pönicke, *August der Starke ein Fürst des Barock* (Göttingen, 1972).

5. J. Gierowski, *W cieniu Ligii Północnej* (Warsaw, 1971); 'From Radoszkowice to Opałów: the History of the Decomposition of the Leszczyński Camp, an Aspect of the Great Northern War', in *Poland at the XIth Congress of Historical Sciences, Stockholm* (Warsaw, 1960), 217–317, J. Gierowski, J. Kalisch, ed., *Um Polnische Krone: Sachsen und Polen wahrend des Nordischen Krieges 1700–21* (Berlin, 1962).

6. J. Szujski, 'Układy pod przewagą Moskwy w Warszawie . . . Sejm warszawski jednodniowy niemym zwany (1716–17)', *Dzieła,* iv (Cracow, 1894), 281–6; L. B. Roberts, 'Peter the Great in Poland', *Slavonic and East European Review,* v (1926–7), 537–51.

7. On the absolutist designs of August II, see J. Gierowski, 'La France et les tendances absolutistes du roi de Pologne, August II', *Acta Poloniae Historica,* xix (1968), 549–70.

8. Eugeniusz Starczewski, *Możnowładztwo polskie na tle dziejów* (Kiev, 1916), 2 vols.; M. Tobias, *Szlachta i możnowładztwo w dawnej Polsce* (Cracow, 1946). Teresa Zielińska, *Magnateria polska epoki saskiej; funkcje urzędów i królewszczyzn w procesie przeobrażeń warstwy społecznej* (Wrocław, 1977).

9. Jan Wimmer, *Wojska RP w dobie wojny północnej, 1700–17* (Warsaw, 1956); S. Herbst, 'L'Armée polonaise et l'art militaire au XVIIIème siècle',

Acta Poloniae Historica, iii (1960), 33–68; T. Korzon, *Dzieje wojen i wojskowości w Polsce: epoka przedrozbiorowa* (Lwów, 1923), 3 vols.

10. See Leonard Ratajczyk, 'Problems of the defence of Poland in view of the threat of loss of independence in the late eighteenth century', in *Military Technique, Policy and Strategy in History* (Warsaw, 1976), 295–346; also ibid. *Wojsko i obronność Rzeczypospolitej, 1788–92* (Warsaw, 1975).

11. See H.R.H. The Crown Prince of Siam, *The War of the Polish Succession* (Oxford, 1901); R. Lodge, 'English neutrality and the War of the Polish Succession', *Transactions of the Royal Historical Society,* xiv (1931), 141–73.

12. See J. Szujski, 'Podupadła sprawa Leszczyńskiego dzwiga konfederacja w Dzikowie', *Dzieła,* iv, op. cit., 341–3.

13. W. G. Whittaker, *The Cantatas of J. S. Bach* (Oxford, 1959), 659–74.

14. Quoted by Alfred Durr, *Die Kantaten von Johann Sebastian Bach* (Kassel, 1971), ii, 668–9.

15. P. Boye, *La Cour polonaise de Lunéville 1737–66* (Paris, 1926); M. Langrod-Vaughan, *Stanisław Leszczyński: philosophe, politique, souverain nominal et administrateur bienfaisant en Lorraine, 1737–66* (Nancy, 1962); Jadwiga Lechicka, *Rola Dziejowa Stanisława Leszczyńskiego oraz wybór jego pism* (Toruń, 1951).

16. Jean Bernouilli (1744–1807), *Mitgliedes Reisen . . . 1778–8* (Leipzig, 1780), quoted by J. Gintel, ed., *Cudzoziemcy o Polsce* (Cracow, 1971), ii, 51–74.

17. See Maria Danilewicz, *The Libraries of Poland* (St. Andrews, 1943).

CHAPTER 18. AGONIA

1. No period of Polish history has received more attention than the reign of Stanisław-August. The extraordinary, classic work is Tadeusz Korzon, *Wewnętrzne dzieje Polski za Stanisława Augusta* (Warsaw, 1897), 6 vols. Emanuel Rostworowski, *Ostatni król Rzeczypospolitej: geneza i upadek Konstytucji 3 maja* (Warsaw, 1966), provides a modern interpretation. The standard introduction to diplomatic events in English is Lord Eversley, *The Partitions of Poland* (London, 1915), which can also be followed in L. Lewitter, 'The Partitions of Poland', *History Today,* viii (1958), 873–82; ix (1959), 30–9. Extracts from Korzon's writings and the polemics which they provoked have recently been republished as T. Korzon, *Odrodzenie w upadku,* ed. M. H. Serejski, A. F. Grabski (Warsaw, 1975).

2. Frederick/Solms (St. Petersburg), 31 Dec. 1766. Quoted by H. Kaplan, *The First Partition of Poland* (New York, 1962), 68.

3. Gladys S. Thomson, *Catherine the Great and the Expansion of Russia* (London, 1947); Ian Grey, *Catherine the Great* (London, 1961).

4. Frederick borrowed the artichoke metaphor from Victor Amadeus of Savoy who used it in connection with his designs on Milan. See W. Konopczyński, *Fryderyk Wielki a Polska* (Poznań, 1947).

5. S. K. Padover, 'Prince Kaunitz and the First Partition of Poland', *Slavonic and East European Review,* xiii (1935), 384–98.

6. Biographies of Stanisław-August, mostly sympathetic, include titles by

R. Nisbet Bain (1909) in English, Jean Fabre (1952) in French, J. P. Palewski (1946) in French, and H. Schmitt (1920) in Polish. Fabre's study, *Stanislaus-Auguste Poniatowski et l'Europe des Lumières* (Paris, 1952), places the Polish Enlightenment within the general European context.

7. *Recueil des actes diplomatiques, traités, et documents concernants la Pologne*, ed. K. Lutosłański (Warsaw, 1920), 2 vols., Vol. I: *Les Partages de la Pologne: recueil des documents*, No. 2, 15/27 Dec. 1763.

8. 3/14 Oct. 1767. Ibid. No. 20.

9. See above, Chapter 11, note 31.

10. See P. T. Tron'ko ed., *Koliivshchina 1768: Materiali* (Kiev, 1970).

11. The standard work covering the first years of the reign of Stanisław-August is W. Konopczyński, *Konfederacja Barska* (Warsaw, 1936–8), 2 vols. On the role of the Confederation of Bar in inspiring the Polish romantic tradition, see *Przemiany tradycji barskiej: studia* (Cracow, 1972).

12. Lutosłański, op. cit. No. 34, 5 Aug. 1772. See O. Halecki, 'Why was Poland partitioned?' *Slavic Review*, xxii (1963), 432–41.

13. See Marian Serejski, *Europa a Rozbiory Polski* (Warsaw, 1970) (with French summary), which surveys the entire historiography of the Partitions and of European attitudes to the fall of Poland.

14. Burke's exact words were: 'Pray dear sir, What is next? These powers will continue armed. Their arms must have employment. Poland was but a breakfast; and there are not many Polands to be found – Where will they dine?' Letter to A. H. von Borcke, 17 January 1774, *Correspondence* (Chicago, 1960), ii, 514.

15. Quoted by S. Kot, *Rzeczpospolita Polska w literaturze politycznej Zachodu* (Cracow, 1919), 231.

16. W. Kalinka, *Ostatnie lata panowania Stanisława-Augusta* (Cracow, 1891), 105.

17. Quoted by W. Zawadzki, *Polska stanisławowska w oczach cudzoziemców* (Warsaw, 1963), 528.

18. Bogusław Leśnodorski, *Les Jacobins polonais* (Paris, 1965); also 'Les Jacobins polonais (1794)', *Annales historiques de la Révolution Française*, xxxvi (1964), 329–47; *Kuźnica kołłątajowska: wybór źródeł*, with introduction (Wrocław, 1949).

19. S. Staszic, *Uwagi nad życiem Jana Zamoyskiego* (Notes on the life of J. Zamoyski, 1787). See also Czesław Leśniewski, *Stanisław Staszic, jego życie i ideologia w dobie niepodległej, 1755–95* (Warsaw, 1926); Barbara Szacka, *Stanisław Staszic: portret mieszczanina* (Warsaw, 1926).

20. J. U. Niemcewicz, *Powrót posła: oraz wybór bajek politycznych*, 7th Edition (Wrocław, 1970); see J. Dihm, *Niemcewicz jako polityk i publicysta* (Cracow, 1928).

21. The numerous biographies of Kościuszko include titles by Monica M. Gardiner (1920) in English, K. Sreniowska (1964), and J. Dihm (1969).

22. See Bogusław Leśnodorski, *Dzieło Sejmu Czteroletniego 1788–92: Studium historyczno-prawne* (Wrocław, 1951). Two of the classic works on the Four Year Sejm are available in western languages, i.e. W. Kalinka, *Die Viejahrige polnische Reichstag 1788–91* (Berlin, 1896–8), 2 vols., and J. Klotz, *L'Œuvre législative de la Diète de Quatre Ans* (Paris, 1913); also E. Rostworowski, 'La Grande Diète, 1788–92, réformes et perspectives', *Annales*

historiques de la Révolution Française, xxxvi (1964), 308–28.

23. Quoted by L. Ratajczyk, 'Problems of the defence of Poland . . .' in *Military Technique, Policy and Strategy in History* (Warsaw, 1976), 295 ff.

24. A. Wolański, *Wojna polsko-rosyjska 1792 r* (Cracow, 1920–2), 2 vols.; J. Łojek, *Upadek Konstytucji 3-ego Maja* (Wrocław, 1976).

25. On the diplomacy of the Second Partition, see R. Lord, *The Second Partition of Poland: a study in diplomatic history* (Cambridge, Mass., 1915); also H. De Montfort, 'La politique de Prusse en Pologne de 1780–92', *Revue de l'Histoire Diplomatique,* lx (1946), 47–70; J. Łojek, *Przed Konstytucja Trzeciego Maja: z badań nad międzynarodowym w latach 1788–91* (Warsaw, 1977).

26. Lutoslański, op. cit. Nos. 101, 128, and 131, provide the texts of the treaties of partition, cession, and (compulsory) alliance.

27. Wojciech Bogusławski, *Cud mniemany czyli Krakowiacy i Górale* (Wrocław, 1956), ed. M. Rulikowski.

28. Szymon Askenazy, 'Przysięga Kościuszki', *Bibliografia warszawska,* lxxii (1912), 477 ff.

29. On Kościuszko's social policies see J. Kowecki, *Uniwersał Połaniecki i sprawa jego realizacji* (Warsaw, 1957).

30. See Jan Kiliński, *Pamiętniki,* ed. S. Herbst (Warsaw, 1958); W. Tokarz, *Insurekcja warszawska, 1794* (Warsaw, 1950); A. M. Skałkowski, 'Legenda i prawda o Kilińskim', *Przegląd Wielkopolski,* ii (1946), 65–73.

31. Philip Longworth, *The Art of Victory: the life and Achievements of Generalissimo Suvorov, 1729–1800* (London, 1965); K. Osipov, *Alexander Suvorov: a biography* (London, 1944). In present-day Poland the destruction of the Polish state after Kościuszko's Rising and the Massacre of Praga by the Russian Army, are subjects of special political sensitivity. Works on them rarely pass the censor.

32. Lutosłański, op. cit. No. 157.

33. 12 Nov. 1794, PRO-FO 62/8.

34. 1 Jan. 1795, PRO-FO 62/9 No. 1. In this same correspondence, letter No. 3 reports that 'Prince Riepenin informed his Polish Majesty that this Kingdom and Republicke no longer existed'. These words are strikingly reminiscent of Molotov's statement to the Polish ambassador in Moscow on 17 September 1939.

35. 18 Jan. 1795, PRO-FO 62/9. Unnumbered.

Index

(NB. The entries are in English alphabetical order, not Polish. Place-names are entered in their present-day form.)

Aberdeen 278, 279
Abramovitch, Eleazer 129
Academy of Sciences of USSR 16
Acre 88
Act of Incorporation of Royal Prussia (1457) 124, 179
Adalbert, Bishop, see St. Wojciech
Adam of Bremen 92
Adelaide, Queen 102
Adrianople, see Edirne
Adriatic Sea 107
Africa 260, 454, 525
Agriculture 49–50, 261–5, 279–85
Albania 192
Albert (Wójt) 94
Albert, G. von 374
Albrecht von Hohenzollern, Grand Master of Teutonic Order 139, 143
Aldona, Queen 102, 116
Aleksander Jagiellon, King (1501–6) 138, 139, 141
Alexander 'the Doctor' 131
Alexander the Great 207
Alexandria 101, 312
Alexei, Tsar 176, 459
Alfonso II d'Este, Duke of Ferrara 421
Alfred the Great, King of Wessex 61, 91
Altmark, Truce of (1629) 416
Altranstadt, Treaty of (1706) 450
America 280, 525; see also United States
Amsterdam 186, 258, 260, 275, 278, 289, 380
Andreas II, King of Hungary 108
Andrusovo, Truce of (1667) 176, 345, 395, 407, 459, 466, 471
Angevin dynasty 93, 105, 106, 108, 112, 138
Ankwicz, Józef 540

Anna of Cilli 123
Anna of Habsburg, Queen of Poland 436
Anna Jagiellonka, Queen (1576–87) 142, 308, 416, 417, 423, 436
Anna Piast, Princess 308
Anna Vasa 179, 310
Annalium Poloniae, of Wespazjan Kochowski 7
Anonymous Gaul, see Gall Anonim
Antitrinitarians, see Arians
Apprenticeship 298, 299
Aqua, A. dell' 445
Aquinas, Thomas 79
Arabia 373
Aranda, Count of (Don P. P. Abarca de Bolea) 398
Archaeology 20, 38–45
Architecture 148, 246, 305, 310–13
Argenson, Marquis d' 368
Arians (Antitrinitarians, Unitarians, Polish Brethren, Racovians, Pichovians, Socinians, Samosatenians, Farnovians, Sabellians, Budneans, Theists, Ditheists, Tritheists) (religious sect) 168, 177, 184, 185, 186, 187, 188, 191, 197, 198, 199, 322, 357, 397
Aristotle 391, 413
Armenians 166, 170, 190, 199, 205, 305, 379, 381
Armourers Guilds 298
Army 3, 335, 339, 425–6, 478, 513, 527, 528, 533, 534, 536; see also Lithuanian Army
Arnold, Stanisław 15, 16, 17
Arpad 107, 108
Arpagon, Vicomte d' 384
Asch, Baron von 543

Asia 446, 459, 525
Askenazi, Dr Solomon 421
Askenazy, Szymon 13
Association of Marxist Historians 15
Atlantic Ocean 38
Attila 46
Auchy, Baron d' 398
Augsburg 62
August II Mocny (Augustus the Strong),
   King (1697–1733) 181, 237, 240,
   311, 347, 383, 385, 408, 409, 492,
   493, 495, 496, 497, 499, 500, 501,
   503, 504
August III, King (1733–63), Elector of
   Saxony 195, 237, 313, 347, 409,
   504, 505, 506, 507, 509, 510
Augustus II the Strong, see August II
   Mocny
Aukštota 31
Aurora, Countess of Königsmark 495
Auschwitz, see Oświęcim
Austrian Succession, War of (1742–48)
   288, 507
Avars 43, 46, 57
Avaux, Comte d' 399
Avignon 98

Babice 418
Bach, Johann Sebastian 506
Bakhchisaray 456
Balk, H. von 88
Baltic Affairs 256–92
Baltic Sea 23, 26, 31, 34, 35, 38, 43,
   46, 47, 53, 56, 80, 260, 274, 289,
   290, 393, 433
Balts 29, 44
Balzer, Oswald 13
Banking 129
Bar (Palestra) 350
Bar, Duchy of 508
Baranów 148, 246, 262, 298
Barcelona 260
Barclay, Gvillaume 364
Barclay, Jean 365
Bari 145, 374
Bari, Duchy of 389
Bartos 'Głowacki', Wojciech 539
Bartosz of Odolanów 109
Baruch, Jawan 194
Basil II Emperor of Constantinople 74
Basle 357
Bastardy 233
Bathory, Andrew 338

Bathory, Gryzelda 252
Bathory, King Stephen (1576–86),
   (Stefan Batory) 165, 179, 237, 272,
   286, 308, 334–5, 336, 337, 362,
   364, 390, 397, 421, 422–32, 435,
   436, 439, 445, 447, 455, 462, 474
Batoh, Battle of (1652) 474
Batu, Khan 57, 87
Bautzen, Treaty of (1018) 83
Bavaria 35, 341
Bazylic, C. 184
Beaumont, J. 277
Behem, Balthazar 128
Bela IV, King of Hungary 70
Belgard, see Białogard
Belgium 542
Belgrade 142, 163, 480
Bellotto, Giovanni 311
Bełz 104, 112, 138, 352
Benedictines 168
Berdyczów 171
Beresteczko, Battle of (1651) 465
Berezina, river 35
Berlin 33, 181, 462, 495, 514, 515,
   523, 527, 532, 546
Bernouilli, J. 509
Bertie, R. 189
Berucci 150
Béthune, Marquis de 399, 402, 403
Beza, Theodore 357, 365
Biała 520, 521
Białogard (Belgard) 84
Białoruś, see Byelorussia
Białystok 19, 29, 154, 190, 246
Bielino 312
Bieliński, Marshal Franciszek 312, 314
Bielitz, see Bielsko
Bielsk 29, 187, 188
Bielski, Marcin, (Wolski), historian 6,
   192, 362, 363
Bielsko (Bielitz) 481
Biernat of Lublin 149
Biren dynasty 454
Biskupin 38, 49
Bismarck, Otto von 525
Blache, Vidal de la 26
Black Death (1348–51) 96, 109
Black Sea 23, 31, 35, 43, 56, 80, 86,
   111, 446, 459, 528
Blandrata, Bishop G. 185, 422
Blank Family 297
Blank, Capt. M. 275
Blessed Kinga, Princess 70

Blois, Château of 489
Blue Water (Battle of) 115
Bobińska, Celina 15
Bobrzyński, Michał 9, 11, 13
Bochnia 304
Bodecker, van 302
Bodin, Jean 357, 363–4
Bogusław, Duke of Słupsk 99
Bogusławski, Wojciech 538
Bohemia 44, 51, 63, 69, 81, 85, 91, 93,
    104, 108, 120, 138, 142, 170, 288,
    360, 384
Bohomolec, Franciszek 530
Boleslaus Premyslid, see Boleslav
    Premyslid
Boleslaus the Brave, see Bolesław I
    Chrobry
Boleslaus II the Bold, see Bolesław II
    Szczodry
Boleslaus III the Wry-mouthed, see
    Bolesław III Krzywousty
Boleslaus IV the Curly, see Bolesław
    IV Kędzierzawy
Boleslaus V the Shameful, see Bolesław
    V Wstydliwy
Boleslav Premyslid, Prince of Bohemia
    (Boleslaus Premyslid) 57
Bolesław I Chrobry (Boleslaus I the
    Brave) (992–1025) 62, 63, 66, 67,
    69, 71, 74, 80, 81, 82, 83, 85, 86,
    92, 115
Bolesław II Szczodry, King (Boleslaus
    II the Bold) (1058–79) 62, 70, 71,
    86
Bolesław III Krzywousty, King (Bole-
    slaus III the Wry-mouthed) (1102–
    38) 5, 9, 62, 71, 72, 84, 93
Bolesław IV Kędzierzawy, Prince
    (Boleslaus IV the Curly) (1146–73)
    72
Bolesław V Wstydliwy, Prince (Bole-
    slaus V the Shameful) (1243–79)
    70, 79
Bolesław-Jerzy Trojdenovitch, Prince
    of Ruthenia 87
Bolinów 295
Bolkenhain, see Bolków
Bolko, Duke of Świdnica 99
Bolków (Bolkenhain) 246
Bologna 257, 489
Bonaparte Napoleon I, see Napoleon I
    Bonaparte
Boner Family 129, 297

Boner, Johan (Jan) 128, 129
Boner, Seweryn 129
Bonifraters 168
Bonneau 543
Boratini 329, 469
Bordeaux 275
Borodino 329
Borromeo, C., Archbishop of Milan 419
Borune 171
Borussia see Prussia
Boscamp-Lasopolski, Karol 540
Bosnia 109
Botero, Giovanni 363, 364
Boucher, Jean 365
Bourbons 106
Bourgoin 419
Bowes, Sir Jeremy 386
Boyars, Lithuanian 119, 211, 216
Boyars, Russian 361, 362
Bozow, H. von 92
Bożydar 312
Bramont 416
Brandenburg 49, 63, 81, 120, 290, 399,
    462, 515
Brandon, Catherine, Duchess of Suffolk
    189
Branicki Family 224, 246, 247, 502,
    504
Branicki, Franciszek-Ksavery 520, 526,
    529, 535
Braniewo (Braunsberg) 90, 190, 295,
    448
Braunsberg, see Braniewo
Braunschweig, L. von 95
Brda river 265, 269
Brehon Laws 208
Breslau, see Wrocław
Brest   (Brześć-nad-Bugiem,   Brest-
    Litovsk) 173, 295
Brest (France) 533
Brest, Synod of (1596) 173, 174, 176,
    439
Brest-Litovsk, see Brest
Brethren of Christ's Militia 146; see also
    Knights of the Sword
Bretislav, King of Bohemia 85
Bridgettines (Brygidki), Order of 172
British relations with Poland 274–7,
    278–9, 288–90, 402–5, 489,–90,
    544–6
Brno 481, 482
Brodawka, Izaak 129
Brody 445

Broglie, Comte de 381
Bromberg, see Bydgoszcz
Brotherhood of Dobrzyn 88, 90
Brouage 260
Brückner Aleksander 207
Bruhl, Count H. von 194, 507
Bruhl, Countess 195
Brun, W. 278
Brutus, Junius 365
Bryansk 141
Bryce, James 334
Brygidki, Order of, see Bridgettines
Brzeg 50
Brześć-nad-Bugiem, see Brest
Buchholtz, Ludwig von 543
Buczacz, Battle of 479
Buczacz, Treaty of (1672) 471
Buda, see Budapest
Buda, Treaty of (1355) 102
Budapest (Buda, Pest) 108, 114, 141, 142, 396, 495
Budiszowice 295
Budneans, see Arians
Budny, S. 185, 187, 191, 192
Budziszyn, see Bautzen
Bug (river) 26, 29, 34, 265, 536
Bukovina 144
Bulgaria 62, 109
Bulgarians 43, 45
Bull of Gniezno (1136) 67
Bummeln, van 302
Buonacorsi, Filippo, see Kallimach, F.
Burghers 126, 201, 205, 212, 297, 302–3, 304, 305, 306, 311, 314, 315, 319, 335, 356, 534; see also cities
Burgundy 102, 107
Burke, Edmund 524
Bursa 164
Burzyński, T. 410
Butler, Jakub 228
Buxhovden, Albrecht von 146
Byczyna (Pitschen) 435
Byczyna, Battle of (1588) 435
Bydgoszcz (Bromberg) 28, 38, 294, 304
Bydgoszcz Canal 265
Byelorussia (Białoruś, White Ruthenia) 31, 35
Bytau, Bytów Duchy of 385, 407

Cache, Benedict de 543
Cadiz 260
Callimachus, see Kallimach, F.

Callot 489
Calvinists 166, 167, 177, 179, 182, 183, 184, 185, 187, 188, 190, 197, 198, 212, 217, 397, 439
Cambridge 190
Cameduli 170
Cammin, see Kamien
Campanella, Tommaso 366–7
Canning, George 546
Canon Law 349
Canterbury 374
Canute the Great, King of England 74
Capitation Registers 203, 205
Capuchins, 170, 311
Carew, G., diplomat 394
Carlsbad (Karlove Vary) 543
Carlyle, Thomas 124, 168, 492, 516, 523
Carmelites 170
Carolingians 62
Carthusians 168
Carwise, Burghermeister of Toruń 180
Casimir I the Restorer, see Kazimierz I Odnowiciel
Casimir II the Just, see Kazimierz II Sprawiedliwy
Casimir III the Great, see Kazimierz III Wielki
Casimir IV the Jagiellonian, see Kazimierz IV Jagielloṅczyk
Casstrom, Samuel 543, 544
Castellans (Kasztelan) 335, 349
Catalania 466, 542
Catherine of Austria, Queen of Poland 146, 397
Cathérine de Médici, Queen of France 413, 417, 419, 420
Catherine (II) the Great, Empress of Russia 240, 368, 388, 410, 411, 510, 515, 516, 517, 518, 519, 524, 526, 527, 528, 529, 533, 535, 537, 540, 541
Catholics 19–20, 67–70, 116, 125–6, 146, 160–72, 174, 175, 176, 177, 179, 180, 181, 183, 186, 188, 189, 190, 192, 194, 195, 197–200, 205, 219, 224, 302, 305, 335, 342, 350, 430, 447, 496, 500, 514, 518, 544
Cecora, Battle of (1620) 313, 460
Cecora, Treaty of (1595) 379
Cedynia (Zehde), Battle of (972) 82
Celts 44, 45
Cereals 128

Cesarini, Cardinal, G. Papal Nuncio 161
Ceuta 260
Chamber of Envoys 330, 331, 359; see also Sejm
Chancellors (*Kanclerz*) 335, 349
Charis, C. M. de 382
Charlemagne 61
Charles of Lorraine 401, 481, 483, 485
Charles IV of Luxembourg, Holy Roman Emperor 98, 99, 100
Charles V, Holy Roman Emperor 373, 374
Charles Martel, King of Naples 108
Charles Robert, King of Hungary 94, 95, 108
Charles V le Sage, King of France 99
Charles IX, King of France 391, 397, 413, 414, 417, 420
Charles X, King of France 536
Charles II, King of England 160, 379, 402, 480
Charles III, King of Spain, 398
Charles IX, King of Sweden (Duke of Sodermanland) 434, 437, 448, 456
Charles X, King of Sweden 365, 399, 400, 407, 450, 454, 465, 473
Charles XII, King of Sweden 383, 408, 455, 497
Charles Vasa, Duke of Sodermanland, see Charles IX, King of Sweden
Charles, Count of Anjou 106
Charles Edward Stuart, Prince 489–90
Charnace, M. de 399
Chassidim, see Hassidim
Chaucer, Geoffrey 92, 93
Chazars 79, 166
Chełm 112, 171, 540
Chełm, Bishops of 329
Chełmno (Kulm) 90, 95, 199, 218, 219, 269, 521
Chernyshev 514
Cheverny, Count P. de 417
Chmielecki, S. 446
Chmielnicki, Bogdan, Hetman 10, 176, 193, 340, 345, 346, 437, 463, 465, 466, 467, 470, 473
Chmielnik, Battle of (1241) 87
Chmielowski, Revd. Benedykt 367
Chocim 474, 479
Chocim, Battle of (1621) 175, 460, 468
Chodkiewicz Family 177, 184
Chodkiewicz, Jan, Grand Hetman of Lithuania 153, 165, 175, 342, 445, 448, 458, 460, 461, 474

Chodza, Efendi (Saad-ed-din) 163
Chodza, Kazer, Ottoman soldier 163
Choiseul, duc de 515
Chojnice (Konitz) 295
Chojnice, Battle of (1454) 124
Chortyca 470
Chreptowicz 226
Christmasse, trumpeter 404
Chronica Polonica of Marcin Kromer 6
Chronica Polonorum of Maciej Miechowita 6
Chronicle of the Whole World, see Kronika Wszystkiego Świata
Cicero 151
Ciechanów 246
Cieszyn (Teschen, Tešin) 84, 104, 481
Cistercians 168
Cities 77–8, 205, 293–320, 350
Clarendon, Earl of (Edward Hyde) 402
Clauder, J. 506
Clement VIII, Pope 173
Clement, J. 420
Clergy 126, 201, 205, 212, 335, 356, 428
Cleves, Marie de, 416
Climate 35–8
Clothes 247
Cmielów 38
Colberg, see Kołobrzeg
Colbert, Jr. 400
Collaborators 526
Collegium Nobilium 532
Colloquium of Cracow 301
Colloquium of Love (1645) 179
Comenius, J. A., see Komensky
Commission of Finance 513
Committee of Public Safety 543
Committee of Two Nations 534
Communism 14
Condé, Prince L. 401
Confederation (*Confederatio, Konfederacja*) 339–40, 513, 518, 525, 534; see also Rokosz, Right of Resistance
Confederation of Bar (1768) 369, 410, 519, 520
Confederation of Gołębie (1672) 479
Confederation of Szczebrzeszyn (1672) 479
Confederation of Targowica (1792) 530, 533, 535, 536, 540, 542
Confederation of Thorn (1767) 518
Confederation of Warsaw (1573) 160, 167, 179, 183, 187, 198, 200, 414, 416, 436

Confederation of Warsaw (1704) 497
Congress Kingdom 24, 56
Conrad II, Holy Roman Emperor 71
Conrad III, Holy Roman Emperor 74, 83
Conrad of Mazovia, see Konrad Mazowiecki
Conring, Herman 365
Constance, Council of (1414–18) 124, 166
Constance of Austria, Queen of Poland 187, 188
Constantine Porphyrogenitus, Byzantine Emperor 45
Constantinople (Istanbul) 46, 61, 86, 120, 138, 159, 172, 173, 174, 379, 382, 404, 446, 470, 473, 520
Constitution of 3 May 1791 325, 410, 530, 531, 532, 535, 537
Constitutional History 74–5, 111, 118–20, 132, 147–8, 152–5, 211–12, 321–72, 375–8, 444–5
Conti, Prince L. 399, 492
Copenhagen 260, 275, 381
Copernicus, N. 150–2, 181, 257–8
Corn 306
Corps de Génie 533
Corps of Cadets 517, 532
Corpus Christi 248
Cortes, H. 374
Corunna 374
Cosel, Mme 495
Cossacks 30, 144, 164, 171, 174, 175, 176, 177, 198, 345, 377, 421, 425–6, 445–7, 450, 459, 462–8, 470, 541
Council of Four Lands, the 320
Counter-Reformation, the 311, 358
Courland (Kurlandia) 31, 56, 147, 378, 454, 493, 497, 517, 521
Courtship 3
Coutts, A. 277
Coyer, Abbé Gabriel 368
Cracow (Kraków, Krakau) 19, 27, 28, 33, 34, 38, 44, 45, 50, 61, 62, 67, 69, 78, 80, 85, 87, 94, 95, 96, 98, 99, 109, 111, 112, 114, 117, 118, 143, 148, 149, 165, 170, 171, 185, 191, 201, 252, 256, 257, 272, 273, 297, 298, 301, 304, 307, 308, 320, 329, 331, 374, 380, 383, 384, 389, 390, 402, 404, 413, 416, 432, 435, 437, 441, 451, 452, 453, 456, 469, 476, 481, 486, 491, 492, 497, 504, 505, 510, 520, 538, 540
Cracow, Congress of (1363) 99–101
Cracow, Treaty of (1339) 95
Cracow School, see Kraków School
Crell, J. 187, 199
Crete 35
Crime 234–6; see also Murder, Rape
Crimea 191, 382, 389, 431, 465
Crimean Tartars, see Tartars
Croats 43, 45, 107
Cromwell, Oliver, Lord Protector of England 186, 200, 466
Cromwell, Thomas 200
Crown Lands 218
Crown Register 346
Crown Secretariat 346
Crown Tribunal 323, 326, 337, 354, 349, 425
Crusades 138
Crutta, A. 379
Csanad 396
Cudna, mistress of Kazimierz III 102
Culter, H. 277
Cultural History 78–9, 98–9, 148–52, 509–10, 530–2
Culvensis, A., see Kulwieć, A.
Currency 80, 130, 152, 439–40, 479
Customary Law 243
Cyprus 101, 260, 373
Czarniecki, P. 452
Czarniecki, S., Hetman 344, 445, 452, 453, 473
Czarnolas 152
Czartorysk 298
Czartoryski Collection 12
Czartoryski Family 177, 224, 246, 362, 409, 502, 508, 516, 517
Czartoryski, Adam Kazimierz 518
Czech 61
Czech Brothers (Bohemian Brethren) 183, 188
Czechowic, M. 185, 192
Czekanowski, J. 39
Czechs 43, 85, 93, 94, 95
Czerniaków 147, 312, 345, 408, 458
Czernich, J. 180, 181
Czersk 246, 307
Czerwińsk 211, 268
Częstochowa 19, 78, 171, 172, 402, 451, 520
Czetwertyński Family 177, 502
Czetwertyński, Adam 540

Czirenberg, merchant of Danzig 260
Czop, Colonel 343, 344
Czorstyn 246, 292

Dąbrowka (Dubravka), Princess 4, 85
Dąbrowski, General, Jan Henryk 541
Dalmatia (Tina) 396
Dancing 251
Daniłłowicz Family 311
Daniłłowicz, Stanisław 477
Dantiscus (Dantyszek), Bishop J. (Hoeffen J. von) 260, 373, 374, 375, 388, 391
Dantyszek, see Dantiscus
Danube, River 46, 66, 85, 87, 91, 95, 107, 291, 445, 483
Danzig, see Gdańsk
Daugavpils (Dyneburg, Dvinsk) 31, 429, 454
Defoe, Daniel 236
Dękart, Jan 314, 320
Dembolecki, W. 159
Denhof, Countess Maria 495
Denmark 146, 147, 384, 400, 433, 434
Desna, River 32
Desportes, P. 413, 416, 419
Diderot, D. 509
Dietines (Sejmiki) 342, 347, 359, 488, 525, 537
Dijon 102
Dionysius of Halicarnassus 396
Diplomacy 373–412, 447–62, 542–6
Dirschau, see Tczew
Ditheists, see Arians
Divov 543, 545
Długosz, Jan (Longinus) 5, 6, 139, 209
Dmitri I, First Pretender 397, 456
Dmitri II, Second Pretender 456
Dnieper (Dniepr), River 23, 30, 31, 35, 39, 40, 43, 49, 56, 66, 82, 115, 124, 144, 176, 265, 377, 396, 406, 408, 445, 465, 470
Dniester (Dniestr), River 30, 32, 35, 57, 120, 144, 195, 403, 460, 521
Dob Baer 193
Dobrzyn Duchy of 95, 102, 230
Dobrzyński Family 230
Doctors 205
Dolgoruky, Prince G. 410
Dominicans 168, 170, 179
Döring, Captain J. 274, 275
Dorofei 430
Dorogobush 141

Dorohajski Family 184
Dorpat, see Tartu
Dracula, Hospodar of Wallachia 161
Drang nach Osten 47–9
Dresden 409, 493, 495, 498, 538
Du Bellay, J. 150
Dubiecki 353
Dubienka 536
Dubno 226
Dubravka, see Dąbrowka
Dubrovnik (Ragusa) 109
Ducal Prussia (East Prussia) 515
Dudith, A., Bishop of Pecs 361, 391, 396, 397
Dudycz, A., see Dudith, A.
Dunajec (river) 49, 54, 265, 292
Dunajów 139
Dunikowski, Samuel 457
Dunkeld 490
Duval, H. 495
Dvina, River 31, 115
Dvinsk, see Daugavpils
Dvornik, F. 40
Dyneburg, see Daugavpils
Dyvilino, Truce of (1619) 458, 459
Dziakel (tribute in kind) 215
Działyński, P., Castellan of Dobrzyn 392, 393, 394, 398
Dzieje Polski Potocznym Sposobem Opowiedziane (Poland's Past Recounted in a Familiar Way) 9
Dzieje Polski w Zarysie (Poland's Past in Outline) 10
Dzieje Wewnetrzne Polskiza Stanisława Augusta (Poland's Internal History under Stanisław-August) 12
Dziekanka 312
Dzierzek, K. 379
Dzików Confederation of (1734–5) 504

Easter 248, 249
Eberdine, Princess of Bayreuth, Electress of Saxony 493
Ecclesiastical Courts 348, 350
Economic history 80, 128–30, 256–92, 315–20, 439–40
Edirne (Adrianople) 163
Education 98–9, 118, 148–52, 165, 167–70, 183, 188–9, 236–7, 444, 509, 528, 530–1; see also Volume II, Chapter 8
Edward VI, King of England 189

Efraim of Międzybóż 441
Egypt 164
Elbe (Łaba), River 26, 47, 49, 82, 506
Elbing, see Elbląg
Elbląg (Elbing) 90, 123, 190, 277, 294, 295, 393, 425, 448, 454
Elections, see Royal Elections
Eleonora of Austria, Queen of Poland 398, 402, 471, 472
Elizabeth of Austria, Queen of Poland 256
Elizabeth I, Queen of England 189, 387, 392, 429
Elizabeth, Empress of Russia 515
Elizabeth of Słupsk, Princess 98
Elżbieta (Elizabeth) Łokietkówna, Queen of Hungary, Regent of Poland 109
Eminilda, Queen 74
Encyclopédie 368, 530
Enghien, Duke d' 400
England, see Great Britain
English Civil War (1642–7) 466
Enlightenment 532
Ennoblement 233, 237
Entail, Law of (Ordinacja or maioratus) 225
Erasmus 374
Eric XIV, King of Sweden 434
Ermeland, see Warmia
Ernest, Archduke of Austria 414, 422, 436
Escorches, P. d' 542
Estates of Royal Prussia 330
Estergom (Gran) 107
Esterle, Countess d' 495
Esther, mistress of Kazimierz III 102
Estonia 115, 448
Eternal Treaty (1634) 459
Euphrates River 35
Executionist Movement 141, 183

False Pretences 235
Farnovians, see Arians
Faro 260
Fatima, mother of Count Rotowski 495
Faur, G. de Pibrac de 413
Fehrbelin, Battle of (1675) 480
Feodor, Tsar of Russia 172
Ferdinand of Habsburg, King of Bohemia 142

Ferdinand II of Habsburg, Archduke 422, 423
Ferdinand, King of the Romans 390
Ferdinand and Isabella, of Spain 148
Ferrara 419
Fersen, Ivan 541
Feudalism 16–18, 203, 214, 279–87
Ficke, merchant of Danzig 260
Figulus, see Jabłoński, D. E.
Finance 80, 129–30, 260–1, 426–8
Finch, Sir Edward 404
Finkel, Ludwig 12
Finland 115, 146, 433
Fiol, Szwajpolt (Swejbold Vehl) 149
Firlej Family 127, 298
Firlej, J., Crown Marshal 414
Firlej, Mikołaj 327
Fleming, Count 492
Flensburg 275
Fleury, Monsigneur de 387
Flucker, F. 278
Fordon 269
Foreign relations 82–93, 99–101, 116–17, 120–4, 134–48, 335–6, 373–412, 413–14, 428–32, 433–5, 447–62, 478–91, 492–3, 495–502, 504–5, 521–5, 526–7, 535–7, 541–2, 542–6
Foreign views of Poland 91–3, 236, 363–9, 473, 492, 511
Foresyth, Joseph 238
Forster, G. 390
Fort James Island 454
Foss, H. 278
Four Years' Sejm 320, 529, 531, 533
France 50, 61, 78, 92, 106, 170, 192, 260, 274, 275, 289, 315, 370, 381, 383, 390, 391, 395, 399, 403, 413, 414, 416, 417, 466, 479, 513, 520, 527, 532, 537, 540, 542
Francis I, King of France 374
Franciscan Minoresses (Poor Clares) 170
Franciscans 170
Franco, F. 187
François, Prince of Alençon 417
Frank, E. 195
Frank, J. (Lejbowicz, J.) 194, 195
Frankfurt-am-Main 195, 413
Frankfurt-am-Oder 413
Frankists (Jewish sect) 192, 194
Franz-Ferdinand, Archduke 37
Frauenberg, see Frombork

Frederick I, Barbarossa, Holy Roman Emperor 72, 83
Frederick II, Holy Roman Emperor 90
Frederick III, Elector of Brandenburg, King of Prussia as Frederick I 408
Frederick II (Frederick the Great) 124, 367, 368, 388, 410, 507, 511, 514, 515, 516, 517, 519, 520, 521, 523–4, 528, 530
Frederick-William I, Grand Elector 385, 462, 465
Frederick William II, Grand Elector 385, 386, 536 '
Frederick William III, of Prussia 528, 535, 537, 540
Fredro, Andrzej Maksymilian 346–7
French, the 49
French relations with Poland 159, 363–6, 367–9, 399–401, 413–20, 475–6, 479–80, 508, 535
French Revolution 530, 533, 535
Frevort, Corry 238
Freytag, A. 445
Friedrich-Christian, Prince 510
Frombork (Frauenberg) 150, 257, 295, 448
Fronde 466
Frontiers 32–3, 63–7
Frycz-Modrzewski, see Modrzejewski, A. F.
Fryderyk (Frederick) Jagiellon, Cardinal 138
Fugger Family 389
Fugger, Georg (Jerzy Fukier) 310
Fukier, Jerzy, see Fugger, Georg
Furniture 247
Furstemberg, von, Grand Master of the Knights of the Sword 146, 147

Gabor, Bethlen, Prince of Transylvania 460
Gac 262
Gada, Izabela del 374
Gadebusch, Jakub 363
Galicia (Galicja) 28, 114, 536
Galicia, Spanish 542
Galicja, see Galicia
Galitzin, Prince A. 457
Gall Anonim 5, 61, 74, 78, 84
Gallus Anonimus, see Gall Anonim
Gambia, 454
Gameren, Tylman van 311
Gardner, William 543, 544, 545–6

Gatinara, Imperial Chancellor 389
Gatka z Dobrzyn, Andrzej 125
Gaudentius, see Radim
Gawrock, merchant of Danzig 260
Gdańsk (Danzig) 19, 29, 38, 56, 67, 83, 91, 95, 123, 127, 129, 147, 149, 177, 182, 190, 256, 257, 258, 260, 261, 265, 266, 267, 268, 269, 270, 271, 272, 273, 274, 275, 277, 278, 279, 280, 286, 288, 289, 290, 291, 292, 301–3, 307, 310, 373, 377, 380, 383, 390, 392, 398, 400, 402, 408, 423, 425, 434, 435, 436, 439, 445, 450, 477, 479, 492, 504, 506, 508, 521, 528, 536
Gdecz 81
Gedymin, G., Duke of Lithuania 112, 115
General Charter of Jewish Liberties 79
Geneva 184
Genoa 260
Geography 34–8
Geopolitics 23–6
Georg-Wilhelm von Leignitz, Brieg und Wohlau, Prince 104
George I, King of England 181, 274
Gepids 43
Gercken, T. 288, 289
German Language 305
Germans 40, 47, 49, 82, 182, 384, 391
Germany 34, 50, 51, 63, 77, 80, 82, 85, 90, 92, 93, 96, 106, 108, 114, 374, 380, 384, 388, 391, 397, 273, 276, 288, 292, 413, 448, 453, 467, 493, 495; see also Holy Roman Empire, Saxony, Prussia, Bavaria, Brandenburg
Gervase of Tilbury 92
Ghettos 213, 308, 313
Gimbutas, M. 40
Girej, Davlet 423
Girej, Izlam 477
Glanville, B. de 92
Glasemeister, Capt. J. 275
Gliński, Michał 142
Gniński, Jan 389, 394, 404, 479, 480
Glogów (Glogau), Siege of (1109) 83
Głowszczyzna, see Head money
Gniewa 269
Gniezno 4, 19, 20, 27, 61, 63, 67, 71, 81, 85, 86, 102, 107, 129, 273
Goering, Reichsmarschal Herman 37
Golden Age of Poland 148

Golden Bull of Andreas II (1222) 108
Golden Bull of Rimini (1226) 90
Golden Freedom 11, 215, 341, 347, 348, 356, 360, 361, 367, 371, 513, 514, 517, 519, 523, 537
Golden Horde 87, 141
Gomel, see Homel
Gomułka, Władysław 19
Gonesius, P., see Piotr z Goniąz
Gonta, Ivan 520
Gonzague, L. de, Duke of Nevers 417
Gopło, Lake 343
Góra Kalwaria (Gur) 295
Gordon, Henry de 238
Gorka Family 127
Gorka, Łukasz 317
Górnicki, Łukasz 150
Gosiewski, A., Starosta of Wieliz 457
Goślicki, Wawrzyniec 150, 363
Gostomski, Hieronym 341
Gostyń 457
Gothenburg 275
Goths 43, 45, 46, 57
Gotland 120
Gower, J. 92
Grabowieczki 131
Gran, see Estergom
Grana, Marquis de 384
Grand Duchy, see Lithuania
Grange d'Arquien, Marie-Casimire de la (Marysienka) 475, 477, 481–3, 484–6, 488, 489
Graz 341
Great Britain 59, 61, 92, 120, 181, 186, 189, 193, 369, 374, 391, 392, 396, 402, 404, 260, 264, 276, 277, 286, 433, 466, 515; see also England, Scotland, British Relations with Poland
Great Northern War (1700–21) 182, 262, 274, 288, 315, 352, 377, 380, 383, 408, 409, 455, 496, 499, 500, 501, 502
Great Novena, the 19
Great War (1409–22) 120
Greater Poland, see Wielkopolska
Greenwich 392
Grefe, H. 288
Gregory IX, Pope 90, 510
Gregory XIII, Pope 381
Gregory, Archbishop of Lwow 139
Grey, Lady Jane 189
Griesheim, Col. 544

Gripsholm 434
Grochowski, Olbracht 352
Grodno 29, 331, 432, 497, 537, 542, 543
Groicki, B. 132
Groszy 130
Grotius, Hugo 357
Grotniki, Battle of (1439) 125
Grunwald, Battle of (1410) 122–3, 161
Grzegorz Paweł z Brzezin 185
Grzybów 312
Grzybowski, Jan 312
Grzymułtowski, K., Palatine of Poznań 394, 395, 396, 406
Grzymułtowski Treaty (1686) 396, 502
Guardians of the Law 534
Guarini 421
Guilds 298–9, 301, 308–10, 319; see also Merchants Confraternities, Jewish Guilds
Guise, Cardinal de 420
Gustav Eriksson I, King of Sweden 433, 434, 435
Gustavus Adolfus, King of Sweden 286, 399, 448, 450
Guzów, Battle of (1607) 342

Haarlem 25
Habeas Corpus 211; see also Neminem Captivabimus
Habsburgs 104, 106, 138, 142, 341, 343, 360, 390, 396–8, 399, 414, 422, 435, 436, 461, 477, 480, 481, 482, 483, 484, 485, 486, 487, 516
Hadad, Siege of 422
Hadziacz, Treaty of (1657) 468
Hague, The 392
Hair styles 248
Halecki, Oscar 13
Halicz 69, 86, 111
Haller, Jan 149
Hamburg 276
Handelsman, Marceli 13
Hannsen, Capt. D. 275
Hanoverian dynasty 493
Hanseatic League (Hansa) 80, 90
Harder, burgher of Toruń 180
Harmęże 418
Harrington, Sir James 366
Hassidim (Jewish sect) 192, 193, 194
Hautevilles 106
Haxthausen, Baron 50

Head money (Główszczyzna) 234–6, 356, 364
Heidenstein, Reinhold 423
Heilsburg, see Lidzbark
Hel 295
Helena Ivanovna (daughter of Ivan III) 139, 141
Helmed, Battle of (1501) 141
Helvetius 489
Hengist 47
Henri Valois, see Henryk III Walezy
Henrician Articles 334, 342
Henry the Bearded, see Henryk I Brodaty
Henry II the Pious, see Henryk II Pobożny
Henry IV, King of England 93
Henry VII, King of England 138
Henry VIII, King of England 374
Henry II, King of France 413
Henry of Navarre, King of France 165
Henry the Fowler, German King 62
Henry II, Holy Roman Emperor 71, 82, 83
Henry IV, Holy Roman Emperor 71
Henry V, Holy Roman Emperor 83
Henry, Duke 420
Henry, Prince of Prussia 521
Henryk I Brodaty, Prince (Henry the Bearded) (1228–38) 70, 77
Henryk II Pobożny, Prince (Henry II the Pious) (1238–41) 72, 87
Henryk IV Probus, Prince (1289–90) 94
Henryk III Walezy (Henri Valois), King of Poland, also of France as Henry III 159, 365, 384, 390, 399, 413, 414, 415, 416, 417, 418, 419, 420, 437
Heraldry 208–10, 216
Herburt, Jan Szczęsny 355
Hermannstadt, see Kolozsvar
Herodotus 43
Heron, M. de 383
Hetman 335
Hetman's Courts 349
Hewel, Merchant of Danzig 260
Hewelka, G. 286
Heyder, burgher of Toruń 181
Hippeum 151
Hirtenberg, Joachim Pastorius von 237
Historia Narodu Polskiego (a history of the Polish Nation), of A. Naruszewicz 7

Historia Polonica, of Jan Długosz 6
Historia Polski (History of Poland of PAN) 18, 22
Historical Geography 23–60
Historiography 3–22, 532–3
Historiya Howożytna (Modern History) of Tadeusz Korzon 12
Hitler, A. 57
Hobman, W. 277
Hochfeld, Kasper 149
Hodo, Margrave of the Ostmark 82
Hoeffen, J. von, see Dantiscus, J.
Hohenstaufens 106
Hohenzollern, Albrecht von 385, 461, 462
Hohenzollern, Joachim, II von, Duke of Brandenburg-Anspach 461
Hohenzollern, Prince L. von 407
Hohenzollern, Ludwig von 488
Hohenzollern, Wilhelm von, Archbishop of Riga 146, 147
Hohenzollerns 182, 183, 384, 406, 407, 408, 411, 428, 434, 495, 515
Holęndry 313
Holland 189, 272, 276, 277, 289, 392, 454, 544, 569; see also United Provinces
Holy Land 161
Holy League (1683–99) 402, 408, 487, 491
Holy Roman Empire 120, 361, 366, 369; see also Germany
Homel, (Gomel) 521
Horn, Count 452
Horodło, Agreement of (1413) 119, 135, 211, 216
Horsa 47
Horsey, Sir Jerome 217
Hosius, S., see Hozjusz, S.
Hospitality 249–50
Hospitallers, The Knights 165, 177
Hospodars of Moldavia, see Stephen of Moldavia, Petrylo
Hoverbeck, J. von 406, 407
Hoym, Mme, mistress of August II 495
Hozjusz, S. (Hosius, S.) Bishop of Warmia 167, 378, 396
Huber, Ulryk 366
Huelva 260
Humań, see Uman
Humanism 148
Hume, David 368
Hungarians, see Magyars

Hungary 87, 93, 94, 102, 106, 107, 108, 111, 112, 113, 120, 125, 138, 142, 159, 225, 230, 360, 396, 397, 486
Hunia, Ataman 446
Huns 43, 46
Hunting 249
Hurst Castle 536
Hus, Jan 125
Husaria (Hussars) 425
Hussars, see Husaria
Hussein Pasha 379
Hussites 135
Hybertsson, H. 448
Hyde, Lawrence 402, 403, 404, 405

Iagiellonus, see Władysław II Jagiełło
Ibrahim -Bey (Strasz, J.), Ottoman envoy 379
Ibrahim-Ibn-Jakub 3, 38
Igłów, Castellan of 426
Illyrians 40, 44
Iłowski 150
Indygenat (Naturalization) 237–8
Inflanty, see Livonia
Inflation 129, 318, 319
Ingelstrom, Baron Osip Andreivich von 543
Innocent XII, Pope, see Pignatelli
Innsbruck 489
Inowrocław 50
Institute of History of the Polish Academy of Sciences 18
Invasions 314–15
Iranians 40
Iroquois Indians 524
Isaac ben Abraham of Troki 191
Isidore, Cardinal-Metropolitan 172
Iskender, Pasha 450
Islam 159, 191, 194, 477; see also Muslims
Israel ben Eliezer 193
Isserles, Moses 444
Istanbul, see Constantinople
Istoriya Pol'shi 16
Istvan I, King of Hungary, see Steven I
Italians 141
Italy 79, 93, 120, 170, 192, 272, 374, 380, 391, 396, 532
Ivan III, Tsar 32, 139, 141
Ivan IV, 'The Terrible', Tsar 58, 143, 147, 154, 252, 337, 360, 361, 362, 386, 387, 421, 428, 429, 432, 456
Iwaszowicz, Jan 477

Iwno People 38
Izmir, see Smyrna
Izraelowicz, Aron 185

Jabłonna 246
Jabłonowski Family 224, 502
Jabłonowski, Hetman 481
Jabłoński, D. E. (Figulus) 189
Jabłoński, Henryk 15
Jacob, Joseph Ha-Cohen 193
Jacobins 530, 539
Jacobsen, J. 258
Jadwiga, Queen of Poland (1384–99) 112, 113, 116, 117, 118, 135, 211
Jadwiga of Żagań, Queen 102
Jagiellończyk, see Kazimierz IV
Jagiellonian Dynasty 99, 113, 134, 138, 142, 144, 148, 149, 152, 155, 308, 399, 434
Jagiellonian University, Cracow 20, 118, 148, 151, 473, 531
Jagniński, S. 262
James I, King of England and Scotland 159, 186, 454
James Edward Stuart 489
Jan, Prince of Hungary 102
Jan Kazimierz (John Casimir), King (1648–68) 315, 328, 376, 378, 385, 387, 400, 401, 406, 407, 435, 439, 450, 454, 462, 463, 465, 466, 469, 474, 475
Jan III Sobieski, see Sobieski, Jan III
Jan Olbracht Jagiellon (John Albert), King (1492–1501) 138, 139
Janicki, Klemens 150
Janko of Czarnków, Vice-Chancellor 103, 109
Janowiec, Battle of 342
Jansen, Capt. H. 275
January Rising (1863) 11
Janusz III, Prince of Mazovia 104
Janusz the Elder, Prince 307
Janusz Piast 308
Jarlach, Danzig merchant 267
Jarnac, Battle of (1569) 413
Jaroslavsky, A., Governor of Suzdal 387, 388
Jarosław 111, 225, 262, 265
Jarosław, Archbishop of Gniezno 109
Jasiński, Jakob 540, 541
Jaskier, M. 132
Jasło of Tęczyn, Castellan of Wójnik 112

Jasna Góra, Monastery of 451, 452, 453, 471, 520
Javcourt, Chevalier de 368
Jaworów 315–18
Jaworów, Treaty of (1675) 399, 479–80
Jazdów 307, 308
Jazdżewski, K. 39
Jedlno 211
Jedlno, Statute of (1430) 135
Jędrzejów 168
Jefferson, Thomas 370
Jelgava (Mitau) 454
Jeremiah, Patriarch of Constantinople 172
Jerusalem 88
Jesuits 167, 168, 170, 179, 180, 198, 433, 435, 436
Jewellery 247
Jewish Council 338
Jewish Courts 349
Jewish Guilds 299
Jewish Tribunal of Lublin 131
Jews 79–80, 96, 126, 130–2, 190–6, 197, 198, 199, 200, 201, 206, 213, 254, 290, 297, 298, 303–4, 306, 308–10, 318, 319, 335, 350, 439, 440, 444, 447, 467, 519; see also Kahal, Ghettos
Joanna, Queen of Naples 109
Jogaila, see Władysław II Jagiełło
Johanisburg, Meeting at (1698) 386
Johann Sigismund, Duke of Brandenburg 462
John Casimir, see Jan Kazimierz
John III Sobieski, see Sobieski, Jan III
John I Lackland, King of England 106
John of Luxembourg, King of Bohemia 92, 95, 99
John III, Vaza King of Sweden 414, 422, 434, 435, 436
Johnstone, J. 190
Joint-Stock Companies 129
Joli Bord, see Zolibórz
Jomsburg 82
Jonge, F. H. de 258
Joppes, Capt. D. 275
Jordan, Bishop of Poznań 67
Jordan, Spytek 219, 327
Jordanów 38
Joseph II, Emperor of Austria, H.R.E. 195
Julian Calendar 338

Julius Caesar 207
Jungingen, Ulrich von 122
Justice 214, 235, 243, 302–3, 338; see also Head Money, Customary Law, Law of Magdeburg, Law Enforcement, Law of Lübeck, Crime
Justinian, Emperor of Rome 46
Jutland 453

Kadłubek, W., Bishop of Cracow (Bl. Wincenty Kadlubek, Master Vincent) 5, 70, 78, 230
Kahal 127, 131, 195–6, 349
Kajdany 183, 190, 450
Kaleczyn 312
Kaliningrad (Koenigsberg, Krolewiec) 29, 90, 123, 143, 184, 257, 274, 276, 277, 290, 317, 400, 450, 471
Kalinka, Walerian 9, 12
Kalinowski Family 447
Kalisz 20, 27, 196, 453, 497
Kalisz, Treaty of (1343) 95
Kalkstein 407, 471
Kallimach, F. 139, 150, 364, 381
Kalmar, Statutes of 436
Kalmar, Union of 433
Kaluga 518
Kambie, Captain 274
Kamenets Podolskiy (Kamieniec Podolski) 124, 294, 395, 471
Kamien (Cammin) 84
Kamieniec 38
Kamieniec Podolski, see Kamenets Podolskiy
Kańczuga 225, 262, 263
Kaniów 526
Kapitulna 312
Kara Mustafa, Grand Vizier 395, 480, 482, 484
Karaites (Jewish Sect) 191, 192
Karamzin 523
Karaya, Beyler-Bey of Anatolia 163
Kardowski 249–50
Karlovitz, Treaty of (1699) 229, 487
Karnkowski, S., Primate of Poland 423, 435
Katarzyna Jagiellonka, Queen of Sweden 147, 434
Katowice (Kattowitz) 19, 28
Kattowitz, see Katowice
Kaufmann, Pavel 129
Kaunitz, Wenzel Anton von 520–1
Kazan 58

Kazanowski, Col. M. 457
Kazimierski, Mikołaj 327, 337, 338
Kazimierz I Odnowiciel (Casimir I the
    Restorer), Prince (1040–58) 71, 74,
    86
Kazimierz II Sprawiedliwy, Prince
    (Casimir II the Just) (1177–94) 5,
    70
Kazimierz III Wielki, King (Casimir III
    the Great) (1333–70) 62, 74, 81,
    84, 87, 93, 95, 96, 98, 99, 100, 101,
    109, 111, 116, 129, 203, 211, 307
Kazimierz IV Jagiellończyk (Casimir IV
    the Jagiellonian), King (1447–92)
    138, 211, 256, 272
Kazimierz 85, 267, 388, 410
Kazimierz Dolny 148, 266, 291, 305
Kaźko, Duke of Słupsk 102, 104
Kazonowski Family 311
Kehlman, Capt. M. 275
Kenworthy, J. 277
Kęsowski, Abbot of Oliwa 400
Kettler, Gotthard von 147
Kettler, Duke J. 454
Kęty (Liebenwerde) 171
Kiejstut, G. D. of Lithuania 112
Kiejsztutowicz, Zygmunt 135
Kielce 28, 38, 80
Kietlicz, Henry, Archbishop of Gniezno
    70
Kiev (Kijów) 30, 34, 61, 86, 115, 147,
    153, 172, 175, 176, 218, 294, 345,
    360, 396, 407, 408, 459
Kiezgajllo Family 216
Kijów, see Kiev
Kiliński, Jan 539
Kinke, merchant of Danzig 260
Kircholm, Battle of (1605) 445, 448
Kirkcaldy 275
Kisiel, Adam 177
Kissinger, H. 400
Kiszla, J. 177, 187
Kitaygorod 457, 458
Kleinfeldt, E. 258
Klemens 128
Kleparz 293, 441
Klewan 298
Kliszów, Battle of (1702) 497, 503
Kłobuck 453
Klonowic, Sebastian 56, 268, 269,
    291
Klushino, Battle of (1610) 445, 456
Knights of the Sword 146; see also
    Brethren of Christ's Militia

Kniprode, Winrich von 116
Knyszyn, Castle of 154
Kobyłka 541
Kochanowski, Jan 150, 151, 152, 172,
    241, 378
Kochanowski, Piotr 6, 165
Kochowski, Wespazjan 7
Kodeks Dyplomatyczny Polski 12
Koenigsberg, see Kaliningrad
Kolberg, see Kołobrzeg
Kolbuszowa 262
Kolivshchyzna 519
Kołłotaj, Hugo 531, 534
Kołobrzeg (Kolberg, Colberg) 69, 84,
    275
Kolowrat, Bishop 482
Kolozsvar (Hermannstadt, Cluj) 108
Kolseć 441
Komensky, J. A. (Comenius J. A.) 188,
    189
Konarski, A., Bishop of Kujawy 413,
    415
Konarski, Stanisław 509
Koniecpolski Family 311, 447
Koniecpolski, S., Grand Hetman of the
    Crown 445, 450, 460, 463, 465
Konitz, see Chojnice
Konrad Mazowiecki, Prince (Conrad of
    Mazovia) 1241–43 62, 86, 87, 88,
    90, 94
Kopernik Family 258
Kopernik M., see Copernicus, N.
Koperniki 258
Kordecki, A., Prior 452
Korniakt Family 351
Korniakt, Michał 354
Kornik Library 12
Korolówka 194
Korsuń 294
Korsuń, Battle of (1648) 465
Korzon, Tadeusz 12, 13, 343
Kos, R. 187
Kościuszko, Tadeusz 530, 533, 535,
    536, 538–9, 540, 541, 543
Košice (Koszyce), Slovakia 112
Kosina 262
Kosiński, Ataman 446
Kossakowski, Józef 526, 535, 540
Kossakowski, Szymon 526, 535, 540
Kostrzewski, J. 39
Koszyce, see Košice
Koszyce, Statute of (1374) 9, 111, 113,
    211
Kot, Prof. S. 190

Kowel 361
Kozin 144
Kozłowski, L. 39
Koźmian, Kajetan 242, 244
Krak, King 61, 269
Krakau, see Cracow
Kraków, Statute of (1433) 135
Kraków School 9, 13
Kraków University, see Jagiellonian University
Krasicki Family 246
Krasicki, Ignacy 227, 530–1
Krasiczyn 148, 246, 298
Krasiński Family 519
Krasiński, Jan Dobrogost 311
Krasiński, W. 168
Krasnik, Salmon 131
Krasny Gorodek 408
Krassau, General 497
Krechetnikov 520
Krevo, Union of (1385) 118
Królewiec, see Kaliningrad
Królewski (Royal) Canal 265
Kromer, Marcin 6, 203, 249, 363, 364, 378, 382, 391
Kronika Wszystkiego Swiata (Chronicle of the whole world) of Marcin Bielski 6
Kronstadt 274
Krosno 111, 172
Krumhausen, merchant of Danzig 260, 302
Kruszwica 28, 61
Krystyna of Rokičana 102
Krzemieniec 441
Krzemionki 38
Krzyztopór 246
Kudak 445, 446
Kujawy (Cuiavia) 28, 88, 93, 94, 95, 102, 109, 274, 333, 349, 521
Kukiel, Marian 13, 14
Kulm, see Chełmno
Kulwieć, A., (Culvensis, A.) 179
Kunicka, Lady 471
Kurbsky, Prince A. 173, 361, 362, 363
Kurbsky, Michał Dymitr 362
Kurfurst, Battle of 480
Kurland, Prince of 329
Kurlandia, see Courland
Kurozwęcki Family 109, 224
Kutrzeba, Stanisław 10, 13
Kwarta (Quarter Tax) 121, 427
Kwartalnik Historyczny, Historical Quarterly 12

Kwidzyń (Marienwerder) 90, 91, 190, 511
Kwidzyn, Battle of (1629) 450

La Rochelle 260
Labiau, Treaty of (1656) 462
Laboureur, Jean de 251
Ladislaus I Herman, see Władysław I Herman
Ladislaus II the Exile, see Władysław II Wygnaniec
Ladislaus I the Elbow-High, see Władysław I Łokietek
Ladislaus Jagiello, see Władysław II Jagiełło
Ladislaus III of Varna, see Władysław III Warneńczyk
Ladislaus IV Vasa, see Władysław IV Waza
Ladislaus Jagiellon, see Władysław Jagiellończyk
Ladislavs von Oppelń 135
Ladoga, lake 430
Lancius, M., see Łęczyca, M.
Lanckorona 194
Łańcut 354
Land Holding 211–13, 218–24, 228–33; see also Crown lands, Latifundia
Landa, Salmon 131
Languages 47, 61, 67–9, 115, 236–7, 315, 378–9; see also Slavs
Lasch, Samuel 351
Laski, Adalbert 421
Laski, J., Primate of Poland 183, 356, 373
Laski, J., reformer 125, 126, 141, 148, 149, 183, 189
Latifundia 224, 228; see also Land Holding
Latin 236–7
Latvia 115
Lauenberg, Duchy of (Lębork) 385, 407
Lausitz people, see Lusatian people
Law 96, 132, 211–12, 234–6, 348–55, 425
Law enforcement 351–2
Law of Lubeck 295
Law of Magdeburg 78, 243, 295, 304, 317
Ławrynowicz, M. 168, 199
Lazarists 168
Łazienki Palace 311, 312, 313
Lebus, see Lubusz

Lech 61
Lechfeld, Battle of the, 955 AD 62, 107
Łęczyca 88, 94, 102, 333
Łęczyca (Lancius), M. 168
Łęczyca, Synod of (1180) 70
Legends 61–2
Leghorn 260
Legnica, Battle of (1241) 72, 87
Łęgonice, Treaty of 328, 334
Lehr-Spławiński, T. 39
Leibnitz, Gottfried 366, 489
Leipzig 505, 506, 538
Leith 275
Lejbowicz, J., see Frank, J.
Lekno 89
Lelewel, Joachim 7, 9, 214
Lemberg, see Lvov
Lemovii 45
Lenin, V. I. 14
Leningrad (St. Petersburg, Petrograd) 193, 275, 409, 410, 500, 510, 514, 516, 521, 523, 528, 532, 535, 544
Leo X, Pope 126
Leopold of Austria 462
Leopold I, Emperor of Austria 481
Leopold II, Emperor of Austria 536
Lepunov 457
Lessenau, B. von 265, 266
Lesser Poland, see Małopolska
Leszczyński Family 183, 184, 246, 312, 395
Leszczyński, B. 189
Leszczyński, R. 183
Leszczyński, W. Bishop of Warmia 394
Leszczyński, King Stanisław (Stanislaus Leszczyński) 189, 383, 400, 497, 504, 508, 509
Leszek I Biały, Prince (Leszek I the White, 1202–27) 70, 86
Leszek II Czarny (Leszek II the Black, Prince 1279–88) 94
Leszek I the White, see Leszek I Biały
Leszek II the Black, see Leszek II Czarny
Leszno 183, 188, 189, 190
Lewartów 298
Leyden 190
Libau, see Liepaja
Liberum Veto 11, 339, 345–8, 365, 367, 513, 518, 519, 534
Lidzbark (Heilsberg) 90, 374
Liebischau, see Lubieszów
Liepaja (Libau, Lipawa) 56, 260

Lind, von der 302
Linkoping, Battle of 437
Linz 481
Lionne, H. de 401
Lipawa, see Liepaja
Lipomano, Ieronimo 363
Lisbon 260, 458
Liske, Ksawery 12
Lismanino, F. 185
Lisowski, A. 456
Liszki 418
Literature 267–8, 374–5, 423–4, 460–1
Lithuania (Grand Duchy) 31, 32, 56, 59, 60, 105, 112, 115, 124, 166, 172, 177, 182, 184, 187, 190, 191, 192, 198, 199, 217, 218, 277, 281, 295, 322, 323, 331, 336, 349, 362, 378, 379, 382, 387, 388, 394, 397, 436, 439, 440, 447, 450, 454, 459, 487, 496, 501, 502, 503, 509, 511, 520, 547
Lithuanian Army 217, 362; see also Piechota Wybraniecka, Husaria, Military History
Lithuanian Council 141
Lithuanian Statutes:
    Second (1566) 216
    Third (1588) 322, 436
Lithuanian Tribunal 349, 425
Lithuanians 49, 87, 93, 95, 378
Litta, Lorenzo 543, 544
Littlepage, King's Secretary 238
Litwa, see Lithuania
Livonia (Inflanty) 31, 49, 56, 90, 124, 146, 308, 329, 343, 383, 399, 416, 422, 423, 428, 430, 431, 434, 447, 448, 450, 454, 465, 480, 482, 496, 521
Livonian War 146
Locci, Augustyn 310–11, 489
Lolling, Capt. G. 275
London 181, 189, 274, 275, 380, 398, 405, 410
Longinus 509
Longinus, see Długosz, Jan
Lorraine, 416, 504, 508
Lothar of Supplinburg, Holy Roman Emperor 84
Louis the Great, see Ludwik Węgierski
Louis XI, King of France 138
Louis XIV, King of France 383, 385, 400, 401, 402, 479, 480, 489
Louis XV, King of France 515

Louis XVI, King of France 538, 543
Louis XVIII, King of France 536
Louis Jagiellon, King of Hungary and Bohemia 142
Louis of Anjou 115, 117, 211, 339
Łowicz 295
Łowmiański, H. 50
Łoziński, Władysław 350, 351
Lubart, Prince 112
Lubartów 260, 265
Lubawa Castle 219
Lubeck 90, 260, 275, 390
Lubieszów 425
Lublin 18, 26, 129, 152, 188, 294, 304, 331, 332, 349, 390
Lublin, Union of (1569) 58, 152−5, 197, 201, 216, 217, 308, 322, 330, 334, 375, 378, 386, 392, 397, 414, 436, 470
Lubomirski Family 224, 225, 261, 502
Lubomirska, Princess, mistress of August II 495
Lubomirski, Prince 180
Lubomirski, Aleksander Michał 225
Lubomirski, Jerzy 343−5, 395, 466, 468, 469, 473, 474, 475, 476
Lubomirski, Piotr 209
Lubomirski, Stanisław Hetman 224
Lubomirski, Stanisław Herakliusz 312
Lubomirski Estates 225
Lubomirski Rebellion 328, 343, 401
Lubrański, Bishop Jan 149
Lubusz (Lebus) 69, 83
Luchesini 536
Łuck 187
Łuck, Congress of (1429) 135
Ludwik Węgierski (Louis), King of Hungary, and of Poland (1370−82) 99, 100, 102, 103, 104, 108, 109, 111, 112, 113
Łukasz 131
Łuków 29, 273
Lumbres, Antoine de 399, 400
Lunéville 508, 509
Luria, S. 444
Lusatia (Łużyce) 63, 81, 82, 493
Lusatian People (Lausitz people, Łużyczanie) 38, 39
Lusignan, Pierre de, King of Cyprus 99, 100, 101
Lustracje (Surveys of Royal estates) 52ff, 315−18
Luther, M. 193, 373

Lutherans 143, 166, 167, 177, 179, 180, 182, 191, 197, 198, 305, 439, 498
Luxembourg Dynasty 93, 95, 113, 138
Łuzyce, see Lusatia
Łużyczanie, see Lusatians
Lviv, see Lvov
Lvov, (Lwów, Lviv, Lemberg) 30, 34, 69, 111, 166, 170, 190, 294, 298, 304, 305, 350, 394, 403, 404, 406, 479, 497
Lwów, see Lvov
Lyblich, Joseph 131
Lynar, Count 520
Lyon 419

Mably, Gabriel Bonnot de 369, 410
Macaulay, Thomas Babington 525
Machaut, G. de 92, 99
Machiavelli, N. 392
Maciejowice 541
Maciejowski, Samuel 341
Macrobius 509
Maczek 288
Madaliński, Antoni Józef 538
Madrepore 317
Madrid 374, 381, 388, 389, 402, 493
Magdeburg 63
Magnates 139, 216, 221−8, 261−5, 266, 300, 311−13, 335, 342, 346, 347, 353, 359, 360, 426, 427, 439, 461, 470, 487, 492, 527, 531
Magnus Vasa, Duke of Ostergotland 434
Magyars (Hungarians) 46, 57, 62, 95, 107, 108, 112, 161
Main, river 82
Mainz 107, 413
Maires, D. de 258
Małachowski, Stanisław 533, 534
Malaga 260
Malaspina, G. Papal Nuncio 246, 436
Malbork (Marienburg) 123, 124, 219
Malbork, Treaty of 425
Malherbe, François 314
Malinowski, J. ben Mordecai Ha Qodesh 192
Mallet du Pin, Jacques 525
Małopolska (Lesser Poland, Polonia Minor) 27, 28, 37, 76, 86, 88, 93, 96, 109, 112, 165, 170, 185, 187, 219, 257, 265, 267, 285, 298, 304, 349, 521
Malta 165

Mamelukes 461
Mandeville, Sir John 93
Manifesto of Połaniec (1794) 532, 539
Manorial Farming 128
Manteuffel, Tadeusz 18
Marescotti, G. 401
Margaret of Savoy 419
Maria, Princess 109, 112
Maria Dobronega, Princess 74
Maria of Anjou 117
Maria-Theresa, Empress of Austria 516, 520, 521
Marian Fathers, Order of 171
Marianite Sisters 170
Marie-Louise Gonzaga, Queen 394, 400, 463
Marienburg, see Malbork
Marienstadt 312
Marienwerder, see Kwidzyń
Marieville (Marywił) 314
Marinius Polonius, see Sachs, Johann
Maritime Commission 147
Marjoribanks, A. 277
Marseilles 540
Martin the Pole 79
Marx, Karl 7, 14–19, 535
Marxism–Leninism 14–19
Mary Perkunatele, St. (Festival of) 124
Mary Stuart, Queen of Scotland 413
Mary Tudor, Queen of England 390
Marymont 310
Marysieńka, Queen of Poland 311, 399, 402; see also Grange d'Arquien, Marie de la
Marywił, see Marieville
Massalski, Ignacy 526, 540
Massalsky, Prince V. 458
Master Vincent, see Kadłubek, W.
Matathia, R. 191
Mątwy, Battle of (1666) 343, 466, 474
Mauritzburg 495
Maximilian I, Holy Roman Emperor 373, 380
Maximilian II, Emperor 400, 419
Maximilian, Archduke of Austria 435
Mazovia, see Mazowsze
Mazovia, Princes of 295
Mazowsze (Mazovia) 28, 45, 67, 86, 88, 93, 95, 104, 196, 218, 228, 229, 235, 264, 288, 295, 298, 306, 349
Mazuria, see Mazury
Mazury (Mazuria) 29
Meaux-sur-Marne 271
Medieval History 61–141

Mediterranean Sea 61, 260
Meissen 81, 493
Melanchthon, P. 183
Melsztyński Family 109, 127, 224
Mendoza, Don F. de 398
Mercantilism 319
Merchants Confraternities 299–300, 301; see also Guilds
Merkuriusz Polski 20
Merseburg, Congress of (1033) 71
Meseritz, see Międzyrzecz
Mesko, see Mieszko I
Methodism 193
Metz 413
Miasecki, Stanisław, Bishop of Płock 232
Michael F. Romanov, Tsar 458, 465
Michael K. Wiśniowiecki, see Wiśniowiecki, Michał Korybut
Mickiewicz, Adam 9, 52, 230
Middleton, Archibald Patrick 238
Miechowit, Maciej 6, 149, 364
Międzyboz 193
Międzyrzecz (Meseritz) 69, 193, 311
Mielnik, Agreement of (1501) 141, 211
Mieszko I Prince (960–92) 3, 4, 21, 59, 62, 63, 67, 74, 80, 81, 82, 83, 85, 92
Mieszko II King (1025–34) 71, 72
Military History 80–2, 121–2, 213–14, 425–6, 445, 502–4
Military Service 213–14, 215
Millenium 19–22
Miller, W. 277
Milsko, see Milzi
Milton, John 473
Milzi (Milsko) 82
Minerals 212
Miners 205
Mińsk Mazowiecki 541
Miński, Stanisław 252
Mint, The 329, 426
Mirabeau, Comte de 525
Mitau, see Jelgava
Mniszek, J., Palatine of Sandomierz 377, 456
Mniszek, Maryna 456
Moab, burgher of Toruń 180
Modrevicius, see Modrzejewski, Andrzej Frycz
Modric 482
Modrzejewski, Andrzej Frycz (Modrevicius) 150, 356–7, 363, 364, 368
Mogilnica 295

Mohacs, Battle of (1526) 142, 380
Mohyla, Peter, Metropolitan of Kiev 175
Mohylev (Mogilew) 295
Moldavia (Moldawia) 32, 109, 139, 144, 175, 211, 361, 416, 470
Moldavians 108
Monarchy 3–4, 61–2, 70–4, 82–3, 93–5, 102–4, 106–7, 109–13, 116–20, 132–4, 135–48, 152–5, 331–6, 341–3, 355–67, 375–6, 414–15, 422–4, 444–5, 474–5, 497–502, 516–18, 544–6
Monasteryszcze 446
Mongolia 80
Mongols 10, 46, 87, 93, 115, 120; see also Tartars
Monitor 530
Monluc, J. de, Bishop of Valence 391, 414
Monmouth, Duke of 404
Montelupi Family 297–380
Montelupi, Walerian 350–1
Montesquieu, Charles Louis de Secondat 367
Monti, Marquis de 383, 409
Montwy, see Mątwy
Monumenta Poloniae Historica 12
Moors 161, 164, 461
Moravia (Morawy) 38, 45, 51, 85, 87, 91, 188, 419, 481
Moravian Anabaptists 185
Moravians 62
More, Sir Thomas 374
Morgan, W. 277
Morison, Fynes 363
Moroni, Cardinal 396
Morrow, Captain A. 275
Moscorovius 186
Moscow 120, 173, 174, 176, 381, 382, 389, 391, 396, 406, 454, 455, 456, 458; see also Muscovy
Moses 468
Motława (Mottlau), river 292
Mottlau, see Motława
Mścisław, see Mstislav
Mstislav (Mścisław) 141, 515, 521
Muhammad IV, Sultan of Turkey 471
Muller, General 451, 452, 453
Municipal Courts 293, 350
Munster 190
Murad II, Sultan 163, 164
Murad the Conqueror 487
Murano, Belotti da 312

Muranów 312
Muratowicz, S. 379
Murder 235–6
Muscovy, Grand Duchy of 134, 139, 142, 143, 146, 147, 217, 310, 329, 337, 343, 344, 345, 361, 423, 426, 428, 431, 480, 487
Muskata, J., Bishop of Cracow 94
Muslims 190, 199
Myszkowski, M., Castellan of Radom 382
Myszkowski, Piotr 327, 341
Myszyniec 295

Najburg 269
Nakowski 34
Nalewajko, S. 174, 446
Namier, Sir Lewis 370
Naples 380, 381
Naples, Kingdom of 106, 108, 109
Napoleon I Bonaparte, Emperor of the French 57, 411
Narbutt, B. 171
Narew, river 265
Naruszewicz, Bishop Adam 7, 12, 104, 241
Narva 58, 147, 430
National Education Commission 320, 526; see also Vol. II, Chapter 8
Naturalization, see Indygenat
Neapolitan Sums 145
Nederle, L. 40
Neisse, see Nysa
Neminem Captivabimus 211, 327, 359
Nero Emperor of Rome 45
Neu Sandez, see Nowy Sącz
Neumark 120
Neumarkt, see Środa Śląska
Nevers-sur-Loire 469
New England 370
New Galicia 542
New South Prussia 542
Newcastle 275
Ney, Marshal 233
Nicholas I, Tsar 491
Nicholas the Pole, of Montpellier 78
Niemcewicz, Julian Ursyn 531, 540, 541
Niemcza (Nimtsch) 83
Niemen, river 31, 115, 265
Niepołomice 262, 417, 432
Nieświez 189, 191
Nieszawa 211, 268
Nieznakowski Island 269

Nihil Novi, Statute (1505) 10, 132, 141, 211, 331
Nikitin 492
Nikolsburg 481
Nikon, Patriarch 176
Nile, river 35
Nimtsch, *see* Niemcza
Noah 207
Nobility (*Szlachta*) 126, 127, 132, 201, 206, 207–55, 326, 335, 343, 350–6, 359, 360, 425, 427, 513, 519, 535, 537
Nogat, river 269
Norbertanki, Order of, *see* Premonstratensians
Nordstrom, Captain J. 275
North Sea 26
Norway 433
Noteć, river 83
Novgorod 58, 61, 120, 154, 429
Nowa Huta 50
Nowe Leszno 312
Nowodworski, B. 165
Nowodworski Gymnazium, Cracow 473
Nowogródek, *see* Nowogrudok
Nowogrudok (Nowogródek) 172, 187, 526
Nowomiejski, Adam 328
Nowy Sącz (Neu Sandez) 78, 521
Nowy Świat 312
Nowy Targ 52, 521
Nyjmegen 404, 480
Nysa (Neisse) 34, 39, 294

Obertyn 144
Obertyn, Battle of (1531) 461
Obodritians (Obodryci) 63
Obrona Potoczna 144
Observantists 170
Ocieski, Joachim
O'Connor, Bernard 363, 364–5
Oder, *see* Odra
Odra (Oder), river 23, 26, 27, 28, 34, 35, 38, 39, 43, 47, 61, 82, 83, 413, 504
Odrowąż Family 127
Oels, *see* Oleśnica
Ogiński Canal 265
Ogiński Family 177, 246, 502
Ogiński, M., Hetman 509, 520
O'Kelly, Hugo 238
Olbracht, Alexander 211
Olbracht, Jan (John Albert), King 211
Old Byelorussian Language (*Ruski*, Ruthenian) 115

Olesko 473
Oleśnica (Oels) 104
Oleśnicki Family 183
Oleśnicki, Cardinal Zbigniew 125, 135, 138, 148, 224
Olgierd 115
Oliński 143
Oliwa 436, 448
Oliwa, Abbey of 425
Oliwa, Battle of (1627) 448
Oliwa, Treaty of (1660) 180, 181, 395, 400, 407, 454, 455, 462, 466
Olkusz 80
Olomouc (Olomutz) 87, 481, 482
Opacki, Cup-Bearer 267
Opaliński, Jędrzej 232
Opaliński, Krzysztof Palatina of Poznan 7, 244, 360, 363, 394, 395, 450
Opaliński, Łukasz 7, 354–5, 361
Opatów 262
Opava (Troppau) 481
Opole (Oppeln) 104
Oppeln, *see* Opole
Oppeln, Ladislavs von, *see* Ladislavs
Oprichnina 348, 361
Order of the Brethren of the Sword 90
Order of the Immaculate Conception, the 240
Order of St. Stanisław, the 240
Order of Virtuti Militari 240, 536
Order of the White Eagle 240
Ordinacja, see Entail, law of
Orleans 107
Orosius, P. 91
Orsetti Family 329
Orsha (Orsza) 167
Orsha, Battle of (1505) 143
Orsza, *see* Orsha
Ort 130
Orthodox Church 166, 172–7, 182, 183, 186, 190, 195, 197, 198, 199, 205, 216, 335, 447, 513, 514, 518
Orzechowski, Stanisław 150, 167
Orzelska Countess, Princess of Holstein 495, 509
Ościk 426
Osiek 262
Osman II 460, 461
Ossig 190
Ossoliński Family 246, 311
Ossoliński, H. 183
Ossoliński, Chancellor J. 159, 352, 394, 463
Ossoliński, Mikołaj 351

Ostrogoths 46
Ostrogska, Princess 176
Ostrogski estates 226
Ostrogski Family 215, 447
Ostrogski 139, 143, 153
Ostrogski, Prince J. 177
Ostrogski, Prince K., Palatine of Kiev 173, 177, 444
Ostrogski, Konstanty 336, 362
Ostrołęka 538
Ostroróg 173
Ostroróg, Jan 125, 139, 299
Oświęcim (Auschwitz) 78, 85, 113, 138, 195, 288, 381, 405, 411, 418, 466, 487, 503–4, 516, 520, 528, 535–7, 542–3
Otto I, Holy Roman Emperor 62, 72, 82, 107
Otto III, Holy Roman Emperor 63, 67, 71, 82
Otto, Bishop of Bamberg 84
Otto, Duke of Bavaria 99
Ottokar II, King of Bohemia 90
Ottoman Empire 394–5, 449–51, 471–2, 476–7, 478–87, 491; see also Turkey
Ottoman Turks 142, 144, 360, 476, 478–9, 480, 481, 482, 483, 484–7
Ottomans, see Turks
Otwock 15
Outlaws 326, 339
Oxford 168, 189
Ovid 509
Oxenstierna, E. 400
Ożarowski, Piotr 526, 540

Pac Family 177
Pac, Jan Michał 519
Pacta Conventa 331, 335, 375, 401, 436
Padovano, Giovanni Maria 150
Padua 257, 396
Padua, University of 151, 370, 422
Paine, Tom 192
Painting 148
Palanga (Połąga) 56
Palatines (Wojewoda) 335, 362
Palej's Rebellion (1703) 497
Palestine 373
Palestra, see Bar
Paley, William 368
Pallavicini, Monsignor 402
Palloni 489

Pamiętnik Historyczno-Polityczno-Ekonomiczny (Historico-Politico-Economic Record) 530
Panin, Nikita 515
Pańszczyzna (labour services) 280, 284
Papacy, see Vatican
Paprocki, Bartosz 209
Parandier, Citoyen 543
Paris 79, 159, 274, 381, 394, 395, 410, 413, 416, 417, 458, 466, 530, 533, 536
Parkany 486
Partitions of Poland 9, 13, 291, 410, 411, 510, 511, 515, 517, 527, 535–7
First Partition (1772) 521–6, 528, 537
Second Partition (1793) 323, 331, 348, 526, 537
Third Partition (1795) 9, 320, 323, 526, 530, 541–2, 544
Partitions, Treaties of
(1772) 513
(1793) 537
(1797) 542
Pasek, Jan C. 7, 243, 245, 267, 328, 329, 332–3, 343
Paston letters 350
Pastor, A. 185
Patkul, J. R. 383
Patras 165
Patriotic Party 534
Patronage 210
Patz, Johann Jakub 544
Paul II, Pope 159
Paul of Krosno 373
Paulmy, Marquis de 409
Pavlovo 329
Pawiński, Adolf 13
Pawłowski, S. 34
Pawluk 446
Payden, M. de 271
Peasants 126, 201, 206, 212, 228, 242–5, 261, 279–87, 335, 356, 359, 534, 539
Pecs 396
Pękosławski 336
Pellison 314
Pels, M. 258
Pels, P. 258
Penzańce 374
Perejasław, see Pereyaslavl
Pereyaslavl (Perejasław) 167, 295, 465

Periodization 5, 7–11
Perkun 116, 124
Permanent Commission 528, 540
Persia 379
Peter I, Tsar of Russia 386, 389, 406, 408, 410, 455, 495, 499, 500, 513
Peter III, Tsar of Russia 408, 515, 516, 517
Peter's Pence 95
Peterhead 275
Petrarch 150
Petrograd, see Leningrad
Petrylo, Hospodar of Moldavia 144
Petty Nobility 221, 228–33, 335, 342, 353
Pfaffendorf, see Szamocyn
Philip II King of Spain 390
Philosophy 149
Piarists (Pietists) 168
Piasts 61, 62, 63, 66, 71, 74, 82, 86, 91, 103, 104, 109, 111, 134, 155, 208; see also Mazovia, Princess of
Piechota Wybraniecka (selected infantry) 425
Piedmont 542
Piegłowski, District Supervisor 267
Piekarski, Anselm 328
Piękosiński, Franciszek 13
Pieniążek Family 52
Pieniążek, J. 52
Pieniążek, P. 52
Pietists, see Piarists
Pignatelli, Monsignor (Innocent XII Pope) 401
Pilau, see Piława
Piława (Pilau) 448
Pilgrom, A. 258
Pilica, river 265
Pilsnitz (Pilczyce), Congress of 536
Piłsudski, Józef 14
Piltyn, see Ventspils
Pinchovians, see Arians
Pińczów 183, 184, 226
Pińczów, Synod of (1556) 183
Pińczów, Synod of (1562) 184
Pińsk (Pinsk) 30, 171, 295
Pinsk, see Pińsk
Pinto, A. L. 260
Piotr z Goniąz (Gonesius, P.) 185
Piotrków 211, 331, 349, 453
Piotrków, Sejm of (1555) 139, 183
Piotrków, Synod of (1551) 167
Piotrowski, A. 182

Pisarski, Eustachy 333, 334
Pitschen, see Byczyna
Plague 154, 313, 314
Plautus 456
Pless, see Pszczyna
Plettenberg, von 141
Pliny 45
Płock 69, 78, 104, 268, 269, 291, 295, 306
Plymouth 374
Pobóg-Malinowski, Władysław 13, 14
Pociej, A., Hetman of Lithuania 503
Podkova, Ivan 426
Podlasia, see Podlasie
Podlasie (Podlasia) 29, 153, 185, 187, 218, 228, 229, 446
Podolia (Podole) 30, 35, 59, 124, 147, 193, 194, 229, 265, 282, 395, 446, 471, 481, 487
Podoski, Gabriel, Primate 368, 526, 540
Podskarbi (Treasurers) 335
Pokucie 144
Polabians 43
Połąga, see Palanga
Polanians, see Polanie
Polanie (Polanians) 4, 27, 44, 45, 61, 67, 69, 85
Polanovka, river 459
Polanów, Treaty of (1634) 23, 463
Polanowski 333, 334
Pole, Reginald, Cardinal 396
Polesie, see Pripyat
Polignac, Abbé, M. de 399
Polish Brethren, see Arians
Polish Language 47, 67, 69
Polish People's Republic 14
Polish Republic 1918–39, 13, 535
Polish–Russian War of 1609–12, 455
Polish–Russian War of 1617–19, 455
Polish–Russian War of 1632–4, 455
Polish Succession, War of the (1733–6) 288, 504, 505
Polish–Swedish War (1654–60) 198, 262, 290, 315, 343
Polish–Turkish War of 1620–1, 460
Polish–Turkish War (1672–99) 478–87
Political Institutions, see Monarchy, Sejm, Sejmiki, Confederation, Rokosz, Liberum Veto, Royal Elections
Political Theory 321–2, 338–41, 346–7, 355–72, 389–92
Płock, see Polotsk

Polonnoe 193
Połotsk (Płock) 115, 147, 171, 174, 295, 429, 431, 515, 521
Poltava, battle of (1709) 408, 455, 497, 508
Pomerania, see Pomorze
Pomeranians (Pomorzanie) 69
Pommern, see Pomorze
Pomorzanie, see Pomeranians
Pomorze (Pomerania, Pommern) 27, 28, 39, 45, 49, 67, 72, 80, 81, 82, 83, 84, 89, 91, 93, 94, 95, 108, 399, 400, 276, 462, 465, 497, 507
Poniatów 298
Poniatowski Family 224, 246, 298, 502
Poniatowski, Michał 540
Poniatowski, Józef 494, 502, 533, 541
Poniatowski, Stanisław-August (Stanislaus Augustus Poniatowski) King (1764–95) 237, 240, 311, 312, 358, 379, 409, 492, 511, 516, 517, 518, 523, 527, 528, 529, 530, 531, 532, 534, 535, 537, 542, 543, 545
Poniński, Adam 315, 523
Poor Clares, see Franciscan Minoresses
Popiel, Prince 61
Portsmouth 402
Portugal 260, 466
Posen, see Poznań
Possevini, A., Papal legate 172, 430, 431, 433, 434
Potash 212
Potemkin, Prince 528
Potis, H., Bishop of Brest 173
Potkański, Karol 13
Potocki Family 224, 311, 447, 488, 502, 508, 519
Potocki, Stanisław-Szczesny (Felix) 526, 529, 535
Potocki, Wacław 6, 7, 245, 254, 460
Potsdam, Conference of (1945) 66
Poznań (Posen) 4, 27, 67, 69, 78, 81, 165, 167, 272, 294, 304, 305, 350, 413, 499
Poznania, Prussian 541
Praga (in Warsaw) 313, 541, 543, 544
Prague 33, 85, 91, 98, 99, 102, 104, 390
Prehistory 38–52
Premonstratensians (Norbertanki), Order of 172
Premyslids 94
Preobrazhenskiy, Treaty of (1699) 495
Printing 148–9

Pripet (river) (Prypeć) 30, 31, 265
Pripet Marshes, see Pripyat
Pripyat (Pripet Marshes, Polesie) 29, 34, 429
Processions 251–2
Proszowice 326, 327
Protestants 166, 167, 168, 177, 190, 198, 199, 342, 404, 467, 514, 518; see also Reformation
Provana, P. 380
Provence 107
Provinces 27–33
Prussia 29, 45, 49, 58, 80, 85, 88–91, 92, 108, 115, 120–4, 143, 146, 177–82, 190, 198, 218–19, 256–92, 297, 315, 329–30, 374, 378, 384, 385, 400, 402, 405, 406–7, 408, 410, 411, 428, 434, 448, 451, 454, 461, 462, 477, 479, 488, 492, 493, 495, 503, 504, 507, 508, 515–16, 521, 528, 535, 536, 537, 540, 542, 503, 504; see also Ducal Prussia, Royal Prussia, New South Prussia
Prussians 398, 400, 405, 407, 408, 462, 507
Prussian League 256, 295
Pruth, river 460
Prypeć, see Pripet
Przegląd Historyczny (Historical Review) 12
Przemyśl 44, 304, 350
Przemyśl II, King (1295–6) 94
Pskov 120, 430
Pstrokoński, Maciej 341
Pszczyna (Pless) 418
Ptolomy 27
Puck 450
Pufendorf, Samuel 363, 364
Pułaski, Casimir 520
Puławy 246, 291
Pułtusk 167, 295
Pułtusk, Battle of 497
Pushkin, G. G., Governor 387

Quadro, Giovanni Battista 308

Raba (river) 52
Racibórz (Ratibor) 481
Racławice 539
Racovian Catechism 186
Racovians, see Arians
Raczyński Library 12

Radim (Gaudentius), Archbishop of Gniezno 67, 69
Radom 118, 211, 331
Radom, Sejm of 141
Radoszkowice 147
Radziejowska, Elzbieta 314
Radziejowski, envoy 389
Radziwiłł Family 177, 183, 184, 189, 215, 224, 311, 377, 426, 502, 504, 509, 513
Radziwiłł, Barbara, Queen 145, 155, 217
Radziwiłł, Bogusław 333
Radziwiłł, Charlotte, Princess 407, 488
Radziwiłł, Janusz, Grand Hetman of Lithuania 341, 342, 346, 450
Radziwiłł, Prince, Karol Stanisław 226
Radziwiłł, 'Thunderbolt', Prince Krzysztof, Hetman 177
Radziwiłł, Prince Mikołaj, the Red 153, 216–17, 429, 430
Radziwiłł, Prince Mikołaj Krzysztof 'the black' 184, 217
Radziwiłł estates 225
Ragazno 94
Ragusa, see Dubrovnik
Rahoza, M., Metropolitan 183
Rahts-Herrn, (Senators) of Gdansk 302
Rakocsi, George, Prince of Transylvania 465
Raków 185, 187, 190
Rape 235, 236, 350
Raskol (Schism), the 176
Ratibor, see Racibórz
Ravcour, Pierre 238
Rawa 138, 329
Rawicz 305
Rebellion 340
Referendaria Koronna 349
Reform 320, 511–13, 526–30, 533–5
Reformation 143, 146, 305; see also Arians, Protestants, Calvinism, Lutheranism
Reformists 170
Regalists 340, 341, 342, 358
Regensburg 394
Regents (Interrex) 331
Reichenbach (Dzierzoniów), Congress of 536
Reimer, S. 506
Rej, Mikołaj 150, 184, 234, 242, 243, 250–1, 357
Rejtan, Tadeusz 526

Religion 4, 19–20, 67–70, 115–16, 124–6, 159–200, 248–9, 439, 514
Religious toleration 145, 206–7, 339, 514
Rembowski, Aleksander 13
Renaissance 148–52, 246; see also Golden Age of Poland
Repnin, Prince Nikolai 410, 518, 519
Retyk 150
Retz, A., Marshal de 417
Reval 436
Revenue, Public 427–8
Revenue, Royal 426–7
Rheims (Reims) 99
Rhine, river 26, 35, 49, 291
Rhineland 542
Rhodes 142
Rhône, river 291
Richard I, King of England 106
Richelieu, Cardinal 378, 399
Riga 90, 146, 147, 260, 295, 319, 407, 434, 448, 496, 497, 480
Right of resistance 365, 371, 534; see also Confederation, Rokosz
Right of Storage 310
Robertello 151
Roberts, J. 275
Robespierre, Maximilien 538
Rodgers, Captain 274
Roesner, Burgermaster of Toruń 180, 182
Rokosz 340, 342, 343–5, 354
Roman, Prince of Ruthenia 86
Rome 61, 62, 67, 94, 95, 98, 107, 171, 172, 173, 175, 370, 380, 381, 391, 394, 435, 458
Romer, Eugeniusz 34
Ronsard, Pierre de 150
Rorte, de 378
Rossano 145
Rostock 390
Rotowski, Count 495
Rousseau, Jean-Jacques 43, 369
Royal Canal, see Królewski canal
Royal Castle, Warsaw 307, 308, 331
Royal Courts 212, 301, 349, 351, 353
Royal Elections 145, 314, 331–5, 366, 367, 382, 414, 421–2, 423, 435, 470–1, 474, 492, 504, 517, 519, 534
Royal Prussia (West Prussia) 138, 150, 151, 211, 218, 295, 297, 320, 330, 515, 521

Rożana 232
Rozyński, P., Prince 456
Rudav, battle of 116
Rudki 44
Rudolf II Emperor 435
Rugii 45
Rurik, Prince 61
Ruriks 86
Rus 61
Rus, see Ruthenia, Kiev
Ruski, see Old Byelorussian
Russia 35, 50, 51, 53, 57, 58, 61, 114,
    172, 173, 198, 273, 292, 315, 345,
    347, 348, 369, 377, 379, 381, 383,
    387, 403, 405, 406, 407–11, 433,
    434, 447, 454, 455, 458, 459, 463,
    468, 487, 495, 496, 497, 499, 500,
    501, 502, 503, 504, 511–46; see
    also Russians, Muscovy, Soviet
    Union
Russian Army 515, 535, 536, 537, 541
Russians (Muscovites, Great Russians)
    182, 189, 377, 384, 386, 391, 406,
    416, 447, 450, 457, 458, 459, 462,
    465, 466, 492, 497, 507
Russo-Polish War (War of the 2nd Parti-
    tion) 240, 530, 535–6
Russo-Turkish Wars 348, 447, 529
Ruthenes 43, 447
Ruthenia (Ruś) 63, 67, 69, 74, 81, 86,
    87, 93, 95, 111, 112, 115, 120, 135,
    172, 190, 224, 229, 238, 298, 352,
    387, 423, 525
Ruthenian, see Old Byelorussian
Rutkowski, Jan 13
Ryazan 120
Rycheza, see Ryksa
Ryki 260
Ryksa, Queen (Rycheza) 72
Rzeczpospolita (Republic) 322
Rzemien 262
Rzeszów 44, 111, 354
Rzewuski, Seweryn Hetman 526, 529,
    535
Rzucewo 38

Saad-ed-din, see Chodza Efendi
Saal (Saale) river 66, 83
Saarburg 413
Sabbateists (Jewish sect) 192, 194
Sabellians, see Arians
Sachs, Johann (Marinius Polonius) 363
Sacramentalist sisters, order of 171

Sacz 304
Sądowski, Col. 451, 453
Sagan, see Żagań
Sahajdaczny, Ataman 446, 460
St. Andrews 190
St. Andrzej Bobola 171
St. Bartholomew's Eve Massacre of
    1572 200, 413
St. Boniface 82
St. Bronisława 70
St. Cloud 420
St. Cyril 62
St. Isidore 171
St. Jacek (Hyacinth) 70, 170
St. Jadwiga, Princess 70
St. Jan Kanty 171
St. John, Order of 165
St. John's Cathedral (of Warsaw) 307,
    311, 358
St. Jozefat Kuncewicz, Uniate Arch-
    bishop 171, 173
St. Kazimierz Jagiellończyk, Prince
    138, 171
St. Louis IX, King of France 106
St. Luke 451
St. Mary's Church, Cracow (Kościół
    Mariacki) 305
St. Methodius 62, 69
St. Petersburg, see Leningrad
St. Salomea, Princess 70
St. Stanisław Kostka 171
St. Stanisław of Szczepanów, see
    Stanislaw, Bishop of Cracow
St. Thomas Becket, Archbishop of
    Canterbury 374
St. Wenceslas (Vaclav) 63
St. Wojciech (Adalbert, Vojtech) 67,
    69, 78, 85, 172
Saladin, Sultan of Egypt 88
Saldern, G. de 411
Salonika, see Thessaloniki
Salt 129
Salza, H. von, Grand Master 90
Samogitia (Żmudź) 31, 116, 120, 123
Samosaterians, see Arians
Samotuły (Samter) 190
Samter, see Samotuły
San Lucas de Barrameda 260
San Clemente, G. de 435
San river 27, 44, 265
Sanderson, John 301–3
Sandez, see Sącz
Sandomierz 28, 87, 262, 294, 331, 333,
    342

Sandomierz, Confederation of (1704) 497
Sanguszko family 153, 177
Sanok 111, 172
Santagucci 150, 310
Santiago di Compostella 374
Sapieha Family 177, 184, 215, 352, 487, 496, 502, 519
Sapieha, J., Starosta of Uświat 456
Sapieha, Kazimierz Jan 487–8
Saratoga 533
Sarmatians 43, 45
Sarmatists 367
Sarnowo 38
Sartawice 269
Saska Kępa 313
Savoy 504
Saxe, Maurice de, Marshal of France 493, 495
Saxon dynasty, see Wettin
Saxons 93, 108, 492, 499
Saxony 107, 315, 377, 413, 492, 493, 497, 499, 501, 503, 504, 505, 506, 507, 544
Schaff, Capt. A. 275
Schenck, W. 258
Schlawe, see Sławno
Schlusselberg 543
Schluter 489
Schultz, burgher of Torun 180
Schultz, H. 258, 260
Schultze, H. 278
Schwartsburg 123
Schwenkfeld, C. von 190
Schwenkfeldians 190
Schwerdfeger, Capt. M. 275
Science 149
Scotland 59, 275, 279
Scriptores Rerum Polonicarum 13
Scythians 39, 43
Segeth, T. 190
Seine river 35
Sejm 132, 145, 151, 152, 154, 211–12, 232, 237, 238, 240, 305, 308, 311, 312, 319, 320, 323, 326, 328, 329–34, 335, 336–9, 341, 342, 343, 345, 347, 349, 362, 364, 421, 425, 429, 432, 473, 480, 488, 511, 513, 518, 519, 523, 525, 526, 528, 529, 535, 536, 537, 538, 540
Sejmiki (dietines) 132, 152, 323–8, 330
Semigalia 147, 454
Senate 141, 151, 211, 219, 330, 335, 342, 359

Senators 211, 336, 421
Serbia 109
Serbs 43
Serfdom 228, 229, 350; see also Peasants, Feudalism
Setubal 260
Seven Years War (1756–63) 288, 409, 507
Sforza, Bona, Queen of Poland 141, 145, 149, 179, 195, 308, 374, 379, 380, 382, 434
Shapoli 329
Sheremetiev, B. P. 406, 407
Sheyn, Michael B. General 458
Sheytan, Ibrahim 479
Shneor, Zalman ben Baruch 193
Shuyski, Prince Ivan Petrovich 430
Shuyski, Prince Vasily 456, 457
Siberia 49
Sicily 35, 106
Siciński, Jan 346
Siechnowice 533
Siedlikowa, D. 196, 197
Sieluń 232, 233
Siemienowicz General K. 445
Siemiginowski 489
Sieniawski Family 488, 502
Sieniawski, A. M., Hetman 503
Sienicki Family 298
Sienicki, Michał 185, 422, 481
Sienkiewicz, H. 470
Siennica 298
Sieradz 88, 94, 102, 112
Sierakowski 539
Sieuertt, merchant of Danzig 260
Sievers, Jakub Jan 543
Sievers, Baron Y. 411
Sieviersk 32, 141, 408, 458
Siewierz, Duchy of 224
Sigismund I King, see Zygmunt I Stary
Sigismund II King, see Zygmunt II August
Sigismund III King, see Zygmunt III Waza
Sigismund of Luxembourg, Prince of Brandenburg 111, 112, 117, 135, 138
Silent Sejm (1717) 172, 499, 500, 503
Silesia, see Śląsk
Silesians (Ślązacy) 69, 84, 85
Silver 129
Simnel, L. 456
Simokata, Theophilactus 151
Sinope 446

Skarga, Piotr 172, 173, 199, 341, 357–60, 361, 439
Skaryszew 312
Skierniewice 224
Sładkowski, Piotr 329
Śląsk (Silesia, Schlesien) 28, 32, 33, 39, 81, 84, 85, 86, 88, 93, 94, 95, 108, 141, 165, 190, 197, 257, 273, 276, 380, 398, 451, 466, 481, 507, 515
Slavs 3, 40, 43, 44, 46, 47, 61, 62, 63, 82, 83, 86, 107
Sławieński, General Piotr 315
Sławno (Schlawe) 83
Słomniki 183
Słonim 246
Slovakia 108, 111, 488
Slovaks 27, 43, 107
Slovenes 43
Slovenia 380
Słuck 183, 190, 518
Słupca 38
Słupsk (Stolp) 83
Smedyno 361
Smith, Adam 368
Smogorzów 267
Smoleńsk 32, 115, 142, 147, 345, 407, 408, 418, 456, 458, 459
Smoleński, Władysław 12, 13
Smółka, Stanisław 13
Smotrycki, M. 174
Smyrna (Izmir) 194
Sobieska, Clementina 489
Sobieski, Jakub, Palatine of Ruthenia 460, 473
Sobieski, Prince Jakub 407, 488, 489, 492
Sobieski, Jan III King (1674–96) 160, 170, 179, 248, 310, 311, 315, 318, 352, 364, 368, 379, 381, 388, 389, 395, 396, 398, 399, 402, 403, 404, 406, 407, 408, 473–90, 491, 492, 493, 499
Sobieski, Marek 474
Sochaczew 138
Social History 75–8, 126–8, 201–55, 279–91, 297–8, 439, 441–4
Socinians, see Arians
Socinius, F., see Sozzini, F.
Sofia 163
Sokiliński Family 184
Soła river 44
Sołtyk, Bishop Kajetan 518, 526
Somyło 422

Sopot (Zoppot) 400
Sorbs 43, 83
Sośnica 354
South, Revd Robert 474–85
Soviet Union 16; see also Russia
Soz river 35
Sozzini, F. (Socinius F.) 185
Sozzini, L. 185
Spain 120, 168, 170, 288, 369, 374, 380, 391, 392, 466, 523, 543
Spake, Capt. M. 275
Spanish Netherlands 398, 406
Speier, Treaty of 422
Spenser, Edmund 150
Spisz (Zips) 516, 521
Spławiński-Lehr, see Lehr-Spławiński
Spytek of Melsztyn 125, 339
Śreniawa, Heraldic Clan of 353
Środa Śląska (Neumarkt) 304
Stadnicki, Stanisław 353–5
Staekelburg, Baron O. 411, 523, 526
Stańczyk Group 9
Stangebro, Battle of (1598) 437
Stanislaus Leszczyński, see Leszczyński, Stanisław
Stanislaus-August Poniatowski, see Poniatowski, Stanisław-August
Stanisław, Bishop of Cracow (Saint Stanisław) 70
Stanisławów 308, 312
Stankar, Prof. F. 184
Starhemberg, Rudigen von 481, 482, 485
Staristsa 430
Starodub 176
Staroleski Family 351
Starosta 335, 349, 352
Starowolski, Szymon 7
Staszic, Stanisław 531
Stęczyc 421
Stęczyna 342
Stefan Batory, King, see Bathory, Stefan
Stephen of Moldavia 144
Stepney, G. 386
Stettin, see Szczecin
Stevan I (Istvań) King of Hungary 74, 107
Steward, Capt. A. 275
Stockholm 33, 147, 260, 433, 434, 436, 448, 450
Stolberg, Louisa von 480
Stolp, see Słupsk

Stoss, Weit, see Stwosz Wit
Strabe, Piotr 148
Stradom 441
Strasz, J., see Ibrahim Bey
Straszowna, R. 397
Strobandt, merchant of Danzig 260
Strzygom 165
Stuarts dynasty 62, 489–90, 493
Stumdorf Peace of (1635) 399, 450, 463
Stwosz, Wit (Weit Stoss) 139
Suchywilk, J., Chancellor 98, 109
Sudovia 115
Suleiman the Magnificent 142
Sulimirski, T. 39
Sułkowski Family 189, 226, 502
Sully, M. duc de 159
Suprasl 173
Suvorov, Field Marshal Aleksander 195, 520, 535, 541, 543, 544
Svatopelk, Grand Duke of Kiev 86
Sven King of Denmark 74
Sweden 146, 286, 303, 310, 314–15, 352, 370, 373, 393, 399, 405, 408, 430, 433–69, 480, 496, 503, 515, 527, 528, 543, 544
Swedes 189, 383, 385, 398, 400, 408, 434, 447, 448, 450, 451, 452, 453, 459, 462, 465, 466, 496, 497
Świdnica (Swidnitz), Duchy of 84, 96
Swidnitz, see Świdnica
Świdry 38
Świdrygiełło 135
Świętosława Storrada the 'Proud' Queen of Sweden 74
Świnka, Jakub, Archbishop of Gniezno 70, 94
Syphilis 149
Szamocyn (Pfaffendorf) 315
Szamotulski Family 127
Szapolyai, John 142
Szary, Florian 209
Szczara river 265
Szczebrzeszyn 476
Szczecin (Stettin) 29, 84, 260, 497
Szelag 130
Szembek, Stanislaw 249–50
Szlachta, see Nobility
Szlichtingtowo 305
Szmulowizna 313
Szujski, Józef 9, 10, 11
Szuyski, Vasyl, Tsar 310
Szydlowiecki Family 224

Szydłowiecki, Krzysztof 129, 149

Tacitus 45, 391
Tamka 312
Tangier 260
Targowica 535
Tarło Family 502
Tarło, A. 504
Tarnogród, Confederation of (1715) 499
Tarnopol 471
Tarnów 265, 298, 304, 305
Tarnowitz, see Tarnowskie Góry
Tarnowski Family 109, 127, 224, 226
Tarnowski, Jan, Grand Hetman of the Crown 121–2, 129, 144, 298, 461
Tarnowskie Góry 481
Tartars 57, 90, 112, 118, 144, 160, 164, 166, 205, 352, 377, 379, 389, 402, 403, 409, 416, 423, 445, 446, 447, 459, 462, 463, 465, 467, 470
Tartu (Dorpat) 147, 167, 431
Tartu, Fortress of 361
Taxation 154, 295
Tczew (Dirschau) 295
Tęczyński Family 109, 127, 415, 422, 423
Tęczyński, Andrzej 128, 326
Tęczyński, Count J. 415, 417, 418, 419
Tenen, Capt. A. 275
Tepper Family 297
Tepper, Piotr 314
Terence 456
Terlecki, C. 173
Teschen, see Cieszyn
Tetiev 225
Teutonic Order 58, 59, 83, 88, 90, 91, 92, 93, 94, 95, 115, 120–4, 134, 135, 138, 139, 142, 143, 146, 151, 161, 165, 166, 211, 256, 307, 323, 373, 374, 385; see also Prussia
Thames river 35
Theists see Arians
Theophano 63
Thessaloniki (Salonika) 194
Thibaut, G. 258
Thietmar 92
Third Crusade 88
Thirteen Years War (1454–66) 120, 123, 256, 257, 307
Thirty Years War 1618–48 188, 288, 361, 397, 448, 450, 461, 462, 467
Thoreau, Henry 371

Thorn, see Toruń
Thorn, Statute of (1520) 212
Thorn, Treaty of (1411) 123
Thorn, Treaty of (1466) 124, 143
Thorn, Tumult of (1724) 180, 181, 182, 501
Thracians 40
Thynne, Thomas 236
Timber 20, 306
Time of Troubles (1605–13) 377, 455, 456, 457
Tina, see Dalmatia
Tintoretto 419
Tisza river 85, 107
Titles 239–40
Tobago 454
Tokes, Capt. H. 275
Tokoly 482
Toll, General 543
Tomicki, Piotr Bishop 125, 148
Torgau 413
Tormasov, Gen. 539
Toropets 141
Toruń (Thorn) 19, 78, 90, 123, 127, 129, 150, 179, 180, 181, 190, 257, 268, 269, 294, 298, 311, 383, 404, 405, 536, 537
Toruń, Protestant Synod of (1595) 179
Trąbą Mikołaj Archbishop 125
Trade 129, 256–92, 315–16, 318, 326
Transport 128, 265–9
Transylvania 88, 108, 185, 315, 361, 429, 432, 462
Treasury, Royal 203, 328
Trebizond 446
Treitschke, Heinrich von 523
Trembowla 479
Trencin 45
Trent, Council of 167, 171, 396
Trepka, Walerian Nekanda 233, 234
Tritheists, see Arians
Troki 191
Troppau see Opava
Trubetskoi Prince D. 458
Trzciniec 38
Tulln 481
Turin 419
Turkey 120, 138, 194, 361, 383, 389, 391, 395, 399, 404, 426, 429, 459, 519, 520, 521, 527, 528, 529, 536; see also Ottoman Turks
Turks (Ottomans) 101, 108, 160, 161, 164, 172, 379, 388, 391, 395, 398,

402, 407, 408, 409, 416, 447, 459, 461, 463, 470, 471, 472, 491
Turzon Family 297
Turzon, Jan 129
Tuscany 107
Tushino 456
Tuszów 262
Tuszyn, Battle of (1618) 165
Tver 120
Twardowski, Samuel 6
Tweenhuysen, H. von 258
Tymff, J. 329, 469
Tyniec 44, 69, 219
Tyshkovitch, I. 187, 188

Ujazd Palace in Warsaw 310
Ujście 360, 450
Ukmerge, battle of, see Wilkomierz, Battle of
Ukraine (Ukraina) 30, 31, 33, 49, 59, 174, 176, 213, 273, 282, 344, 345, 346, 395, 407, 408, 422, 440, 445, 446, 447, 459, 463, 466, 467, 468, 470, 471, 487, 497, 519, 541; see also Rus, Ruthenia, Kiev
Uman (Humań) 519
Uňetice 38
Ungeler, Florian 149
Uniates 174, 175, 176, 197, 198, 199, 205, 335, 447
Unitarians, see Arians
United Provinces 369
United States of America 370–2
Upita 346
Uppsala 437
Urban, Pope 98
Uścilug 265
Ushviata 431
Ussuri (river) 26

Vaclav, King of Bohemia 99
Vaclav II King of Bohemia and Poland (Wacław II) (1300–5) 78, 86, 94
Vaclav III (Wacław III) King of Bohemia 86, 94
Valois, Henri 247, 334, 364, 421, 426
Vandals 46, 56
Varangians 61
Varna 138, 163
Varna, Battle of (1444) 163
Varsevicius, see Warszewicki
Vasa dynasty 310, 433, 434, 454, 461, 462; see also Sweden

Vatican (Papacy) 70, 90, 93, 135, 166, 168, 171, 397, 401, 402, 430, 544
Vedoni, Monsignor, papal nuncio 401
Vedrosha, battle of 139
Veer, H. G. de 258
Vehl, Swejbold, see Fiol, Szwajpolt
Velizh 431
Venedians 39
Venetian Republic 109, 412
Venice 88, 91, 101, 185, 260, 363, 365, 370, 373, 374, 375, 380, 389, 390, 396, 419, 493
Ventspils (Piłtyń) 329, 454
Veresovic, Count (Jan Weihard) 451, 453
Vernon, R. 274
Versailles 395, 508, 533
Viatka 120
Vielikie Luki 429
Vienna (Wien) 33, 101, 104, 142, 364, 380, 381, 382, 395, 398, 399, 404, 419, 422, 436, 460, 480, 488, 492, 505, 523, 527, 532
Vienna, Congress of (1515) 142, 373, 380
Vilna, see Vilnius
Wilnius (Wilno, Vilna) 93, 115, 118, 124, 134, 142, 145, 147, 166, 167, 179, 183, 187, 193, 217, 295, 297, 305, 308, 349, 360, 380, 390, 467, 497, 539, 540
Virgil 391
Vistula (Wisła) river 23, 26, 27, 28, 29, 35, 37, 38, 39, 40, 43, 45, 46, 49, 61, 78, 83, 141, 144, 256, 257, 258, 265, 267, 269, 272, 279, 286, 288, 291, 292, 306, 307, 308, 313, 418, 421, 465, 506
Vistula Trade 256, 257, 258, 261, 279, 280, 285, 286, 287, 288, 289, 291, 448, 450, 463
Vistulanians (Wislanie) 44, 62, 67, 69, 85
Vitebsk (Witebsk) 167, 295, 515, 521
Vitellon, see Witello
Vitovt (Witold) Grand Duke of Lithuania 119, 122, 135, 144, 191, 216
Vitry, Marquis de 381, 383, 399
Vladimir, Principality of 86
Vladimir, Grand Duke of Kiev 74, 86
Vladimiri, Paulus, see Włodkowic, Pawel
Vlaminck, C. 258

Vojtech, Bishop, see St. Wojciech
Volga river 58
Volhynia (Wolyn) 30, 59, 147, 153, 173, 218, 265, 298
Voltaire, François 192, 368, 511
Vorksla, Battle of 118, 124
Vorontsov 511
Voyrknecht, J. 258
Vratislava, see Wrocław
Vratz, Captain 236
Vyazma 141
Vyborg 260
Vyshegrad 95, 99, 102

Wacław II, see Vaclav II
Wacław III, see Vaclav III
Walce (Walzen) 83
Waldeck 485
Waldemar IV, King of Denmark 99
Waldemar of Brandenburg, Prince 91
Waldstein, Count 481
Walkinshaw, Clementina 490
Wallachia 108, 109, 175, 426
Walzen, see Walce
Wanda 61
Wapowski, A. 415
Wapowski, Bernard 149, 155
War of Chocim (epic poem), see Wojna Chocimska
War of the Second Partition, see Russo-Polish War
Warbeck, P. 456
Warmia (Ermeland)
Wars 288–9, 428–31, 447–62, 471–2, 478–87, 496–501, 504–5, 519–20, 535–7, 540–1
Warsaw (Warszawa) 19, 28, 33, 35, 37, 38, 95, 104, 168, 174, 180, 187, 188, 194, 195, 196, 268, 271, 291, 292, 294, 295, 297, 306, 315, 320, 332, 333, 347, 360, 377, 378, 380, 381, 382, 383, 384, 385, 386, 387, 388, 396, 398, 400, 401, 402, 405, 406, 407, 409, 410, 411, 414, 446, 451, 453, 463, 471, 474, 476, 479, 497, 500, 504, 509, 510, 511, 530, 532, 536, 538, 539, 540, 541, 542, 544, 546
Warsaw, Battle of (1705) 503
Warsaw, Duchy of 25, 56
Warsaw Legation, British 546
Warsaw Positivists 12, 13

Warszewicki, K. (Varsevicius) 363, 390, 392, 396
Warszewicki, S. 390
Warta river 27, 83, 265
Washington, George 370
Water Power 128
Watzenrode, B. 257
Wehlau, Treaty of (1657) 407, 462
Wehlungen, Edict of, see Wieluń, edict of
Weiglowa, B. 191
Weihard, J., see Veresovic, Count
Wends (Wendowie) 63
Wendon 429
Weser river 82
Wesley, J. 193
West Point 533
West Slavs see Slavs
Westerplatte 49
Westphalia, Treaty of (1648) 384, 462
Wetka 176
Wettin dynasty 347, 492, 499, 501, 503, 504, 517
White Ruthenia, see Byelorussia
Whitsun 248
Wichman, merchant of Danzig 260
Wichman, Count of Saxony 82
Wielhorski, M. 369, 410
Wieliczka 80, 98, 129, 304
Wielkopolska (Greater Poland, Polonia Maior) 27, 28, 83, 86, 93, 94, 96, 109, 112, 188, 190, 264, 285, 304, 320, 340, 349, 395, 450, 520, 537
Wielopole 312
Wielopolski, Jan 312
Wieluń 451, 453
Wieluń (Wehlungen), edict of (1424) 125
Wieprz river 265
Wierzynek, N. 99
Wietor, Hieronim 149
Wightman, J. 277
Wilanów Palace 311, 488, 489
Wilhamowice 78
Wilhelm von Habsburg, Prince of Austria 112, 117
William of Moerbecke 79
Williamson, Sir Joseph 402
Wilno, see Vilnius
Wilkomierz (Ukmerge), Battle of 135
Wilson, R. 277
Winchester 390
Windau, see Windawa

Windawa (Windau) 454
Winkelbruch, Johann von Koln 425
Wisła river, see Vistula
Wiślica 20
Wisłok river 265
Wiśnicz 225, 262, 445
Wiśniowiecki Family 153, 177, 362, 447, 470, 502
Wiśniowiecki, Prince 495
Wiśniowiecki, Dymitr, Grand Hetman 470, 480
Wiśniowiecki, Jarema, Palatine of Ruthenia 465, 468, 470
Wiśniowiecki, Michał Korybut (Michał K. Wiśniowiecki, Michał K. Wiśniowiecki) King (1669–73) 332, 398, 402, 470, 471, 472, 474, 479
Witaszkowo 39
Witebsk see Vitebsk
Witełło (Vitellon) 79
Witold, see Vitovt
Witoszyński, Haras 351
Wladislavia 81
Władysław I Herman, Prince (Ladislaus I Herman) (1079–1102) 72
Władysław II Wygnaniec, Prince (Ladislaus II the Exile) (1138–46) 72, 83
Władysław I Łokietek, King (Ladislaus I the Elbow-High) (1306–33) 62, 72, 75, 78, 86, 93, 94, 95, 96, 300
Władysław II Jagiełło (Jogaila), King (1386–1434) 116, 117, 118, 119, 122, 124, 135, 211
Władysław III Warneńczyk (Ladislaus III of Varna), King of Poland and Hungary (1434–44) 135, 138, 161, 163, 164
Władysław IV Waza (Ladislaus IV Vasa), King (1632–48) 168, 177, 179, 199, 240, 286, 310, 311, 318, 360, 388, 394, 406, 435, 450, 457, 458, 459, 462, 463
Władysław Jagiellonczyk, King of Bohemia and Hungary (Ladislaus Jagiellon) 138, 380
Władysław, Duke of Opole 99, 109, 111, 112
Władysław Biały, Duke of Gniewków 102, 103
Włodkowic, Paweł (Paulus Vladimiri) 148, 166
Włodyk, Katarzyna 327, 328

Wogan, Charles 489
Wojciechowski, Tadeusz 10, 13
Wojna chocimska 460−1
Wola Field 332
Wola Justowska 225
Wolan, A. 184
Wolff, D. van der 258
Wolin (Wollin) 69, 82, 84
Wołłowicz, Ostafi 153
Wolmar 361
Wolsey, Cardinal T. 374
Wolski, M., Crown Marshal of Poland 277
Wolski, Michał 232
Wolski, Mikołaj 252
Wołyń, see Volhynia
Wransowicz, M. 441
Wrocław (Breslau, Vratislava) 19, 28, 38, 50, 69, 78, 80, 83, 87, 294, 304, 319, 380, 396, 397, 466
Wyczański, Andrzej 228
Wyśmierzyce 333
Wysocki Mrs. 197
Wyszyński, Cardinal Stefan 19

Yam Zapolski, Peace of (1582) 431
Yangtse river 35
Yaphe, M. 444
Yarmouth 275
Yaroslav the Wise, Grand Duke of Kiev 86
Yriarte, Dominic, Don d' 543−4

Zaborowski, Tymon 149, 150
Zabrzeski, Prince P. 441
Zadruga 208
Żagań (Sagan) 104
Zagorsk 456
Zagość 165
Zajączek, General Józef 540
Zajączkowski, A. 51
Zakopane 52
Załuski, Aleksander (Bishop) 329, 389
Załuski, Andrzej S. K., Bishop of Cracow 509
Załuski, Józef A., Bishop of Kiev 509, 510
Zamość 151, 265, 266, 298, 445, 477
Zamoyski, Andrzej, Chancellor 509, 517
Zamoyski, Jan, Chancellor 150, 151, 152, 175, 209, 252, 298, 312, 326, 327, 336, 337, 338, 341. 377, 378, 390, 414, 416, 422, 423, 425, 426, 429, 431, 435, 436, 439, 444, 456
Zamoyski, Jan 475
Zamoyski, Stefan 452
Zamoyski, Tomasz 379, 477
Żarnowiec, Battle of 124
Zator 262
Zawisza Czarny z Garbowa 112
Zawisza of Kurożwek, Bishop of Cracow 109
Zbaraż 441
Zbierzchowski 483
Zbigniew, Prince 72
Zborowski Family 397, 415
Zborowska, Barbara 353
Zborowski, Aleksander 457, 458
Zborowski, Andrzej 415
Zborowski, Jan 327, 328, 336, 337, 415, 425
Zborowski, Krzysztof 327, 328, 336, 337, 415
Zborowski, P. 415
Zborowski, Samuel 326, 336, 415, 426, 431
Zbytkower, Szmul 313
Zebrzydowski, Michal 170, 341, 342, 354, 358
Zebrzydowski, Mikolaj 252
Zebrzydowski Rebellion (1606−7) 439
Zehde, see Cedynia
Zełecki, Franciszek 249−50, 342
Zeleżniak, Maksym 519
Zenowicz Family 184
Zieleńce 536
Zieliński, Marian 350
Ziemowit III Prince of Mazovia 99, 102, 104, 112
Zips, see Spisz
Złota 38
Złoty 130
Żmudź, see Samogitia
Zofia, Jagiellon 138
Żolibórz 312−13
Żółkiew 298, 404, 477
Żółkiewski, Stanisław, Crown Hetman 252, 342, 445, 456, 457, 460, 477
Żółte Wody, Battle of (1648) 465
Zórawno 403, 404, 479
Zórawno, Truce of (1676) 395
Zug, Simon 311
Zurich 185
Zygmunt, see Sigismund

Zygmunt I Stary (Sigismund I the Old)
King (1506–48) 130, 134, 138,
141–4, 147, 149, 308, 373, 374,
375, 380

Zygmunt II August (Sigismund) 131,
144, 149, 152, 154, 155, 179, 183,
199, 213, 235, 308, 315, 356, 361,
378, 379, 386, 397, 413, 434

Zygmunt III Waza (Sigismund III) 168,
175, 179, 310, 317, 340, 341, 342,
358, 376, 379, 387, 356, 434, 435,
436, 437, 439, 440, 447, 456, 459

Zyndram z Maszkowic 122

Zyzka 122